JAZZ

Volume I

TRANSATLANTIC

JAZZ

Volume I

TRANSATLANTIC

The African Undercurrent in Twentieth-Century Jazz Culture

GERHARD KUBIK

University Press of Mississippi / Jackson

Publication of this volume was made possible in part by a generous
donation from the Manfred Bukofzer Endowment of the American
Musicological Society, funded in part by the National Endowment for
the Humanities and the Andrew W. Mellon Foundation.

www.upress.state.ms.us

The University Press of Mississippi is a member
of the Association of American University Presses.

First printing 2017
∞

Library of Congress Cataloging-in-Publication Data

Names: Kubik, Gerhard, 1934– author.
Title: Jazz transatlantic, Volume I : the African undercurrent in
twentieth-century jazz culture / Gerhard Kubik.
Other titles: African undercurrent in twentieth-century jazz culture
Description: Jackson : University Press of Mississippi, [2017] |
Series: American made music series | Includes bibliographical
references and index. |
Identifiers: LCCN 2017026673 (print) | LCCN 2017029150 (ebook) |
ISBN 9781626746596 (epub single) | ISBN 9781626746602 (epub insti-
tutional) | ISBN 9781626746626 (pdf single) | ISBN 9781626746633
(pdf institutional) | ISBN 9781628462302 (hardcover : alk. paper)
Subjects: LCSH: Jazz—African influences. | Africans—Music—History
and criticism. | Jazz musicians—United States.
Classification: LCC ML3508 (ebook) | LCC ML3508 .K83 2017 (print)
| DDC 781.6509—dc23
LC record available at https://lccn.loc.gov/2017026673

British Library Cataloging-in-Publication Data available

CONTENTS

PREFACE

This book is about musical innovators and the hidden family relationships of their thoughts. Its title occurred to me in a kind of midnight flash of thought on March 26, 2008, after Craig Gill of the University Press of Mississippi had written to me in a letter dated February 20: "I am curious about your current research...."

What was my current research? It was not particularly focused. I was just out of hospital and on crutches, after a hip replacement operation on February 4, which would have to be repeated only three years later. Shortly before, however, jazz had been my principal preoccupation, in experiences with our band from southeast Africa on several concert tours to Tanzania, to the European Union, and in 2006 to Brazil. We had been learning about different people's reactions to a kind of music they had never heard before: how they enjoyed it; how they danced to it in some places, notably in Dar es Salaam and São Paulo; how some observers were trying to find a slot in a system of preconceived categories: Was it jazz? Was it revival of South African street music of the 1950s? Why are they unplugged? Why don't they use "modern" instruments? Sure, this must be "world music." But there are those weird harmonic patterns. And there is the twelve-bar blues form. So what?

A book on "Jazz Transatlantic" was a persuading idea. But what kind of book would I want to write? About our concert experiences globally? About jazz and its derivatives outside the United States? On the African side of the Atlantic? In Europe? Elsewhere?

Luckily, the word combination "Jazz Transatlantic" has its own iridescence. So I decided to leave things to their internal propulsion, and let the book evolve largely by itself, as if I functioned merely as an observer of the process.

As soon as I had returned to my desk in Chileka, Malawi, in June 2008, I began to work on it in the compound of Moya A. Malamusi's Oral Literature Research Programme with its library, museum, and other facilities. I saw that it was a huge undertaking. The experience to be covered would need about twenty chapters balanced against one another within three large parts of the book.

During the next few years I was in contact with institutions and colleagues round the world, with musicians, notably in South Africa, with the International Library of African Music (Director: Diane Thram) at Rhodes University, S.A., and with jazz institutions in Italy, Germany, and elsewhere in Europe. In November 2011 I traveled once again to the United States, reading at the formidable library of the Center for Black Music Research, Chicago, with the wonderful assistance of Suzanne Flandreau, librarian, and in fact, the entire staff of the CBMR. I met again my oldest American friend, Donald Hopkins, author of *Princes and Peasants: Smallpox in History* (1983), celebrating our fiftieth anniversary of friendship (since the "jazz days" in Vienna 1961). I was with my good friends and colleagues Kazadi wa Mukuna, Ted and Carol Albrecht at Kent State University, Ohio, before proceeding to Philadelphia to the annual conference of the Society for Ethnomusicology, where I received honorary membership on November 19, 2011.

Almost flattened by the Jupiter-size gravitational force of the jazz literature that had accumulated worldwide by 2013—beyond anything an individual can process—I realized that I had to be reasonably selective. Naturally the present work is full of lacunae, and it has taken a long time to be completed. At last, however, in June 2013, I heard a sound like "klook mop" at the door of my house in Chileka; and a voice seemed to say: "Done! Take it or Leave it!" The print-out of the manuscript was on my desk.

—Gerhard Kubik
Chileka, Malawi, June 30, 2013

ACKNOWLEDGMENTS

In writing *Jazz Transatlantic*, books I and II, I have had help from many friends and colleagues. Most of my thanks go to Yohana Malamusi, who not only retyped the entire manuscript on the computer and integrated the figures and the photography but contributed essentially to its content, resolving some pressing issues concerning jazz in South Africa. Also of great help was his sister Dayina Malamusi, who helped me establish telephone contact with jazz musicians in South Africa, such as Tete Mbambisa, Cape Town, and Johnny Mekoa, Gauteng Music Academy, Daveston. Moya A. Malamusi, head of the Oral Literature Research Programme, Chileka, Malawi, and the flutist and guitarist Sinosi Mlendo of our Malawi jazz band were to me like permanent consultants, available round the clock. During the writing process, I have repeatedly sent drafts of the chapters to colleagues and friends in many places for comments and criticism. The following have been very helpful in reading through parts of the manuscript and often also providing or pointing out additional source materials, thereby allowing me to improve my earlier drafted versions:

Lynn Abbott, Hogan Jazz Archive, New Orleans
Giorgio Adamo, University of Rome "Tor Vergata"
Kofi Agawu, Princeton University, Princeton
Ted Albrecht, Kent State University, Ohio
Fernando Arenas, University of Michigan, Ann Arbor
Kelly Askew, University of Michigan, Ann Arbor
Daniel Avorgbedor, Ohio State University, Columbus
Wolfgang Bender, University of Bayreuth
Jonathan Eato, JISA project, Cape Town
David Evans, University of Memphis
Donald Hopkins, Carter Center, Atlanta
Kazadi wa Mukuna, Kent State University, Ohio
Tete Mbambisa, Cape Town
Paul Schauert, Indiana University, Bloomington
Mitchel Strumpf, University of Dar es Salaam
Tony Thomas, MFA, Sunny Isles Beach, Florida
Diane Thram, ILAM, Rhodes University, Grahamstown

Valuable photography was contributed by friends and colleagues, among them Gottfried Chmelar, Vienna/Johannesburg; the late Maurice Djenda, Central African Republic; Helmut Hillegeist, Vienna; Mose Yotamu, Kabompo, Zambia, and others.

To all of you my sincere thanks!

In addition, I have had support in this project from a number of institutions:

Of invaluable help was the chance for me to study in the library of the Center for Black Music Research, Chicago, under invitation by the director, Samuel A. Floyd Jr., first for three months in 1997 on a Rockefeller Research Fellowship, and then in November 2011 for a few days under Executive Director Monica Hairston O'Connell, with all the kind attention received from the personnel, especially also librarian Suzanne Flandreau. She never tired of responding to my insatiable reading requests.

We have also had modest financial assistance from various other sources. I gratefully acknowledge that the Goethe-Institut Dar-es-Salaam under the directorship of Eleonore Sylla financed the participation of our music ensemble—including Moya A. Malamusi, Sinosi Mlendo, Christopher Gerald, and me—in the 6th International Ethnomusicology Symposium, July 30–August 4, 2012, organized by Mitchel Strumpf and Imani Sanga at the Department of Fine and Performing Arts, University of Dar es Salaam. On that occasion I presented some of the results of my transatlantic research in a keynote address, and composer-musician Sinosi Mlendo discussed composition in our jazz band. I also gratefully acknowledge an invitation to a symposium on mbira music convened by Klaus-Peter Brenner in the context of the 15th International Conference of the Society for Music Research, at the University of Göttingen, Germany, September 4–8, 2012. Although I was unable to participate in person, I submitted a paper on Scott Joplin's "Bethena" waltz, which is also a subject of discussion in this book.

Finally, I would like to express our research team's gratitude to the Wissenschaftsfond FWF Vienna, for financing Projects 23834-G15 and P 26080-G21 on individual histories of African musician-composers. Within this project involving Regine Allgayer-Kaufmann, August Schmidhofer, Moya A. Malamusi, and Yohana Malamusi at the Institute of Musicology, University of Vienna, I have been able to refine the biographies of some artists who are part of the jazz tradition in southern Africa.

INTRODUCTION

In a lecture given in commemoration of Thomas Henry Huxley* on December 14, 2007, anthropologist Adam Kuper of Brunel University, UK, declared that "the original sin of anthropology was to divide the world into civilized and savage" (Kuper 2008: 717). He was concerned with young Charles Darwin's unfavorable reactions in 1833 to observing the inhabitants of Tierra del Fuego. Kuper added: "To compare civilized and primitive is to compare two imaginary conditions" (720; see also Kuper 2005).

Obviously, the underlying framework of thought has been lingering on in surrogate terminology until the present, and has been a long-term impediment to the social sciences and the study of culture. Anthropologists still conceptualize grades of societal complexity; some assume that Western societies are "individualistic" and African societies, by contrast, rigidly community oriented. In the mid-twentieth century, Claude Lévi-Strauss (who celebrated his 100th birthday on November 28, 2008, before he died Oct. 30, 2009) once divided world cultures into "hot" and "cold," one supposed to be dynamic, the other stagnant. Since Marcel Mauss's concept of "reciprocité" in *L'Essai sur le don* (1925), the game of binary concept formation—also in Lévi-Strauss's "the Raw and the Cooked" (1964)—has been irresistible, and not only in French intellectual circles. H. C. Triandis (1990) created the opposition "tight cultures" versus "loose cultures"; and Ulf Hannertz (1992), trying to avoid "primitive," "traditional," etc., came up with the notion of "small-scale" communities.

All these schemes tend to lump together, in the abstract, the alleged behavior of millions of people, drawing artificial dividing lines through humanity. In essence, many of these schemes of thought are based on a hidden formula Marshall Sahlins (1976: 216) identified as "The West and the Rest." The "West" and those who are aspiring to be or to become part of its economic hegemony are self-classifying as dynamic, enterprising, market-oriented, individualistic, etc., while the "Rest" is supposed to be a world apart, variously described as "third," even "fourth," and thought to be stagnant, rural, overly dependent on tradition, collectivistic, folkloristic— "developing."

---

* Huxley (1825–1895) was a physical anthropologist in the vein of Charles Darwin, Herbert Spencer, and other contemporaries.

There is no question that such conceptualizations have affected approach and methodology in cultural research, including the study of music, besides their psychological effect upon those who were the object of such research, with ensuing political consequences some generations later. Until recently, these concepts have been an ever-present undercurrent in popular discourse about culture. The dichotomy "individualistic" versus "collectivistic" often translates in music research into a tenacious belief that music in Africa is primarily a community expression, rigidly attached to social events and ultimately a product of an "ethnic" creative spirit with few individual composers to be traced, e.g., "the mbira of the Shona people of Zimbabwe." Rooted in fragmentary observations across time and space, such beliefs ignore the tremendous investment of individual self-training, contemplation, and organizational talent that is necessary for acquiring instrumental skills, constructing vocal polyphonies, and organizing performance. It is something completely different from activating a cellphone or an electric switch.

I am making these superfluous remarks to remind us that we ought to pay attention to the kind of ideological background glow that may have negatively affected the study of transatlantic cultural exchanges from the sixteenth to the twenty-first centuries. We can only be successful in our endeavor if we learn not only to focus on group phenomena but also on individual contribution and achievement in all the cultures concerned. Luckily, when I began to do field research in Africa in 1959, my previous familiarity with some of the exigencies of jazz performance, and the life histories of its cultural carriers, made me seek individual instruction in Africa from the beginning, by Evaristo Muyinda in Uganda and by Duro and Gboyega Ladipọ in Nigeria. Indirectly, and nonverbally at that time—purely through personal behavior—I declared my defiance of all unilinear and binary schemes aimed at dividing us.

In the 1950s and 1960s, the idea of Africa as a repository of stagnant, age-old traditions had in fact already been shattered. Archaeologists such as Frank Willet in Nigeria, historians, and linguists had begun to patch together a dynamic picture of Africa's cultural history. The study of musical genres and the individual works of their exponents was important in unraveling the dynamics behind stability and change, as well as identifying intra-African streams of influence, besides trans–Indian Ocean contacts (Alpers 1975) and those across the Atlantic.

◆ ◆ ◆

Jazz Transatlantic is essentially a culture-contact and syncretist project. The prefix *trans-* means "across" and implies "crossing" as a process. Along imaginary trajectories we are then crossing and recrossing the Atlantic in different directions and historical periods in pursuit of a music termed jazz, from Africa to America and back. Indeed, it is this theme of crossing and recrossing that is central to this book. I am focusing on something that spreads, and that thing is more than sound; it includes language, and with it concepts, world views, beliefs, experiences, attitudes, commodities, and what is most important: knowledge and expertise.

In a 1971/72 article under the title "Jazz—the round trip," Atta Annan Mensah alluded to the image of someone having purchased a roundtrip ticket upon departure from Africa to New World destinations, with the intention of coming back one day. Whether it takes the form of a search for cultural "roots" or for one's personal genealogy, the fact is that by whatever pressures the original migration may have come about—economic constraints, slavery, kidnapping, curiosity, desire for adventures—there remains something unspoken that binds immigrants to the lands where their ancestors came from. And the great-grandchildren of those who have remained behind in the countries of origin, by fortune or design, are sometimes ready to welcome back the offspring of those who "have been lost." In southeast Africa there is a verb in the Cinyanja/Chichewa language, *kutchona*, describing the state of being hooked up in foreign lands, getting stuck somewhere without thinking of returning. In a song composed in 1978 by Daniel Kachamba, "Kutchona Bambo" (Getting hooked up, Man!) such a state is described in the context of labor migration to South Africa.*

Obviously, Jazz Transatlantic has a certain span of meanings to be covered. One is the implicit reference to a multilateral historical process involving jazz. The music we call jazz has been a transatlantic phenomenon from its start, and it was the result of a constant flux and reflux of ideas embedded in contemporaneous late nineteenth-century musical events in Europe, Africa, Latin America, and elsewhere. This exchange started long before the famous 1893 World's Fair Columbian Exposition in Chicago that brought musical troupes from Dahomey, the Middle East, and many other places to the United States. To separate jazz history from related developments on the other side of the Atlantic is therefore ill-advised.

In the 1920s a first reaction to jazz, by many musicians and composers rooted in the Western classical tradition, was to consider it a fascinating aberration from normal musical practice that meant always playing from written scores. Anything else was "fake music," and so was jazz. But they hailed the apparent syncopation. It was also thought to be characteristic of jazz that the so-called weak parts of a

---

* I recall the late Daniel Kachamba's composition only from our joint concert tour in 1978, after he first performed it at a concert in the town of Waiblingen, near Stuttgart, Germany, on September 1. The tour was organized by the Africa House of Arthur Benseler in Freiberg am Neckar. I was fascinated by a modulation Daniel had introduced in that composition, switching between two keys. The concert was privately recorded, probably by Roland Voitl, Tübingen, but it is not known whether the tapes still exist.

4/4 meter were to be accented. And certain notes sounded to the observers like minor thirds over a major chord. Those apparent deviations from Western tonality came to be called blue notes.

Unfortunately, these assessments derive from heavy reinterpretation of unfamiliar phenomena. Actually, accents in jazz can fall on any point of the meter, on or off-beat, depending on the rhythmic shape of the voice lines. The beat can be organized incorporating sound accents, e.g., on 2 and 4, or no accents at all. And the so-called blue notes are not meant by blues singers to be deviations from anything; they are the hidden legacy of another, non-Western tonal system with cognates in some areas of the West African savannah, even in East Africa.

A good auditory demonstration example of this background is Charlie Parker's instrumental blues performance with John Lewis on piano in his composition "Parker's Mood" recorded in New York, September 18, 1948. There is an introductory frame in minor, then Parker's theme and variations in the twelve-bar blues form.

Hidden in Parker's discourse is the blues tonal system, which is related to African tonal systems that are based on the exploration of partials over a single fundamental. Parker on his alto sax was acutely aware of partials, up to partial 11 at 551 cents, which in the mold of Western tunings can be rendered approximately as a flatted fifth, an interval important in bebop. It is therefore erroneous to link the harmonic structure of his music to Arnold Schönberg or others whom Parker professed to have been an inspiration for him. Rhythmically, there is no such thing as syncopation; Parker evolves his discourse over two simultaneous referential pulse-lines, one dividing the beat by three, the other by four. Accents can fall on any point of either pulse-line, depending on the structure of the melodic phrase to be articulated.

Generally, in jazz there are three simultaneous reference levels of timing. These are shared with most African music. The first (a) is what we now call the elementary pulsation or "fastest pulse," which is like an infinite string of minimal time-units. Sometimes two elementary pulse-lines in a certain ratio, e.g., 3:4, are simultaneously present and integrated in the mind for the musician to shift between. Next (b) is the beat or gross-pulse which is simply the dance beat for the audience, if they want to follow it. And finally (c) is the length of the cycle. In African music short cycles dominate; in jazz it is the twelve-bar blues form, the AABA chorus form, and other forms. A jazz musician developing his improvisatory art navigates within all three reference levels, without actually thinking about them; they are only present subliminally. More consciously he is aware of the sequence of chord changes within the cycle, unless of course the themes are modal (as in some work of Miles Davis, John Coltrane, etc.), or even based on just one fundamental (as in some blues by Ornette Coleman). All this is internalized early, when learning to improvise. It then operates in the mind like an auto-pilot, so that a soloist would never go astray, whatever rhythmic or harmonic disorientation effects are run up by his partners.

Such audio-psychological facts, however, were not yet understood by analysts in the early twentieth century. Even the renowned musicologist Erich Moritz von Hornbostel was at a loss for coming to terms with basics in jazz when he first heard it in the 1920s. And yet it was he who earlier had identified what he called "neutral thirds" in recordings on wax cylinders brought by Günter Tessmann (1913) from Cameroon. Hornbostel acknowledged the existence of specific African tonal systems based on principles different from those of the Western scale.

In some areas of Africa, not only may neutral thirds appear in instrumental tunings, but there may be tuning systems that incorporate thirds of different size that clash—if you wish, major and minor—such as I recorded in a mourning song by a Tikar-speaking woman in central Cameroon in February 1964. She was accompanied by a man in Chief Ngambe's entourage playing a five-string polyidiochord stick zither, tuned pentatonically but incorporating one narrow interval (Track 27 on the CD accompanying the Italian edition of *Africa and the Blues*, Kubik 1999a [2007]).

In spite of the great variety of expressive forms that we associate with jazz history, the music's tonality and organization has remained part of an African culture world. This is not to downgrade the share of other musical cultures in fueling and refueling the creative process in the historical rise of different jazz styles, nor does it deny the status of jazz as an intrinsically American development. But it is evident from the bulk of our historical data that innovative stimuli have originated primarily with those artists in the United States (and more recently also in southern Africa) who in one way or another have carried on concepts and aesthetics from African music. Such understanding corroborates the composer George Lewis's idea of an "historically afrological" character of jazz and other African American music. Jazz can be composed and performed by anyone who has learned its vernacular, but from the moment one is successful—irrespective of one's place of birth, genealogy, and social background—he or she has irrevocably changed one's personal cultural profile, and now belongs to the jazz culture, so to say. George Shearing, Lennie Tristano, tenor saxophonist Winston Mankunku Ngozi from South Africa, and many others—with their birth places scattered around the globe—all equally belong to it, as much as Jay McShann and John Coltrane.

I might perhaps elaborate a bit on what I have said elsewhere: that we no longer think of individuals having a lifelong "cultural identity" conferred upon them by the communities in which they grow up. Socio-psychological studies suggest that no one is actually nailed down to a culture, let alone to membership in an ethnic group, although social pressure demanding conformist behavior can be intense.

Not only do we change our personalities gradually during lifetime, we also change our cultural allegiances, as a result of learning. The transformation begins with contacts outside the individual's earliest social environment, and particularly with learning other languages. Therefore, we speak today of a person's momentary, transient cultural profile* rather than "cultural identity."

In some persons this profile is subject to incisive changes during their lives, particularly if they constantly widen their contacts, or migrate somewhere else, or just travel a lot. This new model also makes superfluous earlier concepts relating to music, such as "bimusicality," because any additional knowledge or skill acquired by the individual is integrated with all previous experiences and learning. Benny Goodman playing swing and also Mozart on his clarinet was not "bi-musical." He simply expressed his personal affiliations, which happened to include swing, Mozart, and some other classical stuff, as much as Bunk Johnson expressed his, which included ragtime and blues, two very different traditions.

The study of European classical and contemporary "art music," and by extension the adaptations of American jazz within that realm, is therefore also a legitimate part of transatlantic exploration. This has actually been well-covered in musicology. Jazz harmony has been studied intensively from the viewpoint of Western music theory—implicitly, however, subscribing to the idea that it is all based on European harmonic traditions. Jazz musicians in Europe have also been the subject of intensive stylistic and biographical work, including Django Reinhardt, George Shearing, or Albert Mangelsdorff. The Jazz Institute in Darmstadt, Germany, has devoted an entire volume to jazz in its interaction worldwide with other musical traditions, in short, jazz in global perspective (*The World Meets Jazz*, Knauer ed. 2008). In Chicago, the Center for Black Music Research (CMBR), under the directorship of Samuel A. Floyd Jr., carried out an extensive survey of the relationships, analogies, and common logic of African American musical styles in the United States and in the Caribbean. A broad panel of relationships was identified at the CBMR conference in Miami, June 9–11, 2000, on "Music and Linguistics in the Caribbean and Other African Diaspora Cultures." Maureen Warner Lewis of the University of the West Indies, Jamaica, gave an answer to the important question why it was that in the Americas, certain long-dormant Africanisms would often erupt suddenly and be creatively used in new musical or other artistic manifestations. She stressed that the so-called Africanisms are often transmitted within small groups, even

---

* I first proposed this new model in 1992 at a conference in Miami organized by Gerard Béhague on so-called "black ethnicity" (Cf. Kubik 1994a: 17, 21).

just families, without people in the mainstream culture being aware of their existence. Then at some stage in history, conditions can become favorable, and suddenly some of these traits in hiding surface to broader public awareness. Lewis presented her observations as an alternative to the popular hypothesis of "cultural memory." She stressed that many African traits in New World cultures had survived somewhere on the periphery of the mainstream culture until, at some point in history, they made it to the center.

In our research we have combined historical methodology with participant observation, enhanced by psychological argument involving both audio-psychology and the psychology of culture contact. We will point to "family resemblances" between musical styles across the Atlantic, as first conceptualized by my good friend, the late Ernest Brown. In fact, there are many hidden family relationships. We want to get a glimpse of the subliminal, how the human mind operates when creating new forms of expression, connecting between them, musically and extra-musically.

Recently, in a preface to Freddi Williams Evans's book *Congo Square* (2010), J. H. Kwabena Nketia has shared with us some of his experiences in 1958 when he first came to the United States and into contact with African American cultural expressions, in Harlem and later in so called "storefront churches" in Chicago, where Melville J. Herskovits was taking him. He points out that there are areas of instant understanding between adherents to African and African American cultures and "that the relationship between African and African American cultures is on a deeper level than their surface manifestations, and that what needs to be identified are the deep structures or the roots that generate the surface features as well as the specific roles, functions, and meanings assigned to them" (x). He cites jazz musician Max Roach's three-month stay in Ghana studying drumming and xylophone music, and emphasizes that Roach's "intention was not to go back to America and reproduce what he learned. On the contrary, his interest lay in acquiring a better sense of the organization and generative processes of this music which he could use creatively in his own way" (x). The same, of course, can be said about European composer György Ligeti (1923–2006), who was deeply interested in the composition techniques of the court music of the Kingdom of Buganda (cf. Ligeti's interview in *Die Zeit*, Feuilleton, 57, no. 5, 1988) but never plagiarized the music.

During the last few decades the geographical range of field research in African and African American cultures has been considerably widened. While our much revered predecessors were focusing at the most on four to five different geographical areas in their data gathering—Melville J. and Francis Herskovits on Surinam, northeastern Brazil, Dahomey, Haiti, etc., or Nicholas G. J. Ballanta on Liberia, the US, and West African coastal traditions—our generation has been fortunate to work in a multitude of societies comparatively, widening the geographical coverage. I myself, with associated researchers on numerous fieldtrips, notably Maurice Djenda, Fortunato Pereira Gonçalves, Mario Ruy de Rocha Matos, Helmut Hillegeist, Donald Kachamba, Kayombo kaChinyeka, Moya and Lidiya Malamusi, Mose Yotamu, and others, have made some twenty-eight thousand field recordings in eighteen African countries over a span of fifty-three years. This collection is considerably larger than anything one could have accomplished in the 1930s and '40s with the equipment then available. In addition to our African field recordings, three of us have covered parts of Brazil, a bit of Venezuela, and in the 1990s it was possible for Moya A. Malamusi and me to work with David Evans, University of Memphis, who took us on joint field trips to the southern United States. Besides our studies of the jazz and blues literature in the library of the CBMR in Chicago in 1997,[*] these trips were an essential experience resulting in my book *Africa and the Blues* (1999a).

Using this database we can now reconstruct historical sequences. Sometimes we can also do so through the comparative study of artifacts and instrument-making technology. There are large collections of African musical instruments in museums around the world, comprising specimens from the early nineteenth to the mid-twentieth centuries. They testify to tremendous technological expertise and power of innovation. I have carried out one such study on lamellophones, variously called *mbira*, *nsansi*, or *kalimba*, which constitute one of the most important African instrumental inventions in history (Kubik 1998d, 1999b, 2002a). The study included some New World derivatives, from nineteenth-century Brazilian specimens that are preserved in the Völkerkunde Museum, Vienna, and in the Pitt Rivers Museum, Oxford, to the ubiquitous Caribbean *marimbula*.

This wealth of information made me realize that there are certain pathways in human creativity that display remarkable resilience, while some others are experimental, even ephemeral, but may yet be pursued further by later generations. It is important to sort that out systematically, case by case, and prognosticate rates of survival.

In the realm of tuning systems, for example, we found that partials-based tonal systems, such as occur in certain musical cultures of the West African savannah, or in East Africa among the Wagogo and in South Africa, are particularly resilient. In a situation of culture contact they tend to impose their structures on other tonal worlds, subverting them. That happened in the United States in the late nineteenth century, leading to the blues; and it has also happened independently in the rise of *mbaqanga* and modern jazz in South Africa.

---

[*] We gratefully acknowledge that our work at the CBMR, Chicago in 1997 was carried out with a Rockefeller stipend. The Center hosted Moya A. Malamusi, two of his children, and me while in Chicago.

Among the traits of considerable resilience in African music, there is also the ubiquitous call-and-response organization in many musical genres, as well as other polyphonic devices: riff patterning, parallelism, interlocking, etc. Further, there is the general tendency to independent phrasings of melodic accents in songs, following speech patterns by stringing words and sentences according to the principle of one syllable per elementary pulse-unit, irrespective of the underlying meter or dance beat. This is very different from the formation of Greek verse, for example. It results in accents that cross the beat, "off beat phrasing of melodic accents," as first described by Richard A. Waterman in 1952. These age-old developments in the music of sub-Saharan Africa are shared with jazz.

The same applies to an audio-psychological phenomenon such as swing, so important in various definitions of jazz. Swing is age-old in African music, but it is an effect only aimed at in certain African musical styles. It is not a universal phenomenon in the music of sub-Saharan Africa. Possibly swing as a kinemic-auditory phenomenon was first discovered in early West African savannah agricultural societies through women's work, such as grinding millet. Archaeology and genetic research of plants suggest that millet agriculture (sorghum, pearl millet, etc.) and that of other African cereals developed ca. 5000–1000 BCE, according to J. E. G. Sutton, Professor of Archaeology at the University of Ghana, Legon (cf. map in Murray 1981: 43). That gives swing a possible time span.

A recording I made by chance in a remote area of central Cameroon on February 14, 1964, demonstrates this kind of integration of voice and work rhythm. In a lonely hamlet on a thirty-kilometer walk through the savannah in the company of one youngster, we bumped into a Tikar-speaking mother with her child, as she was kneeling on the veranda of her house while grinding maize (in earlier times it was millet), and singing a song of complaint in blues-like tonality. Tremendous swing was emerging from the accents in her grinding rhythm. It was the result of sound kicks that fell on the last elementary pulse-unit of each series of triplets. I have discussed her song in greater detail elsewhere (Kubik 1999a: 73–78).

Historically connected with rhythmic organization that generates swing is a second principle of construction in some African music, which may have originated from work division in pounding, when two, sometimes three women gather around a mortar with their pestles, and strike alternately while sharing a song. I recorded one example among the Chamba in northeastern Nigeria in 1963 (Kubik 2010: 11; CD track 3). Each singer relates the song's accents to her own pestle strokes, thereby operating from a relative, individual reference beat. This is probably how the interlocking technique, found in many African xylophone styles and some drumming (first documented by A. M. Jones in Northern Rhodesia in 1934; Jones 1949), may have originated in remote history. It actually takes only a short evolutionary step to transfer the millet-pounding organization of strokes to drumming and log xylophone playing in duple- or triple-division interlocking style. If the alternating strokes combine to suggest a cycle of twelve or twenty-four underlying pulse-units, with accents anticipating the song's dance beat, the result is a lilting effect in the rhythmic structure that swings.

Also from savannah communities in Cameroon is an example I recorded in 1964 of another kind of music generating an enormous feeling of swing. Omaru Sanda, a musician at the court of Vute Chief Emtse, created variations on a large *timbrh* raffia-manufactured lamellophone by using his thumbs in a fast, alternating left/right movement, always sounding two adjacent lamellae at once with the same thumb. The lamellae were tuned in octave pairs. However, what one hears (and that is universal, it does not depend on one's cultural background) is far from a mere rippling of fast notes; it is something the performer has not played, although he designed the structure so that such an effect would emerge. The total image of his playing action splits into auditory patterns perceptible at different pitch levels. For the audience it is as if two to three independent, interwoven melodic-rhythmic lines were coming up in the variations, one in the bass, another in the middle range, another in the higher pitch range. This is the so-called inherent pattern (i.p.) effect, which I have described on various occasions (Kubik 2010: II: 107–30) as an audio-psychological illusion effect, aimed at and explored by various African music composers. As a compositional device it is concentrated in southern Uganda (e.g., xylophone music in Buganda and Busoga), but also is found among the Tikar and Vute chief musicians in central Cameroon, and in some other places of Africa. Many people have been amazed at Omaru Sanda's performance, whenever I play those recordings in lectures. People cannot believe that it is generated by a single person with only two thumbs (Track 5, CD in Castagneto ed. 2007).

Looking at jazz from the background of our African data opens up a special terrain of research. On several occasions in these books I will invite readers to time-travel from Africa to the United States and back, learning about a Ghanaian brass band instructor, visiting nineteenth-century New Orleans on the trail of Marie Laveau, and delving into a photographic riddle concerning Buddy Bolden's only known picture taken of him and his band around 1900. Much of the space available will be devoted to a presentation of our own field research as it relates to the topic and to attempted historical reconstructions.

It is not possible to cover all the fascinating topics relating to the transatlantic approach in two books. This particularly concerns the second part of Mensah's "round trip": the "return" of African American music to Africa, not only jazz but a great variety of genres. Calypso records were already on sale in the former Gold Coast during the 1920s. From the 1940s to the 1960s, jazz proper caused reverberations in nearly all urban areas of Africa, but was soon eclipsed by the much stronger impact of other African American genres: rumba, pachanga, chachacha, and merengue in Central Africa; the twist in eastern and southern Africa during the early 1960s, etc. Soul music, especially by the Godfather James Brown, conquered several West African cities in the 1970s and '80s as a result of his tours, and reggae as well as Rastafarian culture have left a permanent mark in southern Africa and elsewhere.

To be accurate, however, it is fair to say that, in terms of mass audiences, jazz had a spotty presence in most parts of Africa, even at the height of its worldwide popularity after 1945—with the exception of South Africa. There, the impact was particularly strong. Elsewhere it was usually celebrated and studied by small circles of fans and urban musicians with access to jazz records and instruments, such as in Dakar and St. Louis, Senegal, where an annual jazz festival was initiated in the 1960s and is still held. Other such places were Addis Ababa in Ethiopia (Falceto 2001) and Accra in Ghana (Feld 2012), particularly after Louis Armstrong's 1956 visit. And yet the word "jazz" is almost universally current in Africa, though often with decisively altered connotations.

As to those fringe cases of the presence of jazz in Africa, they are now mostly history. If I listed them all, it would inflate our subject without adding essential information. Instead, I will concentrate in the second volume of *Jazz Transatlantic* (Mensah's "return" or "round trip") on southern Africa and South Africa in particular, where several forms of jazz, from swing to post-bop modern jazz have left an indelible historical mark and generated specific South African versions that were carried by personalities such as Abdullah Ibrahim (Dollar Brand), Winston Mankunku Ngozi, Duke Makasi, Gideon Nxumalo, and many others. The contribution by South African musicians to jazz history is significant and underlines the extent to which we may consider jazz to be part of a larger transatlantic family of musical styles.

The subject is not easy to tackle, however, as was pointed out by writer Lewis Nkosi in 1966 in a paper "Jazz in Exile," published in the magazine *Transition*. Referring to Chris McGregor's Blue Note quintet with Dudu Pukwana on alto sax and to a Johannesburg recording of his big band (*Jazz—the African Sound*, Gallotone/New Sound NSL 1011), especially to "Pondo Blues," Nkosi points to "some fructifying explorations of the indigenous African idiom." Mentioning what we would now call Short Cycle Form as a major contribution by South Africans to jazz, he emphasizes the existence of

a harmonic tension based on the overlapping of solo and chorus lines which may lead to the singing of two melodic lines simultaneously, and a very complex metric organization in which some beats are longer than others and accent is constantly being shifted, thus bringing about an element of frequent surprises for both players and dancers. For instance a song played in 4/4 time may suddenly seem to have shifted into 6/8 or 3/4. A number of South African jazz musicians are now going back to this African heritage for new ideas. It is interesting to note that by doing so they arrive at the same point where post-bop musicians like John Coltrane now find themselves though using different routes. (Nkosi 1966: 36)

Such analysis was already available in 1966 by a South African writer born 1936 in Durban, with engagement and intensive knowledge of jazz history.

As an illustration to Lewis Nkosi's thesis, I will also focus in *Jazz Transatlantic II* on a group of musicians I have admired since 1969, when I first came across their music thanks to the late Irene Frangs, who used to frequent all jazz spots in Johannesburg, defying apartheid restrictions. The group was the Soul Jazzmen from Port Elizabeth, with Duke Makasi on tenor sax, Tete Mbambisa on piano, Psyche T. Ntsele on bass, and Mafufu Jama on drums. Their composition "Inhlupeko," which means "suffering" or "distress," is a precious example of how a mbaqanga cyclic theme was integrated into an AABA jazz form. This was post-bop jazz, in the tradition of John Coltrane, but with a remarkable South African tinge.*

Lewis Nkosi arrived at an interesting explanation of why jazz caught on so decisively in that part of Africa:

> The industrial culture in South Africa especially, more than anywhere else on the continent of Africa, provides an ambiance where fusion between the Western and the African heritage has gone so far as to produce a new urban idiom. *Mbaqanga*, upon which South African modern jazzmen are constantly feeding, is really a fusion of American jazz forms with some of these African strands I have enumerated. On any day in Johannesburg you can see shabby unemployed young Africans dancing on the pavements of the city to this jive music which is relayed by loudspeakers from inside record shops. If they survive the constant police raids, some of these kids, like Miriam Makeba, have gone on to conquer the world stage. (Nkosi 1966: 36)

Apart from the common African origins of much of their vocabulary and structure, all the expressions of jazz in Africa share transatlantic family relationships. Within that framework they are being created and re-created in never-ending contacts and exchanges.

---

* I am grateful to Diane Thram of the International Library of African Music, Rhodes University, Grahamstown, South Africa, for having copied for me the LP on which this title was first published in 1969.

PART A

Jazz—The Word and Some Other Words

In 1960 cultural anthropologist Alan P. Merriam published an article under the title "Jazz—The Word" in *Jazz Review*, vol. 3, March–August. Decades later it was reprinted with some corrections, supplementary notes, and an updated bibliography (Merriam and Garner 1998: 7–31). Its principal objectives were (a) to examine the literature from 1917 to 1958 for ideas about the origin and meanings of the term "jazz," and (b) to establish when the word was first used in connection with a specific type of music.

Summaries dealing with some of these questions had appeared before, by Osgood (1926), Blesh and Janis (1950), and others. But it was Merriam who took the trouble to look through the earliest then available sources and systematically compare them. His survey begins with Walter Kingsley's 1917 article "Whence comes jass? Facts from the great authority on the subject" in the *New York Sun*.

Scrutinizing the bibliography compiled by Merriam and Garner (1998), one is faced with the question of which are primary sources and which are not. The danger is always that one may give too much weight of credence to retrospective accounts, as compared to commentary from the period concerned, and also fall into the trap of mistaking secondary material—often diluted, heavily reinterpreted—for the original. The same applies, of course, to recorded music and, for example, to the ultimate source of the theme of "Livery Stable Blues" recorded by the Original Dixieland Jass Band for Victor in New York in 1917 (Charters 2008: 142–48). The controversy about copyright between Yellow Nunez and Nick La Rocca might even have an unaccountable twist, if it ever turned out that the theme and some basic variations had been borrowed from unknown musicians in New Orleans who were lacking the education or possibility of legal assistance to register and defend their legitimate claims.

In their article on sheet music and the commercial ascendancy of the blues (Evans 2008: 49–104), Lynn Abbott and Doug Seroff have pointed out that US copyright laws were anathema to the creative process of folk-blues construction, which relied on the unrestricted recombination of commonly shared rhymes, metaphors, themes, etc. This was the contradiction that played out in the case of "Livery Stable Blues." Ultimately it brought into question the very notion of copyright claims, if—in fact—oral tradition was so much involved. (On "Livery Stable Blues" see also Abbott and Seroff 2007.)

After the first jazz recordings on disc appeared in 1917, there was a wave of anonymous commentary in periodicals such as the *Literary Digest*, the *Music Trade Review*, and *Current Opinion* about the new music. Both the music and the word stirred reactions, and one of the queries raised by those who were convinced of belonging to an advanced civilization was: "Why 'jazz' sends us back to the jungle" (*Current Opinion* 65: 165, September 1918). A mixture of factual observation and wild speculation made it into the media. One of the earliest substantial jazz commentaries was the article "Jass and Jassism," which appeared in the June 20, 1918, edition of the New Orleans daily *Times-Picayune*, attracting many letters by readers.

In 1924 a movement gained momentum to abolish the word "jazz" because of "undesirable" by-meanings and immoral influence upon young people. Other words were proposed for its replacement, but none was adopted by the public. In the 1930s "swing" took over temporarily, investing itself into the then-current youth culture, just as jazz had done a generation earlier. In 1949 another attempt was made, this time by the editors of *Down Beat*, probably as a promotional gimmick, to replace the word jazz which in the meantime had gained new currency due to the New Orleans revival promoted by researchers in jazz history. It was in vain; the word jazz stayed on. But some of the other words proposed by those who wanted to get the thousand dollars offered for the winner of the contest survived into the future to become attached to new musical genres: hip → hip hop; freestyle → free jazz; beatpoint, beatfelt, etc. → beat music. "Freestyle" now refers to an improvisational type of rap. There was no trace in the proposals sent to *Down Beat* of a term like rock 'n' roll, which would rise to prominence within the next few years, designating a blues-derived music with a strong appeal to the next young people's generation.

Earlier iterations of "rocking," and "rolling" in relation to blues and gospel song, were, of course, plentiful (see the song index of *Blues and Gospel Records 1890–1943*), but *Down Beat* readers participating in the contest did not take up those leads. In the 1950s, some jazz terminology was adopted in rock 'n' roll, such as "doing the bop" and "Bopping the Blues," the title of a Carl Perkins rockabilly record.

In America and elsewhere, since 1917 the word "jazz" had conquered the sheet music and record market. In Europe the word "jazz" had also irrevocably caught on. Many writings in French, and the founding of the Hot Club de France in Paris in 1932, were instrumental in promoting the word. But its use was now restricted to what French jazz fans called "le vrai jazz" (the true jazz), in contrast to cheap commercialized alterations.

Earliest Known Printed Sources

Before we proceed any further, it is important to lay bare—on the basis of present-day knowledge—where the earliest known printed sources of the word "jazz" can be found. Here something came up that was a surprise for jazz historians: (1) the earliest known printed appearance of the word was in connection with sports, not with music; (2) it was traced to newspapers in San Francisco and Los Angeles, and not to New Orleans or any other place in the South; (3) the word erupted all of a sudden in 1913 to become part of a quickly spreading sports jargon that was used by reporters on the West Coast with reference to baseball.

Early hints that the word was known on the West Coast had appeared in an anonymous article published in 1919 (cf. Merriam and Garner 1998: 22). This news received support in another anonymous article in 1924 (*Etude* 12: 517–18, 520; 595–96, August/September). Eventually, in 1939 a text by the noted San Francisco etymologist Peter Tamony clarified the matter:

Late in February, 1913, the San Francisco Seals went into training at Boyes Springs.... Mr. Slattery, a sports editor, had heard the word jazz in craps games around San Francisco. It is a Creole word and means, in general, to speed up.... Mr. Slattery, with a sports-writer's sense of the striking, began to use "jazz" as a synonym for "ginger" and "pep." In a few days the novelty was taken up by other writers and the people around the camp, and was used in all descriptions. On the field the players were full of the old jazz, and there was jazz in the effervescent waters of the springs. Everything was jazzy, including the music Art Hickman played for the entertainment of the players and visitors.... The music he provided was his stylization of the ragtime of the day. It was an immediate hit. James Woods, manager of the Hotel St. Francis, heard Hickman while on a visit to Boyes. After Hickman opened at the St. Francis, national use of the word was only a matter of time. (1939: 5)

Henry Osborne Osgood (1926: 18), in his book *So This Is Jazz*, referred to a panel of possible uses of the word jazz in San Francisco:

Speaking of different meanings, Ferdie Grofé ... tells of a peculiar use of the word jazz in San Francisco, which does not seem to have obtained anywhere else. Out there in the years just preceding the War there were certain large and popular cafés which maintained orchestras and also a regular pianist, and gave cabaret performances, limited, however, to singing by young women. Each one had a solo to sing and occasionally they joined in an ensemble. They did not sing their solos from the stage where the pianist was stationed. It was part of their duties to mingle with the guests and join them at table. Whenever one of them heard the pianist begin the prelude to her number, she would rise wherever she happened to be and sing, but when the pianist decided it was time for an ensemble, he would announce, "The next number will be jazz," and they would all troop back to the stage. There was no extra "pepping up" or rhythmic exaggeration in these choruses, and the word appears to have had no special significance as regards the music, simply meaning that it would be sung *tutti* instead of solo. (1926: 18)

In the periods after Merriam's original 1960 article, research on the origins of the word did not come to a standstill. Some of the new findings have been summarized in chapter 1 of Lewis Porter's book *Jazz—A Century of Change* (1997) under the title "Where did the word *jazz* come from?"

In a well-researched article, "Our Word Jazz" published in *Storyville* 50 (December/January 1973/74), Dick Holbrook, an expert in this field of study, gave credit to Peter Tamony for having found the earliest printed reference to the word in the *San Francisco Bulletin*, a daily newspaper, dated March 3, 1913, in a story by Edgar "Scoop" Gleeson on the sports pages, in which the latter was hailing the achievements of McCarl, a member of the San Francisco Seals baseball team. The word reappears again in Gleeson's baseball stories throughout the month of March, albeit with no specific reference to music, except a casual mentioning of ragtime.

Very soon, one of Gleeson's colleagues, Ernest J. Hopkins, would produce a feature article on the new word jazz. Published in the *San Francisco Bulletin* on April 5, 1913, Hopkins begins by calling the word "futuristic." He said that it had become current in the office of the *San Francisco Bulletin* to an extent that there were quarrels between the employees about its spelling, "jazz" or "jaz," and that there were two factions on the staff violently opposed to each other. He gave a long list of related meanings to the word, from vigor, verve, virility, to happiness, and examples of its actual usage. It was then almost incessantly used in conversations about sports, and eventually about everything. The writer stressed that "anything that takes manliness or effort or energy or activity or strength of soul is 'jaz.'" He added: "The sheer musical quality of the word, that delightful sound like the crackling of a brisk electric spark, commends it. It belongs to the class of onomatopoeia. It was important that this vacancy in our language should have been filled with a word of proper sound" (quoted from Porter 1997: 7).

Here one begins to prick one's ears. If there was a vacancy to be filled in the English language, then "jazz" or "jaz" could not be English and should have arrived from somewhere, even from far away, perhaps from a tone language, because of its musical, even percussive quality (due to the buzzing "z" sound). That it was an onomatopoeic ideophone, as we would say today, was observed correctly. An ideophone is a short sound structure used symbolically to describe a state, an action, a manner, quality, idea, even a smell. As a denominator it operates outside grammar, and can be used as an adjective, verb, noun, or intensifier of any other verb. An ideophone can be monosyllabic like "jaz," but also composed of several syllables, and many are onomatopoeic.

The use of such a word, almost overnight, by many people is a sure indicator of its novelty in the place concerned. It had started to be used in San Francisco that year in baseball reviews, expressing qualities of concentration and energy that experienced players had possessed in the past, but the present generation had still to acquire, in the sense of pep and enthusiasm. The "old jazz" was like a magic parcel that could get lost and then only "jazzless" San Francisco Seals would remain. But "jazz" might be brought back to them in a "jazz wagon" ...

How the word got associated with music was discussed by the same sports writer E. T. "Scoop" Gleeson in an article published twenty-five years later in the *San Francisco Call Bulletin*, September 3, 1938. The popular band of Art Hickman, indelible in American music history and also mentioned in Peter Tamony's account a year later, was performing ragtime-based music for dancers at Boyes Springs, where the San Francisco Seals then practiced. Apparently the word, which was associated with dice, was then applied to Hickman's orchestra, which was described as "the jazziest tune tooters in all the Valley of the Moon." Gleeson claimed that he remembered all this.

Recently, researcher Lawrence Gushee (2005: 132, 299) has been intensively engaged in the search for the historical background of the word. He discovered in an April 1912 edition of the *Los Angeles Times* what seems to be the oldest written source testifying to the musical application of the term, still in the realm of baseball. And in 1913 a band going to play in the training camp for the San Francisco Seals was described as a "jazz band." Bands that sit in the grandstands at sports events are still known as "pep bands," David Evans tells me. "Pep" means sexual stamina, and more generally, energy (personal communication, May 10, 2012). So there is also this string of associations between "jazz band" and "pep band" with other implicit meanings.

The next series of sources in the chronology takes us to another city: Chicago, to where the word spread either from the West Coast shortly after 1913, or was already established there for some time and of other, unknown provenance. In interviews with members of Tom Brown's Band, the New Orleans ragtime band that was invited to play in Chicago at Lamb's Cafe in 1915, its cornetist, Ray Lopez (born 1889), reported half a century later how the word "jass" (in this spelling) had made its appearance that year. The musicians were used to calling what they played ragtime and blues (in the sense of "slow drag"). They were surprised to find that in Chicago their music would be given a different name. Their attention to the new word was drawn during a demonstration against them outside the café by people denouncing the noisy sounds produced by the band and the fact that they were not members of the musicians' union in Chicago.

According to what bandleader Tom Brown remembered, there was a placard carrying the message "Don't Patronize This Jass Music." Obviously, a word like "jazz" or "jass"—mostly with unfavorable connotations—was known in Chicago by 1915 (Charters 2008: 114–18).

Here we might add that the mere fact of invitation of a New Orleans–based group to Chicago suggests that ragtime and blues-related music had been known in Chicago for some time and that entrepreneurs in Chicago were fascinated by the novelty of New Orleans music and its commercial potential. One should also not forget that in 1893 Chicago was for six months the venue of the World's Columbian Exposition, a cultural and trade fair, with musical groups from many parts of the United States, and even overseas, being heard. Within the vaudeville theatre circuits musicians from New Orleans, St. Louis, and many other places were also regularly traveling all over the United States from the 1890s on. (See also Abbott and Seroff 2002.)

In his book *Pioneers of Jazz: The Story of the Creole Band* (2005), Lawrence Gushee reports about a letter by Ray Lopez, the band's cornetist, in which he said that once, when they had just finished playing a conventional number, "Hawaiian Butterfly," a man from South Side Chicago shouted at them: "jazz it up, Ray!" Thereafter the band played some up-tempo piece, "jazzing it up," meaning play with more vigor and energy, and also play loud (Gushee 2005: 138). That means that the word was definitely also used as a verb. More recently, Lewis Porter (1997: 8) has pointed out that "Some of the original uses of the word jazz still survive. People still use it to mean 'lively' or 'energetic' as in 'That's a real jazzy outfit' or 'Let's jazz up this party.'"

As a noun, the word was intriguing for the proprietors of Lamb's Café. Forthwith the band was advertised as "Brown's Dixieland Jass Band, Direct from New Orleans, Best Dance Music in Chicago" (Charters 2008: 118). So in 1915 New Orleans had already become a trademark city for musical quality. That the use of the word "jazz"—with the *zz* spelling—had come up in sports circles in San Francisco in 1913, and then surfaced in Chicago two years later with an *ss* spelling in connection with improvised ragtime played by a band from New Orleans, poses many questions that go beyond the search for clarifying the word's etymology. Apart from the date of its first appearance in Chicago, it would be crucial to know: in which kind of social environment, in which kind of community was it first used in Chicago, before the arrival of that band train-ferried all the way up from the South?

No one among the members of Tom Brown's Band in Chicago could have provided information of that kind, and such a question was not even posed. They were foreigners in Chicago, guest workers without union support, "sans-papiers." Tom Brown's Band had been hired in New Orleans by an entrepreneur from Chicago, Joseph Gorham, based on the band's sound as it existed in New

Orleans. Although we do not know what they sounded like, dance was equally important as an aspect of acceptance by northern audiences. It is clear that there was a gradually emerging colony of New Orleans musicians in Chicago. How they adapted to local tastes did affect perceptions of what constituted jazz during the period 1915 to 1920. All of a sudden, it seems, the word "jazz" was there, used by somebody who had picked it up from someone else, and that person again picked it up somewhere, and so on. Since no jazz researchers were yet active in 1915 to witness its early uses and contexts and start inquiries after the word first appeared—they could not have anticipated how important it would be—memory and oral tradition are the principal type of sources we have. And oral tradition of this kind, according to Lawrence Gushee, seems to hold that New Orleans musicians first heard the word in Chicago, and that it became current in New Orleans only after the Original Dixieland Jass Band had recorded in 1917 in New York.

That can be disputed. Dick Holbrook (1976), in his story of Ray Lopez, reports that the latter mentioned a nonmusical use of the word by William Demarest while rehearsing a vaudeville act in a Canal Street theater in New Orleans, ca. 1910. This statement seems to correct the assumption by Gushee that the word was unknown in New Orleans prior to the 1917 recordings by the Original Dixieland Jass Band. Some important written information relating to that period has been retrieved most recently by Lynn Abbott and Doug Seroff in their book *Ragged But Right* (2007). From there emerges the importance of the traveling shows by African Americans during the first two decades of the twentieth century, preparing the terrain for the rise of blues and jazz. The vaudeville circuits and circus enterprises turned out to be a significant background to the competitive ascent of African Americans in theatre and show business, and a breeding ground for the further development of band ragtime and blues toward national recognition. Just a year after the Tom Brown event in Chicago, an African American newspaper, the *Indianapolis Freeman*, testifies to the fact that by 1916 the word "jazz" in various spellings was common in the Midwest, and had become a fashionable word for a new style of playing ragtime.

The October 28, 1916, issue of the *Freeman* advertises John H. Wickliffe's Ginger Orchestra: "Styled America's Greatest Jaz Combination, Now at the Regent Theatre, Indianapolis." It is hailed as "the first orchestra of Colored players that has appeared at that house." All its members and their specialties are then introduced and the page ends with the statement: "Just can't keep still when the Jaz combination plays. It will appear at the Washington theatre Saturday evening." (See original reproduction and picture of the eight-piece orchestra in Abbott and Seroff 2007: 172). It is most interesting that by 1916 the word "jazz," in whatever spelling, was beginning to give rise to derivatives, such as "Jaz combination." With trumpet, trombone, clarinet, and banjo, Wickliff's Ginger Orchestra matches what had become a kind of standard instrumentation of groups that would be associated with the word "jazz."

Published ragtime compositions and W. C. Handy's blues were an indispensable part of the repertoire of African American musical groups appearing in the so-called "annex" or sideshow tent of circus companies. P. G. Lowery and his orchestra traveled from 1899 on with various circus companies, including the famous Wallace-Hagenbeck Circus in 1910. R. Roy Pope and his circus annex band was another group active by 1911, using brass instruments and drums. Prof. James Wolfscale's Concert Band was one of the most notable and widely recognized groups, shortly before World War I. "Wolfscale opened the 1914 season with a concert band of thirty-two pieces," writes the research team Abbott and Seroff (2007: 168). Thus the circus bands demonstrate that the concept of the big band was not as remote in the 1930s as has been thought. There are parallels in organization and the status of the leader. By 1916 the circus band, though versatile in its repertoire, had a significant portion of proto-jazz in it. Abbott and Seroff (2007: 170) write that "Blues and emerging jazz were increasingly significant in Prof. Wolfscale's musical program during the 1915 and 1916 seasons."

It was in these years that the term jazz became current. James Wolfscale's son Roy, cornetist, had joined the John Wickcliff's Ginger Band of Chicago in 1916. They had an engagement at Schlitz Palm Garden in Milwaukee and the Grunewald Café in Minneapolis (Abbott and Seroff 2007: 171–72). Introducing the new style of dance music to audiences in the Midwest is an important commentary signed by H. Jones in a column called "Cream City News" in the *Indianapolis Freeman*, December 22, 1917: "J.H. Wickliffe and his famous Ginger Band will settle all questions with the Dixieland Jazz Band about who are the originators of the jazz music. At least Milwaukeans, both white and colored, have decided among themselves that there is no better bunch of real musicians for playing anything from Tannhauser to the Livery Stable Blues than Wickliffe's Ginger Orchestra" (cited in Abbott and Seroff 2007: 170–71).

As a leading fun maker in Prof. Wolfscale's company, Slim Mason had a share in the rise of jazz. His most successful jazzy feature "Walking the Dog" was the hit of the day and was performed in 1916, besides "Dancing the Jelly Roll" and other "dance craze" hits.

In the 1917 circus season, Wolfscale's aggregation was active presenting a new female actor, the diminutive Princess Wee Wee, on the show *Moonlight on the Levee*. In this context the word jazz appears in two spellings (a) with reference to "Princess Wee Wee And Her Jass Band" in the *Indianapolis Freeman*, December 1, 1917, and (b) in a delightful advertisement in the *Philadelphia Tribune*, February 3, 1917—several months earlier—as "Princess Wee Wee and Jez Band Co." (Abbott and Seroff 2007: 173–74).

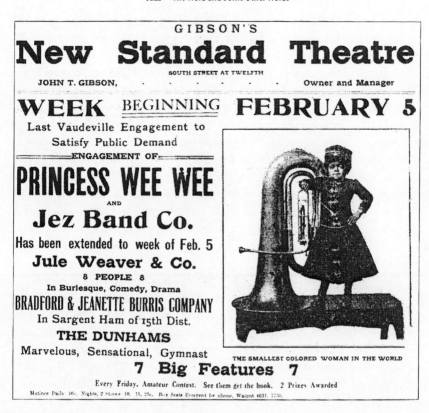

Fig. 1.1. Advertising Princess Wee Wee and Jez Band Co., *Philadelphia Tribune*, February 3, 1917 (reproduced from Abbott and Seroff 2007: 174)

The ambivalence in spellings of the new word, "jazz" or "jaz" or "jass" or "jez," is most significant psychologically, since it indicates that there was a struggle in the public's collective mind to come to terms with its contents.

Meanings and Historical Connections

In the introduction to his book, Lewis Porter (1997) pointed out that, during the 1920s, "the word *jazz* was applied to a much wider range of music than it is today. In the 1920s, white observers writing about jazz used to refer to the written songs of George Gershwin and Irving Berlin just as much as to the recordings of such black artists as Duke Ellington and Louis Armstrong" (11). This wider meaning was also shared in many places in Europe, where any dance band in Germany between World War I and II playing sequences of foxtrot, shimmy and Charleston, besides tangos and waltzes, and after 1930 also rumba, would be called a jazz band. Some Germans began to pronounce the word as *yats*, according to German pronunciation rules.

But during the dictatorship of the National Socialist German Workers Party, 1933–1945, the word *jazz* came to be replaced by swing, as it was in the United States, and consequently, youngsters who liked this music were denounced as "Swing Heinis." In France it appears that the concept of "le vrai jazz" had already taken over in the late 1920s, and so the situation was different.

Our next task is to delineate the semantic field of the word, both as a noun and as a verb, in different contexts of its usage across time. Since usages change greatly, sometimes abruptly, this set of inquiries is also essentially historical. A new word is normally used by people without giving thought to its origins, but simply because it sounds attractive, alludes to something, or applies to events that startled everybody, such as the appearance of Tom Brown's Band at Lamb's Café in Chicago in 1915.

Alan P. Merriam was carrying out a thorough scientific job, supplemented by Fradley H. Garner, the 1998 editor of the reprint of "Jazz—The Word." Merriam divides his survey into sections, each devoted to a different set of assumptions and queries by various informants and authors about the origin of the word "jazz": 1) from personal names; 2) as a minstrel or vaudeville term; 3) from a language other than English.

"As derived from personal names": Here a famous story by an anonymous writer that appeared in the *Music Trade Review*, June 14, 1919, is quoted. This was two years after the name had appeared on the 78 r.p.m. records of the Original Dixieland Jass Band:

Chicago, Ill., June 9. Roger Graham, Chicago music publisher, has his own pet theory of the origin of jazz music and firmly believes it to be the true one. Five years ago, in Sam Hare's Schiller Cafe on Thirty-first Street, "Jasbo" Brown and five other alleged musicians, members of what might have been called, with the aid of imagination, an orchestra, dispensed "melody" largely for the benefit of Sam Hare's patrons. Jasbo doubled with the piccolo and cornet. When he was sober Jasbo played orthodox music, but wrapped around three or four glasses of gin Jasbo had a way of making his piccolo produce strains of the wildest, most barbaric abandon. Strange to say, though, Mr. Hare's patrons, if they could help it, never allowed Jasbo to maintain sobriety while on the job. They liked the thrilling sensation of the piccolo's lawless strains, and when Jasbo put a tomato can on the end of his cornet it seemed as if the music with its strange, quivering pulsations came from another world.

Patrons offered Jasbo more and more gin. First it was the query "More, Jasbo?" directed at the darky's thirst; then the insistence, "More, Jasbo!" directed at the darky's music, and just plain "more jazz!" (Anon. 1919c: 32)

This story was immediately picked up by other writers, and like a folktale it was told and retold with numerous variations during the next twenty years (see Merriam and Garner 1998: 8–11 for other versions). It contains a credible testimony to the use of the technique of "muted cornet" (with a "tomato can") around 1914 at Sam Hare's Schiller Café on 31st Street, Chicago, by that legendary Jasbo Brown and his group. They were obviously playing some unusual music besides the "legitimate" stuff. King Oliver and others later popularized the "muted cornet." The story also testifies to the involvement of African Americans in the Chicago music scene by 1914. But in 1903 musicians such as Charles Elgar, a Creole violinist and clarinetist, already were active in Chicago. There was considerable African American musical activity before 1914. Jasbo Brown, it seems, was a somewhat restrained personality who needed a drink to excel himself, not unusual with musicians of that generation. Obviously, Jasbo is a nickname, someone who has "jass."

Later writers have often dismissed the Jasbo Brown anecdote as a fairy tale, but there is substantial, even unique information in it that cannot be brushed away. From broad, worldwide studies of oral tradition we know that anecdotes, legends, even rumors are not necessarily baseless; not even fairy tales are. There are certain patterns in the workings of the human mind, how it condenses material into a story. Factual history may well end up being distorted, diluted, misunderstood, and mixed up, but there is always some kind of system behind it. A word may be changed in its meaning, its use may be shifted to another occasion (different from the one remembered), two persons or places or events may be superposed and merged into one. That is why we may ask the question whether there was perhaps one identity between the protagonists "Jasbo Brown" and "Tom Brown" in the two different stories, in view of the fact that both names are part of events supposed to have taken place in 1915 and 1914 respectively, and in Chicago (synchronicity of time, identity of place, similarity of venue and of the names of the protagonists).

Or does Jasbo Brown stand for an African American counterpart of Tom Brown in another café in Chicago, doing all those gimmicks which were imitated by later bands to earn publicity? The fact that union members and their sympathizers demonstrated against this band from New Orleans, denouncing its music as "jass," implies that some comparison was being made with music to which "jass" or even "jazz" (in this pronunciation) had been applied before. In other words, did Tom Brown and his group have a shadow in Chicago?

Almost a hundred years have now passed since the story quoted from music publisher Roger Graham (who had published the Ray Lopez/Alcide Nunez iteration of "Livery Stable Blues") appeared in the *Music Trade Review*, June 14, 1919, and it is still a source of much controversy. One opinion is that there was (by implication) no Jasbo Brown at all, but that it refers to the Original Dixieland

Jass Band. Lynn Abbott has written this (personal communication, March 14, 2012):

> Schiller's Café was where the original incarnation of the Original Dixieland Jass Band first held forth in Chicago. A portion of the article not quoted by you goes on to say that, before they arrived in Chicago from New Orleans, "Jasbo's' band was known as the 'Pup Jazz *Band*!'" It seems safe to say that this refers to the Pup Café in New Orleans, where the original incarnation of the Original Dixieland Jass Band was working when they got the offer to go to Chicago. Finally, regarding the tomato-can mute reference, an early photograph of the Original Dixieland Jass Band has LaRocca posing with a sugar-can mute. But, the reference to "Jasbo" as a "darky" doesn't jive with anything else in the article.
>
> Period references to "Jasbo" that predate the *Music Trade Review* article come from as early as 1913, when a tune called "Jasbo Rag" was listed on a program performed by a concert band in Tulsa, Oklahoma. By 1919 there were many "Jasbos" in American popular entertainment.

Another claim for the first appearance of the term "jazz" with reference to music was made by bandleader James Reese Europe, who said in 1919 that there was a band of four pieces about fifteen years before in New Orleans, called "Razz's band" for short, and then this got changed to "Jazz's band." This is a simple, less intriguing story and perhaps more easily interpreted. Since the word "jazz" had after 1915 begun to taste sweet on everyone's lips, similar names would then easily be converted into the popular term. The psychology behind this process is analogous to what happens in cross-language jokes, in which a foreign word or phrase is "understood" as if it were a term in one's own language. Such jokes were prominent in colonial Africa, and sometimes displayed in a theatrical sketch. In 1958 Hugh Tracey recorded one such verbal play from actors Stephen R. Gumbo and J. G. Zimivara in Fort Victoria, Southern Rhodesia (now Zimbabwe), in which one speaker pretending to be poor at English transferred the phonetics of all English words thrown at him into phonetically similar words in the Shona language. The connections in meaning thereby created caused roaring laughter in the audience (Hugh Tracey, *Sound of Africa Series*, AMA TR-80: track A1, "Faulty Translation").

"As a minstrel or vaudeville term," a section in which Merriam and Garner analyze expressions such as "jaz her up" in vaudeville jargon and used on the circus lot before World War I, according to Kingsley 1917 as the primary source: "Curiously enough the phrase 'Jaz her up' is a common one to-day in vaudeville and on the circus lot. When a vaudeville act needs ginger the cry from the advisers in the wings is 'put in jaz,' meaning add low comedy, go to high speed and accelerate the comedy spark. 'Jazbo' is a form of the word common in the varieties, meaning the same as 'hokum,' or low comedy verging on vulgarity" (Kingsley 1917: III, 3: 7).

This earlier source does not necessarily contradict or devalue the Jasbo Brown story given by the anonymous reporter in 1919. In fact, it makes us understand why the legendary performer in a Chicago café would have received the nickname "Jasbo" by his audience. In this context we learn from David Evans (1999: 182) that African American players in the southern United States often call the kazoo a "jazz horn" or "jazzbo," so that word was also projected onto an instrument that represents the sound of a muted trumpet or similar device.

There is one more large area of meanings from the vaudeville circuit that was suppressed in the early twentieth-century literature, rarely making it into print: sexuality. There are many ambiguous and sexually-imbued names in the jazz and blues culture, from "Jelly Roll" to "Winin' boy" (Morton) to "licking stick" (James Brown). Musical terminology is no exception.

Lewis Porter mentions a possible etymology of the word "jazz" favored by researcher Dick Holbrook, that it was derived from *gism*, rarely mentioned in English-language dictionaries, which meant "enthusiasm," but also definitely could mean "semen." Actually, these connotations were familiar to many people in America in the 1920s, and they contributed to the rejection of both word and music in upper- and middle-class families fearing that their offspring might start to associate with age-mates across social and "racial" boundaries.

Gism carrying the meanings of energy, spirit, and enthusiasm is an early "Americanism" of the English language. A related word that appeared in nineteenth-century novels is *jasm*. Dick Holbrook (1973/74) strongly believes that there is a connection in meanings and phonetics between these words and the emerging word *jazz*. He quotes a proverbial slang remark printed in the September 1886 edition of *Harper's Magazine*: "Willin', but hain't no more jas'm than a dead corn-stalk."

Such symbolic descriptions of male impotence and the (desireable) opposite could have been a background glow to several meanings that eventually condensed into *jazz*.

The sexual connotation of the word *jazz*, and words like *jasm* and *gism* that may have preceded it, has been mentioned by many informants familiar with slang expressions in the United States, notably in the South. This kind of meaning was even addressed in an article in the *Journal of Abnormal and Social Psychology*, 1927: 14–15 (Gold 1975). Holbrook interviewed old alumni of his college who seemed to remember that the word was used as a slang term for sexual intercourse in several parts of the western United States, allegedly since 1904, and from 1910 on in Chicago with the same kind of meaning.

In a letter dated April 20, 2012, David Evans has given me a candid and realistic assessment of this issue:

Jazz (the word): I'm quite certain that the word is derived from *jizz* or *jizm* (alternate spelling *gism*). It means literally "semen." I remember hearing this word from (white) schoolmates when I lived in Dallas, Texas, in the late 1950s when I was about 13–14 years old. It was considered a "dirty" word. I think it comes from African American slang usage and is possibly derived from a word in an African language. In any case, it seems to have taken on an expanded meaning of "energy, pep," still with a rather sexual or physical meaning. Then evidently it was applied to a type of music that was associated with energy and pep, and also with African Americans. Among some (but not all) whites, especially outside the South, its sexual connotations probably became lost or obscure and it just functioned as a novel slang term for a new music. The controversy surrounding the word is because many people are still aware of its original sexual meaning. Some of the proposed alternative etymologies are probably attempts to sidestep the word's sexual associations.

This would explain why it became a taboo word in some circles during the 1920s. It might also explain why the proprietors of Lamb's Café in Chicago 1915 chose the spelling "jass" to advertise Tom Brown's band and why the record company Victor in 1917 opted for the "ss" spelling in presenting the Original Dixieland Jass Band on their label. But the motivations in the two cases were probably different. The proprietors of Lamb's Café, well aware of the ambiguity of the word "jazz," wanted to stimulate those by-meanings in young people, though not overtly, in order to attract them to their venues. The "ss" spelling was preemptive, making those meanings less obvious. On the other hand, the Victor company in New York wanted to suppress all possible "inappropriate" associations to make sure that their records would not be rejected by the cash-equipped sections of the public. The *zz* spelling and pronunciation was felt as endangering their business. Very soon, however, the problem faded out by itself, because people were rushing to buy this new American dance music anyhow.

Although it is speculative, I tend to believe that in the same manner as has happened to some words in African languages that later became popular terms in young people's jargon, the word "jazz" could have been a secret slang term known in some tight circles of New Orleans for a long time. When this word reached San Francisco in 1912 or before, it had lost its explicit sexual connotations, with the idea transposed into a more abstract rendering, i.e., energy, pep. In that rendering the word became acceptable in wider circles, such as in sports. The same would apply to its appearance in Chicago. This is my "Freudian" interpretation of the matter, without relying on written sources. The ambivalence in pronunciation—"jazz," "jaz," "jez," "jass"—seems to confirm that there was some suppressed by-meaning.

Another claim of the word's sexual connotation was made in a 1945 comment by Darnell Howard about events in Milwaukee that took place around 1917, after the ODJB's publication of "Livery Stable Blues." (Howard erroneously put 1913 into his text). "I first heard the word 'jazz' used musically in reference to the Original Dixieland Jass Band. . . . The same year, while I was playing with the John Wecliffe band in Milwaukee, the band's press agents erected a huge sign above the dance hall where we were playing. The large flashy letters read: JOHN WECLIFFE'S JAZZ BAND. This caused quite a commotion, for the word 'jazz' at this time was a rather shady word, used only in reference to sex. This was Milwaukee; quite a few miles north of Chicago" (Anon. 1945: 5). Three things are made clear by this account: (1) how quickly business took up the new word, just because it had these "shady" connotations; (2) that it had existed as a slang term in the area probably even long before it was used as an advertising gimmick; (3) that a word with hidden sexual connotations would lend itself ideally to be tagged upon a kind of dance music with an African American background because it confirmed the entrenched stereotype of the male "Negro" as sex-obsessed. (On the psychology of such beliefs. see Fanon 1952 and Cleaver 1968.) As always, it was in the interest of business to stimulate stereotypical projections, especially at a time when conventional moral standards were crumbling. The era would soon be called the Jazz Age and the Roaring Twenties.

This section in Merriam and Garner's article summarizes hypotheses that the word "jazz" originated in some other language, e.g., an African language, Arabic, or French. A possible French link is proposed by an anonymous writer in 1958, tracking the word "jazzbo" to a term that was popular in New Orleans during the 1830s: "In pre–Civil War days, Georgia Negro men competed in strutting contests for their choice of cakes, and ladies, in cake suppers. The strutting contest became known as the Cake Walk, and the winner was dubbed Mr. Jazzbo. Further research traced the word to New Orleans during the 1830s, when *chasse beaux* was a popular French expression denoting a dandy, or a hip Gallic Don Juan" (Anon. 1958: 10). The problem here is the obvious historical discrepancies. The cake walk was mainly a phenomenon of the post–Civil War era, and how a term from New Orleans would have come to be used in Georgia opens up further questions. And yet there are elements in the story that make it difficult to dismiss categorically as a figment of the author's imagination.

The name Jasbo (Brown) for the notorious Chicago musician of 1915, is so close in phonetics to the French word for a dandy, Chasse Beaux, even implicitly in its meaning, that I would not dismiss the possibility of a cross-language connection between the two terms.

The advantage of both Jasbo stories, the one ca. 1914 in Chicago and the one from the pre–Civil War era in Louisiana and Georgia about the strutting contests that became the Cake Walk, is that they connect the term to a specific musical event, thereby explaining how and even why some startling reactions within small groups of fans should have impressed themselves as a key word on the memory of many people.

And yet the formulation of the claims in the 1958 anonymous article is so poor and devoid of hard evidence, that it inevitably invites criticism, even categorical rejection. Lynn Abbott has warned me about being too lenient here (letter March 14, 2012):

> Regarding the 1958 anecdote about pre-Civil War strutting contests, is there anything from the pre-Civil War period to confirm the existence of such contests or to support the notion that the winners of such contests were "dubbed Mr. Jazzbo"? And where is the "further research" that links this name to the French expression *chasse beaux*, and what is there to confirm its currency in 1830s New Orleans? As far as I know, not one of the New Orleans jazz musicians interviewed by Hogan Jazz Archive intimated that there could be a French-language connection to the word "jazz." This in spite of the fact that more than a few of them grew up speaking French. Phonetic similarity and vaguely connective meanings notwithstanding, it requires a mighty leap of faith to get from a 1830s chasse beaux to a 1910s "jasbo."

Paul Whiteman's account also explores the "Jasbo" lineage: "I am often asked, 'What is jazz?' I know of no better definition than that given by Lieut. Comm. John Philip Sousa, USNRF. He derives the word from 'Jazzbo,' the term used in the old-fashioned minstrel show when the performers "cut loose" and improvised upon or 'Jazzboed' the tune" (Whiteman 1924: 523).

Tracing the word to West Africa, however, as was first suggested by Walter Kingsley in his 1917 article, has definitely turned out to be a blind alley. This is what he proposed:

> The word is African in origin. It is common on the Gold Coast of Africa and in the hinterland of Cape Coast Castle. In his studies of the creole patois and idiom in New Orleans Lafcadio Hearn reported that the word "jaz," meaning to speed things up, to make excitement, was common among the blacks of the South and had been adopted by the creoles as a term to be applied to music of a rudimentary syncopated type. In the old plantation days when the slaves were having one of their rare holidays and the fun languished some West Coast Africans would cry out, "Jaz her up," and this would be the cue for fast and furious fun. No doubt the witch doctors and medicine men on the Congo used the same term at those jungle "parties" when the tomtoms throbbed and the sturdy warriors gave their pep an added kick with rich

brews of Yohimbin bark that precious product of the Cameroons. (Kingsley 1917: III, 3: 6–7)

The source of Kingsley's information was supposed to be Lafcadio Hearn, but subsequently the reference could not be tracked. In addition, his line that "some West Coast Africans" in the slavery days on plantations would cry out "Jaz her up" is about New World language usage, and not necessarily about Africans from the West African coast. The rest of the Kingsley paragraph is ethnographic imagery.

Another African connection was proposed by Henry George Farmer. He wrote: "The term *jazz* ... is derived from the Arabic jaz', a term used in the oldest Arabic works on prosody and music, and meant 'the cutting off,' 'the apocopation.' It passed with numerous other Arabic musical terms and customs, to the peoples of the West Coast of Africa, to be handed on, in the course of time to America" (Farmer 1924: 158).

Farmer was a great authority on Arabic and by extension North African music (see his beautiful book in the Series "Musikgeschichte in Bildern" edited by Werner Bachmann in Leipzig, Farmer 1966). However, if one's work is concentrated so much in just one cultural region, North Africa in Farmer's case, one may easily get carried away by the assumption that one's favorite region could be the source of everything.

No doubt there are retentions of Arabic-Islamic traits in certain forms of African American music in the United States, notably in variants of the blues (Kubik 1999a: 93–94), but the case for transmission of classical Arabic musical theory to New World destinations with learned people (perhaps accidentally) ending up as victims of the slave trade is difficult to make. Whether Arabic musical terminology could have been transplanted at all to New World destinations at different historical periods was also the subject of a recent controversy triggered by a claim made by Karl Gert zur Heide (2005: 13–14) that the word "rag" as in ragtime derives from Arabic *raqs* (dancing, dance). Zur Heide believes that the moments of contact with Arabic and Turkish music could be traced to the 1893 fair in Chicago, and even earlier to African American crew traveling on ships to the Mediterranean and the Near East. The problem here is that contacts alone cannot be taken as evidence for processes of borrowing and adaptation. Zur Heide would also have to account for the considerable phonetic differences between the two words, and why *raqs* would have been phonetically altered in the manner supposed to transform into the American term. The same applies to words like "jazz."

There is no end to freewheeling speculation and probably will never be. Recently, it has become fashionable on the internet to postulate a Celtic origin of *jazz*. Soon it will indeed be a globalized "jazz—the round-trip." But the most serious example of neglecting the bounds of scientific methodology was provided by Clarence Major (1994: 255) in his notes on the origin of *jazz*. Most of the words he quotes from African languages do not even exist in those particular forms, and to say that *jazz* was "very likely a modern word for *jaja* (Bantu)" only demonstrates the author's ignorance.

"Bantu" is not a language, but a term meaning "people" that was adopted by linguists as a tag to put under an umbrella a great number of related languages in central, eastern, and southern Africa (within Joseph Greenberg's "Benue-Congo" or I.A.5 family). Bantu languages were comprehensively classified by Malcolm Guthrie (1948, 1971). Ideophonic forms such as *jaja* can occur in countless African languages with a variety of meanings. Here, some warnings by Joseph Greenberg (1966) should be heeded by etymologists working on transatlantic connections. Greenberg formulated three fundamentals of method for establishing genealogical relationships between lexical items: "The first of these is the sole relevance in comparison of resemblances involving both sound and meaning in specific forms. Resemblances in sound only, for example the presence of a tonal system as such, or in meaning only, as in the existence of morphemes (meaningful) forms indicating sex gender but without phonetic similarity, are irrelevant. The second principle is that of mass comparison as against isolated comparisons between pairs of languages. The third is the principle that only linguistic evidence is relevant in drawing conclusions about classification" (Greenberg 1966: 1). "Classification" in a wider sense also means to find out what belongs together, what can be related and what is unrelated.

Another idea for a non-English origin came from an article by Irving Schwerke (1926), who derived the word from French *jaser* (to chat, to chatter):

> Le mot jazz est d'origine française et son application à la musique est la fidèle image de son sens littéral. Il y a 250 ans, la civilisation française trouva un solide point d'appui dans les provinces (plus tard devenues États) de la Louisiane et de la Caroline du Sud. Dans les villes cultivées du Sud (la Nouvelle Orléans et Charleston), le Français fut pour un certain temps la langue dominante, et, dans les plantations possédées par les Français, c'était la seule langue dont on usât. Les esclaves au service des Français furent obligés d'apprendre la langue de leurs maîtres, ce qu'ils apprennent, des inflexions et des modifications propres a leur race.
>
> S'il faut en croire Larousse, le verbe français *jaser* signifie *causer, bavarder, parler beaucoup*. Dans la littérature française, *jaser* s'applique souvent à une conversation animée sur divers sujets, alors que tout le monde parle ensemble; et, souvent aussi, *jaser* traduit plus spécialement un "chuchotement badin sur de petits riens." (Schwerke 1926: 679)

One may add here some of the meanings given in the *Larousse Dictionnaire Usuel Illustré* 1981, page 988: "*Jaser* [ʒaˈze], v. intr. 1ᵉʳ gr. 1 Causer, babiller, bavarder.

Jaser à tort et à travers 2 Révéler des secrets. 3 Médire, critiquer. *Cette femme fait jaser.* 4 Jacasser. *La pie jase.*"

This chain of associations may have some validity, perhaps because the connotations could all be descriptive of a public perception of jazz performance. Merriam says: "It should also be noted that the translation of Jaser, 'chatter' may have some vague connection with the idea held by Kingsley and others that jazbo and jazz have something to do with 'speeding things up'" (Merriam and Garner 1998: 19).

Schwerke's derivation of "jazz" from *jaser* (a French verb) has been given much credence in the literature. However, in contrast to other theories linking the word to a vaudeville term or to the "jazzbo" stories, it lacks all specific circumstantial background. No particular incident, no particular event is cited from observation in which the French word *jaser* was actually used either in New Orleans or Charleston or elsewhere in connection with music. One could also throw suspicion on Schwerke that he was perhaps motivated by French nationalistic feelings, and in addition that his conclusions are not field-based, that he was merely checking the *Larousse* Dictionary for a French verb that would come close to "jazz" in its phonetics. Had Schwerke known the *chasse beaux* story and its alleged association with contests in Cake Walk, he could even have found a shortcut to claim the word "jazz" as deriving from French.

In spite of these reservations, one must admit that his claims of origin remain at least within the boundaries of US cultural-geographical history, in contrast to schemes that seek the origins of the word in some distant language. The importance of French, respectively French Creole in parts of Louisiana is indisputable. However, Lynn Abbott's reservations quoted earlier also apply to the proposed *jaser* connection.

And there are more reservations. One of my readers pointed out to me that according to oral history from conversations with Paul Barbarin and others, Creole French was dying out in New Orleans households at the same time that the word *jazz* was emerging (see also Anthony 1978).

But another question comes up: What could have been the trigger for the French word *jaser* to become associated with a new kind of music? Could it be African concepts that music is essentially a form of conversation between the performers?

Due to the historical distance evoked in Schwerke's proposition it would, of course, be difficult to obtain the kind of additional, circumstantial evidence that is needed by tracking down the word's use in specific events. However, there is one nineteenth-century source with an unexpected detail from another part of the world about what may happen when the French verb *jaser* is used within an English-language sentence. *Jaser* was rendered in English orthography as "jazzing." The credit for having discovered this belongs to the late William Safire, known for his numerous enlightening columns on language usage in the *New York Times Magazine*, many of which were also reprinted in the *International Herald Tribune*. In April 1981 he reported about his finding:

> In a chapter on the Belgian crisis of 1831, historian Ridley quotes this private letter from Palmerston: [Henry Palmerston was prime minister of England in the 1850s.] "I am writing in the conference, Matuszevic copying out a note for our signature, old Talley jazzing and telling stories...." Wow. I zipped the evidence off to Robert Burchfield, chief editor of the Oxford Dictionaries, known to wordsmen as "Superlex."...
>
> "If Palmerston's word has been read correctly by Jasper Ridley," writes Mr. Burchfield... "it must be an isolated Anglicized spelling of French *jaser* 'to chatter, to gossip.'" (William Safire, "On Language," *New York Times Magazine*, April 1981)

There we are. Irrespective of time and place, the important point is that if someone in the mid-nineteenth century could have used the French word *jaser* in an English-language context and rendered it as "jazzing," the same mechanism could have occurred in other parts of the world as well, e.g., in Louisiana. Because the example appears to be isolated in written records, more likely it may have occurred in conversation between English speakers who were fond of fashionable French words. And that would particularly apply to the Napoleonic and post-Napoleonic era and to places in the world, such as New Orleans, that are known as contact zones between these languages.

Common Denominators?

Readers will have noticed that most of the schemes that derive the word *jazz* either from attributes, epithets, or nicknames of a person or usages in some performance context are based on anecdotal narratives. Often their inspiration is a specific event or series of events, stirring up intensive emotions and a creative response in spectators. However, when those stories are told and retold, their contents gradually change. As in any oral tradition, actual events become paraphrased, persons may be exchanged for one another or renamed, so that eventually we lose track of what the real, original story was. I suggested that the 1915 Jasbo Brown story from Chicago might even be a merger of two separate happenings and that the namesake Tom Brown had slipped in somehow, though he was not a "darky" and he did not play piccolo besides trombone, and that Sam Hare's Schiller Café was different from Lamb's Café. But could all those stories, opinions, worthwhile hints, and blind alleys be brought under an umbrella? Is there a common denominator? Are there any structural patterns or formal characteristics to be detected in all those explanations?

Here it is perhaps advisable to change one's entire research strategy. Looking through variants of the stories, we may discover that the structure of a plot is often retained. If we can learn a little from Claude Lévi-Strauss's analysis of myth (Lévi-Strauss 1964, 1967), we find that the structure of the first recorded Jasbo Brown anecdote (as told by the anonymous writer in 1919), for example, contains five meaningful entities: a) there was a "darky" considered to have unusual instrumental skills, making unusual music, playing with a five-piece group of his own in a café; b) his personal name or nickname incorporated the syllable "jaz" or "jas," with its own suggestive meanings; c) he had to get drunk first in order to carry out his gimmicks on piccolo and "muted" cornet; d) audiences got excited and called out to him, shortening his name to the first syllable (as much as Mitchell may become "Mitch" and David may become "Dave"); e) the abbreviated and modified name of the person got tagged onto his activity, in this case his music. There is a pattern in this and it conforms with what we know from human behavior. If people are confronted with something amazing, something they have never seen before, they often construct a name or transfer an existing term from matter to person, or from person to matter (see also Evans's 2008 article on nicknames in blues musicians).

But these transfers are not stable; they may change at least within two generations. As to the rise of variations in oral transmission, we have also learned something from our field experiences in the twentieth century. We know some of the factors that stimulate change in form, meanings, etc., with one caveat relative to an environment such as America in the late nineteenth and twentieth centuries: carriers of an oral tradition may inadvertently begin to draw upon printed information. It need not be that the narrator has read anything himself or herself; to produce significant alterations it is sufficient that just one person in the chain of transmission has done so. Others, asked by an interviewer, would then unknowingly produce a mixture of information from orally transmitted eyewitness accounts and secondary, written sources.

In Merriam and Garner's second section of their article deriving the word *jazz* from a vaudeville term, there is also a recurring pattern. Verbal renderings of "jazz" a) have movement connotations; b) symbolize the dispersion of energy; c) are slang expressions with sexual allusions; d) are basically ideophonic.

Osgood (1926) took pains to discredit most of the stories collected by others as unreliable. Schwerke (1926: 619) denounced the Razz's Band anecdote as "equally ridiculous." Nearly everyone has shown their preferences as to which story they confer credibility on and which ones they consider to be false. Merriam and Garner give preference to the "French connection," i.e., *jaser*, although they warn us that "evidence for one is for the most part no better than for another" (21). Then they add: "The relationship to the French *jaser* remains a distinct possibility, given the French influence in the Southern United States and in New Orleans in particular, as does the early idea that jazz as a minstrel term involved notions somewhat similar to the French translation of that word. The reference to the French *chasse beaux* is indeed an intriguing one which should be vigorously pursued" (28).

On the other hand, they dismiss the Chicago Jasbo Brown story as baseless stating that "the stories of variously named musicians probably have little basis in fact. . . ." Here I beg to disagree; the Jasbo Brown story seems to be precisely one of those based on firsthand observation. I recognize in the portrait of Jasbo Brown a character that can hardly be fictitious. Anyone who has done fieldwork in certain communities of the world, notably in Africa, is familiar with the "Jasbo syndrome" of behavior. The story is simply too tightly knit and psychologically convincing to be dismissed as baseless. Its weakness is not just its components, but the retroactive dating of it from perspectives of 1919.

Merger of Meanings

Perhaps instead of searching for a unilateral derivation of the word *jazz* from some earlier term, we should consider the multiple, conflicting origins that have been suggested not as mutually exclusive but as a network with its own inherent dynamics. Discussions seeking to establish which of the stories are true and which are wrong perhaps miss the point. I propose, therefore, that we embark from the opposite pier, assuming that all these crumpled and ragged stories are somehow true and may have converged in history. At least that prevents us from throwing away information. We may now juxtapose all the information available and see whether any patterns emerge. Each of the stories and etymological conclusions brings up a different facet of the whole. By putting them together we can try to construct a kind of etymological space.

It is not even the overt meanings alone that constitute the complete picture. There are patterns of language behavior that cross times and cultures; they can be fed into the whole to discover analogies. In some African languages, for example, there is—as in most of the world's languages—a verb similar in meaning to *jaser*, implying the idea "to converse," often in a leisurely manner, "small talk," often excessively, and by extension, even the idea "to visit" somebody. In English, "chat" can also have the sense of "visit." In Lucazi, an Angolan language, it is *kwandama*; in Chichewa of Malawi the verb is *kucheza* (word stem: *-cheza*) and may be used to express talk, for example, between family members, but it may also be used as a polite reference to express the real purpose of someone visiting an acquaintance of the other sex. Nowadays, on the radio it may also be used to implicitly warn, in polite language, of the dangers of HIV infection.

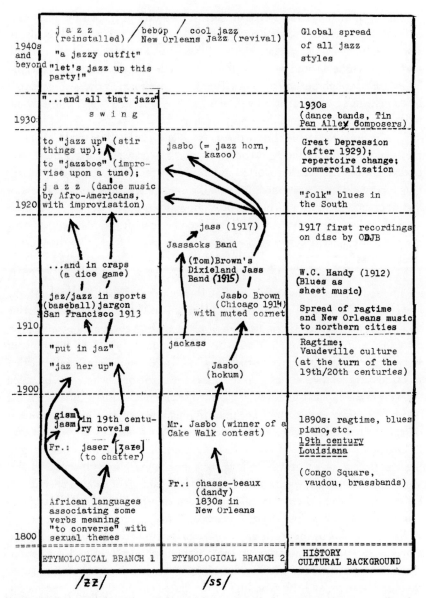

Fig. 1.2. Hypothetical chronology and convergence of words that appear to be connected to the term "jazz"

This verb, therefore has a delicate halo of by-meanings. But it may also have musical implications. Normally, playing music is called *kuyimba* (literally, to sing) in Chichewa. But the late Donald J. Kachamba (1953–2001) used the verb *kucheza* when he wanted to call us for a rehearsal. The idea was that we would "converse" through our instruments. The imperative form of the verb, *cheza!*, is by coincidence even phonetically similar to "jazz," and so is "chat." But I would warn about making a grand theory out of that.

The "genealogical table" I have drawn (see Fig. 1.2) visualizes the kind of synthesis I propose. In chronological order we can, in fact, lay out most of the derivatives (or antecedent terms) reported and show how the various parallel meanings may eventually have converged. I divide the emerging picture into two etymological branches. Strain 1 includes words phonetically characterized by the presence of [z] leading to the spelling "jazz." Strain 2 includes words incorporating the phoneme[s] such as in "chasse-beaux," "jackass," etc., leading to the ODJB's spelling "jass."

In its visual layout the table reveals numerous connections by association that are not easily detected by simply reading through the sources. For example, the term "jackass" reappears in the name "Jassacks Band" as a metathesis referring to a trio in the "South" (no indication of place or year) composed of a banjoist, a vocalist, and a player of an "empty tin can" (Anon. 1919b). And the ghost of Jasbo Brown with his "muted cornet" in Chicago rematerializes in the fact that in kazoo bands of the southern United States the kazoo or jazz horn can be called "jasbo" (Evans 1999). Moreover, allusion to sexual relationship, in some of the words for "conversing," seems to be trans-linguistically valid. While no phonetic or lexical relationships with African words can be postulated for any of the terms in English or French listed in the table, a conceptual element was probably spilling over from a variety of African languages spoken in eighteenth-century Louisiana and elsewhere. They are buried in hidden meanings of some French terms, e.g., *jaser*, and from there they may have been transferred to English-language vaudeville usages, e.g., "put in jaz," "jaz her up," etc.

We can say that by the 1800s different language groups in the southern United States had a word incorporating a syllable with the phonetics [ʒaz], [ʃas], or variants, with different but associated meanings. A process of condensation would then have started, and the meanings of the various phonetic allophones began to converge and be reduced to a specific context: entertainment (Cake Walk, vaudeville, circus) and eventually the music that came out of ragtime during the first decade of the twentieth century.

Figure 1.2 reconstructs what essentially was a fluctuating process of changes between phonetically similar ideophonic compounds, adaptable to similar meanings and reinforcing one another. In that sense, all the stories quoted by Merriam and Garner (1998) are part of a larger mosaic. All these verbs and names, Jasbo and Jassacks, are connected by assonance and have converged under specific circumstances. They may have functioned across time and space as materialization of a common idea that is perhaps embodied in the phrase "jazz her up": speed connotations, sexual connotations, etc., and ultimately related to both French terms: *jaser* (verb) and *chasse beaux* (noun). From the 1920s on, pronunciation and writing was streamlined, and the (z) pronunciation and /zz/ writing taking over.

Tags and Fashions

Research experiences can be channeled into a theory, and from theory we can deduce recipes for further research. As to etymology, however, there is one important caveat: Phenomena and their designations are never married for good. Around 1915 the music called ragtime had somewhat changed and got divorced from its name. Forthwith it was called jazz; and in the 1930s, in response to further changes, it was called swing. By 1945 the term jazz was firmly reinstated. The name ragtime remained attached to the "classical" piano style of the turn of the twentieth century and "ragtime pianists."

Was it all an accident of history? Such questions are to be taken seriously when we try to reconstruct historical sequences. Regarding the persistence of the word, whose meaning was contested in the debates on terminology and definitions of style during the 1930s and 1940s, I recommend Bruce Boyd Raeburn's recent book *New Orleans Style and the Writing of American Jazz History* (2009a), which includes discussion of competing versions of jazz aesthetics and historiography in different ideological camps and the schism related to swing and bebop. It is advisable to follow words and the phenomena to which they are attached separately, like separate strands. Sometimes cultural commodities, specific forms of human behavior, even ideas are adorned with fashionable tags for a while. But verbal attributes also get frequently replaced for social, psychological, commercial, and other reasons. They also change their invested values, sometimes from negative to positive (as in the case of "jazz") sometimes in reverse, until they are replaced by a more neutral term. The latter may also end up coming under pressure, especially if their hidden references are not changed.

When an object, commodity, or knowledge begins to migrate, it may get dissociated from its designation, and the two strands migrate independently. In the 1950s, George List found Raphael Terán, a player of a mouth-resonated musical bow in Palenque, Colombia, on the Atlantic coast, who called his instrument *marimba* (List 1966, 1983: 72ff.). This is a term from Bantu languages in southeastern Africa, applicable to two distinct instrumental categories: xylophones and lamellophones. The term is based on the -RIMBA/-LIMBA word stem, with a prefix to be added, such as the cumulative prefix ma-, pointing to a certain number of notes (xylophone slats, lamellae, etc.) It could not serve as a designation for a mouth-resonated (or any other kind of) musical bow.

On the Pacific coast of Colombia it is still applied correctly to those large, table-size xylophones with bamboo resonators replacing the African gourds, instruments whose organological details reveal that they are ultimately of Zambezi origins. They can be found in communities of African descent along the Pacific coast. Colombian musicologist Fidelita Hereira visited these communities in the late 1970s, crossing steep mountains on foot to get there. But as to the musical bow at Palenque, the original name was long forgotten, and locals called it *marimba*, expressing the only historical knowledge of the bow's origins that had survived: that it was "African." Otherwise, musical bows in Latin America are regularly, and we believe erroneously, considered to be an Amerindian heritage. Actually, I was able to trace George List's mouth-bow of Palenque to its likely culture area of origins, Gabon, southernmost Cameroon, and adjacent areas in southeastern Nigeria (List 1983: 79).

How an object or event or expressive form is named is therefore one (transient) matter, the object or form itself another. The two can be associated for a long time, but they can also get divorced quickly.

A term can also change its meaning and its semantic field within a short time, as it migrates from place to place, from community to community. For this reason it is never possible to give a universally accepted answer to the question what jazz "is," what it is "genuinely," which music may be called jazz, and which music should be excluded. Is Miles Davis's fusion experiment of the 1980s to be called "jazz"?

Some scholars will dismantle the dispute quickly by saying that all jazz is fusion. I normally do the same thing in ending tiresome discussions around the fashionable notions of "hybridity" or "hybrid cultures." I argue that all existing cultures have never been anything else but hybrid, and that we are not in need of borrowing terminology from genetics to apply them to phenomena that are essentially the result of learning.

Such questions have no scientifically defensible answer. All answers depend on the framework of references from which one operates. In 1938 Jelly Roll Morton in a letter to the *Baltimore Afro-American* (with a copy sent to *Down Beat* magazine) protested a radio program by Robert Ripley that had declared W. C. Handy the originator of jazz, stomps, and blues. Jelly Roll was furious. He also denounced all the present-day "Kings, Czars, Dukes, Princes" of the current Swing Era and then stated that "Swing is just another name for jazz" (Lomax 1952: 214–15). For him the common traits linking New Orleans jazz polyphony, as he understood and propagated it, with the recent, more homophonic musical arrangements in big bands by Count Basie, Cab Calloway, Duke Ellington, and others, whose music Morton rejected and even hated while he was in New York, were still obvious to him; so he insisted that swing was jazz. And at one stage he even tried to catch up with the imperatives of Swing Era arrangements with "Mister Joe," "Gan Jam," "We Are the Elks" etc. (Russell 1999). On the other hand, Morton set jazz apart from ragtime and explained the difference at length in conversations with Alan Lomax (Lomax 1952: 216ff., and the magnificent *Complete Library of Congress Recordings of Jelly Roll Morton*, by Alan Lomax in 1938, published on eight CDs by Rounder, John Szwed, ed., 2005).

Bunk Johnson, who was brought back to music by jazz researcher Bill Russell in 1939, had a concept of the word *jazz* somewhat wider than Morton's. He included ragtime. In a recorded conversation with Bill Colburn on May 1, 1943, at the latter's home in San Francisco, talking about Pete Lala's cabaret and Dago Tony's honky-tonks in New Orleans at the turn of the century, he pointed out that the names of these facilities were later changed to "night club." But that did not change the substance of what these places were for, he added, just as "we had years ago ragtime, and they later changed it to jazz, and later they have changed it to swing, but it's going back to jazz, it's going right home to ragtime, that's where things were started" (*American Music*, LP 643, "Bunk talking"). Bunk was underlining the identity of the music across times, in spite of all style and name changes.

By the time of Bunk Johnson's conversation in San Francisco, a new word, *bebop*, had come up in Minton's Playhouse, in Harlem, New York, to signify a new, by many almost immediately vilified, jazz style. While that word had long been rehabilitated, it was now bebop and the kind of music it stood for that became a scorn, as soon as the media grasped it, even among musicians who had actually created that style. They preferred to refer to their music simply as "new jazz." The pressure from public opinion became so strong that Leonard Feather, author of the book *Inside Bebop* (1949), reluctantly had to change the title of his book to *Inside Jazz*, partly because the publisher was expecting much better sales under that title. He knew that many people resented the word *bebop* or were not familiar with it, just as some others in the 1920s had resented *jazz*.

Scientific definitions of a word's semantic field by historians are not excluded from the processes we have discussed; they will in themselves deviate from time to time, according to the historians' ideological standpoint. It is not so long ago that opinions clashed seriously at the advent of bebop in the early 1940s, arguing whether that was "still" jazz or not, and even more so in the 1950s with Ornette Coleman's "free jazz," let alone Miles Davis's "fusion" attempts in the 1980s that still stir discussions.

Methodologically, therefore, it is hazardous to postulate meanings by drawing on the etymology of a word, because those meanings may have changed. But as mentioned earlier, there are comparable patterns and analogies in the handling of one's language across cultures, parallels in the construction of a framework of references. Recently, cognitive psychologist Lera Boroditsky (2011) has dealt with some of these questions.

There is a realm within which African American and African cultures are linked subliminally, at a structural level that evolves beneath the obvious relationships that can be discovered though anthropological trait-by-trait analysis. This subliminal level is manifested, for example, in the approach to word creation, or term creation as such, and in turn this is connected to an individual's general approach to language, to language learning, and to verbal play, powerful cultural determinants of human behavior.

Neither the words *bebop* nor *boogie-woogie*, for example, can be directly traced to any specific African language, nor could they probably be traced to African American terms in earlier centuries. They are all twentieth-century neologisms. But a specific approach to word innovation is revealed by them, a pattern of construction and retention of the new term that is comparable to analogous behavior in many speakers of African languages, in the past and present. David Evans points to phonetic parallels in the terms *vip vop* (1930s), *be bop* (1940s), and *hip hop* (1980s) (conversation, May 10, 2012).

Many of these neologisms are ideophonic; some are even onomatopoeic ideophones, such as the term "jaz" in its historic ramifications. African languages are full of ideophones, those short, sometimes composite syllabic patterns that are not subject to any grammatical variation, cannot be prefixed or suffixed, or subjected to declination or conjugation. They stand alone, transmitting an idea; hence linguistics calls them ideophones (cf. Fortune 1962; Nurse 1968, 1974). In Lucazi, an eastern Angolan language, the ideophone *vwi*, often used in exclamation, conveys the idea of absolute darkness, and *ndwa* accompanied by a slap on one's inner palm expresses the idea that something fits together, for example in size ("I have found a girlfriend, size *ndwa*!").

The cognitional process of expressing oneself in ideophones survives to a great extent in African American English. It is not merely retention, but a constant process of expansion and reinvention, for instance *honky tonk*. As to the jazz culture, the lexical items *boogie-woogie* and in some ways also *bebop* are ideophonic. All are relatively recent, but the method of their formation and the underlying thought processes that gave rise to them reveal a continuity linked to African cultures. Thus, a term can also be the result of a convergence of ideas and speech behavior in now separated culture areas.

Boogie-woogie is descriptive of a rocking movement and feeling that is intensively created by a boogie-woogie pianist by left- and right-hand interaction. There is also the term "booger rooger," which to Blind Lemon Jefferson means a dance event. Pine Top Smith also seems to mean a dance. In addition to the best-known exponents of boogie-woogie piano such as Meade Lux Lewis, Jimmy Yancey, Albert Ammons, and Pete Johnson, I would recommend for audition a lesser-known recording, composed and performed by Kansas City pianist Jay McShann and his orchestra, and recorded on AFRS Jubilee Shows March 1944: "Vine Street Boogie" (reissued on Stash, CD ST-CD-542, track 20). It includes an impressive bass solo by Gene Ramey of McShann's band.

Bebop, of course, is also a word without verbal meaning, used as syllable mnemonics. In this case, verbal meaning was projected onto it later. The origin of the term, according to oral tradition, is that it had a function during instructions between musicians: phrases in disjunct intervals were articulated with those syllables, "bu–ree–bop." It somehow stuck in the mind and eventually became a tag for this new style of jazz. Even this, however, is perhaps an attempted rationalization by musicians for a term that may yet have deeper, but less specific meanings.

Jitterbug is another example of a term, not ideophonic in this case, that may suggest analogies to word formations in some African languages. Alan Lomax, in his book *The Land Where the Blues Began* (1993) thought that "jitterbug," as a term for a forties dance style, was based on African analogies. He said the "root of the word seems to be African" (348). "It seems to refer to a little bug or a small child, crawling on the floor." If the term's implications are considered, it would refer to a bug that gives jitters, anxiety. In the United States, the word also survives in other contexts. Napoleon Strickland, in the Mississippi blues area, used to call his one-stringed heterochord zither a "jitterbug" (Evans 1970, 1978c).

Lomax's reference to the "root of the word" is, of course linguistically vague, apart from the fact that "African" is so universal a term that it has no practical meaning for any historical reconstruction, even if the precise location of those roots could be found; and it is probably not "the root of the word" at all, because the root of a lexical item is something well defined in linguistics, and in the case of "jitterbug" there are two roots. A phonetically identical sequence of sounds in another language can of course become relevant for our research, but only if an identical meaning can be traced in the two forms compared. Ideas concerning bugs that crawl on the ground are not unusual in African cultures, but to construct from that fact alone a historical line of relationships to a term in American slang is a tenuous undertaking. (For comparison, see the discussion of the etymology of "jitterbug" in Evans 1970: 240.)

Word creation has been an important aspect of the jazz culture, as much as sound creation. It is an essential heritage from the blues tradition that jazz is not only an instrumental, but also a literary art. Jazz performance may appear to be abstract instrumentally, but behind the phraseology—and not only in muted trumpets obviously talking like a human voice—there are often hidden verbal associations, much as there are in African music. In addition, the manner musicians use to talk to each other, how they express and formulate principles of performance, often uses special in-group speech of a distinctive literary quality.

Samba—for Comparison

What can we Africanist researchers contribute to the unraveling of the origins and history of certain terms? I asked my nephew Yohana Malamusi for an opinion. He was born in Malawi in 1987 and is a widely traveled young man. With his father and me he was already on fieldtrips in Namibia when he was five years old. In 1997 we were all based in Chicago for three months, on the invitation of the CBMR (Center for Black Music Research), Columbia College, and he now studies musicology at the University of Vienna. I asked him what he thought about analogies in human behavior, how new names for musical genres or stylistic directions are created. He replied that new names tend to come up spontaneously in a group facing an extraordinary event, often within a moment. That was so, he said, with words like hip hop, rap, samba, boogie-woogie, kwela, and also jazz. In response to something amazing, someone in an audience or performance group gets a sudden idea. It can even be a silly idea, or a form of irony, and he or she calls out the new word. If the term catches the imagination of others, it sticks and is taken up within a short time, and then it spreads. "In most cases," Yohana said, "a new term can therefore be traced to a specific event that has impressed people" (conversation, December 2011).

That would go well with the Jasbo Brown story, for example, and many others. A recent example for such a spread, even if it is not a word but a phrase, is how quickly 44th US President Barack Obama's 2008 campaign slogan "Yes we can" was picked up around the world even in the most unlikely quarters, after he had first used it (*The Inauguration of Barack Obama*, DVD, 2009, NBC Universal). Sometimes several strands of spontaneous word creation come into play simultaneously, and a competition arises between them, with "survival of the fittest word." Fashionable words or phrases, however, tend to fade out after some time, and disappear as suddenly as they had appeared.

A common pattern in word creation is rooted in what may be called substitution *res pro persona*, as in the Jasbo story, in which the person's name, often reduced to a formula, becomes the designation of what he or she has produced. Another pattern is that the witty idea by someone in the audience manifests itself as a verb, for example, signifying some specific act or movement. Both processes may apply to the origins of the word *jazz*. Under the impression of a startling event, its characteristics or its outcome may become its tag, often assuming the form of a noun.

An example of the first pattern can be cited from Brazil. The term *capoeira* for the celebrated *jogo* (meaning "play" in Portuguese) or fighting game probably has multilateral origins. But one association that cannot be easily dismissed is quoted by Waldeloir Rego (1968: 27–29), among other suggested etymologies from early nineteenth-century street life in Rio de Janeiro. The young boys who were carrying chicken coops—"capoeiras de galinha" in Portuguese—to the markets, were not in a particular hurry. House slaves in Rio had an enviable life of little manual labor and much leisure, in contrast to those poor fellows working on the sugar-cane plantations. So these youngsters with their chicken coops going to the markets had a habit of taking a rest on their way, putting their loads down to engage with peers in a playful fighting game. Apparently there, and also in more organized, sometimes secret meetings behind the master's Casa Grande, originated what came to be known as capoeira. Johann Moritz Rugendas (1835) made a drawing of a performance he witnessed in the 1820s in Salvador/Bahia. Through metonymy the term capoeira, meaning "chicken coop," was conferred upon the activities of these young men. As I point out in my book *Angolan Traits* . . . (Kubik 1979), "capoeira" was also a code name for the more secret training by some young men for possible insurrection. (See also Kubik 1991 [2013: 109–15].)

The associative mechanism in exchanges of names res pro persona can work in different directions: it can be a transfer from person to product, from product to person, from an object to a personal activity, or the reverse. In the 1970s, while I was working on the Angolan background of Brazilian cultural traditions, I discovered that the term "quimbanda" was used in a unique manner. In Angola, *kimbanda*, a word in the Kimbundu language (*ocimbanda* in other languages), is the designation for a medical practitioner, a healer, herbalist, also psychotherapist if you wish. He or she can communicate with the spirits to solve a client's problems. Accordingly, the work, the medical practice, is called *umbanda* (an abstract noun), especially in southwestern Angola from where both the term and the practice were exported to Brazil during the era of the slave trade. In 1965, during fieldwork in Angola, I made the acquaintance of Emilia Kakinda, a renowned *kimbanda*; she also played *ngoma pwita*, a friction drum, during her sessions (Kubik 1979).

However, when both terms were introduced in Brazil in the late eighteenth and early nineteenth centuries with enslaved people from Angola, these words began to be reinterpreted by people rooted in the Catholic faith and in Portuguese culture. *Umbanda* was accepted, but increasingly understood as an alternative religion with special healing power. By contrast, the person responsible for umbanda, namely the *kimbanda*—male or female—was bedeviled in Brazil. The term was literally "depersonalized." Written "quimbanda" in Brazilian Portuguese, it changed its meaning, and began to denote evil magic, witchcraft, precisely what the Christian public associated with an Angolan healer. From this emerged an intrinsically racist symbolism that has survived until now: "umbanda" has been equated with *magia branca* (white magic, positive healing power) and "quimbanda" with *magia negra* (black magic, witchcraft) (Braga 1961; Kubik 1991 [2013: 136–50]).

The schism of colonial Brazilian society could not be better demonstrated. Ironically, we could say that Brazilian culture has appropriated the Angolan knowledge about healing as embodied in the term *umbanda*, but has rejected the healer, the kimbanda, the owner of this knowledge, even deprived him or her of existence as a human being. A new black/white dichotomy, one with positive, the other with negative connotations, was created using Angolan words. I see parallels to this in early US jazz history: appropriation of the creative product, but concealing or downgrading the originator.

A reaction, analogous to the creation of the phrases "jaz her up" or "put in jaz" in vaudeville jargon as reported by Kingsley (1917: III, 3: 7), can possibly be detected in the rise of the term *samba* in late nineteenth century Brazil. Earlier researchers in Brazil thought they had found its origins as deriving the word from the Kimbundu term *semba* for a musical genre, also known as *rebita* in Luanda. But apart from the anachronism involved—because these are early twentieth-century Angolan developments—the connection also does not work on phonetic grounds. Brazilians nasalize the word samba, while *semba* with a clear [ε] would not lend itself to nasalization. The Brazilian term therefore can only derive from a word exactly the same in some Bantu language. Actually the word stem SAMBA occurs in many of these languages, including Luganda (of Uganda), Cinyanja/Chichewa (of Malawi), and most Angolan languages, with a variety of meanings. It is striking that it always has some movement connotation. It usually occurs as a verb, but is also part of a variety of noun formations. It is probably indisputable that the term samba for Brazil's most important contribution to African American music, originally came from Angola—as much as rumba was introduced to Cuba by speakers of Central African Bantu languages, notably in the Congo.

The problem is to reconstruct the avenues along which this process of diffusion unfolded. One advantage is that in contrast to the word *jazz*, the Brazilian and Cuban terms have survived directly from African languages.

In Angola, a verb *-samba* exists in many local languages, but under various meanings, depending on the tonality of its pronunciation. For this reason we have to be careful. In eastern Angola—a geographical area seriously affected by the Ovimbundu/Portuguese slave trade after 1800—the verb *kusamba* means to skip, gambol, jump, in the Ngangela group of languages (Pearson 1970: 305). Mose Yotamu, my co-researcher from northwestern Zambia and a native speaker of Luvale and Lucazi, gave me an example: "Vambambi vekusamba ngwe kuli kalunga wamundende" (The antelopes gambol when there is light rain) (conversation, December 3, 1978). Yotamu also told me that there was an old dance in eastern Angola, around Kazombo, called *sambakalata*. In Gabela, Povoação do Assango, another area of Angola, in Kwanza-Sul Province, the verb *kusamba* means "to clap hands" (*kusamba apando* = *bater palmas*). I learned this from Angolan cineaste Antonio Paulo de Oliveira in Luanda in a conversation on January 14, 1981.

It is conceivable therefore, that in early nineteenth-century Brazil at the height of dance performances by Angolans, their audiences would have used the imperative "Samba!" inciting a dancer, to "skip," "gambol," or alternatively, demand from vocal participants to put more vigor into their hand clapping.

In all these scenarios the verb would have been used in the imperative form. That would be analogous to "jaz up" some things. In eastern Angola, Samba is also a name. In 1992 at the Okavango River, we made acquaintance with an Angolan refugee who was an excellent dancer. His name was Samba Katolo (Video document no. 15, near Rundu, October 1992, Culture Research Archive Kubik/ Malamusi, Vienna). In a variant pronunciation, *Tsamba* in the Ngangela group of languages means "first-born" and is therefore part of many personal names.

There is also stylistic evidence in the music that points to an Angolan origin of many patterns that converged to form Brazilian samba. A diagnostic marker is the nine-stroke, sixteen-pulse timeline pattern that characterizes much of the music in the eastern half of Angola (Kubik 1979: 16–18).

Outside the Angolan culture area, the verb *-samba* occurs as far east as southern Uganda, where it also has movement connotations, for example in the Luganda phrase *bijjabisamba endege* (they are stamping with their *endege* leg rattles). This is also the title of a song. And then there is the twentieth-century reflux to Africa of the word "samba," besides rumba, jazz, mambo, merengue, pachanga, soul, reggae, and many other African American terms that became current in popular African music of the twentieth century. The term *samba* arrived via Brazilian gramophone records in the urban centers of Angola and Moçambique in the 1940s and 1950s, at first among the Portuguese and the so-called "assimilado" population in cities like Luanda and Maputo. It may have undergone further reinterpretation on the basis of local meanings. An interesting discovery was made by Moya A. Malamusi on one of his fieldtrips in 1988 to the border area of Malawi/ Moçambique. He bumped into a novel musical group led by a Moçambiquan named Mário Sabuneti, then about twenty years old, who had constructed an eight-drum chime, a set of eight drums tuned to a scale, which he called *Samba Ng'oma Eight*. He played all the drums by himself like a single instrument, in an elaborate patterned movement of his hands. The question arose: Had Mário at some stage picked the Brazilian term samba from a record, a radio program, or from hearsay? Did he then use it to give his invention an attractive name?

Ng'oma means drum(s). When asked by Moya, however, he did not confirm any radio inspiration of his choice, but said that the term samba had occurred to him because of the rapid movement of his hands when playing the drums; it looked as if he were bathing! *Kusamba* in Chichewa/Cinyanja means to bathe. And yet it is possible that Mário also heard the Brazilian word somewhere (e.g., on the radio) but reinterpreted it in terms of the dominant local language, although actually he himself was an Elomwe speaker. Two meanings, the musical meaning and the Chichewa meaning (washing one's body all over with one's hands), would then have converged.

As a term for a remarkable new music played with tuned drums, Samba Ng'oma caught on quickly in southern Malawi during the late 1980s. A few years after Moya's discovery we found a folkoristic group that had picked the name and appropriated it, giving a performance in the French Cultural Centre, Blantyre, announced as "Samba Ng'oma." By then, the originator, Mário Sabuneti, had disappeared and was never heard of again. The only testimony to his existence are Moya's recordings and his article (Malamusi 1991).

This story contains lessons for jazz research, its intricacies and pitfalls, showing the ephemeral nature of spontaneous inventions by a genius who disappears after a short while without trace. We are aware of the many blind alleys in historical developments, the discouragements and the dying.

The Word *Jazz* in Africa

For the last sixty to seventy years the word *jazz* has been entrenched in Africa, from Ethiopia to the Congo, Accra, and Dakar, even where local popular music does not have a grain of resemblance to anything that could be called jazz. From the 1930s on, numerous musical groups playing dance music began to incorporate the word into their band names. A brief glance at a contemporaneous discography, such as the one in Wolfgang Bender's book *Sweet Mother* (1991, 2000), brings to light that many dance band names across Africa contain the word: Bembeya Jazz National in Guinée, Prince Nico Mbarga & Rocafil Jazz (Nigeria), Juwata Jazz Band, and Mwenga Jazz Band (Tanzania), Franco and his O.K. Jazz (Congo), etc. All these groups were playing music in their own specific styles. Besides band names, other word combinations were also created, such as Ethio-Jazz for the music of Mulatu Astatke in Ethiopia who had studied at the Berklee College of Music in Boston. He is regarded today as the "father of Ethio-jazz" (Falceto 2001, 2002; Brunner 2009).

The list has no end, especially as concerns bands of youngsters playing with homemade instruments in rural areas across southern Africa. During the 1970s and 1980s in Zambia we recorded bands of youngsters, with the word "jazz" being part of their band names, such as the Kasazi Boys' Jazz Band in Mawewe, Kabompo District, playing homemade banjo and guitar. In Zambia such bands were precursors of *kalindula* music (Malamusi and Yotamu 2001). In Malawi one of the bands of adolescents, the Fumbi Jazz Band, was recorded in the 1980s by Moya A. Malamusi, then filmed by me on November 5, 1987. (See also review of the film by John Baily, 1988.) *Fumbi* means dust. Their music was oriented towards the then popular *chimurenga* (liberation struggle) music of Zimbabwe.

Fig. 1.3 and Fig. 1.4. Fumbi Jazz Band with homemade guitars and percussion. Chileka, Malawi, November 1987. Photos: Moya A. Malamusi

Over the years Moya has recorded a hundred of those banjo bands across southeast Africa, whose performers were mostly in their teens. This has led to a large collection of teenage musical activities in rural and semi-rural areas. Some of it was published on the CD *From Lake Malawi to the Zambezi* (Malamusi 1999a) and more recently on the DVD/CD *Endangered Traditions—Endangered Creativity* (Malamusi 2011) and on the DVD (with PDF booklet) *The Banjo Bands of Malawi*, published in 2015 by Stefan Grossman's Guitar Workshop (Vestapol 13135).

Most characteristic, however, is that those bands in a broad belt across Africa incorporating the word *jazz* in their band names would never use that word to describe their music. By contrast, in South Africa, performers from the 1960s on who began to develop competence in playing modern jazz would indeed call their music by that name, but rarely incorporate that word in song titles or in their band names.

It was from Europe rather than from the USA that the word *jazz* spread to the colonially divided African continent in the 1920s and '30s, and with meanings it had acquired in the environment of ballroom dancing in Europe. Soon, the word was synonymous with same kind of dancing in colonial Africa. It is this meaning that also became current in the Belgian Congo.

In an article first published in *La Revue Coloniale Belge* 143 (September 1951) and reprinted in the *African Music Society Newsletter* 1 (5): 42–43 (June 1952), "Rumba Congolaises et Jazz Americain," Jean Welle, a Belgian visitor to the bars and nightclubs of Leopoldville, as it was then called (now Kinshasa), describes his impressions of the music played in one of them.

The picture he paints of Leopoldville at night is very different from what Kinshasa, overcrowded, dilapidated and full of crime, looks like these days (according to a conversation I had with Prof. Kazadi wa Mukuna at Kent State University, Ohio, November 14, 2011). It was then a well-kept colonial town of a bit more than 130,000 inhabitants, with the so-called Cité Indigène quite accessible to visitors from overseas. This was a township illuminated by millions of kerosene lamps, with much activity at the market in the late evenings but no worry for a visitor about getting attacked. In the middle of this calm between oil lamps, all of a sudden a dance hall could be seen, well lit by electricity, with sounds of trumpet, clarinet, saxophone, and guitars to be heard.

What were these musicians playing? The word "jazz" appears in the title of Jean Welle's article, evoking some expectations in the reader. Actually it was a word well known among young Congolese in Kinshasa townships, but its meaning was much broader than in the United States, in conformity to what it was in Belgium and all across Europe in the 1920s, referring to dance music that included foxtrot, "slow fox," and tango. That was before the post–World War II redefinition of the word among young Europeans drawn to swing, boogie-woogie, and jitterbug dancing. In South Africa that culture had arrived on time, but not so in Leopoldville in the 1950s, and it never would thereafter.

What did that "orchestra" in Leopoldville (Kinshasa) play, with its members in colorful uniforms? Dance numbers, first a tango piece. The dancers belonged to a rising Congolese bourgeoisie, well-dressed men in suits and ties, females in shoes with high heels, demonstrating a class of successful Congolese "evolués," with a European or more precisely a Flemish Belgian lifestyle.

It seemed to the observer that the tango was soon transformed into a lullaby, with no variations or improvisatory exploration added to the theme. But all of a sudden, things in the band changed. Another rhythm, more vivid, came up from the drums; the young musicians played a rumba piece. Here the visitor correctly noticed that something new had been coming up in the townships. On the basis of those rhythms the musicians were obviously exploring a new kind of music that belonged to them and could not be taken for mere imitation of Caribbean and South American patterns. The observer Jean Welle had a name for it: "La rumba congolaise." But he also provided an important supplementary note to this image of Kinshasa township music in 1950: "En revanche, je n'ai jamais entendu de musiciens congolais jouer du jazz—j'entends du vrai jazz, á la façon des noirs américains. On m'a même prétendu que l'audition de disques d'outre-Atlantique les laissait insensibles. Et de fait lorsqu'ils dansent aux son d'un pick-up, ce sont des enregistrements de romances, airs de slow-fox ou de valse lente, que les Congolais affectionnent" (Welle 1952: 43). The observer was startled by this apparent indifference among urban Congolese to any form of American jazz. The musicians had been exposed repeatedly to jazz records by friends, without any positive response. Jean Welle had no explanation for this indifference. He was dwelling on what he thought was a paradox because "enfin, le jazz est d'origine nègre."

Regrettably, "nègre" is no cultural qualifier. Musical reasons, besides others, why jazz was rejected in the Congo, include the strong blues scalar basis of jazz melodic-rhythmic patterning, historically linked to the West African savannah, not to the Congo, where a different, more homophonic understanding of multipart harmony existed. Another reason was the unfamiliarity with jazz form such as the AABA chorus form and the twelve-bar blues form in the Congo. Older genres of music across the two Congos have little resemblance in form, pattern, and timbre of the human voice to historical jazz styles, which sounded weird and dissonant to many Congolese. They have more in common with the music of Cuba, also because of the latter's frequent use of Short Cycle form. Why rumba caught on in the Congo and jazz did not resonate was therefore in part the result of selective processes by the Congolese "ear" on the basis of stylistic affinity. Rumba music, its themes and rhythms, was perceived as part of a Central African continuity on both sides of the Atlantic, in Cuba and in other parts of the Caribbean, as much as samba demonstrated continuity of patterns from Katanga and Angola in Brazil.

The predilection for certain imported 78 r.p.m. records by the Congolese public in the late 1940s, e.g., Xavier Cugat and not Woody Herman, was steered by instant recognition that rumba, chachacha, and pachanga patterns matched age-old Congolese traditions. The new development they had taken overseas, with those glittery instruments used in performance and the element of show business included, were impressive to young people in the townships in search of something to emulate that would be theirs, but chic, advanced, and devoid of the stigma of "primitive music." Jean Welle observed that, besides rumba, the urban Congolese "preferred without hesitation the tender voice of Tino Rossi to the trumpet of Louis Armstrong." The writer then ends his article saying that he would leave this "paradox" to be solved by others more competent than him (Welle 1952: 43).

The rise of the new rumba-based Congo music, both in Kinshasa and in Brazzaville on the other side of the river, is well documented (Kazadi 1979–80, 1992) and was recorded from the start by a Greek firm in Kinshasa, the Jéronimidis Brothers, on their NGOMA records. Their work has been documented in detail by Wolfgang Bender (cf. CD *Ngoma, the early years, 1948–1960*). Following local usage, rumba, chachacha, and pachanga-based band music of the 1960s and 1970s in Kinshasa and Brazzaville was often referred to as "Congo jazz," even in the literature. Other names included "musique zairoise," "African jazz," and "Soucous." Bender (1991: 42) stated that "Congo jazz became known in the 1950s when it was disseminated on the first labels of Congo-based record companies—all of them in Greek hands—and by Radio Brazzaville." This suggests that record companies and the mass media in general had their share in popularizing the word *jazz* in connection with various Congolese groups as a label for dance music, even if it involved the cherished bel canto singing style (by Tabu Ley Rocherau and others) prevalent in Kinshasa music of the 1960s, which is like an antithesis to anything a jazz singer would do.

By the 1930s the word *jazz* had spread to nearly all the urban centers in sub-Saharan Africa, and was readily adopted by young people who began to play dance music for the entertainment of their peers, using Western musical instruments or locally manufactured versions. After the end of World War II ballroom dance music, and in particular rumba, came to Kenya with returning soldiers who had been recruited to serve in the British Army during the Burma Campaign against the Japanese military. In West Africa, notably on the Gold Coast (Ghana), calypso from Trinidad became popular.

In nearly all these instances, from West Africa to the Congo and to Tanzania, there were few actual jazz traits in the music of the dance bands, even if we stretch the term to its limits. But occasionally in Ghanaian highlife of the 1950s, there are certain hidden, heavily reinterpreted, jazz elements, as in voice lines of the reed and brass instruments arranged in a homophonic set and in E. T. Mensah's playing of the muted trumpet. His jazz-like phrasings and intonation cannot be ignored. And yet, when Louis Armstrong visited Accra in 1956 and their bands met, the more gentle, sometimes even rhapsodic phrasings of Mensah as compared to the macho style of Armstrong's trumpet were all too obvious.

It seems that along the West African coast, jazz phraseology was adopted more readily on wind instruments than elsewhere, in Nigeria perhaps even more so. Roy Chicago's alto saxophone solo in "Sere fun mi baby" (recorded July 13, 1961, Philips 420011 PE) displays a timbre clearly derived from cool jazz, although I would not link it unilaterally to Stan Getz, Paul Desmond, or others. In addition, both Ghanaian and Nigerian forms of highlife in the 1950s and '60s were much more strophic in concept than short-cyclic, as compared to Congolese dance music of the period. Many highlife themes were relatively long, in ABA or AABA form, with a bridge. When I first entered eastern Nigeria in August 1960, hitchhiking all the way from East Africa, the Congo, and through Cameroon, my attention was immediately attracted by these differences in form. John Collins, the author of many indispensable writings on West African popular music, including a seminal biography of Mensah (1986), has dealt more comprehensively with the question of "Jazz Feedback to Africa" (Collins 1987).

Kikoongo in French-Speaking New Orleans (Early Nineteenth Century)

The Transatlantic "Congo" Theme

"Congo Square" in New Orleans, where for half a century enslaved persons from Africa gathered on Sundays to perform songs and dances in various African traditions, has become a symbol of African cultural resilience in the United States. Freddi Williams Evans in her 2011 book *Congo Square: African Roots in New Orleans*, gives the following assessment: "In Congo Square on Sunday afternoons, to different degrees over time, African descendants spoke and sang in their native languages, practiced their religious beliefs, danced according to their traditions, and played African-derived rhythmic patterns on instruments modelled after African prototypes. This African population also bought and sold goods that they made, gathered, hunted, much in the style of West African marketplaces" (1). Referring to similar practices in Haiti, Cuba, and elsewhere in the Caribbean, she goes on to say that the "parallel performance styles and practices witnessed in those locations provide a picture of the persistence and consistency of African cultures in the Americas. They also demonstrate New Orleans' previous relationship with Caribbean countries and Congo Square's influence on the perpetuation of African cultural traditions in North America. . . . While not every African-derived cultural practice that occurred in New Orleans took place in Congo Square, the repeated gatherings and long-term perpetuation of African cultures that existed there established the location as ground zero for African culture in New Orleans . . ." (2). Indeed, New Orleans with surroundings was culturally part of the Caribbean, and in a sense has remained so, including sharing the region's natural disasters such as Hurricane Katrina, which devastated the city in August 2005.

F. W. Evans has carried out a thorough assessment of Congo Square's history, and in her book has a timetable as a guide to existing sources. However, the source situation—as she points out herself—is not very good as concerns the activities of people of African descent in Louisiana from the seventeenth to the nineteenth centuries. Eyewitness accounts of African activities in New Orleans during the era of slavery are rare. Most of what is on record are casual reports. All written observations are by cultural outsiders. Reports by people that were part of the culture are nonexistent, or—if we prefer to be optimistic—have not yet been discovered.

After the Civil War era there are some firsthand accounts of the African cultural presence in New Orleans, also concerning the legendary *vodu* priestess Marie Laveau, obtained in interviews conducted in the 1930s and 1940s for the Federal Writers Project. The thirty-one volumes of ex-slave narratives collected in the project also contain precious information on homemade and other musical instruments used in African American communities from the 1840s to the 1860s. Another major body of material was collected at the same time by Harry Middleton Hyatt and published in five volumes. Robert B. Winans (1982 [1990]) has meticulously researched these sources, and confirms that in Louisiana fiddle, banjo, and some percussion instruments were the most popular.

The late nineteenth century, however, was also the time when Congo Square and other aspects of antebellum life in the South were elevated to legendary proportions. Travelers, writers, and musicians all became interested in the subject of "slave songs," and some tried to notate them, "arranging" them for piano and voice. Journalists and illustrators, attracted by the subject of Congo Square, portrayed the culture as if they had personally shared in it; but they were not born when those gatherings were taking place regularly. Often they reproduced hearsay, frequently copying from each other, rarely indicating their exact sources. One example of this practice was identified by F. W. Evans in the writings of Hélène d'Aquin Allain (1883). That author has often been quoted in the literature, but she never witnessed the dances in Congo Square. Many of these authors, including George Washington Cable, were relying on a book about Santo Domingo, not New Orleans, by Moreau de St. Méry, first published in 1797, projecting those descriptions upon New Orleans.

George Washington Cable's two comprehensive and richly illustrated articles in *Century Magazine* (1886a and b), "Dance in Place Congo" and "Creole Slave Songs," have been cited so often in the jazz literature that one wonders what else could be deduced from them that nobody has discussed before. One feasible approach is to see if their contents can be placed into a wider transatlantic context.

The Congo theme actually comes up in many communities of African descent in the New World besides nineteenth-century New Orleans, such as in Cuba, Venezuela, Panama, and elsewhere.

There are historical counterparts to the "Dance in Place Congo" of New Orleans, not only in other places across New World cultures, but even in eighteenth- and nineteenth-century slave gatherings off the coast of Central Africa, in places of transit that served commercial ships as a gateway to transatlantic destinations with merchandise from Congo, Cabinda, and Angola. One such turntable was the islands of São Tomé and Principe, off the coast of Gabon.

In a little-known paper originally presented at the first Reunião de Arquelogia e História Pré-Colonial in Lisbon, October 23–26, 1989, P. António Ambrósio reported about "O danço Congo em S. Tomé, e as suas origens." Enslaved people of Congo origin, waiting for their transportation across the Atlantic on São Tomé island, would regularly organize dances during leisure hours. Such gatherings paralleled those in New World cultures, notably in early nineteenth-century New Orleans, as well as the more formal events in Brazil, such as the "Congada" or Election of a King of Congo (Kubik 1991: 116–20).

This raises many questions; for one, why did people identifying as Congolese organize themselves in such a manner in all those places? Was it because of a feeling that they had come from a once powerful Central African state, the Kingdom of Koongo, with which Portugal had exchanged ambassadors in the sixteenth century? Or was "Congo" just a blanket term to cover several Central African ethnic groups which communicated in Kikoongo? Or, otherwise was it merely a prevalent feeling of liaison with an identifiable African culture, Koongo culture?

Kikoongo (H.16 in Malcolm Guthrie's classification of the Bantu languages, 1948) actually is a dialect cluster, spread over a wide area from northwestern Angola across the Lower Zaïre River, to the Bafioti in Cabinda. It is a five-vowel language and includes two tonemes, and a specialty: reinforced consonants.

Obviously, from its many uses in the literature on Africa and New World African populations, "Congo" became not only a trademark but, from the eighteenth century on, a self-explanatory stereotype, sweet on the tongues of observers, while in New Orleans the protagonists of the dance events in Congo Square were a mixture of speakers of many different, often unrelated African languages. This is suggested by reports saying that the groups performed their dances separately, within the spaces available. In spite of the scarcity of primary sources, we can try to study some of these traditions. Stylistic evidence can perhaps be matched with linguistic evidence provided by surviving vocabularies and phrases as reported in the literature.

The name "Congo Square" is a "folk" appellation of the place where Africans used to gather for their dances. The original name was "Place du Cirque" (in various translations "Circus Park," Circus Place," and "Circus Square"). From the moment in 1724 when—under French rule—the so-called Code Noir was enacted in Louisiana in conformity with Catholic ideas, slaves were required to observe Sunday and other holidays of the church. This included toleration of recreational activities in the afternoons. On the plantations the *kalinda* dance was often performed. Gradually, one location in New Orleans prevailed as a place of gathering and was later nicknamed "Congo Square." The Sunday dances, however, were not the only activity; there was a market, and there were also other gatherings. Under changing governments, French, Spanish, and then American, it functioned as a location for all sorts of festivities. Early in the nineteenth century Cayetano's Circus from Habana opened up there. It was also the place of executions, whippings, etc., between 1803 and 1834.

Various other names of the place are known: Congo ground, Congo green, etc. (F. W. Evans 2011: 20). The authorities, however, were not necessarily happy with any of the popular designations and usually referred to the place as "Circus Square" in official documents. In 1851, after it had become the location of military drills, it was renamed Place d'Armes (in French). But the popular name prevailed.

That the "Congo" theme was coming up in so many communities across New World African American cultures is probably due less to specific cultural similarities of those involved than to transcultural parallels of a specific psychological situation. Koongo was an anchor to hold to, identifying with something like a mythological home culture. And for outsiders the word served as a convenient label that could be pasted on an assortment of African cultural expressions.

In earlier centuries, the Kingdom of Koongo was one of the most powerful, and later in many ways legendary, pre-colonial African states. It was also one of the first to enter into a relationship with a European power. Portuguese ships reached the Zaïre River in 1483. The visitors were welcomed at the court of Mweni Nzinga aNkuwa, the King of Koongo, who became interested in establishing trade relations. In return, he accepted to be converted to Christianity and was baptized. In the year 1506 he was succeeded by Nzinga Mbemba, also known in the literature (through his many letters of friendship with King Manuel of Portugal) under his Portuguese name, Affonso I. In Brazil, the *folguedo* (folk drama) called *Congada* revives the memory of the installment of a King of Koongo.

Portuguese trade soon expanded and began to include the forceful recruitment of people to be employed as workers. The Portuguese began to buy captives for enslavement to work for them on the sugar plantations of São Tomé and Principe. This "trade" soon included subjects of the Kingdom of Koongo to be taken to Brazil and elsewhere for similar purposes.

Affonso I did not sell his own people, but in exchange for European goods, including military equipment, he agreed to supply captives from other ethnic groups, notably from Koongo's southern neighbors, including Ndongo, the country of Kimbundu-speaking people of King Ngola. The name of that king was misunderstood by the Portuguese as the name of a country, and that is how the name Angola originated.

However, Affonso I soon realized that he had committed a mistake. In 1526 he began to complain to his friend King Manuel that Portuguese traders were disregarding his authority and entering separate agreements with various chiefs along the coast. He castigated the greed of the traders, complaining that his country was running the risk of being depopulated.

In 1569 the situation deteriorated completely when Koongo was invaded by armies of the Yaga, groups of warriors split off from the Lunda Empire further east; and he had to ask for Portuguese military assistance. This increased Koongo's dependence, and the state's capital Mbanza Kongo (renamed São Salvador) became part of a territory controlled by the Portuguese and extending all along the coast with the ports of Luanda (founded in 1576 by a commander called Paulo Dias de Novais) and Benguela, down to the Kunene River.

A hundred years later there appeared rivals to the Portuguese: Dutch traders. The King of Koongo, Garcia II, complained once again about the evils of the slave trade, in vain (Davidson, Mhina, and Ogot 1967: 269–71).

By the early nineteenth century a large population of descendants from Koongo, Angola, and even Moçambique was living in Brazil, as is testified by many detailed written and pictorial sources (Kubik 1979, 1991: 32–35). We can reconstruct the ethnic composition of those who were deported, Bakoongo, Imbundu, Ovankhumbi, and Ovahanda in particular. The slave trade in Angola had shifted to the southern and eastern parts of the country in the late eighteenth century, affecting the Vangangela (people of the aurora, people of the lands of dawn; cf. Kubik 2000a). Ovimbundu slave traders purchased them from chiefs who wanted to get rid of "undesirables"; occasionally women and children were kidnapped at lonely places such as at a riverside or while working in the fields. They brought them to Portuguese merchant ships on the coast, notably to Benguela from where they were taken to Brazil and other destinations. The trade now affected all of eastern Angola (Kubik 1979, 1991: 32–35).

During my first fieldwork among Ngangela-speaking people in southeastern Angola in 1965, I found that Ovimbundu slave traders, called *vimbali* by those affected, were commemorated among the Vambwela and Vankhangala in the form of two masked dancers called *Kambinda* (the slave trader) and *Chindele* (the white man) always appearing together in a public performance (cf. pictures in Kubik 2000a: 130).

By comparison, the situation in Louisiana was somewhat different from other New World destinations of the transatlantic slave trade. French colonial presence had started with La Salle's exploration of the Mississippi region in 1682 and the construction of various forts. In 1718 New Orleans was founded. A year later some 450 Africans were landed at Biloxi, brought over directly from West Africa, where the French had a firm bridgehead in Senegal. In 1638 they had established a station in what became known as St. Louis, north of Dakar.

Gwendolyn Midlo Hall's research (1992, 2001, 2005) has been of paramount importance in unraveling the historical ethnic background of enslaved Africans in Louisiana. Under French rule, between 1719 and 1731 the initial wave came mainly through ports in westernmost Africa, Ile de Gorée, etc. They were people identified as Wolof, Fulɓe, Bambara, Mandiŋ, but also "Mina," Fõ, "Nago" (Yoruba from the Guinea Coast), and even Chamba from the hinterland in northeastern Nigeria, besides a few from the Kongo/Angola region. Hall estimates that two-thirds of them originated from Senegambia (1992: 29, 34–35, 41, 159). It seems that this founding contingent in the colony underwent primary processes of inter–West African transculturation in Louisiana, blending languages and customs, which gradually evolved into a Creole culture and language. When a wave of Koongo/Angola people was brought to Louisiana under Spanish rule after the treaty of Fontainebleau 1762, they adjusted to a certain extent to the Creole culture that had been developed. (See also Sublette 2008 on that subject.)

As deplorable as it is from a humanitarian point of view, the hard facts about the transatlantic slave trade were dictated by economics. Workers were needed on the plantations, including skilled workers, with specialist knowledge in the agriculture of tropical environments. And since they would not come voluntarily—in contrast to twentieth-century labor migration, when information about work opportunities could be obtained through the media—they were selected and taken against their will by agreements (contracts) with those in power. They were "drafted," so to say, into bondage. After the first cargo of enslaved Africans arrived in Louisiana in 1719, it soon became clear what kind of workers were really needed on the plantations. In an essay on agriculture and the African presence in colonial Louisiana, Thomas M. Fiehrer (1979: 10) has stressed that enslaved Africans "themselves constituted the specialists who brought the crops along." The responsible Company of the Indies instructed the captains of slave ships to purchase barrels of rice from Africa and recruit people who were knowledgeable in cultivating those crops. Rice became an important crop in Louisiana and later a staple in Cajun cuisine, all as a result of this economic policy. It is now a staple in several Louisiana traditions—Cajun, Creole, New Orleans. Not only manual labor was imported from Africa, but knowledge, technology, and also many food items such as watermelons, okra, pigeon peas, and domestic animals such as guinea fowl (Fiehrer 1979). In some other places ship carpentry was a desired African specialists' knowledge, as is suggested in the context of a recent genealogical study by Donald Hopkins (2011; Hopkins and Bamberg 2011). As to rice cultivation in the New World, there is an important study by Judith A. Carney (2001) of its African sources with reference to the Bambara rice cultivators in West Africa.

French rule of Louisiana lasted until 1766 when, at the end of a protracted colonial war between Britain and France, the treaty of Fontainebleau in 1762 provided for the cession of Louisiana to Spain. However, Spanish rule did not last, and—apart from leading to a stronger Koongo/Angola presence of people in Louisiana—it may have had the least permanent impact among all the cultural influences absorbed in New Orleans.

In 1800 Spain agreed to cede Louisiana back to France. It appears that this was part of a wider political arrangement. France did not keep her former colony. Napoleon Bonaparte, in serious need of money and a feasible working relationship with the United States, sold Louisiana to the States in 1803. Roger Cohen, in the *International Herald Tribune*, April 11, 2007, called the Louisiana Purchase an "astonishing transaction." He says that President Thomas Jefferson had really only wanted New Orleans because of its port. "When his envoys were offered all of Louisiana in a bargain, they could hardly believe . . . In fact, for a mere $15 million, much of it borrowed from British banks, the United States acquired a land mass stretching from the Mississippi to the Rockies, and from the Gulf of Mexico to the Canadian border. . . . Napoleon, under military pressure in Haiti and elsewhere . . . thought he'd done all right. 'I have just given England a rival that will sooner or later humble her pride', he commented."

A year later in Haiti, an insurrection began against French rule by the dominant African population, resulting in independence from colonial rule of a first African state in the New World, under "Emperor" Jean-Jacques Dessalines. (See also Henry Louis Gates Jr.'s illuminating account of Dessalines's rule and fortifications in a recent documentary DVD, 2011.) In 1806, following political events in France, Haiti was declared a Republic, but two years later the eastern part of the island with a strong Spanish-speaking population seceded. A wave of refugees poured into Cuba and from there into Louisiana, especially to New Orleans. Among them there were many speakers of Kikoongo and their masters who did not want to live under "Arada" rule, i.e., under the Haitian majority of descendants from the Fō of the Kingdom of Dahomey.

Between the years 1791 and 1804, as a result of the insurrection in Haiti, some people fled directly from the island to New Orleans, seeking asylum. But the majority of those who did not want to live under the new rule fled later, first to Cuba, which is much closer. Based on statistics given in an article by Paul LaChance (1992), Freddi Williams Evans gives the following assessment of what happened (F. W. Evans 2011: 25): "In 1809, however, with the outbreak of war in Europe between France and Spain, officials expelled French refugees from Cuba and other Spanish colonies who did not pledge allegiance to the Spanish crown from those colonies. Among the thousands who fled to Louisiana from Cuba, 3,226 were enslaved Africans, 3,102 were free people of color, and 2,731 were white. The majority of these immigrants remained in New Orleans increasing the city's population from 17,001 in 1806 to 24,552 in 1810." Such a significant increase of the African or Afro-Caribbean population in the city also inflated the numbers participating in Congo Square gatherings. In 1811, and again in 1817, however, a City Ordinance was passed which restricted all gatherings for recreational purposes to Sundays, until sunset. The 1817 Ordinances also restricted dancing on Sunday afternoons to one public place as appointed by the mayor, i.e., to Congo Square, and placed the gathering crowds under police observation. Dances called "bamboula," "calenda," "congo," and "counjai" (so written in French orthography) flourished in New Orleans during that period.

Fear of rebellion was acute in all the New World colonies, French, Spanish, Portuguese, etc. For Louisiana this explains the haste of the installment of restrictions concerning free assembly, but also the ambivalent attitude of the authorities as to the extent of allowing the enslaved subjects some form of recreational activities, involving games, music, and dance. Some of the authorities speculated that music and dance could have a soothing effect on people, and thereby help the system survive, because energy was dispensed by those in bondage that would otherwise be used for organizing resistance and insurrection. This viewpoint was repeatedly expressed, for example, by City Mayor Girod in his exchanges with the City Council of New Orleans in 1813 (F. W. Evans 2011: 140ff.). The ambivalence of the authorities is expressed in the often contradictory ordinances that were passed by the City Council during the next few decades concerning music and dance activities in the place called Congo Square.

As to the ethnic composition of the Africans in New Orleans, primary sources are in short supply, but there are some rare statements from the times of Spanish rule. Bishop Cyrillo de Barcelona is quoted in C. M. Chambon's book *In and Around the Old St. Louis Cathedral of New Orleans* (1908: 33) as having issued a pastoral letter in 1786 denouncing "Negros" who assembled and danced in a green expanse called "Place Congo." They were dancing "bamboula" and performing rites imported from Africa by the "'Yolofs,' 'Foulahs,' 'Bambarras,' 'Mandingoes,' and other races." If this is authentic—though to me it sounds like a late nineteenth-century transliteration of African names by a French speaker—it would mean that the dominating ethnic groups before 1800 in New Orleans were speakers of I.A.1 languages (Wolof, Fulɓe) and I.A.2 languages (Bambara, Mandiŋ) in Joseph Greenberg's classification of African languages, all of them "blues people" so to say (Kubik 1999a), while Congolese are not mentioned. This may reflect the accents of the French transatlantic slave trade of the period, by which a majority of West African savannah people were among the captives. But the "bamboula" dance was most certainly associated with people of Koongo background.

The presence of West African savannah musical traditions in New Orleans at that time is also suggested in a diary entry dated February 24, 1799, published by Fortescue Cunning in *Sketches of a Tour to the Western Country* (1810); he refers to drumming, fifing and fiddling. This is corroborated by Bergquin-Duvallon's *Travels in Louisiana and the Floridas in the Year 1802*, published 1806, in which the fiddle is specially mentioned. One-stringed fiddles, variously called *gogé, gojé*, etc. are a continuing, vibrant tradition in the West African savannah, as is confirmed in Jacqueline Cogdell DjeDje's in-depth field study *Fiddling in West Africa: Touching the Spirit in Fulbe, Hausa, and Dagbamba Cultures* (2008), an important book also in connection with the background to African American fiddling practices in the eighteenth and nineteenth centuries.

Christian Schultz in his *Travels on an Inland Voyage* (1810) visited Congo Square in New Orleans two years earlier and saw Africans engaged in some twenty different dance groups; this can be taken as an indication that they were split along ethnic traditions. It is also suggested by the wording of his note that they all had their own "national music." He does not, however, name any ethnic groups.

Schultz saw long drums "of various sizes, from two to eight feet in length, three or four of which make a band." This hints at a Koongo background. Such drums have been collected in Belgian Congo during the late nineteenth and early twentieth centuries and can be found, for example in the Musée Royal de l'Afrique Centrale, Tervuren, Belgium (Boone 1951: 1: 71), and in the City Museum, München, Germany (Kubik, Malamusi, and Varsányi 2013). The historic New Orleans drums are perhaps also comparable to those documented in 1977 in Paul Henley's film *Cuyagua* in Venezuela (cf. my review, Kubik 1988). Unfortunately, Schultz does not give any information about the type of tension for the skin used on the Congo Square long drums. If we knew the technology it would be easier to identify the likely regional African inspiration to their making.

Even without direct references to ethnic groups by New Orleans visitors in the early nineteenth century, we can assume that the share of Bantu language–speaking people from the Congo/Angola region was at first relatively small, but increased with the influx of refugees from Haiti and Santo Domingo in 1808, besides the Haitians who were descendants of Fō-speaking and *vodu*-practicing Dahomeyans. In the United States the importation of slaves was forbidden after 1808 by the US Constitution. Some illegal importation persisted, however, up to the Civil War (1861–65).

Also, patterns of the transatlantic slave trade were changing after Britain's declaration in 1815 that the Equator would be a line of demarcation, north of which Britain would attack any slave ships encountered, liberate the captives, and resettle them in places like Freetown, Sierra Leone. In Sigismund W. Koelle's *Polyglotta Africana* ..., first published in London 1854, we have a linguistic documentation of the ethnic origins of recaptives settled in Sierra Leone in 1848 (see also map in Curtin 1969: 245–46) with an overwhelming share of people from the Bight of Benin (Fō, Yoruba, Nupe, Bini, 63.7 percent) and the Bight of Biafra (Igbo, Efik, Ibibio, etc., 20.2 percent). This means that the share of West Africans from the Guinea Coast arriving at New World destinations must have decreased significantly after 1815, while the traffic of people from Congo, Angola, and increasingly also Moçambique through the Portuguese trade—in collaboration with local ethnic groups such as the Ovimbundu in Angola and the Wayao in northern Moçambique—was filling the gaps in the supply of human manual labor.

Another aspect concerning musical traditions in the southern United States emerges from reports such as James Creecy in his book *Scenes in the South* (1860), about his visit to New Orleans in 1834. He describes a performance in Congo Square, referring to separate groups "in different sections" of the square, mentioning "banjos, tom-toms, violins, jawbones, triangle," which indicates contemporaneous developments. Like others he emphasizes that the dancers were wearing bells, shells, etc., around their legs and arms.

In 1834 reverberations from the emerging blackface minstrelsy were beginning to influence the choice of musical instruments among African Americans. As much as blackface minstrels in the United States were portraying the "negro" by mimicking what they thought was "his ways," so did some of those affected internalize the portrait and begin to act exactly in the manner they were portrayed.

A kind of feedback took place from blackface minstrelsy. Homemade banjos and fiddles, jawbones, etc. and their playing techniques had been picked up by young "whites" from African Americans in the first place, but those instruments also thereby gained enhanced visibility in the broader population. From "bones" to jugs to gut buckets, washboards and "jazzbos" (kazoos), those homemade devices would all become a fashion, reflecting back on African Americans of the antebellum generation.

In Africa, by the mid-nineteenth century the slave trade—clandestinely or openly—had shifted from West Africa to Bantu language–speaking cultures in central and southeast Africa, notably Angola and northern Moçambique, as witnessed by David Livingstone in 1866 in the Nyasa area. Most of the East African slave trade was in the hands of Zanzibar Arab traders and part of the Indian Ocean trading network. But some people ended up in on Portuguese slave ships crossing the Atlantic.

Many references in the literature of the nineteenth century (cf. Kubik 1979, 1991 [2013] for Brazil) speak of people from Angola and the Congo as gentle, docile, and adaptive, of slaves from Gabon as suicidal, of coastal West Africans as rebellious, and of Mandiŋ speakers as practitioners of evil magic. In Brazil the designation "mandingueros" for people from that part of Africa has survived until the present.

Due to a convergence of all these political, economic, and social factors, the presence of people with a Central African ethnic background also increased in New Orleans during the early decades of the nineteenth century. Philip D. Curtin (1969) in his seminal study *The Atlantic Slave Trade*, however, warns us that slave imports into Louisiana are difficult to assess with accuracy (82–83). He says that "the total slave trade to Louisiana up to 1803 can be estimated very uncertainly at about 28,300" (83). It is likely, therefore, that the increasing presence of people with a Bantu language background, e.g., Kikoongo, was due to an influx from the Caribbean rather than the result of human supplies directly from Africa, by slave ships clandestinely operating south of the 1815 equatorial demarcation.

One of our earliest sources for the reconstruction of a tentative cultural picture of Africans in New Orleans is the often quoted journals of Henry Benjamin Latrobe from the years 1799 to 1820. What did Latrobe really see in New Orleans and what were the circumstances of his observations? His background was in architecture and engineering; his curiosity remains undisputed.

The observations were made in 1819 on a Sunday afternoon. Besides writing them down, he took pains to draw sketches of the musical instruments he saw being played in Congo Square. Latrobe did not intend to do research on Congo Square culture; he passed there accidentally, probably because he was attracted by the extraordinary sounds emanating from the singing and dancing crowd. He states ironically that he had thought the "noise" proceeded "from some horse Mill, the horses trampling on a wooden floor." But it was drumming. Then he saw a crowd of some five to six hundred persons assembled in an open space or "public square." From others he learned that such meetings were regular on Sundays. He identified the people as "black" and described the crowd as disciplined and peaceful.

Latrobe was in no way hindered from approaching and joining the crowd. Drawing near to see the performances, he noticed that there were several distinct clusters of people with the performers in the middle of the circles. He "examined" four of them, but there were many more. In the middle of these circular clusters of onlookers there was a ring, "the largest not 10 feet in diameter." The first ring revealed two women dancing. The women "held each a coarse handkerchief extended by the corners in their hands, and set to each other in a miserably dull and slow figure, hardly moving their feet or bodies." The music for these women was provided by two drums and a stringed instrument. "An old man sat astride of a cylindrical drum about a foot in diameter and beat it with incredible quickness with the edge of his hand and fingers. The other drum was an open staved thing held between the knees and beaten in the same manner. They made an incredible noise. The most curious instrument however was a stringed instrument which no doubt was imported from Africa. On the top of the fingerboard was the rude figure of a man in sitting posture, and two pegs behind him to which the strings were fastened. The body was a Calabash. It was played upon by a very little old man, apparently 80 or 90 years old" (204). Latrobe made drawings of these instruments. These drawings have been published so often (cf. Epstein 1977, F. W. Evans 2011) that we need not reproduce them here. The gourd-resonated two-stringed lute, according to the description in the text, however, appears in the drawing as if it had three strings. His impression that the instrument was imported from Africa implies that the "Little old man, apparently 80 or 90 years old" who played it would have been allowed to carry it along from his African home on a slave ship. A chordophone such as the one depicted could be tentatively linked to a West African savannah culture, although the carved figure at the top would appear to be unusual. And so are two more organological traits: a flat neck and two vertical tunings pegs. When I showed the drawings to Moya A. Malamusi (conversation, December 1, 2014) he reacted instantly that he did not know any sub-Saharan stringed instrument of that type, rather it may have been based on some kind of Arab lute. That would shift the original source of the inspiration to the Maghreb, possibly even to Spain or Portugal. It seems to indicate decisive processes of transculturation at work in Congo Square meetings by 1819. In any case, it is surprising that this instrument should have been played together with two loud drums. The one drum upon which the man was sitting seems to have a type of cord-and-peg tension that is found only with cylindrical drums.

The second drawing of a drum is sketchy. We cannot be certain about the type of string tension, and whether it is single-headed or perhaps double-headed. Obviously, Latrobe made his drawings after the visit, from memory. Some details may have been forgotten or altered, which makes it hazardous to try and allocate these instruments regionally to any known African cultural tradition, besides tentatively suggesting West African savannah cultures.

The text continues by describing that the "women squalled out a burthen" (probably trills, ololyge) "to the playing consisting of two notes" and he compares this to the response in worksongs by urban "negroes" in a leader/chorus organization. Then he goes on to describe the next group. He mentions that all the circles had "the same sort of dancers," but one was larger, accommodating "a ring of a dozen women walking by way of dancing round the music in the center," i.e., around the instruments (204). After stating that those instruments were of a different kind in this group, he describes and draws a hand-held slit-gong that was beaten on the side with a short stick. This could tentatively be linked with Koongo cultures (cf. small hand-held slit drums discussed in Kubik, Malamusi, and Varsanyi 2014: 28). This instrument was played together with a square drum "looking like a stool." A woman musician was also involved, beating a calabash studded with brass nails.

Although it is equally difficult to link this second tradition as a whole to any specific regional culture of Africa, it can be said that the circle dance could point to an Angolan tradition, or other traditions in south-central Africa. Instruments similar to the hand-held gong were reported in northern Angola and the southwestern Democratic Republic of Congo (Janata 1975: 14). They were found among the Bayaka and Bakoongo. Two specimens are kept in the Museum für Völkerkunde, Vienna.

Latrobe saw performances that were clearly examples of African music and dance traditions with yet little New World modification, and (as he says) the songs were sung in African languages. But his report is disappointingly inconclusive. It is not possible with any degree of certainty to place the two ensemble traditions observed into the vicinity of any known historical African culture. Nevertheless, Latrobe's diary notes are a testimony to the retention of African music and dance traditions in New Orleans' Congo Square by 1819.

A new set of sources became available from the 1840s on in the form of casual reports in the New Orleans newspaper *Daily Picayune*. In an anonymous report that appeared under the title "The Congo Dance" on October 18, 1843, the reporters say that they had never seen this kind of dance before "until last Sunday." Then they report: "This ball—this black ball, was a public one, and was held in a yard of a house in the Third Municipality. The company was numerous and ranged from ebony black to quateroon yellow." Describing the musical instruments, they mention "a long neck banjo, the head of which was ornamented with a bunch of sooty parti-colored ribbands." Clearly this instrument was homemade. It was accompanied by another musician who "beat the jawbones of an ass with a rusty key," while a third musician had a homemade "petit tambour, on which he kept time with his digits, and the fourth beat most vehemently an old headless cask that lay on its side, ballasted with iron nails."

Such a description is detailed enough to allow for tentative conclusions about the kind of music that was played. Clearly, the functional organization was similar to that of small groups playing for dance even today in certain rural areas of (for example, southeast) Africa. The functional division is clear from the *Daily Picayune* description: the cask was functioning as a bass drum, the "petit tambour" player was probably marking a fast pulse, perhaps the elementary pulsation, while the "jawbones of an ass"—if they were not used as a scraper agitated with that "rusty key," but struck—would point to the use of some kind of timeline pattern, perhaps a version of the ubiquitous eight-pulse pattern in its cinquillo or tresillo shape. On top of this percussion basis, the virtuoso banjoist was free to introduce the melodic themes of the songs and probably work out many variations, all of it improvisatory.

The article also describes the three dancers'—one male, two female—corporeal equipment. It mentions that "their male partner had on a pair of leather knee caps from which were suspended . . . metal nails, which made a jingling noise that timed with the music." A "general chorus," i.e., joint singing, is mentioned.

Stylistically, this music may represent an original mid-nineteenth-century African American small group innovative development in New Orleans, coming out of previous traditions by Bantu language speakers. Therefore, the label "Congo Dance" is not far-fetched.

More such reports came up from time to time in the *Daily Picayune*, as in an article on June 24, 1845, under the title "Scenes in Congo Square—Regular Ethiopian Break Down." The word "Ethiopian" would later become important as a synonym for African or black in sheet music. Some of the songs sung at Congo Square were in English, and are mentioned by their titles.

Leg rattles of the dancers are also mentioned in another report, during the 1840s, by a visitor to the "Congo Green" who was African American (cf. Schweninger 1984). This visitor, James Thomas, clearly describes a possibly Angola-derived tradition: "they indulged in dancing with music made by thumping on the head of a barrel with skin stretched over it. The performer would thump on it and carry on a chant. Another would beat the sides with two cobs or sticks. The dancers used to wear pieces of tin or some substitute on their legs to make a sort of jingle. I judged it was African music" (109).

Striking a drum on the sides with sticks is a clear indication of the use of a timeline pattern. The Bantu background in James Thomas's account can be taken for granted. The description reminds me of my field documentation in 1979 in Capivari, Estado de São Paulo, Brazil of a *batuque* performance by an eighty-year-old expert drummer, Benedito Caxias (Kubik 1990).

Markers for Historical Connections

What are the most reliable indicators allowing us to reconstruct historical connections between New World musical styles and their African antecedents? In previous research (Kubik 1979, 1998c, 2008a) I have pointed to asymmetric timeline patterns with their inherent mathematics as markers of indisputable value for establishing links with specific African regions (see also map in Kubik 1999a: 101). I also point to technology, as in specific forms of drum skin tension, particularly wedge-and-ring and cord-and-peg tensions (Kubik 1998c: 218–20) and to certain tonal-harmonic concepts (see chapter "The African Matrix . . ." in this book). On the other hand, I warn students that polyrhythm, off-beat phrasing of melodic accents (Richard A. Waterman's useful term) and call-and-response organization are so ubiquitous across the panorama of African music that they cannot, in most cases, serve as markers or indicators of specific cultural genealogies.

By now the list of markers is quite extensive. It can be expanded beyond technology and musical structure to include concepts in the perception and handling of space and time (as in ideographs of eastern Angola, Kubik 2010: II: 275–322). This includes movement organization, in both their auditory and senso-motoric aspects, from playing attitudes such as squatting astride a long drum, which is generally held to indicate a Koongo background, to dance styles. Dance styles in various forms of African American music are not only a core phenomenon in New World cultures, they are also genre-specific, as they are in Africa, and regional as concerns the African historical background.

In a wide area covering eastern Angola into northwestern Zambia and Katanga (in the Democratic Republic of Congo) with branch-offs in some directions (Koongo, Zambezi Valley, etc.), there are female solo dance styles in which the performer hardly moves in space, shifting her feet just a little, in tiny steps, but the minute, barely visible actual movement experience is concentrated in the performer's pelvis. In eastern Angola this technique is learned in the *chikula* girl's initiation rites at puberty, and there are two prominent movements: *mutenya*, a "pelvis circle," a slow, circular movement of the pelvis; and *kukoka* (to pull), which consists of a set of pelvis jerks, as if writing a square (a figure with four corners) into space to the rhythm of the drums. I have a cinematographic documentation of all these female movement patterns from my 1965 research in eastern Angola, during performances of *makisi avampwevo* (women's masks) (Culture Research Archive Kubik/Malamusi, Vienna, Ciné-film No. 4 and 5, Angola).

By contrast, some cattle herders in the Sudan and in East Africa, for example, emphasize the "high jump" in their dance styles, while dancers among the Fō in West Africa concentrate on spectacular movement of shoulder and shoulder blades in the *achyā* and other dances. Are there any sources in the literature about Congo Square and African dancing in New Orleans that would suggest the presence of any of those styles mentioned? In fact there are, because organization in all African dance styles was so unusual for European eyes, especially from the angle of European-American idiocultural upbringing in the eighteenth and nineteenth centuries, that visitors' attention in Congo Square tended to be regularly drawn to dance performance. Reactions, however, were extremely varied, ranging from aesthetic rejection to curiosity and analytic interest. Benjamin Latrobe in 1819 called the performance by two women in one of the circles "a miserably dull and slow figure, hardly moving their feet or bodies." It is almost certain that these women were carrying out some intra-corporeal, pelvis-centered movement, which gives us a clue as to where the antecedent ideas could possibly be placed on the map of Africa.

Other observers have been more explicit in their descriptions. F .W. Evans (2011) has collected some elucidating accounts in her chapter on 'The Dances" in Congo Square. Citing just two such reports seems enough to be conclusive.

(1) In a letter to Henry Krehbiel in New York in 1885, Lafcadio Hearn observed women's dance movement in a backyard of a New Orleans house, dancing the "Congo" accompanied by homemade drums. He writes: "As for the dance—in which the women do not take their feet off the ground—it is as lascivious as is possible. The men dance very differently . . . leaping in the air."

This is almost certainly a reference to female movement patterns involving the "pelvis circle" and/or pelvis jerks. Movement of this kind would inevitably impress a middle- or upper-class observer in those days as "lascivious." This changed radically after 1893 with Egyptian belly dancers' success at the World Fair in Chicago. It then contributed indirectly to the social "rehabilitation" of such movements, including ones from African American traditions, facilitating their later acceptance in jazz and popular dance. However, the man's movement behavior in Hearn's account point not to an eastern Angolan culture but to a movement tradition inherited from southwestern Angola, an area with a strong cattle-herder cultural complex.

(2) In more detail, this composite picture is confirmed by a report from Alceé Fortier (quoted in F. W. Evans 2011: 92), who in an article published in 1888 describes a dance he saw in the 1860s on a plantation in St. James Parish, and which he calls "Pilé Chactas" (Fortier 1888: 136–40):

> The woman had to dance almost without moving her feet. It was the man who did all the work turning around her, kneeling drown, making the most grotesque and extraordinary faces writhing like a serpent, while the woman was almost immovable....
>
> The musical instruments were, first, a barrel with one end covered with an ox-hide—this was the drum; then two sticks and the jawbone of a mule, with the teeth still on it—this was the violin. The principal musician bestrode the barrel and began to beat on the hide, singing as loud as he could.... The second musician took the sticks and beat on the wood of the barrel. While the third made a dreadful music by rattling the teeth of the jawbone with a stick. Five or six men stood around the musicians and sang without stopping.

Even more revealing than the description of the dance is the detailed description of the use of the homemade musical instruments. Most certainly, there was no "violin," but the jawbone of a mule, with the teeth still on, was used as a scraper. Bamboo scrapers have been used into the twentieth century in traditions of Kimbundu speakers in coastal Angola. The jawbone with the teeth can be understood as a substitution instrument in a place where no suitable bamboo could be grown. Once again the custom of striking a stick pattern on a drum's corpus, points to the Koongo/Angola region, and indicates the presence of the concept of a timeline, most likely asymmetric.

The dance style of the woman fits the picture we have gathered from the same cultural region, but "Pilé Chactas" could not have been based on a Ngangela (eastern Angolan) tradition, for the simple reason that men and women do not dance together in that area, except lined up in two opposing front rows, from which a male and a female person may step out and approach one another before retreating. Either it was an adaptation of a European pair dance to Central African aesthetics, or it is linked historically to a southwestern Angolan tradition, in which a man and a woman may interact in a close-up manner. In the southwestern

Angolan *nkili* dance, for example, the male partner, approaching the woman to receive him, jumps up high and is supported in air by her hands, as if she were lifting him into near horizontal position. Such a figure has not been reported in the Louisiana sources we have. F. W. Evans (2011) has stressed the need for a comparative approach in analyzing all these sources: "The commonalities between and among these descriptions of Kongo-Angola-influenced dances in Louisiana are significant considering the span of years between observations, the fact that the observations took place in different parts of the state, and the fact that most writers only made brief journal entries or incidental observations, not detailed illustrations. It is important to distinguish between accounts of the dance as Holmes offered and the more descriptive reports of the dance as Latrobe, Hearn, and Fortier provided" (92). ("Holmes" here refers to a brief account by Isaac Holmes in 1821 in a rural location outside New Orleans.)

From our present-day knowledge of dance-styles in twentieth-century Central Africa, including the former Kingdom of Koongo and all Angola, it is clear that what has been described as "Congo Dance" in various nineteenth-century sources about Louisiana and New Orleans refers to several surviving Central African dance traditions, which the external observers were simply summarizing under one label.

We can compare some of those descriptions with our Angolan field material—in spite of the time difference separating those traditions—and establish possible historical links. At least we have been able to narrow down the range of possible historical connections in the constituent elements of the music and movement patterns of the so-called "Congo Dance" to specific regions in Central Africa. That some of these Angolan movement patterns have survived, reconfigured, into twentieth-century African American dance cultures, in shimmy and many other forms, has been extensively documented (cf. sources quoted in F. W. Evans 2011: 93ff.)

The Fat Chickens

An overview of the ethnic panorama of antebellum Africans in New Orleans, which appears to be reasonably comprehensive, is found in George Washington Cable's two 1886 articles in the *Century Magazine*.

As a historical source, George Washington Cable (1844–1925) has been dismissed as unreliable, irrelevant, even plagiarizing. Obviously, many of the things he reported he could not have observed himself, because they relate to circumstances in the first half of the nineteenth century, before he was born. This also applies to the impressive drawings by Edward W. Kemble that accompany Cable's articles.

Cable has been accused of excessively relying in his writings on a book by Mederic-Louis-Elie Moreau de Saint-Méry on Santo Domingo, published in Philadelphia in 1797, and that he might have mixed data from St. Domingo and Haiti with observations made by others and by himself at a later date in New Orleans. Indeed, Koongo drumming and ritual traditions have been preserved even until now in the Dominican Republic by a small community of sixth-generation descendants from the area of the Kingdom of Koongo, as is demonstrated in Henry Louis Gates Jr.'s 2011 DVD *Black in Latin America*, and as was researched on several field trips by Martha Ellen Davis (1994).

The problem is that Cable does not separate meticulously what is based on firsthand personal observation from hearsay and from information gathered from the writings by others, with the exception of one definite reference to the writings of Moreau de St. Méry concerning a certain *vodu* ceremony (reproduced in Katz 1969: 56–60). Gilbert Chase, author of the book *America's Music: From the Pilgrims to the Present*, rev. 3rd ed. (1987: 65), thought that Cable either directly copied or paraphrased Moreau de St. Méry. He calls Cable's two articles "fictionalized hodgepodge."

And yet, in view of the scarcity of sources, and the rich detail in Cable's accounts, one should not wrap his peelings too quickly and throw them into the dustbin. Cable was a native of New Orleans, although at one time he was forced to leave the South due to his writings about mistreatment of African Americans. He also fought in the Confederate Army. By the time he wrote the two articles he had absorbed enough information from elderly fellow citizens in New Orleans—who did have firsthand experience of the Congo Square meetings— that we should at least give George Washington Cable some recognition as a carrier of oral tradition. Some was mixed up with readings, of course, but there is a substance of original information. In Africa, when we work with informants, asking them to write down what they know about local history, we get a comparable "hodgepodge," but we have learned from Jan Vansina (1965) and others how to sort out oral testimonies. As with other, in part secondary sources, we have no choice but to use such data—some based on firsthand observation, some secondary—as well as we can, if only with caution, and interpret them from the angle of our present knowledge of African cultures and their New World extensions. Here it is important to keep in mind that the two articles published in 1886 attempt to paint a cohesive historical picture of a cultural world some fifty to seventy years earlier, during a period just after the Louisiana Purchase of 1803.

What struck me first when scrutinizing the Cable texts was the inclusion of so many words from African languages. That leaves no doubt about the authenticity of some of his observations, whatever their ultimate source may be. In "The Dance in Place Congo" (Cable 1886, reproduced in Katz 1969: 37) there is an enumeration of ethnic group names by which are identified the regions from where enslaved people were taken to Louisiana. Describing the people who gathered for a dance at Congo Square, he mentions Cabo Verdians (Senegalese); "Mandingos" from Gambia, with their special skills in metal working and trade; Soso people in Guinée, i.e., speakers of Susu, a I.A.2 Mande language; and many other groups also from the Guinea coast. The names must be transliterated, of course; sometimes they indicate only the place where these people were kept for shipment across the Atlantic, e.g., "Minas" from near El Mina Castle in Ghana (Gold Coast). "Nago," as in Brazil, refers to people speaking Yoruba, and "Fonds" (in this spelling) cannot be anything else but Fõ from Dahomey and Togo. The slave trade, of course, extended further east. It included captives speaking Igbo and many Central Africans. "Angola" in Cable's text refers to Kimbundu-speaking people, while "Ambrice" is a port in northeastern Angola, on the periphery of the former Kingdom of Koongo, from which many people speaking Kikoongo or Kimbundu were shipped away. Each of these groups was also "tagged" describing its reputation. These tags were similar to those known, for example, from Brazil (cf. Kubik 1979: 10, 1991: 17–33). For example the "Angola" group, including Koongo, is described by Cable as "good-natured," and he writes that "these are they for whom the dance and the place are named." On the other hand, the "Arada" from the Dahomeyan/Togolese coast are vilified as "half-civilized and quick-witted but ferocious" and as "the original Voudou worshiper" (Cable 1986a: [37]).

The patterns of nomenclature are structurally similar to those in Brazil and probably in other parts of the Caribbean. Ethnic names and the names of ports had actually served as trademarks, characterizing the value of a slave from the regions in question. But Cable's account also testifies to processes of reinterpretation of the African words, in particular nouns denoting ethnic groups. It includes an instructive example of a phonological transfer in one of these designations, namely "poulahs"—so written in French orthography—for the Fulɓe people of the West African savannah (see also map of their distribution in DjeDje 2008). In Louisiana the word turned into "poulards" (fat chickens) (Cable 1886: 522). The pattern here is that an African term is phonetically reinterpreted by speakers unfamiliar with African languages and "understood" accordingly in their own tongues.

Cable's note about the Fulɓe in Louisiana presents, of course, a slightly different case. Whether it is based on his personal or someone else's observation does not really matter. The observation as such is valid. *Fula* ("foulards") was a term that could be misheard as "poulards." This must have amused many people, because of the implicit joke. Fulɓe people are normally quite slim in stature, never "fat." So it may have alluded to a quality considered to be hidden in their nature.

Bantu Linguistic Connections

There is more related to linguistics in Cable's second text "Creole Slave Songs," while it is, unfortunately, not certain that all this only refers to New Orleans, Louisiana, since he mentions contemporaneous writings about the "African-Creole dialect" based on French from several parts of the Caribbean. But he also mentions two colleagues, Dr. Armand Mercier, "a Louisiana Creole," and "Professor James A. Harrison, an Anglo-Louisianian," as writers on the subject, without indicating, however, to what extent he had used their works.

He clearly refers to Louisiana in his example of how the French verb *dormir* was changed into *dromi*. After citing a number of phonetic changes introduced into French by people of African descent, he goes into the interesting case of grammatical structure—without, however, being able to find out what kind of African language memory is behind it.

He takes the word *courir* (to run) as an example, and gives the following forms in French-based Creole:

mo courri (I run)
to courri (you run)
li courri (he/she runs)

no courri (we run)
vo courri (you all run)
ye courri (they run)

That is certainly plain Bantu in structure. Unknowingly, Cable therefore has testified to how Africans with a background in Bantu languages—not the "poulards"—and who were most likely Kikoongo speakers had modified French conjugations to conform with their own language's patterns. The French personal pronouns "moi" (instead of "je"), "tu," and "il" were turned into Bantu prefixes *mo-* (first person), *to-* (second person), *li-* (third person), no gender distinction in the singular, with an unchangeable verb stem *courri*.

To try out how linguistic and musicological inquiry could be combined, I scrutinized the song texts in his articles, those that were in African languages and apparently associated with *vodu* ("voudou") ceremonies (Cable 1986a "Creole Slave Songs," cf. Katz 1969: 59).

There are two songs in Cable's second article (1986b [59–60]) introduced to the reader as associated with "Voodoo" ceremonies, and apparently sung in New Orleans during the early decades of the nineteenth century. The first one is printed under a picture of the famous *vodu* priest Marie Laveau, who died in 1881 and who is commemorated in Cable's article by Kemble's illustration. Cable introduces the subject by saying that both the dance and the song "entered into the negro worship. That worship was as dark and horrid as bestialized savagery could make the adoration of serpents" (Cable 1886b [56]). Obviously, he did not understand the significance of a central *vodu* image in this Fō-originated religion, incorporating *aido hwedo* (the rainbow snake), an ouroboros figure, or *Dā*, the snake spirit. He goes on saying: "So revolting was it, and so morally hideous, that even in the West Indian French possessions, a hundred years ago [i.e., in the last decades of the eighteenth century] with the slave trade in full blast and the West Indian planter and slave what they were, the orgies of the Voodoos were forbidden. Yet both there and in Louisiana they were practiced."

Then he refers to St. Méry, that the latter had written that the "Aradas" introduced them. But for this information he also quotes one of his own informants in Louisiana, the late Alexander Dimitry, a "learned Creole scholar." He also explains that he once saw "in her extreme old age, the famed Marie Laveau. Her dwelling was in the quadroon quarter of New Orleans, but a step or two from Congo Square, a small adobe cabin just off the sidewalk . . ." (Cable 1886b [57]).

After mentioning a "Voodoo ceremony" that took place "on the night of the 23rd of June, 1884," suggesting that he had actually seen it, he reverts to St. Méry, talking about these ceremonies in a general manner, apparently with reference to St. Domingo, and describing what appears to be an initiation ceremony. Then he says (still referring to St. Méry): "The queen shakes the box (with the snake) and tinkles its bells, the rum-bottle gurgles, the chant alternates between king and chorus:

Eh! Eh! Bomba, honc! honc!
Canga bafio tay,
Canga moon day lay,
Canga do keelah,
Canga li——

He adds that "honc! honc! honc!" was "Hen! Hen! "in St. Méry's spelling for French pronunciation, and in a footnote states that it expressed "a horrid grunt." The comparison shows that Cable knew St. Méry's text notation. To what extent his own notation of the song (reproduced above) is simply a transfer from French into English orthography, or comes from an independent source in New Orleans, is not easily clarified. My guess is that he checked Méry's transcription with a New Orleans informant.

For many years this song in Cable's article had attracted my curiosity. When in 1977 my musician friend Donald Kachamba and I were invited to tour West and Central Africa for concerts and lectures under the sponsorship of the Goethe Institute, Germany, in cooperation with local universities, it was an opportunity to take the Cable articles with me and show them to people in a dozen African countries, and discuss the song texts with students and colleagues to obtain their opinions.

But before we started the trip, I transferred the English orthography in Cable's rendering of the text into a kind of standard African orthography based on Bantu languages. Since it did not sound like a Guinea Coast or other West African language, I abstained from applying a phonetic orthographic system as in Ewe, Fō, and other I.A.4 languages. The system I used was this: c became → nk, ay → e, oo → u, ee → i, ah → a. For /c/ I could have chosen /k/, but I was aware of the fact that Europeans in those days often had problems with homoorganic consonants in African languages, and therefore one would always find the nasals dropped in their renderings. So I opted for reinstating the nasal before /k/.

A rather tricky line in Cable's text was the third one written "Canga moon day lay," perfectly well according to English phonology. But its meaning remains obscure, unless one realizes that "moon day lay" has nothing to do with the moon, or the day, but is a single word, well-known across west-central Africa: *mundele* = white person. I had discovered this by myself, even before setting out to Africa, but in order not to influence their judgments, I did not reveal this to the students or to any other potential informant to whom I read the text on our journey. The text was then in this shape:

Ee! Ee! Bomba honc! honc!
Nkanga bafiote
Nkanga mundele
Nkanga dukila
Nkanga li—

In countries along the Guinea Coast (Côte d'Ivoire, Ghana, Togo, and Nigeria), there was no conclusive reaction by anyone. But on December 13, 1977, I read the text to students in Kinshasa, Congo, at the Institut National des Arts, during a lecture we gave on "L'influence du Jazz en Afrique." The reaction by the students was instantaneous. The exclamatory "honc! honc!" in the Cable text described by him as a "horrid grunt" was considered by the students to express "quelque chose de ruche," implying mysterious, secret sounds. And there was general agreement that the text was from Kikoongo. The students then proposed the following translation into French, with my English translation adjoined here:

(French)	(English)
Ee! Ee! Cache! honc! honc!	Ee! Ee! Hide! honc! honc!
Arrête les petits (blancs)!	Stop the small ones (whites)!
Arrête le blanc!	Stop the white person!

Arrête le poisson dukila	Stop the *dukila*-fish!
Arrête—	Stop—

This translation is, of course, not more than a suggestion. But it gives a reasonably coherent meaning, centered around the idea of a situation of conflict involving a white person, with the key words "hide!" and "stop!" Although it is certainly hazardous to elicit meanings from texts written down a hundred years earlier by someone who had no participating access to the culture and language in question, I feel that the experiment was worthwhile. Here I have to thank my colleagues Prof. Kazadi wa Mukuna and the late Kishilo w'Itunga for introducing me to the Kinshasa students in the first place. Participation by the students was enthusiastic, and I think that methodologically the exercise was superior to working with an individual informant. The translation and text interpretation was the cooperative effort of some thirty students in the classroom, male and female, with different language backgrounds. The result is a common denominator of the opinions, and probably a fair approximation to the real meaning and atmosphere of the song, even very accurate in the first three lines.

However, while I am certain that the text falls within the Kikoongo dialect continuum, many new questions are raised by the result. Both St. Méry and later Cable were describing *vodu* ceremonies in St. Domingo and in Louisiana respectively, introduced by the "Andras" from Dahomey, speakers of an I.A.4 (Kwa) language. But this song, cited in connection with a *vodu* initiation ceremony, is definitely in a Bantu language. Is it not highly unlikely that Bantu language speakers in bondage would have become so deeply involved in the Fō religion that they would have imposed their language on the group? Segregation between different African ethnic groups in such a realm was often rigid, though it did gradually break down even in highly secret rites, with the gradual loss of competence in African languages. And yet, something seems to remain unexplained. What made the *vodu* practicing community adopt a song in Kikoongo? The songs must have contained a special message that was of central concern to everyone in slavery, across language differences. There are indications that it was a very old and widespread song text.

Gradually a picture emerges confirming that it was interregionally known, in several parts of the Caribbean. Louis E. Elie, in *Histoire d'Haiti* (1944), has claimed that this song was composed by initiates of "voudou" in 1734, under the leadership of Thélémaque Canga, who was involved in one of the early slave insurrections, and that it was a revolutionary song.

In 1977 I did not have this information when taking the text to Kinshasa, but it fits the students' translation, which goes perfectly together with the revolutionary meaning as the song's central idea. *Mundele* (white person) is self-explanatory. A question, however, arises whether my transliteration of "Canga" in the original text in French orthography, as *nkanga* was justified, in view of the fact that "Canga" is also the name of the revolutionary. But inserting his name into the text makes no sense, especially in conjunction with *mundele*, unless the text wants to say: "Kanga is (our) 'white man' (= our leader)." In any case, the explanation, that the song was adopted and even composed within *vodu* reunions, would be that *vodu* initiation had begun to be used by everyone preparing for insurrection. In a sense, *vodu* had developed a "military arm" besides its religious context; it had become a symbol of identity for all Africans in slavery on the island. In that context Africans from other ethnic groups were accepted, notably Bakoongo, who were numerous. This would explain the text in Kikoongo. Writing it down, Louis E. Elie in 1944, half a century after Cable, used French orthography, and this is his version:

> Eh! Eh ! Bomba!
> Heu! heu!
> Canga! fafio té!
> Canga, monne dé lé!
> Canga, do ki la!
> Canga li!

We can compare it with St. Méry's writing, which was the earliest printed version of the song, in his book about St. Domingo and Haiti (1797: 49):

> Eh! Eh! Bomba,
> Canga bafio té
> Canga moune dé lé
> Canga do ki la
> Canga li.

Louis E. Elie, the author of *Histoire d'Haiti*, certainly knew this earlier source, but it is likely that he used it to make inquiries, confirming the song's survival in Haiti by the mid-twentieth century, and leading to the information given in his book and his slightly variant rendering of the text. The same, we have said, applies to George Washington Cable's version, which was probably not merely a transliteration of St. Méry's French spellings into English orthography, but was checked against a local informant's pronunciation, who sang the song to him. After all, Cable had learned many slave songs directly in New Orleans. He was part of a circle of musicians and composers seriously interested in such songs: Henry Krehbiel, Louis Gottschalk, Lafcadio Hearn, and others. Occasionally, he gave a show singing those songs in public, as is confirmed in an article under the title "Twain-Cable," ironically comparing him to Mark Twain, in the Fort Wayne *Daily Gazette*, February 6, 1885.

The various sources testify that the song was widely known. Although it was part of the song repertoire of *vodu*-practicing groups, it could not have been composed by an original Fō speaker, but must have been the idea of a Kikoongo-speaking person associated with the emerging revolutionary movement in Haiti around 1734. After the revolution's final success in 1804, the song became an emblem, a signature tune for the revolution, as happens in many revolutionary cultures across history. In that capacity it must have reached New Orleans with refugees from Haiti and St. Domingo in the late eighteenth and early nineteenth centuries. I think we are safe assuming that in view of its wide distribution across the Caribbean, the song was also sung in Congo Square as a popular revolutionary song.

F. W. Evans (2011) has tried to track it down across the Caribbean. She quotes a connoisseur of the music of Puerto Rico, Alex LaSalle, interviewed in 2009, who "reported hearing the lyrics to this song in Puerto Rico, which is where the Kongo-derived music and dance style known as Bomba originated (76)."

Another of F. W. Evans's interlocutors, Ned Sublette (see also her own writings on Cuban music, 2004, and *The World that Made New Orleans* 2008) told her that the term *bomba* was recognizably Kikoongo, meaning "secret." That would corroborate the meanings given by the students in Kinshasa. As to the song's historical presence in New Orleans, Evans quotes Ausettua Amor Amenkum, founder and director of Kumbuka African Dance and Drum Collective, who told her in an interview on July 13, 1998, that an elderly New Orleanian, Lydia DeCastro, had passed down the song to her and that gatherers sang it in Congo Square on Sunday afternoon. Here some precaution may be recommended. Voodoo had already become a veritable "industry" in the 1930s, and—in a kind of wish-fulfillment—imported Caribbean, even African elements were often projected on New Orleans.

With the language of the second song from Cable's article, "Héron mandé, Héron mandé, Tiguili papa . . ." (Cable 1886, repr. in Katz 1969: 60), written in French orthography, and the song's melody transcribed, we unfortunately were not successful in 1977 on our tour of West and Central Africa, although in this case I was even able to sing it to potential informants. And yet the reaction was gaping stares. Thinking that it was perhaps associated with *vodu*, I discussed the matter with Dahin Amagbenyō Kofi, my Fō-speaking friend in Lomé, Togo, who is a *vodu* initiate. I even recorded the song for him in my rendering of what I could reconstruct from the notation. But he quickly excluded any of the languages he himself spoke: his first language Fō, then Ewe, etc. He said, it sounded to him like a language from the savannah hinterland, e.g., northern Togo, possibly a Voltaic

I.A.3 or a Mande I.A.2 language. This would be plausible, because many people were taken into slavery from those areas of the hinterland, off the Guinea Coast. In Kinshasa, the students also reacted with indifference to the second song.

Congo Square and Jazz

One question that has often been posed concerns the extent to which late nine-teenth-century innovative developments in the music of New Orleans leading to jazz can be linked historically to the earlier music/dance gatherings in Congo Square.

Is there any clear-cut cultural-genealogical line to be postulated besides the somewhat romantic statement about "roots"? An inscription in stone at the site of Congo Square, informing visitors that "Congo Square was listed on the National Register of Historic Places on January 28, 1993," seems to suggest vaguely such a link:

> Congo Square is in the "vicinity" of a spot which Houmas Indians used before
> the arrival of the French for celebrating their annual corn harvest and was consid-
> ered sacred ground. The gathering of enslaved African vendors in Congo Square
> originated as early as the late 1740's during Louisiana's French colonial period and
> continued during the Spanish colonial era as one of the city's public markets. By
> 1803, Congo Square had become famous for the gatherings of enslaved Africans who
> drummed, danced, sang and traded on Sunday afternoons. By 1819, these gatherings
> numbered as many as 500 to 600 people. Among the most famous dances were the
> Bamboula, the Calinda and the Congo. These African cultural expressions gradually
> developed into Mardi Gras Indian traditions, the Second line and eventually New
> Orleans jazz and rhythm and blues.

Comparative research in African and African American culture history, however, reminds us to be careful in postulating unilinear developments from something into something. No doubt there are continuities, but not always can they be understood as forms of development in which something new emerges directly from something that preceded it. Sometimes there are ruptures, broken-off branches, blind alleys, and also eruptions of something long repressed that had a kind of underground existence for a hundred years, as a code rather than an overt manifestation. In societies in which a functioning economy depends on extreme forms of social stratification, with inextricably linked forms of repression and exploitation, it happens that some talents within the stratum of the subjugated parts of a population constantly reinvent themselves. However, they identify with their original inventions for only a short time, then leave it all behind, abandoned and neglected, as fodder for others who eagerly take possession of the gems, directly or by "sampling." At the latest, it is the great-grandchildren of the originators who discover the output of their ancestors that their own children had declared as irrelevant for them, while embarking on something else.

These are patterns we can detect in much of the history of African and African American cultures. While nineteenth-century memory of the Congo Square gatherings was fading, some of it was flowing into later developments, including Mardi Gras manifestations and even jazz, although one cannot claim that jazz would in any way present a continuity of these earlier African American cultural expressions. The post–Civil War generation most certainly rejected the earlier culture. In some ways, jazz was a fresh start, not from a vacuum, but aberrant and dissident as to earlier manifestations, with Buddy Bolden's horn challenging the legitimate music of the John Robichaux Orchestra in the New Orleans of the late 1890s. And yet there are genealogical lines that link jazz to earlier traditions, across different intermediate forms and stages. The various strands were twisted in many ways.

It is probably realistic, therefore, to assume that by the mid-nineteenth century there existed several strands of African American music, eventually leading to the rise of ragtime, jazz, etc., by the turn of the century, all of them genealogically related to African traditions in different parts of the African continent, besides the Caribbean feedback (e.g., the "Latin tinge") and European popular music.

a) The strain that culminated in the development and rise of the blues, especially in the Mississippi Delta area, can be traced to eighteenth-century West African savannah musical cultures. In America, essential elements from there were perpetuated vocally in field hollers, for example, and also in stringed instrument performances, an experience that was gradually transferred to the guitar (Oliver 1970; David Evans 1970, 1982, 1990, etc.; Kubik 1999a). At the turn of the twentieth century, the blues experience began to be taken up by African American singers in vaudeville and circus contexts (Abbott and Seroff 2002, 2007); it entered emerging jazz band and piano playing in New Orleans, and was soon incorporated into sheet music compositions (W. C. Handy, etc.), implanting the twelve-bar blues form into the mold of multi-strain formal composition. (For blues in sheet music, see also Peter Muir, *Long Lost Blues* [2010].)

b) An independent, but essentially syncretist development, in that it incorporated Western Sudanic, Central African, and European (British, Scottish) elements from ballads, etc., was the tradition of homemade, later factory-manufactured banjos, solo or in small entertainment groups, often in combination with fiddles (homemade or violin), "bones," and other percussion utensils. This African American tradition was soon adopted by European Americans in the South and extensively used in blackface minstrelsy. As such it soon reflected back upon African American musical practice. Eventually, banjo rhythmic-melodic patterns began to be transferred to jig piano playing, probably around the 1880s, giving rise to early forms of African American piano playing (necessarily unrecorded at that time), in forms close to short strophic cycles. This strand was then used by composers with formal training in European music (Scott Joplin, Tom Turpin, etc.) and worked into multi-strain compositions. The process would result in a wave of generally available sheet music versions for piano under the name ragtime. Separately, the popular, banjo-based strand would also continue in bands of poor adolescents, spasm bands in the streets of New Orleans and elsewhere, around the turn of the century, perpetuating the shorter, strophic song forms in their music.

c) "Congo Square" drumming, and dance traditions as a third, important strand of the African continuity in the southern United States, would survive indirectly, e.g., in some forms of jazz percussion patterns, coming to the surface only gradually in subsequent jazz periods. There is in this context Eddie S. Meadows's (1999) elucidating study of Warren "Baby" Dodds's (1898–1959) drum language and history of his style. In his final remarks, Meadows states:

> I cannot prove that Dodds purposefully emulated West African rhythmic concepts, it is my belief that the frequency and diversity of his use of melodic-rhythmic concepts is a family resemblance based upon drumming. The fact that African musical concepts were employed in Place Congo/Congo Square through the late nineteenth century, ending only two years before Dodds' birth; Dodds' ability to trace his family's musical roots to Congo Square through his maternal great grandfather who taught him African drum language; Dodds' generic use of melo-rhythmic phenomena to fit both individuals and groups; and the make-up of his drum set furnish adequate proof of a family resemblance. Dodds' drumming concepts are, in fact, the strongest indication to date of an African family resemblance in early jazz. (204)

With each new jazz style another African element that had remained dormant since the days of Congo Square erupted—for example, in Kenny Clarke's development of a new way of drumming in the era of bebop in the 1940s, which gave him the nickname "Klook-Mop" (Gillespie 1979 [2009: 99]). Some of the memory of Congo Square also seems to survive in Mardi Gras "Indian" celebrations in New Orleans. No doubt all the generic traits of African music first outlined by Richard A. Waterman (1948, 1952) were present in the traditions of Congo

Square in the nineteenth century, and they would continue in jazz and other twentieth-century African American music.

The three strands isolated above are not to be taken for an exhaustive enumeration. There are many more strands of African-based traditions in the United States, for example vocal styles and organization in churches. They would sometimes interfere with each other, be intertwined in various ways, leading to re-creation of earlier forms with new means, methods, names, and in new combinations. By the 1920s boogie-woogie piano came up as a new approach to piano playing, reviving some of the techniques and compositional processes in African xylophones and lamellophones, but now within the twelve-bar blues form, while African-derived pulse-lines structured within cycle number twelve were retained. Thereby boogie-woogie pianists, particularly Meade Lux Lewis, were able to rediscover polymetric divisions of the beat—a veritable eruption of African traits that had been dormant for a long time, but were now reconfiguring and reorganizing to create something that was unheard-of before.

Vodu—Vaudou—Voodoo— and Jazz's Spirituality

African religious concepts—ideas about the "supernatural," about *omina* (omens) and taboos, practices of magic and witchcraft, reverence for and possession by spirits—have been an indelible background to the rise of African American cultures from the eighteenth and nineteenth centuries and into the twentieth and beyond. There has been ample testimony to these beliefs and practices, for example, in the blues world. Although jazz musicians usually retreat behind a wall of silence in public discourse about unorthodox beliefs, there is direct and indirect testimony to the power of such ideas provided by individual musicians.

Most African worldviews consider human existence to be part of a broader universe of immaterial relationships involving transcendental beings and metaphysical forces from which humans may benefit, or by which they may be harmed or destroyed. Whoever is able to access these forces has opened up for himself or herself vast resources of energy to be used constructively in cooperative engagement with others, in art, literature, and musical interaction, or destructively towards other people's work and achievements. Personal success, and one's destiny, even the survival of one's musical group, its coherence or dissolution, may depend on arrangement with invisible forces.

However, under pressure from adverse ideologies or religious systems, this worldview often retreats to express itself by displacement, within the fold of institutions of the mainstream culture, for example in Christian worship. In contrast to some other places in the New World, such as Brazil, Cuba, or Haiti, African religions in the United States did not merge with Christian beliefs to the extent of forming a creative syncretist amalgam. And yet many of its practices (e.g., catharsis) did find some continuity within Christian forms of religious expression.

Any popular suggestion of effectuality of magic and witchcraft, or acknowledgment of the forces behind these phenomena, is usually dismissed as imagination, both from the viewpoint of rational, "modern" scientific thought and that of age-old Christian beliefs. Belief systems divergent from those of Christianity were not only ridiculed as "superstitious," but their substance was denied any reality.

The result of the repression was that African belief systems, if not overtly persecuted as idolatrous or blasphemous, were forced to retreat to an underground existence. Paradoxically, however, those who categorically rejected African spirituality, who ridiculed even the belief in omina and brushed away any idea assuming endo-psychic, automatic punishment for violating a taboo, still tended to undertake precautions, developing defense strategies that are also purely magic, such as avoiding certain places or certain actions (on taboo studies, see Kubik and Malamusi 2002). The beliefs are thereby only deleted from consciousness and relegated to the unconscious, shifted away from public awareness, while the symptoms of anxiety and anticipation of danger and misfortune continue to haunt the person. This has affected the lives of many jazz musicians and their social surroundings, as will be discussed in a chapter further on.

Religious beliefs on the one hand and practices of magic and witchcraft on the other are in fact two rather different phenomena within their social fabrics, though they have often been equated by observers, while they are clearly differentiated in African languages. Religion is based on personal allegiance to "supernatural" forces, anthropomorphic or abstract. By contrast, magic is a device that works automatically, within the principle of cause and effect, between a generating force and its targets. Its application is in the hands of experts who have learned the tricks to unleash those forces. No spirit, no *vodu*, no "god" or "devil" has to be involved in the process, although some *vodu*, such as Legba, may be helpful as protectors against evil magic exerted by others. Witchcraft or evil magic is rooted in a projection of negative wishes against others, and motivated by jealousy, greed, desire for revenge etc. In Africa its operating terrain is the extended family.

This chapter tries to navigate through some of these phenomena beyond folkloristic or popular questions such as whether magic "really exists" or not. It exists as a psychological reality, and from this perspective our study includes the issue of circumstances under which music and dance can be used as a device that may trigger, for example, extraordinary states such as trance (cf. Rouget 1980) or other forms of affective response.

In the United States the term *vodu* for a religious system is written as *voodoo* and originally refers to practices in New Orleans. Eventually it was corrupted into "hoodoo," which describes, as a derogatory term, a different realm of human interaction, persons or things that bring bad luck. The original term *vodu* embraces a system of religious thought that originated among the Fō people of the Kingdom of Dahomey in West Africa, a territory now within the borders of the République du Benin, between Nigeria and Togo on the Guinea coast. Fō is a so-called I.A.4 or Kwa language in Joseph Greenberg's 1966 classification of African languages, and is also spoken among the same people in neighboring Togo. With the French slave trade in the eighteenth century, many Fō speakers and adherents to the *vodu* religion were deported to New World destinations, notably to what later became Haiti.

External observers of *vodu* practices have written down the name in a variety of orthographies, according to their own first languages: "Vaudou," "Vodou," "Voudou," "Voodoo" etc., up to alterations of the word and its meanings in the term "hoodoo." In addition, the original Fō religious thought system, in its New World encounter with Christian, notably Catholic, beliefs and also with Central African (Bantu) religious concepts, underwent a process of syncretism. This has further contributed to misunderstandings of the term *vodu*. It began with observers including Moreau de St. Méry, and later George Washington Cable, who represented "voodoo" rites as intertwined with witchcraft, also reinterpreting it as "snake worship." Abominable and terrifying ideas were circulated among the broad public about *vodu* in Haiti, Martinique, Guadeloupe, and Louisiana. In the 1930s and 1940s, Hollywood cinema contributed a share to these ideas by popularizing the ghost images of "zombies," actually derived from concepts not linked to *vodu*.

This chapter in our jazz book is based on my 1960 fieldwork in Dahomey, 1970 in Togo, and later. In 1970 I had a prolonged stay in rural Fō-speaking communities up the Mono River, in the village of Sada Gbonjɛnji, administrative area of Atakpamé, Togo. This was the birthplace of my friend and companion on this research, Danhin Amagbenyō Kofi, who also was briefly with our research team in Ghana in 1981 after he had undergone treatment by a *bokɔnō* (healer) in Togo against the effects of witchcraft. The healer removed a mysterious set of sharp metal objects from his right ear, after which Amagbenyō regained his health.

All this is a silent but indispensable background to my writings, as well as the many conversations I had with another friend, the late Hubert Kponton, founder and curator of the Musée Historique et Artistique Kponton, in the Rue Kuassibrouce, Lomé, Togo (see my report, Kubik 1986). My first encounter with Fō culture was in 1960, when I visited Abomey, the king's palace in Dahomey, jointly with Ulli Beier of the University of Ibadan, and made many photographs, while collecting information. In this chapter, however, I will rely predominantly on an unpublished manuscript on *vodu* religious concepts, written for me in French by Amagbenyō and completed in 1986.

Vodu and Òrìṣà

The term *vodu* in the Fō language is analogous in meaning to *òrìṣà* in the Yoruba language of Nigeria, belonging to the same language family (I.A.4, Kwa, within the Niger-Congo languages, Greenberg 1966). In many details the thought systems are related historically, and some details are even identical as to the organization of the religion and its rites. The figure of the *bàbálòrìṣà* among the Yoruba corresponds with that of the *vodusi* (vodu priest) among the Fō, and the figure of the bàbálawo (Yoruba) corresponds with that of the *bokɔnō* in Fō.

Fig. 3.1. The *vodusi* Kenu Elimo, 60, of Sada Gbonjɛnji village, east Mono River area, Togo, January 1970. Photo: author (G331)

Fig. 3.2. Entrance to the shrine of *Pakosu*, with the figure of *lisa* (the chameleon) into which *Mawu* (the highest principle) can transform. Outskirts of Abomey, Dahomey (today République du Benin), August 13, 1960. Photo: author (A511)

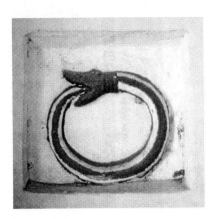

Fig. 3.3. *Aido hwedo*, also called *Toxɔsu* (the rainbow snake); a mural inside the royal enclosure of the King of Dahomey (now a museum), at Abomey (République du Benin), August, 13, 1960. Photo: author (A 522)

As in Yoruba culture, a Fō or Ewe woman can proceed to the *fa* (= same word as *ifa* in Yoruba, and usually translated as the "oracle board") to find out to which *vodu* her child will be linked throughout its life. For example, if it turns out that it will be devoted to the *vodu* of its grandmother, one says that the child has taken the *hŋkā* of its grandmother. This is symbolized by a string of beads the mother will wear.

The late Hubert Kponton (1905–1981), who founded a private ethnographic museum in Lomé, Togo, once discussed with me the function of the *hŋkā* headband worn by women among the Ewe to express the *vodu* to which her child is devoted. "When a woman gets a child, she has to ask the *fa* (oracle) in order to know which *vodu* the soul of the child will choose for its life. For example, if it takes the same *vodu* as its grandmother, on the mother's side, one says that the child has chosen the *hŋkā* of its grandmother. *Asɔ amɛ mamā be hŋkā* (to take the headband of its grandmother). A woman can also delay having her child devoted to a *vodu*. She can even go to the diviner when it is three years old. When the child is ill she also goes to the *vodusi*" (conversation in Lomé, January 1970).

Some prominent *vodu* among the Ewe include *Hɛvyɛso* (thunder and lightning), *Sakpatɛ* (the *vodu* of smallpox), *Ɖa* (a *vodu* in the shape of a snake), *Agboe* (a creature living in the sea), and others. "When lightning has struck someone, the *vodusi* will say that it was Hɛvyɛso. This *vodu* is a natural force, it is not a person" (Hubert Kponton, January 1970).

Vodu in Fō Society

Like any other culture in West Africa, Fō culture, including its religious concepts, has changed constantly since the seventeenth and eighteenth centuries. The genealogical list of the kings of Dahomey begins with Dako (or Dakodonu), ca. 1625–ca. 1650, and Wegbaja ca. 1650–ca. 1685. Although one of our most valuable eighteenth-century sources, Archibald Dalzel, does not say much about the "Dahoman religion" (Dalzel 1793, p. VI), some inferences on Fō religion of earlier centuries have been made from later research.

According to oral traditions collected by Danhin Amagbenyō, the Fō idea of the universe is that of a closed calabash whose shape corresponds with the sky and the earth. *Mawu* in Amagbenyō's definition is the highest principle existing in nature, from which the world was created. *Mawu* can take various visible shapes, for example that of a chameleon (*lisa*), demonstrating that this principle is iridescent, changing, and cannot be grasped within the limits of human understanding. The sky and the earth are connected by the figure of Ɖa in the shape of a snake. Next in the hierarchy come the *vodu* beings, which are the subject of religious activities.

Among the Fō the most important *vodu* include: 1. *Sakpata* (the *vodu* of smallpox), belonging to the Kaja clan; 2. *Xebioso* (thunder and lightning), controlled by the Anyam clan; 3. *Bosikpō*, a *vodu* of the Jago clan; 4. *Aido hwedo*, also called *Toxɔsu* (the rainbow snake). Each *vodu* in any village has its special caretaker called *vodusi*. All the *vodusi* within a particular clan and a certain geographical area are placed under a superior who is called ɣŋbono (= chief of the *vodusi*).

A *vodusi* is distinguished from ordinary "free" people in that he has to observe numerous rules and prohibitions, which make it impossible for him to be mixed up in ordinary people's lives. For this reason *vodusi* undergo an initiation process

Fig. 3.4. House of Sakpata (the *vodu* of smallpox) at Hundenyɔ Sɛlokpa, east Mono River area, Togo, January 1970. Photo: author (G 244)

that lasts up to three months and takes place in the so-called *huxoe* (or "house" of the *vodusi*), where they stay in seclusion during that period. The novice receives tattoo incisions. A *vodusi* can never be ill-treated by anyone in the community, a female *vodusi* can never be sexually abused—such acts would be considered a provocation of the *vodu*.

In Fō villages off the main road one can hardly walk five hundred meters without coming across some religious installation, such as the *vodu* house devoted to Sakpata that stood in a neighboring village to Amagbenyō's birthplace in the 1970s, before the population was moved further east from the Mono River because of the construction of a dam. The painting of a lion on the house wall was to remind onlookers of the power of Sakpata to bring the disease of smallpox to humans. The lion has been an important symbol of power in Fō culture since the famous words by King Glele (1858–1889): "I am a young lion who spreads terror from the very moment his first teeth appear." (On the worldwide history of smallpox and some associated beliefs, see Hopkins 1983 [2002] and 2008.)

Atimɛso—wooden sculptured poles—are often encountered in Fō country. These are carved statuettes stuck into the ground, usually in front of the entrance to a house. They are regarded as figures of protection to invoke an evil force, "nail it to the spot," and thereby neutralize it. They are planted on the advice of a *bokɔnō* (healer, diviner, discoverer of witchcraft) when the inhabitants complain

Fig. 3.5. An example of *atimɛso* (wooden sculptured poles) stuck in the ground for the purpose of protecting a compound and its residents. At Hundenyɔ Sɛlokpa, east Mono River area, Togo, January 1970. Photo: author (G 306)

about terrible dreams and nightmares. The *atimɛso* figures bar "vampires of human blood" (Amagbenyō 1989: 130) from the houses. Households where one finds *atimɛso* statuettes were often plagued by the effects of witchcraft or other evil forces. The owners have had dreams, unexplained deaths, and so on. The head of the family then goes to the traditional healer, called *bokɔnō* in Fō (in French they often call him "le charlatan"), who makes a sacrifice (animal sacrifice, drinks, food, etc.) and sets an *atimɛso* figure in front of the house to block the way to a sorcerer's "bloodsucking" devices.

A *bokɔnō* who cures the sick (*azōzōnu* in Fō) usually keeps iron objects called *saɲny*. In Amagbenyō's view (1989: 130), *saɲny* is also something like a *vodu* in principle, and could be called so because it radiates a "supernatural" force. The pot found below a *saɲny* serves to prevent wizards from manipulating and neutralizing the *saɲny* during the night when the owner sleeps. When one of these iron objects is planted in the courtyard of a *bokɔnō*, the latter then makes an animal sacrifice every year, which—if well received by the *vodu*—will help make the harvest of that year abundant.

Saɲny are iron objects of various shapes, whose meaning is known only to the *vodusi*. The blacksmith (*flotutɔ*) contributes the technical skills of making

Fig. 3.6. *Saɲny* (iron *vodu* objects) in front of the house of a senior *bokɔnō* (traditional medical practitioner) at Hundenyɔ Sɛlokpa, east Mono River area, Togo, January 1970. Photo: author (G 250)

them but does not know much about their meaning. The *saɲny* consist of an iron stem that fans out into several "branches" on the upper end, upon which rests a circular iron plate. From the edges hang *aja* (brass jingles or other brass objects). In the middle of each plate there is a brass figure, for example a goat (*okpɔ*), a fish (*tɔmɛla*), or a gun (*otu*). The round plates of the *saɲny* serve to receive parts of the sacrificed animals and also foodstuffs such as *tevi* (pieces of cooked yam), *agu* (from millet), and *agbaju* (= *moi-moi* in Yoruba, made from beans). This is put on top of the iron discs by the *bokɔnō*.

Amagbenyō (1989: 128) reports that in the past, pregnant women used to go to those *saɲny* that represent the *vodu* called Sakpata (= *vodu* of smallpox), from the Kaja clan, to learn about the fate of a child about to be born. It was also customary to bring a sick child and beg the *vodu* Sakpata to save its life. One would never touch a child from the Kaja clan with a broom, for fear that the child would attract smallpox. Smallpox was seen as being conferred upon a person by Sakpata as a punishment for anyone who did not observe the taboos connected with this *vodu*. All those who have smallpox scars are called *daa*, a name which can also be given to that *vodu* (Amagbenyō 1989: 128, manuscript 1986).

Fig. 3.7. Legba cement sculptures along the road from Contonou to Abomey (République du Benin), August 1960. Photo: author (A 509)

Fig. 3.8. Representation of Tolegba, the "communal" Legba, center, surrounded by smaller Legba clay figures. At Hundenyɔ, east Mono River area, Togo, January 1970. Photo: author (G 247)

The religious world of the Fō, like that of the Yoruba, includes a panel of different characters with different attributes and different roles. The songs performed during vodu ceremonies (cf. Kubik et al. 1989: 132–35) are full of metaphors, proverbs, and symbolic phrases of all kinds that are descriptive of these beings. This poetry is analogous to the *oriki* among the Yoruba. Besides the vodu already mentioned, there is one character at the lowest level of the hierarchy who seems to be particularly important. He is called Legba and parallels Eşu in Yoruba culture. In Fō country every household possesses, in principle, clay figures that represent the vodu called Legba. Usually one finds these mud sculptures behind houses, but also along the street. Sometimes each inhabitant of a house has his personal Legba. Amagbenyō (1989: 130) thinks Legba is always considered a "positive" force among members of the vodu religion.

Legba has various functions, such as announcing to people (through dreams) what is in the offing, early death for example. Legba used to warn people about forces of affliction through dreams; he induced people to go to the *fa* ("oracle") to find out about the nature of the threat and be saved. Thus there are connections between *fa* and Legba.

There are two types of representations of Legba. Besides the smaller clay figure found behind houses, there is also the so-called Tolegba. This is a very large sculpture and is sometimes surrounded by smaller Legba figures. According to Amagbenyō, Tolegba can be called the joint or communal Legba of a village. By clay-modelling a Tolegba figure, the intention is often to protect the whole village against disease and arson. Even destructive insects are prevented from entering a village. Since he is to protect the whole village, he is placed strategically a few hundred meters away from the houses, for example at the roadside. Tolegba is always portrayed as male, as a being from whom nothing can be hidden, not even the sexual organs. Therefore, his penis, sometimes of considerable length, is visible. In fact, all the organs of Legba's body are imagined as large and exaggerated. Amagbenyō says that the sexual organs are portrayed in extraordinary dimensions to allow people to mock each other and Legba and laugh at him. According to Amagbenyō, Legba is almost masochistic; when people laugh at him and insult him, he is delighted. Often useless objects and all sorts of debris such as an old hat, worn-out shoes, torn shirts, drums of inferior quality, damaged ceramics, etc., are placed next to Legba figures (Amagbenyō 1989: 130). When an animal is sacrificed, children aged six to eight are invited to eat up the meat, and then the children form a circle around the Legba figure singing:

Legba nde mado emisito!	Legba, we have nothing!
Ogin do do we do emisito!	Only a penis, nothing else!
Kpoli kita kpoli jin jin	Kpoli kita kpoli jin jin
Oljo kpoli kita kpoli jin jin	Oljo kpoli kita kpoli jin jin*

---

* The last two lines of the song are onomatopoeic: playful, dance-inspiring sound syllables with no explicit verbal meaning.

New World Transformations

The Kingdom of Dahomey in the eighteenth century was one of the chief collaborators with the French transatlantic slave trade. This is why, soon after independence from France in 1960, governments of the tiny country on the West African coast resented the name Dahomey and changed it to Benin, which added another historical-geographical confusion to the map of West Africa, after the Gold Coast in 1957 was renamed Ghana, which was an early precolonial state on the borders of Senegal, Mauritania, and Mali (Davidson, Buah, and Ajayi 1970: 35–44). To maintain clarity, we will refer to Dahomey as a historical state but to the present-day country of the Fō, the Gū, and many others with its French name République du Benin, while the name Benin remains reserved for the historical state of the Bini or Edo-speaking people in western Nigeria.

The religious concepts of òrìṣà (in Yoruba) and vodu (in Fō) were transplanted through the Atlantic slave trade to several parts of the New World, òrìṣà notably to Brazil and Cuba (as well as other places), vodu to Haiti and many other French possessions in the Caribbean. The Fō system of religious thought was significantly modified, however, in content and terminology, in processes of amalgamation that Melville J. Herskovits (1941) described as syncretism, in this case under the impact of Catholic beliefs and a significant shot of Central African (Koongo) religious concepts. The translatability of Yoruba religious concepts into Ewe, and Fō, and vice versa was one of the factors that facilitated the process of fusion and syncretism between religions in the New World cultures, with Yoruba elements dominating in one place, Fō and Ewe elements in another.

There is no term in any European language to correspond to the notion òrìṣà. It is not "gods," it is not a polytheistic idea or the like. In European languages òrìṣà can only be described, not defined. The same applies to vodu. It is evident that this must have created considerable cognitive dissonance (cf. Festinger 1957) in people living within a cultural contact zone which the "New World" had become from the beginning of the Atlantic slave trade and European settlement. It is most interesting to observe how such cognitive problems were gradually overcome by the process of selection and reinterpretation (Herskovits 1941).

In Haiti the equivalent term for òrìṣà and vodu is *loa*, a word whose origins have not been verified with certainty. The religious cults are referred to with the Fō word "vaudou" (French spelling). David Welch (1977: 340) describes Haitian "vaudou" as "an extremely sophisticated religion that accommodates and integrates various religious beliefs (African, Native American, Catholic), philosophies, social conditions, and cultural and artistic values. It is a system of concepts concerning human activities, the relation between the natural world and the super-natural, and the ties between the living and the dead, having its own cause-and-effect order to explain otherwise unpredictable events. It provides guidelines for social behaviour and demands that the gods be responsive. In short, vaudou attempts to tie the unknown to the known, and establish order where there might otherwise be chaos."

The concept of vodu also reached Louisiana in the nineteenth century, mostly with the so-called secondary proliferation of African peoples, in this case migrants to Louisiana from the Caribbean. The concept thereby gained a presence in part of the United States, together with many other African religious concepts and those relating to magic. The US term "voodoo" has developed derivative meanings and has undergone many transformations, assimilating elements from other belief systems and various concepts relating to witchcraft and magic. In some places voodoo became a kind of "underground religious sect that has often merged with or borrowed from Christianity in its use of the crucifix and saints as religious symbols" (Ferris 1989: 492). "Voodoo doctors" is the term often heard in the South, for what in Africa would be referred to as *bàbálawo* (Yoruba), *bokɔnō* (Fō), *kimbanda* (Kimbundu of Angola), etc. In role and world-view these doctors of the southern United States are still comparable to various ancestral African counterparts.

An interesting concept widely current in the southern United States and elsewhere is the so-called "mojo hand." It is the "vehicle through which a spell is placed or removed" (Ferris 1989: 492). "The mojo hand is a small cloth sack that is carried in a wallet or purse and may contain parts of insects, animals (especially lizards), birds, and items that have had intimate contact with the person being hexed (underclothing, feces, fingernails, and hair)" (Ferris 1989: 492). This shows how African concepts have been intermingled, because the mojo hand and the ideas attached to it belong to the practice of evil magic and defense arrangements the individual can make to be protected. In many African cultures, when a person suddenly dies and is supposed to have been killed by evil magic, a traditional medical practitioner will ask his client (perhaps the husband of the deceased) to bring him objects that were intimately associated with the deceased, such as mentioned above, to enable him to "see," through these objects, who might have killed the person.[*]

---

[*] David Evans has suggested that "mojo" is derived etymologically from "mal de ojo" (evil eye) often symbolized as an eye within a hand. (See *The NPR Curious Listener's Guide to Blues*, 224.) The term "mojo" doesn't appear to have been used before the 1920s. The latest scholarly study is Katrina Hazzard-Donald, *Mojo Workin': The Old African American Hoodoo System* (Chicago: University of Illinois Press, 2013).

Voodoo in New Orleans

With refugees and other immigrants to Louisiana from St. Domingue (Haiti and Santo Domingo), several versions of the vodu belief system and also practices of magic and witchcraft filtered into the region of New Orleans. This was the principal point of entry for the awareness of vodu, especially after 1806. By that time vodu as a system of religious beliefs had already undergone many modifications in Haiti and elsewhere, incorporating Christian and some other African elements. And yet, in New Orleans vodu was almost immediately interpreted by locals as "snake worship" and categorized as "satanic orgies."

Vodu did not arrive in New Orleans in one stroke in 1806. A little earlier the knowledge had spread with enslaved people resold from various parts of the French-dominated Caribbean islands, notably from Martinique, Guadeloupe, and St. Domingue. Although there are few contemporaneous sources to be consulted, it is at least testified that two governors of Louisiana, Bernardo de Gálvez in 1782 and Baron de Carondelet—who was governor from 1792 to 1797—explicitly forbade the plantation owners and slave traders to bring people from Martinique and St. Domingue respectively, because of their "addiction to 'voodooism'" (Asbury 1936: 254). Thus, there were serious reservations and safety concerns. This fear was founded in a perception that vodu was developing a political, in fact revolutionary form of expression, and that those carriers "might foment rebellion among the Louisiana slaves" (Asbury 1936: 254).

Starting soon after the Louisiana Purchase in 1803, the American government, it appears, was more relaxed considering immigration, and after the successful Haitian revolution against French colonization and slavery, a stream of refugees poured from Santo Domingo into New Orleans between 1806 and 1810. It is with this massive immigration that "vaudou"—soon to be rendered as "voodoo" in English orthography—gained a permanent foothold in the ritual and religious life of people in New Orleans, gradually developing into a transcultural phenomenon involving African refugees, free and enslaved, and other elements of the New Orleans population in the ritual meetings. The priesthood was normally in the hands of free people of African descent or with both African and European ancestry.

In New Orleans one personality, however, began to stand out prominently, usually referred to as the "voodoo queen." In the 1820s original vodu of the Fõ had long transformed into a syncretistic phenomenon, involving followers with all kinds of backgrounds. It is possible that the phenomenon of a female leader of the rites was adopted from other West and West-Central African religious systems, and can perhaps be linked to people in some of those areas with a matrilineal social structure. In West Africa the Anyi, Fanti, and other peoples on the

Guinea Coast are matrilineal, and in south-central Africa, from Angola across the continent to Lake Malawi, matrilineal systems affecting the status of women are prominent.

Besides the voodoo queen there was the so-called "voodoo doctor"—male or female—probably a Louisiana version of the *bokɔno* among the Fõ. Both of them functioned as healers, psychotherapists, and religious coordinators, controlling a great number of ritual objects, charms, amulets, and magical powders employed in therapy sessions to help people with a variety of psychological problems. It is clear that such knowledge also contributed considerably to income earned by the "queen" and the "doctor," much as modern psychotherapists make a living out their knowledge from remunerations by their clients.

Herbert Asbury (1936) has characterized "Voodoo" in New Orleans during the early nineteenth century as follows:

> Both the queens and the doctors . . . derived substantial incomes from the sale of charms, amulets, and magical powders, all guaranteed, according to the incantations pronounced over them, to cure the purchaser's every ailment, to grant his every desire, and to confound or destroy his enemies. All of these sorcerers, especially the Voodoo queens, were popularly supposed to possess vast knowledge of, and to dispense with great abandon, strange and subtle poisons, which defied detection and caused the victims to waste away and die of exhaustion. But there was never any evidence to justify this supposition, nor proof that anyone in New Orleans died at the hands of the Voodoos, although it is probably true that deaths have been hastened by fear of the sorcerers' supposed powers. (Asbury 1936: 255)

For those who study healing practices in Africa and the ways traditional healers dismantle witchcraft spells in some of their patients, or identify wizards and witches (Malamusi 1999b, 2003, 2016; Soko 2002), this is familiar terrain. It must be stressed about the practice in New Orleans that this particular aspect of "voodoo" is pan-African, not anything restricted to or specifically characteristic only of vodu as we know it in West Africa. In fact, a good part of it is defensive magic, not witchcraft. Exuvial magic, i.e., using bodily products (exuviae) of the victim, and other offensive practices to harm others are not part of the vodu system as a religion. In New Orleans it was mixed up with what can better be summarized with the Central African term *wanga*, a term also heard in New Orleans.

"Ouanga"—so written in French spelling of New Orleans—is not a vodu term. It comes from several Koongo/Angola languages where we write it either as *wanga* or *vwanga* according to pronunciation in the various languages. Pierre Gwa, aged eighteen, a guitarist whom Maurice Djenda and I recorded in 1966 at Linjombo on the Upper Sangha River in the Central African Republic, had written the word *wanga* on the body of his homemade guitar to frighten away people

Fig. 3.9. Pierre Gwa, about 18, Pomo-speaking guitarist in a village on the Sangha River, a confluent of the Kongo or Zaire. The word *wanga* can be seen inscribed on the body of his homemade guitar below his right hand. Pierre Gwa can be seen and heard on my 1995 DVD *African Guitar*, published by Stefan Grossman's Guitar Workshop, Sparta, NJ Linjombo, Nola District, Central African Republic, May 1966. Photo: author

with witchcraft intentions against him. This demonstrates the intensity of the concept for musicians and individual attempts that are made for self-protection. In Gwa's case it also had sexual connotations, because he clearly felt threatened by a certain elderly woman. The term *wanga* covers the idea of an offensive medicine, including poison, that also can be used prophylactically as self-defense. The word is well-known in the Bantu languages of Zone H (in Malcolm Guthrie's 1948 classification), which includes Kikoongo, Kimbundu etc., and in the spelling *vwanga* in the Ngangela group of languages in eastern Angola, with meanings identical to those observed by Cable in Louisiana: "bad charm," "evil magic," designed to kill. However, in Louisiana "voodoo" became a blanket term for various activities and ideas associated with underground religious beliefs, and also the practice of magic, both evil and defensive, as aphrodisiac, etc.

Its presence confirms an equally important, significant Koongo/Angola background of African cultures in New Orleans during the early nineteenth century. George Washington Cable (1886b; Katz 1969: 60) provided evidence that this Bantu conceptualization existed, although he mixed it up with "voodoo": "A planter once found a Voodoo charm, or *ouanga* (Wongah); this time it was a bit of cotton cloth folded about three cow-peas and some breast feathers of a barnyard fowl, and covered with a tight wrapping of thread."

Gwendolyn Midlo Hall's (1992: 162–63) research also underlines the presence of the term *wanga* in Louisiana, referring to magical charms of ritual objects.

The connection to people of Koongo descent (including Angolans) is obvious; these groups seem to have contributed great awareness of magical practices to Louisiana culture.

Another term that has achieved popular currency in the American media and by extension worldwide via Hollywood cinema in the twentieth century is "zombie." This term also comes from west-central African Bantu languages. It is a corruption of a word appearing in many variations and variously written as Njambi, Zambi, Nzambi, Nchambe, etc. Among people of the Upper Sangha River area (Central African Republic, Republic of Congo), Nchambe is a mythological person capable only of doing good things, as opposed to Bembi. There are many stories about the two opponents (cf. Djenda 1994). Missionaries in the Congo and in Angola used the term to translate their Christian concept of God, so it changed its original meaning across the centuries in west-central Africa. In Angola, Njambi is often equated with Kalunga, another concept often used by Christian missionaries to translate their idea of a "High God" into local languages.

But in the negativistic environment of slavery-dominated New World cultures, a contrary development of those meanings took place. In analogy to the "blackening" in Brazil of the functions of a traditional healer called *Kimbanda* in Angola, in Haiti the Kikoongo term Nzambi also received a "negative charge." This is not surprising because in Haiti and St. Domingo Bakoongo people in the enslaved population were at the bottom of the social hierarchy. Corrupted phonologically, "zombi" was then used to describe a bewitched being leading a strange shadow existence between life and death, capable of moving out of the cemetery, frightening and haunting people. The idea itself (without the term "zombi") is of course, based on a concept widespread in Africa. In his work on *using'anga* (healing practice), Moya A. Malamusi (1999b, 2016) has described the case of a boy from Moçambique who had been bewitched to lead such a shadow existence.

Cable paints a reasonably accurate picture of mid-nineteenth century witchcraft practices in New Orleans. While the voodoo religion was disappearing, the need for protection against evil magic was on the increase:

> But whatever may be the quantity of the Voodoo worship left in Louisiana, its superstitions are many and are everywhere. Its charms are resorted by the malicious, the jealous, the revengeful, or the avaricious, or held in terror, not by the timorous only, but by the strong, the courageous, the desperate. To find under his mattress an acorn hollowed out, stuffed with the hair of some person pierced with four holes on four sides, and two small chicken feathers drawn through them so as to cross inside the acorn; or to discover on his door-sill at daybreak a little box containing a dough or waxen heart stuck full of pins; or to hear that his avowed foe or rival has been pouring cheap champagne in the four corners of Congo Square at midnight, when there was no moon, will strike more abject fear into the heart of many a stalwart negro

or melancholy quadroon than to face a leveled revolver. Many a white Creole gives them full credence. (1886b: 60)

This quote reveals the extent to which concepts of magic and witchcraft had become part of the general New Orleans culture. "Professionals" could be paid—just as Jelly Roll Morton has described his part of the "hoodoo" experience—to "make a work," i.e., to weave a spell, to kill somebody by magic. Such a person was then referred to as Voodoo "monteure" (60). But there were also many protective medicines to avert witchcraft; "an Obi charm will enable you to smile defiance against all such mischief," writes Cable (60).

Asbury (1936) on his part mentions that the charms and amulets were

composed of such queer ingredients as nail parings, human hair, powdered bones, and dried lizards. Even the celebrated "gris-gris," the most feared—and incidentally the most expensive—of all Voodoo magic, was seldom anything more than a little cotton or leather bag filled with powdered brick, yellow ochre, and cayenne pepper, with the occasional addition of nail parings, hair, and bits of reptile skin. Left on a doorstep in the dark of the moon, the "gris-gris" was supposed to work incalculable harm to the occupants of the house. That it never did was ascribed by the Negroes to the fact that a man who found a "gris-gris" on his premises hurried immediately to a Voodoo queen or doctor and procured a counter-charm, which invariably worked. Any Voodoo sorcerer, it appears, could always overcome the efforts of another. (255)

From our African research we possess large collections of similar objects. One of my collections from Angola (not yet evaluated) is kept in the Museu de Etnologia, in Lisbon; another collection, given to me by the Prophet (Nchimi) Chikanga Chunda in Malawi (Nyasaland) in 1962, is kept in our Culture Research Archive, Vienna.

In spite of the separation of such "voodoo" practices from *vodu* proper, a "voodoo queen" or "doctor" in New Orleans would make available to their patients many counter-charms to alleviate unbearable states of anxiety. They were consulted by people of the most diverse ethnic backgrounds, and many with serious psychopathological problems sought therapy, including among the "white" and "mulatto" population. Treatment sessions, however, were not rarely raided by police, so it happened that in the year "1855 when Captain Eugene Mazaret of the Third District police invaded a house of the Voodoo doctor Don Pedro, he found a dozen white women and as many Negro men, the former naked except for thin camisoles, and all busily amusing themselves and one another under the direction of the magician. They were all arrested and fined, although Doctor Don Pedro protested that they were simply undergoing treatment for rheumatism. Next day the husband of one of the women committed suicide" (Asbury 1936256). Many working today in psychotherapy can only have a good gloat over this, imagining the stern looks of those defenders of law and order. It reminds me of a scene that happened during apartheid in South Africa in the 1970s when police invaded the Johannesburg apartment of our colleague Professor John Blacking, sniffing at his blankets and bed sheets to find out whether someone from another "race" had been with him.

What raises our curiosity, however, is what kind of therapy was actually used by Don Pedro on "white" women who were obviously suffering from some kind of conversion neurosis described as rheumatism. That was thirty years before Josef Breuer handled the famous case of Anna O., a young woman in Vienna whose problems he tried to tackle with a method he called "catharsis" (Breuer and Freud 1895). Was Don Pedro employing a "cathartic" method or even a precursor of cognitive behavioral therapy methods such as "flooding," exposing those women to the object of their anxiety? Was music involved? Unfortunately lacking details, we have been deprived of the study of "voodoo" therapy methods in New Orleans in the nineteenth century that were used on upper-class New Orleans women in a society with a racist structure. It is credible that many women, imprisoned in the mores of their time, would have sought solace in voodoo therapy.

The first voodoo doctor in New Orleans whose name is on record was an African. He called himself Doctor John and was active during the 1840s (Asbury 1936: 257). He was also involved in the famous case of Pauline, a woman executed under the provisions of the notorious Code Noir. After his retirement he was succeeded by an enslaved person known as Doctor Ya Ya. Some of the histories attached to these personalities are known from police records and newspapers (cf. Asbury: 258). Each of them had their specializations, e.g., love charms, magic cure-all medicines, etc., some of which cost up to twenty dollars.

For the actual "voodoo" religious rites, however, the supreme authority was not the "doctor" but the "voodoo queen." She organized the meetings and also the grand festival in New Orleans on the night of June 21, continuing into St. John's Day (St. John, the Baptist). Syncretism between vodu transcendental forces and the power of Catholic saints developed in New Orleans in a way to a certain extent similar to elsewhere in the Caribbean, and to South America.

As in Dahomey, an important part of the ceremonies was the rite associated with a spiritual entity called *Aido Hwedo*, *Toxɔsu*, or Ɖa in Fõ and represented with a large serpent. An ancestral ritual place of that kind occurs in Ouidah, Dahomey, where I photographed the keeper of the snake in 1970. In New Orleans, one of the earliest remembered voodoo queens was Sanité Dédé, who was active immediately after Louisiana had become part of the United States. She was a free woman from Santo Domingo (Asbury 1936: 260). From her time there is one fascinating eyewitness report by a fifteen-year-old boy in New Orleans who witnessed part of these ceremonies in 1825 (Asbury 1936: 261). The description includes that of a music/dance performance during the rite. It appeared in J. W. Buel 1882.

An entrance door was opened at the call of Dédé, and I witnessed a scene which, old as I am, no passage of years can ever dim. The first thing which struck me as we entered was a built-up square of bricks at the upper and lower end of the shed, on each of which was burning a fierce fire, casting a lurid light over the scene. Along the four sides of the parallelogram of the building, were sconces, with lighted dips placed at equal distances, which barely added to the darkling light of the two pyres. . . . Each man and woman had a white kerchief tied around the forehead, though the heads of the latter were covered by the traditional Madras handkerchief, with its five, nay, its seven artistic points, upturned to heaven. In a little while the company, some sixty in all, had assembled. There were males and females, old and young, negroes and negresses, handsome mulatresses and quadroons. With them half a dozen white men and two white women. . . .

Near where I stood was an oblong table about eight feet in length and four in width. On its right end stood a black cat, and on its left a white one. I thought them alive, and having a certain fondness for cats, stretched out my hand to stroke the nearest. The touch, that most philosophical of all the senses, soon satisfied me that they were fine specimens of negro taxidermy. Admirably stuffed they were, too. In the center of the table there was a cypress sapling, some four feet in height, planted in the center of a firkin or keg. Immediately behind the cypress, and towering above it, was a black doll with a dress variegated by cabalistic signs and emblems, and a necklace of the vertebrae of snakes around her neck, from which depended an alligator's fang encased in silver.

At the side of this table I recognized an old negro by the name of Zozo, well known in New Orleans as a vender of palmetto and sassafrass roots; in fact, he had a whole pharmacopoeia of simples and herbs, some salutary, but others said to be fatal. He seemed to be the corypheus of these unhallowed rites, for the signal of the beginning of the work came from him. He was astride of a cylinder made of thin cypress staves hooped with brass and headed by a sheepskin. With two sticks he droned away a monotonous ra-ta-ta, ra-ra-ta-ta, while on his left sat a negro on a low stool, who with two sheep shank bones, and a negress with the leg bones of a buzzard or turkey, beat an accompaniment on the sides of the cylinder. It was a queer second to this satanic discord. Some two feet from these arch-musicians squatted a young negro vigorously twirling a long calabash. It was made of one of our Louisiana gourds a foot and a half long, and filled with pebbles.

At a given signal the four initiates formed a crescent before Dédé, who was evidently the high priestess or Voudou queen. She made cabalistic signs over them, and sprinkled them vigorously with some liquid from a calabash in her hand, muttering under her breath. She raised her hand and Zozo dismounted from his cylinder, and from some hidden receptacle in or behind the large black doll, drew an immense snake, which he brandished wildly aloft. . . . He talked and whispered to it. At every word the reptile, with undulating body and lambent tongue, seemed to acknowledge the dominion asserted over it. In the meantime, with arms crossed and reverent eyes, the initiates had now formed a crescent around Zozo. He now compelled the snake to stand upright for about ten inches of its body. . . . In that position Zozo passed the snake over the heads and around the necks of the initiates, repeating at each pass the words which constitute the name of this African sect, "Voudou Magnian." (522–30)

Sanité Dédé's reputation was even greater than that of Bras Coupé, the unsuccessful revolutionary, once a remarkable athletic "bamboula" dancer at Congo Square. In 1834, after he was accidentally shot and his right arm amputated, he organized a kind of "maroon" gang in the swamps of Louisiana. He was thought to be invulnerable until April 6, 1837, when he was fatally wounded by two hunters near the Bayou St. John (Asbury 1936: 246–47).

Sanité Dédé was succeeded by the eminent Marie Laveau, who became the most celebrated New Orleans voodoo queen in history. Her reign lasted more than forty years. Marie Laveau was born in New Orleans about 1796, of African and European parents. She was a hairdresser by profession, and of impressive beauty, so says oral tradition. Having had access to the homes of the most fashionable upper-class ladies, she rose to a personality with unusual tasks, comparable in many ways to African charismatic healers, such as Emilia Kakinda, the *ocimbanda* I met in southwestern Angola in 1965, and male healers and prophets such as Chikanga Chunda of Malawi (cf. Kubik in Soko 2002). Significantly, she was a practicing Catholic but had become a member of voodoo as a young lady. Asbury related the story of how Marie Laveau made the decision of her life:

> For several years after she became queen of the Voodoos, Marie Laveau spent much of her time in a flimsy shanty on Lake Pontchartrain, which was sometimes used for meetings of the cult. One day while she was there a hurricane passed over New Orleans and the lake, and the shanty was torn from its foundations and hurled into the water. Marie Laveau sought safety on the roof, but when several of her followers tried to rescue her, she discouraged their efforts, crying out that the Voodoo god wanted her to die in the lake. She was finally induced to accept assistance, however, and according to the tale which was freely spread among the Negroes, the moment Marie Laveau reached the shore the fury of the storm abated and the lake became as smooth as the surface of a mirror. (266)

Thereafter, New Orleans people invested great spiritual powers into Marie Laveau, especially after she had magically saved the son of a wealthy merchant

Fig. 3.10. The keeper of a *vodu* snake and his dwelling in Ouidah, Dahomey (République du Benin), 1970. Photo: author

Fig. 3.11. Marie Laveau and her successor Malvina Latour (standing), shortly before her death, in a painting by Edward Kemble. Reproduced from George Washington Cable 1886b [Katz 1969: 59]

from being convicted innocently for a crime. During her reign as voodoo queen, the vodu tradition went through an intensive period of adaptation. Marie Laveau was struggling to find common ground between vodu and Catholic beliefs. While serving as a voodoo queen, organizing various rites, she never forgot to attend mass at the cathedral. She revised voodoo practice by including reverence of the Virgin Mary and Catholic saints, a trend that is familiar to us from various patterns of syncretism in the Caribbean and in South America. Almost all the ancestral beliefs of vodu were effectively reinterpreted, creating a semblance of a new religion.

Gradually Marie Laveau gained recognition by the wider society and voodoo worship began to lose its negative connotations. At the same time, voodoo become popular in the sense that the annual festivals on St. John's Eve, which were open to everyone, attracted spectators from any part of the population. Even in the nineteenth century such events began to assume a folkloristic character, a trend that also affected the dances in Congo Square. Asbury (1936: 268) notes that "frequently the white spectators outnumbered the voodoos." And yet there was an inner circle, and some voodoo meetings were secret. Many of these meetings were privately financed and clearly had a psychotherapeutic purpose. One of these meetings was described in the *New Orleans Times* of March 21, 1869, four years after the end of the Civil War. It was an aphrodisiac rite, arranged for a European American girl who was striving to regain the affections of her lover, and it was carried out mostly by women, some dressed in bridal costumes. The venue was the lake chapel. Here again snakes were involved. The article states: "As they danced in a circle, in the center of which stood a basket with a dozen hissing snakes whose heads were projecting from the cover, each corybant touched a serpent's head with her brand." It describes a scene in which the young girl fell in trance, but suggests this was not successful, because "The girl was torn half-dead from the scene, and she has never been restored to her faculties" (cited in Asbury 1936: 270).

Soon after that event Marie Laveau resigned and was replaced by a younger queen, Malvina Latour. But Laveau did not abandon her work, while retired, she continued to function as a spiritual adviser in the Catholic tradition, notably in the Paris Prison, among captives awaiting execution. It seems that she retired finally from all engagements about 1875 and retreated to a little cottage on St. Ann Street, where George Washington Cable visited her a few months before her death (cf. Cable 1886b; Katz 1969: 57–58).

After the death of Marie Laveau in 1881, Malvina Latour turned back many of the changes her predecessor had introduced, casting out the Catholic elements in the rites. She also abolished the use of snakes during the annual festival. The voodoo cult movement began to split into rival factions. Asbury (1936) reports about the state of voodoo in late nineteenth-century New Orleans: "By the time Malvina Latour retired as a queen of the Voodoos about 1890, the word itself had been corrupted by the Negroes into 'hoodoo,' and the cult has split into a score of small groups, each with its own titular head and its own ritual and ceremonial forms . . ." (282). The sale of hoodoo medicines continued as an unbroken industry, especially with regard to love-potions and powders to induce employers and others to grant special favors.

An important early article on women healers as cultural carriers in New Orleans was Susan Cavin's "Missing Women: On the Voodoo Trail to Jazz," *Journal of Jazz Studies* 3(1) (Fall 1975): 4–27. More recently, since the book *Swing Shift* (2000) and especially her article "Big Ears: . . ." in *Current Musicology* 2001/2002, Sherrie Tucker has been in the forefront of the study of gender issues related to jazz. In a project contracted by the National Park Service called "A feminist perspective on New Orleans jazz women," Tucker examines the question why "we seldom see women presented as central to jazz culture." She analyzes the factors that have led to a low profile of women in jazz history books:

Interestingly, the primary reason is *not* that the authors of earlier jazz history books intentionally excluded women. Oftentimes, as in other areas of social life, women did not have access to roles that historians are accustomed to using in their criterion for historical importance. Women may have been excluded from the most prestigious activities, for example from playing cornet in 1920s jazzbands, but may have been critical players in other areas; for example as singers, non-soloing pianists in the 1920s jazz bands, or as cornetists at private parties, in all-women bands, or vaudeville shows. . . . Women's careers may not have been documented to the extent, as were men's *during the times in which they lived*, so historians relying on evidence such as recordings may be simply replicating the biases of social life, rather than critically including those sex-specific differences as part of the experiences of people, both men and women, in history. (Tucker 2004: 3)

This last statement is extremely important for our studies. Due to the social circumstances under which the data were collected and published, written and sound-recorded sources are often highly selective, with part of the observable material suppressed, remaining unreported. In other words, much history disappears in a memory hole before we can get access to it.

Niches of Feminine Spirituality

Would it be scientifically acceptable to compare twentieth-century jazz pianist Mary Lou Williams in her spirituality with voodoo queen Marie Laveau in nineteenth-century New Orleans? Can one postulate analogies between blues singers such as Ma Rainey or Bessie Smith or gospel singer Mahalia Jackson's charismatic impact upon audiences, and that of female traditional healers in various societies of Africa? If we said yes, we would probably get quick disapproval from several quarters. The connections seem far-fetched, the similarities not clear-cut, a historical source basis difficult to procure, and the fact that both Marie Laveau and Mary Lou Williams, for example, were deeply involved in Catholicism seems coincidental. The geographical and time differences, moreover, between blues singers, female jazz pianists, and alleged counterparts across the Atlantic in Africa appear to be unsurmountable, even between the individuals compared within the confines of the United States. Marie Laveau was born in New Orleans and spent all her life there. Mary Lou Williams grew up in Pittsburgh and was a child prodigy on the piano. In her drawing of a "jazz tree," representing the history of jazz (see below), New Orleans does not even figure as a name. Jazz history in her view proceeds directly from ragtime to Kansas City swing, in which Mary Lou was actively involved. So what?

Indeed, as much as there is no hard evidence that significant elements from the music of Congo Square in New Orleans were perpetuated in jazz (see also Kmen 1972 on this question), so may it be regarded as tenuous to assume that African religious spirituality with its associated healing potential would have been retained in a veiled form in African American Christian worship and found expression in jazz, blues, and soul music.

However, human cultural achievements are not easily dismantled and removed from the world map; they are resilient. Under pressure they transform or migrate, reappear in a modified, but structurally identical shape somewhere else, reconfigured, "reinvented" at different historical periods. The reasons why this field of study is so hard to come by are many:

(a) One is researchers' validation of written sources as more trustworthy than oral tradition, even in music that is not normally written down. Unfortunately, however, one cannot reconstruct the history of "Buddy Bolden Blues" by taking the first appearance of a semblance of this melody in sheet music for its compositional origin. (See Jelly Roll Morton's remarks on this question, Lomax 1952 [1959: 63].)

(b) The same applies to the historiography of social and religious phenomena. Relying on nineteenth-century written sources alone gives a hazy picture. Self-censorship in the media—including African American journalism after the Civil War—was ever present, preventing the mere mention of perceived African connections in certain Christian religious practices in the United States, because it would have threatened the "pristine condition" of the Christian faith.

(c) In the post–Civil War era, most people living in African American communities were first trying to internalize values they thought represented a higher culture, thereby hoping to earn acceptance by the economically dominant majority. Anything that might "implicate" African Americans in "primitive" African beliefs, i.e., "hoodoo" would arouse anxiety, and be quickly removed from conscious discourse. Many African Americans in the post–Civil War era even thought to suppress their association with, and memory of, slavery. African American achievements, women's achievements (cf. Tucker 2004: 3), orally transmitted knowledge, and the like were systematically underreported.

Thus, the discussion of certain transatlantic analogies in religious practices had to wait for later times. One area in which the historical parallels are particularly eye-catching is the periodic rise of charismatic female personalities with quasi-medial abilities in art, religion, and also in the realm of statesmanship. These are females with strong inner convictions and leadership qualities. (Cf. the nineteenth-century figure Sojourner Truth, who gained the ear of President Abraham Lincoln and was also a feminist leader.)

Not always were they successful, however; often they were doomed to social annihilation. But it is obvious that across the Atlantic divide a common socio-psychological "turf" must have existed promoting the periodic rise of female personalities with a spiritual engagement and a "prophetic" message to society. From that perspective, voodoo priestesses such as nineteenth-century Marie Laveau in New Orleans appear to be part of a wider phenomenon, in fact contemporaneous impersonations of something structural, or at least what could be called a long African tradition that used to keep certain intellectual spaces of activity open for females. Why is it that a name such as Ma Rainey makes perfect sense in eastern Angola?

Before the impact of European kinship terminology, consanguine and affinal, women in African societies did not adopt the names of their husbands after marriage. Such a custom, absolutely normal in Europe, was out of the question in most pre-colonial sub-Saharan African societies. Names are always indicators of relationships and identities. In eastern Angola, for example, personal names and thereby identities were indeed changed more than once in life, but along different lines. During initiation boys would have a secret name within their group of novices. After return to the villages their childhood name (*lizina lyavunike*) would be lost forever, and they would receive an adult name. The next change for both sexes would occur in connection with childbirth, not marriage. When a first child is born it usually takes the name of an ancestor in the family, thereby symbolizing reincarnation. The woman who has given birth and her husband would then be addressed politely as "Mother of . . ." (with the prefix *Nya-*) and "Father of . . ." with the prefix *Sa-*, with the name of the firstborn following, for example NyaLikumbi, SaMuyandulu, etc. If the first-born died, the name of the second or third child would be used. In other African languages very similar prefixes would be used to express the new status. Among the Wapangwa of Tanzania we met Mama Sofia; Mama can be reduced to *Ma-*. Had she ever visited those parts of Africa, Ma Rainey's name would have been understood that way.

African concepts such as these are based on specific forms of spirituality and perceptions of the place of human beings in a wider, visible and invisible universe. Parts of these African traditions reach into the Caribbean and South America. A voodoo queen in New Orleans can be compared therefore, even be equated with what is called Mãe-de-Santo in Brazilian candomblé. She can also be compared with religious healers in African societies.

During half a century of ongoing fieldwork, I have come across many charismatic female personalities in Africa; sometimes they were powerful chiefs, endowed with extraordinary wisdom and capabilities beyond the average. Historical examples of such leaders are plentiful. They include eighteenth-century Anna Nzinga of Matamba, who resisted the Portuguese occupiers, and sixteenth-century Queen Luweji of the Lunda Empire in inner Angola, who succumbed, however, to the allure of a young Luba hunter, Chibinda Ilunga, eventually depriving her of her reign. One might include Empress Taitu (wife of Menelik) in Ethiopia, who led a division at the Battle of Adwa (1896), and earlier queens (Sheba, Yodit). In the second half of the twentieth century I met great spiritual healers, such as NyaVungamba among the Mbwela-speaking people of eastern Angola in 1965. These women had medium power and would do for their patients the hard work of falling into trance, during a *lihamba* spirit possession ceremony (cf. documentation Kubik 2003: 140–52; 1991 [2013: 148–49]).

In music and dance there were also charismatic female personalities. Often they were the organizers of a secret society, such as *tuwema* (the flames) in eastern Angola. This society gave a beautiful spectacle at night in front of the chief's compound, singers and dancers writing ideographs into the sky with sparks of fire produced by glimmering barkcloth. In the Central African Republic in 1966, there was another secret society, *akulavye*, in the hands of young women (Kubik 2000b: 389–95).

And then there is the universal phenomenon of female instrumentalists. In many societies of the world, gender division as concerns musical instruments is rigid. Women may be dominant in one area, while men are in another. In Africa certain instruments are exclusively reserved for women; some instrumental technology may even be secret. On the other hand, it can be regularly observed that women are excluded from playing most kinds of aerophones, notably horns, trumpets, and oboes. It is striking that there has been a somewhat comparable gender division in jazz, with many women pianists, vocalists, and stringed instrument players in blues (e.g., Jessie Mae Hemphill), but rare presence of women as players of wind instruments. As always, there are, of course exceptions: Melba Liston, trombonist and arranger; Clora Bryant on trumpet and flugelhorn; Vi Redd alto and soprano saxophone, etc. However, women's involvement on such instruments was often relegated to specific social contexts, e.g., private parties and all-women bands (cf. Tucker 2004: 3). In the Central African Republic in May 1966, Maurice Djenda and I recorded an ensemble of four adolescent girls playing *efu*, single-note pipes made from the green branches of a papaya tree, alternating between vocal (head-voice) and instrumental sounds.

There are also areas in which parity may have been negotiated. Solo song and the participation in a choir are open to both sexes, though in a choir there may be separate sections due to voice range. But if the lead singer is a woman, she is also in control of the group she is with. This was the case with many blues singers. Bessie Smith in her 1927 recording of "Back Water Blues" had James P. Johnson to accompany her on piano; she did not accompany him with her voice. In 1966 in the Central African Republic the girls of the *akulavye* secret society employed boys to accompany their public performances but would not admit them as members. Very often, in African and African American musical groups, the one in control of the song's words assumes a leadership role, even if the band runs under someone else's name. When Sarah Vaughan recorded "Lover Man" on November 5, 1945, with Dizzy Gillespie on trumpet, Charlie Parker on alto sax, and Al Haig on piano, the Gillespie Sextet temporarily became the singer's accompaniment, the same day they had recorded "Shaw Nuff," "Salt Peanuts!," "Hot House," and other titles themselves. This underlines not only an African concept of primacy of the human voice, but also the ultimate vocal and verbal focus of most African music, even if it is played instrumentally.

In southeastern Africa can be found another amazing phenomenon of interest for those engaged in gender studies, that of female log xylophone players. The region where it is found includes Madagascar, off the east coast, where August Schmidhofer researched the subject in great detail (Schmidhofer 1991). In 1962, when I first came across a female *mangwilo* (log xylophone) player in the Mitukwe Mountains of northern Moçambique, I thought this was an anomaly. But later, in 1983, Moya A. Malamusi and I bumped into an entire school of female log xylophone players among the Yao in a village compound north of Yao chief Makanjila's residence in Malawi. And most recently, on May 3, 2012, Moya discovered two more female log xylophone players, Mrs. Selina Jiya, ca. fifty, and her younger sister Magdalena, in a village in the Madimba area of northern Moçambique. They were expert performers using the method of interlocking, for which purpose they would sit opposite each other in front of the xylophone keys spread out over two banana stalks.

Mary Lou Williams (1910–1981)

The experiences of several African xylophone styles have converged in New World cultures to contribute essential ideas to the motional and harmonic organization of jazz piano, from stride piano playing to boogie-woogie to accentuation through chord clusters. Mary Lou Williams, in league with many other female jazz pianists, e.g., Lil Hardin Armstrong, was perhaps the most innovative pianist in twentieth-century jazz history, a great American composer with a unique status as a carrier of a spiritual message, especially during the second half of her life. Mary Lou's message to posterity, the result of intensive work and meditation in the expressive realm of Christianity, can be seen as an embodiment of several strands of African female leadership. If she had had a former life, she could well have been a *mangwilo* log xylophone virtuoso, then transforming into a pianist, but she could also have been a spiritual healer in an African community, then transformed into a Catholic.

Fig. 3.12. S. Muhua, in a village of the Mitukwe Mountains, northern Moçambique, playing *mangwilo* log xylophone. October 14, 1962. Photo: H. Hillegeist (Culture Research Archive Kubik/Malamusi Vienna)

In the background of her life story I see the gradual self-realization and inner discovery of a mission as a spiritual leader who works through the medium of music. In her 1962 jazz composition *Black Christ of the Andes*, devoted to the memory of a sixteenth-century Afro-Peruvian friar of the Dominican order at Rosary Convent, canonized by Pope John XXIII in 1962, she recorded fourteen tracks (republished on CD by Smithsonian Folkways). There are moments that may induce in a listener a near-trance state, especially in parts where the George Gorden Singers are involved, as in tracks 5 ("Anima, Christi") and 14 ("Praise the Lord"). The lead singer employs various trance-inducing techniques, as known from many African American churches. But also in some of her trio performances, Mary Lou Williams, accompanied by Percy Heath on bass and Tim Kennedy on drums, transmits an essentially spiritual message.

Mary Lou Williams's remarkable transformation from a jazz pianist and arranger in the Kansas City group of Andy Kirk and his Clouds of Joy, in which she played from 1929 to 1942, into a different person occurred in Paris in 1954, when she suddenly decided to walk away from all musical job offers and retreated to a year-long seclusion. She found solace by prayer in Our Lady of Lourdes, a Roman Catholic Church in Harlem that was near her apartment. Under guidance by Fr. Anthony S. Woods, a Jesuit, she was baptized (at the age of forty-seven) into the Roman Catholic Church on May 9, 1957 (cf. liner notes by Fr. Peter F. O' Brien, S.J.: 9). Soon thereafter she began to integrate her life as a jazz pianist with her spirituality. When Fr. Peter F. O'Brien met her for the first time in 1964, it was a memorable encounter he describes in the liner notes to *Black Christ of the Andes*:

> I was about to encounter a most enduring and abiding soul-mate. . . . The music poured from the piano. On a large platform inside the oval mahogany bar at New York's Hickory House, the last surviving establishment offering jazz on West 52nd Street, "Swing Street," an authoritative African-American woman in early middle age sat at the piano, eyes mostly closed, her face registering every nuance in the music she was creating, back straight, her hands lying flat as they moved on the keys. . . .
>
> The emotional experience of the music and the woman herself was so strong that my life at once took on a permanent new direction. There was no confusion or doubt in me, and although I could not possibly have known the full consequences of that night's depth of feeling, I had found my purpose. I was finally at home . . .
>
> I slid off the bar stool and walked nervously toward her and told her my name. She asked me, "Are you a priest?" I told her, "No, I'm a Jesuit seminarian and I will be a priest." She was subdued—almost mute. I had been especially moved by one piece she played and asked her what her third-to-last number was. She replied, "Oh, that was just a blues." (O'Brien 2004: 4–5)

Fr. Peter F. O'Brien thereafter became involved in helping steer Mary Lou's musical career, from 1970 to her death in 1981. Today he is executive director of the Mary Lou Williams Foundation. In the second half of her life, Mary Lou Williams transformed not only into a composer of religious works, but also into a healer, a music therapist in a sense. There is her remarkable vision of a "jazz tree," drawn by her together with David Stone Martin, showing her perspective of the history of jazz as springing up from an eternal background of suffering. It is curious that there is just one female artist included: Lovie Austin, in some ways a precursor to Mary Lou. Austin was a theater pianist, piano accompanist to Ma Rainey and others, jazz band leader, and song writer in the 1920s. But what about Ella Fitzgerald? Billie Holiday? In the drawing there are also broken-off branches, besides the two permanent streams of the blues running up on both sides of the tree, the left stream passing the area of chopped-off branches which she names as follows: (1) "classical books" leading to "exercises," (2) "avant-garde" leading to "cults" and 'black magic" and (3) "commercial rock."

Mary Lou Williams's vision of jazz is perhaps best represented in her own words, in which she emphasizes jazz as a music that arises from suffering, with a spiritual message. However, if that message is lost, jazz would degenerate to mere "mechanical patterns." She also sees jazz as a form of conversation, very much as we do in Africa "talking to each other." And finally she points to the therapeutic effect of jazz.

From suffering came the Negro spirituals, songs of joy, and songs of sorrow. The main origin of American jazz is the spiritual. Because of the deeply religious background of the American Negro, he was able to mix this influence with rhythms that reached deep enough into the inner self to give expression to outcries of sincere joy, which became known as jazz. . . .

The moment a soloist's hands touch the instrument ideas start to flow from the mind, through the heart, and out of the fingertips. Or, at least, that is the way it should be. Therefore, if the mind stops, there are no ideas, just mechanical patterns . . .

The spiritual feeling, the deep conversation, and the mental telepathy going on between bass, drums, and a number of soloists, are the permanent characteristics of good jazz. The conversation can be of any type, exciting, soulful, or even humorous debating.

Your attentive participation, thru listening with your ears and your heart, will allow you to enjoy fully this exchange of ideas, to sense these various moods, and to reap the full therapeutic rewards that good music always brings to a tired, disturbed soul and all, who dig the sounds. (From a mimeographed handout under the title "Jazz for the Soul," which Mary Lou Williams gave audiences in 1963 and 1964; reproduced in the liner notes of the CD *Black Christ of the Andes*, 2004: 11)

PART B

Retention, Resilience, and Reinvention of African Instrumental Techniques in the United States

Writing on the social history of the Zimbabwe "marimba," a type of xylophone first constructed at Kwanongoma College in Bulawayo during the 1960s, Claire Jones (2012) has shown how validation can influence the fate of an invention. In Zimbabwe and elsewhere in south-central Africa, the highest ratings today are assigned to a certain technology. If the cherished technology is present in a musical performance, the event is pre-rated favorably—regardless of the performers' actual competence. If technological expectations such as a specific sound amplification, stage lighting, etc., are not met, the group on stage will not even be recognized as musicians.

Claire Jones quotes from a conversation that her acquaintance, Nicholas Manomano (then teaching "marimba" at Prince Edward School), had with the manager of a local hotel in June 2000. When he told the manager what kind of instrumentation his group of performers would use, the answer was "no, we want real music." Asked what he meant by that, the man was explicit: "Real music, like with amplifiers and electric guitars" (51–52).

The matter comes down to a proposition that any other manifestation should be disqualified and considered below what "real music" entails. Many different forms of musical practice in Zimbabwe would then fall outside the category of "real music." The "marimba" is in any case quickly dismissed as "schoolboy stuff" in street conversations, and some other music is only referred to under specific labels such as "church choirs," "school choirs," or by the adjective "traditional." All these genres seem to rank below "real music," without a chance of ever reaching mass popularity. In fact, they are often denied dissemination by the media because "no one is keen on that stuff." Zimbabwe's best-known popular musicians in the early twenty-first century, Thomas Mapfumo and Oliver Mtukudzi, are aware of this dictatorship of values, and they have been living up to the standards imposed, in order to be successful, even as Thomas Mapfumo included the *mbira dza vadzimu* in his shows, and Oliver Mtukudzi—in an experiment a few years ago—included several Kwanongoma "marimba" (see picture in Jones 2012: 32).

Lower-ranking genres in south-central Africa today include the once-popular music for acoustic solo guitar. At least this kind of music, however, is described politely as a "precursor" to the "real music" or as "an earlier stage" of it, or simply as "a style of the 1950s." The same is said about jazz, if it is played unplugged, thereby depriving audiences of the electric bass guitar's vibrations in their chests. It is then classed as "American music of the past," even if the ensemble introduces new compositions and shows brilliant experimentation with form and tonality.

Social Interaction

There is good reason for assuming that declamatory validations of this kind are not just a phenomenon of our times, although the mass media, the internet, and manufacturing industries contribute to their preeminence. They are a pan-human legacy that has affected musical production in the past as it does in the present. In a time journey back into the 1940s and beyond, there would be no sign of "real music, like with amplifiers and electric guitars"—and yet there would be music, and there were ratings. During the era of bebop, as it emerged at Minton's Playhouse in Harlem, the saxophone as an instrument enjoyed high status, higher than the clarinet, which had come to be associated with swing à la Benny Goodman, unacceptable in those avant-garde circles. Such validation guaranteed that an alto or tenor saxophonist at the door would probably be admitted for a jam session, after a brief test of his performance skills. Later, the instrumental panel of what was acceptable in jazz was further widened with John Coltrane's use of the soprano saxophone in ways that were different from earlier usages (cf. *My Favorite Things*, CD, Atlantic 1361, 1961).

How did domineering value systems influence behavior in New World social environments? What was the situation in these places a hundred, a hundred and fifty, two hundred years ago? To what extent would tightly knit New World communities with their religious beliefs exert pressure on individuals?—These are some of the questions to keep in mind in the comparative study of culture contact and its effects on the use of musical instruments.

For example, in New Orleans at the turn of the twentieth century, the word "music" had a much narrower semantic field than it has nowadays. It explicitly referred to musical notations. Written scores, i.e., sheet music, were valued highly; it was music as such, and a musician was someone who had learned to read and play from them. Anything else was "fake," including Buddy Bolden's variations on his cornet. (Here a look at the wordings New Orleans veterans used in talking about the city's music can be instructive: Shapiro and Hentoff 1966, *Hear Me Talkin' to Ya*; Charters 2008, *A Trumpet around the Corner: The Story of New Orleans Jazz*.)

Selection and Reinterpretation

Culture contact triggers many reactions. Sometimes the outcome is a prolonged struggle between different value systems. Strong convictions may form in people who are certain that they represent the only conceivable world order. In the realm of art it is thereby often determined what is going to succeed and what is going to perish.

In a strict sense, of course, all value systems are merely sets of entrenched beliefs, inaccessible to argument or contrary evidence. They are "logic-tight compartments" of the mind, as Michael Shermer (2013: 71) has called the phenomenon, "modules in the brain analogous to watertight compartments in a ship." Cultural resilience and the ensuing processes of retention and reinvention, therefore, can often be understood as expressions of resistance by people within one belief system to the claims of universality by another.

The cognitive realm is perhaps the most important one in the study of culture contact. It was opened up by Melville J. Herskovits (1941) with his descriptive terms "selection," "reinterpretation," and "syncretism." How do these concepts explain the fate of African musical instruments and their playing techniques in New World cultures?

On lecture tours through Europe, Africa, and South America in the 1970s, our research and performance group observed repeatedly that people in a general audience whose musical training was Western would react in surprisingly uniform ways to our presentations of African instruments. After a lecture, some people would come up from the floor to see and touch my eight-note *malimba* lamellophone from southwestern Tanzania. This instrument has a "buzzer," a chain such as was used in the colonial days by men to carry a pocket watch. It is laid out across the lamellae to vibrate like an automatic rattle. Those curious people, however—if they had not already mistaken my lamellophone for a mousetrap, as has happened many times—would inevitably remove the chain from the lamellae before trying to play.

It is precisely here that African perceptions about music diverge from those of adherents to some other musical cultures. The snail shells or bottle tops attached to the gourd resonator of a Zambezi lamellophone, the raphia vibration needles on the *timbrh* of the Vute of Cameroon, the membranes of a spider's nest-covering glued onto the vibrato holes of a xylophone's resonators, all are essential timbre-modifying and sound-amplifying devices. For people unaccustomed to their aesthetics, such devices appear to be just noise-producing, disturbing, and superfluous.

When industrial enterprises discovered a business potential in making African instruments, the first intervention was to streamline the elements of construction, thereby deviating considerably from the original designs. On xylophones and lamellophones they would not include any buzzers, but aim at a uniform, clear timbre for all notes. The sound of each note would be "pure." The tuning would be Western, mostly diatonic.

By contrast, manufacturers in African villages used to give each note individual timbre, as if these wooden or metal notes were voices in a family or community. The sound would not be streamlined. "Everyone" would speak with his or her individual voice, the "girls" among the notes, the "boys," the "elders," and the "chief," each voice represented by one lamella or one key of a xylophone. Pie-Claude Ngumu (1975/76) told me that on southern Cameroonian xylophones in his home area, the lower notes were conceptualized as males, but each of them with his "wife" (octave) in the upper part. There was also a chief or family headman among the notes to start the tuning process. Each instrument manufactured in a village was unique, identifiable by the maker's style.

This may be surprising to hear because of prevalent stereotypes, which hold that African societies are less individual-oriented than Western ones but rigorously community-centered, with individuals defined by their social roles and functions, and only a narrow margin for personal initiative. One social psychologist, Paul Parin (1983: 153ff.), even claimed that the Dogon in Mali had a "group ego" and thereby a psychology different from that of "people in the Western world."

The truth is that community organization and social roles within a community do not necessarily curtail individualism and personality. If musical concepts and behavior reflect social structure, as Alan Lomax has shown, based on the results of his worldwide Cantometrics Project (Lomax 1968), then there must be something wrong with singling out African cultures as "collectivistic" in contrast to the alleged "individualism" of Western societies. Ironically, Ngumu (1975/1976: 15), reflecting on the social order displayed in the tunings of southern Cameroonian xylophones, found that one note was always a "spoil-sport" (*esandi*)—one could say a dissident within the culture.

As to timbre, Rudi Blesh in his *Shining Trumpets* (1949 [1958: 20–21]) was one of the first to recognize a general tendency in African music to aim at a variety of specific sound spectra in the performance on instruments and the use of the human voice. Blesh describes these timbre concepts in the context of African American music. In a table of "African survivals" (20), he points to "vocalized instrumental tone" in jazz and other African American traditions, and within this heading to "great variety of unorthodox tone qualities" and to "hot tone."

Timbre concepts seem to rank among traits that are tenaciously resistant to acculturative changes. During the last few decades timbre has been studied repeatedly by musicologists from various scientific angles, in different musical cultures. Much of this is highly relevant to jazz research and African American music in general. Timbre research was recently summarized in a volume edited by August Schmidhofer and Stefan Jena (2011).

Jazz Instrumentation

Jazz is considered to be mostly instrumental music, though the contributions made by singers, particularly female, since the 1920s have been enormous. From Ma Rainey, Bessie Smith, and others interpreting blues to Ella Fitzgerald, Billie Holiday, and Sarah Vaughan, their share in jazz history has been intensively researched and appreciated (cf. Abbott and Seroff 1996; Friedwald 1992; zur Heide, 2004; Martin 1994; Santelli 1993; Spencer 1993; Titon 1977, 1993) Male vocalists have also had a significant share, with the unforgettable voices of Louis Armstrong, Jelly Roll Morton, Thomas "Fats" Waller, Cab Calloway, and others.

In its predominantly instrumental repertoire, however, jazz differs from most (though by far not all) African music in which vocal parts are essential, either as a soloist's voice a call-and-response schema, or in interlocking polyphony. One function of the instruments in African music is to support these vocal arrangements or represent them. In many African societies it is also the text of a song that is of primary concern to audiences. The relevance of a song is often judged in terms of its literary appeal, plus its movement-inspiring instrumental support.

That does not mean, of course, that there is no concept of instrumental music in Africa. On the contrary, prominent instrumental formations have included xylophone and horn ensembles in several former king's courts in East Africa, the *entenga* twelve-note drum chime played at the court of the Kabaka of Buganda (Anderson 1977, 1984), the set of nine tuned drums used to accompany masked dances of the *nyau* secret society among the –Maŋanja of Malawi, and the Hausa and Fulɓe court music in northern Nigeria, Niger and Cameroon, to give only a few examples. But even in purely instrumental performances, words are often hidden in the instrumental renderings of songs, since most African languages are tone languages. The emphasis on instrumental performance in jazz was inherited from "orchestral ragtime," brass band, and dancehall music in New Orleans and elsewhere at the turn of the twentieth century, as well as from piano ragtime; and yet it is possible to find analogies in some African instrumental traditions, pointing to hidden syncretism in jazz, rather than connecting early jazz band lineups and instrumental resources exclusively to Western models. Alfons M. Dauer (1985) pointed to one possible transatlantic family line leading back to the *ganga/algeita* (drum-and-oboe) complex in court music ensembles among the Hausa and Fulɓe in the West African savannah.

If jazz is predominantly instrumental, it is not necessarily in the European sense of the word, as for example a symphony orchestra or chamber music ensemble. There is in jazz an underlying reliance on speech-like expression. As in African musical cultures, instrumental variations in jazz can in part function as an extension of vocal articulation, in that jazz melodic-rhythmic phrases may be verbalized in the mind. Anyone intensively involved in jazz performance will have discovered by themselves that sometimes one thinks of certain phrases in colors, sometimes in short spoken sentences, or in syllables of no verbal meaning. Such associations may also occur to people in audiences who are not at all speakers of tone languages.

In Central Africa a soloist player of a board zither, a lamellophone, or a guitar produces a complex instrumental soundscape beneath his vocal line, as if he were conducting a lively conversation between his voice and the sounds emerging from the instrument. In some African languages there is no terminology to distinguish singing and the playing of an instrument. For example, in Chichewa of Malawi there is just one verb, *kuyimba*, meaning both vocal and instrumental sound production. Accordingly, *zoimbaimba* (the things that constantly sing) are musical instruments. In other African languages, however, a sharp distinction is made between vocal and instrumental production, for example, in Mbwela, Luchazi, and other languages of eastern Angola within Bantu Zone K, Group 10. The verb *kwimba* means to sing (by mouth), while *kusika* is used to express playing of an instrument. There is, however, an important difference in the semantic field of *kusika* and "playing" as conceptualized in European languages. *Kusika* in Mbwela/Lucazi is a specialist term, only used to express instrumental musical performance. In that language one cannot use the verb for "playing" (as in games), *kuheha*, to express action upon instruments. One does not "play" an instrument.

The human voice can be instrumentalized in many ways, for example, in the technique of overtone singing (or diphonic singing), as found in Mongolia and among the –Gogo of Tanzania and the –Xhosa of South Africa. There are many voice-disguising techniques, especially in African initiation ceremonies, and the voices of spirits may be represented by an unusual instrumental sound such as that of a bull-roarer. We have comprehensive field data on initiation, e.g., from Liberia (Stone 1982, 1988), Côte d'Ivoire (Zemp, 1971), Dahomey (Rouget 2001), and Angola (Kubik 1993a, 2002b; Tsukada 1988, 1990a). Both verbalization on the one hand and instrumentalization on the other have survived in jazz, though in somewhat different, non-ritual contexts, from Ella Fitzgerald's scat singing to the "jungle style" of muted trumpets in Duke Ellington, to the very name that came to be associated with a new music in the early 1940s, bebop, and to Kenny Clarke's "klook-mop" percussion.

The brass and reed sections of a 1940s swing band, such as that of the formidable Jay McShann of Kansas City, can interact in their compact, homophonic lines as if they were two instrumentalized sections of a vocal group. There is good reason to assume that on Jay McShann's performance of his favorite tune "Jump the Blues" the musicians, subliminally, were feeling it that way (recorded ca. March 1944, *Early Bird*... CD, track 21, Stash ST-CD-542). Jazz uses instrumental resources inherited from European music—reed and brass instruments, string bass, piano, guitar, a modified marching drum ensemble that became the jazz drum set—expanded by nineteenth-century instrumental novelties such as the saxophone, which rose to prominence in the 1920s. Then came twentieth-century innovations such as the vibraphone, electric amplification for the guitar, etc.

However, one can also say that African musical instruments were reinvented by using trumpets, trombones, clarinets, and saxophones like molds around which different playing techniques were constructed, which ultimately came from the transmitted experience of African music in New World cultures. Patterns originally associated with xylophones and lamellophones in African music had survived, struck by children on household objects or even just encoded as body movement. They began to enter piano playing in ragtime, and more so in boogie-woogie and various jazz piano styles. In the 1930s when the vibraphone was introduced into jazz, it was like a metallized offspring of gourd-resonated xylophones, even if it was invented in response to Amerindian adaptations in Central America. When Willie Cornish, the last surviving member of Buddy Bolden's band in New Orleans around 1900, described Bolden's cornet playing in an interview with researcher William Russell in the late 1930s, he enumerated techniques we know from African aerophones, from the *vandumbu* secret horns in southeast Angola to gourd trumpets across Africa. Ramsey and Smith (1957: 14) summarized the conversation as follows: "Willy Cornish, the only member of the original [Buddy Bolden] band living today, played a piston (valve) trombone. For a mute, Cornish used an empty bottle. Bolden, who always played with an open horn, sometimes used a rubber plunger, water glass, half a cocoanut shell, derby hat, a piece of cloth, or his hand, for muted effects." What was important for Bolden was different from that of musicians who were playing "legitimate" music from notations. Key changes, for example, apparently were not important for him.

In several ways African instrumental techniques have resurged and been implanted into the playing of European musical instruments. Some techniques have been reinvented in jazz and other African American traditions, often in disguise. Initially, some of these "survivals" would stay in hiding, used on tools available in small African American communities, families, etc., as long as mainstream American culture had a monopoly of instilling values. Decisive changes would only be brought about in the 1940s and 1950s, from the moment a new generation of musicians—more assertive and conscious of its rights—would refuse to identify with many of the mainstream values. This is illustrated by some of Dizzy Gillespie's, Don Cherry's, and others' instrumental inventions.

Before that, instrumental techniques with an obvious African background would survive predominantly in small communities, offstage, among economically poor musicians, "amateurs," in rural areas or in the urban social underground. A way of discovering how culture-specific skills of long ago were retained and transmitted is to look at such tightly knit communities that often existed in self-imposed isolation. On farms in the Deep South, and among owners of small plots and homesteads, one could encounter in the 1980s and '90s extraordinary personalities with sometimes "strange" habits, skills, and technical knowledge, as David Evans has shown us on joint field recording trips in 1993 and 1997. Our encounter with storyteller and "home philosopher" John Milton Alexander in his farmhouse at Byhalia, Mississippi, March 1, 1993, will remain unforgettable, as does our visit to "bo diddley" player Glen Faulkner in Senatobia, Mississippi, February 27, 1993. Complete transcriptions of all recorded conversations have been made by David Evans, University of Memphis. Esoteric knowledge such as uncovered in these conversations has always been a stimulus in African American history, for experimentation, for trying out something unusual.

The same applies to so-called gang cultures in US inner cities, youths socially isolated from the mainstream who form separate, in some ways even "secret" societies which require certain rituals for admittance. In such social environments emerge behavioral traits, concepts, skills, and forms of creativity that are usually rejected, ridiculed, even criminalized by the dominant society, but because of that they develop substantial in-group resistance and self-encouragement, defining a separate identity. Break dance came up like that.

In the nineteenth century, drums and other African instruments were suppressed by the authorities in the South and soon abandoned by people of African descent. But their techniques and their conceptual basis were retained and eventually recreated with tools such as household articles that were not destined for destruction. Thereby a memory of otherwise lost cultural resources was kept alive and eventually revived. In a brilliant article on Warren "Baby" Dodds, Eddie S. Meadows (1999) has uncovered an astonishing number of concepts and patterns of behavior traceable to African cultures, which New Orleans jazz's most prominent drummer had preserved in his mind. That is why the few descriptions we have of African musical instruments on US territory in the eighteenth and nineteenth centuries can be instructive "missing links" in recovering aspects of jazz history.

Fiddle, Banjo, and Percussion

Robert B. Winans (1982 [1990]) scrutinized the thirty-one volumes of the ex-slave narratives collected by the WPA in the 1930s (cf. Rawick 1972) to statistically assess all references to mid-nineteenth-century musical instruments as played by African Americans in the United States. In addition, he searched through the Virginia Narratives (Purdue, Barden, and Phillips 1976). These were oral testimonies by people born between 1830 and 1860, therefore referring to the situation in the southern United States in the mid- to late nineteenth century.

Among the instruments most often mentioned, according Winans's table (44), the fiddle is in first place with 205 entries, the banjo second with 106, various forms of percussion (75), quills (30), etc. At that time the guitar was still occupying a minor role in African American music, but is more often mentioned by narrators from Mississippi than from elsewhere. Fiddle playing was prevalent throughout the South, especially in Mississippi and Georgia, but also in South Carolina, Texas, Alabama, Virginia, and Louisiana. The same picture emerges for the banjo, probably because the two instruments were often played together; but in the table Virginia has a higher rate (14) than other states for the banjo, with the exception of Georgia (26).

Winans (1990), however, warns us about direct comparisons of the figures. He points to problems in obtaining a conclusive picture about the frequency of the usage of particular instruments "because the quantity of the data varies considerably from state to state. The reasons for this involve the number and length of interviews per state and the kinds of questions asked by the interviewers, about which each state organization made its own decisions.... North Carolina, for instance, was a great disappointment, since, while it had a significant number of interviews, the questions asked rarely elicited the kind of information I wanted. Georgia interviewers, on the other hand, regularly brought out information about instrumental music" (45). He then gives advice for how to cope with this situation: "For instance, if one is interested in comparing the relative strength of the black banjo-playing tradition in various states, comparing the absolute numbers of references to the banjo in each state is not a valid approach. But the ratio of banjo references to fiddle references for each state, expressed as percentage, allows for a rough comparison. This percentage is highest for Virginia (14 over 10, or 140 percent) and North Carolina (100 percent), suggesting that black banjo playing was especially strong in these states" (46). He proposes that "A similar ratio approach to other instruments would suggest that the use of percussion was strongest in Louisiana, South Carolina, and Georgia, and that quill playing was more common in Georgia and South Carolina than elsewhere" (51). Finally, he summarizes the cultural contact situation in the southern United States in antebellum times, from ca. 1830 to 1860, in a most interesting paragraph:

> The final topic I want to discuss is black-white musical interaction. In the narratives, one finds references to blacks listening to white music, and, as just noted, whites listening to black music. One can also find a few references to whites teaching blacks

how to play an instrument, mostly the fiddle. Quite frequently, black musicians are noted as playing for white dances as well as their own. Much less expected are the references to whites playing for black dances, which apparently was not all that rare. The usual situation involved a plantation owner who loved to play the fiddle and who regularly played it for his own slaves' dancing. All of these interactions, plus the instruments the black musicians most often played, the kinds of dances for which they played, and the repertoire noted above [referring to a song list given earlier in his article], indicate that in the mid-nineteenth century, just before the Civil War, black instrumental music traditions represented a considerable amalgamation of white and black elements.

The Gumbé (Frame-Drum)'s Transatlantic Roundtrip

In an article in the journal *African Music*, Rachel Jackson (2012) of SOAS, London, tries to reconstruct the three-hundred-year transatlantic history of a square frame drum variously described in sources from Jamaica to Sierra Leone, and other places in West Africa and in the Caribbean, as *gumbe*, "goombah," etc. The earlier history of these frame-drums can be traced to Arab cultures, notably of the Maghreb, and their extensions into the Iberian peninsula (cf. the *adufe* in Portugal, Veiga de Oliveira 1964 [2000: 267]). During the eighteenth century this type of instrument became associated with Maroon (runaway slave) communities in Jamaica. The earliest known account (by Long) dates to 1774.

Because of the example provided by the successful Haitian revolution in 1793, there was great fear of a slave insurrection in British-dominated areas of the New World, which actually happened tentatively in Jamaica in 1793 and 1795. Kenneth Bilby (2007, 2011) has done considerable research on the legacy of slavery and emancipation in Jamaica. A year before Jackson's article he published a paper on what he has called "Africa's Creole Drum," the *gumbé*, as "vector and signifier of Trans-Atlantic Creolization" (Bilby 2011). Both Bilby and Jackson have used the term "creolization" as defined by Ulf Hannerz (1996: 66).

In her own survey, Jackson traces the spread of this drum from Jamaica to the Bahamas and from there to Freetown, Sierra Leone, and other places along the West African coast. The mid-twentieth-century presence of the *gumbé* in Freetown is well documented, for example. The eminent Krio singer and guitarist Ebenezer Calender in his *maringa* music used it occasionally (Bender 1991: 111ff.). Even the pandeiro used by the West African Instrumental Quintet (WAIQ) from the Cold Coast, recorded in 1929 (cf. *Jazz Transatlantic* II), may have been an extension of the *gumbé*-playing tradition.

Jackson (2013) also points to the interesting case of New Orleans. While the city has been recognized as "the ultimate Creole society," it "poses a problem.

There is evidence that gumbé reached the Louisiana settlement yet it did not survive despite the presence of a valid Creole culture" (147). However, she points to Benjamin Henry Latrobe's 1819 publication about his visit to Congo Square and his description of a recreational meeting of slaves at that place. Latrobe's "square drum, looking like a stool" (1819 [1905]: 181) is considered by Jackson to be a clear reference to the presence of a *gumbé* drum. This puts early nineteenth-century New Orleans more firmly on the circuit of transatlantic exchanges.

> Cuban music arrived in Africa in the 1930s and is often hailed as the proto-typical
> "returned" Caribbean music. Prior to Cuban forms, Trinidadian calypso arrived
> on Ghanaian shores in 1873, transported by English speaking West Indian troops
> stationed there by the British during the Anglo-Ashanti wars. Yet, stretching
> even further back, . . . it was in fact *gumbé* that first "returned" to the continent in
> 1800. . . . Unlike Cuban music, yet similar to the spread of Trinidadian calypso in
> Africa, *gumbé* spread throughout West and central regions via real people not via
> recordings. The nature of *gumbé*'s diffusion demonstrates the existence of a modern
> and cosmopolitan music scene long before the first vinyl records were introduced by
> Western record labels. (Jackson 2013: 128–29)

However, as always in historical research, it is important to keep separate the consideration of phenomena and their designations. It is not certain that calypso as we think of it existed this early to arrive on the Gold Coast in 1873. What existed is something that present-day researchers have decided to call calypso. The same applies to the cross-cultural projection and widening of the word *gumbé*. Its semantic field is highly susceptible to changes across time and space.

The Marimba Brett

In "The Dance in Place Congo" (1886a), George Washington Cable describes leisure activities of Africans in New Orleans during the first half of the nineteenth century, especially as these gatherings were concentrated in the famous Congo Square. He mentions dances such as "bamboula" accompanied by drums, "counjaille," "calinda," and others, using the French spelling. Some of this information may have come from his own observations during childhood, although the Congo Square meetings were suppressed after 1843. It is clear that no direct continuity binds these neo-African interethnic dances in New Orleans to the rise of jazz at the beginning of the twentieth century. But it is also evident that certain patterns of behavior, a certain worldview, and a certain approach to movement and sound persisted to be remolded, eventually reconfiguring in new contexts.

In Cable's day this process of transculturation had not yet reached discernible proportions, although it actually started in the days of blackface minstrelsy. A remarkable description of African musical instruments in New Orleans in the early nineteenth century is found in Cable under the heading "Grand Orchestra," as they were used in the Congo Square dance meetings. His descriptions of long, single-headed drums laid on the ground with the drummers in striding position using "fingers, fists and feet" point to Congo drums, as known from several museum collections in the world (for specimens in the Musée Royal de l'Afrique Centrale, Tervuren, cf. Boone 1951). Probably they were of a type similar to those filmed a century later in Venezuela by Paul Henley (cf. review of his film, Kubik 1988). That the "wooden sides of it are beaten with two sticks" suggests the use of a timeline pattern, I daresay probably an eight-pulse variety, as it occurs also in the batuque of Brazil (Kubik 1990). Cable also mentions what may be a mouth-resonated musical bow and then goes on to describe a "queer thing," adding that the "West Indies" were the place "whence Congo Plains drew all inspirations" (1886a: 34). He then describes a lamellophone. Although it is not clear whether Cable or others had actually seen this instrument in New Orleans, or whether he even quotes from observations made in other parts of the Caribbean, the find is remarkable, if only for the curious name: *marimba brett*. The term contains the well-known Bantu designation *marimba*, but also an attribute written "brett," which seems to be a German word (exact in its spelling) meaning "board." Since Cable refers to a lamellophone, its notes mounted on a board-shaped corpus, the attribute makes sense. But the mystery lies in the fact that the word is German. Even if it had been incorporated into local jargon, how would a German word get into this composite designation? Here we can only guess. If the observation was indeed made in New Orleans, as I tend to believe, it was in a city that already was cosmopolitan in the nineteenth century. There were many Germans in various professions. Cable might have written down the term "marimba brett" from the spelling of a German informant who accompanied him on an excursion to the Congo Square. If so, the name would be secondhand information, not obtained directly from the performer. It is also possible that Cable just saw the instrument in a local German's collection.

Marimba is a term that originally came from Bantu languages of southeast Africa (Moçambique, Zimbabwe, etc.) to New World destinations. It is based on the -LIMBA (or -RIMBA) word stem with a cumulative *ma-* prefix, expressing the idea that the instrument consists of several sound-producing agents. In southeast Africa the word stem -LIMBA/-RIMBA appears in designations for both xylophones and lamellophones. For centuries it has been used with various prefixes such as *kalimba* (small lamellophone), *malimba*, *lulimba*, *ilimba* etc., to express specific ideas associated with these instruments. There are also phonetic

116

variations, e.g., *madimba* in northern Angola for gourd-resonated xylophones. Sometime between the sixteenth and eighteenth centuries the term *marimba* was picked up by Portuguese traders, travelers, and mariners, and it became a well-established lexical item in the Portuguese language. Its original meaning, however, was cramped to refer specifically to gourd-resonated xylophones, such as the type depicted by Girolamo Merolla (1692) from the Kingdoms of Koongo, Ndongo, and Matamba, in what is today northeastern Angola.

It is this meaning that was exported to New World destinations with two major organological types of xylophones: (a) a Koongo type that survived for a long time in the southern Brazilian festivities of Congada (installation of a "King of Congo") and (b) a Zambezi type, surviving with modifications, e.g., the replacement of gourds with bamboo resonators, for example in Colombia on the Pacific coast (cf. CD Group Naidy). Xylophones called *marimba* are still known across the Caribbean and South America, in countries such as Guatemala, Nicaragua, Panama, Colombia, Ecuador, etc. Occasionally this knowledge was borrowed by members of the Amerindian population, who then claimed the tradition to be their own, pre-Columbian heritage.

The technique of constructing lamellophones, especially some types from the so-called Slave Coast, also came to the New World, notably to Cuba, as we know from Fernando Ortiz (1952: 86–123). They seem to have come mostly from the area around Calabar in eastern Nigeria. An intermediate form in Cuba could have been the gourd-resonated *marimbula de güira* depicted in Ortiz (99. From those models a large type was developed in Cuba. Drawing on the word *marimba*, it was then called *marimbula* in Spanish. In the 1930s English-speaking musicians began to call it "rumba box" because of its association with son or rumba music. The marimbula was well established in the nineteenth century in Cuba, and in the early twentieth began to spread all over the Caribbean (see, for example, George List's find in Cartagena, Colombia, List 1966, 1983). At the end of the nineteenth century it also spread to the West African coast, in particular to Lagos, with a wave of Brazilian and other *retornados* from the Caribbean after abolition in 1888 in Brazil. In Lagos it gave rise to the development of the Yoruba *agidigbo* (the name comes from the fighting game *gidigbo*, possibly related to capoeira in Brazil) and a similar large lamellophone type in (Portuguese-speaking) Guinea-Bissau (cf. Kubik 2002a: 321–22). This is another case of a transatlantic "loop" such as described for the *gumbé* frame-drum by Rachel Jackson (2012: 128). The retornados from Brazil also introduced a Brazilian architectural style in western Nigeria.

Cable's report of a lamellophone among Africans in New Orleans must be seen within this wider transatlantic loop. Perhaps the knowledge had come directly from Central Africa or eastern Nigeria to New Orleans, but more likely is that it had spilled over from the Caribbean, as he himself seems to suggest.

Diddley Bow and Unitar

In his short paper "Afro-American one-stringed instruments" (1970), David Evans first demonstrated to what extent one-string instrumental techniques from various regions of Africa had survived in the southern United States. They include those of the Central African monoidiochord zither surviving in the organology and playing technique of African American instruments variously called "diddley bow," "jitterbug," "unitar," etc. He also examined African American musical bows, all single-fundamental, something like a homemade jew's harp and quills that seem to be related to pan-pipes and their blowing techniques as found in the lower Zambezi Valley (southeast Africa) (Evans 1994; Graham 1994; Malamusi 1992, 1997).

One part of the remote history of slide guitar playing can be explained in this context: the use of a slider for stopping the string, thereby creating glissando sounds, is probably based on a discovery that was originally made in the so-called raffia zone of west-central Africa. This is an equatorial forest area where the raffia palm, even today, is one of the most often-used plants for making household utensils, chairs, tables, beds, and some musical instruments. Among the latter are so-called mono-idiochord zithers. These are instruments made from the length of a raffia leaf stem from which a single strand of fiber is "peeled off." Nowadays they are children's instruments; perhaps they also were in the remote past. One boy strikes the string with two sticks, while the other changes the pitch using a knife or other object as a slider (field photograph in Kubik 1999a: 18).

Knowledge of the instrument's manufacture and how to play it was exported to New World destinations with people from that region of west-central Africa, notably to Venezuela, where the locally made *carángano* is virtually identical to the Central African models. In the United States it turned from idiochord to heterochord. The single string is a wire mounted either on the wall of a house or on a length of board. It is played solo. Eddie One-String Jones, Glen Faulkner, and many others have provided good recorded examples of the African American derivatives. (Cf. CD *Bottleneck Blues*, David Evans and Pete Welding, Testament TCD 5021. See also Glen Faulkner on David Evans's CD *The Spirit Lives On*.)

Recently, recordings of another one-string man, Moses "Doorman" Williams (born 1919) in or near Itta Bena, Mississippi, have been published, and his life history and music has been discussed in great detail by David Evans (2012). It is important here to mention that in the African American versions of the mono-chord zither, in North America at least, the string can be strung vertically, as in "Doorman" Williams's case, and the playing attitude is then vertical. Also, it is always a solo instrument, in contrast to the frequent work division between two boys encountered among the Central African adolescents.

The technique of slide guitar playing derives in part from the experience of the mono-idiochord and mono-heterochord zithers. It could be that the technique was first transferred to the guitar by sailors who had picked up the knowledge in Central African ports. They were then traveling to many parts of the world, including Hawaii. There the technique developed within the so-called "Hawaiian guitar" by the 1890s. While a maritime diffusion pattern is likely, it is almost impossible to reconstruct details of the chronology of its diffusion (or even parallel invention). The slide technique is also found in India and Japan, but later stages of its application to the guitar are definitely in connection with Hawaii.

Mantle Hood (1983), based on research by his colleague B. C. Deva in India, refers to the slide technique "being applied to forms of tribal bamboo zithers" and that the "ancient slider technique of India" is "preserved on the *gottuvadyam* and the Hawaiian steel guitar." Following findings in Java and from India by Deva dating to 600 CE, he infers that "the principle of the slide could be as ancient as 200 BCE." If that is so, a similar minimal antiquity could be realistically assumed on ecological grounds for the same technique on mono-idiochord zithers in the west-central African raffia zone.

During the 1940s, records of Hawaiian guitar music were massively sold in southern Africa. Local guitarists like Ndiche Mwarare in Nyasaland (Malawi) would then reproduce the sounds with the slider technique they remembered from the monochord zithers that were once widespread in southeast Africa, including Moçambique (cf. picture in Margot Dias 1986: 171–72, fig. 133 of *nkungulandi* from the –Makonde). In Zimbabwe, South Africa, and Malawi the style was then often called *hauyani*. The word comes from "Hawaiian."

More recently, the technique has spread from the guitar back to one-stringed instruments. During the 1990s and thereafter Moya A. Malamusi, on numerous research trips, recorded bands of adolescents in Malawi with homemade banjo, guitar, percussion, and a very large bass guitar, laid horizontally on the ground. Its single string would be stopped with a slider, usually a glass bottle or similar object. (Cf. recordings of the Makambale Brothers Band, August 3, 2005, tracks 16 and 17, *Endangered Traditions . . . Endangered Creativity*, CD/DVD pamcwm 801, Frankfurt: Popular African Music, 2011.)

The Skiffle Bass

Age-old African playing techniques also resurged on another New World string instrument, first in a homemade variety, then in the transfer of the playing technique to factory-manufactured instruments: the string bass. In contrast to the African mono-idiochord zithers, the playing attitude here is vertical.

The ancestral African instrument is the ground-bow. Its New World derivatives include (a) the washtub bass, or "gut bucket," made from household articles, (b) the plucked string-bass in jazz bands. Unfortunately, our documentation comes exclusively from the mid-twentieth century. We do not know in which manner the African techniques survived and in which local communities. David Evans tells me (conversation, February 2013): "I'm not aware of any instances from the slavery era. In fact the earliest American versions I know are from the 1930s." The question arises whether linear continuity traceable to specific African places can be assumed at all. One-string bass devices were also known, for example in Haiti (Courlander 1960). Did the knowledge spill over from the Caribbean? In that case, it would have been secondary proliferation of an African trait.

The African prototype of the skiffle bass, as recorded by us on many occasions in Uganda, Tanzania, Central African Republic (Djenda 1968a; Kubik, Malamusi, and Varsanyi 2013: 189), etc., depends on a dug-out pit that serves as a resonator. Usually it is covered with an animal skin, weighing it down on all sides with stones, or nailing it to the ground. Alternatively, a metal sheet can be used. A strong single string (rope) is threaded through a hole in the center of the skin or metal sheet and its lower end is knotted to a nail or small piece of wood. The string's upper end is connected to a young tree or tree branch, perhaps a meter high, and a bit flexible, but firmly rooted in the ground.

Playing this device, the performer can change the string's tension by pressing with his left hand against the string-bearer, i.e., the tree branch, thereby obtaining different notes when plucking or "slapping" the only string with the right hand. There are many different playing techniques used by instrumentalists in different areas of Africa, but this is a basic one.

Historically, the idea is probably related to spring pole snares, a common type of trap in East Africa. I discussed the matter with Moya A. Malamusi. In terms of origins, he said, human beings in the remote past would probably first have invented this kind of trap called *chilapu* in Chichewa and—accidentally playing around with the string—they would have later discovered that it was giving a sound that could be manipulated (conversation, January 28, 2013).

The ground-bow was once widely known in Central and East Africa, and it was here that our research team made several photographic, auditory, and cinematographic shots showing its manufacture. In Buganda, for example, the instrument is known today. It is called *sekituleghe* (Video document no. 60, February 6, 2000 at Lutengo village, northeast of Mukono, Uganda; Culture Research Archive Kubik/Malamusi, Vienna).

In the United States the ground-bow and its technique continued to be used, though in modified forms:

a) as a "gut bucket" or washtub bass (such as was played by Clarence "Pops" Davis, photo in Kubik 1999a : 168) or as a skiffle bass, with a box resonator. In all these cases the pit was simply replaced by a portable resonator, such as a pail or wooden box; otherwise essential details of the construction remained stable, within a variation margin also present in the African examples.
b) by transferring the ground-bow's playing technique to the established Western double bass. This step was taken by musicians in the earliest jazz bands. The plucked string-bass in jazz bands is a curious "out-of-context" survival from European string ensembles, in an environment otherwise dominated by brass and reed instruments. Toward the end of the nineteenth century, in "orchestral" or dance-band ragtime, the double-bass was still bowed. In the only photograph of the Buddy Bolden band so far known, we can see Jimmy Johnson with a bow in his right hand. One day, however, someone began to "slap" the bass. William Russell and Stephen W. Smith in *Jazzmen* (Ramsey and Smith 1957: 20) reported the following story tracing the event to Freddie Keppard's

> Original Creole Band, the first important group to leave New Orleans. Organized by Bill Johnson, they started on a series of vaudeville tours as early as 1911. Bill Johnson was one of the earliest string bass players. One time, when playing up in Shreveport, his bow broke; so he had to pluck the strings the rest of the night. The effect was so novel and added so much more swing and flexibility to his playing, that he took to slapping his bass entirely thereafter.

In anecdotes reported by jazz veterans and others (see the earlier chapter on the word *jazz*), something new like an important technical change is often traced to a specific event. So Bill Johnson is said to have been the "first" jazz musician to "slap" or pluck the double bass. Such accounts also emphasize that the new idea would have occurred as a result of an "accident," something that was missing or had been broken or spoiled, leading to a compensatory reaction.

Essentially, such anecdotes may be true, but they are rarely the full story. They represent what an observer may have picked up in a recent, critical moment, not the earliest incident or the moment of invention. In the present case, later research has turned up statements by Sid LeProtti about first exposure to "slap style" bass from William Manual Johnson in 1908–09, well before formation of the Original Creole Band (Tom Stoddard 1982 [1998]). For information on Mexican heritage musician Martin "Chink Martin" Abraham also utilizing "slap style" in New Orleans ca. 1908, see Bruce Boyd Raeburn: "Beyond the Spanish Tinge: Hispanics and Latinos in Early New Orleans Jazz" (2012b). Therefore, the technique of slapping the double bass had probably been tried out several times and independently, by several musicians including Bill Johnson, long before the particular events that have been reported. Musicians in New Orleans did have knowledge of what is described with the Italian term pizzicato in classical music. But the giant step was reinterpretation in terms of the African ground-bow technique whose basic idea has survived in the gut-bucket bass in the southern United States.

The slap technique is also somewhat different from the ground-bow technique, but it is closer to it than it is to pizzicato. This can be gathered by watching how a jazz bass player's right-hand fingers act, in their specific modes of attack and release, a movement pattern very different in its kinetic structure from pizzicato, which is usually considered to be a special effect, not a dominant technique. This manner of bass playing appears to be shared across jazz styles, if one compares, for example, Slow Drag Pavageau (New Orleans jazz) with Walter Page (Kansas City swing) and with Larry Gales in the Thelonious Monk quartet, 1966. There are several photographs and some cinematographic shots that can be studied.

Many novel playing techniques that came up in jazz had most certainly been used by the musicians before they were first seen by the broad public. When established bands displayed those novelties, they naturally claimed to have invented them. We can safely assume, however, that what comes up before our eyes is often only the most recent link in a chain of events. From the viewpoint of observers outside the culture—taken by surprise—it appears to be a quantum leap in innovation, while from the viewpoint of a historically informed Africanist observer, it is often like déjà vu or the warming up of a well-known dish.

Brass and Reeds

Nineteenth-century European, factory-manufactured instruments—notably aerophones as used in military music—became widely available to African Americans after the Civil War. From the first, however, they were used by some musicians who were outside the tradition of Western notation, in manners and techniques very different from those for which these instruments had been designed in the context of European classical music. In a sense, African Americans in the United States and elsewhere in New World cultures reinvented African musical instruments by using the factory-manufactured instruments in a functionally analogous manner, even if the overall context was radically different. Playing techniques associated with African music organization, responsorial schemes, timbre sequences, vocalization, etc., were incorporated into the replacements. Trumpets, clarinets, saxophones, double bass, and piano became representations of lost African musical instruments.

This process was not restricted to North America, of course. It is a transatlantic phenomenon, a background also to contemporary developments in the aftermath of colonialism in Africa. No South African musician playing jazz on a saxophone, no Central African using an electric guitar for his music would agree to accusations that his was "not African music." It is African music, he would say, with new tools.

In the process of adopting factory-manufactured instruments for performance, rigorous processes of selection were involved. Violins, for example, did not usually make it into jazz, needing someone like Stéphane Grappelli of Django Reinhardt's Quintette du Hot Club de France to demonstrate their potential ("Minor Swing," recorded Nov. 25, 1937, Matrix no. OLA 1990–1). And yet, with a variety of background, e.g., in ragtime, there were notable violinists in New Orleans. Emile Bigard, Peter Bocage, and Louis James must be mentioned. The mid-1920s recordings of Lonnie Johnson and James "Steady Roll" Johnson may also provide insight into alternative fiddle aesthetics from New Orleans players.

Why did oboes and bassoons not become jazz instruments, while double-reed instruments have been common among the Hausa and Fulɓe in the West African savannah? The first choices in jazz—trumpet, trombone, clarinet, etc.—were circumstantial, since these were the main lead instruments in dance and marching bands, and had become generally accessible after the Civil War. And they also enjoyed a high status as military musical instruments in an era when war was still perceived as a matter of male glory and honor.

The introduction into jazz of the saxophone in the early 1920s shows perhaps a slightly different pattern of adoption, motivated in part by an emerging ideology requiring performers to be up to date, "fashionable" by using the latest technology, though it had been invented in the nineteenth century. Under certain social circumstances, symbols of social upward mobility had become important. But the saxophone also caught on very quickly for musical reasons: it was ideal for infusing into jazz many of the inherited African timbre-modifying techniques, vocalization, etc., in connection with the increasing importance of long solo performance parts. It lost some of its prominence only when jazz as a popular music began to be replaced by other forms in the 1960s.

Selective processes, at work in each historical period, are extremely complex and not easy to disentangle in their multiple functions and motivations, in the middle of changing value systems and techniques. By the nineteenth century a selection of available European musical instruments (e.g., the violin, which later lost popularity) already had begun to function in African American cultures not merely as substitutes for African instruments but as "reincarnations." Somewhat earlier, household implements had been the available material for construction. Some of the homemade fiddles in the nineteenth-century United States, and by extension the factory-manufactured instruments, represented aspects of the West African *gogé* or *goje* (DjeDje 1981, 1984) and other one-stringed African fiddles (Minton 1996). The mouth organ as used in the blues was factory-manufactured and inexpensive, so it became available to African Americans in the late nine-teenth century. In blues and dance music traditions of the Deep South, it began to echo the *algeita* oboes of the west-central Sudanic belt in tone and articula-tion. It also absorbed the panpipe technique of alternating blown and whooped notes. In Africa this technique is prominent among Nyungwe pan-pipe players in the Lower Zambezi Valley, both in solo performances and the *nyanga* pan-pipe dance (Andrew Tracey 1971; Malamusi 1992) and it also exists in many other African pipe traditions.

Alfons M. Dauer (1985) looked into the possibility that some technical, orga-nizational, and conceptual traits that characterize several horn, trumpet, pan-pipe, and other wind instrument traditions in various parts of Africa could have been transmitted and re-created in jazz. He thought that heterophony, which dominates multipart organization in New Orleans street brass bands, could be connected with West African savannah orchestral ensembles, while the New Orleans jazz dance band music with its functional polyphony and responsorial schemes, its breaks and stop-time choruses, showed principles of organization closer to Guinea Coast styles (Dauer 1985: 173). He asked whether different parts of the New Orleans jazz repertoire might be rooted in different African tradi-tions. In his analysis of Bunk Johnson's version of "Panama," a composition in AABACC multi-strain form, published in 1911, he postulated that the first strain (A) reflects the heterophonic "street band style," followed by the polyphonic and responsorial "dance hall style." (174). (For comparison, see also Gushee 1994.)

Notwithstanding some criticism he received from colleagues, Dauer's merit is that—following various leads—he tried to unravel the remote history of jazz in relation to prominent wind instruments used in the court music of Islamicized societies across the Sahel and Savannah belt of West Africa, notably among the Hausa (see also Gourlay 1982; Ames 1973) and Fulɓe (Kubik et al. 1989: 82–85). It is important, however, to realize that this is just one strand of possible histori-cal connections. Unilinear explanatory schemes seldom work in history; instead, a multiplicity of social, personal, and other factors converge in determining trends and choices.

The court music tradition among the Fulɓe and Hausa includes an orches-tral ensemble incorporating double-headed snare drums called *ganga* and played with bent sticks; the long trumpet called *kakaki* in Hausa, *gagashi* in Fulfulde; and oboes, variously called *alghaita, algaita, algeita*, etc. These instruments derive from prototypes found in the Maghreb that were brought to west-central Sudan from the thirteenth century on with trans-Saharan trade. They became court music instruments in the political hierarchies of the emerging city-states from the middle Niger River to Lake Chad.

Specific instrumental techniques traceable to this region survive in jazz and other forms of African American music. But they tend to be operational as

Fig. 4.1. Royal musicians at the court of the Lamido of Toungo, ruler of the Fulɓe (Fulani) in northeastern Nigeria. This court music ensemble included three double-headed snare drums called *ganga*, two *algeita* oboes, and one long trumpet (*gagashi*), all played by professional musicians under the guidance of Prince Sarki Bandawa Toungo (standing in the picture, right). At the entrance to the court of the Lamido of Toungo, northeastern Nigeria, November 25, 1963. Photo: author

Fig. 4.2. Close-up of *ganga* drummers. There are snares across the drum skin. The performers use hooked sticks for striking the drums.

clustered traits, i.e., they operate, appear, and disappear together from individual musical styles.

What is perpetuated in the United States of African techniques and characteristics can probably best be analyzed within such a theoretical framework. We think that clustered traits, in contrast to a mere agglomeration of single traits arbitrarily thrown together, made the journey across the Atlantic easily, i.e., as sets of interdependent, functionally connected traits. If you cancelled out one, the cluster would first tend to disintegrate, as if an organ was removed from a body. In any case there would soon be some reconfiguration. If, however, only one or two traits in such a cluster survived and became prominent in a New World culture, even after a pause of a hundred years, the missing traits in the cluster would be reinvented; they would reinstall themselves. For example,

Fig. 4.3. Close-up of *gagashi* (long trumpet) player. Observe circular breathing!

Fig. 4.4. Dizzy Gillespie using circular breathing. Courtesy of the Institute of Jazz Studies, Rutgers University Libraries.

circular breathing, which is prominent in the playing of *alghaita* oboes among the Hausa and Fulɓe, was used in various contexts by Dizzy Gillespie. He did not pick up the technique by studying Fulɓe court music ensembles in Nigeria and Cameroon, although Gillespie was a widely travelled man often on State Department circuits, and even played trumpet for a cobra in Karachi, Pakistan (cf. the show-biz photograph, Gillespie 1979 [2009: near page 338]). He rediscovered the advantages of circular breathing.

John Coltrane's technique of timbre manipulation on his soprano saxophone (cf. "The Promise," recorded at Birdland, October 8, 1963, and many other recordings) produces sound sequences similar in articulation and timbre of *algeita* (oboe) players, such as at the court of the Lamido of Kontcha, northern Cameroon, where I recorded in the same year three praise songs by Hamadicko and court musicians, with one *algeita* (oboe), two *ganga* (drums), and the praise singer's recitations. (Orig. tape no. 29, recorded November 29, 1963, at Kontcha, copy in Phonogrammarchiv Vienna, B 8911–13.)

A question arises in all these instances: Should such analogies be taken as historically conclusive? Or merely as a result of the nature of those instruments, producing similar timbre qualities, here double-reed oboe, there single-reed soprano saxophone? The court musicians of the Lamido of Kontcha, as well as those of the neighboring Lamido of Toungo, just across the border in eastern Nigeria, were contemporaries of John Coltrane. Other *algeita* players had been recorded in Nigeria before, and some had been on the record market since the 1950s. Is it possible that the late John Coltrane could have been listening to some Hausa or Fulɓe recordings? Though transforming such an experience into a skilled personal technique on another instrument is not the same as casual acquaintance, there is evidence from Coltrane's late period, 1965 to 1967, that he was interested in and tried to assimilate musical patterns from cultures in Africa and Asia in his compositions "India," "Africa Brass," and "Meditations."

Here we are posing principal research questions. If Coltrane had actually studied such recordings—which were available in the 1950s and '60s—and found inspiration in the Fulɓe *algeita*, it would be fine. Everyone is free to find inspiration anywhere. But if that was not the case, one answer to our question (above) would be that there could have been something like a code on stand-by to be ready at a certain moment in history for a musician to tackle certain problems, unknowingly in analogous ways across time and space. Such a code would incorporate the remains of a trait cluster that was once transmitted. If it is activated so that one specific musical problem finds attention and is solved, other components of the original trait cluster would be activated as well, allowing a creative musician—two hundred years after the forced transplantation of some of his great-grandparents to New World destinations—to reinvent some of their modes of expression, with another tool, on another instrument.

Fig. 4.5. John Coltrane playing soprano saxophone. Courtesy of the Institute of Jazz Studies, Rutgers University Libraries.

I am not a follower of the theory of "cultural memory," which in essence is a Lamarckian concept; we proceed from the observation that culture is learned, not genetically transmitted. But I suggest from many years of research in African and African American cultures, notably in Brazil (Kubik 1991: 188ff.), that a culture trait can sometimes be preserved and transmitted in communities, families, between peers, etc., in a coded form. A code can be absorbed by the mind without being explicitly formulated. Rhythm patterns, for example, have a mathematical code, and when people are deprived of the instruments (e.g., drums) to play such patterns, the code may survive as such in some other expressive manifestation, e.g., in a visual pattern, or body movement, or in the unusual handling of some tool. If the social situation of the community changes, after some generations, and a moment in history arrives introducing a new set of tools, instruments, or means of expression, it may happen that the code resurges in some kind of reconfiguration: people begin to experiment and—klook-mop!—one of them reinvents the pattern. There is in sound many implicit number games, much mathematics, not only in rhythm but also in tonal systems, in timbre preferences, sound clusters, etc.

Codified representations of behavioral patterns can be learned and thereby retained and transmitted in families down the genealogical lines, including among children and adolescents. Portions of a cultural heritage, dormant for a long time, may then all of a sudden resurface in another environment, in a different era, on another continent. Perhaps when new styles of jazz suddenly erupted were such moments.

Resilience, Survival, and Reinvention

Culture is learned, and there are many different scenarios of cultural transmission. Musical education can take place within families, within peer groups, by informal contact with friends or instructors in the neighborhood, or more formally in a music school. What actually happens and how the individual processes the input depends on multiple factors, such as the technological resources available at the time, the social position of those involved, and also on the degree of spontaneity of the encounters and opportunities. On both sides of the Atlantic, at different periods, we are faced with heterogeneous traditions, different musical languages, and idiosyncratic individuals. In New Orleans at the turn of the twentieth century, there were channels of transmission for different musical styles and ideas. It was a cosmopolitan city. Some musicians uptown may have started off in a spasm band as adolescents, and remained essentially autodidacts, while others in the city went through the procedures of conservatory-based educational systems. An example is the so-called Creole school of jazz clarinetists, the outstanding case being the Tios family. The rise of the Tios is intimately connected with pedagogy that was conservatoire-based and rooted in nineteenth-century European musical aesthetics (cf. also Kinzer 1996). From that background arose one distinctive jazz clarinet style in New Orleans, which—incidentally—greatly surprised jazz fans in Europe during the 1950s when they first heard recordings of Alphonse Picou playing "High Society," etc. Other New Orleans instrumentalists had learned their instruments in the context of marching music, another European strand, adapted for parades, funerals, and various civic events that allowed for a greater margin of improvisation and divergence from written scores. This is where African concepts crept in; Afrologic reinterpretation took over. When William Russell recorded in New Orleans during the 1940s, the tradition of marching bands was in decline. Trying to preserve it, he set up sessions with Bunk Johnson, Kid Shots Madison, and others at clarinetist George Lewis's home (cf. "In Gloryland," Bunk's Brass Band, recorded May 18, 1945, American Music 101, Matrix no. 903). It was the start of a revival, with some modifications; subsequently, as in the Eureka Brass Band of the 1950s and '60s, alto and tenor saxophones were included.

By the mid-nineteenth century most African musical instruments had disappeared in the United States without any obvious traces left behind. Some had "migrated" into different populations, as was the case with mouth-resonated musical bows, surviving mostly as a European-American tradition in the Appalachian Mountains (Graham 1994; Kubik 1999a) or as a single-fundamental variety—unusual for African bows—in the case of Eli Owens (Evans 1994; Kubik 1999c). Other instrumental techniques, such as playing the mono-idiochord zithers in central and southeast Africa, survived with new materials and modified playing techniques (cf. the diddley bow, Evans 1970, 1999: 385). Some African instruments and their techniques rematerialized in household objects that began to assume the role of representations of the lost instruments.

However, the prevailing process of resilience and survival was expressed in the fact that tonal ideas, playing techniques, and aesthetic concepts from African music were gradually transferred to the factory-manufactured instruments from European traditions on which such techniques had never been tried. That happened as soon as such instruments became accessible to African Americans, i.e., after the Civil War (1861–65). At the end of the war many brass band instruments turned up, second-hand, in shops. Their often unusual handling by African Americans, in many cases without formal training from European-style music schools, often created amazement and hidden admiration in observers.

This must be considered against the backdrop of a certain fluidity in relations between different ethnic groups in the South, notably in a city like New Orleans, and how it affected individual enculturation and stylistic preferences. In a paper entitled "Stars of David and Sons of Sicily: Constellations beyond the canon of early New Orleans jazz" (2009), Bruce Boyd Raeburn has unraveled the intricacies of historical terminology in New Orleans concerning ethnic groups. He pleads for a nuanced treatment also of "white" ethnicities and how they affected the rise of New Orleans jazz. This includes the premise that Jews, Sicilians, and some immigrants from Latin America were not even considered to be really "white" in early twentieth-century New Orleans. Therefore, as was also characteristic of South Africa in the mid-twentieth century under apartheid (cf. *Jazz Transatlantic II*), "whiteness" was a negotiable commodity. Raeburn mentions that there are "passe blanche" stories in oral tradition. As much as people of African descent cannot be jumbled up as an undifferentiated ethnic block, so has the European segment of the population in cities like New Orleans to be given the same level of elucidation. He points out that Northern Italians and Sicilians, for example, represented dramatically different cultural tendencies. That this also reflected on the receptivity of individuals to various cultural elements of African provenance is undeniable.

What originally had been a creative transfer of African ideas of movement and sound, of timbre, polyphony, etc., to an instrumentarium of European provenance (selectively, because some instruments proved to be more, some less suitable) soon appeared to be something like a novel, alternative culture from the viewpoint of young people. And they were keen to make it their own.

The use of bamboo scrapers in some African music, for example in *nkhwendo* of Moçambique and Malawi, or in *semba* or *rebita* of the City of Luanda on the Angolan coast, transforms in early jazz into the use of the washboard. We could say the washboard stands for the "forgotten" or abandoned African counterpart. There is perhaps even more to it historically. In 1967 in Malawi, I recorded a young man who used his own ribs as a scraper, rubbing them with the knuckles of one of his hands. The villagers said he was "psychologically disturbed"; I did not look in the DSM (Diagnostic and Statistical Manual of Mental Disorders), but instead took note of the fact that the knowledge of the scraper could also be transmitted as a body experience.

In a famous interview series for the Library of Congress, Jelly Roll Morton in 1938 told Alan Lomax that he had introduced the fly-whisk in drumming (Lomax 1952). If that is so, he must actually have reinvented it. Its transatlantic counterparts can be found in West Africa, for example, in the playing of a large gourd (ògó) among the Fõ with a soft leather flap (*afafa*) held by the player in his left hand. (Recordings January 1970 at Hundenyo Selogba, Mono River area, Togo, orig. tape no. 130, Culture Research Archive Kubik/Malamusi, Vienna.)

King Oliver is known to have popularized—though not invented—the muted playing of the cornet or trumpet, which is also paralleled in some handling of aerophones in African cultures. The most intriguing story, however, is that of the jug, as used in jug bands in the United States. The knowledge of producing sounds from a vessel held vertically in front of the player's mouth, blowing at its rim, is widely known in Africa and often practiced using Coca-Cola or Fanta bottles, not however as part of a musical performance. I do not remember having ever recorded something like a jug band anywhere in Africa. But David Evans (1999: 382) refers to the Ocora OCR 35 LP *Musique Kongo*, side B/tracks 4 and 5, a recording from the Babembe in which wooden figures with holes in the back are used like jugs in a ritual context. About the American history of the jug, he writes:

> Jug. This instrument is also derived from African prototypes of hollow vessels that
> serve as voice disguisers or spirit voices. In one example from the BaBembe near
> the mouth of the Congo River four hollow wooden effigy figures with holes in the
> back serve this purpose, symbolically representing spirits of father, mother, son, and

daughter. The instrument is played by making a buzzing and flapping sound with the lips facing the opening of the vessel. In the United States this instrument usually is simply a ceramic, metal, or glass jug, at one time a common household object, used as a novelty bass instrument in combination with other instruments. It is thus a counterpart to the kazoo in the bass register. There exists, however, a report from 1888 of a band of four boys in Palatka, Florida, all of them with jugs and possibly a harmonica and kazoo. Reports of similar ensembles of four instruments of this type come from Haiti and the Dominican Republic. But around this same time the jug was becoming a bass instrument in string ensembles, as can be seen in a photograph taken in 1898 in Atlanta. By the 1920s, jug bands of this sort, with a single jug as a bass instrument, recorded as urban novelty ensembles from the cities of Louisville, Memphis, Birmingham, Dallas, Cincinnati, and Chicago. The jug had thus undergone a process of reinterpretation from its African prototypes similar to that of the kazoo. (282–83)

Representations of a forgotten African instrument or instrumental technique either through common household objects or through a factory-manufactured instrument were therefore the most common pathways for resurgence of African musical characteristics in jazz. Sometimes such representation works even across organological differences. This includes cymbals, Chinese woodblocks, and other percussion devices.

Conversely, a Western instrument, if out of reach for aspirants due to their limited purchasing power, could be temporarily represented by homemade devices close to African models. Kazoos, often called a "jazz horn" by blues musicians, and flageolet flutes, for example, would be used by kids in New Orleans that formed a "second line" in brass band parading to represent those brass instruments in their own imitations. The same phenomenon gave rise to *malipenga* ("bugles") parading in East Africa after World War I.

Gradually, in the twentieth century, therefore, the African instrumental experience resurged step by step in American cultures, on fashionable industrially manufactured instruments, to the amazement of musicians in the classical European tradition, who found the new timbre qualities thrilling, sometimes "dirty." But young Euro-Americans in the 1920s and earlier became attracted and started to imitate and appropriate those "dirty tones" and how they were produced.

From the 1920s on, this was no longer a parody of the "black man's ways," as it had been in the days of blackface minstrelsy. It was now all meant in earnest. The "white cats" identified with those "black" musicians who in a sense became their role models, but they also wanted to produce something of their own. An early attempt at trying something slightly different from the kind of jazz that had been recorded between 1917 and 1923 was Bix Beiderbecke on cornet in Frankie Trumbauer and His Orchestra, 1927, with Trumbauer on C-melody saxophone

Table 1: Some African instrumental retentions through substitution processes in jazz, blues, and other African American music.	
United States retentions and reinventions	**African regional counterparts**
washboard	(a) bamboo scrapers such as *dikanza* from the Angolan coast; (b) *igbá*—a gourd used for percussion among the Yoruba, the player wearing iron rings on eight of his fingers (thumbs excluded)
"bones" (in nineteenth-century groups)	concussion sticks used in Angola and elsewhere
gutbucket and slap bass techniques	one-stringed ground-bow found in many regions of Africa
"jitterbug," diddley bow	west-central African monochord zithers
jazz drums, cymbals, etc. (Chinese) woodblocks	various African membranophones and idiophones with comparable sound spectrum, e.g., raft rattles, small slit-drums, etc.
banjo	west-central Sudanic spike lute traditions
guitar	techniques from several African stringed instruments: bridge-harp, polyidiochord stick zither, etc.
"hot" violins	*gogé* and *gojé* (one-stringed) fiddle traditions among the Hausa, Dagomba, and others
some trumpet techniques, especially "circular breathing" (e.g., by Dizzy Gillespie)	Hausa and Fulɓe playing techniques of various wind instruments (*kakaki*, *algeita*, etc.)
"muted" trumpet ("jungle style" in Duke Ellington's band, etc.)	voice-disguising techniques in African initiation ceremonies and secret societies
mouth-harmonica playing in the blues	*algeita* (oboe) and its stylistic traits from the west-central Sudanic belt; also, panpipe techniques of "whooping"
piano (sometimes with "buzzing" addition or sound-modifying devices like tacks on the hammers)	techniques of playing gourd-resonated xylophones, such as *madimba* in Angola, *balo* in northern Guinée, Senegal, Mali, *gyil* in northern Ghana, whenever the bass is in the musician's left hand
mouth-bow (with single fundamental)	jew's harp as recorded by David Rycroft in South Africa; rare single-note mouth-bows
quills	bamboo panpipes, e.g., *nyanga* in the lower Zambezi Valley; used by alternating blown notes with "whooping"
vibraphone	xylophone playing techniques, even with four beaters, as in some areas of the southern Sudan; secondary inspiration from New World "marimba"
kazoo, comb-and-paper, etc.	African mirlitons used for voice disguising; also, *luvimbi* used by children in eastern Angola (Kubik 2010: I: 336–39)
saxophone (general jazz techniques)	"moan" used on some kazoos, flutes, and oboes in various parts of West Africa (e.g., Cameroon, northeastern Nigeria)
saxophone (timbre alterations and manipulation of overtones, e.g., by John Coltrane)	Hausa and Fulɓe playing techniques of the *alghaita* (or *algeita*) oboe

(cf. "Singing the Blues—till my daddy comes home" recorded February 4, 1927, Okeh 40822, Matrix no. W-80393-C). Trumbauer would also have a notable influence on Lester Young and his development of a "cool" tone on tenor. Beiderbecke in his short life experimented greatly. Particularly in his solo piano playing he was able to integrate creatively his love for jazz with his interest in the harmonic and tonal world of Claude Debussy. In jazz he was in personal contact with Louis Armstrong, discussing the tricks of variation. There was a multiplicity of other influences on him: LaRocca, Emmet Hardy, who was a student of Afro-Sicilian Creole educator Manual Manetta in New Orleans, and others (Raeburn 2012a).

Soon the interest of musicians would focus on arrangements and, by the 1940s, on some of the complex harmonic changes that were developed in late swing (Kansas City) and bebop. That was the case of someone like tenor saxophonist Stan Getz of Woody Herman's Second Herd. He was hanging around 52nd Street in New York and Minton's Playhouse to hear and learn from Charlie Parker. "Four Brothers" and Ralph Burns's composition "Early Autumn" for the Woody Herman Herd with Stan Getz's solo against the background of this new harmonic understanding, are timeless achievements in jazz history.

I give a summary of the transatlantic instrumental connections in the form of a table (see Table 1) about the most important African instrumental retentions and adaptations in twentieth century African American musical practice. Though far from complete, it will give the reader an idea of the hidden ways by which cultural knowledge reinvents itself in the most unexpected contexts.

Theory

The theoretical underpinnings of what I have tried to outline in this chapter are mainly to be found in the work of Melville J. Herskovits, Fernando Ortiz, recent publications by David Evans, and my own writings on the psychology of culture contact. Herskovits had a good feel for cognitive processes in acculturation, the reactions of groups toward one another, and defensive reactions if a group felt threatened, fearing to lose its cherished values and cultural identity. David Evans (1990, 1999) has stressed that Herskovits's concepts—retention, survival, reinterpretation, syncretism, and cultural focus to describe processes in culture contact—are as relevant today as they were seventy years ago when they were first formulated.

In an article on the reinterpretation of African musical instruments in the United States, Evans further elaborated on Herskovits's concept of reinterpretation, as it describes "mental and/or behavioral processes," a concept that is "applicable to situations of acculturation anywhere in the world" (Evans 1999: 379). With reference to the concept of syncretism, he regrets that it was often misunderstood. He says that it originally meant "a process whereby an African cultural trait is equated with or likened to a European or Euro-American trait encountered in the New World on the basis of some perceived similarity between the two traits" (380). One may add that this process is universal and can, of course, be detected in any cultural encounter of some duration.

Expanding on Herskovits, Evans (1999) identified three patterns of reinterpretation in the African American instrumental scenario:

the use of found, discarded, or commercially made objects, often viewed as "junk" in the making of musical instruments, with a consequent minimal use of special fashioning such as carving, casting, or decoration . . .

the accommodation of African instruments to European instruments in their forms, names, and materials of construction, with the instruments in America sometimes taking on a novelty and/or humorous function.

the use of these reinterpreted instruments in distinct African American types of music rather than purely African music. (208)

After an exposition of the choices Africans in the United States made in order to come to terms with the obstacles they encountered, Evans expands Herskovits's terms in what he calls the "middle range" of the ensuing processes of social and cultural adaptation, introducing the concepts consolidation, substitution, subversion, and accommodation.

Consolidation, he says, "is a process that must have occurred in earlier centuries when people from different African ethnic backgrounds, placed together on plantations in North America, realized that their ancestral musical traditions shared a number of traits in common" (209) Among these Evans enumerates (a) leader/chorus antiphonal organization of songs; (b) hand-clapping to mark a steady beat; (c) the organization of many pieces of music in short repeated melodic-rhythmic phrases commonly called "riffs."

Then he explains that "in the realm of musical instruments, consolidation is often aided by substitution. In North America a common household object, such as a jug or washboard was substituted for the variety of African vessels and scrapers. Or a simple commercially manufactured kazoo was substituted for the variety of African voice-activated vibrating membrane instruments" (209).

Finally, he writes that "Subversion and accommodation as acculturative patterns in African American music are really just two sides of the same coin, of the same phenomenon. One term places emphasis on the change, modification, or destruction of a western musical trait, while the other term places emphasis on the acceptance and adaptation to it" (210). He gives the following examples:

"Western chord triads and typical tonic-subdominant-dominant harmonic progressions are subverted by a legacy of parallelism from many types of African music. Blues guitarists and pianists also accommodate to and at the same time subvert western three-chord harmony by playing series of tone clusters of two or three notes chosen from the tune's scale rather than making chord changes in the manner of western functional harmony" (210).

The underlying processes are sometimes veiled by the fact that many African American musicians began to describe their special instrumental techniques in Western music terminology, thereby insisting upon their legitimacy. When five of us, David and Marice Evans, Moya A. Malamusi, Richard Graham, and I recorded Glen Faulkner with his *bo diddley* in 1993 at his home near Senatobia, Mississippi, we were surprised about the techniques he used while explaining his one-stringed instrument that he had constructed in the shape of the body of an electric guitar. He also showed us an earlier model he had made. Both ideas ultimately derive from the Central African monoidiochord zither made of raffia, something Glen Faulkner's generation could no longer be aware of.

The reaction pattern described by David Evans under the term subversion can be explained psycho-dynamically. At the start of this process is the acute experience of repression. An individual—and by extension many individuals, a group, a community—within an oppressive dominating society that claims cultural superiority, is subjected to regular degradation, disregard, snubs, etc., in relation to its expressive forms and its very existence by the dominant group.

The dominant group targets the individual's way of talking, way of movement, and specific cultural practices, music, dance, etc., declaring it to be worthless or ridiculous. If such discrimination becomes a daily experience, the individual has four options to cope with the terror: (a) suicide, either literally or symbolically, directly or by immersing oneself into risky behavior, alcoholism, drugs, unsafe sexual practices, etc.; (b) flight into physical and virtual "marronage"; (c) internalizing the oppressor's standpoint and adapting oneself to his ways and ideology; or (d) acting as if adopting it, but finding avenues of hidden forms of expression of what has been repressed. This last reaction, if successful, is subversive, and aims at tumbling the structures cherished by the oppressor. Psychologically, it is the healthiest one. Most often it is unconscious, or the "subverter" might have some awareness of it but never acknowledge it, even to intimate friends and family members.

Jazz musicians have had a share in all these reaction patterns. Some African Americans in their centuries-old struggle adopted option (c), only to discover that they were still not fully accepted by the other half of the society, in spite of all personal effort. An instructive example is the case of an African American pianist who had advanced to one of the world's best performers of the piano works of Mozart, Beethoven, Chopin, and other European composers. And yet, some audiences in the depth of their hearts still rejected him, accusing him of denying his "true identity"! Concert agents would therefore insist that someone looking like him should also perform some piano works pertaining to "black culture," even if it were only something out of George Gershwin's *Rhapsody in Blue*. Indeed, audiences would feel reassured that this pianist had no intent to upset the world order, and that he observed the identity ascribed to him. It is interesting to compare this reaction with how Western audiences rooted in classical music normally react to a young female Japanese pianist playing Mozart. She would get a standing ovation. Another example is operatic singers such as Marian Anderson, Leontyne Price, etc., who almost always feel an obligation to include one or two spirituals in their recitals.

Some jazz musicians who are aware of or somehow feel the subtleties in the psychology of culture contact have found elegant solutions to demonstrate familiarity with sacred works of the "superior" culture, while at the same time displaying "black" identity. They simply insert some blues tonality and rhythmic patterns not known in classical music. John Lewis and his Modern Jazz Quartet were perhaps the most successful group navigating in such hazardous seas.

Option (d) has been tried out most frequently in the United States. It works like this: One maintains one's ways, if one still possesses such resources, but infiltrates the other culture, using its instruments, theories, tonal resources as a vehicle, while converting their meanings, even subverting them to express what has been repressed.

I need not emphasize that these reaction patterns are not necessarily explicit strategies by those involved, worked out in an office and applied to their social surroundings. They come about at a psychological level that is subliminal. The best strategy of subverting the other culture is discovered by the individual in a process of trial and error, as if learning how to swim and survive in dangerous waters. Once this avenue is opened up, it is pursued almost automatically, reaction by reaction, event by event; nobody would therefore theorize about the matter.

A surprise of option (d) is the outcome: the self-declared dominant culture, thereby subverted, begins to accept its own subversion and rewards the artist for his act by conferring stardom upon him or her. Still, acceptance as an artist does not necessarily include acceptance as a member of the dominant society. At least a minority among its members will continue to insist that from time to time the intruder should declare his "identity."

Ragtime

Term and History

Although the term *ragtime* for a type of late nineteenth-century African American piano music became well known in 1896, it was probably around in the Midwest for several years. The music itself was practiced and taught by African Americans in eastern Kansas before Ben Harney first played ragtime in New York in 1896 (Abbott and Seroff 2002: 447).

Ten years earlier, George Washington Cable, in his writings about New Orleans's Congo Square, spoke of a "ragged" rhythm, describing a particular event in which the dancers of "Bamboula" changed steps to perform "Counjaille" (*Century Magazine*, XXXI, February 1886: 40, reprinted in Katz 1969): "The bamboula still roars and rattles, twangs, contorts, and tumbles in terrible earnest, while we stand and talk. So, on and on. Will they dance nothing else? Ah!—the music changes. The rhythm stretches out heathenish and ragged...."

Ragtime as a composite term has its specific history in association with music. The first component, however, the monosyllabic word "rag," has various connotations in English and has been used both as a noun and a verb. Something that is ragged (adjective) may be "old and torn" or "unfinished and imperfect" or "with uneven edges or surfaces" (*Longman's Dictionary of Contemporary English* 1990: 856).

Usually a "rag" is a small piece of old cloth; an old worn-out garment can be called a "rag." But there is a second meaning, especially in British English: "an amusing procession of college students through the streets on a special day," which is called "rag day" (ibid.). This second meaning as a social occasion also continued in the United States, as we shall learn later in this chapter. *Rag time*, therefore could also be understood as "time for a rag, a certain social occasion with dance, amusements." Such double meanings are always favorable to the rise of a new, fashionable term, which can then be understood either way.

Describing the off-beat rhythms in African and African American music in terms of "ragged" time was a formulation that would be catchy in the late nineteenth century, because of its by-meanings. Publishers of sheet music in "Ethiopian two-step," "coon songs," "cake walks," and eventually "ragtime" were calculating on these ambiguities: (a) by reducing the composite term to the noun

Fig. 5.1. Sheet music covers of some of the first ragtime publications. (Reproduced from Blesh and Janis 1950 [1971])

Fig. 5.2.1, 5.2.2, 5.2.3. Three portraits of Scott Joplin: (1) ca. 1900, (2) ca. 1904, and (3) ca. 1911. (Reproduced from Blesh and Janis 1950)

"rag," thereby activating associations of something like torn pieces; then (b) by suggesting that, in the new piano music, meter was torn up by the pianist's right-hand phrasings, and thereby the melodies were in bits, like pieces of rags. This had the attraction of novelty. Using the word literally, publishers were also cashing in on the surprise effect that something called "rag" could be worthwhile and enjoyable. The cover of Jerome H. Remick & Co.'s sheet music of Scott Joplin's "Original Rags" (which was the title of one piece by Joplin) in 1899 shows a person picking up rags in front of a dilapidated house with a broken door, watched by a hungry dog. The words on the cover, across the roof, read: "Original Rags," and on a poster nailed on the house wall the sentence is continued: "Picked by Scott Joplin. Arranged by Chas. N. Daniels."

In search of a publisher, young Scott Joplin had actually traveled from Sedalia to Kansas City, where he was at last successful selling some of his compositions to publisher Carl Hoffman, who was assisted by a "professional" arranger, Chas. N. Daniels. Luckily, nothing was really "arranged" by the latter; all the compositions were from Joplin's hand. And yet, the cover suggests that he had picked the melodies like rags from someplace. Therefore, the melodies (so it is implied) could not all be his; perhaps they were folk melodies picked up and rearranged, just like the person in the picture was picking real rags from the ground. The idea of this new music as scraps (rags), i.e., something put together, is similar to the term W. C. Handy used for folk blues: "snatches of song," i.e., bits of melody/lyric used as the basis or an element in larger compositions (David Evans conversation, Vienna, May 10, 2012). The cover of Tom Turpin's "Harlem Rag Two-Step" also shows ragged clothes, hanging down from a laundry line.

Strategies of double meaning can be very effective in business. The word "rag," in the majority of midwestern and southern households owning the cherished piano in their parlors, was both demeaning and attractive. Ragtime, from the moment it was available in print, became a fashion almost overnight. Word and music both hit some hidden tendencies in the bourgeois society, especially among young people who were secretly identifying with the alternative African American culture and creative impulse of the underprivileged. Fashion strategies often work with the method of inverting an existing scale of values. In the twentieth century this has been applied repeatedly, as in the 1970s when all of a sudden blue jeans from a patchwork of rags, even torn in some places were thrown on the market worldwide. Young people soon identified with the new culture.

In all those cases, the underlying psychological process is that the renaming of an article or fact makes it eligible for expressing an idea hitherto withheld, e.g., identification by individuals with something forbidden, or expression of criticism. It is the social undercaste that is seriously victimized by barriers in a stratified society. Maybe it was more than coincidental, therefore, that between January 1889 and December 1895, when ragtime came up, almost a thousand lynchings were executed on African Americans in the South (Abbott and Seroff 2002: xi). On the other hand, this was also the time of cultural and trade fairs, such as the 1893 World's Columbian Exposition in Chicago, from which incidentally, African Americans were excluded from representing themselves as an ethnic group. By contrast, besides the reconstruction of a Cairo bazaar, bellydancers from Egypt, and Turkish music, sub-Saharan Africa was "represented" by a French organizer who had hauled a Dahomeyan troupe of drummers and Amazons (Fō-speaking female warriors) via Paris across the Atlantic to freezing Chicago, to exhibit them as part of "Afrique Occidentale Française." Sudan and Haiti were also "represented."

Nevertheless, African American music had begun to stir international attention. In the same year, the Czech composer, Antón Dvořák (1841–1904) declared that the future of American music was to be found in "negro melodies." Suddenly there was a rush to get a ticket on that particular intellectual train.

Social barriers, although they can be temporarily reinforced (cf. the Jim Crow ruling of 1896, which seriously affected Creole musicians in New Orleans) tend to break down after some time, and a new societal compromise is negotiated. Centripetal forces take over, because the dominant class also begins to discover a liking for the cultural products of those it has cordoned off. It gradually realizes that it has only constructed its own social prison.

The manner in which African Americans had begun to play the piano in the late 1880s, whenever they got access to such instruments, was secretly admired in upper-class families who had such an instrument in their parlor. There was a dramatic increase in rhythmic complexity. But the places where those people from the underclass normally got a chance to practice their art, i.e., in brothels, honky-tonks etc., were off-limits for most people of social standing. So they had to limit themselves to the "legitimate" music. On the other hand, young males in the "sporting life" would patronize brothels, and others attended cake walks.

I estimate that for at least two decades before the word *ragtime* was first used, the kind of music associated with it, i.e., strophic themes incorporating off-beat accenting, had been played, first on banjos and fiddles, then on piano by African Americans in midwestern towns. But these pianists had not studied classical music theory and were not used to writing down their music. It is likely that multiple-strain form was not used in these early expressions of aurally transmitted ragtime. In order to be accepted in the parlors of the upper-class families, the music had to be written down and "arranged."

Pressure by publishers made it conditional that sheet music would follow certain compositional conventions. In earlier decades of the nineteenth century, there would always be someone from outside their own class and culture who would do that, the likes of Gottschalk and Krehbiel. They would "arrange" the "Negro" slave songs for upper-class consumption. But in the last two decades of the nineteenth century, something unexpected happened that became a new factor, although at first it was still the "white man" who—encouraged by a variety of factors—appropriated the "Negro" stuff and wrote it down (or tried to) under their own names and copyright. But what little edge, commercially, they still had on African Americans vanished. They were only one year ahead. African American pianists learned to "arrange" this music by themselves, and they were closing in.

Ben Harney published "You've Been a Good Old Wagon" in Louisville in 1895, and in January 1897 publication begins under the name *ragtime* with Krell's "Mississippi Rag," announced as "the first rag-time two-step ever written and first played by Krell's Orchestra Chicago." The picture on the cover of the music sheet is revealing, however. It shows precisely one of the sources of ragtime, by depicting a gathering of African American dancers at the Mississippi River, in front of a musical group involving a banjo as the central instrument (see Fig. 5.1 reproduction of the "Mississippi Rag" sheet music).

Perhaps these early publications of written versions of the new music would not have been brought about had this music not been popularized on the sidelines of the Chicago World's Fair in 1893 with many pianists congregating in that city. In 1897 it took just a few months more until Thomas Million Turpin's "Harlem Rag" was also published in December. Two more years, however, passed until in March 1899 Scott Joplin was able to publish his "Original Rags" and, in September, the seminal "Maple Leaf Rag" with publisher John Stark.

Scott Joplin was born November 24, 1868 (perhaps 1866), near Texarkana, Texas. His life history stands for an era in which perhaps for the first time, in some isolated cases, friendship and cooperation in equity between an African American and a person of European descent became possible in the United

States. Theodore Albrecht of Kent State University, Ohio, has pursued the question of who taught musical notation to the young Scott Joplin in Texarkana. A hint given in 1949 by Lottie Stokes Joplin, widow of Scott Joplin (who had died in 1917), in conversation with Rudi Blesh and Harriet Janis, authors of *They All Played Ragtime* (1950), was taken up by Albrecht. Lottie had told her interviewers that the young Scott had received his first music lessons on the piano from a German professor living in Texarkana when he was eleven years old.

Albrecht began an intensive search in the area, also securing the 1880 census records and conducting interviews. He determined that Scott Joplin's teacher in all likelihood was Julius Weiss, a "professor of music" born in Sachsen, Germany, ca. 1841 (Albrecht 1979: 97). In a more recent publication, Albrecht (2008) writes:

> Weiss had come to Texarkana in ca. 1877 or 1878 as the tutor to the family of lumber manufacturer Robert Wooding Rodgers (1820–1884), and lived as a roomer in the Rodgers' spacious house on the Texas side of town. The Joplin family lived not far away, on the Arkansas side, in a neighborhood that included many working-class black families.
>
> Weiss gave piano lessons to the girls of the Rodgers family and violin lessons to the boys. He also instructed them in musical literature.... When Weiss was sent to New Orleans to purchase a new piano for the Rodgers family, their old square instrument was somehow passed on to the young Scott Joplin, probably paid for by his father Giles working in the Rodgers lumber mills. (216)

The part of the story dealing with young Scott Joplin's musical education is formulated by Blesh and Janis in their book (1950 [1971]) in this manner:

> Scott grew up with two brothers, Will and Robert, and two sisters in a household that, though poor, could afford music. His father played the violin, and his mother sang... and played the banjo as well. Will played the guitar at first, and under his father's instruction the violin later, while Robert's boyish voice gradually deepened into a notably rich baritone.
>
> By the time he was seven, Scott was already fascinated by a neighbor's piano. Whenever he was allowed to touch it he showed clear signs of musical promise. Giles Joplin, despite a desire, natural in near poverty, for his son to learn a trade or like himself to work for the Iron Mountain and Southern Railroad, nevertheless scraped the money together to buy a somewhat decrepit square grand. Scott was at this out-of-tune instrument every hour he could manage, and before he was eleven he played and improvised smoothly....
>
> Scott's self-taught ability began to make him the talk of the Negro community and the surrounding countryside. Such news seeped eventually into the white houses through servants' talk, perhaps even through the stories of a mother about

Fig. 5.3.1, 5.3.2, 5.4. Contemporaneous photographs of Arthur Marshall, Scott Hayden, and Marshall's home in Sedalia, Missouri. (Reproduced from Blesh and Janis 1950 [1971])

the exploits of her child, for Scott's mother was a laundress. An old German music teacher heard of young Joplin, and what he heard interested him.

The opportunity came for the boy to play for the old teacher. As a result he received not only free lessons in technique and sight reading but also an initial grounding in harmony. The professor conceived a real affection for the little black boy and would play for him and talk of the great European masters, and particularly of the famous operas. In later years Joplin never forgot his first teacher and sent him occasional gifts of money up to the time the older man died. (37)

It is likely that young Joplin's experience of a loving, positive relationship with a teacher who treated him as a capable human being, intellectually mature enough to understand the greatest composers of the world the teacher adored, was consequential. The boy passed an initiation period into intellectual equality, an experience permanently molding his approach to life. This must have contributed greatly to Joplin's psychological balance through most of his life and his success. Later, he transferred the positive relationship with his own teacher to a forthcoming relationship with two young students, Arthur Marshall (1881–1968) and Scott Hayden (1882–1915), whom he promoted on a basis of comradeship. This can be seen as duplicating Joplin's earlier experience with his German teacher. Another positive relationship Joplin developed was with the music publisher John Stark, who was willing to share profits equally. At least initially, Joplin always received royalties on the basis of a proper publishing contract, something seldom heard of in late nineteenth-century business relationships between publishers and African American authors.

In the 1940s Arthur Marshall proved to be an invaluable source of information on Joplin's life, when Blesh and Janis contacted him. He cultivated a deep sense of reverence for his former teacher, just as Joplin had carried along the same feelings for Mr. Weiss.

Blesh and Janis (1950 [1971: 93]) have confirmed that the term *ragtime* in relation to a new form of "syncopated" African American piano music became current around 1896. Shortly before that and sometimes thereafter, this piano style as played in the honky-tonks and bars was called jig piano. But the music did not start with any of these terms. It was developed as soon as African American youngsters got a chance to experiment with pianos.

By the late 1840s European Americans had tried piano renderings of African American music in Louisiana, when "The Banjo" and "Danse Nègre" were composed by Louis Moreau Gottschalk (1827–1869) from songs he may have heard in New Orleans' Congo Square. "The Banjo" with secondary rag figure was published in 1855. Of course, we can never be sure about ultimate sources. Such music was probably performed in various areas of New Orleans, not only at Place Congo. Blesh and Janis (1950 [1971]) have pointed out that "Syncopation began to invade American printed music with the rise of popularity of the coon songs in the nineties, though there were many songs dating back at least to the beginnings of minstrelsy that had a measure of syncopation here and there, or a general feel of off-beat accenting" (93). Black-face minstrelsy had begun to spread considerably after 1848, four decades earlier. In many parts of the South, the actors of these burlesques of "Negro" behavior, executed from an angle of stereotyped thinking, were reinterpreting a lot of banjo- and fiddle-based African American street music, simplifying it and also exaggerating certain structural components they needed in order to portray them as "characteristic of the Negro," to the applause of their audiences. As to the "Coon song" craze and its often synonymous use with the term "ragtime" after 1897, Lynn Abbott and Doug Seroff have unearthed a vast amount of documentation in their book *Ragged but Right* (2007). Earlier, with reference to the parallel "Cake walk" craze of the 1890s, Blesh and Janis took the following note: "In many of these songs the syncopating comes from the vocal part rather than the piano treble, so that if the right hand plays the vocal part over the bass as printed, a fair sort of ragtime comes out of it" (931).

After Ben Harney, from Middleboro, Kentucky, made a hit with piano ragtime in New York in 1896 at the age of twenty-five, it was recognized in a review in the *New York Clipper*, February 17, 1896, that Harney had earned the public's "favor through the medium of his genuinely clever plantation Negro imitations and excellent piano playing" with his hit song "Mister Johnson Turn Me Loose." But European American song transcribers at first had big problems grasping the rhythms of African American piano playing in the honky-tonks, and Harney apparently received some help after he had first learned the art orally. For this reason it can be assumed that all ragtime sheet music is to a certain extent a slightly simplified version of the rhythms and factual accentuations executed by competent African American pianists in the 1880s and 90s, including even the Scott Joplin and Tom Turpin rags. A case in point is Scott Joplin's own hand-played versions of his "Maple Leaf Rag," "Something Doing," and "Weeping Willow Rag" on piano rolls, of April and May 1916. Some music critics have pointed out that "Maple Leaf Rag" as played by Joplin himself, deviates from the sheet music version he had published in 1899. Some have even stated condescendingly that this was probably due to Joplin's "old age" or "advanced syphilis" in 1916. However, the piano roll version has rhythmic subtleties that are missing from the sheet version, and therefore, may be considered even closer to how ragtime was played around the turn of the century—"never too fast," as Joplin warned (cf. CD *Scott Joplin "The Entertainer": Classic Ragtime from Rare Piano Rolls*, Biograph BCD 101, 1987, track 1). And Joplin was himself part of the traveling circuits in the late nineteenth century, playing music from memory without recourse to notations in various locations. His performance in 1916 can be favorably compared with interpretations of "Maple Leaf Rag" by others in later years, such as Dick Hayman's hasty and ostentatious rendering, recorded in 1975 (*Jazz—The Smithsonian Anthology*, 2010, disc 1, track 1).

Accent patterns and minimal rhythmic deliberations in a performance that are impossible to notate, because they do not lend themselves easily to representation within the Western notational system, probably account for what Jelly Roll Morton later declared to be the difference between ragtime and jazz. The rigidity of the ragtime scores and some of their reproductions on piano rolls, however, was within the margins of understanding by the broad public (i.e., Americans of any ethnic background). As a first access to the African American musical world, the tradition had to be simplified a bit to become successful. The fact that an

Afrologic approach to rhythmic and accentual treatment of themes and melodic patterns was packaged into European multi-strain form adopted from marches, polkas, mazurkas, etc., and that harmony (in contrast to jazz developments later) largely still followed the rules of Western classical composition as transmitted in music schools, were important factors in making ragtime acceptable to upper-class audiences in a private music parlor.

By "elevating" ragtime to a written tradition, and transferring the music originally heard from anonymous African American piano virtuosi into the molds of nineteenth-century European popular form and harmony, composers such as Scott Joplin, Tom Turpin, and others created what has been called "classical ragtime." There was a difference between written ragtime played from notations and the music played by pianists in the bars. Orally transmitted ragtime by unknown composers—and one can, of course, be a composer without writing down a line—can perhaps no longer be reconstructed. But some inferences can be made from recordings by jazz musicians, particularly Jelly Roll Morton's repertoire recorded in 1938 by Alan Lomax for the Library of Congress (cf. the complete collection on Rounder 11661-1898-2) and later documentary recordings by Alonzo Yancey, the elder brother of Jimmy Yancey.

In spite of being celebrated as "originator" of ragtime, Ben Harney's status did not remain undisputed. James McIntyre and Thomas Heath, veteran entertainers, contested Harney in 1916 as to who "invented" ragtime. Blesh and Janis (1971) write: "James McIntyre stated in an interview that a buck dance with handclapping to the tune of an old 'rabbit' song he had learned from southern Negroes was ragtime. This dance he had brought to Tony Pastor's in New York in 1879. McIntyre . . . stated that ragtime originated with the Negroes and that it was taught to him in the South while he was working with Billy Carroll in a circus in the 1870's. An old Negro taught him a song that his grandfather had brought from Africa, an African chant in true ragtime syncopation . . ." (226). James McIntyre probably did learn the old "rabbit" song, but, of course, it would not have been called ragtime. Important is that the rhythm patterns were already there at that time, if McIntyre's observations are correct.

The controversy made Ben Harney a little uneasy, and according to Blesh and Janis, he retreated

> to a more tenable position. "Real ragtime on the piano, played in such a manner that it cannot be put in notes," he said, "is the contribution of the graduated Negro banjo-player who cannot read music." He expanded this with some pertinent observations: "On the banjo there is a short string that is not fretted and that consequently is played open with the thumb. It is frequently referred to as the thumb string. The colored performer, strumming in his own cajoling way, likes to throw in a note at random, and his thumb ranges over for this effect. When he takes up the piano,

the desire for the same effect dominates him, being almost second nature, and he reaches for the open banjo-string note with his little finger. Meanwhile he is keeping mechanically perfect time with his left hand. The hurdle with the right-hand little finger throws the tune off its stride, resulting in syncopation. He is playing two different times at once." (1971: 226–27)

As the years went by, many more sources have been uncovered and secured to confirm that during the 1880s there must have been some home-bred input from the music of itinerant string band players on how the piano began to be handled by African American musicians in the Midwest and elsewhere. One researcher, Eric Thacker (1973), even holds that banjo melodic-rhythmic patterns were "one of ragtime's prime ingredients":

> Examination of just a few bars of "Maple Leaf Rag" (first strain) reveals several elements which could only have been derived from the banjo tradition—off-balancing rests at the beginning of and during measures, intervallic phrases echoing the open-strings technique, simultaneous octaves, thirds, sixths, and other intervals struck in contrast to the single notes, quaver-crotchet snaps, repetitive figures. And they are all set against the regularity of the striding bass, much as the banjoists' syncopations moved against the solid thump of his accompanying foot, or—to take it a step or two further back—as the kora player's finger-picked patterns moved against the ostinato of his thumb-notes.
>
> The rag pianists—Joplin is the obvious example—aimed at a sort of formal sophistication but preserved the folk element in an odd kind of purity simply because they were not recollectors merely, nor conscious imitators, but natural identities to the tradition they transmitted, to a degree, perhaps, unwittingly. (6)

By all accounts, Joplin was an accomplished pianist who traveled for many years through the Midwest performing in various entertainment establishments, even during the time he had settled in Sedalia, Missouri, ca. 1896. He had absorbed all the refinements of the accent techniques on the piano, and internalized the rhythms of banjo playing in his parents' home by his mother. His piano rolls, the only direct evidence we have of his "touch," transmit an intensive feeling of swing.

In retrospect it is startling to learn that "jig piano" playing would rise to popularity in the United States—albeit under a new name—within less than twelve months in 1897, after the publication of Krell's "Mississippi Rag" in January and Tom Turpin's "Harlem Rag" in December. There may have been some additional triggers, besides the stimuli from the Chicago World's Fair 1893 and Anton Dvořák's pronouncements in New York. But how the word *ragtime* came to be attached to the new piano music is still a subject of controversy.

Blesh and Janis (1950 [1971: 129]) state that the term was coined by the so-called roustabouts, those doing the hardest manual work, carrying heavy loads to the ships along the Mississippi River and to the railroad trains.

Cake walk had also suddenly come up to national, and indeed international, recognition in 1896. Actually, Blesh and Janis claim that "ragtime" was the name those workers were giving to "cakewalk" (129). Recent research has pushed the first appearance in the United States of the word "rag" in the context of music, dance, or festivity further back in time. In their monumental collection of data on African American music between 1889 and 1895, *Out of Sight* (2002), the authors, Lynn Abbott and Doug Seroff trace the first printed reference of the word "rag" to a place in eastern Kansas and to the year 1891. In a note in the *Topeka Weekly Call*, August 16, 1891, within the "City News" there was this illuminating complaint: "The Jordan hall 'rags', which are held in Tennesseetown weekly, are a nuisance and should be abated." Similar complaints appeared in subsequent issues of the same paper. On October 4, 1891, it is stated more specifically what was so annoying to people: "Those 'shin-digs' who were passing through Tennesseetown going home from a dance Monday night, ought to have muzzles on their mouths so they will not annoy people who wish to sleep." On another occasion the "Patrol wagon was called to Jordan's Hall to quiet a row." There was also something like a "theme song" young girls were fond of singing at that time, about a famous racehorse named Proctor Knott (Abbott and Seroff 2002: 202).

Someone unfamiliar with the causes of the excitement, reading these newspaper remarks today, will come to the conclusion that both "rags" and "shin-digs" must have been slang terms, otherwise they would not have been written under quotation marks. In the meantime these words are found in dictionaries, but "shin-dig" is listed in the *Longman Dictionary of Contemporary English* (1990: 965) as an abstract noun, informal, old-fashioned, and its meaning is given as "noisy party," "dance," "a noisy quarrel or disagreement." By contrast, how this word is used in the October 4 note, is in reference to a noisy group of people, walking home from such an occasion.

Equally, the word "rags"—clearly meant to be in plural form—refers to (noisy) dance gatherings, parties taking place every week, etc. Abbott and Seroff (2002) give the following assessment of life in that particular township:

Tennesseetown, scene of the notorious "Jordan Hall rags", had sprung up on the western edge of Topeka during the 1870s as an "Exoduster" enclave, the final destination for hundreds of African American refugees from deteriorating racial conditions in the South, mostly from Tennessee and Mississippi. During the 1890s "living conditions in Tennesseetown were substandard by any criteria" [Thomas C. Cox, *Blacks in Topeka, Kansas, 1815–1915: A Social History* (Baton Rouge: Louisiana State University Press, 1982), 31, 145.] Further complaints about the "Jordan Hall nuisance" and cryptic comments about Tennesseetown and its inhabitants give some notion of the general ambience. (202)

In another part of their book they cite later sources, from the statement of Ben Harney's ragtime instructor who claimed that "ragtime" could be literally translated as "Negro Dance Time" to Rupert Hughes's 1899 essay (quoted in Blesh and Janis 1950) that the "Negroes call their clog dancing 'ragging' and the dance a 'rag.'" However, they warn us not to take these statements literally, and point out that articles and reports in newspapers such as *Topeka Weekly Call* and the *Kansas City American Citizen* in the 1890s indicated "that a rag was not just a particular sort of 'shuffling dance,' but a kind of grassroots social function, sometimes integrated, at which black string bands provided music for dancing. Before the word 'rag' came into fashion, 'breakdown' was most often used to describe similar dance affairs" (Abbott and Seroff 2002: 443). Scrutinizing newspapers of the Midwest, Abbott and Seroff found ample instances of use of the word "rag" in that sense, and they say that both words "seem to have evolved into slang for a back-country hop, and also a *type* of dance music" (443). Most interesting among the many written sources uncovered is a note in the *Kansas City Star*, December 29, 1893: "When an Atchison fiddler plays at a rag he always sits near the door so that he can get out when he hears the first fighting word." So much about the circumstances.

Most recently, the earliest printed evidence of the use of the word *rag*—without quotation marks—has even been traced further back in time. In the *American Music Review* 15/1 (Fall 2010): 11–12, Fred Hoeptner introduces a note from the *Kansas City Star*, dated February 4, 1881, under the headline "Crittenden's Rag." Thomas T. Crittenden was the newly elected Missouri governor. The word does not appear again in the text of the short article describing the governor's reception at Jefferson City as "one of the finest ever held at Missouri's dingy capital," but its use as a title gives it particular weight.

Obviously, the word "rag" already was current in the Midwest in 1881, and it was used in the sense elicited by Abbott and Seroff as "a kind of grassroots social function." That it was applied in the headline of a note describing a reception by the governor lasting "from eight to one o'clock" in the night, was most probably a journalistic *coup de bec* to introduce a bit of irony into the matter. This point of view seems to be shared by Hoeptner (2010), who concludes: "A feasible explanation is that the reporter simply borrowed a widely known slang term to lend a touch of flippancy to his piece. The article contains certain other allusions which would lend credence to this theory: namely, he or she refers to Jefferson City as 'pneumonia bluff' and 'Missouri's dingy capital'" (15).

The earliest known reference so far was unearthed by Pen Bogert, who shared the discovery with Doug Seroff, from whom it was later received by David Evans and me. David Evans wrote in a letter: (April 20, 2012):

Just yesterday I received a newspaper article from the Louisville (Kentucky) Daily Courier, January 7, 1852, page 1: "From the Athens of the West. The Grand Fancy Rag Ball." This was sent to me by Doug Seroff, who got it from Pen Bogert. Pen was the one who unearthed it. The word "rag" occurs only in this title. The article itself is a very detailed description of the high society white people attending a costume ball in Lexington, Kentucky, on December 31, 1851, described as a "great carnival." It seems to have been a benefit for the poor people of the city and was attended by about 700 people in costume. To me this suggests that "rag" originally referred to a dance where people wore costumes or "fancy" clothes. "Rags" are often used as a slang expression for clothes, often ironically for fancy clothes as in the expression "glad rags." Perhaps the term migrated into black usage and came to refer to dances where people would "dress up," such as the cakewalk. And from there it becomes attached to the type of music performed at such dances, eventually to include the syncopated music we know as "ragtime."

When David Evans visited Vienna on a concert tour, in May 2012, I was able to tell him that a term with analogous meanings even existed in German, describing such dance gatherings: *Lumpenball* (Lumpen = rags; ball = ball, dance event).

The Auditory Reception of Ragtime

For an ordinary piano player and listener, the novelty in ragtime was in rhythm. The compositional technique of repeatedly interpolating chains of 3/8, respectively 3/16 units (according to notation) in the pianist's right hand, over a left-hand, mostly regular 2/4 (or 4/4) beat, with an apparent accent on beat-units 2 and 4, had its attraction. The left-hand stride piano effect was achieved by structuring the bass line so that on 1 and 3 mostly a single note or octaves would be played, while on 2 and 4 a chord appeared. The right-hand melodies therefore often produced the effect of a transient "bimetric" tension in relation to the 4/4 bass. Another tension arose from cross rhythm, i.e., rhythm patterns with their own accents shifted horizontally against the piece's meter. Early twentieth-century music critics interpreted these compositional devices as "syncopation." On the other side of the social barrier, audiences without formal musical training found the term "rag time" to be a better description, since it seemed as if the melodic lines on the piano were constantly torn apart, but then quickly restored to fit the meter, as if little rags had been used to stitch together a cloth that, in the end, would also make up the complete thing.

The larger parameters of this music were established by European-derived multiple-strain form and dominant-to-tonic harmonic changes. Since pianists, African American and European American, had both learned to use contemporaneous popular forms, as in mazurkas, marches, polkas, etc. in their piano lessons, the natural thing to happen was that the street-music "syncopations" within short strophic form would then be applied by "learned" composers and performers to extended form, arranged in two, three successive strains. W. C. Handy's blues adaptations would later follow the same principles (cf. "St. Louis Blues," 1914 etc.) He would integrate the twelve-bar blues form as at least one of the strains into his compositions.

That was the start of the rise of a national American music that incorporated many principles of rhythmic and melodic shaping ultimately inherited from African traditions, but embedded in forms of the current, late nineteenth-century European-style popular music. Considering the variety of resources used by individual ragtime composers and the rise of different styles of ragtime piano— e.g., a New Orleans style was quite different from the way ragtime was played in Sedalia, the "cradle," and other towns in Missouri—the African components in ragtime deserve a closer and more detailed investigation.

"African" is a vague term. Obviously, ragtime makes use only of a selection of African principles of rhythmic formation, in fact only from some places and musical cultures in Africa. These were radically different from resources that contributed to the salient traits in much of the blues (Kubik 1999a). Considering the structure of many ragtime themes and ragtime melodies, we observe that the 3/8 (respectively 3/16) interpolations are always "chained." They form patterns of a certain length, and it is these patterns, not any single units, that are driven against the regular left-hand bass. This fact invalidates all descriptions of ragtime as "syncopated." A syncope in Western music is a particularistic entity: it refers to a note that anticipates the beat and is then held on. Syncopes are always tied to the main accents in a European-type meter. But the rhythmic structure in ragtime and other African American music follows a different principle. First, the beat as such is not pre-accented in the musician's perception; only acoustically are accents placed and they may fall on 2 and 4 of a 4/4 meter brought about by the clustering of notes (chords) in those places of the pianist's left-hand bass. Second, in the right-hand part there are recurring patterns with often heterometric and asymmetric structure, standing against the regular left-hand beat. As in many forms of African music, these patterns are in a polyrhythmic relationship to other parts of the composition. Syncopation is not a polyrhythmic device, but invariably tied to the concept of unilinear, divisive rhythm. If a piano player who has grown up within the tradition of Western classical music has difficulty performing ragtime and begins to accentuate the patterns as if some of its notes were syncopes, the result is what is called "corny." The principle of ragtime polyrhythm is demonstrated in most of the renowned works, from Scott Joplin's "Maple Leaf Rag" to a hundred other published compositions.

From its early beginnings ragtime was a piano style, but soon bands and orchestras adapted the published pieces. A remarkable later attempt at reconstruction of ragtime band performances as they sounded in the early twentieth century can be heard in Bunk Johnson's recordings of December 1947, with a group of musicians who were from a different tradition but able to read music and willing to cooperate with Bunk, following his instructions (cf. Bunk Johnson, *Last Testament*, Delmark Records 1993). I recommend listening to tracks 2 "Hilarity Rag," 4 "The Entertainer," and especially to track 10 "Kinklets," composed in 1906 by Joplin's star student Arthur Marshall.

Filling heterometric chains into a 2/4 or 4/4 meter, the patterns must be rounded off after two or three repetitions, by adding a supplementary metrical particle. This is what makes ragtime rhythm asymmetric. The important point is that those heterometric interpolations are transient. Within the limits of three to four consecutive 3/8 (or 3/16) interpolations, there must be a compensatory link in the chain, to add up to 16 elementary pulse units—the usual length of such patterns. Each pattern therefore, normally covers two measures, and is then followed by another one often with a differently structured make-up, so that listeners would not lose their 4/4 (respectively 2/4) bearings.

Can the essentials of ragtime rhythms in the style that emerged in Sedalia, St. Louis, and Louisville be explained in ethnomusicological terminology? What demonstration examples could we use from the hundreds of ragtime compositions in the period 1897 to 1917?

Scott Joplin's Piano Exercises

The best way to pursue this task will be to follow Scott Joplin's own approach in getting ragtime's basic ideas across to the student. We therefore concentrate on composition principles he himself expressed, with the caveat that our findings should not be generalized light-heartedly to "explain" all ragtime. We only want to get a glimpse of some ragtime compositional devices, albeit important ones.

In *The School of Ragtime—Six Exercises for Piano*, a short but essential tutor that appeared in 1908, Scott Joplin was trying to summarize his ideas. From the six Joplin exercises it is obvious what he was expecting his upper-class piano students to have major difficulties understanding: it was in the realm of rhythm, how to integrate left and right hand finger movements, maintaining a constant playing speed (no rubato) and accentuation, and how best to transmit the intra-culturally accepted ways of this music to learners.

Blesh and Janis (1950 [1971]) have given the following assessment: "Studying the six Joplin Études, one is immediately struck by the subtle time divisions and the way in which the syncopation and the 'three over four' are built in, so to speak, in the music itself. The Études virtually need only to be played to swing by themselves: the very arrangement of the notes tends to throw the accent from the main beats to where it belongs" (141).

Joplin's first four exercises cover four measures each, and they are all based on the following chord changes (allowing for small variation): 16 [F/F♯° → C → G → C] Strangely, if this sequence were used to encompass an entire musical theme, to be followed by variations ad libitum over the same chord progression, it would be almost identical with one of the common short cycles in twentieth-century African music.

In Joplin's exercises no. 2 and 3, this cycle is harmonically varied. In addition, some chord changes are placed off-beat or "tied over" across implicit beat-units, as in example no. 2, all of which is familiar procedure in African music. In exercise no. 2 the functional sequence V → I (dominant chord → tonic) is modified, as was the practice in many ragtime compositions and by extension in New Orleans jazz pieces. Here it is C/A⁷ → D⁷/G⁷ → C. Melodically, the D⁷ → G⁷ step allows for a note E which is elegantly resolved downward into the tonic, a precursor of what would become common in jazz.

Such chord changes were no problem for pianists trained in Joplin's day, and diminished chords were also well established in nineteenth-century European music, e.g., in Frédéric Chopin's (1810–1849) mazurkas, polonaises, etc. In New Orleans, however, the use of diminished chords in blues piano, would give them a different meaning; they would sound like they were accommodating the lower (e♭) and middle (f♯) blue notes of the non-Western blues tonal system.

Joplin in his Études does not talk about chord changes. Apparently he anticipated that they did not present any problem to his students. Instead he concentrated his discourse on the realm of rhythm. Here, he employs an interesting pedagogic device: a separate line is placed at the top of every notation example, and there he transcribes the right-hand piano part without any ties. With this he not only eliminates the syncopation idea, but establishes a string of semiquavers as a kind of reference pulsation (cf. exercises no. 3, 4, and 6). In African music theory we call such a grid the elementary pulsation (cf. Kubik 2010: II: 31–35).

It is fascinating that Joplin gets this idea across, visualizing it, teaching students that these notes are supposed to be an internalized perceptual reference grid, not a prescription for playing: "The upper staff is not syncopated, and is not to be played" (Joplin, quoted in Blesh and Janis 1950 [1971: 142]).

What, for lack of a better term, he calls "syncopation" in ragtime Joplin then explains this way: "It is evident that, by giving each note its proper time and by scrupulously observing the ties, you will get the effect. So many are careless in these respects that we will specify each feature. In this number [referring to Exercise no.1] strike the first note and hold it through the time belonging to the second note." Then he says: "Play slowly until you catch the swing, and never play ragtime fast at any time" (142).

Thus, from the start he gives a definition of "syncopation" that is slightly different from what is written in European music theory; and he uses the word "swing" many years before it became a common term for a manner of playing and dancing to jazz in the 1930s.

We can make Joplin's ragtime rhythmic structures visible by retranscribing his exercises in impact notation, a system I developed in the 1960s for the transcription of xylophone and other African music from the analysis of cinematographic shots (Kubik 2010: II: 59ff.). Impact notation proceeds from the idea of representing a musical performance not in terms of durational note values, as implied by the Western staff notation system, but in terms of action units, strokes (written x) and non-strokes (written .). Both signs have the same time value, namely one elementary pulse-unit.

The strokes can be delivered on a xylophone key, a lamella, a string, or in the present case on a piano key. Since we are not primarily concerned here with chord progressions and melody, we only notate the impact points of the action as such, for the right hand (r.h.) and left hand (l.h.). In this context we are suppressing information on how the fingers are used for each action and which ones are employed. We know, of course, that for a ragtime or jazz pianist it is not all the same which finger is used to hit a particular key, and the action of certain fingers, e.g., the index finger alone or in combination, tends to form movement patterns, creating kinemic* entities. For the moment, however, we disregard this dimension of piano playing and transcribe the left and right hands' parts as if they were to be produced by a hammer (see Fig. 5.5).

Fig. 5.5. Scott Joplin's Exercise no. 1. (Reproduced from Blesh and Janis 1950 [1911: 142])

---

* Following Kenneth Pike's (1954) etics/emics differentiation of standpoints in cultural research, which was modeled on the difference between phonetics and phonemics, we proceed by analogy to a differentiation between kinetic and kinemic studies: *kinetics*, the comparative study of movement across cultures, worldwide; *kinemics*, the study of meaningful movement within a specific culture and cognitive system.

Retranscribing in impact notation the rhythm expressed in Joplin's exercise no.1 we first have to put an encircled number at the start of the layout; this is the cycle number expressing the number of elementary pulse-units covered by the theme. Our x-ray hammer image of Joplin's first exercise then appears as shown in Figure 5.6.

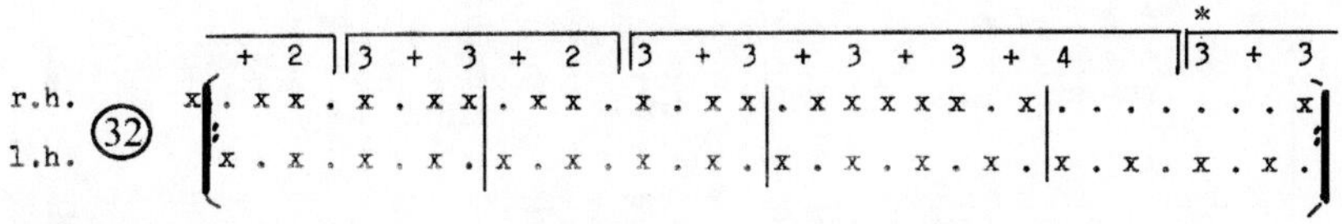

Fig. 5.6.

What appears like "syncopation" in the Western notational system reveals its true nature in impact notation. The example shows, that in this case the right-hand part starts off with an 8-pulse unit, structured as 3 + 3 + 2, which is repeated across the bar-lines, thereby establishing a gentle cross rhythm. This is followed by a new phrase in threes, rounded off by one four-pulse unit. The entire asymmetric cycle, which can be seen as starting at the point I have marked with an asterisk (*), reads: (3 + 3 + 2) + (3 + 3 + 2) + (3 + 3 + 3 + 3 + 4) = 32, In fact, this is the sequence of two well-known asymmetric rhythm patterns from African music, superimposed on a regular 4/4 beat. The first one, 3 + 3 + 2 is familiar from a host of Latin American traditions, son, rumba, etc., in Spanish called *cinquillo*. The second is found, for example, in bossa nova, and as a transient pattern in jazz, even in commercial big band jazz of the 1940s as in Glenn Miller's theme "A String of Pearls" (Glenn Miller, *American Patrol*, CD, FABCD 186, track 18, Acrobat Music & Media, 2003).

In appreciation of these timeless African rhythm patterns there are, however, pitfalls of understanding. Ragtime is full of recurring asymmetric figures, all of them age-old African devices, but they are not used to function as timelines as in certain other forms of African American music across Latin America and the Caribbean. They appear in the form of transient interpolations, constantly modified, interchanged and frequently interrupted by short melodic runs in European-style metric division. This last fact is not explained in the Joplin exercises, because he knew that the European-style divisive rhythms were of no difficulty for his students. The superimposition of heterometric and asymmetric figures, executed by the pianist's right hand over a regular 4/4 beat in the left, creates tension that is enhanced by melodic off-beat relationships and independent kinemic patterns formed by the action of each hand's fingers on the piano.

The next exercise, Joplin's no. 2 (see Fig. 5.7), depicts another source of ragtime polyrhythm. Joplin considers it difficult "especially for those who are careless with the left hand, and prone to vamp. The first note should be given the full length of three sixteenth, and no more" (Blesh and Janis 1950 [1971: 142]). Joplin insists on precision: "The second note is struck in its proper place and the third note is not struck but is joined with the second as though they were one note." Actually they are one note.

Fig. 5.7. Scott Joplin's Exercise no. 2 (Blesh and Janis 1971: 143)

If this were played today to surviving mid-twentieth-century Central African guitarists for listening (such as those on my DVD *African Guitar* 1995, or on our recent CD *Central African Guitar Song Composers*, Schmidhofer 2010), they would probably say that Joplin's exercise no. 2 is a kind of rumba. Here, however, the right- and left-hand parts duplicate each other rhythmically, and in harmonic content one is an extension of the other. In the first two bars the chords appear in the bass line, the parallel octaves in the right-hand part; in measure three it is the other way around. Both parts are structured as 3 + 3 + 2, with the diminished chord appearing in the bass crossing the bar line. The exercise demonstrates that the *habanera* bass that seems to give the music a "Latin tinge" (Roberts 1979) was known in Missouri and along the Mississippi River before Jelly Roll Morton popularized the concept. Example no. 2 is simpler in structure as compared with no. 1, though not for a player who is unfamiliar with asymmetric divisions of the meter. But at least in this exercise the pattern does not trespass bar lines. It is also repeated through all three measures without change before its conclusion in the fourth (see Fig. 5.8).

		3 + 3 + 2	3 + 3 + 2	3 + 3 + 2	4 + 4
r.h.	(32)	x . . x . x x .	x . . x . x x .	x . . x . x x .	x . . . x . . .
l.h.		x . . x . . x .	x . . x . . x .	x . . x . . x .	x . x . x . . .

Fig. 5.8.

Exercise, no. 3 may be a surprise, but it only reconfirms the presence in ragtime of many of the essential rhythmic devices from Africa, notably I would say from Bantu-language speaking areas. It has been claimed that none of the asymmetric timeline patterns current in coastal West African and Central African music occur in North American blues, jazz, ragtime etc. This is true, but it is important to know that a timeline pattern is primarily defined by its function. The same rhythms that constitute a timeline can be used in other contexts, as is the case in ragtime and jazz. A timeline pattern can be symmetric or asymmetric, and it is characterized by the fact that it is repeated throughout a musical piece.

Transient structures, patterns that are repeated once or twice in melodic shape on percussion instruments before another pattern takes over, are not to be considered timelines, although their structures may be identical. We only call them timeline patterns when they are repeated throughout a musical piece as an orientation guide. The West African seven-stroke twelve-pulse standard pattern (cf. Jones 1959; Kubik 2010: II: 72–84) survives in New World cultures, e.g., in the Brazilian candomblé (orixa) religious meetings. But nothing like that can be found in ragtime. This particular pattern is out of the question, because it would not fit into forms that are based on cycle numbers sixteen, thirty-two, or its multiples. Such cycles are not divisible by three or six.

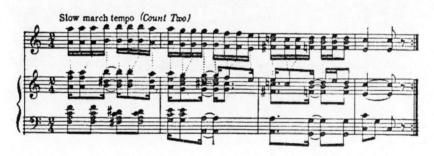

Fig. 5.9. Scott Joplin's Exercise no. 3.

Through the magnifying glass of our impact notation system we can detect in Joplin's exercise no. 3 (see Fig. 5.9) an asymmetric rhythm that in sum is congruent with the well-known nine-stroke sixteen-pulse timeline pattern called *kacha-cha* in eastern Angola, also prominent in the music of Katanga (Shaba Province, Democratic Republic of Congo) and in Brazilian samba. In Joplin's no. 3 exercise, however, its structure is merely hinted at; because from measure 1 to measure 2 it jumps from the left hand into the right-hand part. In the left hand it is discontinued in measure 2 after the fourth pulse-unit. I have encircled the constituent notes of this pattern in the notation in Figure 5.10. In measures 3 and 4 the rhythm

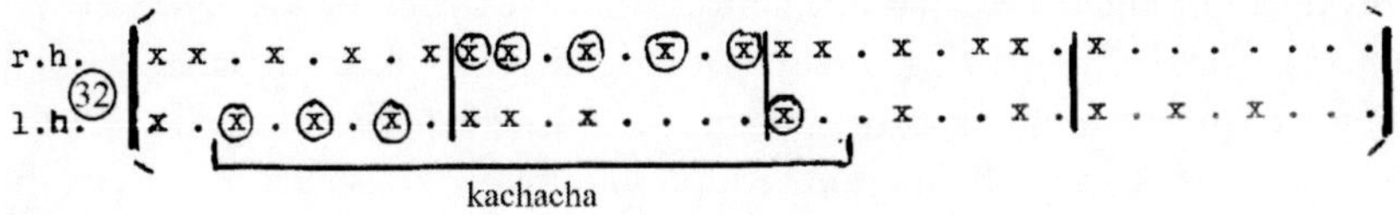

Fig. 5.10.

is totally changed. Measure 3 displays a combination of tresillo in the bass and cinquillo in the treble, but the two are combined in a non-interlocking way.

Exercise no. 4 (see Fig. 5.11) shows another application of the technique of transient interpolation of heterometric or asymmetric patterns. Here we find a floating melodic pattern that is phrased so that the last note of the upward melodic run always falls on the last elementary pulse-unit before beat 3 of the left-hand part throughout the first three measures. This off-beat rhythmic kick is reinforced through octave duplication of that note. Consequently, the right-hand treble notes develop a 3 + 5 structure that is repeated twice, covering the first three measures. It is followed up by a concluding 4 + 4 division of measure 4. (In the Joplin exercises the last measure always serves to bring about some kind of conclusion by returning to a regularly divisive, "European" treatment of the meter.) Accordingly, we follow the divisions created by the octave-enhanced strokes to mark the underlying rhythmic idea (see Fig. 5.12).

Fig. 5.11. Scott Joplin's Exercise no. 4.

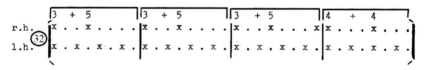

Fig. 5.12.

Exercises no. 5 and 6 are longer; they cover eight measures each. Here, Joplin introduces the learners to other forms of accent placement. Explaining exercise no. 5 he speaks of a *ragtime effect*, using the term in its literal meaning that "time" is torn at some point. He writes: "The first ragtime effect here is the second note, right hand, but instead of a tie, it is an eighth note rather than two sixteenth with a tie." What he means here is made clear by the notation; because the anticipated note does not fall before a bar line, it does not have to be tied over. Actually the difference between this "ragged" effect and those in the previous example is only a result of the western notational system used. The great value of the Joplin exercises is that they show the "ragtime effect" in different constellations. Here, the left-hand beat is regular, but it carries an accent on 2 and 4, due to the fact that on 1 and 3 the left hand plays single notes or octaves, whereby on 2 and 4 it plays chords. The accent on 2 and 4 is merely a result of the "thickness" of the sound and the pitch; the chords falling on 2 and 4 are considerably higher in pitch than the single or octave notes on 1 and 3 marking something like a bass drum.

We are already in the territory of stride piano, which would become prominent in early jazz. Against this left-hand bass, the right hand develops patterns in threes that are grouped in the manner shown in my rendering of the structure in Figure 5.13. In impact notation in Figure 5.14, I have tried to express the idea of the left hand's part, using a capital X for the acoustically prominent beat units 2 and 4. I have retranscribed only the first four bars.

Fig. 5.13. Scott Joplin's Exercise no. 5.

$$
\begin{array}{c|c|c|c}
3 + 3 + 3 + 4 & 3 + 3 + 3 + 3 + 4 & 3 + \\
\text{x x . x x . x x} & \text{x x . x . x .} & \text{x x . x x . x x} & \text{. x x . x . x .} \\
\text{x . X . x . X .} & \text{x . X . x . x .} & \text{x . X . x . X .} & \text{x . X . x . x .}
\end{array}
$$

Fig 5.14.

The pattern interpolated by the right hand has the structure $(3 + 3 + 3 + 3 + 4) = 16$ and is repeated three times to fill six bars of the extended form, followed by two concluding bars. From our analysis, so far, we can also tentatively postulate that in 2/4 or 4/4 ragtime the interpolated asymmetric patterns are usually either eight or sixteen elementary pulse-units long. Such a pattern can then be repeated in melodic transposition following the chord changes within the adopted form, or it can be replaced further on by another pattern of the same kind, as we have learned from Joplin's exercises no. 1 and 3, for example.

Joplin's last exercise, no. 6 (see Fig. 5.15), is aimed at training students to use right and left hands in parallel movement, here melodically in parallel octaves. This is probably not coincidental. Octave parallelism is characteristic of many theme presentations in certain African xylophone styles, and also in *timbrh* lamellophone music of the Vute in central Cameroon.

Fig. 5.15. Scott Joplin's Exercise no. 6.

The line of notes on top of Joplin's score is, moreover, a perfect visualization of the underlying African concept of elementary pulsation. Obviously, Joplin wants to inculcate the idea in all his students, and to say that only if there is this internalized reference grid in a performer's mind can he or she play ragtime. He takes pains to make that clear by relating all the notes in the exercise to the top line that is not to be played.

```
  ⌈3  +  2 + 3  ⌉⌈3  +  3  + 2 ⌉⌈3  +  2 + 3  ⌉⌈3  +  3  + 2 ⌉
③② |x  .  . x x x  . x|x  .  .  x  . x x  .|x  .  . x x x  . x|x  .  .  x  . x x  .|
                                              *
   + 3  +  2 + 2  +3  +  3  +  2 + 2 + 2 + 3  +‖2    4    +   4
   |x  .  . x  . x  . x|.  x  .  .  .  x  . x|x x  .  x  . x x  .|x  .  .  .  x  .  .  .|
```

Fig. 5.16.

The rhythmic structure of this exercise can be laid out as shown in Figure 5.16. The numerical structure of the first line is characterized by two permutations of a pattern whose constituent elements we can call a and b, forming this combination: $(b + a + b) + (b + b + a)$. $a = 2$, $b = 3$. It covers sixteen pulse-units and is repeated over the length of four measures.

The second line (measures 5 to 8) displays the most complex structure so far introduced by the Joplin exercises. If we deduct the "resting bar" at its end (4 + 4) from it, the pattern of the second line can be seen as covering twenty-four pulse-units. To understand its internal order, however, we have to take the stroke I have marked with an asterisk as its starting point and think of the pattern as circular. Then it reveals itself as based on the principle of an arithmetic progression: $(a + b) + (a + a + b + b) + (a + a + a + b) = 24$, or: basic → doubled → tripled (but discontinued). The difference between the successive terms is a + b which is adjoined to the previous term so that each element adds up to its own kind, a joins the a's, b the b's. However, while this is clear in the abstract, the progression is discontinued due to the constraints imposed by the length of the three bars. In order to get resolved within the twenty-four-pulse frame, the pattern cannot continue as it would, if the principle of an arithmetic progression were to be maintained. So the last b is not tripled.

This example should underline the mathematical background of asymmetric interpolations in ragtime. The long note chain over twenty-four pulses plus eight resting units in the second line of Joplin's exercise no. 6 is quite remarkable, and it is also phrased deceptively across the bar lines between measures 5, 6, and 7.

Melodic Split and Cross Rhythms

Impact notation has helped us systematize rhythmic structures in ragtime as provided in Scott Joplin's piano exercises published in 1908. We emphasize that ragtime's rhythms cannot be described as syncopation, but have to be understood in terms of the pattern structures of asymmetric, heterometric interpolations into a regular 2/4 or 4/4 beat. By contrast, syncopation in European music history is a particularistic phenomenon and may be understood as an anticipation, a shifting of a note to a "weak" part of the meter from where it is tied over to the following "strong" part. While such an idea works for European music with its historical background in Greek verse syllables, it cannot be applied to rhythmic structures based on an African understanding of timing, and its extensions in New World cultures. There is no concept of "strong" and "weak" parts of the meter in the African traditions, hence no concept of metric pre-accentuation, although meter as such is important and must be recognized by dancers. Accents in the melodic-rhythmic lines of a musical piece have their own structure inherited from speech patterns in African tone languages, and consequently, may fall anywhere on-beat or off-beat, just like the syllables of a spoken sentence. Between themselves, these accents, melodic, timbric, agogic, etc., form patterns. The right-hand pattern formations in ragtime are of restricted length, usually not exceeding sixteen elementary pulse units (two bars) before a new pattern is introduced, or the same pattern is repeated in melodic transposition. Advanced pattern formation was presented by Joplin in his last exercise for students (no. 6), covering twenty-four pulses plus the 4 + 4 divisive fillout following it, to resolve into a thirty-two-pulse line.

Cycle number	Pattern structure		Number of additive components	Reference number
2 ·⑧	[3 + 3 + 2]	or (3 + 5]	three (or two)	I
⑯	[3 + 3 + 3 + 3 + 4]		five	II
⑯	[3 + 2 + 3 + 3 + 3 + 2]		six	III
⑯	[2 + 2 + 2 + 3 + 2 + 2 + 3]		seven	IV

Fig. 5.17.

It is startling that most of the repertoire of linear rhythmic sequencing in ragtime can be schematized and condensed into just four basic models within ragtime's sixteen-pulse cycles (see Fig. 5.17). That is what there is in asymmetries, besides stretches of divisive European-style rhythms that are also abundantly used.

A composer has plenty of freedom in using these patterns. While they all cover eight or sixteen elementary pulse units, they can each be turned around internally with the same number of possible starting points. In addition, they can be shifted against the left-hand regular bass, also in sixteen possible relationships. One of the knacks of ragtime composition (and jazz for that matter), in fact, is that the bar lines implied by the metric reference scheme can be crossed by any of these patterns.

Because ragtime compositions are almost exclusively based on cycle number 16 (and its multiples thirty-two, forty-eight, etc.) and very rarely on twelve-pulse schemes (Joplin's "Bethena" is the most notable exception), asymmetric West and Central African rhythm patterns based on cycle numbers twelve or twenty-four do not appear in the ragtime tradition, while, by contrast, they occur abundantly in many forms of Afro-Latin American music.

The eight- and sixteen-pulse asymmetric patterns shown in Figure 5.17 are indisputably African in their provenance. On the Guinea coast and in large parts of Central Africa (Congo, Angola, down to the Lower Zambezi), they are essential. Often they are used in those cultures as timeline patterns, i.e., as a rhythmic orientation screen that is repeated throughout a song or musical piece. In ragtime they are not used in that function. Instead they are interpolated as ever-changing blocks; each block is transient, repeated two or three times, often in melodic transposition, then to be replaced by another block.

It may be surprising that there should be just these four different asymmetric structures that can be melodically filled up and inserted into the 2/4 marching time framework. But a simple mathematical equation can show the limits for the sequencing of 2s and 3s within a-sixteen-pulse cycle. If you ask yourself "How many 2s and how many 3s can I mix and add up to get 16?" you will discover a surprising answer: that there are only two possibilities: two 2s with four 3s (rhythm III in fig. 5.17), or five 2s with two 3s (rhythm IV). Mathematically, this can be expressed by the equation $2x + 3y = 16$, with x or y your unknown variables. You will then find that there are only two solutions that give you whole numbers (and no fractions).

One cannot change the structure of the patterns shown in Figure 5.17. If you try to change their inner order, you will not get any "new rhythms," as you might have been hoping for, but only the same numerical content reshuffled. For example, if you shift the first of the two 2s in pattern III shown in our table, by one step to the right, then you get this permutation: $[(3 + 3 + 2) + (3 + 3 + 2)]$; but it is the same as the first rhythm in the table (see Fig. 5.17). Conversely, if you shift the 2 at the end of the pattern by one step to the left, then you get the form $[(3 + 2 + 3) + (3 + 2 + 3)]$, which is once again the tresillo rhythm shown under reference no. 1, only now with a different starting point.

However, one fact to be learned is that the structures shown under ref. I, II, and IV are all optimal distributions of an uneven number of strokes over a cycle with an even number. In a mathematical study (Kubik 2008a), I used the formula shown in Figure 5.18 for calculating how many permutations exist for an uneven number of strokes distributed over an even-numbered cycle.

$$C_n^k = \frac{(n-1)!}{(n-k)! \cdot k!}$$

Fig. 5.18. n = the number of elementary pulse-units in the cycle. k = the number of strokes (or impact points) to be distributed across the cycle.

This formula is applicable to rhythms that are asymmetric, with an uneven number of strokes, such as five, seven, nine, etc., distributed over an even-numbered cycle of elementary pulse-units (eight, twelve, sixteen, etc.) which cannot be divided by the former. It then turns out that the African asymmetric patterns used as timelines represent the most evenly distributed solutions that are mathematically possible. But there are many permutations. A simple pattern such as the habanera or tresillo rhythm (see Fig. 5.17, ref. I) and its cognate, the cinquillo pattern, represents one out of seven possibilities of distributing three or five strokes across an eight-pulse cycle. By comparison, if we take rhythm IV, which is called *kachacha* in eastern Angola, it is the 715th of the possible permutations (n = 16, k = 7 or 9); and rhythm II is the 273rd. This can be calculated with the help of the formula given above (Kubik 2008a).

To what extent however can Scott Joplin's exercises be regarded as representative of the entire repertoire of asymmetric rhythm patterns found in ragtime? Is Figure 5.17 a complete microcosm? Within the limits of this book I cannot, of course, scrutinize each of the hundreds of ragtime compositions published in the late nineteenth and early twentieth centuries and retranscribe the scores in impact notation. But our quick survey of the Joplin exercises has uncovered the essence of the African background in ragtime's rhythmic structures; and at least for cycle numbers eight, sixteen, and thirty-two the microcosm shown is indeed comprehensive. In the actual compositions there may be extensions obtained by some input of divisive and symmetric patterns from European music as well, but as to the asymmetric patterns in ragtime, they mostly resolve within the framework of sixteen elementary pulse-units. Within this schema almost unlimited variety is obtained by shifting, reshuffling, duplicating, filling in particles, etc., which generates a lot of compositional freedom.

There are two more facts about ragtime structuring to be addressed before we go further: (1) The manner in which heterometric chains are coordinated with the left-hand metric scheme often follows the principle of cross rhythm, i.e., the phrase is preferably superimposed with its accents off the beat (see Fig. 5.19). (2) Internal melodic structuring of many ragtime themes and the manner in which pitch values are allocated to specific fingers, especially of the pianist's right hand, also displays a system. There are concepts of motion organization inherited from African traditions. Unlike European-style melodic construction, the individual notes of a ragtime theme are often choreographically allocated to one's fingers, which move as if in a dance. In some cases there is a kind of interlocking relationship, like the tiles laid out to make a roof. French ethnomusicologists have a good word for this compositional technique: *tuilage*. The same principle is found in weaving patterns (cf. Kubik 2010: II: 315–17). Often the right-hand fingers of the pianist act as if each finger were a separate player confined to a certain key or range of keys, or as if this was a group of drummers interlocking their strokes.

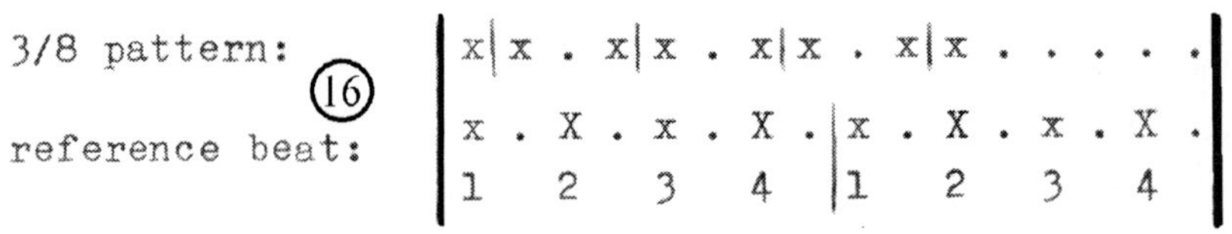

```
3/8 pattern:          │x│x . x│x . x│x . x│x . . . . .│
              ⑯        │                                │
reference beat:       │x . X . x . X .│x . X . x . X .│
                      │1   2   3   4  │1   2   3   4  │
```

Fig. 5.19.

This a principle of construction first described by A. M. Jones in *African Drumming in Northern Rhodesia* (today: Zambia) (1934), and it was soon corroborated by ethnomusicologists as important in many portions of Central Africa, especially in xylophone music. Jones used to call this combination principle

CALLIOPE RAG

Fig. 5.20. First page of James Scott's "Calliope Rag." (Reproduced from Blesh and Janis 1971)

cross rhythm, and we call it now *interlocking (reference) beat* (cf. Kubik 2010: II: 39–40). Many ragtime melodies are structured according to this "drumming" or "xylophone" combination principle, as if the constituent notes of a phrase were to be produced by different agents in interlocking action. Each finger is then strictly allocated to a certain piano key or range of keys, and the allocation of certain parts of a movement pattern to certain fingers is preconceived. When the melody or theme is transposed to another area of the keyboard—following chord changes—the movement pattern is also transferred with it. This fact links rag-time piano with African practices on xylophones and other instruments through the deep-rooted idea that movement patterns have their autonomy, that they are independent of melodic output. One of the secrets of finger movement in ragtime and other African American piano music is the hidden presence of this principle, which should also explain "unusual" fingerings in some jazz pianists (e.g., Thelonious Monk).

To exemplify this principle, I will take the first theme in James Scott's "Cal-liope Rag," composed ca. 1910, and reproduce just one page here (see Fig. 5.20). Apparently, James Scott used to play this piece on the steam calliope at Lakeside Park, between Carthage and Joplin, Missouri (Blesh and Janis 1950 [1971: 297]).

If we look carefully at the right-hand theme played against an [x . X . x . X] left-hand stride piano rhythm, we discover that its constituent notes have a cer-tain order in their recurrence or progression. The rhythmic structure of the theme covering the first four bars, before it is transposed from tonic to dominant, cor-responds in its initial part to a combination of patterns given in Figure 5.17 under ref. no. II and I: (3 + 3 + 3 + 3 + 4) + (3 + 3 + 2) + 8 = 32. But the melody in disjunct intervals is structured so that an inherent pattern (i.p.) effect is created; it falls apart, dissociating into three pitchlines, as if performed by three different players (as in Fig. 5.20), just like three tuned horns playing together in interlock-ing style.

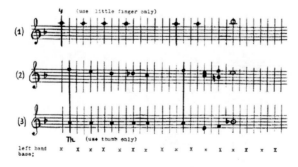

Fig. 5.21. Retranscription of the theme of "Calliope Rag," to demonstrate its internal structure as cross rhythms.

Split in the manner shown in Figure 5.21, we find that the second pitch-line beginning with f, and pitchline 3 in an octave relationship with line l, are both staggered by the value of one elementary pulse-unit in relation to pitchline 1. Only at the start of the fourth measure covered by the theme do the three lines reunite.

The basic motif of "Calliope Rag" covers four measures in the alla breve notation. This rhythmic structure is then repeated in the next four measures in a transposition of the melody to the level of the dominant chord, and so on. If this were played by African musicians combining the pitchlines with three separate instruments of the same timbre, e.g., three flutes, three horns, or three drums, they would operate from a so-called interlocking reference beat. Players 2 and 3 would have their subjective beat reference one elementary pulse-unit behind Player 1.

Tony Jackson's "The Naked Dance" is another good example of hidden melodic cross rhythm (cf. Jelly Roll Morton's performance in New York, December 14, 1939, piano solo, R-2563, Commodore XFL-14942 [LP], and Lomax 1952 [1959: music section, transcription]). In the late nineteenth century the transient bimetric and cross-rhythmic structure of many themes in ragtime stood at a level of rhythmic complexity unheard of by the general public. Out of the broadest spectrum of African-derived polyrhythmic devices of the time, only the relatively simplified forms in tango from Argentina and ragtime had become manageable on the piano in the parlor and in orchestrations by popular bands.

And yet the overall picture was one of large-scale transculturation into new areas of auditory experience. Just one or two principles of rhythmic construction from African music—mostly Central African, Bantu language–speaking cultures—had reemerged in the United States in ragtime, under favorable conditions such as access to pianos by African Americans. But these were sufficient to become triggers for new developments. African Americans began to experiment, often drawing upon clandestine knowledge. The models for transfer to piano came from banjo, fiddle, and other street and plantation music, long reduced to musical forms in which a sung (or treble) melody was accompanied by "vamping" on the banjo or guitar with a straight beat. The relatively complex melodic lines of both voice and instrumental passages over the beat produced by the "vamping technique" owe their unusual rhythmic structures to the fact, that in nineteenth-century African American communities—as in Africa—melodies and rhythm patterns were imagined as verbalized. They implicitly contained a text, sometimes of ambiguous meanings, whether actually sung or not. But words have their own syllabic lengths and pattern structure; they start and end somewhere. Among speakers of African languages, or languages under the impact of African tonal understanding, such phrases played or sung against a regular dance beat will have their tonal accents (which is different from stress accents) and fall on or off beat according to their own pattern structure. This is rooted in language learning within traditions—as by nearly all speakers of Niger-Kordofanian languages (Greenberg 1966)—in which one syllable corresponds to one tonal unit (mora), and chains of syllables are not defined by stress, or in terms of long and short, but in terms of equi-spaced tonal unit, each corresponding to one elementary pulse-unit in music/dance. In addition, nasals such as [m], [n], and [ŋ] may be syllabic. That many singers of African descent in the southern United States have been treating English as if it were an African language is well known. The length of a sung phrase with its internal accents is not subordinate to a meter, as represented for example by hand-claps. Its accents will fall here and there; in some cases an entire text line can be shifted against the beat.

Scott Joplin's "Bethena"

Scott Joplin always tried to explore unknown territory in composition. One of his most remarkable ventures in this sense was a waltz, thereby steering away from the 2/4 or standard ragtime beat. "Bethena—A Concert Waltz" was published in 1905 in St. Louis by Bahnsen Piano Co. It is available on the CD already mentioned: *Scott Joplin "The Entertainer,"* BCD 101, 1987, Biograph Records, track 12, from a piano roll produced in the 1960s by Hal Boulware, a collector, and digitally recorded directly from a 1910 Steinway 65/88 note player.

Michael Montgomery and Trebor Tichenor in the album's liner notes call "Bethena" "one of Joplin's most captivating and ambitious creations. . . . The cover [of the sheet music publication 1905] is graced by a photograph of a lady who may have been the beautiful Bethena herself. Beginning in G, the work flows through a labyrinth of beautiful and sometimes unexpected modulations: G—B♭—G—F—B minor—D, and finally ending with the A theme in G one last time."

Each passage from strain to strain is marked by modulatory lines suspending the rhythm for a short time. The composition is structured this way:

Intro 8 bars
Main theme in G (strain 1) 16 bars 1x
Modulation passage (4 bars)
Strain 2 in B♭, (16 bars) 2x
Modulation passage (8 bars) back to
Main theme in G (strain 1) 16 bars 1x
Modulation passage (8 bars)
Strain 3 in F (16 bars) 2x (modified in repetition)
Modulation passage (4 bars)

Strain 4 in B minor (16 bars) 2x
Strain 5 in D (16 bars 2x
Modulation passage (6 bars)
Main Theme in G (16 bars) 1x
Coda 8 bars

Fig. 5.22. The start of Joplin's "Bethena." (Reproduced from the published score 1905)

Fig. 5.23. Start of main theme (1st strain) of Joplin's "Bethena."

The introduction to the main theme is typically a so-called "false track" passage, triggering a disorientation effect in listeners. This is a composer's trick familiar to us from many areas of Africa. In Joplin's composition, a listener will be inevitably drawn into projecting the reference beat upon the quarter notes. The right-hand chords in measure 5 then seem to enter off-beat, until the introduction comes to a rest. Listeners (from any culture) therefore cannot discover the dance beat immediately. It only emerges when the bass line of the main theme begins.

But is it a waltz?

Most listeners will probably relate the main theme to a 3/4 beat as written by the composer. But when I heard "Bethena" for the first time, as it sounded from the piano roll, my auditory perception reacted differently. From the background of my southeast African musical training, I perceived the right-hand patterns as triple rhythms against a regular 1, 2 beat, with the bass line crossing it. Listening to "Bethena" in this manner, the composition sounds as if it had been inspired by *mbira* music in Zimbabwe, with Joplin's "waltz" bass line actually part of a bimetric setup. It was enjoyable to listen to these wonderful excursions that way, but I wanted to know whether other musicians from the same culture area in southeast Africa would also hear "Bethena" in 6/8 or 12/8 rather than 3/4 time. I asked our guitarist, flutist, and composer Sinosi Mlendo to share with me a brief experience. I asked him to take one of our tin rattles, put earphones on, listen to "Bethena"

Fig. 5.24. The main theme (first strain) of Scott Joplin's "Bethena" retranscribed in "Zimbabwe" 12/8 time with dance beat and rattle pattern supplemented.

from the CD and imagine Joplin to be a pianist in our band. How would the rattle player accompany this composition? (experiment, March 2, 2012).

The result was startling and confirmed that Sinosi's auditory alignment of the theme was identical with mine. Like me, he divided the 3/4 bass by half, marking the dance beat in the appropriate places. To illustrate the implications of this observation, Figure 5.24 reproduces the result of our beat perception experiment in relation to the first four bars of Joplin's "Bethena" main theme. My illustration is to be compared with Figure 5.23. I haven't changed a note in Joplin's theme; what changes is how it is related in the mind to reference lines that are different from those of a waltz.

So, we hear "Bethena" as if it were a *mbira* piece from Zimbabwe transferred to the piano! The question, of course, is whether our perception is merely an example of extreme cross-cultural reinterpretation (in Herskovits's term), or does it uncover a hidden, perhaps unconsciously intended dimension in Joplin's composition?

Perceptual processes are by nature subjective; they reveal how our brain organizes stimuli, and this is greatly modelled by cultural learning processes. This is the question we have pursued from the beginning, and here is the answer. But are there any objectively detectable analogies between the rhythmic idiosyncrasies of "Bethena" and Shona music of Zimbabwe? In fact, the rhythm pattern is basic to the *mbira dza vadzimu* (lamellophone) music and has been transcribed for the "big" tune (i.e., most important song) called "Nyamaropa" (cf. A. Tracey

Fig. 5.25. "Nyamaropa," a theme for the Shona *mbira* in Zimbabwe, transcribed by Andrew Tracey, 1970.

1970: 13). The *mbira* left/right-hand interaction in that kind of song is identical in rhythm with Scott Joplin's main theme in G (1st strain) of "Bethena." The earliest transcription evidence we have for the *mbira* rhythmic combination comes from Tracey's first article, "Mbira music of Jege A. Tapera" (1961: 53) (see Fig. 5.25). In rhythm the combination is identical with Joplin's, except that left- and right-hand parts are exchanged for each other on the *mbira* as compared to Joplin's layout. The 3/4 component of the bimetric scheme is found in the deep notes as it is in Joplin.

While these traits, very basic to Shona music in Zimbabwe and to *mbira* music in particular, are identical in both musical forms, without any evidence of direct diffusion in the late nineteen and early twentieth centuries—no Zimbabwean musicians were invited to the 1893 Chicago Columbian Exposition—a harmonic comparison may perhaps suggest some more, but less clear-cut parallels:

(a) Like Joplin's first-line melodic-harmonic motif in "Bethena," the basic combination pattern for one type of mbira songs (see Fig. 5.22), which Jege A Tapera taught Tracey, carries a minimalist melodic motif through four tonal-harmonic steps. In the Shona example they can be expressed like this: d;G → f♯;B → b;E → a;D, with some intermediate returns to the basic bi-chord. Often they are spread out in a six-step standard arrangement (cf. Andrew Tracey 1961: 51):

$$d;G \rightarrow f\sharp;B \rightarrow b;E \rightarrow d;G \rightarrow f\sharp;B \rightarrow a;D$$

The order in which these bi-chords appear in *mbira* music of southeast Africa has been called the standard progression, and it is also found in themes for *chipendani* musical bow (Brenner 1997).

This order, however, and even the bi-chords themselves may change in different regions (Kubik 2010: II: 210ff.). More consistent, therefore, across heptatonic traditions in southern Africa and possibly elsewhere, seems to be a preference for themes structured along cycles with four tonal steps. This applies even to the handling of the Western "three common chords" in today's popular music in southern Africa. Often they are conceptualized as if it was all a progression through four tonal clusters, the fourth cluster created by strictly using a fourth/

sixth inversion of the tonic. All four chords then have equal, non-functional status. They represent "shifting tonal levels" such as discussed in 1987 by Peter van der Merwe in a conference paper at the 6th Ethnomusicology Symposium of the ILAM, Grahamstown (Van der Merwe 1988: 53–65).

(b) Joplin's four-bar motif has the flavor of such an African cycle. Superficially, the harmonic progression in the first eight bars G → A⁷ → D⁷ → E_m appears to be a functional all-around European pattern; it does not resemble the Shona chords. But if we reduce them to their fifths frame, i.e., to d;G → e;A → a;D → b;E an analogy to the Shona bi-chord repertoire d;G → f♯;B → b;E → a;D is perceptible, with only one bi-chord out of the four, the B/f♯, falling apart and the order of the last two bi-chords exchanged. A present-day pop musician with his electric guitar could easily use A⁷ as a substitute chord for f♯;B.

I have the impression that there is a hidden background to the "Bethena" four-bar nuclear theme, based on vestiges of an African harmonic cycle Joplin either reconceived or heard someone play in a street performance, and then adapted to the rules of late nineteenth-century Western musical conventions.

I do not want to strain my readers' tolerance for speculation, but merely point out that sometimes there is more under the surface than meets the eye. Remnants of African harmonic concepts in Joplin's music would necessarily tend to appear veiled and reinterpreted by the composer under pressure from late nineteenth-century Western musical conventions with which he identified. The main theme of "Bethena" in four lines (sixteen bars) is then developed by Joplin in the European tradition, by transferring the basic line to different tonal levels, with appropriate chord changes.

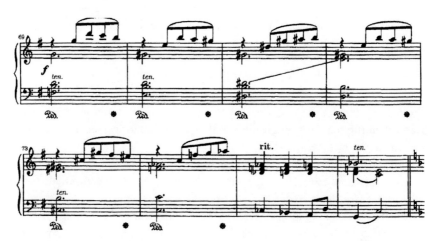

Fig. 5.26. Scott Joplin's modulation from strain 1 in G (repeated) to strain 3 in F. (Reproduced from the published score, 1905)

There is another fascinating detail that can be discovered in "Bethena." The passages pursuing a modulation to a next strain of this "concert waltz" are harmonically far beyond the usual chords in ragtime and other popular music of Joplin's days. There is, for example, this passage linking the main theme in G to strain 3 in F, by modulation (see Fig. 5.26). This sequence of piano chords and right-hand melodic variations could well be part of modern jazz improvisations in the 1940s and 1950s. More twists concerning Joplin's music can be found in Marcello Piras's recent analysis of "Magnetic Rag" (2013).

Treemonisha

During the second half of his life, Joplin ventured into opera composition. His first attempt was the opera *A Guest of Honor*, and apparently he toured with it, accompanied by a small group of performers, through parts of the Midwest in 1903. Then his manuscript was left by mistake in a trunk somewhere and was never recovered.

His second opera, *Treemonisha*, composed between 1907 and 1910, is preserved and was staged occasionally after it was published by Joplin at his own expense in 1911 in New York. *Treemonisha* is a fascinating work whose value has been seriously underrated, and in many ways it is also something like a gateway into Scott Joplin's personality and driving spirit.

In the article entitled "African, autobiographical, and earlier operatic elements in Scott Joplin's Treemonisha" (2008), Theodore Albrecht has undertaken an in-depth analysis not only of the musical and literary content of the work, and the creative processing of various sources of inspiration from European opera, Verdi to Wagner, and Weber with which Joplin was familiar, but of the creative mind and life history of the composer as reflected in the opera's plot. Albrecht uncovered details in the plot that are clearly based on Joplin's own life history. Albrecht's article is the most thorough compilation yet available, placing *Tree-monisha* into the wider context of theatre and music history in the nineteenth century. But what is particularly novel and fascinating is Albrecht's excursion into the psychology of the author of *Treemonisha*, and the symbolism he uses, including the contrasting symbolic use of speech: standard English versus dialect by the protagonists in the play, with all its social connotations. Albrecht's analysis follows a multidisciplinary approach, drawing upon music history, socio-linguistics, and even depth psychology. It has encouraged me to proceed along that path of analysis in this final section on ragtime and the personalities who created it.

The full story of *Treemonisha*, the name of a baby girl found abandoned under a tree, only comes to the surface in bits and pieces during the operatic act. The latter begins when the girl is already eighteen, and the earlier history is gradually reconstructed in flashbacks, through conversations. Albrecht (2008) points out that the early part of the story would by itself form another theatre play, because it "contains dramatic elements that could, themselves, have been developed into a separate opera, much as Wagner's *Die Walküre* sets the dramatic situation for the *Siegfried* of the next generation" (219).

Joplin, however, opted for telling that part of the story, which most certainly was the primary inspiration for his operatic play, in a preface to this "Opera in Three Acts." The text is relatively short, but gives the essentials. An archetypal motif is here, as we find in many variations of folktales, and also within large collections of African stories (cf. Kayombo kaChinyeka's story of the miraculously born young man Kamuvelenge; Kayombo kaChinyeka 2008: 109–10). In all these cases the person born or found under unusual circumstances develops into an extraordinary being, capable of liberating his or her people of a curse or of servitude, as Moses in biblical history.

The start of Joplin's story focuses on a couple, Ned and his wife Monisha, living on a plantation northeast of the town of Texarkana under the conditions prevalent in 1866, after the end of the American Civil War. Ned and Monisha are childless, which in the African and African American traditions inherited by the ex-slaves is an intolerable situation open to ridicule by members of the community. All interventions through magic to address the problem of infertility fail; but one day, by the middle of September 1866 (so writes Joplin), Monisha finds an abandoned baby girl, just two days old, under the tree in front of their little log cabin. They adopt it as their own child, but have to hide the fact from the community. So they undertake a journey to relatives in a far place, in order to create a scenario in which the child appears to have been born in the meantime. The secret of the baby girl's origin is kept tight and will never be revealed. Monisha, so writes Joplin, first transfers her own name to the child, but when the girl is three years old adds a little detail to the name, calling her Tree-Monisha in reverence to the tree under which she had found her. The couple then enters a job with "white" people, with the understanding that the lady of the house would give Treemonisha some education. The opera begins when Treemonisha is eighteen years old, and in the first act shows the family in front of their cabin, with a "conjuror" (witch-doctor, wizard, trick artist, etc.) approaching them and trying to sell Monisha some medicine as defensive magic. The educated Treemonisha intervenes and persuades her mother to reject the offer.

Despite the declaration "story fictitious" on the page above Joplin's preface, Albrecht is of the opinion, with much justification I think, that "the details here and elsewhere in the score suggest that there are many elements of factual or thinly disguised symbolic substance in the opera" (219). I would even go a step further and dare to say, precisely because of the emphatic denial of any factual background of the story and warning audiences not to read anything like that into it, the autobiographical inspiration is indirectly confirmed. Albrecht meticulously pursues this idea in his analysis, relating places and dates mentioned in the preface to Joplin's own time and geographical surroundings, and especially parallels in his family history.

Reading through the text of the preface, I am more and more convinced that it might even be based on a dream Joplin had shortly before starting work on this opera. This would corroborate Albrecht's idea that the events, even their dates in the narrative, reflect very personal events in the author's life.

It turns out to be very likely that Treemonisha, the child found abandoned under a tree, stands for Scott Joplin's Self (in the sense of C. G. Jung's concept of that archetype). The story or even dream illustrates Joplin's reaction to a mid-life identity crisis, offering a solution to the existential question "who am I?" In this scenario, Ned with his drunken habits would represent Scott's father with whom the boy did not want to identify, opening up for himself a way out of the constraints of African American family life through education under the circumstances of the late nineteenth century. Monisha would unconsciously symbolize his mother, with an interesting twist that in the story she passes her name (i.e., her identity) to the girl she found under the tree. But that girl is none other than Scott.

The name Treemonisha is a wonderful construct—I believe that Scott Joplin was either dreaming it or it occurred to him suddenly as a daydream or flash of the spirit. It links the mother's name to the symbol of a tree, which universally is "tree of life" and thereby also a symbol of Self.

The deeper stratum of the *Treemonisha* story is most likely a fantasy by Scott Joplin that it would be fine if it turned out that his parents were not his real parents, a child fantasy he could have cultivated at age eleven when he was beginning to learn piano, that he with his talents and artistic inclinations belonged somewhere else. This idea could have been stimulated in him indirectly through the relationship with his piano teacher, Mr. Weiss from Germany, who probably had a deep affection for the boy beyond a teacher's or father's love, stirring up in the little boy the fantasy: "Actually I am like a girl. I am following my mother, not my father; but I am not from here, I come from somewhere far, like a light-skinned girl picked up under a tree. But I have the strength, the intellectual power to obtain the education to assume a leadership role in my community."

In the operatic plot there is also the symbol of the evil forces trying to prevent just that. The gang of three conjurors with their talismans try to exert their power over Treemonisha at age eighteen, but she resists. At a closer look, however, we find that the plot is not so much about a struggle between superstition and faith within the mold of a Christian worldview. It rather expresses a struggle with evil forces associated by the author with his father, who wants to pull him to his side, to his lifestyle, symbolized by the act of the conjurors kidnapping Treemonisha. Actually, Monisha, the mother, also has strong beliefs that others would call superstitious, like reverence of the tree under which the little child was found. The idea of a sacred tree is paralleled in many African cultures. Monisha's idea is a cognate of the eastern Angolan idea of the *muti wamundzango* (the tree of the assembly pavilion) or foundation tree of a village, which marks the start of a historical period just like Monisha's finding of the little girl.

However, if the Treemonisha story is symbolic of Joplin's own life, then we have perhaps found a key to unlock the secrets of his creative drive and extraordinary achievements. The implication is that the girl Treemonisha is something like Scott's other secret self. Cross-sex identification can be brought about by a variety of circumstances in a person's life. Joplin's father, projected upon Ned in the play, was said to have been an alcoholic.

The young Scott, under the tutorship of Mr. Weiss, found the strength to develop different lines of behavior, identification, and identity. His biological father was no longer a model. In relationship to Mr. Weiss, the young boy was activating a more female aspect of his nature in early adolescence, perhaps even through some earlier identification with his banjo-playing mother; he must have been diligent, intelligent, submissive, the most delightful student one can imagine. Although we cannot directly reconstruct the intricacies of the kind of relationship he had with his tutor, from written or other sources we can infer some likelihoods by psychological insight.

Scott Joplin's work *Treemonisha*, both as a literary and a musical work, is a wellspring of symbolic ideas leading in many directions, personal, autobiographical, and social. This brief analysis can only scratch the surface of the artifacts we have tried to uncover.

Jazz Legends, Facts and Fiction

Cosmopolitan New Orleans

"A city like no other," writes Samuel Charters in his recent book on the history of jazz in New Orleans. For one of his interlocutors, drummer Johnny Vidacovich, talking about his neighborhood in his adolescence, it was "way more than fifty percent immigrants" (Charters 2008: 3). Cosmopolitan aspects of the musical environment were already present by the 1830s, with street criers such as Signor Cornmeal alternating on theatre stages with Italian opera companies from Havana, Cuba (Kmen and Baron 2013). Like in Havana, anything coming up in popular music in Europe was also soon heard in New Orleans. The ethnic diversity of the population was remarkable; many nationalities were present. People lived in often large families within a stratified society, subdivided by language, customs, age groups, and profession. All kinds of music had a chance to find an audience in some place, some home. The range of musical styles spanned those of the French opera house, religious songs in the Catholic Church, a variety of dance and entertainment music, quadrilles, polkas, mazurkas, brass bands, string bands, the shouts of street sellers, and musical activities in the African American communities. Manifestations of the latter, however, were often deliberately ignored and were underrepresented in the media. This contrasts with some places in Latin America, for example, Rio de Janeiro, from where—thanks to visiting painters—abundant pictorial and written material about music played by Africans in the streets and markets is available from the nineteenth century (Kubik 1979 [2013]).

Sheet music was the principal source of private leisure-time musical practice in wealthy families and also in public spaces. A piano was standing in nearly all the better situated homes and in public establishments, with music flowing out of windows into the streets. In spite of the availability of some ragtime piano rolls and cylinder recordings, New Orleans after the turn of the century was still within an era prior to "canned music," as the leader of the most prominent ensemble in the City, John Robichaux, later denounced gramophone records (Charters 2008: 55).

And yet "canned music" was plentiful in the 1890s. Louisiana Phonograph Company marketed cylinders with George Paoletti and Luis "Bebe" Vasnier beginning in 1891, and they were regularly consumed by nickel coin-slot machines at drug stores on Canal Street. These products were popular with audiences across the social strata and for many were a good cure for "the blues" (Brooks 2004). One of the cylinders recorded around 1900 may have contained a performance by Buddy Bolden.

Among the many aspects of live music, from small groups at private parties such as string bands, and the mostly undocumented adolescent spasm bands, street sellers' announcements, etc., marching bands—originally introduced by German musicians—had become a prominent part of funeral ceremonies in Creole-speaking communities. Besides Germans such as Jaeger and Bothe, Italian brass bands such as Joseph Paoletti's were active in New Orleans from the 1870s. Many different styles, covering a wide range of repertoires, were present in the parades.

By the end of the nineteenth century, as stated by pianist Jelly Roll Morton, "New Orleans was the stomping ground for all the greatest pianists in the country. We had Spanish, we had colored, we had white, we had Frenchmens, we had Americans, we had them from all parts of the world, because there were more jobs for pianists than any other ten places in the world. The sporting-houses needed professors, and we had so many different styles that whenever you came to New Orleans, it wouldn't make any difference that you just came from Paris or any part of England, Europe, or any place—whatever your tunes were over there, we played them in New Orleans" (Lomax 1952 [1959: 47]).

Lawrence Gushee (1994 [2002]), in his seminal paper "The Nineteenth-century Origins of Jazz," focuses among other things on the question of formal education, e.g., reading skills among musicians. Examining the 1870 census of the city, he discovered there were 222 individuals registered as musicians or teachers of music. Of those, 80 percent were foreigners: 44 percent were Germans, Austrians, or of Swiss nationality; 15 percent were French, and 10 percent Italian. But ten years later the picture had changed. In 1880 only 45 percent were still foreigners. The remainder was mostly from New Orleans, and about fifty to sixty persons among the music teachers were "Negro." By 1910 the share of African Americans doubled; they were now 30 percent of the music teachers (156–57). This may be in part a reflection of the "racial" reclassification with Creoles by then included in the "Negro" category, in contrast to 1880.

Elsewhere, Gushee (2002) quotes a correspondent to *Metronome* magazine, December 1888: 14, saying "We have some twenty to twenty-five bands averaging twelve men apiece. The colored race monopolize the procession music to a great extent ..." (157). New Orleans composer W. T. Francis is quoted as having compared (in 1889 while in New York City) the musical landscapes of Boston and

New Orleans. He said about Boston that "everything runs to classical music . . ."; but about New Orleans he said: "The most popular music is that which is marked by melody. As a result, every new song and dance which appears in Paris, Madrid, Florence, Vienna, or Berlin appears in [New Orleans] anywhere from six months to two years before it is heard in [Boston] . . ." (Gushee 2002: 161).

However, Gushee (1994 [2002]) also stresses that there is much work still to be carried out on musical developments in New Orleans, especially after 1841, to expand the time period covered by an earlier work, Henry A. Kmen's (1966): *Music in New Orleans: The Formative Years, 1791–1841.*

In the nineteenth century, immigration was a dominant factor in molding and remolding the cultural mix. From the 1840s to the 1850s a flood of immigrants from Germany and Ireland invaded New Orleans. They had left their home countries due to political or economic hardship.

In the 1870s and thereafter came a large influx of people from Italy, particularly Sicily, with all their social and cultural baggage, from south Italian musical traditions to gang organization, mafia-style. Northern Italians from Lombardia, Piemonte, Liguria, and the Veneto, preceded the Sicilian diaspora and also became important in shaping the panorama of New Orleans music and pedagogy (Raeburn 2009b). Barbers, tailors, musicians, cigarmakers, porters, laborers, etc., were common professions among many first- or second-generation immigrants of various ethnic background. Many Germans were photographers, perhaps even the one who made the only known photograph of Buddy Bolden in the 1890s.

By 1900 the population of New Orleans had risen to approximately 278,000. The oldest coherent ethnic group established in New Orleans since the days of French rule was referred to as "free people of color," a term adapted as a translation from the French expression "les gens de couleur libres." The Creole population also included Afro-Italians such as Ernie Cagnolatti and Afro-Sicilians such as Manuel Manetta (Raeburn 2009b). In Latin America populations of comparable genealogical background would be called mulatto. In the francophone Caribbean that included Louisiana, however, intermarriage had taken place between African and French population elements. The creoles began to speak a form of French somewhat comparable to that spoken in Haiti (see also Henry Louis Gates 2011, documentary video from Port au Prince after the earthquake), with elements in grammar and vocabulary from African and other languages.

Gwendolyn Midlo Hall (1992: 194) has pointed out that Louisiana Creole and its folklore was also a means of communication among "whites" in Louisiana who learned songs and the language from their nurses. Like any other term, "Creole" developed a variety of meanings over time. Hall (2001: 81) gives this definition: "The word simply meant people born in the Americas whose parents or more remote ancestors were Africans. This was the normal usage of the word Creole everywhere in the Americas through the eighteenth century." Culturally and in outlook, the Creoles became a distinctive, even distinguished element in the New Orleans social hierarchy, responsible for most of the upper-class musical life in the city. On Sundays public gardens would be flooded by families of the Vieux Carré and the Tremé, and almost every night there were balls. The topographical center of Creole culture was not, however, the so-called French Quarter, now a tourist destination with remnants of the former architecture still visible. It was the so-called Seventh Ward (including Faubourg Marigny), known as the "Creole Ward" with significant concentrations in nearby Tremé and in Algiers on the West Bank. Lower French Quarter in the late nineteenth and early twentieth centuries had some Creoles, but many more Latinos and Sicilians, with a strip of African Americans along Burgundy Street, adjacent to Tremé. The neighborhoods inhabited by the Creoles were summarized as Downtown, i.e., downstream from Canal. Jazz researchers later created the idea of a specific Downtown musical culture, i.e., Creole culture, in contrast to an Uptown musical culture carried by "blacks." This has turned out to be a somewhat simplistic model in the study of New Orleans cultural dynamics. More recent research emphasizes a nuanced presentation of ethnicity, working out contrasts in terms of personalities, individuals' educational background, and views on music and lifestyle.

And yet, identifying with European, notably French culture, many Creoles initially rejected cultural expressions associated with African Americans, including music. Until the mid-twentieth century, racist attitudes were very common in all of New Orleans' segmented communities, and particularly obvious, for example, in the choice of members for musical groups. They sometimes implicitly remained segregated. The Creole community had long become a significant carrier of many aspects of contemporaneous European musical cultures, with opera a major specialty. In the nineteenth century, opera productions rose to be considered the best in the United States. The French Opera House on Bourbon Street was a cherished, almost sacred cultural institution, defining Creole identity. Another distinctive self-identifier of the group was Catholicism, including fringe cases of a merger between Catholic and *vodu* elements inherited from grandparents who had come to New Orleans from Haiti and other parts of the French-speaking Caribbean after the Haitian revolution.

At the end of the Civil War there was a notable influx of newly liberated families from plantations along the Mississippi seeking their fortunes in town. They were now free to move anywhere. Thousands came to New Orleans in search of opportunities but also for reasons of protection in the big city, because the countryside had become unsafe for ex-slaves. After losing the Civil War, hard-core Southerners organized themselves into groups of vigilantes under fanciful names to establish their own "law and order." They roamed the countryside, threatening and harassing African Americans. Only towns could provide security and protection.

The New Orleans administration responded to the challenge of the massive influx by creating new city districts. The areas where most of the people from the plantations then settled were west and north of Canal Street, in what became known as Uptown. The houses that were built were cheap and were called in popular jargon "shotgun" houses, because it was said that one could fire a gun in the front door and the pellets would fly out the back door across the narrow corridor.

An incisive change in the social situation of New Orleans, however, came in 1894, when a new social division was imposed by law, on top of the existing customary divisions and animosities between, for example, the French- and English-speaking populations facing each other across Canal Street, each keeping to its side. The original freedom obtained by African Americans in New Orleans and elsewhere after the Civil War was already eroded in 1890 with the establishment of a "separate car law," segregation in railroad transportation. This was the beginning of the country's descent into an apartheid state that would last for sixty years. In 1894 two segments of the New Orleans population, the "black" and Creole sectors, ended up being lumped together and reclassified as "Negro." This was most traumatizing for the Creole-speaking community, whose attitudes were no less ethnicist than those of other population groups in New Orleans. But precisely because they claimed a birthright to a superior status in the social hierarchy, re-classification gravely hurt their self-esteem. They tried—in vain—to fight back against the new law, which was advertised under the motto "separate but equal," with the lawsuit that led to the Supreme Court decision in *Plessy v. Ferguson*. The United States had been turned into a segregated nation. Cultural cosmopolitanism received a serious blow.

The so-called Black Code of 1894, however, was also a crucial moment for stimulating new artistic encounters, eventually leading to a merger of a variety of "black" and "Creole" traditions, ragtime, blues, brass band marches, "legitimate" dance-hall music played from notation, etc., into something new that was increasingly dominated in style and approach by rebellious Uptown creativity, unconcerned with the values of "polite" society (i.e., music to be understood as something only played from notation). Younger Creoles, growing up after 1894, such as pianist and singer Jelly Roll Morton (ca. 1885–1941),* Sidney Bechet, Achille Baquet, and Freddy Keppard found consolation in reconstituted identities as jazz musicians. They had no choice but to accept the new divisions in their social surroundings. Jelly Roll, the "Winin' Boy," was the teenage darling of fair-skinned girls in the entertainment centers of Storyville, as the red-light district came to be called. Successful Uptown bands like Buddy Bolden's began to trigger a change in musical taste within the broader population.

---

* On Morton's year of birth, see further on in this chapter.

Fig. 6.1. Jelly Roll Morton, ca. 1926. Courtesy of William Russell Collection, Hogan Jazz Archive, Tulane University.

Like nearly everyone in the New Orleans Creole community, pianist Jelly Roll Morton emphasized his French ancestry, and never accepted the "racial" categorizations established by the authorities in 1894, by which even one line of genealogy leading to somewhere in Africa would suffice to categorize that person as "Negro." By contrast, a "white" person might have ancestral lines going back to the Huns who invaded Europe around 360 AD or to Genghis Khan, if that could have been proved in pre-DNA-analysis days, but it would not matter.

Jews were also discriminated against and, for example, excluded from certain educational facilities (Raeburn 2009b). It was the beginning of a peculiar system that has haunted North America. Even in the late twentieth century visitors to the United States would still be required to fill an entry form declaring whether they were "White," "Black," "Hispanic," "Native American," etc.

Six years after 1894, Jelly Roll Morton penetrated the forbidden Storyville entertainment district as a teenage bordello pianist. The system of ethnicity within which he had grown up was still based on the fictitious triangle "White," "Creole," and "Negro," in that order of political power. When it was discarded to give rise to a binary, oppositional system, Jelly Roll would become increasingly ambivalent. Where did he belong? He first tried to use the new divisions to his advantage. Later, during the years of Depression after 1929—in a personal mid-life crisis—he would try to come to terms with the inherited ethnicism among Creoles about which he had feelings of guilt and had also developed a paranoiac idea that he was persecuted by evil magic.

Deeply split as a personality, Jelly Roll must be credited with having been one of the first to try a transcultural approach. He defended the rights of composers and originators of specific tunes on the basis of individual merit, not "race." An example is his fierce attack on sheet music composers who used "folk" or other "floating" materials for their own benefit. He particularly named W. C. Handy, but also the composers in 1904 of "St. Louis Tickle," whose names he did not remember, but who he said had stolen Buddy Bolden's composition "Buddy Bolden's Blues," to include it as one strain in their product. Thereby Morton gave expression to his conviction that both "blacks" and "whites" were borrowing from original composers, including the idols of his youth, Tony Jackson, Buddy Bolden, etc. Of course, he himself also drew from "folk" sources; sometimes he acknowledged it, but sometimes he forgot where he had occasionally picked up a melody.

At mature age Jelly Roll Morton demonstrated a sense of identification with peers beyond the confines of Creole culture and its purported values. Earlier he had learned and assimilated much from the emerging Uptown cultural expressions, without plagiarizing, and created a piano style that—beyond ragtime's rigidity—would embrace accents and phrasings later summarized as "jazz."

Another early jazzman rediscovered in the 1940s, Bunk Johnson (1879–1949)[*] crossed the social barriers from the other side. He deeply identified with the values of Creole musical culture and education across the invisible lines of separation affecting him as a "black" person. Musicians such as those around clarinetist George Lewis, trombone player Jim Robinson, trumpet player Kid Howard, etc., were obviously viewed by him as uneducated and backward, quite in opposition to how his fans, mostly young people in Europe, viewed these musicians.

---

[*] On the queries about Bunk Johnson's year of birth, see two sections further on.

Fig. 6.2. Bunk Johnson and George Lewis in concert, January 1, 1946, Town Hall, New York. Courtesy of Hogan Jazz Archive, Tulane University.

Fig. 6.3. Bunk Johnson, 638 Franklin Street, New Iberia, Louisiana, May 1945. Courtesy of Hogan Jazz Archive, Tulane University.

Eventually, he dissociated himself and began to seek other partners, e.g., pianist Don Ewell (cf. LP *Bunk Johnson and Don Ewell with Doc Evans & His Band*, recorded in Minneapolis, May 3, 1947), and in New York musicians within the stylistic fold of contemporaneous swing, because they were able to read music, follow his instructions, and play pieces taken from his cherished Red Back Book of Rags.

The conflicts between Bunk Johnson and his New Orleans sidemen, especially 1945–46 at the Stuyvesant Casino in New York, have been the subject of persistent commentary. As Bunk "kept trying material that was unfamiliar to the others" (Hillman 1988: 91), his musical predilections were increasingly ignored by them. The result was a quagmire of strained relationships. It is a matter of debate, however, whether this resulted from Bunk's need for demonstrating authority, or should rather be explained as cultural differences between those involved.

Blues Comes to Town

The word *blues* to describe a state of mind has been used by African Americans at least since the 1860s, according to Paul Oliver (Grove DJ 2002: 247), but to describe a musical genre, it came up only after the practices of ballad singing and field hollers from the plantations had somehow converged.

History of the blues as a tradition from rural areas of the Deep South is in a sense separate from jazz history. During the 1890s blues was around as a "folk" tradition—whatever names may have been used—and heard along country roads from itinerant musicians and sung to the guitar or to the accompaniment of homemade stringed instruments. The strange tonality of the blues impressed many people on the vaudeville circuit and also in urban centers. They began to adopt some of the wailing tonality in their own singing and musical practice. Early blues singers were active in minstrel shows and circuses (Abbott and Seroff 2002, 2007).

Blues, as a literary/musical genre, is characterized by specific formulaic, literary, tonal-harmonic, and expressive qualities. Several strophic subtypes were already current by the 1890s, as confirmed by contemporaries, notably Willie Cornish, Kid Ory, and others. They included the songs "Make Me a Pallet on the Floor," "The 219 Took My Babe Away" (later adapted by Jelly Roll Morton as "Mamie's Blues"), and "Carless Love Blues," all of which were in the repertoire of the Buddy Bolden band and possibly that of a predecessor, Charlie Galloway (cf. Vic Hobson 2014: 74–78, for analysis and transcriptions).

There has been some debate, however, about when and in which contexts the twelve-bar form became current, and when exactly it came to New Orleans. Since it seems to have first appeared in print only in 1912 (W. C. Handy's "Memphis

Blues"), it was argued that twelve-bar blues with its associated harmonic structure was of "urban" and "professional" origin, i.e., developed by established composers.

Jelly Roll Morton disputed this idea in 1938. My research in West Africa does not support any such assessment, either. The argument itself is weak methodologically, since it is based on a silent assumption, namely that a publication date reflects the described materials' first appearance. This would relegate all inventions, if unreported, to nonexistence. Sherrie Tucker has raised a similar point about non-recorded women's activities in early jazz.

We have good reason to assume that post–Civil War African American itinerant musicians, responding to the challenge of the new "freedoms," were key actors in creating experimental new song structures, performance techniques, and stylistic trends. But this immense upswing in creativity remained unacknowledged in its details by the media, and—if at all—was reported as a "curiosity" or in a condescending manner, a fate these innovators have shared with, for example, present-day adolescent musicians in southeast Africa who roam the countryside with homemade banjos and guitars (Malamusi 2011, 2015).

As to the twelve-bar blues form, it first needs a more precise definition, beyond its usual description as AAB or as a sequence of chord changes. There are structural variants of the twelve-bar form, often used consecutively in a song (cf. Mississippi Mathilda, "Hard working woman," CD accompanying Kubik 1999a [2007]). The most frequently encountered form can be understood as a framework for song text development in three-line stanzas, each line with an instrumental response, e.g., on guitar. The three lines are structured as STATEMENT, REPEATED STATEMENT, and CONCLUSION. Each statement and most often also the conclusion is bipartite in text construction, with two connected ideas or images, e.g., "it rained five days / and the sky turned dark as night." The first idea also gets a separate, short instrumental response.

1	STATE	/ MENT	RESPONSE
	repeated		
2	STATE	/ MENT	RESPONSE
3	CONCLU	/ SION	RESPONSE

This form is not unknown in West Africa. In my book *Africa and the Blues* (1999a: 42–45), I give an example with full transcription of an *àlọ* story-song I had come across in Oshogbo, Nigeria, in August 1960. Here I should emphasize that I was not specifically on a trip in search of the "roots" of blues. The discovery was by chance. In structure and layout, the song text demonstrates identity with the schema described above. This is the first stanza:

1 Wẹ ná o / wẹ ná baba ol'ódò!	Tere natere
STATEMENT	RESPONSE
2 Wẹ ná o / wẹ ná baba ol'ódò!	Tere natere
REPEATED STATEMENT	RESPONSE
3 Erù òb'ọmọ Ládẹjọ Awẹlé Oniterena	Tere natere
CONCLUSION	RESPONSE

But how would a form structure like this get filled in with Western-style chords? This process that took place in the United States can also be tentatively reconstructed. A key to understanding the American twelve-bar blues form is to realize that the original singer/poet and (probably) guitarist who had the idea of using a chord change at the moment of his REPEATED STATEMENT thought of this as a device for giving emphasis to the textline, in order to re-attract the listeners' attention. So he would change the "floodlight" underneath, i.e., move the tonal level of his accompaniment, the bourdon-centered and partials-based blues column, c, e-386, g-702, b♭-969, a fifth down (or fourth up), transposing it while retaining the melodic ductus of the song's textline. We can infer that he did not conceptualize this change in terms of a progression from "tonic" to "subdominant" in the Western sense. That is the crux of the matter.

For the third line, the CONCLUSION, no special emphasis would be needed, because the different text is self-asserting. So the instrumental commentary on the third line of the twelve-bar form (measures 8 and 9) can even be just one note, g-702, or—if a dominant chord is used in the accompaniment–the voice line ignores it and continues with its blues tonality.

There is no blues-inherent concept of a dominant chord with a leading note. This absence has historical roots. West African savannah pentatonicism does not accommodate the idea of tonal shifts between three fundamentals. Shifting tonality is between two steps, most often a second apart, as demonstrated by Amadou and Mariam, the blind couple from Bamako, Mali, in their song "Mon amour, ma chérie" (CD *Mali to Memphis*, PUTU 145-2, 1999). In the United States the I-IV shift soon took over under the influence of guitar fingering patterns.

This short structural analysis should suffice to explain that, on cultural-psychological and historical grounds, the twelve-bar blues form could not have been invented by a "professional" composer with a background in late nineteenth-century European music.

When blues melodies were transferred to instruments with standard tuning, such as pianos, a musical problem to be solved was how to accommodate a tonal system incorporating notes not represented in the Western scale (i.e., the so-called blue notes). This problem presented itself practically, not in terms of theoretical concepts, because nobody would have postulated at the time that field hollers and intervals intonated in blues-like singing represented a different, non-Western tonal system. To represent those intervals and melisma on instruments, several solutions were found to be practical, e.g., "worrying" or bending a note on the guitar or striking adjacent notes on the piano, but not quite simultaneously (Oliver 2002: 247), to create the auditory illusion of a note fluctuating somewhere between the two.

The blues tradition, being originally rural, plantation-bound, and confined to homesteads and the roadside, had no parallel in cities like New Orleans. Paul Oliver (2002: 247–54) mentions that some Uptown musicians in New Orleans who were born on plantations had absorbed a direct blues influence in their youth before migrating to town. No doubt Uptown musicians were protagonists in the conversion of ragtime dance bands into groups playing as if improvising, with subtle accentuations, off-beat phrasing of melodic accents (cf. Waterman 1952), etc. Soon their music would display a "feel" different from that experienced by anyone playing from notation. The avant-garde incorporated cornet players, such as Buddy Bolden, Chris Kelly, and others who were all known to have played blues, though not only, and preferably so at dances after midnight when the presentable folks had left. Bunk Johnson, who was one of the youngest to be in contact with the original fold, learned to pile up a large repertoire of twelve-bar blues. Traveling a lot with circuses during the first decade of the twentieth century, he was not much seen, however, in New Orleans until he became part of the Superior Orchestra around 1906, together with Peter Bocage, Big Eye Louis Nelson, and others photographed on one occasion.

As to the confluence in New Orleans of various traditions from rural areas and small towns, Paul Oliver (2002: 248) mentions that "pianists who worked in turpentine camps and logging towns in northern Louisiana are known to have visited New Orleans." They must have promoted a variety of male-centered styles. Apparently, Jelly Roll Morton's "Mamie's Blues" reflects yet another early style. He had learned it as a boy from Mamie Desdunes, a female blues pianist residing in New Orleans.

This song, also called "219 Took My Babe Away," was played in Buddy Bolden's band, as is confirmed by his valve trombone player Willie Cornish in the interview conducted by Charles Edward Smith in 1939. Vic Hobson (2014) arrives at the following conclusions:

> "The 219 Took My Babe Away" is an identified twelve-bar blues. . . . It is once again the interview that Charles Edward Smith conducted with Willy Cornish that solves the mystery. Cornish told Smith about the tunes he played with Bolden and said "two tunes you had to know: 'Careless Love Blues' and '219 Took My Babe Away.'" This has profound implications. Jelly Roll Morton performed two versions of this blues (also known as "Mamie's Blues"); the first was for Alan Lomax at the Library of

Congress in 1938. In both recordings he performed a twelve-bar blues with standard AAB stanza lyrics. If Morton's rendition of this blues is as performed by Bolden, then it is clear that not only was the tonality of the blues known to Bolden through tunes such as "Careless Love," but also the twelve-bar form was known to Bolden and his contemporaries. (74)

Blues had come to town. The Mississippi waterway was one avenue for its spread south. With itinerant musicians it was introduced to the streets of New Orleans and soon picked up by local groups. Pianists in the honky-tonks of New Orleans and in other parts of Louisiana were among the earliest. We know the names of some of them who were already famous in New Orleans before the turn of the century. Tony Jackson, for example, picked up on the blues idea. According to contemporaneous testimony, Tony Jackson had a repertoire that included all kinds of popular music, from opera to ragtime to blues. But piano-accompanied blues was his specialty. Jelly Roll cites one text by Tony that clearly has a twelve-bar blues structure (cf. Lomax 1952 [1959]): "I could sit right here and think a thousand miles away. / Yes, I could sit right here and think a thousand miles away. / I got the blues so bad that I cannot remember the day" (53).

One way pianists solved the arising problems of scale, tonality, and phrasing can be demonstrated in piano compositions and adaptations by Jelly Roll Morton. Under the spell of Tony Jackson, he integrated much of the blues tonal experience into his music. "Mamie's Blues" (copyrighted only in 1939 in a transcription by J. Lawrence Cook) is among his 1938 demonstrations for the Library of Congress. "Winin' Boy Blues" and "Buddy Bolden's Blues" (for which he gave Bolden credit as a composer) are two more instructive examples of how blues, as it was articulated in the streets by many unknown rural musicians, was adapted by pianists in the honky-tonks of New Orleans and elsewhere. Blues tonality began to be applied to a variety of strophic, AABA, and other forms beyond the twelve-bar structure.

Jelly Roll Morton's "Winin' Boy Blues," as recorded in 1938 by Alan Lomax (CD of Morton's Library of Congress Recordings, Rounder Records), gives an idea of how blues tonality had become part of piano playing and solo singing as heard in the honky-tonks and brothels of Storyville. With itinerant musicians from Mississippi and Louisiana, blues had increasingly risen to the consciousness of New Orleans musicians as a tonality alternative to that of the opera house music, quadrilles, polkas, waltzes, and marches. Even when blues was accompanied with guitar chords, it tended to circumvent the functional harmony within European heptatonic scales. Not only "black" Uptown musicians adopted blues tonality, e.g., Buddy Bolden on his cornet in the slow dance numbers, but also "Creole" pianists such as Jelly Roll Morton, in a typical phrasing divergent from, and yet strangely in concord with, the underlying chord progressions. I see in

Fig. 6.4.

this integration of blues tonality into the Western tonal system the seed of later harmonic developments, as in the extended and altered chords of modern jazz. The vocal phrase "don't deny my name" in "Winin' Boy Blues" (cf. reissued Alan Lomax recordings CD *Louisiana*, Rounder 82161–1830–2) is like a core idea or premonition of things to come (see Fig. 6.4).

Still a teenager in 1902, Morton got the nickname "Winin' Boy"; and he composed what has since been one of his songs most celebrated among collectors. The name was inspired by an incident involving champagne, in which the young pianist in Hilma Burt's mansion used to pour the "partly finished bottles of wine together and make up a new bottle from the mixture" at closing hours. But the epithet "Winin' Boy" also alludes to "Winding Boy" which was descriptive of a "fellow that makes good jazz with the women" according to guitarist and banjoist Johnny St. Cyr (quoted in Lomax 1952: 51). In this oral testimony we encounter the use of the word *jazz* in the sense of sexual play. David Evans (personal communication, June 2014) adds one more interpretation: "In my opinion the phrase is derived from 'winding ball' (like a ball of yarn), i.e., a rambler. This meaning would be consistent with St. Cyr's."

Not all New Orleans musicians, most certainly not those with a thorough "classical" training, were keen to adopt blues tonality. When Alan Lomax recorded clarinetist Alphonse Picou, born 1879, he noticed that "Picou played a joyous pure-toned Creole clarinet with never a 'dirty tone' or a blue note. Only the phrasing and rhythm reminded one that this was early jazz. As Picou saw it, jazz consisted of additions to the bars—doubling up on notes playing eight or sixteen for one.' This urban New Orleans ragtime, salty with West Indian rhythms, was the inspiration for Morton's best melodies" (Lomax 1952 [1959: 76]). Also, a generation gap must have been at work here. Younger musicians, such as Lorenzo Tio Jr., Sidney Bechet, Freddy Keppard, Johnny St. Cyr, the Baquet brothers, etc., did embrace jazz without compunction. But there are probably more explanations, relating to individual biographies and personal psychology.

By 1902 musical expressions in the bars and entertainment places of the city included what musicians and audiences were identifying as ragtime alongside the common waltzes, mazurkas, quadrilles, polkas, etc. Several oral testimonies paint a vivid picture of the environment of Storyville, the red-light district adjoining Canal Street. In popular talk it was so named because of a 1896 ordinance promulgated by alderman Sidney Story to restrict prostitution to a certain area of the city. Bunk Johnson started to work there in 1897, according to his own narrative. Morton, who was about seventeen in 1902, became acquainted with that milieu as a piano player, in an environment that was defined by many great pianists, the most eminent among them Tony Jackson.

A true novelty for musical practice in New Orleans was the speech-like handling of intonation and melodic phrasing on instruments, a hidden Africa-rooted trait. The practice descended from Uptown. On cornet and other wind instruments, timbre shades and microtonal pitch variations became part of a panel of expressive devices. Therein lay the difference in the handling of a cornet by idiosyncratic artists such as Buddy Bolden and musicians in the Creole tradition Downtown. The Uptown style of handling wind instruments was so contrary to the established aesthetics of playing European musical instruments that it met with resistance. A classically trained violinist would complain that this new style made a "fiddler" out of him, expressing his disgust at "fake music." "Legitimate" musicians would find the new approach that was suddenly gaining a following across New Orleans rough, incoherent, chaotic, unprofessional, whatever contemporaneous vocable was available to express their bewilderment and irritation.

But the inspiration for the new performance style came ultimately from the roustabouts—to use a word that was dear to W. C. Handy—the levee workers, street sellers, spasm bands founded by itinerant adolescents, and blues singers up the Mississippi using melodic patterns of field hollers. Their approach and their system of tonal and timbre-modifying techniques infiltrated New Orleans with the intensifying migration from the countryside. It began to manifest itself in the playing of brass wind instruments that had become affordable to young people. Often with no chance of formal instruction by expensive professional music teachers, these youngsters were left to their own devices. They experimented with sound autodidactically, not taking recourse to notations.

Blues came to town in various expressions and by various routes. Vocal patterns became instrumentalized, blues tonality was transferred to the piano. In New Orleans, I believe, blues was the major catalyst leading to jazz expression. Jazz was not actually a new kind of music but a new expressive form of rendering a variety of musical genres, including brass band tunes and ragtime pieces, whereby the jazzy expression most likely had its important source in rural blues singing and tonality. In dance band performances it was then further developed on wind instruments, notably the cornet. At the same time, the availability and circulation of ragtime sheet music was of unbroken importance during the first decade of the twentieth century in determining the formal basis of early jazz, the prevalence of multi-strain form, all of which was more complex than street ballads, especially also in harmonic progressions.

From 1912 on, Handy's publications contributed to further popularize the blues genre, particularly in the vaudeville and circus milieu, i.e., among singers and instrumentalists who were readers. Important contributions to harmonic refinement and "bluesy" harmony were made.

Musical Transformation: Fakers, Spasm Bands, Blues, and the "Latin Tinge"

"Classical" European functional harmony was the rule in piano ragtime, but in its rhythm composers broke loose from the constraints of uniform metrical accents, by interpolating transient heterometric structures into the melodies, contrasting them with the regular (left-hand) ground beat. That gave ragtime its apparent syncopation. However, they did not invent or originate the trick. The inspiration came from the streets, from banjos, jig piano, and orally transmitted songs and melodic passages by those for whom music was not part of a writing culture. We will never know exactly what these people were playing, because there are no recordings, and even if there were notations they would be unreliable, simplified. In the 1880s, in search of work, African Americans became increasingly mobile and visible on country roads of the South, stimulating greater public awareness of their art. A decade later, sheet music composers would discover its commercial potential.

When in the 1890s blues tonality began to penetrate piano playing in the honky-tonks and other places of entertainment in New Orleans and elsewhere, harmony was also affected. Meanwhile, sheet music composers, encouraged by Antonin Dvořák's statements, were turning to African American "folk" music for inspiration and new material. They sniffed out the new trend and tried to follow it, reinterpreting a strange tonality, as it was later also heard by Ma Rainey from a girl or young woman in front of her circus tent. By the 1890s it could be heard on country roads and along the Mississippi. Luckily this type of tonality was carried on into the 1920s in blues performances and recorded. It contains a characteristic vocal passage involving a so-called third blue note, a wailing tone fluctuating around what to a Western musician sounds like f♯ descending in glissando towards f, in the key of C (see Fig. 6.5). Actually, its pitch value fluctuates

| Start | 3rd bluenote | 2nd bluenote | bourdon basis |

Fig. 6.5. Melodic context of songs involving the third blue note. (For song examples see Titon 1977: 65, 97–99, 118; Kubik 1999a: 146–149, 2008d)

around 551 cents within a glissando frame from 600 down to 500 cents. This gliss tone over a bourdon basis (C) constitutes one toneme, which means individual singers can intonate it a little higher or lower always with a wailing glissando descent—it does not matter; it is not a passage between two tones, but just one pitch area, ca. 600 → 500 cents.

Sheet music composers picked up this characteristic of some blues and reinterpreted it as chromaticism. Ben Harney with "Cake Walk in the Sky," published in 1899 (see also Hobson 2008: 9–10), was perhaps the first who cut out a piece of the cake. The "folk" melodies that seemed to proceed from a fifth to a flatted fifth, and so forth, were novel for Westerners and highly attractive to composers in search of something unusual. Trying to "harmonize" such melodies, the third blue note was reinterpreted as part of a diminished chord, set into various contexts according to the song, for example (in relative notation): $C \rightarrow C^\circ \rightarrow G^7 \rightarrow C$ in the first line of "Cake Walk in the Sky"; or $C \rightarrow C^\circ/G^7 \rightarrow C \rightarrow C^9$ in Jelly Roll Morton's piano accompaniment to the first line of "Buddy Bolden's Blues." Both composers clung to a resolution via a dominant/tonic relationship, while the original blue note's context, if rendered by chords is simply this: $C \rightarrow C^\circ \rightarrow C$.

The source of it all was African American music heard along the roads, levee worksongs, wailing solo blues based on field hollers, and songs at some social gatherings. This background is even indirectly admitted on the sheet music of "The Cake Walk in the Sky" through the text which portrays problems of a "coon," and also in the genre designation of the associated dance: "Ethiopian Two-Step." "Ethiopian" simply stands for African or "black." As little as Harney was the "originator of ragtime," which his agent declared him to be for marketing purposes, as little also was he the originator of melodies like the chromatic descent in "Cake Walk in the Sky." The true originators were poor lads who had never written down anything, and therefore were never rewarded for their music, not even reported. What was reported about African American "folk" music followed the stereotypes of folk anonymity and pentatonic scales as "characteristic" of "Negro" singing. Absence from the media was also the fate of the unknown early ragtime initiators, long before Scott Joplin and others (however ingeniously) adapted some of the patterns heard, transplanting them into the sheet music world. At least, however, Ben Harney deserves credit for "having had his ear to the ground," recognizing and then promoting some of this music, thereby preserving a semblance of it for history.

In New Orleans, Uptown musicians, some with little formal musical training, began to "fake" the popular music of the day. They were reversing a trend, taking musical performance to the realm of oral transmission, but with then modern, industrially made instrumental equipment. That was their key to the success that spasm bands could not have achieved. In the process they were also memorizing sheet music hits besides their own favorites, but playing them with variations and melodic extensions absent from the written scores. On European brass and woodwind instruments new techniques of timbre modification were evolved, abandoning streamlined, uniform timbre. African American musicians in the US South succeeded in accomplishing a transformation that would lead away from "classical" heptatonicism and functional harmonic rules, imposing blues tonality on top of the standardized system. Vocalized intonation would be introduced on brass band instruments, creating what others would call "dirty tone" (cf. Blesh 1949: 20–21). "Legitimate" Downtown musicians at first rejected the new trend. They preferred to stick to time-honored rules.

In rural areas, notably in Mississippi, under the circumstances of plantation life, one cluster of musical traits from a specific West African cultural region, the western Sudanic belt—as it was transmitted mostly in personal music—had had a better rate of survival than others, e.g., those from the Guinea Coast and Central Africa. It included several non-diatonic scalar patterns, speech-tone melodies, use of vocal melisma, and a basis in stringed instruments rather than drums. It seems that it won the selective struggle against other traditions because the latter were also more group-oriented and therefore seriously targeted for suppression by the plantation owners in fear of a slave revolt that could have been organized clandestinely through message drumming. Tonal and scalar concepts from the Sahel and Savannah zones of West Africa had continued unchallenged in field hollers, street advertising of charcoal and other merchandise, lullabies, and many lesser known individual expressions. Chanted sermons and prayers (in contrast to hymnbook songs) were another type of expression preserving these tonal and scalar concepts. Their existence was not impeded by nineteenth-century teaching of church songs, nor by the parallel adoption of European "folk" harmonies in banjo and fiddle music. Different tonal systems often exist side by side in a culture, each limited to certain genres. Another reason for the survival of a Sahel and Savannah West African strand was that perhaps it was best suited to express, by its wailing quality, the states of depression experienced under the impact of slavery. After the Civil War it contributed to articulation of a separate identity by people who had been liberated from slavery, but not emancipated to equal status in the broader society.

African American musicians, of course, pursued many avenues of coming to terms with the new social situation and expressing it in music. Some were still believers in complete acculturation and began to strive for Western-style education. But even this group discovered that there was little reward by the other side for trying a crossover.

In New Orleans four interrelated processes were, it seems, important in the amalgamation of popular music around 1900 leading to what would be called jazz.

(a) "Faking" and "hot" performance

Musicians from Uptown New Orleans who cherished an African-derived approach to music/dance performance began to "fake" ragtime and other set forms, as they were played from notation by "legitimate" bands such as the John Robichaux ensemble. These Uptown musicians played popular tunes from memory, as if it were from notation.

It is important, however, to account for the complexity of individuals' musical backgrounds in New Orleans at the turn of the twentieth century. Not all Uptown musicians were necessarily "fakers." Aspiring jazz performers had a variety of special skills. There were what have been called "readers," "spellers," and "fakers." Spellers could not sight-read notation but could deduct basic chord structures from the written materials and base their variations on them. Educational facilities were varied, and musical education was available even in places like the "Colored Waifs' Home." Most of all, however, there was a lot of private and circumstantial teaching.

Donald M. Marquis (1978) has said that the process of "ragging" or "jazzing" was not so much a quality of improvisation: "It was more a matter of extra touches to the music" (100). Talking about Buddy Bolden, he said that most of his contemporaries attributed his fame "to his ability to fake; if he forgot a passage he would introduce embellishments that his listeners often enjoyed more than the music originally written." In the process, musicians introduced melodic and timbre variations unheard of before. They also made ragtime rhythms more complex, beyond what was suggested in sheet music. They modified instrumental timbre and accent patterns. Soon they discovered that they could play any tune that way, not only ragtime but any popular music including the blues. Now bands of Uptown musicians began to incorporate it into their repertoire. Sheet music ragtime was taken back to its sources, to what it had been in the streets before the appearance of printed versions by established, "professional" composers. Once again in culture history, oral memory reclaimed its share. In interviews with veterans conducted in the mid-twentieth century, there is agreement among New Orleans musicians that ragtime cornetist Buddy Bolden was one of the most innovative and successful persons among the "fake musicians," played the loudest cornet ever heard, and won competitions against bands that played from notation.

According to Jim Robinson (1955: 13, quoted in Gushee 1994 [2002: 152]), jazz was nothing but ragtime played by ear, by "fakers" or "routiniers." This is probably true of bands not only in New Orleans but also in other parts of the country. Johnny St. Cyr, who was fifteen in 1905, mentioned in an interview article "Jazz as I remember it," in *Jazz Journal*, September 6–9, 1966, a band that really played "hot": the Golden Rule Band. Buddy Bolden was not "hot," he said, but had "a little hot lick." Hot musical forms were ragtime and blues-based, played without notation and with unusual instrumental expression. Violin and clarinet were often interchangeable in dance ensembles.

What was new for New Orleans was that African-derived concepts and techniques, as mentioned, began to characterize ragtime playing by Uptown dance bands. In the 1890s they often consisted of this instrumentation: cornet, valve trombone, clarinet in B^b or C, guitar, bowed double bass, and drums. The combination reflected what also was standard Downtown with a violin often included, as in the John Robichaux ensemble. The violinist was usually the leader and a fluent reader of notation. Uptown he could be replaced by a C clarinet player with a similar function who would, if necessary, explain melodies for the other transposing instruments played by musicians with insufficient fluency in reading. Violin and C clarinet were often interchangeable in dance ensembles.

Robichaux played "legitimate" music, always of the most recent sheet music publications, which he obtained from New York publishers. His vast collection of tunes and arrangements is preserved in the Hogan Jazz Archive at Tulane University, New Orleans. Although there was rivalry between Uptown and Downtown dance bands, there are reports that Robichaux occasionally attended performances by his Uptown rival Buddy Bolden. In spite of their competition, the two personalities were not necessarily enemies. In post-*Plessy* New Orleans, rigid social divisions became increasingly blurred within a new generation of young musicians, enabling a high degree of transculturation across the "color line."

Jelly Roll Morton said the following about jazz as compared to ragtime: "Ragtime is a certain type of syncopation and only certain tunes can be played in that idea. But jazz is a style that can be applied to any type of tune. I started using the word in 1902 to show people the difference between jazz and ragtime" (quoted in Lomax 1952 [1959: 64]).

In an impressive piano exercise recorded in 1938, Morton demonstrated how to transform other music into jazz, showing Alan Lomax how he had composed "Tiger Rag" from the strains of an old quadrille, and how he got the idea for the name of the piece.

(b) Blues integration

Popular music around 1900 began to absorb substantial input from blues in the honky-tonks and other locations. Big Eye Louis Nelson has been quoted as saying: "Blues is what caused the fellows to start jazzing" (quoted in Lomax 1952 [1959: 90]).

As I have pointed out earlier in this chapter, blues would have a strong modifying influence on tonal understanding. Among those who readily absorbed blues tonality was Buddy Bolden, and his rendering of blues on the cornet was probably a decisive factor in triggering a breakthrough of the new ways. Later, Bunk Johnson would become heir to Buddy Bolden's blues intonation. Bunk, as contemporaries have compared his style to that of Bolden, is considered to have been softer and more gentle, while Freddie Keppard seems to have continued the other, vigorous side of the Bolden cornet.

With blues came a new individualism in instrumental expression, and it promoted tendencies to stardom. Buddy Bolden became a star and, as it happens, upon his demise the star becomes a legend. Jelly Roll Morton described Buddy Bolden's cornet playing from memory: "Buddy Bolden was the most powerful trumpet in history. I remember we'd be hanging around some corner, wouldn't know that there was going to be a dance out at Lincoln Park. Then we'd hear old Buddy's trumpet coming on and we'd all start. Any time it was a quiet night at Lincoln Park because maybe the affair hadn't been so well publicized, Buddy Bolden would publicize it! He'd turn his big trumpet around toward the city and blow his blues, calling his children home, as he used to say." To be on the safe side of dating, it is important to note that both Johnson Park and neighboring Lincoln Park were opened in 1902. "The whole town would know Buddy Bolden was at the Park, ten or twelve miles from the center of town. . . . They claim he went crazy because he really blew his brains out through the trumpet. Anyhow he died in the crazy house" (Lomax 1952 [1959]: 62).

Musical performance once again transcended mere reproductive craftsmanship and became a creative act in public. This was reviving an idea inherited from both European and African traditions that an important composer may also be a virtuoso, all in one person, and often a "mad genius." The idea became a theme in jazz history. The transformation was in part triggered by one charismatic personality, Buddy Bolden, who in New Orleans after 1900 catapulted himself to stardom because he had developed a new understanding of performance practice, tonality, and instrumental timbre in his music, traits that had their origins mostly in the blues.

(c) The Latin tinge and its effects

One could say that jazz was fusion from its beginnings, an amalgamation of styles, patterns, genres, but selectively so; that is, as much as certain elements were integrated into jazz, others were excluded. Ragtime, brass band instrumentation, popular dances, and blues were the ingredients to form what would be jazz in the first decade of the twentieth century. Some of the musicians interviewed have emphasized a continuity especially from ragtime to jazz, and some have even claimed identity between the two. But one element that came in and made jazz malleable was what Jelly Roll Morton and others have referred to as the "Spanish tinge." Essentially it is nothing particularly Spanish, but denotes certain genres and a general approach to music that became associated in the nineteenth century with people from Spanish-speaking areas of the New World, such as Mexico and in particular Cuba, as well as other parts of the Caribbean.

Here one must take into account that the piano was the most popular instrument in urban areas of the southern United States during the 1890s. Musicians in New Orleans, pianists in particular, but also dance bands, opened up to habanera-based rhythms that had flocked in from Spanish-speaking areas in the Caribbean (cf. Narváez 1994 [2002: 175]). Morton explained in great detail how he had worked it into some of his own compositions, transforming "La Paloma" into the "Ragtime Tango" by changing his right-hand phrasing.

> I heard a lot of Spanish tunes and I tried to play them in correct tempo, but I personally didn't believe they were really perfected in the tempos. Now take La Paloma which I transformed in New Orleans style. You leave the left hand just the same. The difference comes in the right hand—in the syncopation, which gives it an entirely different colour that really changes the colour from red to blue.
>
> Now in one of my earliest tunes, New Orleans Blues, you can notice the Spanish tinge. In fact, if you can't manage to put tinges of Spanish in your tunes, you will never be able to get the right seasoning, I call it, for jazz. This New Orleans Blues comes from around 1902. I wrote it with the help of Frank Richards, a great piano player in the ragtime style. All the city played it at that time. (Morton in Alan Lomax 1952 [1959: 64])

This was probably the third most important factor, in the genesis of a style of performance that would be called jazz. After all, tango as it had emerged in Buenos Aires, Argentina, about the same time, had started a worldwide trip to popularity. In New Orleans habanera-based rhythms were around, including the ubiquitous $3 + 3 + 2$ bassline that had penetrated piano playing in the honky-tonks, elevating some of the music beyond some of the rigid pattern formation in piano-composed ragtime.

As John Storm Roberts (1979) has pointed out, Cuban influences in New Orleans during the nineteenth century mostly came through Mexican intermediaries. In Mexico, the habanera rhythm had been popular since the 1870s. From 1884–85 there was the world's Industrial and Cotton Centennial Exposition in New Orleans to which Mexico had sent the band of the Eighth Regiment of Mexican Cavalry. Many other musicians came. Many musicians in New Orleans had Mexican family relationships. Lorenzo Tio Sr. was Mexican; the wife of Jack "Papa" Laine was Cuban.

Ernest Borneman considered jazz in its early forms to be part of an Afro-Caribbean culture in southern Louisiana. The nineteenth-century so-called

Creole dances, such as counjaille, bamboula, chacta, and juba, had an influence on the rise of jazz, according to Borneman (1969: 103). Jelly Roll Morton's "New Orleans Blues," based on a Creole song, is the most famous example of what came to be called the "Spanish tinge." In Borneman's opinion what preceded New Orleans jazz before 1890 was "Afro-Latin music similar to that of Martinique, Guadeloupe, Trinidad and San Domingo" (104). This music must have incorporated some notion of asymmetric rhythm patterns, while other music popular in late nineteenth-century New Orleans, based on European dance forms such as the mazurka, polka, waltz, etc., and the standard European instrumentation and line-up (perpetuated in early New Orleans jazz ensembles) did not incorporate them. Borneman (1969: 100) postulated that it was precisely during the years when New Orleans jazzmen migrated to Chicago after the closure of Storyville in 1917 that jazz lost its "Spanish tinge" and was reduced to straight 2/4 and 4/4 time. This has met with some criticism, however, because there apparently was no such exodus, with the exception of Johnny Dodds with Mack and Mack, and Dodds was back in New Orleans in early 1918.

Here, one may perhaps add a more relevant factor of influence on developmental directions: that the Original Dixieland Jass Band was the first to appear on gramophone records, gave its version of jazz a lead and model function. After 1917 audiences expected musicians in Chicago to conform with the sort of "improvised" ensemble work, showbiz, and two-beat dance rhythm they had popularized. Once something had become engraved on sound carriers, it was bound to set and propagate a "standard," with audiences exerting pressure on musicians to play and act likewise. The Africa-rooted elements from early New Orleans jazz were relegated to backstage.

After I first met Ernest Borneman at the jazz research conference in Graz, Austria, in 1969, I visited him in Frankfurt in the 1970s and he played me unheard-of 78 r.p.m. records from New Orleans beside some of the better-known titles, such as Albert Nicholas's 1940s recording "Mo 'Pa 'Lemé Ça" in Creole, demonstrating his point. Even as late as that, it showed a surviving style of New Orleans music that had been left aside by the music industry in the 1920s. As Peter Narváez (1994 [2002]) has warned researchers, the music industry following its own selective principles often "neglected the realities of living music in small places" (176). Unfortunately, that is still the case, and it applies even more to sub-Saharan Africa, where fascinating developments are often neglected, if they are unusual, and then killed off by discouragement.

The "Spanish tinge," or "Latin tinge" as John Storm Roberts preferred to call it, was less Spanish or Latin than it was Afro-Caribbean. It had spilled over into New Orleans from the Caribbean, where music had preserved an array of asymmetric patterns from Central Africa and the Guinea coast, determining the structure of melodic lines and also serving as timelines (*clave*, in Cuba).

And yet there was a limit to the adoption of the Spanish tinge in New Orleans. While asymmetries in melodic-rhythmic formation of songs and their variations were present in jazz from its beginnings, and the habanera 3+3+2 bass can be traced not only to Morton's "New Orleans Blues" but also, for example, to the middle part of Handy's "St. Louis Blues" published in 1914, such patterns were not used as timelines. Handy simply incorporated the then-popular tango rhythm. Conversely, the simple eight-pulse pattern did survive as a clapped time-line in some ring shouts recorded in the twentieth century and it may have been present earlier in the striking of "bones" to accompany stringed instrument per-formances. Handy had heard what probably was son in Cuba during a visit. Even Scott Joplin experimented with "Latin" elements, in "Solace" published in 1909. And "Panama" by W. H. Tyers, published in 1911, had a habanera bass in the original piano version. But none of these composers proceeded from the idea of "clave."

Recent work on Latin tinge includes Charles Hiroshi Garrett's analysis of Jelly Roll Morton's recordings in Bruce Raeburn's "Beyond the Spanish Tinge" (2012b).

(d) The "second line" phenomenon and the spasm bands

A fourth factor in jazz genesis in New Orleans could be summarized as the innovative impact of adolescents' street culture. It can be split into two separate phenomena: (1) the "second line" of kids marching with brass bands, (2) the so-called spasm bands.

In New Orleans during street parades by brass bands, a second line, mostly by children, was often forming at the sidewalk, young boys marching or rather danc-ing along (see picture in Blesh, *Shining Trumpets* [1949]). Later, some of these kids grew up to become musicians themselves, but not merely faithful new-gen-eration brass band performers. They would also take to the latest fads, which by the 1890s would be cakewalks and eventually rags. This is how, in instrumenta-tion and form, many elements of an already strongly Africanized brass band style slipped into the emerging jazz culture, including rearranged marches, such as Bunk Johnson's 1942 demonstration of "Moose March," recorded at Grunewald's Music Store, New Orleans, June 11, 1942 (Bunk, tp; George Lewis, cl; Jim Robin-son, tb; Walter Decou, p; Lawrence Marrero, bj; Austin Young, bs; Ernest Rog-ers, dr.). This recording is, in my opinion, representative of the sound of brass band jazz in New Orleans before World War I. A more focused attempt at recon-struction was initiated by Bill Russell in 1945, recording a brass band organized by Bunk with Kid Shots Madison on second trumpet, omitting the saxophones.

Brass band music became more relaxed in the early 1900s in the new perfor-mance style of those grown-up "second line" kids who had dual allegiances: to jazz and to brass band music. Many of them played in both kinds of groups. Brass band music had become dance-like and full of improvisatory variations (cf. later recordings by the Eureka Brassband, etc.). Paul Barbarin stated in an interview that Onward Brass Band began shifting toward a looser, jazz-like configuration and repertoire ca. 1904, when Manuel Perez became leader (Goffin 1946). About the same time, i.e., around turn of the twentieth century, a similar kind of "easing up" development took place independently in brass band styles on the Guinea coast (see ch. 2 in *Jazz Transatlantic II*).

The difference that can be noted between nineteenth-century European brass band music, played from scores, and the ways both African American musicians in New Orleans and African musicians along the Guinea coast had begun to transform it, came about in several successive stages of change. In New Orleans one important factor was that musicians had already started to be "fakers" while employed in brass bands, i.e., they did not always play from the notations that were in front of them, but had memorized their instrumental parts and begun to modify them with occasional fill-ins. In doing so they inadvertently took recourse to aesthetics inherited from Africa, including variation techniques and syntactic principles as described for example by Thomas Brothers's (1994) analysis of Louis Armstrong's 1920s jazz. Such knowledge was still around by the end of the nineteenth century, a hidden legacy from Congo Square and other sources for the young Louis Armstrong, born in 1900, to assimilate. They began to shift melodic phrases rhythmically by minimal values, a bit off-beat, anticipating or retarding them in relation to the meter, and introducing melodic variations to the themes. Brothers has since published two highly recommendable books on Louis Armstrong, his cultural background, relationship with his mentor Joe Oliver, and how he became one of the most influential jazz musicians of the twentieth century (Brothers 2006, 2014).

This underlines the essentiality of the New Orleans cultural background to jazz. In later forms of jazz, i.e., after 1917, in Chicago and New York and most radically in Kansas City, the marching music element disappeared, as did most of the nineteenth-century multi-strain forms associated with march and ragtime.

The other phenomenon, the adolescent itinerant street musicians, was probably a key factor in the eventual victory of "faking" over "legitimate" performance, i.e., reading from scores. Why? Although there is little documentary material about those tightly knit itinerant street bands in Louisiana, usually kids or adolescents with homemade instruments, we can infer a few things from our knowledge of a parallel phenomenon in some parts of Africa even today. In the jazz literature these adolescent groups are usually mentioned under the term *spasm bands*. In an interview Donald M. Marquis (1978) conducted with Ernest "Punch" Miller on April 17, 1962, a musician named Louis Ned was mentioned. He was said to have played cornet in the days before Buddy Bolden's career in

New Orleans, which would mean before the late 1890s. Marquis writes this about Louis Ned: "As far as can be determined, he grew up in New Orleans and played with some of the kid 'Spasm' bands before Bolden's time, but he later moved to Baton Rouge" (85–86).

The implications are that some of these kids eventually became professional musicians with access to instruments such as cornets, clarinets, double bass, etc. This is a scenario that reminds those of us based in southern Africa of a phenomenon we are familiar with. In southeast Africa, for example, a present-day analogy to the New Orleans' kid spasm bands is adolescents with homemade banjos and mobile percussion devices who often walk long distances to earn money at markets, street corners, bus stations, etc. These kids often display incredible technological creativity (cf. Malamusi 2011). Here, as in late nineteenth-century New Orleans, those street youngsters play without any notational device. And also as in Louisiana, there is a constant supply of adolescents from poor families, rural and urban, keen to engage in this age group–related activity. In Louisiana many of these kids eventually migrated to town, and, as adults took up residence Uptown in New Orleans. If, later in life, the person takes up formal music as a profession, the experience of music making in a spasm band inevitably affects his approach. In many a young man who later took some formal musical training, the earlier experience was not wiped out.

Earlier membership in spasm bands was therefore a likely factor that facilitated "fake" musicians' self-liberation from the constraints of European-style classical musical practice and the reinvention in Louisiana of an African approach to music making. From the moment musical instruments are played without the player's eyes fixed on a sheet of paper called "music," a margin of experimentation opens up. It modifies one's kinetic approach to music making. Also, in the spasm bands various Africa-derived techniques of percussion had probably survived, which eventually transmuted into specifics of jazz drumming, and instrumental techniques that were later transferred to or recreated on cornets, guitars, string bass, etc. As concerns jazz history, therefore, the spasm bands in the late nineteenth century can be regarded as an artistic avant-garde and as a pool of surviving African concepts, instrumental techniques, and movement patterns.

Primacy of the Written?

There are areas of jazz research in which the question of written versus oral sources comes up: in the assessment of musicians' personal biographies, in the reconstruction of a chronology of events, in copyright problems, in identifying the originator of a song, or genre, or instrumental technique, etc. If we encounter conflicting information, one oral (eyewitness accounts, autobiographical narratives), the other written (newspaper reports, certificates, notation, etc.), which one are we going to give more credibility? Can there be anything like unequivocal written proof or, conversely, written invalidation of an orally transmitted statement? Is the absence of a written account about a matter or an event sufficient proof that it did not exist or happen?

Jazz historians sometimes proceed implicitly from the assumption of a primacy of written documents over oral testimony. Unless a written document is the obvious result of forgery, it is taken for granted that a real event is encapsulated in the written record, in contrast to the weak memories of people.

However, the relevance of oral narratives, oral tradition, and oral history, as some prefer to call it, as a source of information, has long been recognized in folklore studies and cultural anthropology. In communities without written records, oral tradition may be the only window into the past. A standard methodology of handling oral tradition was published in 1965 by Jan Vansina on the basis of his work in Rwanda. His book *Oral Tradition* has been required reading in many anthropology classes. Ethnohistorians on their part have emphasized source criticism especially with regard to written accounts from the colonial era, as to content, authorship, circumstances of data gathering, idiocultural bias, etc.

In highly stratified societies with class differences, institutionalized or habitual, implicit segregation, and unequal access to educational facilities, the lower class may have few channels to articulate its concerns. In such societies we get parallel strands of information, one that is written (by those in power, issuing certificates, declarations, news, often based on self-interest), the other predominantly oral (expressing its concerns in jokes, anecdotes, folktales, legends, rumors, etc.).

There is good reason to assume that post–Civil War society in the southern United States, from the late nineteenth into the first decade of the twentieth centuries, was very much of that kind. The first strand manifested itself in an abundance of printed information, newspapers, documents, certificates, posters, photographs, sheet music, etc. In two books, *Out of Sight* (2002) and *Ragged but Right* (2007), besides numerous articles in scientific journals, the research team Lynn Abbott and Doug Seroff have meticulously explored late nineteenth to early twentieth-century written records relating to African American popular music, traveling shows, sheet music publications etc. Although the books draw on "black" newspapers, etc., the latter represented and reported especially on the urban literate class within the community and its concerns. This is indeed the cream on top of the bulk, but underneath there is more "out of sight": a second strand, i.e., what the dominating society did not consider worthwhile to report, or did not even have access to. This strand gets expression in oral narratives and, most eloquently, in orally transmitted musical structures. Unless as it happened, established composers surveyed that knowledge, this stratum remains largely unaccounted for until much later in history, when trained researchers, equipped with tape recorders, begin to record in situ. If Henry Edward Krehbiel (1914), in his assessment of "racial and national music," reports no instance of melodic use of a flatted fifth in "Afro-American Folksong," it does not mean that the tonality incorporating it was absent. It simply means that data gathering was limited to certain events, places, people, and performance contexts. It may also reflect bias. Krehbiel's sample turns out to be overwhelmingly diatonic or pentatonic. Blues recordings made soon thereafter, in the 1920s, give a more complex picture of various tonalities (cf. Titon 1977). Before the advent of field recording, very little of the second strand of information made it to general awareness, unless in an edited, heavily reinterpreted form.

In the era after World War I, with the advent of the gramophone, radio broadcasting, and eventually tape recording, this second strand eventually got a chance to articulate itself. The importance of sheet music as a medium receded. But even then, the factors of selection and reinterpretation in the data-gathering process were hardly eliminated. *Selection* is inherently present, as record companies choose whom or what to record, or prescribe a certain instrumentation or repertoire to be put on disc. In the case of interviews, the selective factor is in the choice of interlocutors, the exclusion of others, the willingness of people to talk to the interviewer (some refuse and drop out), the kinds of questions posed, etc. *Reinterpretation* abounds if interviewers, who may be alien to the culture of those to whom they give questions, use categories that are unfamiliar locally (e.g., "What functions does your music have within your community?"), and through leading questions (e.g., "Are you a professional musician, semi-professional, or an amateur?"). Formulations can seriously affect the information elicited, unless the interviewers have become alert to the problem in anthropological field research courses. Interlocutors also assess the interviewers' interests and capacity of understanding and modify or withhold information accordingly.

For our purposes, it is important to recognize the duality of the written and oral strands, as two supplementing, though often conflicting, sources of information, and to realize that information obtained either way does not cancel the other one out. Both strands are subject to error, falsification, neglect, and cross-influences—the oral may influence what is written, the written may reflect back on the oral. To balance it in specific cases is what makes research so hard. Did my interlocutor perhaps read something about the events she describes as from personal memory? The question is justified, but I cannot assume that she did and present my conclusion as a fact.

Late nineteenth-century society in the southern United States was impregnated with a legacy of colonial structures. The training of officials responsible for written records was often haphazard, their enthusiasm bound to be dim if the temperature was above 90 degrees Fahrenheit. In such a society, a relatively reliable source of information on someone's life, including age and place of birth, is family traditions, rather than official documents. This is so because the family is the strongest cohesive social unit, the least likely to abandon its sense of solidarity with relatives or its strong feelings of group identity. To know about its members' genealogy, place, and date of birth serves as an identifying reminder.

For this reason, when Jelly Roll Morton in his talks with researcher Alan Lomax in 1938 said that he was born 1885 or 1886, it has the ring of authenticity even though he was evicted from home as a youngster. It also conforms with the chronology of his travels, his musical engagements, and his other statements, e.g., that he was "about seventeen" in 1902. That he once wrote into his insurance policy that he was born in 1888 cannot be taken as evidence to the contrary, since we do not know the background of the error or for what reason it happened. Nor is Lawrence Gushee's discovery of a baptism certificate, issued many years after his birth, which states that he was born October 20, 1890 (cf. Gushee 1981, 1985), sufficient evidence for a revision of Morton's oral estimate of his year of birth. In the absence of a birth certificate, baptism and also marriage certificates are only ancillary documents, in fact secondary sources with regard to birthdates and places, and they are prone to error.

An illustration of the difficulties encountered by jazz historians in search of reliable chronologies is Donald M. Marquis's (1978) admirable endeavor to unravel the life history of the legendary man of early jazz, Buddy Bolden. In one document unearthed by Marquis (15), the birthplace of Westmore Bolden (Buddy's father) was entered as "Texas," while according to Frederic Ramsey's research, Bolden's family came from Tunica, Louisiana (near Angola Penitentiary). Of course Bolden's father could still have been born in Texas, later settling in Tunica, until the family moved to New Orleans.

In this case Marquis speaks of a "clerical mistake." A marriage certificate of Jimmy Johnson, who was Buddy Bolden's bass player, kept in the New Orleans Vital Statistics Records, and dated February 3, 1904, says that he was born 1884. That also raises doubts, if one looks at the Bolden band photograph. On the other hand, C-clarinetist William Warner's year of birth, given as 1877 according to his marriage certificate, is more credible, even if one dates the photograph to as early as around 1897. Marquis acknowledges more difficulties created by different spellings of "Bolden" (Bolen, Bolding, Boldan, etc.) in various writings: "Some of the documents were made out by ministers and others who were nearly illiterate themselves" (19).

He also recognizes that in the death certificate of Mrs. Alice Bolden of August 11, 1931, her age is given as 54, while she actually was about 76. In 1890 and 1891 Buddy Bolden's mother, Alice, was listed in the City Directory as "widow of Louis," while it is clear that she had never remarried after her husband Westmore had died. Finally, Marquis discovered that when Buddy Bolden's female partner Hattie gave birth to a son, Charles Joseph Bolden Jr. on May 2, 1897, Buddy's age was given as twenty-two and hers as twenty-three in the son's birth certificate. Accordingly, Bolden would have been born in 1875, and not in 1877. By contrast, in 1907 when he was admitted as an "insane person" to the Insane Asylum of Louisiana, his age was given as twenty-six. Accordingly, he would have been born in 1881. With an exclamation mark we may also cite *The Complete Encyclopedia of Popular Music* 1900–1950, published 1974, in which his year of birth was given as 1868. Since Marquis's research was published, Buddy Bolden's birthdate has been generally accepted as September 8, 1877, which is reasonable but by no means certain. It must be pointed out that this information comes not from a birth certificate but from a baptism document, dated March 7, 1884, which—in addition—seems to have disappeared since 1970 (Marquis 1978: 12, n4).

Marquis's admirable work is hardly to be envied, because research on Bolden and some of his contemporaries has been like a walk through a thicket. Marquis, incidentally, gives reasonable credit to Jelly Roll Morton's narratives about early jazz, first published in 1952 in Alan Lomax's book *Mister Jelly Roll*, including what he said about Bolden; Marquis considers some of it "far-fetched" but adds that "they withstand scrutiny if toned down a bit" (8). As to Morton's account of Bolden, he says that he had "a good knowledge of what was going on."

Occasionally, however, Marquis's statements are excessive. He probably would not have anticipated that one of his guesses would have a serious effect on writings about early jazz history: his outright dismissal of much of what Bunk Johnson told his friend and interviewer Bill Russell and others during the late 1930s and 1940s.

Bunk, a key personality in early jazz, was an invaluable source of information as an eyewitness about people, places, social circumstances, and as a musician. After suggesting that he had given a false birthdate to Bill Russell, writing he was born December 27, 1879, in order to substantiate his claim of having played in Buddy Bolden's band after 1895, Marquis simply shifts Bunk's year of birth forward by exactly ten years to 1889, leaving day and month unchanged. Moreover, he then redates the only surviving photograph of the Buddy Bolden band dated by Bunk to ca. 1895, also by exactly ten years to 1905. In his book he introduces the photograph with this caption: "The Bolden band photograph from 1905 . . . ," thereby declaring his estimate as fact.

Here, I feel that scientific methodology has come under stress. Marquis states that "no records have been found to substantiate Bunk's claim of being born in 1879" (6). That may be true, but the absence of a traceable written record does not substantiate the opposite claim either, and does not at all justify that his year of birth should be shifted forward to a fictitious date. Marquis says: "My conclusion, based on dates of photos, the testimony of Pops Foster and Bocage, plus the lack of mention of Bunk being with Bolden by any other musician, is that Bunk was born closer to 1889 and did not play with Buddy Bolden" (6).

As far as we know, neither Pops Foster nor Peter Bocage ever gave any statement about Bunk Johnson's birthdate. In addition, two different topics are lumped together: (a) the issue whether Bunk had "lied" about his birth date, and (b) the issue whether he had perhaps exaggerated his association with Buddy Bolden's band after seeing the only surviving photograph of the group. The two issues are not necessarily connected by cause and effect, and additional speculation is required to assume that Bunk deliberately shifted his birthday back by ten years in order to insert himself into the league of earliest jazzmen.

Allowing for inaccuracies in someone's personal memory, especially as dates are concerned, is one matter, but to accuse someone of having willfully lied for personal gain is another. People do lie sporadically about their birthdates in specific contexts. Normally that context is sexual relationships. Also teenagers may spontaneously lie about their age in order to get access to cigarettes or liquor.

But fabrication by design is a different matter. There are also reasonable tests of credibility in conversations with an interlocutor. For example, if he or she often uses phrases such as "if I am not wrong" or "if I remember well," as did Jelly Roll Morton in the interviews with Alan Lomax, or a phrase like "I might say," as Peter Bocage did when he was asked to specify the year he heard Buddy Bolden, this may be taken to upgrade the narrator's credibility; because it demonstrates critical self-reflection and concern about possibly being inaccurate. Also, if someone feels that he must begin his narrative by stating where and when he was born (as did Bunk in a letter to Bill Russell), it indicates an old-fashioned way of strong attachment to one's birth date as an identity tag, rather than the beginning of a plot of deceit whose details he could not all have anticipated at that stage.

It is also unlikely that someone changes his or her year of birth in the middle of a fluent autobiographical conversation. It would entangle the person in a network of falsified chronology and in complex calculations, such as readjusting all events (in the case of Bunk Johnson by ten, Jelly Roll Morton by five years). The narrator would have to be extremely vigilant to avoid contradictions, resulting in a noticeable loss of fluency in the conversation.

Unfortunately, Marquis's remarks in 1978 have had a domino effect. Not only has New Orleans jazz history, in some of its details, been shifted forward by five to ten years from the 1890s to the first decade of the twentieth century, but they have also promoted an assumption that orally transmitted data are inherently flawed and always in need of adjustment and corroboration by written documents as "hard evidence."

Fresh fuel was poured into the Bunk Johnson controversy by jazz historian Lawrence Gushee, after he found a controversial note in the New Orleans Federal Census of 1900 (Gushee 1987). In the family of Theresa Johnson, 44, which is indeed the name of Bunk's mother, resident at 3523 Tchoupitoulas Street, the street where Bunk's family lived, a ten-year-old lad was listed in a rather illegible

writing which looks like "Geary" or "Gerry," born December 1889. It is persua-
sive to assume that this was Willie Geary "Bunk" Johnson, and Marquis's guess
would turn out to have been prophecy. But it requires a lot of faith to do so.
Bunk himself had told Bill Russell that his parents, William and Theresa, had
fourteen children. There may have been another December-born child called
Geary or Gerry in 1900, while Bunk was long gone, traveling with circus jobs,
and only briefly working in New Orleans by 1900 in Tom Anderson's dance hall.
In any case, if Theresa was 44 in 1900, she was far into child-bearing age in 1879
and could have given birth to Bunk. The fourteen children must have been born
between ca. 1876 and ca. 1896.

Observers have also tried to guess Bunk's age from a photograph that has
been dated variously to 1906, 1908, up to 1910, showing Bunk with the Superior Orchestra, together with Peter Bocage, violin, and Big Eye Louis Nelson,
clarinet. Bunk is slim, looks young, standing in the back row, but to say that he
was eighteen at that time is too much of an inference. The photographs of the
Superior Orchestra with Bunk and the Imperial Orchestra probably were shot
the same day, as pointed out by Karl Gert zur Heide (1999), who has to be com-
mended for his detective work establishing that the two photographs must have
been taken in the same studio, since they show the same drapery and curtain, and
probably on the same day, because Big Eye Louis Nelsen appears in both in the
same attire. "I'm convinced that Big Eye Louis Nelson is wearing the same jacket
and just put on the cap of the orchestra whose clarinet player failed to turn up"
(Zur Heide 1999: 18). A much better estimate of Bunk Johnson's age is possible
from photographs taken of him during his short second career in the 1940s. At
that time he was definitely a "grey eminence," hair white all over, and certainly
not a man in his fifties but well into his sixties. Many times and most recently also,
I have checked and rechecked spontaneous estimates of Bunk's age with a variety
of people from different cultures, notably in Africa. I have asked jazz musicians
in southern Africa to estimate his age from the photographs taken in 1947 on the
CD *The Last Testament*. The answers were unanimous: "about seventy or so." By
comparison, Peter Bocage, in a photograph taken in 1950 (Hillmann 1988: 79),
was estimated as "in his sixties." He was born in 1887 and died December 3, 1967.

Controversies about Bunk Johnson recently have received some unexpected
twists. Mike Hazeldine's research has largely restored Bunk as a key figure in early
jazz, and also as a reliable informant on early jazz history (Hazeldine and Martyn 2000; Hazeldine 2008). The great surprise, however, has been Vic Hobson's
book *Creating Jazz Counterpoint* . . . (2014), with a magnificent photo of Bunk
on the cover. Hobson presents strong evidence that Bunk was indeed a performer
in Buddy Bolden's band, as he had claimed, and he convincingly discredits Marquis's arbitrary shift of Bunk's birth date to ten years later. While not restoring
it to 1879, he comes up with an interesting hypothesis. He detected in Bunk's

narratives one factual mistake concerning an event in New Orleans. Bunk—otherwise demonstrating a phenomenal memory—referred to the Robert Charles riots as an event in 1895 rather than July 1900, i.e., anticipated by five years. Hobson takes this as a cue that, by analogy, Bunk could have "simply adjusted his dates and age to suit." Consequently, he proposes that Bunk's month and year of birth were most likely December 1884, and as a consequence of this adjustment "we now have a consistent narrative that is completely compatible with the available evidence" (Hobson 2014: 39). Whether one accepts this new hypothesis or not, it questions at least one of the worst distortions of early jazz history. One must commend Hobson for having dared to rattle some of jazz historians' entrenched convictions that tend to become fossilized.

Some other controversies nevertheless continue unabated. Beginning in the early 1980s, there was something like a campaign in circles of upcoming jazz historians to discredit narratives by prominent early jazz musicians as collected by researchers Bill Russell, Frederic Ramsey, and Alan Lomax. Even Louis Armstrong became a subject of controversy. Gushee (1985) constructed a revised chronology of Jelly Roll Morton's life and career, based on the assumption of a 1890 year of birth.

Luckily, when Alan Lomax wrote up his experiences with Morton on their joint journey to the past during the recording sessions at the Library of Congress from August to December 1938, the discussions about early jazz musicians' birth dates had not yet started. So we get a fair picture of the chronology of Jelly Roll's life, based on his own dates and his year of birth screened from what family members were telling him when he was a child and adolescent.

Proceeding from this marker, the story evolves without contradictions. He was a small boy when he heard Mamie Desdunes playing blues on the piano. He was about fourteen or fifteen in 1900 when peers, after stealing long pants, first took him to the tenderloin district. This was the time of curfew after the Robert Charles riots. About that time his mother died and he was put under the care of his uncle. At age fifteen or sixteen, after engagements as a pianist in the bordellos, his grandmother evicted him from the house and thereafter he was on his own, trying to survive by piano playing and gambling.

His own testimony is that in the year 1902, when he was "about seventeen," he invaded "the section where the birth of jazz" took place in New Orleans. In the 1938 conversations with Lomax he claimed that he had used the word "jazz" in 1902 "to show people the difference between" playing a piece with "jazz" as opposed to the rigid ragtime style. Such statements should not be dismissed hastily; one cannot discard the possibility that the term was perhaps part of an underground slang in Storyville, a taboo word shared in the bordellos, with strong sexual connotations, long before it became associated elsewhere, e.g., in California, with virile sports, having softened some of its meanings.

If "jazz" was a taboo word around 1902 and as such unacceptable to people of some social standing, then it was certainly never written down and used in print, and could therefore not be found in written records. Even by 1933, religious righteousness was so pervasive in the US South that a text like William Cornish's "funky butt" verses to "Buddy Bolden's Blues" could not be printed, and yet the song existed. Talking to Alan Lomax in 1949 about Jelly's composition, "Winin' Boy Blues," Johnny St. Cyr said that this term was "on the vulgar side" and accurately described its meaning by using the taboo word "jazz" in its bordello signification (Lomax 1952 [1959]: 51).

For Jelly Roll the term "jazz" was a kind of qualifier of the rendering of a musical piece. The later known expression "put some jazz into it" can summarize this process. From Morton's testimony emerges a picture of decisive changes in musical style and manner of ragtime presentation around 1902 in New Orleans. That he had a hand in it can hardly be denied. If he was one of the first who applied the slang term to musical rendering, then he had in a sense even "invented" jazz as he claimed in 1938. Symbolic formulations are not necessarily to be dismissed as baseless.

Of course, it is as impossible to prove anything like that as it is to prove the opposite. Therefore, we had better tolerate all opinions in their diversity as a stock of information that may still be enlarged. Morton realized he had a historical mission. The relationship with his "analyst" Lomax was marked by positive transference and counter-transference, thanks to Alan's enthusiasm, acceptance of his interlocutor as a peer, and gentle methods of asking questions to establish a positive field climate.

There was a point in young Morton's life when he could no longer stand the "swell people." He vividly describes the scenes happening in New Orleans at the Robert Charles riots in 1900, the year he also briefly witnessed a performance by Buddy Bolden and his group that ended with a fight between two people in the audience, with one of them killed (59–60). It is unlikely that he was just ten years old on that occasion.

In 1904 or a little earlier, Jelly Roll left New Orleans, migrating to places like Gulfport and Biloxi, Mississippi. It is here that the chronologies of Jelly Roll and Bunk Johnson intersect for a moment. Johnson, running into Jelly at that time, reports in Lomax 1952 [1959]:

> I played with him in Gulfport, Mississippi, round in 1903 and 1904. He was real young, then, but he was a really good piano man. Had lots of work at the Great Southern Hotel playing waltzes and rags for the white people. Him and me played a date at the Busy Bee Park on Labor Day. I remember it because the longshoremen had two parades—one for the union men and one for the boll weevils, the scabs. (111)

If we accept both musician-composers' own narratives with their years of birth 1879 and 1885 respectively, the anecdote remembered by Bunk makes sense. Bunk was then about twenty-four years old, Jelly about eighteen. This goes well with Bunk's formulation "real young," but "man." If on the other hand we followed the discrediting campaign against these two musician-composers, assuming that Bunk was born ten years later and Jelly Roll five years later, then Bunk would have been about fourteen, and Jelly Roll thirteen at their concert meeting in Gulfport, Mississippi.

Buddy Bolden's Legacy

Charles "Buddy" Bolden, born in the 1870s in New Orleans and deceased August 11, 1931, in a mental asylum, has been called "The elusive man who may have invented jazz" (cf. Michael Cieply, *International Herald Tribune*, April 24, 2007, describing two cinematographic projects about Bolden's life). In contrast to Jelly Roll Morton, Bolden had no chance of staking any such claim. He burned out quickly. Others have assigned that status to him since the appearance of the book *Jazzmen* (Ramsey and Smith 1939), and gradually have erected a formidable mythological construction around his life comparable to those of later-day socio-cultural heroes such as Che Guevara or Bob Marley.

Buddy Bolden has become a culture hero in jazz mythology. But if researchers in the 1940s such as Bill Russell had not rediscovered Bunk Johnson and other New Orleans veterans to tell us about Bolden, the reconstruction of Bolden's life and contribution to jazz would have been even more difficult and more legendary than it is. Like any remote facet of culture history, therefore, early jazz history is based essentially on an interpreted set of oral testimonies. Herein are encased some of the challenges also facing the Africanist researcher who tries to reconstruct missing links leading to the other side of the Atlantic.

Bolden, with a loud and bluesy horn style, "calling his children home" over distances in New Orleans' Johnson Park after 1902, is credited with the popularization of a new "fake" performance style of dance music that was in sharp contrast to music played from notation by contemporaneous late nineteenth-century New Orleans musicians. With a little help from music-reading C-clarinetist William "Red" Warner, his band played a wide variety of dance music items from memory and by head arrangement, as did groups in many Afro-Caribbean cultures and in Africa, thereby exploring alternative avenues of intonation, timbre effects, variation, and off-beat phrasing beyond the relatively rigid ragtime written scores. Instrumental techniques were tried out that were previously unheard-of on Western instruments. Personal experiment revived and reinstated techniques common in African music.

Asked about Bolden in an interview by Allen and Russell on January 29, 1959 (Hogan Jazz Archive, Tulane University), one of Bolden's contemporaries, violinist Peter Bocage, gave this assessment of Bolden's status:

Q. Who do you think was the first band to play jazz or ragtime?
A. Well, I attribute it to Bolden. Bolden was a fellow he didn't know a note as big as this house, whatever they played, they caught, or made up. They made their own music and they played it their own way. So that's the way jazz started. Just this improvisation. And the surroundings were a fast type—exciting! But the old-time musicians, they didn't play nothing but music. [The word *music* in those days was synonymous with written scores.]

Q. When did you hear Bolden?
A. I heard him when I was a kid. I was just fixing to start, you know, a young man. He played over here [meaning in Algiers, N.O., where Bocage grew up] and heard him play. He wasn't old.

Q. You remember about what year?
A. That was around I might say 1906. Now he was a fine-looking fellow and a healthy-looking fellow, but the life, you understand. That fast life just broke him up.

Q. How did he sound?
A. Oh, yeah. He was powerful. Plenty of power. He had a good style in the blues and all that stuff.

Q. Did anybody or does anybody play like Bolden?
A. Keppard, they were most on the same style. The improvisations is always gonna be a little different, no two men alike. . . . He had a good tone, didn't know what he was doing, didn't read. He played everything in b-flat. He played a lot of blues, slow drag, not too many fast numbers. Those fellows played b-flat, e-flat or f . . . but get three or four flats or three or four sharps and they was out of it. Blues was their standby, slow blues. They played mostly medium tempo. [Emmanuel] Perez had a better tone, sweeter than Buddy, he was taught.

The most comprehensive historical study of Buddy Bolden remains Donald M. Marquis's book, first published in 1978 with a revised edition in 2005. Marquis's work is based on thorough, incessant research, using both written sources and a vast amount of oral testimony by musicians and other contemporaries. The written sources include baptism, marriage, and death certificates, police reports, medical reports of Bolden, data in the New Orleans City Directory from 1875 to 1931, and two newspaper clippings from 1906. Marquis also uncovered the invaluable writings of a New Orleans Creole author, E. Belfield Spriggins, in the *Louisiana Weekly*, April 22, 1933, "Excavating local jazz," which contains a first mentioning of Buddy Bolden, based on an interview with the surviving Willie Cornish (1875–1942), valve trombone player in Bolden's band during the second half of the 1890s, with a short interruption due to his service in the 1898 Spanish-American War. Spriggins's work has been further highlighted by Lynn Abbott (1999).

The article appeared prior to the work of the team of Frederic Ramsey Jr., Charles Edward Smith, William Russell, and others in the late 1930s leading to the publication of the book *Jazzmen* in 1939. Donald M. Marquis's monograph on Buddy Bolden is based on partly different primary sources, and it is contextual. The book portrays not only Bolden's family but also his neighborhood, the places he played, and his sidemen and contemporaries. In this process several earlier assumptions have been corrected and traced back to their origins; the legend that Bolden was a barber, obviously was due to condensation into one image of reminiscences about two people, the other a good friend of Bolden: Louis Jones, born 1874, who was indeed a barber, and who had moved to New Orleans in 1894, about the time Bolden had become active as a musician. Bolden, Louis Jones, and Willie Cornish formed an inseparable triumvirate in the late 1890s, young and enterprising, engaging in all sorts of excitements of nightlife. Jones's and Cornish's memories of Bolden have contributed much to the reconstruction of Bolden's personality and lifestyle.

Another earlier assumption, that Bolden was the editor of a scandal sheet called *The Cricket*, was also discarded for lack of evidence. In a conversation with Bill Russell at Preservation Hall on September 12, 1970, Marquis reports that Russell also dismissed the idea as "a figment of someone's imagination" (Marquis 1978: 7).

How easy it is to mix up facts and create fiction—which then spreads at incredible speed, satisfying many people's wishful imagination—can be demonstrated by the balloon ascension story (Marquis 1978: 60–61). There was a "colored aeronaut" called Buddy Bartley, performing in Lincoln Park by 1905. He was sometimes referred to as "Buddy Bottley" and "Buddy Bottle." The phonetic similarity of the names with Buddy Bolden was the basis of a fantasy creation that spread to many people. Campbell and Ertugin in an interview with Edward "Kid" Ory, April 20, 1957 (Hogan Jazz Archive), came upon the story that Buddy Bolden "used to go up in a balloon and play a horn," and as Marquis has commented, some people even "remembered" Bolden playing his cornet while parachuting out of the balloon (Marquis 1978: 61).

Oral accounts by contemporaries are generally quite reliable if they are subjected to interpretation, while two known newspaper reports, for example, dated March 27, 1906, in the *Daily Picayune*, and March 28, 1906, in the *New Orleans*

Item about an incident in Bolden's home, have to be read with caution. Journalists could not have witnessed the incident; they relied on information that came from relatives and the police. There is a core of factuality in them, mainly as to Bolden's condition by March 1906: not that he was "insane" or "in a state of dementia," as is written, but that he had developed a paranoiac syndrome of feeling extremely threatened, convinced that he was being drugged or rather bewitched with some hoodoo from his mother and other relatives (about which the newspapers would not write). Marquis confirms that "in New Orleans it is ticklish to ask questions about such topics." As in some extremely Christianized parts of Africa, hoodoo is brushed aside as "superstition" and denied existence by not talking about it. But Buddy Bolden had developed extreme fear to touch his cornet (Marquis 1978: 123).

Confined to bed, Bolden reacted with a violent outburst. Here the newspaper notes diverge. In one print it is declared that he struck his "mother with a water pitcher," in the other that he "mauled his mother-in-law." The latter, whose name was Ida Bass, is identified as Mrs. Ida Beach (1) in the *Daily Picayune*. The reports were probably based on the police department's arrest record after Bolden was taken into custody.

Drawing on various oral testimonies, Marquis gives a more realistic account of Bolden's condition, the events leading to his demise as a musician (112–22), and his institutionalization and death (123–33).

In Vic Hobson's recent book *Creating Jazz Counterpoint* (2014), Bolden's personal history and circumstances also are given ample space. With access to the large body of interview transcripts of Bolden's contemporaries preserved in the William Ransom Hogan Jazz Archive at Tulane University, Hobson has been able to settle a few queries probably for good. For example: (a) The story that Bolden was a barber came from Preston Jackson. He was no barber, but his close friend and drinking companion, Louis Jones, set up a barber shop in 1899, which confirms Marquis's earlier assessment. (b) A local magazine called *Cricket* did exist in New Orleans in the 1890s, as Bunk had claimed. Hobson traced four editions; unfortunately none of those contained articles by Otis Watts that might throw light on New Orleans' music scene in the 1890s. Bolden himself apparently never wrote in the *Cricket*, nor was he the editor. (c) Hobson also presents evidence based on Willie Cornish and others that a cylinder recording of Buddy Bolden's band had existed and was in possession of a German trader named Oscar Zahn who unfortunately dumped his cylinders sometime in the 1930s. Hobson deplores—and so do we—that Charles Edward Smith was unable to conduct more than one interview in 1939 with Cornish, the last surviving member of Bolden's band.

In spite of meticulous research and the preserved volumes of recorded eyewitness accounts, our only direct touch with Bolden is through an effigy. There is just one surviving photograph, in fact a print of a print, because the original disappeared from Dr. Leonard Bechet's estate in 1959. There are, however, several published versions thereof, one with Bolden's signature and those of the other band members underneath (cf. Rose and Souchon 1967).

This photograph was originally in possession of William and Bella Cornish. No negative has ever been found. It has been the subject of continuing bewilderment, because in whichever way one reproduces it, some of the six people seen appear to be left-handed, while it is certified by their relatives that no one was. Did the photographer pose them that way? In 1985 Alden Ashford, in an article called "The Bolden Photo—One More Time," presented an analysis focusing on the two clarinet players in the photograph: William Warner with C clarinet (seated) and Frank Lewis, B^b clarinet (standing). Based on the Albert system clarinets' construction and the musicians' fingering he was able to ascertain that these two people must have been in the right section of the band lineup (from the band members' viewpoint), as in the original print showing the band members signatures underneath. However, if the photograph is printed that way, guitarist Brock Mumford and bass player James (Jimmy) Johnson appear left-handed or, as I had suspected long ago, mirror-inverted.

Eventually, after taking a copy of the picture to Africa, showing it to musicians and photographers, it dawned upon me that perhaps it was a composite image created by the New Orleans photographer from two square-sized negatives, because whichever way it is printed (compare the two versions in Ramsey and Smith 1939 and Rose and Souchon 1967), exactly half of the musicians appear mirror-inverted, as if an invisible line in the middle separated the halves. From an uncropped reproduction in the Hogan Jazz Archive placed at my disposal by Lynn Abbott, I was able to ascertain that clarinetist William Warner and guitarist Brock Mumford had even been sitting on the same chair, though at different times. This is revealed by the symmetry of a dark line underneath, meeting at a point in the middle, forming a flat v-shape. The meeting point is on the invisible line where the two pictures were joined.

My conclusion was that the unknown photographer of the late 1890s had made two separate shots of the musicians, probably the same day, three people in each, using two square-sized negatives. Thereafter he created a darkroom montage to rearrange all the six in a standard New Orleans band lineup as was expected by convention, and for that purpose he reversed one negative so that the bass player would be shown at the extreme left of the band. Consequently he appears in the photo mirror-inverted. Clarinetist Warner, seated, is depicted correctly propping up his C-clarinet on his right upper leg, while guitarist Brock Mumford now sitting to his left is also side-reversed, and among the players of the brass instruments standing behind them, Cornish is in correct position.

For one shot he would ask clarinetist Warner to sit down on the only chair available in his studio, with B-flat clarinetist Frank Lewis and valve trombone player William Cornish standing behind. For the other shot on a different negative, he would ask guitarist Brock Mumford to sit on the same chair used by the clarinetist before, with Buddy Bolden standing behind him, and Jimmy Johnson with the string bass standing to the right side of Brock and Buddy Bolden. Thereafter, in his darkroom, he turned the second negative round, integrating both shots in the positive print, using exposure techniques photographers had learned long ago, intersecting the two pictures by a margin of ca. 25 percent of each negative. Thereby he was able to create a composite, rectangular print that is absolutely deceptive. The guitarist appears to be left-handed or "posed" (while in fact he is just mirror-inverted with the correct fingering positions on the guitar). He sits next to the C clarinetist with the end of the guitar's neck inserted over the clarinet player's left arm (cf. Kubik 2009 for details).

Musicians' expectations of a certain band lineup and the need for avoiding empty space between the two groups in the final print from the negatives must have motivated the photographer to turn around the second negative, with the result that the three people in the right half of the composite picture are mirror-inverted, not only the apparent left-handers Brock Mumford and James (Jimmy) Johnson, but also—less detectable by a casual observer—Buddy Bolden. No New Orleans cornetist posing for a photograph at the turn of the twentieth century would hold the instrument in his right hand (see pictures of John Robichaux, Bunk Johnson, and others, Kubik 2009). So the correct representation of Buddy Bolden, as we would shake hands with him, would be the one in which he holds his cornet in the left hand. It has been argued, however, that Bolden's cornet in that position appears as if it were "soldered together backwards" (Sager 2010). Although I am not certain that this can be deduced from details that are not particularly clear in the photograph, and Bolden seems to hold his instrument unusually, there may indeed be another hitch.

My proposed solution to the Bolden photograph mystery, so I thought, would make redundant all speculations that assume that the photographer would have asked the string players to pose left-handed or hold their instruments unusually, for whatever reason. The problem that some of the musicians appear mirror-inverted also is not eliminated if one assumes that the photographer used tintype photographic equipment, as proposed by Justin Winston and Clive Wilson (2009). By the late 1890s this technique appears to have been obsolete in a city like New Orleans and superseded by more modern equipment.

However, there may still be some incongruity of another kind in the Bolden photograph. The two persons in the back of the grouping, Cornish and Bolden, look strangely positioned within the picture's perspective. Frank Lewis is real; he clearly steps on the ground in front of the curtain, but where are Cornish's legs and feet? The curtain spreads so much forward, that Cornish appears to have stepped into it—without tearing it down? For Bolden one may concede that his invisible legs are there, hidden behind Brock Mumford's body sitting in front of him; but Cornish looks as if he were in a state of vertical levitation inside the curtain. How can this be rationally explained? Tintype hypothesis will not help here. Was there perhaps another, undetected and even more complex intervention by the photographer in his darkroom art? Could it be that Bolden's and Cornish's portraits were originally separate pictures, copied in? That would make plausible the absence of Buddy Bolden's drummer Cornelius Tillman: no effigy of him was available.

This photograph does not match the other photographs we know of New Orleans bands (cf. Rose and Souchon 1967). It looks composite, as if it were created upon request, to put some of the people together with whom Bolden was playing, for advertising or whatever personal reasons. We also should not forget that the period from the late 1850s to the end of the nineteenth century was high season for composite photography as art, and it was quite common to use even five negatives to create a picture, as for example, Henry Peach Robinson's 1885 photo "Fading Away."

In addition to the photograph and the vanished cylinder recording of marches played by Bolden in 1898, there is Marquis's finding of a painting, apparently depicting Buddy Bolden but without documentation. The provenance and date of this painted portrait remains elusive, besides a stated association with the mother of Alvin Alcorn. To me it seems that it could be an idealized rendering of Bolden's face derived from the only known photograph. If my suspicion is correct, then the painting would have been made after 1939 when the photograph was discovered and copies were made, unless of course another print of the same photograph was circulating in New Orleans earlier in somebody's possession. Since my analysis of the photo suggests that the correct appearance of Bolden is the one with the cornet in his left hand, the division of his hair would therefore appear over the right side of his forehead. In the painting, however, it is drawn at the left side, which suggests that the painter could have worked from the print in Bill Russell's personal collection. In any case, the painting is unlikely to have been made with Buddy Bolden sitting in front of a portraitist during his lifetime.

Very quickly, as a bandleader in his twenties, Buddy Bolden developed an unmistakable personal style with an expressive repertoire of timbre and variation techniques that had come from blues and street music performances, reinstating elements of an African approach to performance that had survived in the cultural underground. The development of a personal style at age twenty or shortly before is normal among those rare, gifted musicians who become founders of a new trend. It was equally important in the rise of eminent twentieth-century musical personalities in Africa. Katanga guitarist Mwenda Jean Bosco, Daniel Kachamba growing up in Salisbury (Harare), and Faustino Okello in a blind school in Uganda (see DVD *African Guitar*, Kubik 1995) all had their unique styles perfected when they were between eighteen and twenty-two years old. Many of these artists remained faithful to those styles all their lives. That Bolden had an inclination to showmanship is no surprise; many jazz musicians in later years also had that in adjustment to market trends, competition, and expectations by young people. In any case, it must have been a factor promoting his popularity among broad dancehall audiences in New Orleans.

What was the sound of the Bolden band? And what was its repertoire?

Besides popular music of the day—waltzes, quadrilles, mazurkas, etc. and a lot of ragtime—Buddy Bolden was renowned for playing the blues, in contrast to his Downtown rival John Robichaux, who worked exclusively from sheet music. "Make Me a Pallet on the Floor" is cited as part of his repertoire by George Baquet in an article in *Down Beat*, December 15, 1940, and around 1904 "Buddy Bolden's Blues" had become his signature tune, allowing musicians, dancers, and audiences to invent further textlines on the spot, often as a sarcastic commentary on current social or political events, e.g., "Thought I heard Judge Fogarty say, thirty days in the market, take him away." Judge John J. Fogarty had become presiding judge of the First Recorders Court in 1904. For minor offenses he used to hand out thirty days of forced labor, to sweep the market with a "good broom." That was one of the topics of the open-ended lyrics to the melody of "Buddy Bolden's Blues," one of the earliest blues in an Uptown band to incorporate the wailing third blue note.

Other songs Buddy Bolden is known to have played include many that became New Orleans jazz band standards somewhat later: "Careless Love Blues," "Bucket's Got a Hole in It," "Just a Little While to Stay Here," and so on.

With regard to its emotional impact, a description of Buddy Bolden's music was given by trombone player Bill Matthews, born ca. 1889:

> He was one of the sweetest trumpet players on waltzes and things like that and on those old slow blues, that boy could make the women jump out of the window. On those old, slow, low down blues, he had a moan in his cornet, that went all through you, just like you were in church or something. Everybody was crazy about Bolden when he'd blow a waltz, schottische or old low down blues. He was the sweetest trumpet player in the world. He'd tell his boys to get low, they'd get low and he'd take it . . . Louis Armstrong, King Oliver, none of them had a tone like Bolden. Bunk Johnson got his style following Buddy with his sweetness, but could never play rough and loud like Bolden. (from Collins and Russell's interview with Bill Matthews, March 10, 1959, Hogan Jazz Archive; reproduced in Marquis 1978: 100–101)

Blues was clearly pivotal in the repertoire of Uptown dance bands from the mid-1890s on, including the Bolden band. I know, of course, that some colleagues insist that "there is really no evidence of blues anywhere until after 1900"; one should add: "on paper." Nor is there any evidence to the contrary. At that time no one could have learned blues from sheet music publications. But that does not mean that Bolden did not play the blues before 1898, when trombonist Willie Cornish had to leave his band for the Spanish-American War. The blues were the essence of his success. In the days before "canned music," a new orally transmitted genre would be present underground for at least ten to fifteen years before someone tried to recognize and appropriate it. That applies to ragtime as it applies to the blues. For blues it came more than a decade later, when W. C. Handy began to publish his adaptations, beginning with "Memphis Blues" (Mr. Crump) in 1912. Ragtime was available in print shortly before 1900 and could be learned with the help of reading musicians, such as William "Red" Warner and Willie Cornish in Bolden's band, though they are not reported to have played any of Scott Joplin's numbers, for example. But for blues, there was no such facility at all. They had to be learned exclusively from oral sources.

Luckily, blues does not involve a system of multiple strains as does marching music, ragtime, and the dance hall music that was current. But there were cognitive problems of a different nature: how to incorporate the characteristic (vocal) blues tonality into a framework of chords within the Western tonal system? To accommodate the blue notes, musicians learned to circumvent the customary dominant/tonic relationships of Western music by a variety of methods, such as extending chords upwards, e.g., C^7, C^9 to accommodate blue note 1 (B♭ 969±) or proceed from C^7 straight to a subdominant F^7 instead of F. Sometimes blue notes were represented by a diminished chord, as in "Buddy Bolden's Blues," to accommodate blue note 3 (f♯ 551±), or by hitting major and minor thirds simultaneously to create some semblance of a neutral third.

Often linear melodic development was pursued in violation of classical harmonic rules. This is demonstrated in recordings from later days, for example by a phrase from George Lewis's celebrated "Burgundy Street Blues" (see Fig. 6.6). The ear accustomed to jazz and blues accepts that Lewis's clarinet melody includes c played over an A^7 chord of the banjo, and f over D^7, thereby creating friction that gives the illusion of c♯ and c, respectively, f♯ and f being one toneme.

Fig. 6.6. Melodic development in George Lewis's "Burgundy Street Blues," measures 8–10.

It can be taken for granted that the re-creation of vocal blues tonality with melodic instruments such as trumpets, clarinets, etc., over a basis of Western chord relationships was tested out in Buddy Bolden's days and by his ways of structuring a melody. Otherwise he would not have had that "moan"!

Bolden did not play like musicians who had grown up in the score-reading tradition Downtown, such as Alphonse Picou, in spite of Picou's cultural crossover somewhat later (cf. Lomax 1952 [1959: 72–76]). Picou, incidentally, stated in an interview with Lomax that Bolden "was best at ragtime." This could imply that he was "not so good" in other genres. It may also indicate that Picou did not like Bolden's blue notes, a device Picou never used himself.

And yet Picou was one of the most sought-after clarinetists by jazz bands, with his "High Society" solo an indispensable attraction. Like Albert Nicholas, Barney Bigard, and others, Picou had a broad background as performer, allowing him to negotiate contrasting band styles and repertoires (cf. Raeburn 2012c). This created modes of transculturation and new models, with many "fakers" eventually deciding also to become acquainted with notation.

There are conflicting opinions about the extent to which Buddy Bolden was a "reading" musician. Many of Bolden's contemporaries have contradicted Peter Bocage's statement that "He didn't read." Most likely he could read, but found it of limited use for his performance. Marquis (1978: 106) suggests that he must have had reading abilities, since he also used to play in brass bands on parades, and their repertoire was always written. Also, in the 1900 City Directory of New Orleans he was listed as a music teacher. Therefore, his approach most likely was similar to some latter-day jazz musicians who are familiar with notation, but would not use it when making music. In contrast to "legitimate" musicians, jazz musicians began to cultivate a different approach to the kinemics of musical performance.

Marquis stresses that it was their cultural background that largely determined informants' views of Buddy Bolden: "Some differences of opinion concerning Bolden's music can be expected simply because of the different values and approaches taken by Creole musicians and Uptowners" (102). When Peter Bocage stated in the 1959 interview that Bolden "didn't know a note as big as this house" and "those fellows" used to play in no more than three keys, it only reveals how Bolden's music was judged by a musician whose views were rooted in the tradition of performance from notations. Although it is a credible assessment that Bolden mostly played pieces in B♭, and some in E♭ and F, that does not mean he was "limited" to those keys. The kind of music he propagated demanded a different focus of attention, phrase development, and timbre within a linear non-transpositional concept of scale, and in the blues with a strong central reference tone. This applies equally to many first-generation African dance band musicians, e.g., in the 1950s. Many African musicians proceed from awareness of absolute pitch when tuning their instruments, whatever kind of scale is used, even with the most unusual intervals from a Western music standpoint. This awareness gets disoriented and weakened if one changes between too many keys from song to song. B♭, E♭, and F are related within a cycle of fifths (or fourths in reverse). Obviously, Bolden had this African approach to music making, and by the 1890s he had the guts to come out into the public with it, discovering that he was successful. Gradually others began to switch to his direction, eventually reaching some kind of syncretist compromise. In that sense, Bolden and his cohorts, especially his friend the trombone player Willie Cornish, were jazz musicians. They could read, but did not need that knowledge for performance.

In retrospective we can also get a glimpse of the kind of music in the days of Buddy Bolden or shortly thereafter, by scrutinizing Bunk Johnson. As is testified by Tom Albert (in an interview September 25, 1959, Hogan Jazz Archive), Bunk used to play from the "Red Back Book of Rags," for example Scott Joplin numbers, and this is also corroborated by his 1947 arrangements of "The Entertainer" and other rags on his final album *The Last Testament*, recorded December 23–26, 1947. But in earlier 1940s recordings he had played superb blues from no book with the George Lewis /Jim Robinson group from New Orleans.

Buddy Bolden may not have arranged Scott Joplin rags for band performance using notation, but Tom Albert and others have characterized his group as a "ragtime band," albeit "with the blues and everything." This shows that New Orleans musicians around 1900 were drawing upon a great variety of sources.

One of the oldest contemporaries of Bolden interviewed, bassist Papa John Joseph (born 1877), stated that "Bolden outplayed Robichaux's band in a way, 'cause they used to play them blues. . . . What made his band different from country bands, was more jazz to it" (interview, November, 26, 1958, Hogan Jazz Archive). This is an interesting use of the word *jazz*, as if it were something quantifiable, a quality, even substance one could put into something in a dosage.

Another facet of Buddy Bolden's music, as agreed upon by many informants, was that he played in the middle range of his cornet, and that musical pieces were introduced in unison, respectively parallel octaves, since the trombone played an octave lower, when they played their special numbers. (This information was collected from Charlie Love, a trumpeter, who had listened to Bolden in his teens, Charters 2008: 89–90.)

Most important, however, and in agreement with what we know from many African traditions, is that Buddy Bolden's early "jazz" (though it was not called by that name) was not improvised, in the sense of "free improvisation," one of the jazz credos of later days, i.e., jazz as "improvised music." As Africanist researchers we have long been suspicious of this concept and believe that the idea is rooted in a reinterpretation by audiences of popular music in the 1920s, who were still accustomed to think of musical performance (opera, concert, etc.) in terms of notation. When confronted with African American musicians who could do without it, they considered the music to be improvised. Gradually jazz musicians began to internalize that viewpoint, and by the 1930s and 40s it was common to improvise solos just following the chord changes.

There are test cases to reconstruct the scope of improvisatory variation acceptable in early jazz. Listen to Bunk Johnson's *Last Testament* recordings, especially the ragtime compositions from the Red Back Book of Rags he persuaded his New York partners to play with him. Of course, Bunk interprets the written melodic lines, i.e., he plays them in terms of his very personal tone and timbre phrasings, but melodically there is little deviation from the theme; not only in the rags, but also when he takes up contemporaneous 1920s and 1930s hits such as "You Are Driving Me Crazy." One may compare two takes of the piece "Out of Nowhere" published on the CD *Last Testament*, Delmark DD 225, recorded in New York, December 24, 1947, to assess the precise amount of improvisatory variation Bunk allowed himself to pursue. Another instructive example is the recordings he made with pianist Don Ewell in New York, June 3, 1946; on one of them—with many repetitions of the theme on the trumpet, he explains to Ewell the kind of piano accompaniment he desires.

Bunk's self-restraint was a tradition. He had not changed his approach or his tone on the horn since ca. 1908 when he had played with the Superior Orchestra. What had changed by the 1940s was that there were no longer musicians in New Orleans who were willing to and capable of playing the kind of music Bunk had cherished in his youth, who would play from the Red Back Book of Rags and also constantly enlarge their repertoire with current song hits.

What Bunk valued as desirable was most certainly similar, if not identical to, Bolden's values. Both were following the trends of their times. Bunk was highly educated musically, with wide interests and yet strict preferences (cf. Bill Russell and Gene Williams's consternation over Bunk wanting to also play current music of the 1940s, which he eventually did). Many New Orleans jazz fans in the 1940s and '50s, however, wanted to freeze and immobilize early jazz to conform with an imaginary purist model, and their reaction in particular to Bunk's *Last Testament* was devastating. They considered his 1947 recordings to be a sellout, because of his choice of (reading) musicians from the environment of Chick Webb and his playing of some current hit songs. He was a traitor to their New Orleans purist faith. Perhaps they would have been equally disappointed and surprised if the alleged Bolden cylinder had surfaced.

We owe Bunk Johnson praise for two aural testimonies of the music played in New Orleans around 1900. The first is a theme he remembered as composed by Tony Jackson, "Baby I'd Love to Steal You," harmonically very beautiful and gently demonstrated by Bunk on the piano (recorded May 7, 1943, in San Francisco at Bertha Gonsoulin's home). The second is Bunk's demonstration of Bolden's musical style by whistling one of his repertoire pieces, on the album *This Is Bunk Johnson Talking* (with Bill Russell, recorded in New Orleans, June 13, 1942).

Bunk was in command of a wide repertoire, but he also believed in authenticity, that one should be faithful to the style chosen, e.g., play ragtime based on what was written, with some margin for personal variation.

The cornet theme Bunk whistled included in its second rendering a diminished chord in arpeggio to fill the break in the middle. It has strophic form, and is one of those thirty-two-bar themes that are divided into two halves, as became common in New Orleans jazz. Bunk whistles it faithfully, allowing himself a modest amount of improvisatory variations. Figure 6.7 gives the melody transcribed from the CD, and the chords under the theme that I have deduced from Bunk's whistling. Measures 15 and 16 would accommodate the break. Most likely Bolden played the tune in B♭ and may have transposed it to E♭ in the course of his performance, as is suggested in the third chorus of Bunk's whistling.

Fig. 6.7. Bunk Johnson whistling a ragtime piece played by Buddy Bolden (first chorus, relative notation).

An experimental guess about how the Bolden band may have sounded has been provided by Samuel Charters from his lifelong involvement in research on the history of New Orleans music. In a chapter called "The Other Side of Town" in his recent book *A Trumpet around the Corner* (2008), he summarizes his talks with musicians in the 1950s and later who were contemporaries of Bolden:

Considering the instruments in the group, the sound had to be considerably lighter in texture than later bands in the city. There was no drummer; the rhythm was a soft-toned, gut-string guitar, which Mumford played in a steady chorded rhythm of four beats to the measure. The bass was played with a bow, and it accented the first and third beats of the measure, just as in the published arrangements for dance orchestras in the period. I asked several musicians who've heard the band to hum or sing what would have been their own part in the ensemble, as they remembered it. When I put together a group to recreate the sound through the notes I'd transcribed, I found that the *feel* of the band was much closer to the surviving recordings of dance orchestras in Cuba and Venezuela from this same period—the textures more reminiscent of the Cuban *danzon* or the Venezuelan *paseo*, with their lighter, more fluid rhythmic pulse, than to the march-oriented music of other American cities. Havana, at that time, was only a short excursion boat ride away across the Gulf. The musicians who thought back to those first years also agreed that Bolden's band didn't improvise. The instrumental parts for their general repertoire, as well as for their speciality pieces were worked out in rehearsals and each player played from memory. (Charters 2008: 90)

Charters's explanation reads a bit like a postscript to the late Ernest Borneman's writings, who was convinced that the earliest expressions of African American music in New Orleans were much more in a Caribbean stylistic mold than the slapstick syncopated rhythms of the Original Dixieland Jass Band and others between 1917 and 1923.

In part this may be true, but Charters's experimental reconstruction also seems to have taken inspiration from the content of the Bolden photograph with two clarinet players and no drummer, although Dee Dee Chandler's affiliation (among others) with Bolden is a fact. Jazz bands routinely have used drummers from the beginning of this music, because dancers needed orientation by a constant beat. And—as I have said further above—the Bolden photograph also appears to be composite, showing some of the people with whom Bolden played, but not his band in a lineup ready for a performance. It is unlikely that a band led by a powerful and charismatic cornet player would have produced the kind of Caribbean-style light music reconstructed. Latin elements may have been there, but most likely there was more of the aesthetics of ragtime, brass bands, and of course, the blues. For a critique of Borneman's views on Creole roots of jazz and jazz going "tangent" in the 1920s, one may also consult Bruce Raeburn's recent article "Beyond the Spanish Tinge" (2012b).

Most certainly, controversies about Bolden and his music will never come to an end. One issue that has recently attracted researchers' attention is whether Bolden composed "Buddy Bolden's Blues." Jelly Roll Morton was explicit in this matter, vigorously defending Bolden as the composer. After playing his piano adaptation of the song, in the Library of Congress 1938, he explained:

Morton: This is about one of the earliest blues. This is, no doubt, the earliest blues that was the real thing. That is a variation from the real barrelhouse blues. The composer was Buddy Bolden, the most powerful trumpet player I've ever heard or ever was known. The name of this was named by some old honky-tonk people. While he played this, they sang a little theme to it. He was a favorite in New Orleans at the time.

> I thought I heard Buddy Bolden say,
> Dirty nasty stinkin' butt, take it away,
> A dirty nasty stinkin' butt, take it away,
> Oh, Mister Bolden, play.

> I thought I heard Bolden play,
> Dirty nasty stinkin' butt, take it away,
> A funky butt, stinkin' butt, take it away,
> And let Mister Bolden play.

Later on this tune was, uh, I guess I'd have to say, stolen by some author I don't know anything about—I don't remember his name—and published under the title of "St. Louis Tickler." But with all the proof in the world, this tune was wrote by Buddy Bolden. Plenty old musicians know it.

Lomax: When?

Morton: Oh, this number is, no doubt, about nineteen-two.

(Source: transcription of the Library of Congress sessions 1938: 51ff)

"St. Louis Tickle," for which Barney and Seymore signed as authors, was published in 1904. It is a multi-strain song hit showing signs of what I call a "potpourri" approach to composition, i.e., that the authors picked motifs from here and there to form their different strains, just as W. C. Handy would do ten years later for his "St. Louis Blues" and other compositions, connecting various street music motifs and ideas to create something that people in their parlors would not find repetitive and boring. One strain in "St. Louis Tickle" shows similarity to "Buddy Bolden's Blues." Jelly Roll Morton accused the composers of plagiarism.

There are various reasons why Morton's accusations are justified, apart from the argument of chronology, if we take Morton's estimate as correct that the tune came up in 1902 in Bolden's dancehall repertoire. One reason is that if, prior to the era of electro-magnetic sound carriers, a tune had become popular in the streets and bars of a city, and shortly thereafter appeared in print in the context of a multi-strain work, it can be taken for granted that the original was the street version. To avoid accusations of plagiarism, "professional" composers would place a tune into a larger context and thereby, if necessary, claim to have "improved" those "folk melodies." Another reason is that in the era of

Bartok, Dvořák, and others the fashionable avenues of inspiration for composers were from "folk" to "serious" music rather than the other way round. Sheet music composers were constantly on the lookout for something exciting, novel. Multi-strain compositions such as "St. Louis Tickle" are particularly suspect of this avenue of appropriation.

Another question, of course, is how to define a song's ultimate originality. Jelly Roll Morton's statement about "Buddy Bolden's Blues" being a "variation from the real barrelhouse blues" suggests that there was something before, a certain background and possibly even multiple authorship of the melody and the text idea. Morton says honky-tonk people "sang a little theme to it." How we interpret this depends very much on our definition of composition, respectively "writing," a concept that has in the meantime been widened as popular music is concerned. In African cultures a song's originality is usually acknowledged by people on the basis of the words, i.e., the song text and not the melody alone. A different text to a similar melody can make it be considered another song. By contrast, observers educated in the Western music tradition tend to consider the words ancillary, and focus on the melody and harmonic background as the important indicators of originality. From the 1920s on it was common among jazz musicians to circumvent copyright problems, by taking just the chord changes of a popular hit and creating another theme on top of it, usually more complex than the original. Famous examples are the numerous compositional derivatives of George and Ira Gershwin's "I Got Rhythm" (Berliner 1994: 76–77).

Vic Hobson (2008) pursues the issue of similarities in the alleged chromaticism of the melody of "Buddy Bolden's Blues" on the basis of the recordings by Jelly Roll Morton (78 r.p.m. discs General 4003-A and Bluebird B-1043) and two sheet music publications: "St. Louis Tickle" by Barney and Seymore, 1904, and the earlier "The Cake Walk in the Sky" by Ben Harney, 1899. He seems to suggest that both Barney and Seymore and Buddy Bolden could have picked up the melody from "The Cake Walk in the Sky":

> One thing, I think, is clear. The melody of "Buddy Bolden's Blues" did not originate with Buddy Bolden. This melody had been published under the title "The Cake Walk in the Sky" in 1899. Unless we are to believe that Buddy Bolden was playing this same melody before this date (and there is nothing that I have found to support this view), then the melody "Buddy Bolden's Blues" was derived from "The Cake Walk in the Sky." (Hobson 2008: 11)

A statement like this cannot fail to trigger contradiction because it is a somewhat hasty conclusion and based on silent assumptions. One assumption is that the similarity between those melodies is real, which is not necessarily so. Also, this issue of "melody" refers just to the first line, i.e., the first four measures (Hobson

2008: 10). Another assumption is that the melody of "Buddy Bolden's Blues" must be derived from some sheet music, while Jelly Roll Morton suggests that it was a "variation" somehow shared in the barrelhouse and honky-tonk milieu, and that there were therefore several contributors. A third assumption is that the "melody" can only be derived precisely from "The Cake Walk in the Sky" (if not from "St. Louis Tickle"), excluding the possibility of any other source. The fourth assumption is a kind of undeclared general premise, namely that sheet music publications were the normal source of musical groups' repertoire around 1900. At length the author tries to investigate whether someone in Bolden's group could have had access to the score of "The St. Louis Tickle" kept and played by a rival band, John Robichaux's Orchestra. Among the "legitimate" Downtown bands in New Orleans, the sources were sheet music publications and Robichaux had piles of it, but this did not necessarily apply to Uptown bands such as that of Buddy Bolden. It is unlikely that the source of "Buddy Bolden's Blues" was any kind of sheet music publication, and likely the inspiration came from elsewhere. According to most testimonies by contemporaries, blues was an essential part of Bolden's repertoire, and "Buddy Bolden's Blues" (so called by Jelly Roll Morton) deserves that genre description. But there were no sheet music blues publications around by 1902. Ben Harney's "novel ditty of a love-sick coon" called "The Cake Walk in the Sky," Ethiopian Two-Step, in "Tempo di Marcia" is—in its published form—miles apart from what could be qualified as blues.

As I have suggested earlier in this chapter, one should more often pose the question where sheet music composers such as Ben Harney got their "melodies" from, rather than speculate whether Bolden picked something from Ben Harney, let alone from the "composers" of "St. Louis Tickle."

"Buddy Bolden's Blues" is blues in essence as much as are "Make Me a Pallet on the Floor" and many other standards played in New Orleans jazz bands, unless someone limits the blues genre to the twelve-bar schema. The flatted fifth to the word "heard" is a wailing blue note par excellence, not the result of chromaticism. Ben Harney, who learned so much from African American music "floating" in the streets for anyone to pick up, had begun to scratch at the third blue note in a song of some unknown "love-sick" individual, and reinterpreted it as chromaticism. Harney's is a weak imitation of blues tonality, while Morton's piano version of "Buddy Bolden's Blues" is faithful, as is his rendering of "Mamie's Blues," learned from the lady whose piano playing he had admired as a boy.

But both Harney and Morton represent the third blue note as part of a diminished chord, which is indeed one of the ways it can be represented within the Western twelve-tone system. Another one, in transposition, and from a later date, would be Thelonious Monk's half-diminished chord (or minor chord with added sixth, as he called it). Anyhow, the source is blues tonality, as heard from singers and musicians who had left their secluded existence on the plantations, traveling for the first time to any destination they chose, thereby increasing their visibility and audibility to Ben Harney and his like.

In its melodic structure "Buddy Bolden's Blues" is most likely based on roadside blues singing, possibly accompanied with a stringed instrument, and not on any sheet music composition. The difference to Harney's rendering is that Bolden and Morton understood the blues essence in its tonality, while Harney did not. The text is a different matter. The inspiration comes from "folk" ditties that started with the words "I thought I heard . . ." followed by sarcastic or humorous, often also obscene criticism of some event or some official character. Starting with the phrase itself expresses the singer's alleged distance from the story, keeping a backdoor open to be used in case the statements offended someone or were not appreciated by the audience. "I thought I heard . . ." implies that I am not even sure that I heard such nasty news. This gives participants in the collective text composition a license to say anything demeaning. It was probably a long-established phrase in African American cultures in the South, possibly even pre–Civil War. Blues singers in the countryside picked it up first, as a post–Civil War reaction by the "liberated" people to a domineering society with lots of moral censorship. Vic Hobson has actually traced a few instances in which the phrase is reported in various contexts. It had inspired countless text poets and singers to comment on a variety of subjects, which is how one can approximately date each new version, something Hobson has skillfully tried to do.

The "funky butt" version definitely originated in Buddy Bolden's time, as contemporaries have agreed upon, and in that sense the tune became Buddy Bolden's "theme song," while the words were probably improvised and first used by Willie Cornish. The descending melody involving a flatted fifth was inspired by blues songs incorporating that note as much as Buddy Bolden played any of the other two blue notes learned from the "roustabouts."

Hoodoo Affecting Jazz and Blues Musicians

The word *hoodoo* is a corruption of the term *voodoo*, and the latter is the English-language spelling of a word that was carried by Haitian immigrants to New Orleans around 1804 or earlier. The original term was *vodu*, denoting the religious practices of the Fõ people, speakers of an I.A.4 or Kwa language, in the ancient Kingdom of Dahomey, West Africa. The *vodu* religion was exported to New World destinations, notably to Haiti. Residents of nineteenth-century New Orleans, aligned with churches, soon reinterpreted the immigrants' religious rites as witchcraft. "Voodoo" became synonymous with "snake worship." Those not involved pronounced it with shivers running down their spines. Soon English speakers changed it to "hoodoo" to express their own feelings of horror, and gradually the new term referred exclusively to evil spells and sorcery, while "voodoo" regained some of its original meanings and legitimacy under the celebrated Marie Laveau and her successors.

Thanks to cultural anthropologists and linguists in the twentieth century, the terminological quagmire has been cleared up. *The Merriam-Webster Dictionary* now acknowledges that the derivative term *hoodoo* in its present usage has a semantic field different from *voodoo*. "Hoodoo" now stands for "a body of magical practices traditional esp. among blacks in the southern U.S." and, in a narrower application of the word, "something that brings bad luck." On the other hand, "voodoo" is correctly recognized as a religion of West African origin, which had spread to Haiti and on to New Orleans. It is acknowledged that "voodoo" as a religion also includes the use of charms and spells.

There is no doubt that this two-pronged system of thoughts about a world beyond rationalist explanation survives in African American cultures in the southern United States and elsewhere, and has contributed to the reinterpretation of some forms of Christian worship as well as Christian symbolism, although it has not resulted in an obvious syncretist merger, as in the Yoruba-derived *orixa* religion in Bahia, Brazil. West African concepts and modes of thought continue in the United States more in the form of abstract schemata rather than West African imagery. Images can always reconfigure in history, while the schema remains, for example, the idea of a liaison with a supernatural power, or force, or person. In one culture the image takes up male, in another female connotations; it can be anything from the mermaid to the "Devil" to the "Big Black Man." These images can transform across time and space, assuming new contents, "modernizing."

It is also important to note that, by contrast, the idea of magic is not based on belief in spirits. No communication with spirits, or sacrifice, is involved. One does not pray or call one's grandmother to make magic work. It works by itself. It is a kind of proto-scientific procedure, on the basis of certain hypotheses about causality. A religion attributes the sources of power to supernatural beings who are often conceptualized in an anthropomorphic shape, e.g., the Christian and Jewish God Father image, animal "gods" in Ancient Egypt, ancestral spirits anywhere, e.g., in sub-Saharan Africa, up to concepts which integrate anthropomorphic images with immaterial properties, such as color, sound, a movement pattern, certain qualities of character, as in the *orisa* and *vodu* religious systems on the West African coast. By contrast, magic is supposed to work automatically along specific lines of cause and effect.

The two worldviews are different, though not necessarily mutually exclusive. All religious systems nurture some magical practices, as can be noticed in the Catholic Eucharist, in the practices of curse and sanctification, and in the existence of taboos whose violation is assumed to be self-punishing (Kubik and Malamusi 2002). It is this automatism, thought to be at work in magic practices, that characterizes them as part of a world vision somewhat different both from religious thought and from the rationalist, often materialistic worldview of modern times, embodied in mathematically based scientific discoveries. While rational worldviews propose relationships of causality to be verified by experiment, repeating the effect-producing arrangement, magic proposes the existence of connections that are not directly reproducible or verifiable in physical terms. In magic, practitioners proceed from four basic hypotheses:

(1) The existence of a non-material dimension of cause and effect across time and space. This implies that ESP effects, telepathy, and meaningful synchronicity as defined by C. G. Jung (1961 [1972: 418ff.]) are considered to be feasible as interaction between living beings.

(2) That symbolic acts can therefore affect real life, irrespective of time and distance; for example, hurting and torturing an effigy, a puppet, even a photograph or some DNA-carrying substance of a person, such as hair or fingernails, is bound to hurt the real person in a remote place. Equally in "love magic," the action of the practitioner can consist of associating or uniting two objects symbolizing the two persons to be linked. James G. Frazer (1890 [1907–15]) coined the terms "contagious magic" and "sympathetic magic."

(3) For magic to work, all depends, of course, on the presence of an agent, a practitioner who has learned magical practices from an expert, sometimes during long periods of apprenticeship. Such learning periods can be followed by amnesia, i.e., the

person does not remember having ever been instructed. According to oral tradition, the power of carrying out magic can also be implanted into a person, notably at a very young age, without the person being aware of his or her abilities.

(4) To uncover an incidence of "evil magic" (sorcery), a professional person is consulted, a seer, healer, diviner, etc.

The pathways of how magic is supposed to work are universal. The most important one however, is by analogy. An analogous scenario is created, expressing one's wishes, libidinous or aggressive, and focusing through intensive imagination on the target. Psychologically, magic operates along thought associations, even if there are plant, mineral, or animal ingredients involved in the practice. It may require activities such as imitation, will-effort, spell (recited or sung words), often using archaic language, mnemonics, syllable constructions, reversal of normal space/time or kinetic processes, e.g., reading a text backward, or writing a symbol left-handed.

Familiar terms for what came to be called hoodoo in America from various African languages include: *vwanga* in several languages of the Congo; *vulozi* in the Ngangela languages of eastern Angola and neighboring areas; *mangu* in Zande of Congo, Central African Republic, and South Sudan; *ufiti* in Chichewa/Cinyanja of Malawi and Moçambique; *uchawi* in Kiswahili (East Africa), etc., all synonymous with evil magic, sorcery that hurts and kills.

Jelly Roll Morton's Fears

Jelly Roll Morton had his first encounter with magic when he was a baby. What relatives told him later about his infancy he summarized for Alan Lomax in the 1938 interviews: "When I was six months old, my godmother—a very dark woman—would take me from my mother and, in absence of mother, would pass me off for her child. It seems she got a special kick out of this because I was a very good-looking baby" (quoted in Lomax 1952 [1959: 14]).

"Good-looking" meant fair-skinned, almost white. He always described his godmother beginning with her skin color. This was normal in a city in which "racial" categorizations had long become a reference scheme synonymous with social divisions. Someone like Morton was upholding a Creole identity, emphasizing his French ancestry. His godmother was not Creole.

But he also remembered her as a professional healer. Eulalie Hecaud (Lomax wrote "Echo") was a spiritualist, herbalist, and soothsayer with a large clientele. In some African communities, by comparison, there is sometimes a saying that such a woman, if entrusted with the upbringing of a child who is not hers, would inevitably implant witchcraft power in the abdomen of the infant. Subsequently,

Fig. 7.1. Jelly Roll Morton, 1904. Courtesy
of Al Rose Collection, Hogan Jazz Archive,
Tulane University.

in adult life the child would unknowingly practice magic in order to outwit others, to be successful, and to accumulate wealth.

According to Jelly Roll Morton's family, it happened once that his godmother passed little Ferdinand (as he was called, after the King of Spain) into the hands of a female acquaintance. "This lady displayed me in saloons, setting me on the bar and so forth . . ." (Lomax 1952 [1959: 14]). Then the sporting-woman was arrested. Six-month-old Ferdinand landed together with her in jail. There, the other inmates began to sing songs for him, and that was, he insisted, when he got his "first musical inspiration" (14).

In another section of his narratives, Jelly Roll said that during his boyhood the City of New Orleans was for him synonymous with "the whole world." At that time he could only speak French. But when his great-grandmother Mimi Pechet brought toys from an overseas trip, he realized that some of the names on maps were indeed place names. He then thought of trying to work hard, for money, to see the whole world one day. He took up the task of washing dishes at school.

When he was eleven years old, in 1896 or 1897, according to his own estimate, he was still in the care of his godmother, who tended to spoil him, he said, by giving him "a little freedom." He was staying with her uptown. She was looking thoroughly after his education and also arranged for his piano lessons and regular practice.

> My godmother, Eulalie Echo, wasn't a handsome woman, but she was very intelligent, had a pleasant personality and plenty money. She used to monkey around with this spiritual business. There were glasses of water around her house and voices would come out of those glasses. Very prominent people would consult my godmother and she would give them stuff like turtle heart—*cowein*—she'd have them swallow that and, afterwards, they had good luck and no one could harm them. (Lomax 1952 [1959: 19])

Once young Ferdinand was enormously frightened; that was during the time of the curfew after the Robert Charles riots, erupting in the summer of 1900.

> New Orleans was a kind of haunted place anyhow, and in those days I was scared to death if I was caught away from home past curfew. I remember one night, when I came back home, I saw a big black man sitting on a fence blowing smoke at me through his nose. The minute I saw him, I started running. Nobody can convince me that there are no such things as spirits. Too many have been seen by my family.

The idea of a "big black man," capable of defiance and fighting back at the racist system upheld by police, was deeply engrained in individuals' imagination. But it could also be transformed into a threatening evil spirit, symbolizing tendencies with which the young Ferdinand could not identify.

Other motifs of spiritualism would also find expression in his stories:

> My uncle met a girl on his way home one night and tried to flirt with her. He asked her if she didn't think it was rather late for her to be out. They talked for a minute and she asked him to see her home. When they got to the graveyard, the gate opened and she walked in and my uncle started running.
>
> I was very very much afraid of those things, in fact I was worried with spirits when I was a kid. Our family home, located on the corner of Frenchman and Robinson, seemed to be full of them. We heard dishes rattling at night, people walking around, the sewing-machine running, chains rattling, etcetera, and we used to keep the house filled up with holy water. I had it tied all around my bed. Even then it seemed like those spirits would touch my toes. I'd look up over the covers and see them and take one jump and be in my mother's bed. (20)

Jelly Roll Morton's childhood was not unusual. Like Port-au-Prince and several West African coastal cities, New Orleans has always been a place with people concerned about the effects of supernatural forces and beings, of "zombies," voodoo, witchcraft, etc. Complex forms of defense, mostly symbolic and for an outsider often bizarre, would be undertaken against those forces.

Many *voodoo*-experienced women in New Orleans, but also men, were professionals. They were able to discover hidden connections and neutralize some of those forces. Eulalie Hecaud, in Jelly Roll's young life, was such person; in Africa we would say she was a traditional healer and consultant, such as a *bokɔnō* in Fō culture, Dahomey, or *ǫrunmìlà*, the wise man of the *ifá* oracle in Yoruba culture, Nigeria, or a *mukwakutaha* (diviner of the *ngombo* oracle basket) in eastern Angola. Such persons were not only experts in the practice of divination, but psychotherapists with a vast knowledge about treatments and medical plants. Jelly Roll's godmother probably acquired her fluency in this domain from her forebears transmitting ancient knowledge from Dahomey or other parts of Africa via Haiti to New Orleans.

At age eleven Jelly Roll appeared to be deeply affected by this alternative world, as were many people in his Creole cultural environment, in spite of nominal Catholicism. For Jelly Roll it became a yardstick for interpreting his future fortunes and misfortunes.

Growing up in the care of his godmother, neither his biological father nor Mr. Morton (actually Monsieur Mouton), father of his younger sister Amède, were role models; he hardly ever met them. Consequently, in the interviews with Alan Lomax he did not focus on Ed LaMenthe (or LaMothe), his father, whom relatives in a later interview identified as a musician fond of the French Opera House, and who played slide trombone. Lomax was convinced "that the legacy of his father's trombone playing came up in Jelly Roll's compositions, in the bass figures written in trombone phrasing" (Lomax 1952 [1959: 41]).

An interesting question is why Jelly Roll adopted his stepfather's surname Mouton in an anglicized version, which is not a translation but merely a phonetic approximation. "Mouton" means mutton or lamb, and there are by-meanings he may have resented.

Jelly Roll's biological mother died when he was about fourteen. Thereafter he spent years with a male caretaker, his "favorite uncle" whom he did not really favor. The environmental component in making him become both an extraordinary, creative artist and a person who later, at middle age, would feel persecuted by strange forces can be traced to his family circumstances and also to the extra-family allegiances within which he grew up. The absence of an acceptable male role model in the extended family was decisive and the source of an early ambivalence in relation to females, resulting in fears about being called a "sissy" by peers. Gradually, he developed a plan to escape domestic domination with the help of his musical activities.

At age sixteen he discovered the "Tenderloin" district of New Orleans, taking up employment as a bordello pianist. In this context occurred the most traumatic event of his young life, which would be the starting signal for his future "rambling" as an adult. It was the sudden severing of all ties to his secure Creole family, and his eviction from their house by his great-grandmother. The reason was that he had taken this job as a pianist. Actually, he was honest about his new occupation, but he was naive enough to talk about it at home. On a Sunday, he came home, dressed in new clothes, meeting his great-grandmother Mimi Pechet as she was returning from church. He told her how he was making money as a musician, and offered to share his earnings with the family. But Mrs. Pechet refused to take anything and told him that he should leave their house forthwith, because he presented a moral danger to his very young sisters Amède and Mimi.

Kicked out like that, Jelly Roll Morton would carry this trauma through life. Alan Lomax, to whom he told the story in 1938 at the Library of Congress sessions, understood very well the import of the event, as is clear from his comments in "Interlude One" of his book *Mister Jelly Roll* (Lomax 1952 [1959: 34ff.]).

Jelly Roll's own narratives about his first professional work as a pianist at age sixteen or seventeen depict the situation and the ensuing drama:

The streets were crowded with men. Police were always in sight . . . Lights of all colours were glittering and glaring. Music was pouring into the streets from every house. Women were standing in the doorways, singing or chanting some kind of blues—some very happy, some very sad, some with the desire to end it all by poison . . . Some were real ladies in spite of their downfall and some were habitual drunkards and some were dope fiends as follows, opium, heroin, cocaine, laudanum, morphine, etcetera . . .

The girls liked their young professor and they worked the customers for big tips for me. I began to make more money than I had ever heard of in my life. I bought a new suit and a hat with the emblem Stetson in it . . . I was wearing these clothes on my way home from work on Sunday morning when I met my great-grandmother coming from early mass.

She looked at me and, I'm telling you, this Mimi Pechet could look a hole right through a door. "Have a good job now, Ferd? Making plenty money?"

Being very, very young and foolish, I told her what I was making. My grandmother gave me that Frenchman look and said to me in French: "Your mother is gone and can't help her little girls now. She left Amède and Mimi to their old grandmother to raise as good girls. A musician is nothing but a bum and a scalawag. I don't want you round your sisters. I reckon you better move."

My grandmother said all this and then she walked up the path to the white columns of the front porch, went inside, and shut the door. (quoted in Lomax 1952 [1959: 33])

In shock, relegated to the status of a homeless orphan by a religious zealot, the boy gasped for fresh air. He traveled to Biloxi, where he began to hang around with peers, older boys who quickly taught him to abuse alcohol in order to become "a real man." Eventually he got a minor job as a pianist in Biloxi for a "white sporting-house woman" whose name was Mattie Bailey (46). It was not a lucrative job, and the place was dangerous. Rumors began to circulate that there was a sexual relationship between the boy and the "white woman," and someone began to threaten that they would lynch him, as happened regularly in Mississippi. Hastily he returned to New Orleans. This was in the year 1902 and he was "about seventeen years old," according to his own testimony.

Back in New Orleans, his "home" would now be in those parts of the city where jazz originated. But he was ill; his hands did not move properly for playing piano (49). An old man named Sona discovered him and said: "Son, you are sick!" Jelly Roll replied that "someone must have put something on me," a remark he later weakened by saying that he was "just kidding." In any case, the boy was wondering how the old man could have known that he was ill. Papa Sona offered to cure him. Jelly Roll had met him before as a small child and remembered that he used to prepare medicines from frog legs and the tongue of a boa constrictor to be used as an aphrodisiac. Papa Sona took the boy to his house, stripped him, and put him in a tub with herbal medicine. He rubbed his body with this medicine, and repeated this treatment on three consecutive Fridays. Thereafter he said that now he would get him a job as a pianist. He said:

> "Take me to the house where you want to work, only don't say anything when we get there. Just touch me. In three days you will have that job."
>
> I took Papa Sona past Hilma Burt's house, which was one of the highest class mansions in the District, and did as he had requested. Three days later at two o'clock in the afternoon I was sitting around 25's and a maid from Miss Burt's house walked in and said their regular piano player was sick. Would I like to make a few dollars? (50)

In that high-class "mansion," pianist Jelly Roll Morton earned a lot of money. But unfortunately, he never thought of remunerating the old man as promised. He did not even thank him. Thirty-six years later, in the interview with Alan Lomax in Washington, D.C., he expressed his regrets: "In a week I had plenty money, but I never thought of paying Papa Sona for what he did, because I never really believed he had helped me. I should have realized that he used some very powerful ingredients. I should have been more appreciative, for I have lived to regret this ungrateful action" (50).

After the loss of what had been home, in spite of his mother's early death, and a secure family background he would not have wanted to miss, he started the odyssey of his life: "Alabama bound," Mississippi, Memphis, Chicago, the East Coast, California, Vancouver. His restlessness, his striving after compensation for the loss of a family, self-decoration with "achievements," diamonds sewn into his underwear and one fixed into a front tooth, surpassing the most notorious crooks in gambling—all that converged upon him. It can be explained as attempts to deny the reality. Sometimes he tried to reconstruct his lost family. In California, after 1917, Anita Gonzales was Jelly Roll Morton's first wife. Like him she was a New Orleans Creole, but somewhat older than Jelly. He composed the piece "Mama Nita" for her. She had six brothers back home and was the only girl in the family. When Jelly Roll was a youngster, he had sometimes visited her brothers, but she never threw a glance at him, knowing about the stigma that he played in a whorehouse. In California Jelly Roll became deeply attached to Anita, even dependent on her. Literally, he "nailed her down" (165), obsessed with fear of losing her. This refers to the years from 1917 to 1922.

Eventually, Jelly Roll Morton had success with something beyond his expertise as a solo pianist, with a band, the Red Hot Peppers. But in 1928 he married again to Mabel, whom he had first met a year earlier while she was working in a club in Chicago in the theatrical business. As if by destiny, it turned out that she was also from New Orleans, even from the same church parish as was his family. Morton, it seems, possessed an inner telepathic scanner that identified as potential partners women representing "home," in his vain attempts to reconstruct the family world from which he had been brutally expelled as a teenager. They toured together in many places in the United States, with Morton's band. By then he was in control of everything, it appears, and they were well off due to the success with his band. But Mabel also reports about behavior that scared her and reveals another side of his restless mind:

> He had a beautiful bus for the band with a sign on the outside—JELLY ROLL MORTON AND HIS RED HOT PEPPERS—but he and I travelled in the Lincoln. I guess the only trouble we ever had was over him going sixty-five around all those curves. That made me very nervous. He used to kid me and say, "May, I'm gonna leave you at home. . . . Don't you know I love myself better than anybody else in the world and I ain't never gonna have an accident when I'm driving the car?" Of course, he never did have an accident; and if a cop stopped him he could smooth-talk his way right out of it just like they were relatives. (188)

During the Depression years came the rise of a different music in the United States. Swing was enjoyed by the young people. Jelly Roll Morton's fortunes decreased. In New York he was sometimes laughed at for his music. Young Harlem musicians in the second half of the 1930s all played swing. They were calling his music "corny," which in a sense was true if compared with Count Basie and the bass of William Page, or with Jay McShann and some others. The Red Hot Peppers may have sounded corny, but not necessarily his solo piano playing.

In 1930 the Red Hot Peppers broke up. The Victor record company revoked his status as a preferred artist. As Alan Lomax has pointed out, Jelly Roll, unfortunately, did not understand the economic factors behind his misfortunes in the years of Depression, after 1929. He interpreted it all as a confluence of evil forces aimed at his person.

He reacted defensively, through projection, attributing others' success to plagiarism of his works. After his band had dissolved, he felt victimized by musicians who in his view had become undisciplined and rebellious, but also by "those white boys" (197) of whom he said he could "hear" them playing his tunes without acknowledgment. When the Waldorf-Astoria Hotel in New York closed its premises to "colored" bands, he interpreted it as a result of "the niggers acting rowdy" (198). Soon he would find New York to be a "cruel city" (200).

Underneath Jelly Roll's reactions and accusations was his simmering indignation about the 1894 reclassification of "Creoles" in New Orleans as "Negro" by a change in the legislative code. But there were also long-accumulating personal misgivings and feelings of guilt. The exuberance of his lifestyle during the rosy years, when he thought he was on top of everyone (as confirmed by Mabel, cf. Lomax 1952) was now shallow memory. His earlier success as a gambler and musician appeared to have been "undeserved" and in contradiction to his Catholic upbringing and the original plans for a decent future for him, envisaged by his various caretakers.

Such feelings—hardly ever articulated consciously—accumulated into anticipation of inevitable doom, into paranoiac fears, resurrecting the ghost of his great-grandmother. Now the whole world seemed to be intent on evicting him from his position in it.

He was passing through the worst crisis of his life. Increasingly, he developed panic feelings and a conviction that people wanted to harm him. Profits and his success as a musician were shrinking, but he stubbornly refused to acknowledge general economic and sociological factors as a cause for the downturn, including the unpredictable changes of fashion in the music business. Instead he reverted to a system of beliefs he had internalized during childhood, and became convinced that witchcraft (hoodoo) was behind his misfortune. This was the "return of the repressed," the beliefs he had pushed backstage in his mind, in favor of Christian views and rationalist thought. Facing those "underground" forces, now turning against him, he revived his earlier interpretive framework carried along since his up-bringing by soothsayer Eulalie Hecaud.

A firsthand account of the strange things that happened to Ferd Morton in New York by 1935 is found in his conversations with Alan Lomax, whose positive reactions to his narratives were a much needed stimulus, even a kind of psychotherapy in the quiet, human-to-human atmosphere of the Library of Congress recording sessions. Lomax's work in the United States, the Caribbean, and Mexico during the 1930s and 1940s—first jointly with his father John Lomax, later on his own—established a golden streak of field research. His documentation of Jelly Roll was further expanded by contact with Mabel, and later through field-work visiting Jelly Roll's family members and many musicians who had known him in New Orleans.

How the past had caught up with Jelly Roll in New York around 1935 is best related in his own words:

> One day I met a frizzly-haired woman who said she wasn't a fortune teller, but that she could work in those fields. If you wanted anybody killed, you would deposit her fee in the bank and she would go to work. She would buy a package of fine meat, tie it up with strings and throw it in a desolate section. In nine or ten days, this meat would decay and, as it decayed, your enemy would be dying. At the end of ten days, the enemy would be dead and she would go to the bank and collect her money. If the person was not dead you didn't owe her a thing. (202)

At that time Jelly Roll was still trying to suppress his earlier belief that sorcery was a reality. But this woman warned him about neglecting that invisible dimension of the world around him. "I didn't believe in those things. I didn't pay any attention when this woman told me that somebody was working against me. She said my Lincoln would be stolen. In three weeks it was gone. When they caught the thief, he wasn't even put in jail. It wasn't long before I wished I had taken this woman's advice" (202).

In need of an assistant partner in the music-publishing business—since more orders than Jelly Roll could handle were arriving, for band arrangements, radio programs, etc.—he bumped into a Caribbean gentleman whom he found trust-worthy. He hired the man and employed him as a typist in his New York office.

But soon there was a conflict. Jelly used to drive him home to Brooklyn every evening; often the man asked him to stop and wait, since he wanted to talk to a certain old guy, apparently a friend. Jelly Roll, waiting in his car and getting impatient, began to listen to their conversation. It turned out that the topic was a woman who "had lost everything," because she did not want to pay the old guy for his services. The employee revealed to Jelly Roll that the old guy "had a book like an encyclopedia, full of charms that never fail"(203). An atmosphere of suspicion was established. Jelly Roll began to believe that the Caribbean part-ner—with the help of the old man—was preparing something "against him." The Caribbean man was also a bad accountant. It then seemed that he had stolen some of the music and sold it to a certain firm. Possibly he had just tried to find a better publisher, but apparently he had not consulted with his employer.

Jelly Roll ended the man's contract, and they began to have an argument. It climaxed in some beatings. The man then cursed him, saying that before long he would lose everything, all his property, all his wealth.

Strange things turned up after the man had left the office, affecting Miss Billy Young, an actress who was working with Jelly Roll:

> After I kicked the West Indian out, she told me she had noticed that people would come to the door, and stop, seemingly unable to step across the sill; that was strange to her, because formerly a lot of people came to the office. We pulled up the rug near the door and there, underneath were four different colours of powder—grey, white, brown and pink. We started searching the office. We found powder sprinkled everywhere, even in the woodwork of the desk. There wasn't a piece of stationery that was clean of it. (204)

After her contact with the powder she continued typing letters, and involuntarily touched her face. "When she took her hands away from her face, her cheeks bursted out in a horrible looking rash. She took a drink out of a paper cup at the water cooler and her lips swelled up as big as the bumpers on a box car" (204). Thereafter he tried to contact the old guy who was a friend of the Caribbean (West Indian). He said he planned to shoot him, but the man was nowhere to be seen. Suddenly he discovered that the garage where he had left his bus for repair had sold it, because payment from Jelly Roll had not arrived in time. Inside was a trunk which had all his contracts and repertoire of songs. The company claimed that no trunk had ever been seen.

In his despair, Jelly Roll—seeking help from the "underground"—contacted a woman named Madame Elise. He paid her a hundred dollars for the consultation and was amazed what he saw there, how "she put her hand on a woman's head and this woman went out like a light and stayed out for thirty minutes." Madame Elise prescribed some baths for Jelly Roll. Some success returned to him for a while, and he organized a new band with bookings through Pennsylvania. But the members of the group were rough and they piled up huge bills for food and drinks in the hotel. Since Jelly Roll had not enough money on him, he had to drive back to New York for some more, leaving behind his trunk with music transcriptions, his fur coats, and many other valuables. Once again strange things happened.

> When I got back to New York, somehow I just forgot to send for that trunk. I always planned to, but I never could get around to it. I just wasn't myself any more. I walked around in a stupor. I went back to see Madame Elise. Pretty soon I was bringing big bags of food to her. Then I got to eating there—I don't think her husband liked that. I told her about the condition in my office—how people couldn't walk in the door. She took some turpentine and scrubbed the walls, but this only made everything

worse. Then I resolved to take action and to beat the West Indian to death, because Madame Elise told me it would help if I caught him and drew blood. But every time I got to the guy I couldn't raise my hands. (206)

By this stage, Jelly Roll Morton's situation had visibly turned pathological, in patterns known from the study of conversion neuroses. Such afflictions are also common in African cultures, where they are usually attributed to the workings of witchcraft. A spell expresses itself in the inability of the victim to act things out as planned, feeling very weak, lacking initiative. Early signs of the problem may turn up in parapraxis, such as constantly misplacing indispensable tools, or unexplained forgetfulness about important obligations, life-saving medication, etc. More serious symptoms include paralysis of the hands, arms, or legs and other physical ailments without an organic cause. Neither protective nor aggressive movements can then be carried out. A famous case from Europe reported in the literature was Anna O., a patient of the celebrated therapist Josef Breuer in Vienna in the 1880s. At the bed of her dying father she had the hallucination of a snake approaching him from behind, but she was unable to lift her arm in order to chase it away and thereby protect her father.

In Morton's case the pattern underlying his anxiety was a program of self-damage and self-punishment, which he carried out with pitiless perseverance. Unaware of the power of these inner forces, he tended to project them outside. He began to accuse Madame Elise that she had decided to work with his enemy:

I realize now that she was helping my enemy, the West Indian. I found this powder all in my hats. Every time I would put one on, it felt like I had the Library of Congress on my head. Madame Elise told me to take my handbags and cut them up in small pieces and throw them into the Harlem River, and, like a fool I did. She personally ordered me to cut up every bit of clothing I had and burn it all. I always had a lot of clothes and the stack I made in my backyard was way up over the top of my head. I poured on the kerosene and struck a match; it like to broke my heart to watch my suits burn. (206)

If we think of Madame Elise as a psychotherapist, her prescription would make sense as a kind of "implosive therapy," in this case allowing the patient to satisfy some of his wishes of self-damage in order to avert the danger of complete (life-threatening) destructive impulses. For a while, however, Morton's impediments continued unabated; he received job offers but could not muster enough energy to hire people for a new band. He lost participation in a Hollywood movie. He remembered: "I spent thousands of dollars trying to get this spell taken off me, but my luck just got blacker and blacker" (206). He continued to hold the "old guy" with his sorcery book responsible; he tried to make a lawsuit against him, contacting the New York district attorney, only to learn there was no law in New York concerned with this kind of accusation. His wife Mabel, in conversation with Alan Lomax for his 1952 book, confirmed these stories in part, except that she had a more rationalizing interpretation of the events. Not subscribing to the idea that the strange powder the "West Indian" had sprinkled over the place was some kind of hoodoo, she maintained that it was insect-killing powder. But she confirmed that after Jelly Roll Morton had started to consult "fortune tellers," he lost everything.

In 1935, when all these events took place, the two different interpretations, Mabel's and Jelly Roll's, became incompatible. This was perhaps one of the reasons that would make him "take leave" from New York and from his wife, relocating to Washington, D.C.

He did, however, discover that there was a hidden conflict in his mind: a struggle with feelings of guilt. That he initially was successful in his life he now attributed to the power conferred upon him by "hoodoo" people. But since he had never acknowledged it, all his accumulated wealth appeared to be undeserved and worthy of destruction. "When I was a young man, these hoodoo people with their underground stuff helped me along. I did not feel grateful and I did not reward them for the help they gave. Now, when everything began to go against me, those underground streams were running against me, too" (102).

This image of "underground streams" is a perfect visualization of forces and tendencies in Jelly Roll's own unconscious of which he had become a victim. Guilt feelings for having preyed upon many people—not the least by gambling—and for taking his success for granted, without acknowledging that it was a gift requiring a gesture of thanks, were now overwhelming. He felt he was being presented the bill for his excesses and shown the reverse side of the benefits he had received.

During his life Jelly Roll made several attempts to undo or at least minimize the power of his great-grandmother Mimi Pechet's verdict. Alan Lomax discovered one such attempt during his visit to the family in 1949, long after Morton's death: that for decades he had sent money and presents to his sisters from whom he had been separated as an undesirable influence.

The "hoodoo" persecution episode, it seems, began shortly before 1935. Thereafter he left New York and was away from his wife Mabel for about two years, working in a small bar in Washington, D.C. During this period many people were getting interested in jazz history, and by playing piano in that bar he attracted fans. They were of two types: one revered him as a historical figure representing New Orleans from the era of the beginnings of jazz; the other found him old-fashioned and preferred the current music of big band swing.

By staying away from New York, however, and playing his piano for those who were interested, he gradually regained much of his self-esteem. He began to fight back at exploitation and promote the cause of an undiluted jazz history that would give credit to its true originators.

He began to talk about the works of Tony Jackson, Josky Adams, Mamie Desdunes, Buddy Bolden, and other musicians and composers whom he had known in New Orleans as an adolescent. Gradually he assumed the role of defender of those composers' rights, as much as his own. He castigated plagiarism and the excesses of the music business. Morton's oral testimonies are very important to jazz history, because they bring up both criticism and valuable information no one else could have provided. Oral history, otherwise irretrievably lost, began to take shape on disc and in print. Often Morton would say bluntly what no one else dared to say. In particular, his controversy with W. C. Handy in the aftermath of a radio program in the spring of 1938 in which Handy was hailed as the "originator" of jazz and blues, helped stir interest in the facts of early jazz and blues, and in his own work, by fans, researchers, and folklorists, including Alan Lomax.

The personal tragedy of Jelly Roll Morton's life is one aspect of history, with all the damages involved. What has not been destroyed, however, is the legacy of his music. Here the recording sessions in 1938 with Lomax at the Library of Congress are paramount, and their complete issue on eight CDs by Rounder Records in 2006, under the tireless efforts of Anna Lomax Wood, Jeffrey A. Greenberg, and John Szwed, must be hailed as a lasting tribute to the work of one of jazz's great personalities.

Lomax's conversations with Jelly Roll Morton, moreover, helped the battered composer overcome recurring depression, regain self-confidence, and restore his personal dignity. The two of them, in the Coolidge Auditorium of the Library of Congress, were definitely on the same "wavelength."

Jelly Roll Morton died in Los Angeles on August 1, 1941, after a brief but intensive second career. The cause of death was asthma and late complications in his lungs due to a knife attack two years earlier, which had occurred at the Jungle Inn in Washington while he was playing piano for the guests.

Gunther Schuller, in *The New Grove Dictionary of Jazz*, vol. 2, has written this posthumous appreciation of the composer: "His accounts, both verbal and pianistic, have the ring of authenticity and revealed Morton as jazz's earliest musician-historian and a perceptive theorist and analyst of the music" (828).

Liaison with Supernatural Forces

Artists everywhere are individuals not necessarily following a society's conventions. In cultures that prize rational thought, presumably since eighteenth-century Enlightenment, an artist's special abilities are usually summarized under the term "talent," a kind of inborn disposition for developing certain skills. Other societies of the world have different views. David Evans (personal communication, July 2013) relates this story: "When I referred to an African American singer's 'talent' in a church setting, I was quickly upbraided and told that it was a 'gift' [i.e., from God]."

In some parts of Africa, any spectacular personal achievement, not only in art, but also in other areas of professional engagement, such as sports, technology, medicine, etc., may kindle assumptions about that person's possible access to some kind of magic, or that he or she could have entered a liaison with a supernatural being. The word *supernatural* here must be taken only as a translation of convenience for a great variety of concepts in African languages expressing this idea.

Such assumptions do not necessarily imply witchcraft. In fact, recourse to the techniques of sorcery is very much the domain of the underprivileged, not the successful person but the disappointed, poor chap who has failed in life and hates his or her more successful peers and relatives. Artists are as often the victims of witchcraft as other people. They are targeted through mischief, scandal, backbiting, etc. (see Daniel Kachamba's experiences with *misece*, Kubik 2010: II: 257–59). They can become suicidal. Artists themselves, therefore, will not normally practice sorcery, although local interlocutors have sometimes declared that a human sacrifice marks the beginning of a successful career. More often the artist will be thought of as having acquired his expertise through apprenticeship, an initiation ceremony, or from a caretaker in childhood who was a traditional healer and/or diviner. If it is through some kind of contract with a supernatural entity, concepts vary from culture to culture. While the structure of such a relationship is a constant cross-culturally, the details are culture-specific.

A musician may decide to confirm what people are saying about him. Away from family members, leading a "rambling" life, he may use those rumors to his commercial advantage. He may even include in his songs details about the alleged relationship with the supernatural, or drop casual remarks to confirm those stories. This is a marketing trick to increase his popularity and also make him appear invincible, because some people will get scared hearing about those forces he apparently commands. To corroborate such a self-portrait, the artist may also adopt a descriptive trademark for his activities or a special personal habit, a dress code or an artist's name that instills fear.

David Evans (2008: 179–221) has studied the subject of nicknames in blues musicians, and in some instances nicknames may be fear-instilling. Normally they depict an alter ego quality the artist wants to project, e.g., names such as Howling Wolf, Rip Top, Papa Lord God, the Devil's Son-in-Law, Hound Head, etc. Evans writes that nicknames

> project the attributes embodied in them as some sort of special, essential, or outstanding feature of a person that is worthy of attention. In other words, they project

a simplified and focused *persona* or image that may or may not be consistent with the actual being, appearance, or personality of the bearer. In the case of blues artists nicknames may be conferred on them by themselves or by family members, friends, audience members or promoters (including record companies). (181)

The same applies to nicknames for jazz musicians, as surveyed by Skipper (1986). Remarkably, however, nicknames in blues artists that would explicitly suggest connections with the supernatural, are rare (Evans 2008: 201), in contrast to what is sometimes said in song texts and through some forms of behavior.

Relationships with a supernatural being or possession of witchcraft are often the subject of songs whose content thereby underlines the status of the artist as someone in command of mysterious forces. In cultures that have been strongly affected by Christian mythology, the artist may express liaison by using such Christian symbols as saints, angels, Lucifer, etc. Many names and nicknames of gospel singers and groups suggest possession of divine power. On the other hand, among Christians, liaison with the supernatural may also be viewed negatively as abuse of spiritual power, good or bad, and therefore he or she is destined for automatic punishment or doom. This idea is perpetuated in modern science fiction, in the motif that humankind tries to compete with God, abusing technology, creating Frankenstein's monster, Godzilla, etc., with inevitable consequences.

In cultures with not only Christian but also Islamic backgrounds, itinerant musicians often rank low on the social ladder. In the West African savannah, trader-musicians carrying fiddles or spike lutes, but also professionals referred to as "griots" in French, often have an unsavory reputation. They are believed to practice sorcery and to have demonic associations. This picture is perpetuated in New World cultures, for example, in the term *mandinguero* in Brazil (cf. Kubik 1979), which derives from Mandiŋ (a person from Mali or Guinea speaking a Mande language). Mandingueros are thought to be sorcerers. Under Islamic law, as imposed for a few months in 2012–13 in the ancient cities of Timbuktu and Gao on the Niger River in Mali, all musical activities besides live music, including CD players, iPods, and even cellphone ringtones, were forbidden as un-Islamic.

What is it that makes ideas about musicians having a liaison with the supernatural so popular in some places? There can be a variety of reasons, depending on ideology, religion, even social structure. In the Christian US South of the 1920s and '30s, the lonely, unmarried alcohol-dependent musician who was drawn to prostitution and gambling represented a dangerous example for young people to emulate. Fundamentalist religious circles in particular would react by isolating him as much as possible, or he would retreat voluntarily from functions, as did Son House, who was a preacher, then resigned from church activities and became a performer of blues. Insisting upon his chosen lifestyle, the artist sometimes takes note of the negative opinions about him, but is not bothered by being a "danger" to normal people's ways. He cherishes his freedom of choice and independence. Often a rebel against established religions and social conventions, he either deletes references to all beliefs from his lyrics, or explains to the public the source of his skills as rooted in a counterculture. What satisfies ordinary people in such stories is the thrill embodied in the projections. The (psychological) term *projection* describes a defense mechanism, i.e., one manner through which we may accommodate to unacceptable tendencies in ourselves: by ascribing them to others. This includes the general desire to break loose from society's restrictions and try something else.

Such tendencies and wishes are massively projected by the public upon artists who seem to demonstrate that they can live it up. Blues and jazz artists also absorb and recreate ordinary people's secret yearnings. Sometimes both text and musical structure reflect the underlying inner conflicts.

In the southern United States, especially among Mississippi Delta musicians during the era of rural blues from the 1920s to the 1940s, there were many "rambling" originals with a guitar in their hands and a lifestyle contrary to anything the churches were teaching They thought of the churches as endorsing the established social order, including segregation, economic exploitation, and social denial. The roaming blues artist in the South, therefore, was a strong statement against this order, because he often rejected all these institutions and their conventions, including soothing stories about God and the afterlife. In "My Black Mama" recorded in 1930, Son House even dared to sing: "Ain't no heaven, ain't no burnin' hell / Where I go when I die, can't nobody tell."

(a) Mamiwata

Along the Atlantic coast of Africa, from Ghana, Togo, Nigeria, and Cameroon down to the Congo, a popular idea is that musicians, painters, and others with outstanding ambitions can acquire power and have success if they enter a liaison with a being in the sea called Mamiwata (Pidgin English for "Mother in the Water").

Mamiwata is understood as an attractive but dangerous spirit, always female, with the upper part of her body a beautiful young woman, the lower part in the form of a fish. The young man who enters into a relationship with Mamiwata is awarded material riches, he will have success in his art, etc. It is said that to enter such as liaison is easy. All he has to do is write a proposal and deposit the letter under a stone near the river. After some time he will find that it is gone, and there may soon be an answer.

There is a famous highlife song of the 1960s from Nigeria about Mamiwata. The composer was Sir Victor Uwaifo and in the song (sung in English) the guitarist engages in a conversation with the spirit: "If you see Mamiwata / never,

never you run away." The reply by Mamiwata is depicted in lead guitar melodies that "speak." This is possible because Igbo is a tone language as are all the other languages of the I.A.4 or Kwa family. "Guitar Boy and Mamiwata" was first published on a 45 r.p.m. disc by Philips, Dancing Time No. 8, 420034 PE.

The Congolese painter Chéri Samba, born December 30, 1956, near Madimba in the Bas-Congo area close to the Atlantic Ocean, has painted several remarkable visualizations of this image. So has another Congolese painter, Cheri-Cherin. In one of the latter's, Mamiwata bursts out of his easel as a haunting image, while he is painting her, overwhelming him.

The Mamiwata myth is not restricted to the West African coast. It has spread further inland to Central Africa. Mamiwata—always called by that name in Pidgin English, sometimes translated into French as "La Sirène"—is thought of as being found in rivers, even in small watercourses. The idea is familiar to anybody in southern Cameroon or western Congo. People have developed their precautions in order not to offend her, especially those living near large watercourses, and a vast oral literature has emerged with a few central themes and motifs.

My friend and colleague, the late Maurice Djenda, sociologist and cultural anthropologist from the Central African Republic, has reported extensively about Mamiwata in the Sangha River area (Cf. Djenda in Kubik 2007b:). He describes how a young man's life with Mamiwata can be a dangerous liaison:

> In order to take "possession" of Mamiwata, i.e. to make her love you, first you have to make a sacrifice; on an evening at about six o'clock you deposit perfume, but especially eggs near the stones at the water.
>
> Next morning you come again, and you will hear whether she loves you or not. If she agrees, you go back to your house and reserve a special room for her. This room must always be locked. No one else may enter . . . Mamiwata will come to you in the night holding a strong light in her hand, but she will first try to find out whether you are courageous; she will transform into a snake, a lion, etc. If you are not afraid, she will remain with you.
>
> Mamiwata makes you rich. But one day, if you cease to love her, you can liberate yourself. You take a basket which is empty and ask her to fetch water. She will be unable to do so, water will always run out of the basket. Then she will not come back again, feeling ashamed.
>
> What Mamiwata demands from you as her husband is "one cock" every year. "Cock" means human being. She will kill one of your relatives every year; it can be your brother, then your mother and so on. If you have lost all your relatives, then she will want one of your fingers every year, first from the hands, then the toes. And when all your fingers and toes are gone, she will take you into the water to die. (Author's translation of Djenda's text originally written in French) (37ff.)

Fig. 7.2. Image of Mamiwata, half woman, half fish, with a red book in her left hand, a magic telephone line leading from a black pot down into the sea, her domicile, red candles placed on a tray and a snake slung around her body. She lures the young man, in this case painter Chéri Samba, into a relationship, but his parents in "Heaven" depicted with wings, implore him to resist. Painting reproduced from Wolfgang Bender (1991) with kind permission.

Peer groups of adolescents in a village exchange tips about how to attract Mamiwata and how to take advantage of her. A common motif within the hundreds of narratives circulating in West and Central Africa is that the liaison eventually ends with the protagonist's death. Mamiwata makes you rich and successful, but in the end she takes your life. She lures you into the sea and you die. A young man's indecision whether he should or should not enter such a liaison is well depicted in the conversation printed on one of Chérie Samba's paintings as in a comic strip: the parents, long dead, warn the young man about such a relationship. Many of Chérie Samba's paintings are like blues texts, juxtaposing conflicting views, orthodox opinions and warnings, and a young man's cravings.

In terms of C. G. Jung's analytical psychology, Mamiwata would represent an archetype of the collective unconscious, although Jung has never written specifically about this West African female spirit. In Jungian terms Mamiwata could be a manifestation of what he called the "anima" archetype, an unconscious feminine element in a man's psyche, "animus" being the male counterpart of the phenomenon in women. The anima archetype may be projected upon any female, including supernatural representations, especially by men who have repressed the female component in their soul, tending to undervalue female qualities and even treat women with contempt. Mermaids in various cultures, from the Sirens of Ancient Greece to the nymphs enticing a man under the water, are common expressions of the "anima" archetype, according to Jung. Being a sailor in an all-male occupation, sometimes with an aggressive view of the other gender, can make the person particularly prone to a reaction of this kind from the unconscious.

Historically, the present-day Mamiwata image along the Atlantic coast of West Africa is probably due to a merger of several related ideas about female water spirits that were once part of the local mythology. The merger must have occurred in the early stages of European maritime trade along the West African coast, i.e., from the fifteenth century on. It is known that some sailing ships had the figure of a siren depicted at the bow. The imported image then merged with local ideas and became syncretized. Characteristically, Mamiwata is often thought of as a "white" woman, or at least fair-skinned.

From all cultures we have sayings that some extraordinary personalities, artists, explorers, political leaders etc., acquired their power from a strange liaison with a female benefactor, sometimes a queen-like woman, sometimes a "femme fatale." Often the narratives emphasize how a male person can be overwhelmed by unconscious forces symbolized by the "anima" archetype, or by the "Great Mother" (Jung).

(b) Pact with the "Devil"

In an article published in 1923, Sigmund Freud analyzed the story of a seventeenth-century painter, Christoph Haitzmann, on the basis of a manuscript preserved by the Catholic church in the library of Mariazell, Austria—a place of pilgrimage for Catholic believers. The manuscript, discovered by a colleague of Freud, reported about the miraculous redemption of the painter by the grace of the Holy Mary. Haitzmann, so it was written, had entered a "pact with the devil" (Teufelspakt) for nine years, which he signed first in black ink and later in blood. With the deadline of the pact approaching in the ninth year, Christoph Haitzmann began to suffer from hallucinatory visions, convulsions, painful sensations all over the body, paralysis of the legs, etc., and he consulted a priest in the village of Pottenbrunn, where he lived.

On September 5, 1677, he was sent to Mariazell with a letter by the priest in the hope of finding help there. Sigmund Freud asks a basic and universally applicable question: Why would someone sign himself up to bondage with the

"Devil"? This question had been posed before, e.g., in Goethe's Dr. Faust, a story based on earlier, ultimately oral literature. In structure, the deal is analogous to that by a young artist in West Africa entering a relationship with Mamiwata, or—for that matter—any (young) person entering a liaison with a spiritual being. As a reward for giving up the immortality of one's soul promised in Christian and other Middle East religions, the Devil offers riches, wealth, power over other people and over the forces of nature, knowledge of magic, and, most of all, pleasure, including sexual pleasures.

Freud then analyzed the personal motivation behind Haitzmann's "pact." He found the answer in a brief note by the artist himself, in which he claimed that Satan appeared before him with a book of magic formulas in his hand. In the pact's text, Haitzmann declared that he was subscribing himself for a period of nine years to be the biological son of Satan (i.e., Satan would take care of him like a father), but at the end of this period his body and soul would belong to the latter.

Freud detected in this relationship the revival of an earlier feminine attitude of the man toward his original father that he had repressed as a boy, i.e., a homosexual, incestuous tendency. Haitzmann revealingly painted the Devil with breasts. Here, the church protocol gives us precious information about the "motivation" for the pact. Haitzmann was neither interested in money—he rejected the Devil's offer in one of his hallucinations when he appeared before him with a bag of gold—nor was he interested in magic or entertainment of any sort. What did he want from the Devil?

He was suffering from depression, and he found himself impeded in his work. He said in the protocol that he had painted the Devil to "drive away the melancholic mood." We could even translate that phrase as "to get rid of the blues." In a second report it is mentioned that the death of his father had triggered the melancholy. Haitzmann entered a liaison with the Devil to be relieved of his depression, electing him as a parental substitute.

Freud has to be congratulated on a formidable interpretive coup, against all odds, considering the time distance between the reported events from a different culture in the seventeenth century and his twentieth-century analysis. A similar situation also affects our work about historical jazz and blues artists and their thoughts, because the artists in question can no longer be involved in analytically oriented conversations.

In Haitzmann's century personal psychological problems were inevitably clad and expressed within Christian mythology. Freud elicited a few universals in behavior from the Haitzmann story, notably the function of the Devil in such a liaison as a substitute for a parent figure, with the candidate's resulting overdependence and loss of personal identity, and the frequency with which individuals of extraordinary talent, such as artists (e.g., Haitzmann) or researchers (e.g., Dr. Faust) seem to be drawn into relationships of that kind.

He identified demonic imagery as the personification of "rejected wishes, derivatives of rejected, repressed tendencies" (Freud 1923 [1997: 173–74]). Humans tend to project their own unacceptable tendencies and wishes onto the external world, on collectively created symbols of fantasy (e.g., the Devil, Mami-wata) thereby experiencing a decrease in the frightening pressures from those inner forces.

A few questions arise concerning the manuscript. Why was this case written down at all by the priests and the manuscript so carefully preserved in the church archives, the pictures of Satan copied? Obviously, it served to put on record and even publicize miraculous healings through the grace of the Holy Mary, confirming the status of Mariazell as a place of pilgrimage. Freud thought that Haitzmann may have even invented his fantasy in a state of hypnotic dependence on the priest whom he had consulted in Pottenbrunn and from whom he expected solace and relief—in fact something like seventeenth-century psychotherapy. Haitzmann's fantasy totally conforms with the worldview of the Catholic church at that time, in which some confessions by clients were regularly interpreted as due to illicit contacts with Satan. Haitzmann may have responded to such suggestions by the priest. Eventually he did find refuge in a monastery and became a monk.

We have also become aware of a small detail in Haitzmann's symbolism, the importance of the number 9 (i.e., nine years of the pact and the year 1669 as its expiry). Such number symbolism is also found in African American folklore, for example in an oral narrative about a banjo player collected from an interview in the US South during the 1930s and '40s (cf. the five volumes *Hoodoo—Conjuration—Witchcraft—Rootwork* published by Harry M. Hyatt [1970]):

370. If a man wants to sell hisself to the devil, why—if he wants to play banjah [banjo] good he's to go to a *four-corner road* [crossroad] nine mornings. You go ever' morning till the ninth morning. He sets along there playing de banjah until after awhile a *lot of things* would come up. They'll *go around him nine times*. And after awhile the last one behin'll ast him what would he rather do, do what dey doin' or serve de Lord. The man said do what they're doin'. He can bang his banjah up and he'll *play on de ball* anywhere. [Deal Island, Md., (121, 33: 2)]

What are the implications for jazz and blues research of these studies in West Africa about Mamiwata or a case from seventeenth-century Europe on the effects of Christian mythology? The results may help us better assess patterns of thought and behavior that are ultimately rooted in psychological universals, but clad in contemporaneous symbolic expression.

Power Projection through the Devil

In the US South from the 1920s to the 1940s, there was a surge among Delta musicians of delight in the macabre. Not everyone, however, shared the trend, and it seems that it started to some extent with Peetie Wheatstraw, born 1902, who called himself "The Devil's Son-in-Law" and also "The High Sheriff from Hell." He was killed on his birthday in an accident in 1941 in East St. Louis, Illinois, when the car in which he was traveling crossed a rail line and was struck by a train. The background meaning of the Devil in the South was a bit different from that in the Haitzmann case. Here the aim of the myth could be described as power projection through an image.

Other prominent blues singers in whose works or lives a relationship with the Devil appears include Tommy Johnson (1896–1956), Son House (1902–1988), and, most of all, Son House's disciple Robert Johnson (1911–1938). As a motif, the Devil also appears in Skip James's celebrated song "Devil Got My Woman" (cf. Kubik in Evans 2008d).

From the late 1920s to the early 1940s, blues was all around on the roads of the South (Evans 1978b). It was a musical culture independent of, but parallel to swing jazz as it emerged in Kansas City and elsewhere. Blues was commercially exploited within the category of so-called "race records" catering to the African American market. Rural blues musicians soon found their records all over the place in juke boxes. This contributed to their popularity and enhanced their self-esteem. The record companies, however, were recording only artists that were commercially promising, leaving many others unrecorded. In spite of that the result has been a valuable body of precious historical recordings. Text censorship also had some effect, perhaps even positively. It became an intellectual stimulus for musicians to express themselves ambiguously, by image substitution or in coded form. Blues audiences easily decodified the texts. Blues was truth. Any topic of pressing personal and social concern was brought to public awareness, even most intimate sexual problems, if only expressed in a veiled, symbolic language. Humor, irony, and despair alternated in the texts.

Along with the commercial recordings, broader interest developed by writers, folklorists, etc., as to the lives and "romantic" careers of blues musicians. The trend started with Howard W. Odum's novels about a (fictional) wandering blues singer. John Lomax and John Work started to record in the South; later this was continued by Alan Lomax. An early account is John and Alan Lomax's 1936 portrait of the singer Lead Belly. W. C. Handy's autobiography appeared in 1941, stirring further interest. But it took a quarter century after the 1940s for scientifically compiled biographies of rural blues singers to appear. A thoroughly researched modern biography, based on extensive fieldwork and interviews with relatives, is David Evans's book (1971) on Tommy Johnson. Here, it must also be noted that many artists would call themselves "songsters" or even "musicianers" rather than "blues singers" or "bluesmen," and their repertoires might include blues, spirituals, and other types of song.

Blues as "Devil's music" was a familiar label in the South, to castigate the roaming blues singers whose music had become increasingly present in juke boxes in roadside bars. Church people rejected this lifestyle and their music. But its stigmatization attracted young men's interest in protest against values that tolerated Jim Crow. Some songsters increased their spell over audiences by deliberately identifying with the negative stereotypes that were cast upon them. They suggested having access to satanic supernatural forces. Reappearance of an age-old African precursor to the roaming blues musician was thereby enhanced, the itinerant string-instrument-playing musician of the West African savannah, often in a similar social condition.

The popular folk myth about making a pact with the Devil gained new currency. David Evans, in his book on Tommy Johnson (Evans 1971: 22), quotes from a conversation with a brother of the blues singer, the Reverend LeDell Johnson, who had played blues as a young man but later renounced it in favor of his church functions. Tommy Johnson, born around 1896 near Terry, Mississippi, came from a family of thirteen children. By the time Evans began his field work, in 1965 and 1966, Tommy was dead, but Evans was able to conduct extensive interviews with family members, notably Mager (born 1905) and the Reverend LeDell (born 1892), besides musicians who had known Tommy Johnson personally.

Reverend Johnson paints a lively portrait of his brother Tommy and how the latter, after he had run away from home as a sixteen-year-old with an older woman in 1912, learned to play the blues. When he returned home (without the woman) in 1914, he was an accomplished singer:

Well, when he left home, he wasn't drinking all that mess and stuff, canned heat and shoe polish and bay rum. He could sit down and just think up a song, which is blues, and make 'em hisself without anybody learning him. I remember since I been here in Jackson. Me and him would play for some white folks here, and he'd just set up and just set there and follow with his box, and he could make a song in ten minutes. Now if Tom was living, he'd tell you. He said the reason he knowed so much, said he sold hisself to the devil. I asked him how. He said, "If you want to learn how to play anything you want to play and learn how to make songs yourself, you take your guitar and you go to where a road crosses that way, where a crossroad is. Get there, be sure to get there just a little 'fore twelve o'clock that night so you'll know you'll be there. You have your guitar and be playing a piece sitting there by yourself. You have to go by yourself and be sitting there playing a piece. A big black man will walk up there and take your guitar, and he'll tune it. And then he'll play a piece and hand it back to you. That's the way I learned how to play anything I want." And he could.

He used to play anything, don't care what it was. Church song. You could sing any kind of tangled up song you want to, and I'll bet you he would play it. [Rev. LeDell Johnson] (Evans 1971: 14)

This is a direct quote by Rev. Johnson of what his brother had told him. Probably, Tommy Johnson had really stated that his guitar expertise came from an encounter of that sort at the "crossroad." However, one has to be careful with such stories. Often they functioned as a way of demonstrating to others, in this case to his religious brother, that there was an alternative path of life, even if society disapproved of it. What Tommy Johnson related, moreover, was in itself a quotation, of something that had been part of the folklore in the South for a long time: the ideas of the crossroad, the Big Black Man (see also the young Jelly Roll Morton's encounter), and recipes for a pact with supernatural beings, as in both African and European traditions. It is impossible to ascertain whether Tommy Johnson just believed in the possibility of such a pact or whether he had actually experienced such an encounter at the "crossroad," or had used the story only to boast to his brother that from now on he had access to resources that he certainly would not share with him.

The image of the Big Black Man was a powerful archetype in African American communities that were under pressure from three directions: (a) a male-centered family system; (b) many children in competition within the household; (c) racist encounters and pressures from the outside upon the intra-family social structure, with the accompanying daily experience of denigration, snubs, discrimination, etc. This powerful male archetype had compensatory function, expressing personified wishes for power. He could instill fear as he did in little Jelly Roll Morton, but could also be perceived as a benefactor, if an adolescent identified with him and learned to come to an agreement ("pact"), as in the story attributed to Tommy Johnson. The Big Black Man is the counter-image of the weak little boy in the household and what the latter strives for. The image is also one of social empowerment, summarizing the unbearable situation in a racially segregated society, in which the word *black* was synonymous with anything undesirable. This is why the Big Black Man cannot be hastily equated with the figure of the Devil in Christian mythology.

A deal or pact made by a blues singer more often focused on the idea of a black Power Man, rather than that of the Christian Devil. The Devil was a speech convention, the result of diction expressing a Christian reinterpretation of the African American dream images describing relationships with the spiritual world. In the 1920s and 1930s this reinterpretation was deeply internalized in African American culture through several generations of Christian believers. In African fieldwork we have found the same kind of reaction in people who had adopted French, and who were living in proximity of Christian missions. For example, *evus* (persons practicing sorcery) in the Faŋ language in Gabon was rendered by the same speakers, once they were using French, as *les vampires*. In another society, the Mpyɛmɔ̃ in the Sangha River area, Central African Republic, the concept of *bidimi* (haunting spirits) was rendered in French as *les diables*.

For this reason, stories about blues singers said to have subscribed to a pact with the Devil are better scrutinized in terms of the hidden African American imagery. The pact, no matter whether imagined or actually made, was in many cases not with the Christian Devil but with the image of a powerful "black" man as a transcendental figure. As such it could appear with a positive or negative charge, depending on the nature of the psychological problem of the "applicant." It would transform into a negatively charged symbol if the applicant was unsure about the relationship, ambivalent, or paranoiac. Then it would also be equated with the Devil.

What has been said above should suffice to demonstrate that there are deeper issues and levels of interpretation than the ones proceeding from nominal Christian terminology, as it was adopted by blues musicians and their communities in rural areas of the South. In addition we can analyze, in terms of family and professional relationships, some spontaneously created Christian-tinged terms serving as nicknames. What does Peetie Wheatstraw's self-identification as the Devil's Son-In-Law really express?

Here, we should look at the term's kinship allusions. Unlike seventeenth-century Christoph Haitzmann, in search of a father substitute, Peetie Wheatstraw postulates a different kind of relationship with the Devil (see Fig. 7.3).

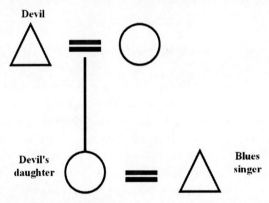

Fig. 7.3. Peetie Wheatstraw and the "Devil"

The Devil has a daughter whom the blues singer married. Since the daughter of an evil principal is supposed to be evil as well, he married the Evil. To whom the Devil himself was married to produce his daughter is left open. But there are sidelights. Peetie Wheatstraw also called himself "The High Sheriff from Hell." So, Satan not only accepted him as an affinal kin, but gave him a professional task. In real life, the High Sheriff was, of course, the enforcer of the southern racist system.

These fantasies created something like an alternative world, mirroring the world on Earth, with family bonds, professions, and concern for security. "High Sheriff from Hell" almost sounds like a precursor in diction to that of the Black Panther movement of the 1960s, e.g., *Essays from the Minister of Defense Huey Newton.*, a pamphlet available for seventy-five cents in 1968 (Culture Research Archive Kubik/Malamusi, Vienna). Like "Minister of Defense," "High Sheriff from Hell" describes a male authority whose task is to guarantee security and maintenance of law and order. That position is claimed by the singer. But fantasy also reveals a wider concern by the singer. As a High Sheriff he is responsible for the welfare of the African American community in the South, by implication proposing an independent self-governing territory, even if it was to be located in Hell.

Paul Garon's biography of Peetie Wheatstraw offers further reading. He apparently did live up to the "devilish" image, being involved in various rackets. David Evans tells me (conversation, May 2014): "I spoke to his relatives in Cotton Plant, Arkansas, all devout church people. Peetie was the 'black sheep' of the family, and children were admonished never to mention his name. Yet he made occasional return visits from his base in East St. Louis, Illinois, staying with a more tolerant cousin and performing at parties of the local white folks, who treated him like the recording star that he was. Truly 'The High Sheriff from Hell'!"

Robert Leroy Johnson

Much has been written about Robert Johnson, who after his death rose to stardom and become an embodiment of tendencies toward the macabre in people writing about his "pact with the devil." To commemorate that pact there is a monument in Clarksdale, Mississippi, at crossroads 49 and 61, with sculptured guitars, for tourists to photograph; the place where blues musicians are supposed to have "sold their soul to the Devil." A symbol has turned into fact, myth has been subjected to business interests to lure people to places where blues artists were active from the 1920s to the 1940s.

In our assessment of the work of singer and guitarist Robert Johnson and the circumstances of his life, it is crucial to keep a few facts in mind that appear separated in his biography. He was born May 8, 1911, in Hazlehurst, Mississippi, to Julia Dodds and Noah Johnson from an extramarital relationship. Young Robert had hardly any male role model during his childhood; he was kicked about by changing parental figures, so he acquired the reputation of a "strong-willed" child. Lacking a model and a firm male identity, he expressed his social ambivalence by taking different names at different times, Spencer, Lonnie, etc. Soon he was a school dropout. Impressed by blues greats of his time, whom he came to know personally or from their successful records, it turned out that records would be a considerable influence on his emerging art.

A traumatizing and therefore consequential event in his life came after he had just started a family in 1929 at age eighteen, marrying Virginia Travis in Penton, Mississippi. In April 1930 his wife Virginia and the baby died in childbirth. Thereafter, partly in friendship with blues musicians Eddie "Son" House, Willie Brown, and others, he began a life of travel. He had begun to play harmonica in 1927, but on the guitar he was still a beginner in 1930. That changed radically after guitar lessons from Ike Zimmermann, taken around 1931. He became a solo performer in clubs, bars, juke joints, and on streets in the Midwest and South.

The only times he was ever recorded were in November 1936 and June 1937 for the Vocalion/ARC label. Like those of other blues musicians, these discs were categorized as "race records," because they were marketed to the African American population. One song from the first recording session became a hit: "Terraplane Blues," describing the workings of an ingenious sex machine which had started to malfunction due to the female partner's unfaithfulness, all expressed symbolically to the point of incomprehensibility for cultural outsiders. By using the image of a "Terraplane"—a low-priced but powerful sedan produced by Hudson Motor Co. from 1933 to 1938 (cf. LaVere 1986 [1990])—the message was transmitted clandestinely. A similar allegory is contained in another of his songs, "Phonograph Blues," recorded twice, with more "mechanized" sexual symbolism, now explicitly complaining about impotence: "you have broken my winding chain," "my needles have got rusty," etc. The cause of the problem is the protagonist's long-standing ambivalence toward women, transferred to any new relationship. The records, especially the first one, became hits precisely because the problem is universal and the real content is so masterfully veiled, that no censorship could have discovered the true meanings, but the African American community had learned to decode blues symbolism.

In those days, having one's music published on records was greatly status-enhancing. After the success of "Terraplane Blues" and some other titles, Robert Johnson became well known, not only in the Mississippi Delta and Memphis but in many places to which he traveled on various journeys, St. Louis, Chicago, Detroit, New York, alone or in the company of musician friends. His bad luck occurred on August 13, 1938, after he had apparently made advances to a woman whose husband was the owner of a bar (jook house) called Three Forks, not far from Greenwood in the Delta. He was poisoned with strychnine or some other substance and within a few days he died, on August 16, 1938.

In his brief recording career, Robert Johnson made forty-one recordings of twenty-nine different songs. Although he played acoustic guitar, his recordings were a seminal influence on the rise of urban blues in the 1940s, electrically amplified on R&B music and on rock 'n' roll. They eventually stimulated serious research to establish the circumstances of his short life, and also much speculation about the man, his nature, and his relationships, initially almost entirely based on the contents of his songs. In a host of publications too numerous to be cited, the idea gained ground among fans and even researchers about an alleged "pact with the devil." This went so far as to become part of a permanent listeners' portrait of Robert Johnson as someone who had lived in a world of "hoodoo" and the "supernatural," for the sake of obtaining power through his music and in his personal life. In part this was patched together through interviews with people who knew him, while the plain facts are much more prosaic. As Pete Welding (1971: 16) points out, "remarkably little is known of Johnson the man."

The story of Robert Johnson's liaison with the Devil originated with blues veteran Son House, who first met the seventeen-year-old Robert in 1930, when the latter had some experience playing blues on the mouth-harmonica, but no command of the guitar. A few years later, when they met again, according to Son House's narrative (Welding 1971), Johnson was about twenty-one or twenty-two years old. He had run away from his stepfather's farm two years earlier, but now he was in possession of a guitar to which he had added a seventh string. Son House and his musical partner met him in a place called Banks, Mississippi, where they performed. Johnson offered to play one number in public. Son House was skeptical, but allowed the young man to carry out his plan. As soon as he had started, Son House and Willie Brown who were ready to laugh at him, "paled" at seeing how the young man had mastered blues guitar in the meantime and how people "went wild over it." In search of an explanation, Son House suggested, perhaps jokingly, that Robert, while away from home for many months, would have "sold his soul to the devil in exchange for learning to play like that." Son House had to come to terms with his own failure of not having recognized Robert's talent a bit earlier. So he offered some generally accepted rationalization. Although he was saying so apparently in seriousness, according to Pete Welding, it was a customary explanation in those days to underline that playing blues meant to be no longer a good Christian. Only Welding (1971) reported this from House; the latter never mentioned the devil pact elsewhere, but simply expressed amazement at Johnson's rapid improvement as a musician. But the idea had been launched and began to proliferate.

Johnson, in fact, had largely adopted House's style, who for him had become a musical father substitute. He had studied hard in the meantime, in reaction to an earlier, painful experience with his mentor: whenever he came to their

Saturday night parties, he would be told by the older House not to make noise with his guitar during the breaks, because it annoyed the audience. It is normal that such a rebuke, repeated several times, evokes a compensatory reaction. So, two years later, when they met again, Johnson wanted to show his mentor what he had learned in the meantime, independently. House declared that it was simply "miraculous" that Robert had widened his knowledge as a blues musician in such a short time.

If this sequence of events had taken place somewhere in coastal West Africa, I am sure people would have said that Robert had made a contract with Mami-wata, or perhaps that he had come into possession of some magical device, for which of course, he would have had to pay the owner of the knowledge whatever the "contract" required. While the idea as such is deeply rooted in African traditions of explaining extraordinary achievement, in this case, in the US South, it was clad in the imagery of Christian religion.

Another description of Robert Johnson in his twenties was given by his friend Johnny Shines, with whom he teamed up in Helena, Arkansas, in 1935, traveling to Chicago, Detroit, New York, New Jersey, etc. Shines said in an interview:

> He was a natural rambler, his home was where his hat was, and even then lots of times he didn't know where that was. We used to travel all over, meet the pay days in the lumber camps, the track gangs—anywhere the money was. Used to catch freights everywhere. Played for dances, in taverns, on sidewalks—didn't matter where, far as he was concerned. Robert was a natural showman; he didn't need no guitar–he could be clapping his hands and have a crowd around him in no time. And they'd give him their money too. (Shines in Welding 1971: 16)

However, the content of their friendship was strictly music. Johnson apparently never talked to Shines about his background, his family, his origins. Apparently he was secretive concerning his past, which is not unusual even in friendly relationships, if the person is under the impression that it does not concern or interest his partner. Shines stated, "I never remember him being close to anyone," which fits perfectly the reclusive character also painted of Johnson by others, and expressed in any of his song texts, products of long cogitating. He characterized Robert Johnson as a "lone wolf" (17). His lack of group association was no doubt his strength, making him an extraordinary musician, and also reflecting earlier experiences in childhood and as a teenager, of isolation, rejection by others, lack of positive bonds with male parent figures. Attachment to anyone besides professional acquaintances was not his way.

Shines had almost a psychologist's look at his friend, and his verbal testimony appears to be reliable through the narrative's internal cohesion:

Close to a split personality, I'd say. You never knew what he was going to do or how he'd react to something. Sometimes he'd be the most mild-mannered, quiet person you'd ever meet; at other times he would get so violent so suddenly, and you couldn't do nothing with him. He was that changeable—different things to different peoples. Of course when he drank—and he was a very heavy drinker—he was most unpredictable.

Money didn't mean a thing to him. He'd give you every cent he had if you needed it, and it wouldn't bother him at all. Likewise, he'd sleep outdoors, anywhere, because he knew he didn't have to. And women—much as he was a woman lover— didn't mean nothing either. If you'd wake him up in the middle of the night and tell him there was a freight coming through, why he'd say, "Well, let's catch it," and he'd get himself ready, take hold of his guitar, and off he'd go—no matter who the woman was he was with. He just left. (Shines in Welding 1971: 17)

Shines had returned to his family in Memphis and Johnson to Mississippi in 1937, before the poisoning event happened. From hearsay, not from personal observation, Shines stated that people attributed Robert's death not only to "poison" (as someone would in terms of a rationalist worldview), but to "the black arts," i.e., witchcraft. This is once again identical with how many people in Africa would have interpreted this case of the sudden demise of a young man. This is the statement from Shines:

He was poisoned by one of those women who really didn't care for him at all. . . . And Robert was almost always surrounded by that kind . . . seems like they just sought him out. That was down in Eudora, Miss., that it happened. And I heard that it was something to do with the black arts. Before he died, it was said, Robert was crawling along the ground on all fours, barking and snapping like a mad beast. That's what the poison done to him. (Shines in Welding 1971: 17)

Shines possibly got some locations wrong; it seems that Johnson was poisoned near Greenwood, not Eudora. Pete Welding's collection of interviews with various people, first published in *Down Beat* in 1966, then reprinted in *Blues Unlimited* 83 (July 1971) is, however, a well-written primary source. He gives this final assessment of Robert Johnson:

However apocryphal (House, for example heard that Johnson had been stabbed to death by a jealous husband, stabbed by a woman, and also that he had been poisoned—all three accounts were circulating at the time), the story certainly details an appropriate end for a man who all through his adult years felt the hounds of hell baying loudly and relentlessly on his trail. In the end, he just couldn't outrun them any longer. (Welding 1971: 17)

What can Robert Johnson's songs tell us about the man? A detailed account of the main themes in the recordings was given by David Evans in *Blues Revue* in 1996. My following remarks will be supplementary, focusing on a few songs.

Fantastic realism (a term used for a post-surrealist school of painters in Europe) and dream imagery are the hallmark of Johnson's blues lyrics. Not always have his images remained undiluted, however, probably not even during street performances, far away from a recording company's expected censorship. For all their exuberance, blues singers like him could not avoid using concepts and categorizations that were familiar to audiences of their times, otherwise the texts would not have been understood. And yet symbolism, allusions, and double-talk abound in the lyrics, often a very personal symbolism.

A general pan-African trait that continued in the rural, solo performed blues accompanied with a stringed instrument (guitar, diddley bow, etc.) is the primacy of the word. The instrumental accompaniment may be startling, attractive, beautiful, harmonically surprising, but both in Africa and in the US South it was the text that the general listener first registered and interpreted. As much as the guitar lines are appreciated and essential, they function as commentary, underlining the verbal statements, with interludes to keep things going, and sometimes catchy accents to attract attention, dramatizing the content of the words.

Sometimes parts of a blues text are directly inspired by a singer's dreams in their imagery, then submitted to the necessities of rhyming in the compositional process, thereby editing the images along "left-brain" verbal reasoning and lines of association, e.g., "dark as night" rhymed with "taken my appetite" in the third line of "Stones in My Passway" or "ride" with "satisfied" in "From Four Till Late" (both recorded June 19, 1937), followed by a thematically more connected rhyme: "no-good bunch and clown" is rhymed with one of his standard phrases: "but tear a good man's reputation down."

Dreams are always subject to self-censorship; so are blues texts. This is why most of the blues texts express central ideas by ambiguity and displacement. They cannot be taken as verbatim accounts of a thought. To understand their real meanings is an exercise in symbol cracking, to uncover the latent dimension behind the manifest images. This exercise is hard for two reasons: (1) all present-day potential analysts, including anyone born in the Delta, have a cultural background different from that in the South a hundred years ago; (2) the authors of the texts, i.e., the blues singers/dreamers, are no longer available for comments.

Sometimes sentences may come up in a text in conformity with church teachings, but their real meaning may be ironic, or just a simulation of righteousness, or they may simply reproduce a situation from a dream (e.g., most likely "fell down on my knees" in "Cross Road Blues," recorded Nov. 27, 1936). As in dreams, opposing ideas may be blended into one and the same image. If the reader, therefore, believes to have discovered a "contradiction" between different lines in a song, it may simply be the presentation of an inner conflict, suggesting ambivalence.

By creating an alternative culture and perception of human life within the harsh realities of the segregated South, blues musicians soon attracted large audiences. Blues lyrics are honest in their choice of topics and the wisdom arising from the harsh facts, renouncing all self-deception. An alternative culture with all its advantages and disadvantages had emerged and was presented to audiences during that period.

What can we learn from a text like "Hellhound on My Trail," recorded June 20, 1937?

Just this one example of Robert Johnson's poetry is sufficient to secure him an eternal place in the history of world literature, alongside Rainer Maria Rilke, Georg Trakl, Arthur Rimbaud, and others. The text starts with a dream image: a wanderer moving on and on. Robert moves through a thunderstorm, hail cutting down on him; blues transforms into hail hitting the exhausted man. As the days pass, it is as if a hellhound were on his trail, pursuing him.

Then the image changes to a scene of sweet wish fulfillment, Christmas Eve with a family. I believe that this recreates the atmosphere before the unfortunate death of his wife and the unborn child in 1930. So Robert is condemned forever to celebrate Christmas Eve only, never Christmas Day.

The next line is difficult to interpret: "You sprinkled hot foot powder, mmm / Mmm, around my door." Stephen C. LaVere identifies the type of powder as "Doctor Pryor's Alleged Hot Foot Powder—for burning or sprinkling" and manufactured by Japo Oriental Incense, Chicago. David Evans (1996: 12) states: "Clearly Johnson is singing here about sorcery," an opinion I share. It is difficult, however, to crack the symbolism of the powder. Is it something like the powder Jelly Roll Morton discovered under the carpet and everywhere in his office in New York in 1935? We do not know for which purposes Doctor Pryor's product was used in Robert Johnson's day in communities of the US South. Apparently it is placed to make someone leave in haste. "You" clearly refers to a female companion, and "daddy" is a common expression for a woman's man or lover, referring to Robert. David Evans suggests this meaning (personal communication, June 2014): "To have a 'hot foot' or to 'hotfoot' (verb) means to leave (or have a desire to leave) quickly."

The song then claims that this act of sorcery, or whatever it was, is keeping him "with rambling mind." The lyrics then change into images of inhospitable landscapes and the singer's yearning for the bliss of a home.

Robert Johnson's song texts would need a book-size psychological analysis of the kind I have only started here. Space does not allow us to include more texts, but it is clear that Johnson, in his songs at least, felt persecuted by bad luck that he interpreted as mysterious forces directed against him. From there originates the image of the hellhound, but also the image of Satan in one of his most famous songs: "Me and the Devil Blues."

In this song Robert Johnson delves deeply into personal misery, discovering that the "Devil" as an evil principle was perhaps lurking in his own soul, unknowingly, and pushing him to do all sorts of awful things, including sadistic outbursts: "And I'm going to beat my woman until I get satisfied."

The song, however, is no testimony of a pact with the Devil; in fact, a pact is never mentioned, but it depicts a state, a personality which has split. The evil, personified as the Devil, is now like Johnson's shadow, inseparable, ever present, walking side by side with him as an alter ego, knocking at the door of consciousness early in the morning, when the dreamer wakes up.

One thing that makes Robert Johnson's poetry so convincing is the many contemporaneous images woven into it. These identify him as a man of the twentieth century, not as an epigone of some literature of the past. He talks about the Terraplane, the phonograph, the V-8 Ford, goggle-eyed perches, and the Greyhound bus. His poem "Me and the Devil Blues" was recorded at the last session, June 20, 1937, and the message is perhaps a premonition of his early death. Mysterious forces in the human mind are often personified in the blues, including "blues" itself. "Satan" is a personification of evil, from the viewpoint of a dualistic morality and worldview. Johnson now believes to have discovered it in his own body. In explicit Christian tradition he locates those evil forces as coming from "deep down in the ground," which is also the actual abode of the Devil, translated: from what has been repressed, pushed underground. The notion of an afterlife is also accepted by the author of this poetry, but within a more African imagery. There is no going to Heaven or to Hell after death. On the contrary, someone who is burdened by many misdeeds in life cannot rest after death. He will roam about, haunting relatives who may fall ill because of the worries inflicted upon them. In eastern Angola there is a name and even a typology for this category of spirits: *mahamba*. They are spirits with a typical unfortunate background in their lives, and they also often belong to specific professions. *Mahamba*, roaming, restless spirits, can afflict a relative with disease, all psychological. The victim can be helped by a professional medium who can make the *lihamba* spirit (singular of *mahamba*) talk to her, and explain the problems. Rejected, neglected, excluded from the pleasures of this life, haunted by people ("hellhounds") intending to do harm, with no chance of a permanent relationship, Robert Johnson suggests in his song that it would be better to bury him right away, "by the highway side," so that his soul could catch a Greyhound bus and keep traveling on. After death he would therefore be a restless spirit, haunting people.

Evans has the right feel when he writes (1996: 12): "Even in death Johnson expects to become a restless soul or a ghost with unfinished business who will haunt others. Certainly there was some truth to this, when one considers the powerful influence his music, songs, and personality have exerted on other musicians up to the present day." Evans also stresses that in this song "there is no mention of an actual pact," while, on the other hand, Robert and the Devil are now "virtual doubles for one another" (12).

In a sense, we who write about him function as media to allow his spirit to speak out his troubles. therefore I feel obliged to correct our contemporaries' fantasy of Robert Johnson's "pact" with the Devil. He was familiar with the myth and it may have even come up in some of his dreams, inspiring him to compose songs like "Cross Road Blues," and he also was sure that such a topic would find an eager audience. But the scene in which he falls down on his knees, at the crossroad, asking God to have mercy and "save poor Bob" is an image describing his defense against the inner forces he had come to acknowledge as evil, not asking for God's help to prevent him from signing a pact with the Devil. Identifying his own tendencies as evil, with an enormous feeling of guilt, was gradually pushing him into a program of self-destruction. Therefore he created the image of asking God to "save poor Bob."

In fact, the text says that in spite of trying "to flag a ride," nobody came to help him. God also let him down. The image "Bob is sinking down" is a dream image, symbolizing a situation in which one is hopelessly exposed to neglect by others, or to negative forces in others, or in one's own unconscious. Either it symbolizes a death wish or is a cry out against the injustice by others who have exercised total neglect. It is very likely that he composed this text following a dream from which he woke up on a certain morning. So in the song he says that his co-inhabitant of the house should run and tell Willie Brown, his friend, that Robert got "crossroad blues this morning" and that he was sinking down.

The motif of sinking down is common in West African stories and *chantefables*, such as *àlọ* in Yoruba (see my analysis of one, Kubik 2001) about a child beginning to sink down due to neglect by his/her mother, very likely also the case for little Robert Johnson. Robert must have been "sinking down" as a child under the family circumstances he grew up with, which were probably the root of all his later problems. But as concerns the alleged pact, this blues text suggests the opposite. No Big Black Man is coming to "poor Bob's" rescue at the crossroad to save this fatherless son, so he is "sinking down."

What I am writing here is only supplementary to the much more extensive analysis of Johnson's texts in their essentials by David Evans (1996). However, both of us are skeptics about Robert Johnson having actually cherished the idea of entering a "pact" with a spiritual being. While the myth of the pact at the crossroads was shared by nearly everyone in the region and the motif haunted musicians in their nightmare dreams, this was not Robert's problem. A proposal, to go to the crossroad at midnight with a guitar and see what happens, is much more likely to spring from the brain of a crazy field researcher than from a blues guitarist who would have been struck by fear of the spell of witchcraft, spirits, etc. I remember a reaction once in Nigeria in 1960 when I proposed to the composer Duro Ladipọ that we go together to the place of an òrìṣà at a watercourse in the forest at midnight. He reacted with absolute horror.

Robert Johnson's song texts are the testimony of a blues singer's worries, of someone who was haunted by paranoiac dreams, fear of being abandoned (by females), haunted by impotence, anxiety about his own tendencies and fear of witchcraft, pushed by a program of self-punishment and self-destruction. Sharing his imaginary world with audiences, he undertook a kind of self-therapy at the time, in compensation of these fears. His songs depict the tragedy of a man experiencing persecution by uncontrollable, mysterious forces in his own psyche. It is unlikely that someone like that would stop at a crossroad to shake hands with those mysterious forces. One does not have to look up the *Diagnostic and Statistical Manual of Mental Disorders* (DSM-V) to detect the structure of Robert's problem, his neurosis. After the death of his wife and child in 1930, he must have started the self-torture with the painful question whether he had perhaps shared the blame? neglected her? There is evidence that Johnson was away from home when his wife and child died. Or was witchcraft behind it? Was the sorcery now on his trail? This is what the hellhound symbolizes. The idea of an evil alter ego in himself is also well expressed in the image (daydream or actual dream) of walking "side by side" with Satan.

Charlie Parker, Thelonious Monk, and the Generous Baroness de Koenigswarter

One of my colleagues at Sigmund Freud University, Vienna, Thomas Barth, who in 2011 completed his doctoral dissertation under my guidance, is both a psychotherapist and a jazz musician. I gave him the following questions to prepare for his "rigorosum" on January 17, 2011: "Psychotherapists have often classed jazz musicians as depressive. What is the state of development in this little explored area of research? Where do those depressions come from?"

Unexpectedly, my colleague submitted a thirty-six-page manuscript with a systematic survey of the literature, pointing to some of the uncertainties introduced into the subject by a number of factors. He identifies them in a methodological process similar to the one he had used in his thesis on "Those who gave Freud ideas" (*Wer Freud Ideen gab*, Barth 2013). He says that there are seven "blurs" in this area of jazz study including interpretive misunderstandings, adoption of a "Bennfeld technique of interpretation," "blurs" due to alleged secretiveness of the artists researched, and "blurs" introduced by the media, such as Thelonious Monk's image of "mad genius" or Robert Johnson's retouched left eye on a photo appearing as a US postal stamp. Barth acknowledges that the greatest obstacle for researchers is that we are approaching an era from where no contemporaneous witnesses to the artists in question would be available any longer.

This touches on issues such as to what extent early separation experience within the parental environment of Charlie Parker or Robert Johnson could be considered main traumatizing episodes. This may be part of a general dispute within psychiatric diagnosis that has increased recently, and been taken up by the media, as a result of the publication of the DSM-V in 2013. Medical doctors and psychologists have warned about "diagnosis" being abused as a kind of labeling.

"Traditionally, a diagnosis is something devised by distant experts and imposed on the patient," writes Blake Charlton (2013). "Moreover, the definition of almost any diagnosis changes as science and society evolve." Charlton concludes: "Diagnostics might have more in common with law than with science. Legislatures of disease exist in expert panels, practice, guidelines and consensus papers. Some laws are unimpeachable, while others may be inaccurate or prejudiced."

In this situation one cannot brush aside one's suspicion that several jazz musician/composers, once they had fallen into the traps of the psychiatric establishment of their days, as happened to Charlie Parker and Thelonious Monk—and independently, to one of my friends, a jazz musician who ended up receiving electro-shocks in a clinic in Nigeria—were not only victims of social pressure, and the usual racist categorizations, but also of Western-style psychiatry.

(a) Charlie Parker (1920–1955)

In his short life, Charlie Parker was in and out of psychiatric clinics and rehabilitation centers for drug abuse. Only one such stay may have had a notably positive effect upon his music, and the name of the clinic will always be remembered because of the piece "Relaxing at Camarillo" recorded February 26, 1947 (CD *Jazz & Blues*, Charlie Parker BN 207, 1998 BIEM STEMRA). The title is almost ironic. What kind of relaxation did Bird experience in that clinic? Anyhow, when he came out, he had put on a lot of weight.

I tend to think that the kind of psychiatry imposed on bebop musicians was a Western "cognitive escape model," in reaction to the incomprehensibility of patterns in African American cultures of the time. Psychiatry tended to explain artists within the dominating society's concepts about what was to be considered healthy and what was a "disorder." With no alternative explanatory schemes, doctors in such a society were unable even to think of the possibility that some of those African American musicians' problems could perhaps be better addressed from a different cultural perspective, e.g., assuming that they were bewitched or haunted by what in Africa would be called spirit possession, e.g., *mahamba* in eastern Angola. A projective interpretation of this kind of psychological

Fig. 7.4. Charlie Parker and Red Rodney watching Dizzy Gillespie and Chuck Wayne. New York, 1947. Courtesy of the Institute of Jazz Studies, Rutgers University Libraries.

Fig. 7.5. Charlie Parker, Carnegie Hall, New York, ca. 1947. Courtesy of the Institute of Jazz Studies, Rutgers University Libraries.

"disorder" is normally understood quickly by the patient and accepted, serving as a cognitive schema to externalize the deep-rooted conflicts and solve them through fictitious model images, e.g., "spirits." The important thing in an alternative therapy of this kind is that the original conflict gets a chance to be replayed in a clinically staged context, such as a spirit possession ceremony, and thereby expressed. That can be done simply through the personification (as spirits) of repressed inner tendencies. In Brazil or Haiti, or even in New Orleans, appropriate treatment for Parker, Monk, and others would have been available, but not in the clinical psychiatrists' culture of the 1950s. The story of Bird's encounters with Western psychiatry is particularly sad, if one lists all that was done to him, shortening his life.

On different occasions, Charlie Parker was diagnosed with substance abuse (heroin or alcohol), heart dysfunction (cf. Reisner 1974: 47), ulcers, syphilis in 1945 and 1954, and schizophrenia (cf. Spencer 2002: 135). In 1945 he spent eight months at Camarillo State Hospital, California, after a "nervous breakdown." He was also treated with penicillin, bismuth, and arsenic for syphilis, and in September 1954 he spent ten days at Bellevue Hospital in New York, in the Psychiatric Division, Ward PQ 3, where he was diagnosed with acute and chronic alcoholism and narcotic addiction. He had been admitted after a suicidal attempt by ingestion of iodine (Reisner 1974: 42). He was reported to show a "passive tendency" and was "ingratiating" and friendly with all physicians. But otherwise he was evaluated as a "hostile, evasive personality with manifestations of primitive and sexual fantasies associated with hostility and gross evidence of paranoid thinking." An alleged "psychoanalytic" diagnosis was also given: Latent schizophrenia (cf. Reisner 1974: 42).

Thomas Barth poses the bewildering question about terminology: "Based on what was 'latent schizophrenia' diagnosed? On what kind of symptoms, their quality, their dimension and by whom?" (8).

A few weeks later, Parker was admitted for a second time to Bellevue Hospital for eighteen days (September 28–October 15, 1954). Apparently he said that he had been severely depressed since his previous discharge, was drinking again, and "feared for his own safety" (Reisner 1974: 42) This time he was admitted with the diagnosis "acute alcoholism and undifferentiated schizophrenia." Thereafter he received electro-shock treatments at the same hospital. A spinal tap (lumbar puncture) was also performed. The collodial gold curve was negative, thereby excluding neurosyphilis. Nurses of Parker wrote that he was "lazy and kept bothering them for doses of *paraldehyde*" (Reisner 1974: 42). Obviously he had been subjected to massive doses of sedative drugs (paraldehyde, etc.) Dizzy Gillespie reported from memory about the last few days of Charlie Parker in the year 1955 (Gillespie and Fraser 1979 [2009: 393]):

Just before Yard died in 1955, he came up to me. Boy, I'll never forget this. I was playing at Birdland; Benny Goodman was playing at Basin Street East, down in the basement on Fifty-second Street, off Broadway. So between sets I went down there because Charlie Shavers was playing with him at the time. . . .

And that night, Yard was in the audience, and he came over to me, and we were talking and he said, "Save me. . . ." Only that one time, just before he died. Gee, Yard was looking bad, man, fat. He walked up to me and said, "Diz, why don't you save me?"

And I saw the expression on his face. It was a pained expression on his face, and I didn't know what to say. I said, "What could I do?" He said, "I dunno but just save me, save me, man." . . .

It hit me pretty hard. I really took that one, but I don't feel that I let him down in any way, not necessarily. . . .

Probably, as soon as he died, Nica called me and said, "Yardbird just died in my apartment."

I said, "It's done . . . ?" No, I couldn't believe it, but it was the truth. That broke me up. I couldn't help it. I had to go down in the basement and cry. . . . It hit me so hard because we were so close, man. We weren't associated musically at the time, but I still had this strong feeling toward Charlie Parker and just couldn't take it when he died. . . .

Charlie was closely associated with three women at that time. He was living with Chan and had a wife, Gerri, who was in jail in Washington. He had Doris. Everybody was wondering what to do with his compositions, so we formed a committee to try and salvage something and put it all together.

Much more negatively tainted is Mary Lou Williams's account of the last days of Charlie Parker. She was realistic about the inevitable fate that had materialized. She hailed Dizzy Gillespie for organizing a proper funeral. "If it hadn't been for him, that poor boy would probably be a cadaver or something, because nobody knew he was dead, and they were taking him to Bellevue Hospital." Then she relates how all the musician colleagues including herself formed a committee to raise the money needed for the funeral. Hailing Dizzy Gillespie and his wife Lorraine's cooperation, she added:

If it hadn't been for Dizzy, you wouldn't ever hear about Charlie Parker now. Because nobody liked Charlie Parker by that time. When I had to go to the agents to collect money—I collected quite a bit of money, maybe two or three thousand dollars—they were mad. They were calling him all sorts of dirty names. . . . It seems when he died, he was just down to the lowest. Nobody liked him; he'd made a lot of enemies. (394–95)

Max Roach, on his part criticized both Dizzy Gillespie's and Mary Lou Williams's individual-focused interpretation of the events. He said:

> I maintain that society is largely responsible for Bird's demise. Dizzy maintains that Bird should've been stronger than to let them destroy him like that, at such an early age. He just discounts this society. But you see Dizzy is a very strong person to have survived in this kind of society with all of the pressures on him. . . .
>
> This is why I say Dizzy is a "fox." He is not going to sacrifice his musical integrity, but he is determined to survive out in this shit, in this maze that black folks have to do, and especially when you're dealing with black culture, because culture is such a powerful weapon. When the musicologists break down Dizzy's contribution, they are going to see the kind of intellect that prevails inside the black psyche.
>
> Afro-American music was here, and no one recognized it more than people like Bird and Diz. They knew that the music is here, and they would hope to add maybe a page to the history that's already been laid down by their predecessors, understand. And so that's the thing they had in common. . . .
>
> On the other hand the difference in the way Bird perceived himself spiritually and the way Dizzy perceived himself spiritually, I believe may be the difference . . . Like Bird's statements were always that the government is responsible for the black people. He'd walk down Harlem streets and say, "Why do you think we've got two bars on every street? Why is it that we can cop drugs anytime we want to? You can buy drugs and whiskey before you can buy milk." That was his political and social perception of what was going on. . . .
>
> There is a concentrated effort to destroy black folks. Billie Holiday I would give credit for that, too.

Twenty-four years later, Michael Zwerin, one of the most prominent jazz journalists of the twentieth century, writing for the *New York Times*, visited Charlie Parker's wife Chan in France (Zwerin 1979). She was staying in Champmotteux with her children. One of Parker's children had died. Chan had married again after Parker's death, to one of his disciples, Phil Woods. But by the time Zwerin visited her in 1979 she was alone, her association with Phil Woods had ended, and she was working on her autobiography, *My Life in E-Flat*, which was eventually published. Chan was also a musician; by 1979 she had written thirty-one arrangements for vocal quintet. Most of her income, however, came from selling tapes she had made privately of Parker's music. Once he had said: "These tapes are your inheritance. They will support you one day." Chan was the daughter of a Ziegfeld girl. After she was introduced to Bird at a place called Three Deuces, they began seeing each other. She related this story about Bird to Michael Zwerin, stressing that she had lived together with Charlie Parker for five years. One good morning he suddenly said to her:

"Pack your valise. Let's go. Right now."—"Where to?" she asked.—"We are going to Paris."—She talked him out of it, but now wonders: "If we had gone that day, he might still be alive. He wouldn't have had all the rejection, frustration, all the bloodsuckers, hustlers and junk connections feeding off him. Bird always loved France. He wanted to live here. He was knocked out by the respect his music was accorded. He wanted Baird [their son] to be brought up in France.

"Bird was so different from the image he has been given. He wanted to live a straight life, but he had been turned on junk at 15 and he never escaped that. Except musically, he could communicate better with straight people. He loved Sunday dinners with my mother and Aunt Janet.

"When we lived on the Lower East Side, he used to go out on the streets and talk to the old Ukrainians, Gypsies and Orthodox Jews in the neighborhood. They all called him Charlie." (Zwerin 1979: 20)

Thirty-nine years after Charlie Parker's death, Mike Zwerin wrote again about him and Chan in an article in the *International Herald Tribune* dated Wednesday, September 7, 1994. At that time Chan's estate was for sale in London. He started his report this way:

It's hard to know whether to laugh or cry. "Bird—The Chan Parker Collection: A Bird's Eye View of the Private Genius" is being auctioned on Thursday by Christie's in London. The auction house hopes that more than 80 items will realize in excess of $100,000 or more than $150,000.

Included are Charlie Parker's driver's license, correspondence, concert posters, Christmas cards, musical scores and the cream acrylic Grafton plastic saxophone (serial number 10265) he played at the Massey Hall "Quintet of the Year" concert in Toronto on May 15, 1953, with Dizzy Gillespie, Bud Powell, Charles Mingus and Max Roach (estimate: 30,000 to 40,000).

(b) Thelonious Monk (1917–1982)

Thelonious Monk, pianist and composer within the movement of modern jazz that started in Harlem in the 1940s, had a personality different from that of Charlie Parker. While Parker's problems could be seen as socially induced during childhood and early youth, Monk suffered from a genetic disposition psychiatrists identify as bipolar. "In a bipolar disorder, a person alternates between the hopelessness and lethargy of depression and the overexcited state of mania. Mania is manifested by hyperactivity and wild excitement" (Sonderegger 1998: 137). It seems that Monk's father had that condition. When Monk was eleven, in 1928, his father left the family, and in 1941 was confined to the State Hospital for the Colored Insane. Like Buddy Bolden, decades earlier, someone confined to that kind of institution would never come out.

Thelonious Monk was a family man, deeply attached to his wife Nellie and his two children: Toot, who became a jazz drummer (and played in Monk's band during the last few years), and Boo Boo (Barbara), who became a dancer. In the mid-1960s both Monk and his drummer Ben Riley would bring their families along to concerts and on small tours (Kelley 2009: 377). His two children showed talent in music/dance at an early age.

Robin D. G. Kelley (2009) has written what can be hailed as the definitive biography of Thelonious Monk using a thousand sources, all meticulously listed chapter by chapter in the notes to his book. When the little girl Boo Boo expressed interest in the piano besides her dancing practice, conversations with her father were centered around "Daddy show me this" or that. Thelonious showed her how to play "Ruby, My Dear." Toot, who in adult life would adopt the name Thelonious Monk Jr., developed a very positive relationship in his childhood, which is also evident in his writings, touching one's heart, for example in the introduction to the precious film material from the 1966 concerts in Norway and Denmark, published as *Thelonious Monk Live in '66* by Reelin' in the Years Production in 2006.

Toot showed interest in drumming, and almost instantly his father contacted bebop's greatest drummers, notably Max Roach, to teach the boy. Monk did not interfere with the teaching process, nor did he give the impression of exerting control; he let things develop as they did naturally and this was precisely the way to let a very positive relationship grow between father and son. Eventually, after a long period of apprenticeship, Thelonious Monk integrated his son into his quartet in a show celebrating Malcolm X's birthday (Kelley 2009: 423). Toot became a regular member of the quartet, his powerful polyrhythms driving the ensemble. He also had the unenviable task, conferred on him by his mother Nellie, to be his father's caretaker and protector from the early 1970s on. Besides monitoring signs of unusual behavior, due to his father's psychological condition, "Toot's job was to keep so-called fans and admirers from giving Monk drugs" (425). In those days it had become a kind of initiation rite in those circles, and "offerings to the king" were customary.

The individual study of the lives of jazz innovators in Minton's Playhouse during the early 1940s—Parker, Gillespie, Monk, Kenny Clarke, etc.—suggests that there was a centripetal cultural process going on that brought many very different individuals together for a common purpose. Such an assessment is perhaps contrary to stereotypes that project certain habits, from sunglasses at night to (bebop) berets, to the use of drugs, etc. upon those involved, thereby creating an imagined "bebop culture." I do not think that there was anything like that. Diversity was the reign, and experiment, also in social relations and the management of relations with the larger society. But some "white" musicians who frequented the bop sessions and learned from them were the most obvious victims of stereotyping, including the belief, e.g., in the case of Stan Getz and others in Woody Herman's Second Herd, that heroin was essential for becoming a creative jazz musician.

Thelonious Monk was not heroin dependent, although Gregory I. Wills writing in the *British Journal of Psychiatry* (2003) insists upon Monk having experimented with a variety of recreational drugs, though he had a particularly adverse reaction to amphetamines. As a psychiatrist working with the DSM-IV categories, Wills (2003: 257) posthumously diagnoses "substance intoxication delirium" in Monk. Robin D. G. Kelley stresses that Monk's problem was instead bipolar disorder, the first signs of which had appeared in the 1940s. In view of the strong public exposure of any jazz star like Monk, such episodes were of particular interest to the media, contributing to the creation of an alleged "personality" of the artist that included expectations about behavior at concert and the nature of his music (weird, dissonant harmonies, etc.). Monk rejected and even ridiculed many of these stereotypes, and often in interviews with journalists he courageously criticized the entire journalistic approach of asking certain questions and subsequent media manipulation of the information gathered to make him saleable to the public. It is obvious that audiences are capable of putting immense pressure on an artist to behave in certain ways, and often these pressures are very uncomfortable. Jazz audiences in the 1960s and '70s expected jazz musicians to be something like improvisational conveyer belts spitting out a "new style" every year, on every concert tour, which would then be celebrated as "the latest" development. It is precisely this mentality that kills art and excludes any possibility for normal, organic development that would gradually lead to stylistic changes. Mass audiences' pressures and massive media intervention were two factors among others that ended American jazz in the 1970s. Musician/composers in Africa now also feel the same sort of pressures, the composer being mistaken for an industrial production machine. No space, no time is granted for individual reflection and nurturing of what has been achieved.

Musicians like Monk knew that; they tried to resist, but failed to educate audiences and the media. Fans expected him to be "continually innovative," lead jazz to "new horizons," and when this was not forthcoming, critics like Leonard Feather began to label Thelonious Monk as "conservative." In the late 1960s a journalist asked him whether he was playing more piano now than when he was twenty. Monk is reported to have said: "Why should I have to create something new? Let someone else create something new!" and to Feather: "How about you as a writer? Are you creating? Are you writing better than you did 20 years ago?" (Cf. Kelley 2009: 378–79). That was his ultimate declaration of defiance, until in his last few years he virtually stopped playing.

Due to a variety of somatic and psychological problems, Monk in the 1970s was put on a schedule of medication, including thorazine and worse, lithium treatment. His wife Nellie tried to counterbalance, putting him on a vitamin (juice) schedule, until her preoccupation assumed an obsessive-compulsive character, making it all a business, grinding carrots at 3 a.m., which caused tremendous complaint from neighbors.

Thelonious's brush with psychiatry in the early 1970s can be seen as the "hoodoo" of his days. The irrationality of the situation is well reported by Dr. Eddie Henderson of Langley Porter Psychiatric Hospital in San Francisco, to which Monk was referred after suffering a severe manic episode on October 24, 1970. Luckily Dr. Henderson happened to be both medical doctor and jazz musician playing trumpet, including with Herbie Hancock. In an interview Kelley conducted with Henderson on January 11, 2004, the latter reported:

> No one knew who he was. I said "Wow, that's Monk!" . . . Nellie brought him in because he was more or less kind of catatonic. . . . He spoke in monosyllables, very abstract. The first thing I'm supposed to ask him, "Why are you here?" That's the traditional thing a resident says. So he shows me his MONK ring, turned it upside down, and it looked like K-n-o-w. He said, "Monk, Know." I knew what he meant but they had no idea of what he was talking about. (Henderson in Kelley 2009: 418)

Monk was then subjected to the usual standard tests: Rorschach or inkblot test (developed by the Swiss psychiatrist Hermann Rorschach in 1921) and TAT, Thematic Apperception Test developed by H. A. Murray.

Thelonious Monk immediately made fun out of these procedures, thereby signaling to the hospital staff that he was not a nut, just fed up with everything:

> The next morning, Henderson found one of his colleagues trying to engage Monk using the standard Rorschach or inkblot test. He wouldn't answer. When she tried the Thematic Apperception Test—a series of ambiguous pictures meant to prompt the subject to tell a story about what she or he sees—the situation went from bad to worse. Henderson recounts what happened: "She showed him a picture of a little boy sitting, grimacing, while his mother and father stand over him. He's like grimacing playing a violin, and the parents are saying, 'Well you better practice,' you know. So Monk looked at me and winked and said, 'Is this motherfucker crazy? I don't see nothing. It's just a picture.' So I fell out laughing. The psychologist kept insisting that he try to interpret the picture. So Monk finally said, deadpan serious, 'Okay, the little boy is really drugged.' 'Well, why, Mr. Monk?' the psychologist asked. Now I'm thinking, 'Oh no.' Monk replies with no expression whatsoever. 'Because his mother won't give him no more pussy.' The psychologist dropped the clipboard and that was the end of that interview."

"That was his sense of humor," Henderson continued, "but the staff thought he was nuts. Besides being sarcastic, he just didn't want to relate on that stupid level." During his nearly two-month hospitalization, he participated in group therapy and was subjected to more tests and to electro-shock treatment. . . . (Kelley 2009: 418–19)

Unfortunately, Monk's various medications included an extreme dose of thorazine, benzedrine, and lithium from 1972 on, which in combination had a negative effect on his work as a musician and composer, causing fatigue, sleepiness, sometimes nausea, even memory impairment, and increasing his prostate problems. In addition, his medical expenses were rising infinitely. Even a prominent musician such as Monk was unable to make enough money to cover those bills, all of which added another serious stress to the family, especially to his wife Nellie, although the generous Baroness de Koenigswarter tried to help as much as she could, eventually taking the ailing Monk into her house for permanent residence.

Audiences and jazz critics had their own needs, projecting them on musicians. Monk was seen as an "eccentric" artist, sometimes called "Mad Monk," sometimes "High Priest of Bebop"; he was also seen as the "mad genius," the "idiot savant," if one reads newspaper comments on his many concerts around the world; eventually he was accused of stagnation, of being conservative, not producing anything new. Occasionally, there was something critics acknowledged, such as his wonderful adaptation of a Japanese composition "Kojo no Tsuki" (The moon over the desolate castle), composed by Rentaro Taki in 1901, which he came to know on a tour to Japan organized by Reko Hoshino.

It is fair to believe that to a great extent, Monk's final withdrawal from "jazz business" was the result of all the medication which doctors were pumping into his body, including some substances he added on his own. But like Parker, he was really a victim of the domineering society's convictions and its predatory capitalism, specifically as concerns touring and working conditions for musicians.

(c) The jazz baroness

Monk spent the final year of his life in the home of Baroness Pannonica de Koenigswarter. On February 5, 1982, he had a stroke and collapsed. He was taken to Englewood Hospital, where he died February 17 from the consequences of the stroke. Even after his death, the family did not come to a rest. In 1983–84, within three months, Toot's fiancée, Yvonne Fletcher, and his sister Boo Boo both died of breast cancer.

This mysterious sequence of events, and the interconnected fates of the two jazz musicians, Charlie Parker (in 1955) and Thelonious Monk (in 1982)—all in the baroness's apartments—have been the subject of much underground speculation. Who, after all, was the generous Baroness Pannonica de Koenig-swarter, called Nica in jazz circles? Was she a witch? Someone who devoured jazz musicians? In 1982 the tabloids were relatively quiet, and in any case, questions about witchcraft would not have been considered appropriate in a society purporting to be rational (with the exception of the irrationality of its racism). The accusations that were directed against the baroness by the media in the 1950s all had the stain of sexist wish fulfillment, but this time they were not repeated, since the baroness had also befriended Nellie, Monk's wife; meanwhile she was a quarter century older, and the times had also changed a bit in the 1980s. But what was it that motivated Nica to be always ready to help those jazz giants financially and psychologically? Monk is reported to have said something significant about his relationship to the baroness in a conversation with Walter Booker, his bassist; the latter reported it in an interview with Robin D. G. Kelley on February 24, 2005:

> One night, he [Thelonious Monk] saw me hittin' on some girl at the club or something. He said to me, "Be sure that you want to have her for a girl or have her for a friend, because if you make love to a girl she ain't gonna be your friend. Because you can have a friend, like Nica's my friend, and I wouldn't touch her. She's the best friend I ever had." (Kelley 2009: 403)

The Baroness de Koenigswarter, a descendant of the powerful Rothschild clan, was an extraordinary personality, on a par with two other European women, Bertha Pappenheim and Anna Freud. The baroness's implicitly anti-racist and anti-segregationist activism in New York during the 1940s and '50s forms a lasting detail in the history of modern jazz.

These three women all had grown up in Jewish families of central or western Europe and had reached prominence during the first half of the twentieth century, reacting to various forms of overt and hidden ethnicist and gender discrimination, the former based on genealogical ancestry (Jewish identity). They reacted with creative engagement compensatory to the terror they experienced, forming their own circles of activity, their own "intellectual families": Bertha Pappenheim (who in the 1880s was a patient of Joseph Breuer in Vienna and is now considered co-originator of psychoanalysis) founded a feminist movement in Germany. Anna Freud (youngest daughter of Sigmund Freud), after their expulsion from Austria in 1938, founded the Hampstead Clinic in London together with her lifelong American friend Dorothy Burlingham, as a center for child therapy. Baroness de Koenigswarter, on her part, founded a circle of art consciousness with African American jazz musicians who had created modern jazz during the 1940s and '50s.

Baroness de Koenigswarter, born Kathleen Annie Pannonica Rothschild, known as Nica (Rothschild) for short, was born on December 10, 1913. She experienced the brunt of Nazi terror in Europe. When the German army invaded France in May 1940, it was advisable for her to leave the country. In fact, not everyone in the Jewish communities shared her justified pessimism, but it turned out to be realistic, and the mother of Nica's husband and many other family members died later in Auschwitz.

Long before that, as a ten-year-old child, she witnessed a tragedy in her own family. Her father, a partner in the family bank, and passionate entomologist, committed suicide in 1923, at the age of forty-six. Nica, who was deeply attached to her father, was seriously traumatized by this event, without being able to come to terms with the facts. And yet she married in 1935, to a peer who like herself was attracted to aviation and had become a pilot: Baron Jules de Koenigswarter.

When they settled in New York, she had good reason to take note of the fact that the very seeds of racism and legalized segregation that were leading to geno-cide in Germany were also present in America. In the early 1950s she began to frequent the spots where modern jazz originated and made the acquaintance of Charlie Parker, Dizzy Gillespie, Miles Davis, Thelonious Monk, and others. She invited musicians to her home and began to sympathize with their problems, largely caused by a nearly unbearable social situation for African Americans dur-ing that period. Gradually she created in her apartment a future vision of Ameri-can society. She refused to identify with the same kind of structures that elsewhere had forced emigration upon her. Gradually her jazz family formed. Sometimes she submitted her friends to three favorite questions: "What are your three wishes?," her own brand of psychoanalytic learning about her musician friends.

In an article in the *International Herald Tribune*, Tuesday, October 21, 2008, Barry Singer announced an exhibition at the Gallery at Hermès in New York opening on October 30, 2008, where her collection of photographs of the musi-cians and their answers to those three questions in her original notebooks were shown.

Baroness de Koenigswarter identified with the problems in African American creative artists caused by segregation, discrimination of all sorts, drugs, suicidal tendencies, etc. She saw these as reactions by the artists' sensitive nature to an adverse social situation. No doubt, her own trauma of expulsion and family loss, including the trauma of her suicidal father, was part of the turmoil within her memories. It is strange, but one of the photographs reproduced in the report by Singer (2008: 17) shows her eyes fixed upon Thelonious Monk as if she were reenacting the little girl trying to attend to her powerful father's wishes. I see this as a visual imprint of a psychological pattern.

She knew that drug addiction could not simply be treated with other psychi-atric drugs, but that alternative methods were needed to tackle the problem. So it happened once in 1958, while she was driving Monk, that they were stopped by police in Delaware. When they did not find anything in terms of sex, they focused on a small amount of marijuana in their car. The baroness took it all upon herself and spent a few days in jail (Singer 2008: 17).

It is clear that earlier experiences she had in her own family in Europe would become a model that would be revived and restaged in a process known in psychology as transference. In part it was a restaging of the "little girl's" relationship with her suicidal father transferred upon Parker and later Monk, who were equally self-destructive. It also served to express her feelings of guilt toward her biological father, as to what she should and perhaps could have done in 1923 to deal with his clinical depression and prevent the suicide. Now, this was played out again, in transference on two of the most revered jazz innovators of the time.

Charlie Parker, in his desperate situation in 1955, due to drug addiction, and his peers refusing to help him, took refuge with the only person on stand-by to "save" him: Nica. He died in her apartment. However, this event sealed her expulsion from the larger society—a repetition of her earlier fate in France—this time not by Nazi ideology, but by the segregation system of the United States during the 1950s. Her revolutionary, subversive behavior was bound to trigger a reaction; all kinds of rumors began to circulate, particularly about sexual relationships. When Parker died in her apartment and the jazz community tried to raise money for his funeral, the media began a vicious campaign against the baroness, centered upon sex, drugs etc. Her husband divorced her a year later, and she lost custody of her three younger children.

Thereafter Nica was alone with her jazz family. Twenty-seven years after Charlie Parker had died on a sofa in her Fifth Avenue apartment in New York, another genius of modern jazz, Thelonious Monk, would collapse in her house in New Jersey, after he had secluded himself for long periods in her world of isolation. And yet, the baroness also accommodated Monk's wife Nellie. She looked after all their needs economically and arranged for psychiatric consultations for Thelonious by many doctors. Her relationship with him must have been a strange replica of the little girl's experience in 1923 as her father was slipping into deep depression. This time, however, she wanted to win against those evil forces and save Thelonious Monk against all odds. But things took their own course.

Backed by her financial resources and through her jazz associations, Nica instigated an overt protest against the society into which she had found herself thrown, after settling in the United States, a society whose structure reminded her of the harassment she had suffered in Europe, as a Jewish person. Identifying with African American artists and intellectuals, she opted for a "private revolution" through behavior, not overt political agitation, simply by associating with "blacks," with jazz musicians, and inviting them into her home. As could have been anticipated, the segregationist society reacted with a campaign of denigration and rumor, as one learns from scrutinizing the press, especially after the despairing, drug-dependent Charlie Parker died in her apartment in 1955. It triggered wide reaction by the scandal-prone media, eventually leading to the breakup of her legitimate family.

Her "crime" was simply that she had violated the racial barrier installed by the authorities in power, through personal relations of friendship with the under-privileged. The only thing that prevented the worst from happening was her wealth and financial independence. As much as the surrounding society disapproved her demonstration of resistance, it could do little legally to stop her.

But what did the baroness represent psychologically for Charlie Parker, Thelonious Monk, and others in the jazz scene? This question is difficult. It could have been followed up easily by short, unfocused conversations with the artists, or through quotation of their casual remarks. Unfortunately, this is no longer possible, apart from the inevitable interference of such conversations with the nature of any relationships. We can only draw tentative conclusions on the basis of behavioral hints and occasional statements that happened to be recorded, such as the one by Thelonious Monk quoted earlier. Particularly difficult is the assessment of Parker's countertransference in relation to Nica. It is certain, however, that relationships with his wife Chan and with Nica were based on very different imperatives.

We can also offer conclusions drawing upon analogies observed in African cultures. Early "white" visitors in sub-Saharan Africa were sometimes identified as ancestors who had returned. This was reported, for example, by Paul Parin et al. (1980) from their research among the Anyi in Côte d'Ivoire. The idea that the dead would become "white" or migrate to a country full of snow is also found in the folklore of eastern Angola (cf. Kayombo kaChinyeka 2013: 131–35). In Angola it was widely believed by 1965 during my fieldwork that if someone died he would become white and go to a place where all dead people who had become white were. The association of "white" with death was also often expressed in initiation ceremonies by painting a face white, expressing that this mask came from the world of the dead. However, color symbolism is multilateral; a researcher has to be extremely careful about carrying meanings into traditions. White caolin (*mphemba*) in eastern Angolan initiation rites also stands for "luck," "resurrection," while red (*mukundu*) stands for "blood," "death," for example, symbolic death in initiation rites.

I can add here a personal experience from another place in Central Africa. In 1966, in Mpyɛm̃ɔ society, southwestern Central African Republic, when people noticed that a close friendship had developed between Maurice Djenda and me and that we were behaving like brothers, even addressing each other "*Mon frère*," some people launched the idea that I was indeed his elder brother who had died a few years ago and who had now returned. I was given a role in Maurice's family.

Could it be that any such thought patterns continued to be transmitted in African American communities? Psychoanalysis seems to confirm it. One thing can be postulated generally: that people in a crisis situation (and this was the case of the two founders of bebop befriended by Mrs. Koenigswarter) would take recourse to thought patterns long repressed. For this reason, I would think that this unusually understanding and care-taking "white" woman had exerted a "magic" appeal upon the two musicians far beyond the realm of practical and economic assistance. Even if they never asked her for an explanation, they were confronted with the question: "Why does this white woman act that way?" (in contradiction to the normal behavior expected from "whites" in those days).

The solution, therefore, is that to Parker and Monk, the baroness represented a kind of mythical, refuge-providing mother figure, perhaps something like Jung's archetype of the Great Mother, always ready to help. Of course, no one can be totally entangled by an archetypal image; there is always some space for humor. For Thelonious Monk the image was often shattered, during his stay in her apartment, by the baroness' feline "children" swarming the place. By the 1980s she is said to have kept over sixty(!) cats in her home. Nica had to keep them out of Thelonious's room, whose door remained closed most of the day. He did not want to share that facet of her neurosis.

Stan Getz (1927–1991)

Jazz musicians have often been associated with drug addiction, especially in the 1940s. It is obvious from individual life histories that, in many cases, alcohol and abuse of addictive substances, in addition to the rigors of performance schedules, travel, and social discrimination to the point of being an "outcast," have been powerful factors of personal destruction. Often musicians have been subject to a kind of self-imposed destruction fueled by feelings of guilt. Many careers were then prematurely ended. The problem, it seems, was particularly serious during the 1940s and 1950s. There is however, no evidence of a causal link between creativity in jazz and substance abuse, which became a powerful myth or stereotype promoted by the media, much as in earlier rural societies the myth was promoted that a relationship with a supernatural being was essential for becoming a successful musician. In the urban cultures of the 1940s and '50s, within a society that claimed to be "rational" in its thought patterns, the supernatural being was replaced by a "supernatural" substance, amphetamines, heroin, etc. Trying to cross over into "black" musical culture, a few "white" aspirants to jazz in Harlem internalized those stereotypes. They unconsciously employed symphatic magic, imitative magic, etc., to transform into their role models. Drugs, particularly heroin, were the "medicines" to achieve those personal transformations.

The outstanding example of this "hoodoo"-like approach was tenor saxophonist Stan Getz. The "white" youngsters who were trying to penetrate the

rising bebop culture were infected by the broader society's beliefs about alternative lifestyles. Their compliance with those beliefs was in part motivated by an
internalized conviction that they did not have that "inborn" feeling of rhythm,
etc., and could therefore never play like their "black" idols. Although this belief
was racist—a kind of inverted schema of earlier beliefs of racial superiority, now
attributing "special abilities" to the other side—all sorts of rationalization and
recipes to deal with it were offered. One was based on the observation that many
of the bop musicians, long before the rise of bebop, as in the case of singer Billie
Holiday, were on drugs, not only marijuana but hard drugs like heroin. The belief
gained currency among those aspiring to become jazz musicians that drugs were
the key to allow them to reach the creative level of their idols.

Woody Herman and his collaborators, mainly Ralph Burns (1922–2001), tried
to update their music according to trends in 1945–46, on the one hand in direction to Western "serious" music (cf. the "Ebony Concerto" by Igor Stravinsky,
recorded August 19, 1946, in Los Angeles), on the other by assimilating bebop,
which triggered the main changes characterizing the sound of Herman's Second
Herd from 1949 on. Several members of Herman's band had been hanging out
with the bebop scene in New York, among them star tenor saxophonist Stan Getz.

In his commemorative liner notes to a reissue on CD of Woody Herman's
Columbia records, Ralph Burns, the composer and principal arranger in Herman's Second Herd, informs us about the situation in 1947, after a year's break:

> The band experienced some monumental changes, resulting in the birth of the "Sec-
> ond Herd." The new incarnation found us on the cusp of "cool," and the new Herd
> sported a crop of first-rate players, including Serge Chaloff on baritone sax, and
> Zoot Sims, Herbie Steward and Stan Getz on tenor. But with the changes came a
> monkey that affected the whole jazz scene: heroin. I'd taken some time off, and when
> I came back, I observed a whole new attitude on the stand. On more nights than I'd
> care to remember, the front-line would be 'cracked out,' as I used to say. Although
> we'd flirted with bebop as far back as 1945, when Neal Hefti composed *The Good
> Earth* . . . the finest examples of the bebop influence that the new guys brought to
> the band can be clearly heard in tunes like Shorty's *Kean and Peachy*, and Al Cohn's
> *The Goof and I.*—On Jimmy Guiffre's classic *Four Brothers*, three tenor saxes and one
> baritone played by Zoot Sims, Herbie Steward, Serge Chaloff and Stan Getz, the
> "four brothers" of early bop, set the stage for the sound of the "second" Herd. This
> recording is priceless, truly the beginning of a new era for Woody's music.

And about Stan Getz in particular, he wrote:

> *Summer Sequence* had become a showpiece for the band, and everyone, but Stan had
> a part. I wrote *Summer Sequence* (Part 4) as a feature for him at Woody's request.

Later, I crafted *Early Autumn*, based on the original solo, as a stand-alone for him to record on Capitol Records. There were a lot of chord changes in it, and he was the only one that could play those chords. (Hooper 1991: 8)

About his childhood experiences as a musician, Stan Getz told Joseph Hooper, an interviewer for the *New York Times*, after his last concert at Carnegie Hall in June 1991 that he had never studied music theory or harmony, but begun saxophone practice at age thirteen.

I became a music kid, practicing eight hours a day. I was a withdrawn, hypersensitive kid. I would practice the saxophone in the bathroom, and the tenements were so close together that in the summertime, when the windows would be open, someone from across the alleyway would yell, "Shut that kid up," and my mother would say, "Play louder Stanley." My folks were proud; they didn't want me to be a street kid. Most of the kids in my neighborhood in the Bronx became members of Murder Inc. or cops. There wasn't much choice. . . ." (8)

He also experienced the brunt of racism, in his case, against Jews. He then dropped out of school in the ninth grade and became a professional musician, playing jazz, because he needed the money for his family. "My father was a mostly out-of-work printer and at that time in the '30s they didn't allow Jews into the printer union, so we had a hard time."

In the early 1940s, Stan Getz became attracted to what was happening at 52nd Street, Harlem, New York, and often visited this laboratory of modern jazz enacted by Charlie Parker, Dizzy Gillespie, Thelonious Monk, and associates. Although Getz at that time played in Benny Goodman's band, he was obsessed with trying to embrace the new style. He was only eighteen years old but "in awe of be-bop," as he said. He also heard Billie Holiday and met Lester Young. He was not allowed to sit in with them, just listen. He was not accepted. Only much later did he once appear jointly with Dizzy Gillespie under the instigation of producer Norman Granz (Jazz at the Philharmonic). It was worse for Getz in the 1960s when he began to feel "reverse racism" during the era of Free Jazz. He reacted by calling it "hate music." But his lack of a positive reception by bebop musicians in the 1940s, Getz eventually believed, was due to the fact that as an eighteen-year-old chap he simply lacked status with the pioneers of bebop (8).

This is quite reasonable. There is no evidence that bebop musicians would have excluded him on other grounds. Bird and Dizzy Gillespie made recordings with pianists Dodo Mamarosa and Al Haig. There was also Dizzy's affiliation with the Boyd Raeburn big band in 1944–45, based on mutual interest and musical appreciation.

Portraying Getz, Hooper writes about the complexities of the general situation:

As jazz left the mass popularity of the swing era, the serious white jazz musician found himself in an anomalous position—an insider (that is to say not black) practicing an outsider's art, an art regarded by mainstream America as too abstract or too vulgar or both. Musicians like Getz and the saxophonist Art Pepper occupied a no man's land, further cut off from "straight" America by certain habits endemic to the working musician. "To be a junkie is to be an outsider," Getz said. (8)

Group pressure was significant. Trombonist Bob Brookmeyer once stated in an interview: "Musicians who didn't drink or take drugs back when Stanley and I came up, you didn't trust them" (8). "We did have this great sense of intensity. Most of us didn't expect to live to see 30."

Stan Getz, according to his own narrative, began to use heroin when he was sixteen, under the influence of older jazz musicians who "wanted to turn a nice kid on." "I didn't even know that smack was habit-forming. In two weeks I was hooked and I spent 16 years trying to get off. A good Jewish boy doesn't take drugs." Hooper comes to the conclusion that "Getz was the classic prodigal son, indulged by a mother who worshipped him, arrested in the warp of anesthetizing chemicals" (8).

But other traits must be inserted into this picture: in spite of being a drug addict for much of his life, he was overly concerned about his health and apparently in constant fear of a health breakdown, a fear he tried to compensate for with lots of pills, vitamins, etc., a dietary regimen, swimming, sauna, massage, acupuncture, etc. Haunted by liver cancer, he also practiced Qi Gong.

Pianist Lou Levy once remembered an interviewer who marveled at how cool Stan Getz looked on stage. Getz replied: "Yeah, but inside I'm a seething mass" (8). He tried all sorts of things, more or less magic. Eventually, he told his last interviewer, Hooper, how he had benefited from Qi Gong: "It's a Chinese visualization process where you push the energy down into your liver. Also, I lie down in bed and then I stand up and do certain movements that look like tai chi. All that stuff works." But then, even Getz surmised that perhaps he would not win this last fight. Stan Getz died at age 64 from liver cancer, at his home in Malibu, California, June 6, 1991.

Tragically entangled in beliefs that psychoactive substances would enable the young man to cross over into the other culture, Getz will always be remembered for his part in the teamwork "Four Brothers" in Woody Herman's Second Herd, and especially for his solo in Ralph Burns's composition "Early Autumn" which is unforgettable as one of the greatest personal jazz renderings by someone in the twentieth century.

Perhaps Stan Getz's most spectacular legacy is his recorded musical interaction with trombone player Jay Jay Johnson, in the October 19, 1957, recording "Blues in the Closet" (Verve MGV8265), with Oscar Peterson on piano. Their performance of long solos, first Johnson, then Getz, with riffing commentary by their partners, culminates toward the end in a collective improvisation, with a hitherto unheard-of polyphony developing between Getz's tenor saxophone and Johnson's trombone, something like the simultaneous, but gradually diverging 100 metronomes in Györgi Ligeti's "Poeme Symphonique." Getz and Johnson's "chase" is a kind of "heterophonic polyphony" resulting from simultaneous linear variations of individual lines, molded together only by the twelve-bar form and the chords provided by Herb Ellis (guitar), Peterson (piano), and Ray Brown (bass) against the driving beat of Connie Kay (drums).

Swing

The Kinemics of a Phenomenon

Kenneth Pike's 1954 distinction of "emic and etic standpoints for the description of behavior" (derived from "phonemic" and "phonetic" in linguistics), and for the study of culture in general, is still relevant in ethnomusicology: emics as the understanding of phenomena in terms of the thought systems, categories, and concepts held by the cultural carriers in their own languages; and etics as the understanding of the same phenomena within a framework of scientific terminology projected from the outside. As seen today, the two "standpoints" are complementary, not mutually exclusive, and a researcher can switch from one to the other. In this chapter we first opt for discussing "swing" in terms of kinemics, the study of movement structures and behavior as experienced and conceptualized by members of the jazz community.

In musical practice there are always principles of organization: organization of tonality and harmonic patterns for example, rhythmic concepts, and even ways and methods of analysis that can be named in local terminology by their exponents. But some other phenomena seem to evade description in a rationalist manner, even if they are considered essential in defining a musical style. A rationalist examination of the category "swing" has been attempted by ethnomusicologists (Hodeir 1956; Schuller 1989; Prögler 1995), but such examinations have not resulted in a comprehensive delineation of the semantic field of the term, i.e., clarifying what "swing" is, in terms of musical structure and auditory perception. It is much easier to define the opposite: whatever can make a performance not swing, such as when it is staged by musicians from outside the jazz culture, trying to "jazz up" some tunes while they are inescapably imprisoned in the classical concept of syncopation, and thereby playing in a "corny" way. In the 1930s popular descriptive terminology in circles of jazz fans included "hot," "sweet," "corny," etc. (Ramsey and Smith 1939). "Corny" is one of those performance terms at the opposite end of a continuum of shades ranging from "swing" and "drive" to an array of negatively charged epithets. While all the qualities along that spectrum of terms are easily recognized, and appreciated or denounced, by jazz musicians and jazz audiences, it is difficult to transmute the basis of their judgments into rational discourse. Even a top jazz composer such as Jelly Roll Morton, and indeed one of the originators of jazz as a way of performing ragtime, was victimized in the late 1930s by critics calling his music "corny" when compared to contemporaneous big band swing.

Peter Townsend, writing on the subtleties of the rhythmic language in jazz and the failure of Western-style musical notation to capture some of its essentials, states in *Jazz in American Culture* (2000):

> Jazz culture itself has not produced an alternative system of notation in which these subtleties of rhythm can be captured, but it has its own language in which to express fine distinctions in this domain. Rhythmic strength and skill in rhythmic expression are considered to be absolutely basic musical values, even more so than the capacity for original improvisation, and a vocabulary has grown up around this crucial set of abilities and perceptions. The two master terms that express the issues for the player and the listener are "swing" and "time." These can sometimes come to the same thing. It can be said that a player does or does not "swing," does or does not "have good time." (21–22)

As performers—and this applies to performers of jazz, African music, and any musical tradition—we are all sensitive about aberrations of that kind among our co-performers and blame them quickly, especially if they are inexperienced. If someone in the group is unstable in his or her timing, worse if it is a member of the rhythm section, a sensation of discomfort lights up in our brain.

In 1967 Daniel Kachamba of Malawi often blamed his rattle player, Josefe Bulahamu, then fourteen, for inverting the beat, playing *ki-chi-ka* instead of *ka-cha ka-cha*, as it is expressed in mnemonics. Josefe took the criticism to heart and began to improve. I remember when in 1956, in my early twenties, still a bit short-tempered, and in full view of the audience I kicked our banjo player off the stage of the theatre in Vienna where we were playing. I was fed up with his erratic slowing down or hastening the tempo. He soon quit the band and was replaced by someone with an "iron" beat, resisting the wildest off-beat accents and retardation effects by the improvising wind instrument players. Sometimes we deliberately challenged him, launching an odd melodic rhythm to test his steadiness of tempo. Miles Davis reports in his autobiography that he was very much concerned with the rhythmic/temporal competence of his co-performers. He once even sacked his own nephew in one of his bands, because "He was always dropping the time, and if there's anything I can't stand in a drummer it's to drop the time" (quoted in Davis 1990: 367).

Obviously "dropping the time" impairs the quality that jazz musicians perceive to be swing. From those anecdotes it follows that swing also depends on a set of conditions such as constant speed and a regular statement of the beat. Steadiness of tempo is paramount in jazz and African music, subjectively however, allowing for miniscule acceleration in the course of a performance.

Rubato-style playing precludes that effect. But such conditions—as important as they are—are ancillary; they do not explain the phenomenon as such. A measurable beat, accurate to a millisecond, as can be produced by a computer or a synthesizer, does not specifically promote the impression of swing; in fact, it even seems to counteract the perception thereof. In 1962 our study of Moçambique log xylophone playing in a frame-by-frame analysis of film showed that deviations of 5 to 10 percent from regular spacing of elementary pulse-units (running at ca. 600 M.M.) is normal. And again, in his reconstructions of *amadinda* xylophone music of Buganda by computer simulation, from some of my field transcriptions, Ulrich Wegner (1990: items 12, 14, 17, etc.) learned that he had to introduce a chance deviation factor in order to make the computer renderings of this music sound "deceptively human." Actually, he succeeded well; upon hearing the recordings, court musician Evaristo Muyinda asked him: "Which group has played this?"

In an interview with Nat Hentoff published in *Down Beat*, Nov. 2, 1955, Miles Davis gave a blunt assessment of the music of some of his contemporaries. About West Coast jazz (i.e., music played by people such as Gerry Mulligan, Chet Baker, Lee Konitz, Clifford Brown, Bud Shank, and many others) he said that he found it monotonous in spite of all the technical expertise of its exponents: "The musicians out there don't give me a thrill. . . . " About Dave Brubeck he bluntly stated that the latter "does not swing." The same thing applied to Brubeck's saxophonist Paul Desmond, he said. Miles added that he preferred Lennie Tristano as well as Dizzy Gillespie even as a pianist to Brubeck! Many West Coast musicians, he said, simply played "too much" on the 88 keys of the piano. "Brubeck has wonderful harmonic ideas, but I sure don't like the way he touches, the way he plays the piano" (13–14).

Miles stated categorically, "jazz has to swing." But "can we put into words what it means to swing?" he asked. "If a guy makes you pat your foot and if you feel it down your back, you don't have to ask anybody, if that's good music or not. You can always feel it" (14). Endorsing subjectivity, Miles refers us to a specific experience of motion, a feeling "down your back," but sees no need for further verbal delineation of the phenomenon. And yet, swing is such an important concept in jazz culture, such an essential characteristic expected from the music and its performers, that we cannot lightheartedly abandon our search for parameters. Kinemics requires from us that we compare many statements by musicians about this basic idea, and collect their pronouncements across time and space, as diverse as they are, to find areas of agreement.

Many of those statements actually come from musicians at the height of the so-called Swing Era (ca. 1935–45), when the genre made a breakthrough to broader, popular awareness, and then became the label of a musical style, temporarily replacing the word "jazz," which was relegated to the older (i.e., New Orleans and Chicago) expressions. Swing made the initial step to public awareness through one of the earliest exponents of what later came to be called Kansas City swing by historians, for the man who started it all: Bennie Moten, with his record "Moten Swing," recorded December 13, 1932.

More than twenty years later, when "progressive jazz" by Stan Kenton was the talk of the day, Count Basie—an original member of Moten's band—gave these assessments in an article in *Down Beat*, May 16, 1956. Basie said that in 1951 he had suddenly come across the new orchestra of Duke Ellington and was amazed, because "the DUKE was swinging . . ." (in contrast to Kenton). Basie was fond of anything that had swing, e.g., Benny Goodman's and Tommy Dorsey's music. "Swing" was his declared criterion for judging jazz to be danced to. This testifies to the power of the concept and its spell that jazz musicians of the time cast on their audiences. It was used like a yardstick to evaluate the abilities of individuals and groups, without any need for defining the term, because everyone inside the culture was supposed to know—in the sense of nonverbal, symbolic knowledge—what it meant.

Jazz critics, however, were not insiders, and as such they had different needs. They were more comfortable with the term "time" taken from European music, in its association with tempo, speed, measure, etc. Ethnomusicologists studying African music also clung to "time," carrying it over into their field, although in African languages rhythm is not described that way (cf. Kubik 2010: II: 276–78). Even Africa's leading musicologist J. H. Kwabena Nketia spoke of "timing"; he also coined the term "time-line" in the 1960s.

Jazz historians and musicologists who were upset by the "mystery" of swing as a performance quality—in contrast to the use of the same word as the designation of a musical genre or style, e.g., big band swing—exerted pressure on the insider community, expecting clarification. Relegating the concept to the realm of rhythm, they tried to come to grips with the kind of rhythmic relationships producing such an effect. But soon many were persuaded to recognize a kind of innate quality or perceptual ability in musicians, which nobody really knew how it was transmitted. This played into the hands of racist ideology. Michael Zwerin, musician, jazz critic, and journalist, who will always be remembered for his articles on jazz personalities in the *International Herald Tribune* (cf. Zwerin 1979, 2001, 2004, etc.) recalled in his book *Close Enough for Jazz* (1983: 4) that when he once performed with Miles Davis, the latter said to him: "You got good time for a white cat." This was intended as a compliment. But it was also embarrassing, since it was based on a tenacious racial stereotype.

The problem of defining swing or time is exacerbated by the fact that audiences do not necessarily agree between themselves whether such and such group "swings" or not, even whether a certain music should be called jazz, rock 'n' roll, pop, or anything else. For me, Bunk Johnson swings a lot, for others he doesn't swing at all, and for others still his music recorded in the 1940s is not even representative of "traditional" New Orleans jazz, but had become something else to be summarized as "revival." In addition, there may be disagreement about the intensity of the presence of swing in different jazz styles. Peter Townsend (2000) reminds us that

> Jazz did not "swing" in the same way in 1945 as it did in 1925 and in 1935. The overall direction of change seems to have been towards a levelling out of the beat. Early jazz, up to about the mid-1930s, used a rhythmic style the "two-beat" rhythm, based on a strong accentuation of the second and fourth beats in the bar. By the late 1930s, the four beats of the bar were being sounded more or less equally, and the standard procedure for drummers was to mark all four beats on the bass drum. In bebop, the marking of beats shifted to the top cymbal, played with the drummer's right hand, a lighter sounding of the beat that made it less emphatic. If the beat in jazz is thought of as a kind of oscillation, what has happened progressively in jazz rhythm is that the depth, the amplitude of the oscillation has become shallower.... (23)

Some authors have tried to link the phenomenon of swing to a certain way of phrasing, especially in the use of a triple division of the meter in a 4/4 scheme; in notations this has often been expressed as sequences of dotted quaver plus semiquaver (dotted eighths plus sixteenth) with the semiquaver (sixteenth) carrying an offbeat accent. This can be quite misleading, as it invites the wrong accentuation; also, these note values do not represent the exact moments of attack. In actual phrasing, musicians may alternate between two simultaneous reference lines, leading to a triple and a quadruple division of the beat, depending on how they place their accents. I believe that this kind of notation, once widespread within the community of jazz musicians, is actually a carryover from the first decades of the twentieth century, when composers of sheet music were struggling to get jazz "syncopation" down on paper; thus the carryover became a convention.

In 1979 the arguments turned up again in an article by Leonard Feather on Jay McShann. In a series of recordings for the album *The Big Apple Bash* (SD 8804), one track by Jay McShann had become celebrated, a blues he sang and played on the piano, accompanied by guitarist John Scofield: "I'd Rather Drink Muddy Water." The piano part of this twelve-bar blues is transcribed for the journal *Contemporary Keyboard* in 12/8 time, rejecting conventional renderings of jazz in 4/4. In an editorial note inserted into Leonard Feather's text, the journal's editor defends his standpoint that notations of blues-based music would be rendered more accurately in 12/8 time, showing the alternative notation in 4/4 of

Fig. 8.1. Jay McShann performing with Charlie Parker. Courtesy of the Institute of Jazz Studies, Rutgers University Libraries.

Figs. 8.2 and 8.3. Jay McShann's piano part of "I'd Rather Drink Muddy Water," transcription by Jim Alkin (reproduced from *Contemporary Keyboard*, October 1979: 80–81). Extract: first two measures only, as rendered in 12/8 time, and as rendered in 4/4 time.

the first two measures and its disadvantages, such as clustering triplets marked by threes (Feather 1979; see Figs. 8.2, 8.3). The editor of the journal explains his choice: (80) "We preferred the 12/8 notation, which in this case is equivalent to 4/4 with each dotted quarter taking the place of a quarter, because it makes the rhythm more apparent to readers who are not familiar with the conventions of jazz notation, and also cleans up the page by eliminating a lot of triplet brackets with little 3's over them" (80).

This standpoint is also shared by those of us who play jazz in southern Africa. In an interview conducted by researcher Linda Williams in Harare, Zimbabwe, on October 19, 1992, with Zimbabwean jazz veteran Christopher Chabuka, the latter commented on the problem:

It's not the triplet rhythm that's important. . . . It's only important when you put it on paper, but it's not that simple. Like in American jazz, people think that in order to swing, you have to place a dot behind the quarter note and play an eighth note, followed again by a dotted quarter note, consequently and repeatedly. That's not it! What American jazz musicians do is take two eighth notes and place an extraordinary emphasis on the second note of each eighth note grouping to create an added tension in connecting each phrase. It's precisely the same element that we find in our music. (cf. Williams 2005: 93)

The implications of Chabuka's statements are noteworthy: (1) swing does not come from a rhythm notated as sequences of dotted note plus half its value, actually dotted quaver plus semiquaver (not "dotted quarter note"); (2) American jazz musicians tend to intonate notes of equal length, e.g., two eighth notes, but the accent is often shifted off-beat on the second one; in other words, they do not think in terms of the "classical" concept of syncopation rooted in a centralized pre-accented meter.

Very few authors, in fact, seem to recognize that the ground beat in jazz is not the ultimate reference level for a jazz performer, and that the development of a "feeling for the beat" (Waterman 1952) is only part of the story. It may have been disproportionately important to some revival Dixieland bands of the 1950s struggling to emulate New Orleans jazz, but generally, jazz clings to a more complex framework of timing. There is an ever-present, deeper reference level in performers, like an infinite grid of smallest time or action units, subliminally carried in the mind and capable of serving as a powerful steering device. It goes beyond Richard A. Waterman's "metronome sense"; it is faster and the units are shorter than the beat. A. M. Jones was the first researcher who became aware of this inner reference grid while working with musicians when he was stationed in Northern Rhodesia (Zambia) during the 1930s. He referred to it as the "smallest units" and used squared paper to represent them visually. I have called it "elementary pulsation" (cf. Kubik 2010: II: 31–35). As a basic grid regulating time awareness, it is ingrained in our brains; but like any inborn special ability, it must be developed during an individual's life span in order to operate. Like language acquisition there are crucial years for its development; otherwise it becomes stunted. In some places of the world musical enculturation promotes such development, whereas in others it hinders the process.

Rather than functioning as a subdivision of the beat, those faster units operate as an autonomous, silent reference line in performers. They have no structure, no accents, no beginning, and no end. Their steering mechanism is activated from the moment the trained jazz player begins to perform. He will then always know (without counting) where he is, even in the most intriguing improvisational contexts. By itself, the elementary pulsation is merely an infinite string of reference points, up to the speed of 600 M.M. It is by nature inaudible, but may of course be objectified in percussion. Only when the ground beat (or dancers' beat) is superimposed as a second, broader reference level do those pulse units congregate to form compounds of two, three, and four units. After a regular number of repetitions of such a compound, even larger entities are formed, the cycles of 12, 16, 24, 32, 36, 48 units, and strophic forms may arise as in the blues, and the chorus form as in jazz. A twelve-bar blues is actually compounded of 12 x 12 = 144 elementary pulse units. These larger cycles, as in blues and jazz, are an important third reference level for the improvising musician; an experienced jazz musician will never get lost within a chorus form, such as jumping one bar or missing a beat. He may even try to tempt his co-players to go astray, by injecting disorienting phrases into his playing. Dizzy Gillespie (1955) reported that Charlie Parker was sometimes doing that:

> I remember how at times he used to turn the rhythm section around, when he and I, Max and Duke Jordan were playing together. Like we'd be playing the blues, and Bird would start on the 11th bar, and as the rhythm section stayed where they were and Bird played where he was, it sounded as if the rhythm section was on one and three instead of two and four.
>
> Every time that would happen Max used to scream at Duke not to follow Bird, but to stay where he was. Then eventually it came around as Bird had planned and we were together again. (14)

This describes an audio-psychological phenomenon I would call cycle disorientation. A soloist, e.g., Parker, shifts a phrase that sounds like beginning another chorus, to an odd bar. Listeners, and more rarely co-performers, can get thrown off the cycle, believing for example, that they are in measure 1 of a new chorus, while the band is still in measure 11 of the previous chorus. In that manner, a soloist may even test the strength of cycle awareness in his co-performers. Jazz musicians learn to resist being thrown off-track by unusual accents and phrase shifting. A mild example for a self-test in this context is perhaps Dexter Gordon's long tenor saxophone improvisations in "Dexter Rides Again" (Savoy 623, Matrix no. S 5879–1). A more advanced test example is "Cool Blues" (Callander West) with Charlie Parker's phrase developments across bar and cycle lines (cf. *Jazz & Blues*, Charlie Parker, BN 207, 1998 BIEM Stemra, CD 2, track 8).

A prevailing observation is that jazz audiences often have little consciousness of the cycles, and therefore that an important aspect of jazz improvisation, the subtle shifting of phrases off-track to strengthen and reconfirm cycle awareness in the band, escapes them. It is not so much the harmonic progressions in modern jazz that present difficulty to the general audience, but phraseology that trespasses the customary boundaries of measures and cycle lengths.

The soloist may also trigger in listeners' auditory perception what I have called the illusion of beat inversion (Kubik 2010: II: 95–107). As a disorientation effect this is similar to cycle disorientation, but takes place at the level of the reference beat, not the cycle. In such a case, if the soloist has used strong off-beat accents, the listener may, for example, take beat units 2 and 4 (more often 4 and 2) for 1 and 3. Experienced jazz musicians, of course, resist the illusion.

The use of disorientation tactics in phrase development, as described above, is a direct legacy from African musical practice continuing in jazz. Numerous examples could be cited from recordings in various parts of Africa.

Jazz theoreticians are not normally aware of the subliminal presence of more than one reference line of timing in performers, and that their interrelatedness is of relevance to the kinemic experience that has been called swing. Swing is an audio-psychological phenomenon to be studied within the psychology of perception. It is somewhat comparable to optical illusions, sensations of tactility, and acoustic illusions, but especially to the so-called phi phenomenon discovered by Gestalt psychologist Max Wertheimer in 1910, which "occurs when you see two adjacent lights alternately blinking off and on and perceive them as one light moving back and forth" (Sonderegger 1998: 48). Similarly, in swing an impulse moves back and forth (swings) between beat and off-beat emphasis.

Gestalt psychologists have long postulated that there are innate, organizing faculties in the brain that steer the processes of perception. And yet it may appear strange to someone not familiar with the psychology of perception to accept that there is a steering device in the mind to process units shorter than the beat or gross-pulse. Most musicians and audiences educated in Western classical music proceed in their musical understanding from a centralized framework of pre-accented meter, e.g., 1–2–3–4. In early jazz this was reinterpreted as 1–2–3–4. To write down music identifying the elementary pulse units that are much faster than the gross-pulse, and replace time signatures such as 4/4 etc. with cycle numbers, at first looks aberrant. However, European classical music differs significantly from some basic concepts of timing in both African and African American musical styles, including jazz. The crux of the matter is that even if a jazz drummer hits 2 and 4 regularly on the hi-hat cymbal, the accent is only acoustic, it is not the meter (the reference scheme) that is accented.

We have so far isolated three simultaneous reference levels of timing both in African and African American music. The first is the elementary pulsation as the most basic subjective grid. It is developed in children and youngsters early on, provided that there is a favorable cultural environment. In some forms of African music and (modern) jazz more than one elementary pulse-line may be present simultaneously, in a relationship of 2 against 3, or 3 against 4 (see Fig. 8.4). The second reference level of timing is the beat or gross-pulse, the dancers' steps. This is a relatively slow reference line, three to four times slower than the elementary pulsation. The beat combines a number of elementary pulse-units, thereby introducing a structuring principle. The third reference level of timing is the cycle formed by repetition of a certain, usually even number of elementary pulse units that are tied together within the spacing of the ground beat. In transcriptions we express cycles with a number that is encircled, e.g., 32, 48 etc., or if the form is strophic 16 x 8 or 32 x 4, etc., as in an AABA jazz form.

This intersected rhythmic and formal module can be observed in all musical styles that display swing. Usually the cycle number of the songs or the musical piece is a multiple of 12, or simultaneously 12 and 16. Therefore, the elementary pulsation in relation to the ground-beat or dance beat resembles triplets, combining with duplets and quadruplets of the second reference line, as is the case in many forms of boogie-woogie. In improvisation, the performer can shift phrasings between the different subjective pulse-lines.

Melodic or other accents tend to fall on the last pulse-unit of a chain of triplets just before beat 1; or alternatively, phrases are interpolated in conformity with two simultaneous reference lines. This gives some variations a kind of transient bi-metric flavor, although no two meters are actually conceptualized by the performer. The concept is to delay, to play behind the beat.

Finally, we note that traditions that exhibit swing do not employ asymmetric timeline patterns, except the short eight-pulse pattern universal in Africa and in New World cultures, variously known as *habanera* or *rumba* pattern, "Latin tinge," cinquillo, tresillo, etc. Mathematically more complex timeline patterns (cf. Kubik 2008a) are not swing-generating. Found across the music of the Caribbean, in Brazil, and of course, in the African areas from where they were exported, these are not employed as time-keeper devices in jazz.

Figure 8.4 shows one possible relationship between three simultaneous reference lines in jazz. Here it is important to keep in mind that these are not "played" notes; the dots are not strokes, but silent pulse-units, although each dot may of course, receive an acoustic impulse, if the performer decides to generate one.

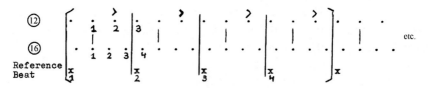

Fig. 8.4. Example: Simultaneous pulse-lines as a subliminal reference scheme in some jazz and some forms of African music (relation 12:16)

The trick of this particular reference scheme is that it allows performers to produce both swing and retardation effects (playing "behind the beat"), because the three reference lines are related here to each other like cross rhythms. This comes about because the twelve- and sixteen-pulse lines have their meeting points (written by me as 1) off the reference beat. That moment, therefore, does not also coincide with the dancer's steps suggested by the beat. It falls on the second pulse-unit of the twelve-pulse reference line that divides the beat into triplets. I have tried to express how the three reference lines interlock by inserting small numbers into the illustration.

Because of this kind of alignment, the sixteen-pulse line runs delayed against the reference beat; pulse-unit 4 occurs a fraction of time behind beats 1, 2, 3, and 4. Swing is triggered by accents on the last pulse-unit in the triplets of the twelve-pulse line. Such accents anticipate the ground-beat and thereby give it a kick. Hence the music begins to swing like the alternately blinking lights in the phi phenomenon.

By contrast, retardation effects are triggered if the performer switches to the sixteen-pulse line, because that reference line is delayed against the beat due to its start on the second pulse of the triplets. Accordingly, I have marked the coinciding starts as 1.

The improviser can stay within the twelve-pulse reference line, but he can also move temporarily to the sixteen-pulse line. In the latter case his melodic phrases will appear to be slightly delayed in relation to the reference beat (marked x in Fig. 8.4). Audiences will say he "plays behind the beat." The figure shows why that is so. One may look at the vertical relationship between the point marked 4 and the x underneath! If we write out Figure 8.4 in Western notation and take the twelve-pulse line as being composed of quavers, the sixteen-pulse line will appear to be shifted and delayed against the beat by the value of a thirty-second note.

It must be stressed, however, that this analysis refers to the structure of the process, but is not necessarily descriptive of a performer's thoughts while playing. The performer does not delay his phrases in terms of counting minimal numerical time values or "microrhythms." While he may operate simultaneously from two separate grids in his mind, he will not analyze their relationship while playing, i.e., that they diverge from each other by a fraction of an elementary pulse-unit. He simply conceptualizes the melodic-rhythmic phrases he plays as slightly behind the beat. This is consistent with research carried out by Giorgio Adamo on movement (Adamo 2008, 2012).

Charlie Parker often switched between simultaneous pulse-lines. An example is "Parker's Mood," with John Lewis on piano, Max Roach on drums, and Curley Russell on bass (recorded in New York, September 18, 1948; *Complete Savoy Masters* 1999, CD 2, track 4). It is slow enough to make these minimal shifts effective.

Accents that coincide with the two pulse-lines' meeting points may enhance the swing by the additional tension created. Proceeding from kinemics to kinetics, the feeling of swing is a pleasant perception of the kind we all once experienced as children when playing on the swings in the park. It is a movement between two apexes, swinging down through a trough. In jitterbug dancing swing also becomes effectively visualized.

However, there is more to Figure 8.4. If listeners are hooked on the triplets, understanding them as a subdivision of the beat, they might believe that the musicians do not divide the beat regularly but place accents somewhere between triplets and quadruplets. Some researchers speak of "micro rhythms." Figure 8.4 should make clear how these miniscule deviations come about. The performer switches between two simultaneous reference lines, sometimes in the middle of a phrase.

In order to come up, swing presupposes a system of timing that is regular, though not necessarily unilinear. The phenomenon is kinetic, acoustic, and perceptual. What the listener notices, however, is predominantly the sound-producing event, not the subjective reference lines that are behind it.

Retardation effects are as important in the rhythmic texture of jazz as is the creation of swing. They are equally based on the existence of more than one simultaneous reference line, as described above. Erroll Garner's piano style became famous for his delight in retardation, with his right-hand melodies slightly behind the chords played with the left. Such effects on piano, trumpet, or any other instrument can only be generated if timing references in the performer are absolutely stable, as a firm grid in the improvising mind. If a musician then seems to play behind the beat, he or she actually play in accordance with either of the subjective reference lines underneath the music, while the percussionist objectifies the reference beat.

Anyone phrasing his improvisatory melodies in retardation to the beat actually phrases them in retardation to one of two simultaneous pulse-lines. In group performance, Miles Davis was a master of this. The same technique is employed

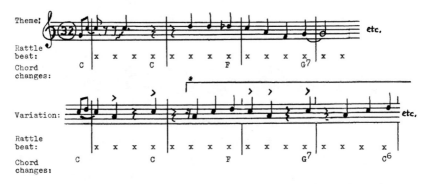

Fig. 8.5. "Simanje-manje D," composed 1973 by Donald Kachamba, Chileka, Malawi. Clarinet variation. Recorded September 30, 1991, for Südwestfunk (Mr. Jacobshagen) radio station, Mainz, Germany.

in some genres of African music, e.g., by a lead singer's or soloist's phrasings. For African jazz practice I gave an instrumental example of a theme and its variation from our own group in Wolfgang Knauer's book *The World Meets Jazz* (2008: 189). It is retranscribed in Figure 8.5, to show that complex relationships can be written down, albeit in a somewhat modified notation system.

In jazz notation we now use cycle numbers, as we do in African music, 16, 32, 36, etc., to express the number of pulse-units underneath. In Figure 8.5 there is only one subjective pulse-line defining the ground beat. But another one comes up implicitly because all harmonic changes are shifted against the beat; they are anticipated by one beat-unit. Thus they occur always on 4 of the 1–2–3–4 metric scheme. The clarinet phrase in the variation part is shifted one sixteenth note behind the beat.

While it is true that jazz culture itself has "not produced an alternative system of notation" (Townsend 2000: 21–22), there was one remarkable attempt in that direction by a jazz musician with no obvious need for sharing his results with others. In 1960–61 Viennese trumpet player Helmut Hillegeist, in his quest for emulating New Orleans veteran Bunk Johnson's music, began to study the latter's recordings phrase by phrase, with an almost spiritualistic empathy. He used to play flügelhorn, which is close in timbre to a cornet. Faithful to the aesthetics of Bunk Johnson's music, he developed a system of notation for his private use that gives minute visual renderings of the rhythmic structure and phrasings in this music. His notations on squared paper proceed from the recognition of two simultaneous reference levels of timing: (a) the elementary pulsation, represented by the vertical lines of the squared paper; (b) the ground beat, represented by reinforcing certain vertical lines at regular distances.

In 1973 Hillegeist gave me two of his transcriptions from his files covering all Bunk Johnson recordings that were available to him in 1960–61. I reproduced them in an article about his system in the journal *Jazz Research* (Kubik 1973). To give an idea of Hillegeist's notations I offer two extracts, in Figures 8.6 and 8.8. The first covers six lines, thirty-six measures of his transcription of the trumpet part of "Iberia Blues" (see Fig. 8.6); the second transcribes the first five lines of "Panama," introduction and the first chorus (see Fig. 8.8). The inception of each trumpet tone is marked by Hillegeist with a small point from which a trail or length of line proceeds to the right, expressing duration and sometimes pitch fluctuations. The trumpet notes are identified by their names, but unfortunately they are in German. Readers should therefore take note of the fact that "des" means d♭, "cis" means c♯, "b" means b♭, while "h" means b. The small numbers seen next to some letters indicate the octaves. A trumpet player, I believe, should be able to understand this notation quickly and reproduce the melodic lines.

More than what could ever be revealed by a spectrogram, Hillegeist's notations by ear demonstrate how Bunk phrased his melodies—not only on or off beat, but

'New Iberia Blues", Bunk Johnson Band, recorded in New Orleans, July 1944; American Music LP AM 257.
Bunk Johnson, tp; transcription H. Hillegeist.

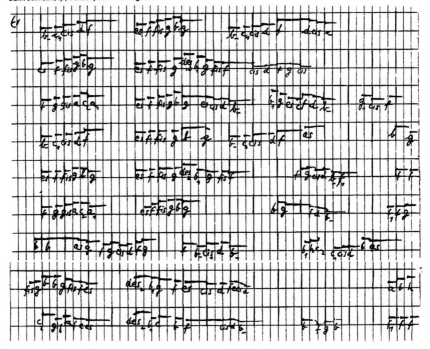

Fig. 8.6.

Fig. 8.7. H. Hillegeist in Moçambique, on the road out of Tete from the north bank of the Zambezi River. October 1962. Photo: author

"Panama", Bunk Johnson's Original Superior Band, recorded in New Orleans, June 11, 1942; JAZZMAN 8. Bunk Johnson, tp; transcription H. Hillegeist.

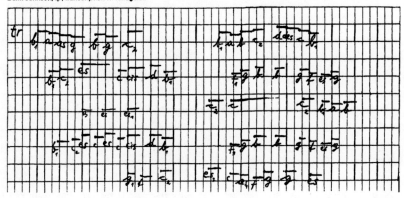

Fig. 8.8.

also on or off the elementary pulsation underneath. Rhythmic subtleties become visible, generated sometimes by minimal retardation of some phrases, which was obviously a concept and technique present from the earliest days of jazz. Bunk could not have introduced it in the 1940s.

If someone attempts to play Hillegeist's notations against a stable banjo beat such as Lawrence Marrero's, he or she will discover that the faithful reproduction swings just like the original.

New Orleans jazz veterans interviewed in the 1940s sometimes commented on the term "swing" or even used it. In an interview conducted by Rudi Blesh and Harriet Janis with New Orleans trombonist George Filhe (born 1872) for their book *They All Played Ragtime* (1950 [1971]), the term "swing" also came up. Filhe gave a statement defining the difference between ragtime and jazz renderings of sometimes the same compositions, and he also suggested when this new manner of performance first appeared: "In 1892—played [solo cornet] with Cousto & Desdunes, Cousto solo cornet, O'Neill cornet, Desdunes, violin & baritone. Played jazz, would always swing the music, that was their novelty. Solo B cornet came in then and replaced the old rotary valve E-flat cornet. They played quadrilles, schottisches, straight. Onward Brass Band Younger musicians about 1892 began to 'swing'. Older men used lots of Mexican music."

Analyzing that statement, Lawrence Gushee (1994) comments: "Filhe was born in 1872, a youngster compared to Sylvester Coustaut, born in 1863, but a near contemporary of Dan Desdunes, born about 1870. What did he mean by 'swing' and 'older musicians,' and how literally should we take the date 1892? In any event, what is really interesting here is the identification of a drastic shift, from Mexican music to a new kind that, by contrast, swung" (17).

I for one suggest that we take 1892 literally, and understand Filhe's use of the term "swing" as an attempt to explain to his interviewers in contemporary language (of the 1940s) how the music had changed. He was sure that they would then understand what he wanted to say when he claimed that by 1892 New Orleans musicians began to swing. He thereby also indirectly declared that "swing" was a defining moment for the new dance music, long before the so-called Swing Era, in contrast to "straight playing" as written.

Casually, the word "swing" would come up a bit later. When the Original Dixieland Jass Band published "Livery Stable Blues" on a 78 r.p.m. Victor record, selling more than a million copies, the following comments appeared in the *New Orleans Times-Picayune* on April 17, 1917, in an advertisement for the Maison Blanche department store's music section which was selling the records: "Made by New Orleans musicians for New Orleans people, it has all the 'swing' and 'pep' and 'spirit' that is so characteristic of the bands whose names are a by-word at New Orleans dances."

The Swing Belt of Africa

With regard to African music, the most often heard comment by jazz fans in the last century was that "African music does not swing." Usually such comments were based on limited knowledge of regional styles and genres, but were articulated with an air of certainty, as if applicable to all African music. The implication is that one essential trait in jazz, namely swing, could not be of African origin.

Even if that had turned out to be true, it would not have impaired our historical research, because—in contrast to Brazilian Candomblé and Cuban Lucumi, largely extensions of Yoruba, Fō, and Ewe religious music, as well as Brazilian samba, with dominant traits that can be traced to the Lunda/Luba historical cultures of Katanga and eastern Angola (Kubik 1979 [2013])—jazz cannot be considered a direct extension of any regional African genre or style cluster. Too many undocumented, intermediate American developments took place in the nineteenth century and later, so that all cultural/genealogical linkages are blurred.

But in spite of the poor source situation, we can still carry out "family" research if we try to follow up single constituent traits such as the presence or absence of certain tonal ideas, instrumental playing techniques, vocal styles, preferences for certain forms, etc. Occasionally we learn that some traits are clustered, each dependent on the presence or absence of other traits. This is very much the case with swing. To swing in performance requires the presence of a certain environment of related traits, while other elements in rhythmic and tonal organization seem to prevent its formation. As in physics, in culture there are laws of attraction and repulsion, in the sense that some traits would never get associated with certain other traits, while other elements easily combine and reinforce one another. Many apparently salient characteristics of music in Africa are regional, and not shared by all African music; in fact, very few are universal. Some are mutually exclusive, such as certain tunings that would not be compatible with principles of harmonic formation. For this reason, the search for swing in Africa may take us to some unexpected destinations.

It was Paul Oliver who, in his book *Savannah Syncopators* (1970), first arrived at a somewhat refined perspective. In 1964, upon invitation by the Department of Architecture, Kumasi University, he traveled to Ghana. First he worked in coastal Ghana, then in the hinterland close to the border of Upper Volta (now Burkina Faso). He found that coastal styles, by the Akan group of peoples, with their emphasis on percussion, polyrhythm, and asymmetric timelines, did not evoke in him any associations to jazz, let alone blues.

In a chapter entitled "Africa and the Jazz Historian," Oliver examines the various theories by authors about transatlantic historical connections. He underlines that for him propositions of relationship between Guinea Coast music and jazz were exaggerated because "jazz developed a different kind of rhythmic feeling with a lifting movement between adjacent beats which the jazz musician identifies as 'rock' or 'swing'" (36). After discussing Richard A. Waterman's seminal 1952 paper, he says that for him, "in the jazz sense, West African drum orchestras simply do not 'swing.' The 'ride' of a New Orleans jazz band, the 'slow and easy' slow-drag of a country blues band, have no counterpart in the forceful thrust of the multilinear drum rhythms" (37).

But as soon as he moved to a village in the north, Nangodi, at the border of Upper Volta, well within Greenberg's linguistic family I.A.3 (Voltaic), things began to look and sound different. The turning point came when Oliver made the acquaintance of two Fra-Fra musicians, fiddle and rattle players Kunaal and Sosira, whom he perceived as playing "a combination of vocal, rhythmic and stringed instruments which hinted at a link with the blues. Here too," he writes, "I heard in person for the first time an African music which could be said to 'swing' in the jazz sense, where the singer and accompanist seemed free to improvise and where the combination of instruments had a certain feeling of syncopation" (38).

He then makes an important proposal: that we should look to the West African savannah hinterland, rather than the coast, for any African retentions in American jazz and blues to be traced.

In the same year, 1964, I also happened to be traveling in the West African savannah. I had started my journey in October 1963 in Oshogbo, Nigeria, on a Solex autocycle (a French bicycle with a small assisting motor). I went north, cycling across the Bauchi plateau into northeastern Nigeria and down to Yola, from Genye/Sugu to Toungo, the seat of a powerful Fulɓe Lamiɗo, recording everywhere on the way. Then I crossed into Cameroon, from Toungo to Kont-cha, Ngaoundere, and Yoko.

On long footslogs through thinly populated areas west of Yoko in Cameroon, I traveled with reduced baggage in the company of only one adolescent from a local school, who had volunteered to accompany me. We passed a few Tikar homesteads, sometimes larger settlements by Tikar-speaking families, places that were still surrounded by ditches as a protection against the nineteenth-century Fulɓe invaders on horseback and slave recruiters. Here I made a fabulous record-ing of a young Tikar woman with her child. She was grinding millet on a grind-ing stone in front of her house with a shuffle rhythm and singing a surprisingly blues-like song of complaint (cf. track 19 on CD accompanying Italian transla-tion of *Africa and the Blues*, Kubik 2007). Any contact with American music was to be excluded; for a hundred kilometers around there were no radios during that period. Further south, walking to Linté, seat of the powerful Vute chief Dimani Garba, and to Emtse, north of Nanga-Eboko, I came across *timbrh* lamellophone music, with ensembles usually composed of two to three timbrh of different size and a flat rattle (*kara*). I was fascinated by this music (track 17), which displayed immense swing.

In brief, the timbrh is a lamellophone made of materials from the raffia palm tree. The lamellae are cut from the hard epidermis of a raffia leaf stem. They are tuned by attaching lumps of black wax at the underside of their ends. On top of each lamella a vibrating needle, also of raffia, is attached by means of black wax. Its sympathetic vibration gives the instrument a buzzing timbre and also pro-longs the duration of each note.

The notes are tuned in octave pairs, and the player, sounding two adjacent lamellae at once with each thumb (thereby creating parallel octaves) produces two fast, interlocking tone-rows through right and left thumb alternation, in disjunct intervals, usually tetra- to pentatonic. The resulting combination at the speed of the elementary pulsation is in a duple movement over a cycle of usually twelve or twenty-four pulse-units. However, this is interpreted by the rattle as a triple rhythm, creating a shuffle very close to what I saw and heard the young Tikar woman do on her grinding stone. The tension in this combination arises from the simultaneous presence of the interlocking tone-rows and the rattle-generated ground beat to be shared by the dancers, combining three pulse units. Strong accents fall anywhere off beat, often forming patterns between them-selves. In some ways this music reminded me of boogie-woogie, though there was no underlying twelve-bar blues form.

The combining left and right thumb tone-rows also produce an auditory illu-sion effect, because the resultant total of twelve notes falls apart in perception into three separate, interwoven melodic-rhythmic lines. Such inherent pattern

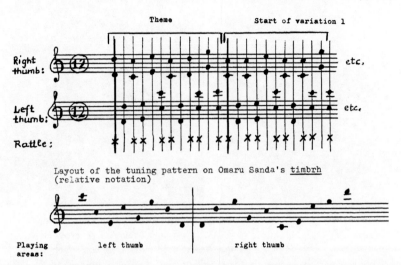

Fig. 8.9. "Manengombe"—Performance on *timbrh* raffia lamellophone by Omaru Sanda and group; recorded at the chief's court, Emtse, Cameroon, February 1964. (Relative notation)

Fig. 8.10 and 8.11. Omaru Sanda, about 30, principal performer in the *timbrh* (lamellophone) ensemble at the court of the Vute chief of Emtse, north of the town of Nanga-Eboko in central Cameroon. The ensemble was composed of three raffia-manufactured lamellophones of different size and a box rattle (*kara*). The young rattle player responsible for the swing of the group is seen in the second picture. At the chief's court of Emtse, central Cameroon, February 1964. Photos: author (C57, C58)

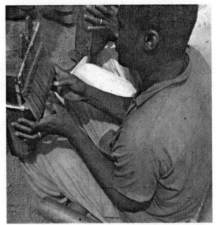

Fig. 8.12 and 8.13. Swinging *timbrh* (lamellophone) music was also part of the court music of the Vute paramount chief Dimani Garba in Linté. As always, it consisted of three *timbrh* and one rattle. The first picture shows the group seated with the responding women's chorus in the back; the second picture shows the left/right thumb interlocking technique with the raffia lamellae tuned in octave pairs. Linté, south of Yoko, central Cameroon, March 1964. Photos: author (C 63, C 64)

effects are the composer's intent. The effect is enhanced in the long improvisatory variations that follow the theme (Kubik 2010: II: 107ff.; 142–44).

Figure 8.9 gives a short transcription of a theme and one variation played by a group of three timbrh musicians—the theme always in unison—and one rattle (kara) player to accompany a women's chorus praising the chief of Emtse village.

In 1964 I did not analyze my recordings in great detail. I merely enjoyed the music. Analysis came only in the 1990s when writing *Africa and the Blues*, and again I consulted Paul Oliver's book and various recordings by ethnomusicologists such as Gilbert Rouget, Artur Simon, and others. The evidence of all this clearly pointed to the fact that there was something like a geographical "swing belt" across the West African savannah from Guinée to Burkina Faso, northern Nigeria, into central Cameroon, and further on to central parts of the Sudan. Musical genres here, displaying swing, would however occur in a scattered distribution. Characteristically, they were found in a population stratum that had been a primary target of the Atlantic slave trade in West Africa during the second half of the eighteenth century. These people were descendants of what anthropologists have sometimes called the Ancient Nigritic cluster. The remote ancestors of those people had developed millet agriculture between 5000 and 1000 BC. When much of the West African sahel and savannah zone became Islamicized from the eighth century AD on, and was dominated economically by merchant

Fig. 8.14. Swinging work rhythm produced by young women of the Chamba ethnic group, north-eastern Nigeria, who employ an interlocking technique of strokes. The woman in back has just hit the millet in the mortar, the one in the left of the picture has raised her pestle to the apex of her movement, while the third woman, in the right side of the picture is about to drop her pestle with the next pounding stroke, as soon as the woman in the middle lifts hers. The alternating strokes are executed in a circular order. At village Disol, near Genye/Sugu, south of Yola, northeastern Nigeria, November 1963. Photo: author

empires such as Mali, Songhai, and later the Hausa city states gaining their power from the Saharan trading network, some of the Ancient Nigritic people retreated to inaccessible mountainous areas.

Many of Rouget's recordings in Guinée in 1952, notably a solo for *seron* (a nineteen-string bridge-harp) played by Mamadi Dioubaté of the Mandiŋ-speaking people, display formidable swing (cf. *Musique de l'Afrique Occidentale*, Gilbert Rouget and Jean Koroma, LP Contrepoint M.C. 20.045). Among the Chamba, a I.A.6 Adamawa-Eastern-speaking ethnic group along the border of northern Nigeria and Cameroon, I made a recording that could potentially reveal how the principle of the interlocking beat was initiated in the remote past in Africa through work division, and with it, how swing first emerged as a by-product. In November 1963 in Disol, a village near Genye/Sugu in northeastern Nigeria, I found three women standing around a mortar in the village, each with a pestle in her hand, pounding millet (see Fig. 8.14). While working, they produced clicking and sucking noises by mouth, giving accents. It was fascinating to watch these young women and learn how the starting stroke of the first performer, establishing the ground beat, was followed by the other two women with interlocking strokes that divided the sequence into triplets. Occasionally, one of the women—instead of dropping her pestle on the millet—hit the rim of the mortar, thereby giving an off-beat accent. Indeed, this was work and music, all in one, and the music was swinging. The click sounds contributed a further line of accents. It was perfect cooperation between three performers of equal standing, each with an analogous task. I spontaneously recorded their performance and

Fig. 8.15. Music in the African swing belt: *Bal* single-note pipes and a gourd horn played by members of a family of the Ingassana ethnic group. At Rumeilik, in the Ingassana Mountains, southwest of Ed Damazin, Sudan, January 26, 1977. Photo: author

the recording can be heard on the CD accompanying *Theory of African Music* Vol. 2: CD 2, track 3.

Although the idea of an interlocking reference beat has not survived in jazz, one result of the original process, namely swing has indeed been transmitted, in contrast to percussion based on asymmetric patterns as on the Guinea Coast, in Angola and other parts of West-Central Africa.

It is interesting to learn that swing can be created in a group, even when each group member produces just one note (tone) at a certain moment of the combination, as is the case in the gourd horn ensembles I recorded in the same geographical area, the *faŋ kure* end-blown gourd horns played for the ancestors among the Kutin (Kubik et al. 1989: 88–89).

The swing belt extends further east into the area of Nilotic speakers within the Nilo-Saharan super-family of African languages. This is demonstrated by Artur Simon's 1982 recordings of the *waza* horn ensemble among the Berta (CD SM 17082 Museum Collection Berlin, 2003; Simon 1989) and my recording of *bal* flute ensembles of the Ingassana, central Sudan, in 1977 (see Fig. 8.15). More recently waza was recorded in Ethiopia by ethnomusicologist Timkehet Teffera, who showed me her video document in 2010.

The waza horn tradition evokes vivid associations of jazz in concept, timbre, articulation of the horns, and the underlying dance beat. It belongs to the most eastern branch of what I call the swing belt of Africa. It is an ancient Sudanic tradition, part of a substratum of styles that once covered wider areas across the savannah and sahel zone from central Sudan to Lake Chad. The Berta, in their practice of waza, have been resistant to Islamic influences upon their musical culture.

In the waza tradition up to ten gourd trumpets serve in the ensemble. The music is polyphonic. Artur Simon (1983) reports that in the village Uffud EI-Nuweiiri where he recorded waza, the trumpets had a length of 60 to 174 cm: "Five of the players each also carried a forked stick on their right shoulder which was struck with a cowhorn held in the right hand. The player of the seventh trumpet played a rattle (*asɔso*) simultaneously while the singing and dancing women wore ankle rattles (*atitish*) made of the capsules of the fruit of a certain tree" (309, my translation).

Each of the ten performers executes just one note on his horn, but the interlocking voice attacks are so coordinated that melodic and rhythmic cycles emerge. While playing, reports Simon, the musicians do not count, but each of them proceeds from a personal movement pattern involving various parts of the body plus the moment of blowing into the horn. The music swings, as Simon's recordings aptly demonstrate. For me this swing is even perceptible in some of Simon's still photographs, especially in the relaxed attitudes of the players in one picture (cf. Simon 1983: 308), each of them holding those heavy horns with ease, using a personal embouchure, and particularly in the way the front horn player stands, or rather moves perpetually, lifting his right knee slightly.

In the now independent South Sudan some music of the Acooli also swings, for example *nanga* zither playing. The swing belt extends into Western Kenya, where lyre music of the Abaluhya sometimes shows a jazz-like beat.

Another area of Africa that frequently turns up swing elements is southwestern and southern Africa. Swing characterizes some polyphonic !Kung bushman music (cf. "Kainta a," Kubik 2010: I: track 27), and it is probably not coincidental that jazz of the1940s was so easily transplanted to South Africa and transformed into *kwela* and other genres. Once the opportunity had arisen through exposure to American cinema and records, something in the South African youngsters "clicked."

Moten Swing

In the *Smithsonian Anthology* of jazz recordings (Burgess 2010) Bennie Moten and His Kansas City Orchestra's "Moten Swing," recorded December 1932 in Camden, New Jersey (Victor 23384, Matrix no. 74847–1), follows James P. Johnson's "You've Got to Be Modernistic," recorded two years earlier, on January 21, 1930 in New York (Brunswick 4762, Matrix no. E-31958).

The contrast could not be greater. Johnson's stride piano and the mannerism of his virtuosity, the directions his music had taken in New York by 1930, and his side-trips into theatre production, opera, and "concert" jazz were all diametrically opposed to what was coming up in Kansas City.

From the first bars of "Moten Swing," listening to the interaction between Count Basie on piano and Walter Page on bass, one realizes that this was worlds different from jazz as played before, including anything that Bennie Moten and His Kansas City Orchestra had recorded five years earlier, in 1926 and 1927 (cf. CD *Moten Stomp*, Rare Sequential 1920's Recordings DSOY 716, Submarine Records, Enfield, Middlesex ENIl 2JA, UK). "Moten Swing" did not get its name by chance; it was an exercise in producing precisely that kind of kinetic feeling that would soon be generalized with the new term *swing*. "Moten Swing" is based on Walter Donaldson's 1930 hit song "You Are Driving Me Crazy" in an arrangement by Eddie Durham (trombone player and guitarist in Bennie Moten's band), using the song's chord progressions. The first few bars in the recordings already transmit that immense feeling of swing. This came about because with Basie, Page, and Eddie Durham, a new generation was taking over. The interaction is only between three people, Basie on piano, Page on bass, and Willie McWashington on drums. The horns come in later. Obviously, one key element is the way the bass player and the drummer handle their parts, in a straightforward driving 4/4 beat without any stereotyped accentuations on 2 and 4. Against that, Basie on piano puts off-beat accents over the bass line that are novel and different in their pattern structure from anything that was previously recorded by jazz pianists. It is an intrinsically non-Western approach both to rhythm and to piano playing, and would initiate a path jazz development would take during the next decade.

Like many other groups, Bennie Moten and his orchestra in the 1920s played dance music in a style that had evolved in the environment of New Orleans jazz migrating to Chicago, with echoes of recordings by King Oliver, Jelly Roll Morton, and the "Austin High Gang" in Chicago: Bix Beiderbecke, Red Nichols, etc. What was it then that generated an incisive change in the Bennie Moten Orchestra's music in 1932, as is also reflected in a few other recordings they made besides "Moten Swing," for example "Toby," "Blue Room," or "Lafayette"?

My impression is that the major driving force, even literally, was the bass player Walter Page, who already had experimented with young musicians including Basie, Eddie Durham, and others between 1926 and 1931. They were calling themselves the Blue Devils. When the Bennie Moten Orchestra absorbed nearly all of these young musicians by 1932, the band began to sound different. Walter Page's 4/4 beat had an impact on the handling of rhythm by the entire rhythm section in Moten's orchestra. Swing erupted literally from Walter Page's bass with Basie's piano patterning in predominantly single-note melodic style.

Five years after 1932, Billie Holiday (born April 7, 1915) would record one of her most beautiful songs, backed up by Lester "Pres" Young on tenor saxophone and Teddy Wilson in a modern, harmonic piano style. Even at a slow tempo as in this song, "Mean to Me," recorded May 11, 1937, in New York, there was an unmistakable, surprisingly "cool" element of swing, extremely economic in the phrasings, extremely effective.

Down Beat magazine took a long time before paying attention to the new trends in jazz, except in connection with boogie-woogie, the other revolution of the period—and so did the rest of the jazz literature, rarely mentioning Kansas City at the time. Unfortunately, one of the pioneers of the new music, Bennie Moten, died on April 2, 1935, due to medical neglect, or even incompetence, while undergoing a tonsillectomy.

The new music would now be increasingly referred to as swing, a word that before 1930 had not been used for a musical genre. Inspired by the title of Moten's successful record, swing as a genre established itself through the competitive work of the bands of Andy Kirk, Jap Allen, Paul Banks, and eventually Count Basie. Moten had employed Basie and other musicians who later became prominent, but the band broke up in 1932, soon after "Moten Swing" was recorded. In effect, Basie took over Moten's band, and reorganized it on slightly different lines. Next to Jimmie Lunceford and His Orchestra, Basie became the leading big band exponent, playing for audiences eager to dance. His arrangements, strongly rooted in a renewed discovery of the blues and a characteristically minimalist piano style, were the foundations of his fame, often symbolized by the success of his "One o'Clock Jump" recorded July 7, 1937 (Decca 1363, Matrix no. 62332-A). With international tours the fame of Count Basie lasted into the 1970s and 1980s, far beyond the so-called Swing Era.

By the mid-1940s, however, another group from Kansas City, unjustifiably neglected, came to broader public attention: the orchestra of Jay McShann (born January 12, 1916), pianist, arranger, and composer. Interest in Jay McShann emerged not only because of the musical quality of his band and himself as a pianist, plus the arrangements, but also because Charlie Parker emerged from McShann's fold. In fact, among many other musical gems, "Moten Swing" was recorded again in 1940 at a private performance by Jay McShann's Orchestra, the so-called Wichita recordings (cf. *Early Bird*, Stash Records CD, ST-CD-542, track 3) and this time the piece included a memorable solo by Charlie Parker, whose music had risen and developed in the same Kansas City cultural environment.

How around 1932 did Kansas City become the turntable of new developments that—in retrospect—appear to have recovered several long lost and ultimately African elements of musical organization, such as in homophonic multipart settings, in certain blues-based harmonic patterns, swing-generating rhythmic principles, and soloist melodic-rhythmic improvisation? Walter Page and Count Basie cannot be the only explanation.

Here, I should perhaps mention that those of us who are based in Africa tend to look at jazz history from a slightly different angle from what is found in some jazz history books. We do not think, for example, that swing was a sell-out of jazz in its core ideas to commercialism, or that it was jazz appropriated by "whites," because Benny Goodman, Ralph Burns, Woody Herman, and others shared in this music and contributed to it. Psychological fixation on "race" actually was breaking down during the Swing Era, in some individuals faster than in others; by the 1930s cooperation between Goodman, Lionel Hampton, and Teddy Wilson was an unmistakable sign of change in American society. Blindness in jazz musicians, notably in the case of 1940s/'50s pianists Lennie Tristano and George Shearing, was also a factor—not to be underestimated—that helped indirectly declare irrational divisions of society irrelevant in jazz.

Kansas City was entrenched in segregation. However, there was also immense motivation for learning and thereby a drive to reach out and transcend class barriers. The young musicians of Kansas City in particular and those who soon picked their style, or just learned from others' experiences, were trying distinctive new ways of organization. Among them was Andy Kirk and his "Clouds of Joy" with composer and arranger Mary Lou Williams on piano (a further sign of barriers breaking down, in her case, gender); constantly on tour was Jimmie Lunceford and His Orchestra, originally from Memphis, born in Fulton, Mississippi—all these groups contributing to the experimental breeding grounds of a new mass-popular music that would appeal to dancers, and thereby also reestablish a liaison between musicians and dancers as there used to be in many African societies. Kansas City was also attractive to itinerant blues musicians.

Consequently, in the 1930s many elements of "classical" European provenance prevalent in popular music of the nineteenth century, which had been absorbed by ragtime and early jazz, were now increasingly abandoned, especially in the realm of form. Jazz got rid of multiple-strain forms, e.g., AABAACC, inherited from European nineteenth-century marches and quadrilles that were emulated by ragtime composers in the Midwest and saloon bands in New Orleans during the 1890s. As much as this was an essential acquisition for ragtime composers, it now began to disappear in favor of shorter, repeating forms, stimulating improvisational skills. With the beginning of the so-called Swing Era, and even earlier in Chicago jazz, multi-strain forms were replaced by three other types (a) thirty-two-bar strophic form divided into halves, the first sixteen measures geared to a dominant chord caesura, the second sixteen leading back to the tonic; (b) the AABA chorus form incorporating an often modulatory "bridge"; and (c) the twelve-bar blues form.

This trend can also be seen as moving in the direction of recovery of African form preferences that are mostly cyclic, and within which tonal-harmonic segments are a constant. Such forms are at the opposite end of European multiple-strain form as in nineteenth-century popular music. Even shortly before World War I, most composers of sheet music were still following that tradition. (See, for example, "Panama," composed by William H. Tyers and published in 1911, but even most blues in sheet music, such as W. C. Handy's compositions.)

Short-cycle form as a characteristic of much African music was largely wiped out in North America in the nineteenth century under the impact of popular European music inherited from ballads, marches, polka, minuet, quadrille, etc. This contrasts with the Caribbean and South America where cyclic form often survived in local genres, even when European musical instruments such as guitars were played. It survived in Cuban son and was reintroduced into some US popular music between the 1960s and '70s from the Caribbean, notably with reggae. However, one thing definitely accelerated the processes of change: a new repertoire of songs became available to jazz musicians to be used for improvisation and dance music arrangements. After World War I American composers, so-called Tin Pan Alley composers in particular, seemed to work in silent agreement with jazz musicians by providing an inexhaustible stock of resources of new "tunes," some of which turned out to be highly suitable for soloist improvisation. New popular songs such as "Dinah" (by Harry Akst, words by Sam M. Lewis and Joe Young, 1925) or "You Are Driving Me Crazy" (by Donaldson, 1930) were frontrunners. They were attractive to jazz musicians (see, for example, Fats Waller's performance of "Dinah" recorded June 24, 1935, Victor 25471), not only because they were popular but because in form and structure they were, perhaps unconsciously, a step closer to African concepts of form. Bipartite strophic form with a caesura in the middle, was, of course, already present in some rags, stomps, struts, one steps, two steps, etc., such as played by Alphonse Picou and even Buddy Bolden around 1905, as was testified by Bunk Johnson in his talk with Bill Colburn in San Francisco on May 7, 1943 (on that occasion he was whistling one of the tunes attributed to Bolden around the turn of the twentieth century).

But now such forms had received a new tinge by the incorporation of either responsorial schemata or thematic riffs such as the transfer of a short melodic motif across harmonic changes. Kurt Weill's "Mack the Knife" is an example, a song picked up later even by Louis Armstrong.

Short cycles were not yet used in the 1930s, but they were sometimes implicit in certain song lines, such as in George Gershwin's "I Got Rhythm," which not by chance became a standard tune for jazz improvisation. By the late 1920s American composers of popular music had internalized elements of the responsorial structure of the blues, so that many of their sixteen- or thirty-two-bar compositions assumed a hidden responsorial structure for each line. Blue notes also became an important structural element, although they were reinterpreted as minor thirds over major chords. The ubiquitous AABA form, usually referred to in jazz as the chorus form, often embraces blues-derived ideas such as the organization of lines into statement and response sections. The AABA chorus form is characterized by four double lines, statement, repetition of statement, followed by a so-called bridge, and a concluding statement (cf. examples in Berliner 1994: 77). It usually appears in a thirty-two-bar version. However, in a sense the AABA form is also a cycle. One could call it a compounded cycle with a "bridge" that often displays modulation. Although this is not found in older forms of African music prior to western and African American influences, it is also fair to say that African music is not always based on short cycles. In some of the oldest eastern Angolan traditions, surviving in initiation songs such as the songs of *kukuwa*, e.g., "Samba papelo," performed by initiates and their guardians, there are compounded cycles with notable strophic tendencies (cf. Kubik 2010: I; Tsukada 1990).

In jazz the use of cycles, specifically compounded cycles, is just as essential as it is in African music, because of improvisation. There must be cyclic repetition to allow for improvisational variation. In this sense, even the long chorus form in jazz perpetuates an important interregional trait from African music. The jazz chorus form was a sort of compromise between the African idea of short cycles and the European strophic song forms.

In swing as a genre, call-and-response organization can take the form of antiphony between the brass and the reed sections of the band. Another African heritage that was rediscovered in swing is extensive use of instrumental riffs. In many forms of African music, especially in the organization of xylophone playing, for example in the Zambezi valley by Asena musicians playing *valimba*, there is a work division between three players, one playing a bass line, another a pattern that is repeated throughout, while the third player is free to develop melodic-rhythmic variations on top of this solid foundation. Such an organization is also the basis of some West African drumming ensembles with a "master drummer" engaging in talking drum narratives. In swing this tradition has been reconfigured into a relationship between an improvising soloist backed by an orchestral riff.

How, by 1930, did certain trends in jazz converge in Kansas City to stimulate new developments? Nathan W. Pearson Jr. gives some answers in his 1987 book *Going to Kansas City*. From the mid-1920s until the end of the 1930s many jazz musicians of the Midwest migrated to Kansas City in search of jobs. They came from Texas, Oklahoma, New Orleans, and Missouri. The most important early groups that formed were those of Bennie Moten, Andy Kirk, the Kansas City Rockets, and later the groups of Count Basie and Jay McShann. These are the names that are generally associated by jazz historians with the term Kansas City jazz. Here, not only the first expressions of what would be called swing developed, but also the grounds for development of what later came to be called modern jazz were laid, especially because of many experiments with harmony and form.

Economy, of course, is always an important factor in making things happen. In Kansas City it is a fact that due to the corrupt administration of the notorious Tom Pendergast, and economic activity based on nightclubs and gambling halls employing musicians, Kansas City survived the years of the Great Depression quite well.

Beneath economics, however, some of the deeper, non-economic factors were addressed in little-known notes by Rudi Blesh in the 4th edition of his book *Shining Trumpets*, first published in 1946. Blesh gained a reputation of being a traditionalist, someone who wanted to subscribe jazz forever to the styles associated with New Orleans and the music of King Oliver, Jelly Roll Morton, Louis Armstrong, etc. He was decried as "the man who wanted to take jazz back to 1926" and his followers were portrayed as "moldy figs."

However, in the years after the first publication of his book, he did in fact pay attention to contemporaneous developments through the 1940s into the 1950s, articulating his thoughts in newspaper articles and preparing radio programs. Cassel & Company, London, the publishers of his groundbreaking book in 1946, gave him a chance to write a twenty-six-page postscript in the fourth edition in 1958. It is interesting how Blesh in the meantime had come to terms with some of the new developments. He was even one of the first to understand the historical significance of what would come to be called Kansas City jazz, and in some ways how bebop, later emerged from it, in Harlem.

Denouncing commercialized big band swing by the likes of Glenn Miller—he did not comment on Woody Herman—he writes:

> So, at the very heart of swing, was a valuable core.... It was a concept of the big band that derived not from any European idea but from the basic impulse that came originally from Africa. This concept ... came to the fore in bands that developed in Kansas City and Oklahoma City, like those of Andy Kirk, Walter Page, Benny Moten, Jay McShann, and Count Basie. Among these must be numbered that of Jimmie Lunceford.
>
> These men are all of the same generation, from Moten, born in 1894 to Basie, born in 1904, the only younger one being McShann.... They are from the same area—Page, Lunceford, and Moten from Missouri, McShann from Oklahoma—except Kirk, born in Kentucky, and Basie, born in New Jersey. However, Kirk and Basie both cast their musical lots in Kansas City over a third of a century ago.
>
> This was that Missouri—neither North nor South, East nor West, nor yet wholly Midwest—which was first the cradle of ragtime and then a focal point for the blues that flowed up from the "deep woods" and the turpentine camps of eastern Texas

and the Mississippi Delta. Historically this may have been a northward migration of music second in importance only to that of New Orleans jazz to Chicago. (356)

Blesh then characterizes the music and the organization of Kansas City bands, pointing to some of the roots of this music in earlier traditions such as gospel songs and blues. He is very perceptive in mentioning gospel and sanctified music, which by the 1920s and early 1930s were often using verse-chorus and AABA forms.

> These bands were big. They did not play improvised counterpoint or intend to play it. They did not play Creole songs or marches or jazzy quadrilles. They rocked with the rhythms of the Sanctified Church, they wailed and shouted the blues, those twelve bars that distilled the freedom songs into a call that nothing as yet has ever silenced. . . .
> The swing of Count Basie's fifteen-piece group was showing us how the big band could exist in jazz. Its brass and reed choirs moving in antiphonal masses were more strongly African than even New Orleans jazz. Lester Young's tenor saxophone and Buck Clayton's muted trumpet leaping out, solo, into the spaces between those great massed movements, sound like the leader shouting to his chorus. (356–57)

"More strongly African than even New Orleans jazz": Blesh seems to have inverted all his earlier premises. What does he mean? Comparing the brass and reed sections to "choirs" in antiphony, he correctly identifies the vocal origins of much of the homophonic harmonic style of the swing bands. That reveals a hidden genealogical link to various African song traditions, notably in Angola, many parts of the Congo, and some places on the Guinea Coast. He also correctly identifies the reinstating of responsorial (leader/chorus) form in swing music's prominent arrangements.

Boogie-Woogie

One of the most accomplished feats of recovery or reinvention of movement structures of African historical background in North America is boogie-woogie. An ideophonic/onomatopoeic sound pattern, the name verbalizes a dance movement which goes with a vibrant piano style that makes full use of the piano's potential as a neo-African percussion instrument, to be placed within the genealogy of gourd-resonated xylophones, *timbrh* raffia lamellophones, and similar instruments. Boogie-woogie came up in honky-tonks and bars in many places, from the Midwest up to Chicago's South Side, during the second decade of the twentieth century. The cultural carriers were mostly migrants from the Deep

South, pianists with no or little background in ragtime. Its blues basis and poly-rhythmic playing technique would also be a strong influence on big band swing during the 1930s.

It is assumed that boogie-woogie, based on the twelve-bar blues form, gradually started as a blues variant in barrelhouses of the southern United States. It seems to have spread quickly to cities like St. Louis, Kansas City, and Chicago at the time of World War I. All the great boogie-woogie pianists represent more or less one specific generation. They were all born within a span of thirteen years around the turn of the twentieth century. Alabama, Kansas City, and Chicago were their birthplaces. The two most senior persons among the boogie-woogie pianists were Charlie "Cow-Cow" Davenport (1894–1955) and Jimmy Yancey (1898–1951). A little younger were Pete Johnson (1904–1967) and Meade Lux Lewis (1905–1964). The youngest was Albert Ammons (1907–1954). Besides those famous ones, others were born in Louisiana, Mississippi, Arkansas, and Texas.

This means that effective musical activities of the boogie pianists began to take shape shortly before 1920. Some of them, still teenagers, were already involved in the vaudeville circuit. The first among them who was recorded—with almost a decade delay—was Clarence "Pinetop" Smith (born 1904) who soon thereafter lost his life tragically in a shooting incident in 1929. Smith was born in Alabama, but had moved as a young person to Chicago. In his fabulous recording "Pinetop's Boogie-Woogie" published 1928, the genre's name first appeared on a 78 r.p.m. record and hit the market. Some jazz historians have ascribed the "invention" of boogie-woogie piano to him.

Meade Lux Lewis and Albert Ammons—the latter earned his living as a taxi driver—used to live in the same building in Chicago with Clarence "Pinetop" Smith. They learned the art of boogie-woogie piano from him, then developed their own style. Later they often recorded together, as a duo.

In Chicago, this music was often part of a house-rent party (Russell 1957). Poor families sometimes had no means to pay the landlord, so when payment was due, the family would throw a party, called "pitchin' boogie"; a pianist played and the entire neighborhood, in a wonderful show of solidarity, would come and contribute money so that the rent could be paid by the family. William Russell reports: "Around five o'clock in the morning when almost everyone was knocked out and things were getting pretty dull and awfully quiet, someone over in a corner came to life and yelled out, 'Let's have some blues.' Then Jimmy [Yancey] obliged with his *Five O'clock Blues*, known as the *Fives* for short. No one called it Boogie Woogie then, but it had all the peculiarities of the piano style known today as Boogie Woogie" (183).

Jimmy Yancey one of the most important, creative pianists of boogie-woogie, was born in Chicago. He is also credited for the introduction of a habanera or rumba bass (3 + 3 + 2) in some of his compositions. Yancey's art was insufficiently

Fig. 8.16. Jimmy Yancey, 1948, in a photograph by Dick Mushlitz published on the cover of Document Records DOCD-1001, a series issued by Johnny Parth, Vienna.

documented by the record companies though he did record commercially following Mead Lux Lewis's recording of "Yancey Special." For this reason we are particularly grateful to young banjo player Dick Mushlitz who visited and made friends with the Yancey family at their home in Chicago, starting in 1948, and eventually made wire recordings of the pianist and his wife Mama Yancey in their apartment, just three months before Jimmy died on September 17, 1951.

Thanks to an initiative by Konrad Nowakowski in Vienna in 1997 with Kurt Hriczucsah and John R. T. Davis, these recordings have been published on Document Records DOCD-I007: *The Unissued 1951 Yancey Wire Recordings*, Jimmy and Mama Yancey & Guests recorded at the Yancey Apartment by Phil Kiely and Dick Mushlitz, June 16, 1951. The CD includes liner notes by Dick Mushlitz and photographs from 1948 and 1951, which represent a real proto-testimony of the event.

Honky-tonk pianists from Missouri down the Mississippi River, deeply rooted in blues, seem to have started the style by experimenting with a strictly twelve-bar, streamlined layout of the blues form. In contrast to ragtime and its multiple-strain textures, the blues form freed the pianist of several limitations, allowing him to work out recurring bass figures with the left hand to be contrasted with ever-changing melodic and rhythmic patterns in the right hand. The choice of a standard form, the twelve-bar blues, also allowed the pianist to develop a stream of hitherto unheard-of variations, uninterrupted by the constraints of linear theme changes with attached harmonic changes and modulations as in other, earlier jazz piano styles. As had never happened before, African

American piano playing came a step closer to patterns of theme development and variation known from African music. And this came to pass within a novelty in form, the twelve-bar blues.

In the US South, around the beginning of the twentieth century, blues singing and its instrumental accompaniment crystallized into a genre and then condensed into a predominant shape, the twelve-bar form. This can be seen as a first step in an Afrologic process (to use composer George Lewis's term) of recovery and reconstruction. The music was moving a bit closer to African form principles.

From the moment instrumental blues accompaniment on guitar, piano, etc., began to condense into a three-line, twelve-bar form, it also provided the stimulus for recovering long lost polyrhythmic and polymetric combination techniques found in several genres of African music, if they are based on cycle number twelve or its multiples. This refers especially to music for xylophones and various other types of idiophones used percussively, across the continent, from West to Central Africa and down the Zambezi.

I am not suggesting that boogie-woogie pianists would have consciously thought of incorporating elements of African music into their style; the ideology of black ethnicity that would promote such an undertaking and the availability of recordings all belong to an era half a century later. Nor would I suggest that there was cogitation about phrasings in mathematical terms. The analogous pathways were simply discovered by practical experimentation along lines of rhythmic, formal, and melodic understanding connected to the African past. That experimental direction was to create something kinemically satisfactory for the player, patterns to be played continuously, as if in meditation, a kind of soloist musical self-therapy common in African cultures.

The boogie pianist's left hand is unequivocally bound to producing a rocking beat with minimal melodic change. It could be like one of the short *timbrh* patterns. The novelty in the boogie-woogie style, however, inspired by the twelve-bar blues form, was transposition: that the basic left-hand pattern, with one component almost like a drone (e.g., the lowest note in Meade Lux Lewis's "Honky Tonk Train Blues"), would be transposed a fifth down in measures 5 and 6, and again into another position in measures 9 and 10. But because the left-hand bass is cyclic and repeating, the pianist is free to explore with the right hand a broad panel of heterometric interpolations that the twelve-bar form allows, due to mathematical provisions, in contrast to a sixteen-measure form and multiple strains such as in ragtime.

The mathematics of the twelve-bar blues form is expressed by the fact that the archetypal number twelve is divisible by two, three, four, and six. No other number (except multiples of twelve) can be factorized that way. The twelve bars in the blues, which consist of a total of 3 x 16 = 48 beats or dance steps, can be simultaneously divided by different repeating units defined by those factors, and they will always resolve within the larger form. In ragtime there were also heterometric interpolations (a characteristic of ragtime melody) into the beat, but they had to be more transient, because ragtime form is not divisible by three and six. In boogie-woogie the implicit elementary pulse lines behind the recurrent ground beat function as a grid in the musician's mind to allow him to create phrases that divide the beat by three (into triplets) or by four (into quadruplets), and within these divisions to create patterns that, in their length and structure, lend themselves to unusual combinations. Since the form is divisible in multiple ways, heterometric passages in the right hand can be sustained for much longer than would have ever been possible in the duple-division structure of ragtime beat. In boogie-woogie it is not rare that a triple overrhythm combining six elementary pulse units is carried across the caesura of the blues form, even stretched out beyond a full twelve-bar chorus. Equally, the reference line appearing as a quadruple division of the beat can give rise to melodic-rhythmic patterns introducing a triple accentuation into the quadruple division (see Fig. 8.17).

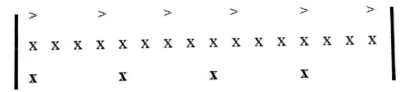

Fig. 8.17.

All this can easily be discovered from listening to or watching any of the great boogie-woogie pianists, Jimmy Yancey, Meade Lux Lewis, Albert Ammons, and others. An instructive example of a three-beat interpolation can be heard on track 1 of the CD of 1951 Yancey recordings (see Fig. 8.18).

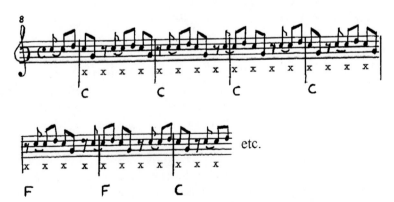

Fig. 8.18. Right-hand interpolation by the performer of "Lux's Boogie," recorded in the Yancey apartment, June 16, 1951. 5th chorus (extract), track 1 CD Document Records DOCD-1007.

The delight of boogie-woogie pianists exploring implicit polymeter in the twelve-bar blues form allows nonstop performance of this kind of instrumental blues for long periods, with endless new variations and reshuffling of melodic accents. Sometimes this sounds like the rolling rhythms of a night train, hopping over the rails—an unforgettable experience for everyone who has slept in a compartment on one of the early to mid-twentieth-century trains that were in use at that time. The experience was musically explored both by boogie-pianists and by African musicians recorded during the mid-twentieth century. The most famous testimony by a boogie pianist is Meade Lux Lewis's "Honky Tonk Train Blues," recorded May 7, 1936, in Chicago (RCA Victor 25541, Matrix no. 06301–1). Lewis recorded it eleven times between 1927 and 1961, as reported by John Edward Hasse in *Jazz—The Smithsonian Anthology* (2010): "Observers recall that Lewis could improvise on this tune for thirty minutes, his fingers cascading over the keys relentlessly rolling out the rhythms, dazzling everyone within earshot" (53).

The train motif also appears in the repertoire of other boogie-woogie pianists, notably in Cripple Clarence Lofton's "Streamline Train." Lofton was a friend of Jimmy Yancey, though their relationship was strained, according to Mushlitz (1997: liner notes and photograph).

From African music we also have several recordings in which a performer/composer processes the experience of train rhythms. In 1952 Hugh Tracey recorded Josiasi Yemba Mate with his *kathandi* (twelve-note lamellophone) in Luanika/Mongu on the border of Zambia and Botswana (then Northern Rhodesia and Bechuanaland). Josiasi played a song he had composed after a long train ride from Livingstone to Bulawayo, depicting train rhythms. He called his song (in the Mbunda language) "Sitima kwenda namoto" (The train that goes with fire). In 1953 he obtained an Osborn Award, 3rd prize, for this composition by the International Library of African Music, directed by Hugh Tracey (cf. AMA TR-184, *The Sound of Africa Series*, ILAM).

On July 15, 1965, I recorded Tokota, a thirty-two-year-old player of the *ocisanzi*, a "board" lamellophone with sixteen iron notes at Munengole village, near Ndindi in Huila (Wila) Province, southwestern Angola. He had composed the song "O andamento do comboio" (The movement of the train) in reaction to those "iron monsters" that were introduced in Angola during the early part of the twentieth century, but specifically referring to the railway from Moçamedes (today Namibe) to Serpa Pinto (today Menonge) (cf. CD, track 18, accompanying Kubik 2002).

It is important, however, to understand that in boogie-woogie the inherent bimetric and polymetric structure is not objectified as a permanent division of the twelve-bar form into different simultaneous meters, as happens in some forms of music in Central Africa. These "meters" are only simultaneous reference lines. In his mind the pianist shifts his phrasings and pattern construction between them ad libitum. The reference lines can be laid out schematically as in Figure 8.20. But there is one permanent bimetric relationship: between the 4/4 ground beat of the music and the 6/4 cycle of the steps in jitterbug dancing to go with boogie-woogie and swing music in general. The dance pattern has its own obscure history, but evidently originated in African American communities of teenagers with flexible young bodies. Jitterbug is a relaxed, swing-enhancing style of dancing that goes with a medium boogie tempo. The tension between the different metric cycles is visualized by experienced partners in how their figures constantly cross the metric division of the blues form generated by the 4/4 ground beat, to resolve at the end of a chorus and start again at the beginning of the next one.

I learned jitterbug dancing as a teenager in 1950 and 1951 in Vienna, when we were living in a district that was part of the post–World War II American Occupation Zone. Since 1946 American military personnel and their families had introduced swing, boogie-woogie, and jitterbug dancing to locals in clubs and at numerous social gatherings. In addition there was the AFRS (Armed Forces Radio Service), the radio station almost exclusively tuned into by young people. It contributed a great deal to the dissemination of jazz in the late 1940s and early 1950s.

In jitterbug dancing as I learned it, the partners perform a cycle of dance steps in mirror-inverted relationship. At a certain point of the six-step pattern (aligned with the ground beat of the music) the girl, often helped with a light push by the boy's right hand in leftward direction, performs a clockwise turn, full circle, returning to the basic position. There are many complex variations that experienced dancers can carry out for a show, but this is the essential movement pattern. Even during the basic steps or taps, the dancer's body appears light, relaxed, flexible, and while the boy does not perform any turns, he carefully coordinates his own spatially defined movements with the fluid action of his female partner.

The joint experience is something like a gentle rocking. It might be a good idea in a future study of the kinemics of swing to involve colleagues in the medical field besides those working on the psychology of perception. One area to be investigated would be to find out the extent to which the vestibular system among our senses might be involved in the sensation of swing. In psychotherapy, for example, it is known that the repeated performance of a rocking movement, e.g., in a rocking chair, which stimulates the vestibular organs of the inner ear, is beneficial to patients. It enhances the feeling of well-being, as it does in normal life—among infants, on playgrounds and last but not least among dancers.

Figure 8.19 shows the basic pattern of the footsteps in jitterbug as I remember them. There are six taps in the cycle, in synchronization with the ground beat of the music. These are shown as r (right foot) and l (left foot) in my illustration. However, the execution of the steps is within a spatial layout. Therefore I have inscribed them into squares, marking the areas for a foot to be set on the floor.

As one dances, of course, the areas (squares) are also gradually shifted. This is not marked in the illustration, because everyone discovers it by themselves, after a short time of practice. I show the step action by marking r or l in an appropriate corner of the squares, with points indicating the areas not touched by foot action at that particular episode.

The steps by the boy and the girl (or young man and young woman) are in mirror-inverted relationship: when the boy uses his right foot, the girl uses her left. The girl's full turn of her body is done clockwise and it is started the moment she has firmly set down her right foot, slightly behind her left (as in the fourth set of squares in Fig. 8.19). At that moment she swings her body around full circle, with her left foot lifted, while her right foot remains on the ground and turns without changing position. On the next beat unit of the music her right foot lands in the basic position (having completed her turn) opposite the left foot tap of her partner.

Experienced dancers will soon learn to accentuate their steps. The boy, for example, may begin to tap the floor with his foot (or just the toes) lightly on beat 1, while dropping his full weight on the foot in action at beat 2 and 4. On beat 1 of the music, he may even just lift his foot without stepping on the ground; then the accent will be a kind of up-beat. Further patterning of the movement takes place by the fact that, when he performs the alternate left-right steps as shown in Figure 8.19 at ground beats 3 and 4 of the music, he will put his foot firmly on the ground, because this is also the moment to support the girl who will perform her turn.

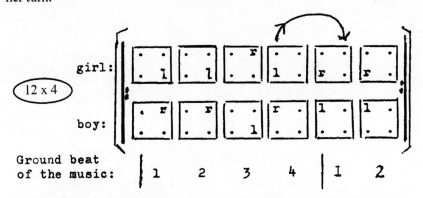

Fig. 8.19. Schema of jitterbug dancing in relation to the music over a twelve-bar blues form.

Apart from the intricacies of its internal spatial structure, this sequence is repeated after completing a cycle covering six beats of the music. In a twelve-bar blues form the dancers therefore complete eight repetitions of this 6/4 cycle across the entire form, to start again with identical steps at the beginning of the next chorus. Thus they produce a perfect bimetric division of the twelve-bar blues form.

Of course, in other pieces played by a swing band that may be based on the thirty-two-bar AABA form, the 6/4 cycle of the dancers does not resolve at the end of each chorus. The forms cross each other, but no dancer finds it uncomfortable. The two "meters" come together only every third chorus performed by the musicians, after sixteen repetitions of the dance cycle.

Simple arithmetic reveals why the combination of the blues form with the cycle of jitterbug dancing is musically so successful and why internal reference lines dividing the ground beat by two, three, and four provide a suitable framework for long periods of heterometric interpolations that create the cross rhythms characteristic of boogie-woogie. Figure 8.20 shows how the different reference lines and the dance movement are integrated. Only the first two measures of the twelve-bar blues form are shown in the diagram; the rest proceeds accordingly. For the dance-steps I have only given the male dancer's part; the female part can be seen in Figure 8.19.

Each reference line consists of a total amount of pulse units that are contained within the twelve-bar form, and all are of course divisible by two, three, four, six, and twelve (ref. line 1: 36 x 2 = 72; ref. line 2: 36 x 3 = 108; ref. line 3: 36 x 4 = 144 units). This gives the right hand of a boogie pianist almost unlimited possibilities of internal combinations, stringing duple, triple, and quadruple units within each reference line to form melodic and rhythmic patterns.

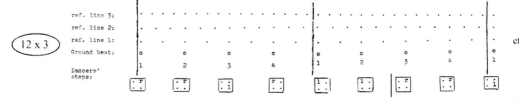

Fig. 8.20. Internal structure of two measures in boogie-woogie (shown by three additional reference lines besides the ground beat).

In order to give readers a concrete example of what I have condensed into an abstract schema in Figure 8.20, I have transcribed the first chorus and beginning of the second of Meade Lux Lewis's "Honky Tonk Train Blues" recorded May 7, 1936, in Chicago (RCA Victor 2554) in our modified staff notation system (see Fig. 8.21), which I have used since the 1970s in transcribing various forms of African music, notably Yoruba àlọ story songs (Kubik 2010: II: 151–209, where the system is also explained in detail). This system is non-durational and highly suitable for piano styles like boogie-woogie with a polymetric texture, with no pedal used by the pianist. Each note's duration fades out by itself naturally or is revoked by the impact of another note. Actions to stop or dampen a note are shown by a stroke (/).

The extract transcribed reveals the relevance of reference lines 1 and 2 of the subjective grid orienting the pianist's playing. Meade Lux Lewis shifts his accents between reference lines, also side-tracking to reference line 3 in the course of his performance.

However, the most controversial problem encountered here, was how I should represent the left-hand part in my transcription. To write the continuous pounding of the left-hand rhythm as dotted quaver plus semi-quaver as is customary among jazz transcribers, was out of the question; it would be misleading, even simply wrong. But how about presenting it as a triplet pattern?. I had a suspicion here that one's auditory perception gets deceived; in the recording it seems as if the left hand were pursuing this rhythm, but not quite. So what is it? Something between? The deception apparently arises from the fact that the listener projects the triplet feel produced by the right hand following reference line 2 upon the left-hand pattern, thereby creating a kind of common meter in perception.

I did not want to get lured into a perceptual abyss, so I asked some help from our guitarist Sinosi Mlendo. He is the one who steers us through the many different rhythms in our Donald Kachamba's Kwela Heritage Jazzband, from Chileka, Malawi. I asked him whether he thought that Meade Lux Lewis's left-hand bass would go with the syllables *ka-cha*, i.e., evolve within an implicit triple pattern with an accent on the third pulse-unit, or whether he thought that the rhythm of the bass line was "straight," i.e., equal-valued. He listened to the CD very carefully, headphones on, tapping the rhythm of Meade Lux Lewis's left-hand bass line on the table. Without hearing what he was listening to, I noticed that he tapped straight. After the second chorus he had made his decision and told me with a smile of conviction on his face that it was *ta-ta ta-ta ta-ta ta-ta*, i.e., straight, the left hand following the internal reference line 1. The auditory deception originates in the off-beat accent.

This is what I have transcribed and it is our joint responsibility (conversation and auditory experiment on February 16, 2012). The purpose of all this was to get closer to what is in the mind of a performer, and obviously, the enjoyable thing is the tension between left and right hand parts by their implicit relationship two against three. And that is also what gives this boogie-woogie an intense swing, which indeed seems to emerge as if from the rocking patterns of a train journey.

Meade Lux Lewis's compositions, like many others in boogie-woogie piano, stimulate us to pose new research questions. Most significant and probably an indicator of African concepts in this particular piece (see Fig. 8.21) is the structure and the movement of the left-hand bass part. The chords are in the so-called second inversion. This is very common in the organization of homophonic

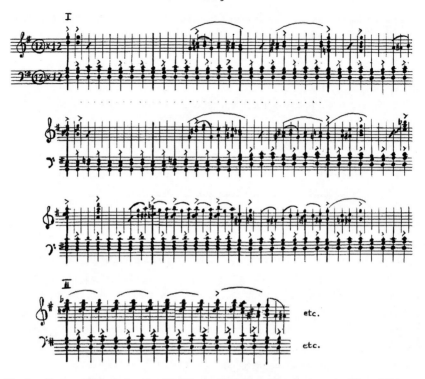

Fig. 8.21. Extract of Meade Lux Lewis's "Honky Tonk Train Blues" transcribed from RCA Victor 25541, recorded May 7, 1936. First and beginning of second chorus.

multipart singing across Central Africa, the fourth is always down, the third is up. This is so because it reflects the order of partials in the natural harmonic series from the third to the fifth harmonic, i.e., g → c → e, rising over fundamental C.

In Meade Lux Lewis's "Honky Tonk Train Blues" in the key of G, there are additional revealing traits. One is that in the left-hand bass D is used as a persistent bourdon (drone) throughout the piece, with the exception of four spots in the two bars using the subdominant chord. I see in this a tendency to recreate a lost heritage, something that goes back to the cultures of the West African savannah and sahel zones (cf. Kubik 1999a). Another possible retention is that the "train" pattern with its tonic chord in the second inversion is transposed entirely and unchanged a fifth down into subdominant position in measures 5 and 6, as if the declaration made in measures 1 and 2 were to be repeated with an even stronger (deeper) voice. And the fact that the pianist superposes a fast triplet line incorporating the blue-note b♭ on top of the dominant seventh chords in the bass, demonstrates that harmonically, boogie-woogie is deeply rooted in the blues tradition.

Also, it is probably not coincidental that, both in boogie-woogie piano and in some African lamellophone playing, the experience of train rhythms is processed

(a) as individual (solo) music. Indeed, one sleeps alone on the train experiencing these patterns in solitude, half in a dream.

(b) that in our sample from southern Africa (Botswana, Angola), train rhythms are expressed especially on iron-note lamellophones, in North America on a piano. These instruments therefore appear to be genealogically aligned. For boogie-woogie it is the relationship lamellophone → piano as analogous; for some other styles, the relationship xylophone → piano, and also xylophone → vibraphone.

The pioneers of the boogie-woogie tradition were exclusively African Americans, which indirectly suggests a strong Afrologic background, an aesthetic very different from what musicians rooted in European traditions would identify with. At the time no one else was taking up boogie-woogie piano; most would have found it repetitive, harmonically restricted, etc. That attitude would change only twenty years after the first recordings were made, and today there are boogie-woogie pianists of any ethnic background. Dancers, however, discovered the merits of boogie-woogie earlier.

The African Matrix in
Jazz Harmonic Practices

In 1998, a flyer was circulated announcing the appearance of *The Garland Encyclopedia of World Music*. On that leaflet, the publishers subjected readers to a test with five questions under this heading: "How Well Do You Know World Music?" The first of these questions in statement form was "American jazz borrows its harmonic structure from European classical music." Readers were supposed to mark whether the statement was true or false. The answer given on the back of the flyer for those still in doubt was "True"—thereby endorsing one of the most tenacious stereotypes about jazz, the all-embracing notion that harmony in jazz and other African American music was European while the rhythm was African. Fortunately, matters are not that simple. From a standpoint in Western music theory claiming universal applicability, it is often difficult to comprehend that jazz musicians have always converted the tonal-harmonic resources provided by the Western instruments that they used to suit their own concepts strongly rooted in blues tonality, which is non-Western. Jazz harmony at its structural and aesthetic level is based on a variety of matrices, many of them African, but it must be added that individual jazz performers, ensembles, and composers vary in the extent to which their harmonic understandings can be historically linked in specific directions and the kind of creative merger achieved. It may vary even from one work to another by the same composer, or from one performance to another.

I am not the only one trying to get a glimpse of the hidden side of the coin. Actually, it was Percival R. Kirby, in his article "A Study of Negro Harmony" (1930), who first detected a structural principle of African provenance in the harmonic patterns of Negro spirituals. Later, in 1951, A. M. Jones wrote on "blue notes and hot rhythm"; and the eminent Richard A Waterman (1952) pointed to common evolutionary roots of harmony in European and African music:

> Harmony . . . appears in aboriginal music nowhere but in the western one-third of the Old World, where it is common in European folk music and African tribal music. . . . There exists a broad intrusive belt of Arabic and Arabic-influenced music which stretches across the middle of the western area, along both shores of the Mediterranean. Since the times of ancient history this alien musical outcropping

has masked the fact of the previous existence of a continuous harmony-using bloc of cultures established earlier in the area. (209)

Although he ignores Polynesia, and his proposal of a former continuous bloc of European and African harmony-using cultures is probably an overstatement—since the "intrusive" nonharmonic sector existed across North Africa and Mediterranean Europe in antiquity (e.g., among Egyptians, Phoenicians, Romans, and Berbers)—it is important that Waterman, like Kirby, recognizes the precolonial existence of harmony in the music of sub-Saharan Africa.

More recently, Thomas Brothers (1994: 490) has drawn attention to melodic anticipation of harmonic schemes in Louis Armstrong's "Big Butter and Egg Man," recorded in 1926. He writes that "Armstrong's F chord comes a measure early, and as a result the phrase structure of the solo collides with the harmonic rhythm of the accompaniment." Brothers, who carried out fieldwork in Ghana, points to the fact that such behavior serves "an African conception of syntax that involves two levels, a fundamental and a supplemental, with the supplemental moving in and out of agreement with the fundamental." Insights like Brothers's open jazz to cognitive investigation. At one level of inquiry it may be sufficient to identify the social processes that promote or inhibit innovation, or to study the sounds and their sequences that musician-composers produce; but at another level, we would like to learn about the implicit thought patterns that fuel and steer those results.

It seems that in jazz history from the start of the twentieth century to the 1970s, different hidden sets of African musical ideas became prominent in succession. Heterophony and responsorial, functional polyphony were dominant in early New Orleans jazz, unrecorded at the time, but later preserved in the testimony by Bunk Johnson and musicians such as clarinet player George Lewis, who had remained "local" (that is, not emigrating to the North during the early 1920s); homophonic multipart structures set the tone of big-band jazz during the Swing Era of the 1930s, while equitonal melodic principles, clustered chords often based on remote partials, and what has been called the pitch area concept in the blues (Evans 1982) staged a breakthrough in bebop in the 1940s. In a sense, jazz history is also like a series of volcanic eruptions. Whenever a new jazz style appeared, it brought to the surface something that had been dormant in the United States for some time. Often we researchers then recognize a principle, an approach, a pattern we have been familiar with from some specific region of Africa with which those contemporaneous American musicians could not have had any direct contact. So what happened? Independent multiple invention of the same thing, a mysterious "cultural memory," spirit possession?

A fascinating hinge of jazz history is that when something new appears, as (most radically) bebop did in Minton's Playhouse in Harlem in 1941, it often seems to re-create concepts, traits, and aesthetic principles central to some African cultures somewhere on the map. However, they erupt in a new disguise, as if remolded or reconfigured with a different type of clay. Thus, a time journey through jazz and blues history is often like an excursion through different African cultures. In one style of jazz or blues, one gets traits familiar from the west-central Sudanic savannah and sahel zone, in another from the Congo and the Guinea coast, and in a third from the Zambezi valley and northern Moçambique. From a viewpoint inside Africa, it is difficult to escape the feeling of déjà vu that periodically arises.

Recorded African Traditions of Multipart Singing

The age-old presence of specific multipart styles and compositional principles, both vocal and instrumental, in the music of sub-Saharan Africa is no longer much in dispute. There are numerous works dealing with the subject. In Africa there are large areas in which only singing in unison and octaves is practiced, such as among pastoralists: the Cushitic and Semitic speakers of northeast Africa, the Fulɓe cattle herders in West Africa, and the Herero pastoralists in Namibia. However, unison and octave styles do not exclude the development of polyphony; the evidence is the instrumental polyphony on xylophones and harps that developed in the pre-colonial kingdom of Buganda in East Africa's interlacustrine region, a very complex serial music with no simultaneous sounds other than octaves allowed (Kubik 2010: I: 58). Octave styles in Africa contrast with large pockets of harmonic traditions, for example, along the Guinea coast, from the ancient city of Benin, the Ijesha- and Ekiti-Yoruba-speaking peoples, to the Côte d'Ivoire and southern Ghana, where harmonic composition techniques among the Fanti and Asante were first described by Thomas Edward Bowdich in 1819. Another large geographical "harmonic patch" covers areas of Congo-Brazzaville, Congo-Kinshasa, southwestern Angola, eastern Angola into Zambia, expanding into the Zambezi valley and other parts of southern and eastern Africa. Although we cannot time travel for verification, there is good reason to assume that Africa was one of the planet's cradles of polyphony. "Bushmen" hunter-gatherers must have discovered the harmonic properties of stretched strings as soon as they had discovered the use of the bow and arrow; and this knowledge has continued until today, with the !Kung', for example, using no fewer than four different kinds of harmonics-producing techniques on hunting bows (Kubik 2010: I: 217–24). The Pygmies of Central Africa developed polyphony probably thousands of years ago—although, in contrast to the savannah-inhabiting southern African "bushmen," not from instrumental techniques but from the formants of speech and vocal techniques such as yodel—long before their forests were invaded by early Bantu-language speakers from eastern Nigeria and the Cameroons between circa 1000 and 400 BC. Some of these immigrants then adopted the Pygmy-style polyphony, while others may have retained different multipart experiences brought along.

In 1946 André Didier and Gilbert Rouget of the Musée de l'Homme in Paris recorded fascinating multipart singing in the then French Congo: heptatonic harmony in lush triadic chord clusters. I reconfirmed the existence of these styles among the Bongili and Bakota in 1964 during my own travels (see transcription outline in Kubik 1998b). In structure and content they had the ring of being long-established practices. In the 1950s Rouget documented an equiheptatonic singing style among the Baule of the Côte d'Ivoire with its characteristic neutral thirds (see, for example, Rouget's recordings *Pondo Kakou*, MC 20.141). And in 1965 in eastern Angola, I recorded homophonic three- and four-part singing in initiation ceremonies and masked performances among the -Mbwela, -Nkhang-ala, -Lucazi, and -Cokwe. This is an area displaying a nonmodal style that involves chord progressions that fluctuate between major, minor, and neutral triads. An impressive example is a song in the women's secret *tuwema* (flames) society (cf. CD accompanying Kubik 2010: I: item 41).

In 1964 I recorded instances of chord clusters shifting by a semitone in the *ṣya* chantefables among the Mpyɛmɔ, an ethnic group settled in the southwestern forests of the Central African Republic. In that culture area, there is a strict par-allelism of individual voices. The method of chord formation in this style could be described as stacking of thirds on top of each other. In principle, this process is unlimited. Sometimes there are only two voices in parallel major thirds. In another performance of the same tune, there might be three voices, forming major triads. In one version of the song "Atɛndɛ," which I recorded at Bigene village in 1964, a fourth singer joined with yet another third on top of the triad. Thereby, the progression turned most naturally into parallel movement between two major sevenths chords, a semitone apart: C^{maj7} to $D\sharp^{maj7}$ and back (see Fig. 9.1).

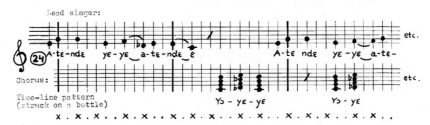

Fig. 9.1. *Ṣya* (story song) recorded at Bigene, Nola District, C.A.R., June 1964. Ethnic group and language: Mpyɛmɔ (complete transcription in Kubik 1998b: 665). Elementary pulsation: 375 M.M. (vertical lines). CD track 20, Kubik 2010: I.

These harmonic traditions used to flourish in places that were relatively isolated. There were no influences from church songs or mass-media music. Probably they were centuries-old local developments, and some of them had restricted distribution areas. In light of the precolonial presence of distinct harmonic practices in many parts of Africa from where people were deported to New World destinations, it would be strange if nothing of the underlying concepts had survived in African American cultures. To be sure, New World cultures were a bedrock of innovation, so things became modified; blues and jazz were developed as new genres in the United States. And yet there was resilience, and there were also contemporaneous parallels across the Atlantic divide.

The Perpetuation of Structural and Conceptual Elements from African Music in Jazz: Five Principles

The remote cultural genealogy of various practices and understandings in jazz links with African cultures of the past mainly at structural and cognitive levels. This makes research on the subject difficult. We are not dealing with phenomena that can be easily measured and verified but with what is hidden, discernible in some forms of behavior that otherwise remain unexplained and in the nonverbal dimension beneath the rationalizations one may get from musicians in interviews. In the area of the visual African arts, the book edited by Mary N. Nooter (1993) is a good introduction to the visual language of secrecy that parallels an auditory language of secrecy perpetuated in jazz.

There are five major principles of organization and conceptualization of tonal-harmonic elements in different regional styles of African music that seem to have continued and been creatively applied in jazz. These organizational and cognitional principles include 1) the span process, 2) the experience of partials-derived systems, 3) blues tonality, 4) the concept of flexible pitch areas, and 5) equiheptatonic concepts.

I would not claim that this list is complete. Thomas Brothers's (1994) discovery of a conception of syntax involving a fundamental and a supplemental level, for example, could be listed as a sixth principle. Africa is a vast continent, and the connecting lines between African American and African traditions crisscross the continent like caravan trade routes (see also Brown 1991). Often it is impossible to disentangle the picture historically because we are compelled to rely predominantly on twentieth-century data, projecting into the past. And yet, I feel it is worthwhile to descend to the basement of the building where foundations become visible that may be totally obscured by the noise and the jargon spoken on the first and second floors.

I. The span process

A span is defined as "a stretch between two limits" according to the *Longman Dictionary of Contemporary English* (1990). Xylophone players in Africa often transfer visual spans over the keyboard; that is, holding a beater in each hand, they strike two keys on the xylophone that are separated by one key and then shift this bichord in parallel hand movement to lower or higher keys. This technique can be seen in Hugo Zemp's (2001) film of Senufo master xylophonist Nahoua Silue.

One would expect such movement to result in harmonic parallelism. It often does, but not necessarily, depending on the tuning of the instrument and the layout (scale or otherwise) of the notes.

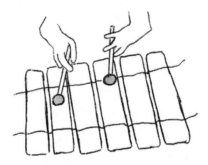

Fig. 9.2. Bichords on a xylophone shifted in parallel hand movement over the keyboard; the combination here is with two notes apart.

If African xylophones were tuned to the Western diatonic scale—they rarely were before factories began to produce the commercialized marimba—the result would be chains of thirds, alternating between major and minor. Lionel Hampton produced them occasionally on his vibes. If, on the other hand, the tuning of the xylophone is pentatonic, such as (from top to bottom) c-a-g-e-d-c, the result of the series of bichords described above would be parallel fourths that are interrupted in one place by a major third. Figure 9.4 shows why that is so.

Figs. 9.3 and 9.4. Transference of a visual span in a simple pentatonic tuning. Span process and resultant simultaneous sounds.

During my earliest work in Africa, from October 1959 to October 1960, I encountered vocal harmonic patterns of this kind in southwestern Tanganyika, among the -Pangwa, -Kisi, -Ngoni, and others. (See, for example, the transcription of the song "Kitandoli matala" in Kubik 2010: I: 200.)

At first I had no explanation for the isolated major third that always appeared in a certain place, until a structural explanation occurred to me. I had chanced upon the "span process" or "skipping process" (as I began to call it) as a generating principle. It turned out to be valid cross-culturally, determining the character of many forms of African homophonic multipart singing (instrumental layouts included).

But let me first explain the terms "homophonic" and "polyphonic" as we use them in African music studies (cf. Kubik 1999a). We distinguish two separate procedures in African multipart organization, vocal or instrumental: (1) homophonic, in which all combining voices proceed in analogous movement; (2) polyphonic, in which the constituent voices are interwoven, and interlock with each other.

In category 1 (homophonic), two or more parts are sung by individual singers in an analogous manner. All parts are rhythmically identical; they start and end at the same point. If the performance is vocal, participants sing the same text. The individual voices usually move together in intervals that are perceived as consonant (i.e., "agreeable"). Motion can be strictly parallel, in which case the participants' voices are always separated by the same interval. Much homophonic singing in Africa, however, is not strictly parallel. There are styles for example, in eastern Angola and northwestern Zambia in which all kinds of movements— parallel, oblique, and contrary motion—are considered acceptable. Homophonic multipart singing is associated in Africa with the call-and-response (leader/chorus) form.

In category 2 (polyphonic), a group of people perform together, singing different text phrases (or syllables) in an interlocking style, without any common starting and ending points. The phrases can have different lengths, and they interlock in various ways. At certain points, some of the voices meet, producing simultaneous sounds. This category of multipart organization is not normally linked to the call-and-response (leader/chorus) form. Besides the polyphony of the "bushmen" and Pygmies, impressive polyphonic styles can be found, for example, in Shona music of Zimbabwe, Sena music of the Zambezi valley, and in many other places in Africa. A great variety of polyphonic principles is applied in instrumental styles, or instrumental commentary on solo singers. The most complex examples can be studied in xylophone, stringed instrument, and other traditions, including horn ensembles and drum chimes.

Returning to the span (or skipping) process, a second singer finds his or her vocal line easily by skipping one note of the scale that they share. The second singer, who may be anyone in the audience or within the performance group, duplicates the pitch line of the first at a different level, most often either two steps down or two steps up the scale. In a pentatonic system such as outlined above in Figure 9.4 (and there are, of course, several types of pentatonicism in Africa), the combination of the two voices will yield characteristic bichord progressions. Like the xylophone player who transfers a visual span, these singers transfer an auditory span that is not defined by "intervals" (e.g., thirds versus fourths) but by an identity in directional movement of the vocal lines combined. This means that what for a Western observer would seem to be an important distinction between fourths as contrasted with thirds is conceptualized in this culture area as an identical linear relationship. The transcription of a story-song in Cinyanja from southern Malawi illustrates this point (see Fig. 9.5).

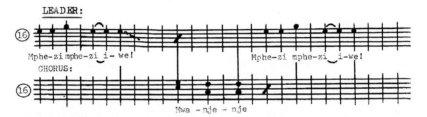

Fig. 9.5. Extract from the story song "Mphezi mphezi" (Lightning), sung by Anasibeko Kachamba with audience participation, Singano village, Chileka, Malawi, March 1967 (full transcription in Kubik 2010: I: 201, recording on CD I, track 14).

In other African culture areas, there are different relationships of sound, as the span process is applied to a variety of tonal systems. When I realized that it was an interethnic, interculturally valid procedure for the formation of simultaneous sounds, I began to test its applicability across Africa. Soon it became clear that the span process was a constant. The most important variable on which the sonic result depended was the structure of the underlying tonal system. What will happen, for example, if one pitch in the simple anhemitonic pentatonic scale that I have just described is altered by a semitone? We do not have to carry out an experiment because such an alteration already exists and has been documented independently in Cameroon and Burkina Faso.

Ever since Paul Oliver's pathbreaking research on the blues and its remote historical links to West African savannah cultures, the so-called west-central Sudanic belt has emerged as a key region for the likely provenance of many of the blues' most salient traits, including the use of bourdon, the strongly centralized tonality, the blue notes, the often declamatory, melismatic singing style, heterophony, and more (Oliver 1970; Kubik 1999a). In December 2000, Hungarian musicologist Andreas Szabo, on one of his numerous visits to Burkina Faso, worked with Mamadou, a xylophone player in the Diabate family settled at Torosso, forty kilometers west of Bobo Dioulasso. Mamadou's xylophone (*bala*), gourd-resonated and on a stand, was tuned to a "bluesy"-sounding pentatonic scale. He played with several younger musicians, Sadama, Sibiri, and Moussa from the same family, all belonging to the Sembla people, a Mande-speaking group. The auditory impression of a blues-like scale arose from the fact that the second degree (from the bottom) of this pentatonic tuning was raised by approximately a semi-tone compared with the more common pentatonic tunings elsewhere. Although Szabo did not make any measurements, my notation in Figures 9.6.and 9.7 should give an idea of the kind of intervals aimed at. The resultant bichords were obtained by the player through the visual span process described above. Szabo's video document was recorded in a village that showed no traces of any "returning" blues influence through Ali Farka Toure or other such artists. Obviously, the tuning was part of an established xylophone tradition. Although I would not propose that the *bala* tradition in this village has remained unchanged since the early 1800s, it also happens sometimes that certain traits show surprising stability. For this reason, it is useful simply to pay attention without imposing premature conclusions. Mamadou, the xylophone virtuoso, then created his bichords by shifting his beaters, held parallel, across the keyboard with one "empty" key between.

Figs. 9.6 and 9.7. Xylophone (*bala*) tuning by Mamadou of the Diabate family, video-recorded by Andreas Szabo, at Torosso, Burkina Faso, December 2000. Tuning (relative notation, intervals fairly accurate; middle section of the xylophone) and resultant bichords struck by player (brackets indicating the span process).

A quarter century earlier, in another key African area, the central Cameroonian savannah, I had recorded a fabulous blues-like grinding song by a Tikar woman. (Cf. Kubik 1999a: 73–78 and CD item 15 accompanying the Italian translation, 2007). On the same trip in 1964, I also recorded a mourning song by another Tikar woman in the local Chief Ngambe's entourage, the scale pattern of which strangely conformed with that of Mamadou's *bala* in Burkina Faso (same CD, item 27, Ngambe, February 1964). She was accompanied by a man playing a polyidiochord stick zither (*mbø loya*). The five strings divided into ten sections by the central notched bridge were tuned (relatively, from top to bottom) e♭-c-a-g-e-e♭-c-a-g-e♭. Within this pentatonic scheme, an interference pattern emerged between the middle e♭ in the performer's right-hand playing area and the e in that of his left hand. This interference accounted for the music's blues-like character. The wailing quality of the female voice and her melodic patterns were other traits. She complained about her husband, who had deserted her.

Ngambe village in Cameroon is about two thousand kilometers from the Diabate family's domicile in Burkina Faso. I think that the incidence of close similarity in tuning pattern found at such a geographic distance is significant and may suggest a certain antiquity of this pattern. The span process is, of course, absent here (in contrast to the music of the Diabate family in Burkina Faso) because the Tikar singing tradition is based on unisons, octaves, and some heterophony, not on harmony-oriented combinations. In harmony-employing African traditions (see the rough distribution map in A. M. Jones 1959), the span process often establishes a functional relationship between harmonic style and tonal system. In these cases, it is possible (as I did on many occasions) to reconstruct the "family relationship" between the constituent tones of a tonal system and the type of chords used in the music, and—vice versa—to predict what chords will be used in a musical culture if one has understood the intricacies of its tonal system.

In eastern Angola, for example, the underlying heptatonic system invites the application of the span process in two directions simultaneously, up and down the scale, proceeding from a middle voice. Thereby it is possible to explain some of the spectacular progressions in triadic chord clusters that are so characteristic of eastern Angola and that can be heard, often all night, sounding from a *mukanda* boys' initiation camp. (See, for example, Kubik 1998b and Tsukada 1990b, 1998 for transcriptions.)

The harmonic system of the -Mbwela, -Nkhangala, -Cokwe, -Lucazi, and -Lwena (-Luvale) in eastern Angola emphasizes stepwise progression. But singers want to preserve a euphonic identity between the emerging triads across the range of the scale, so intonational adjustments are constantly made. The result is flexibility of several constituent pitches of this scale; they can be modified according to harmonic context. The span process, however, operates independently of this fact. Take the upper c (degree 8) as a point of departure, it can be represented as in fig. 9.8.

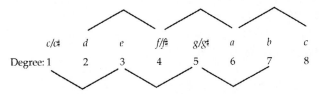

Fig. 9.8. Tonal resources in eastern Angolan multipart singing and the span process of obtaining chords.

It is important to understand that (1) the span process goes in any direction and can be triplicated even to form seventh chords; (2) individual voices tend to move within the margin of a fourth, rarely exceeding the range of a fifth (Kubik 2010: I: 194); and (3) the notes written as c/c♯, f/f♯, and g/g♯ in Figure 9.8 are each to be understood as a single toneme. In the musical language of the Ngangela- and Cokwe-speaking peoples of eastern Angola, the pitch values represented here as c and c♯, for example, are not necessarily conceptualized as different pitch units but rather as two alternative intonations of the same toneme, according to context. Therefore, applying the span process from e downward, the note to go with e can be c or c♯ or even a value somewhere between. The tendency is to intone the "resting" chords, that is, the last bichords in Figure 9.9, as neutral thirds. The songs employ sequences of lush triads, occasionally even seventh chords, and end on bichords that to a jazz ear may sound "altered."

Fig. 9.9. Harmonic clusters in eastern Angolan multipart singing. Examples of southeastern Angolan multipart singing can be heard on the CDs accompanying *Theory of African Music* (Kubik 2010, CD I, tracks 40 and 41) and the LP *Mukanda na makisi* (Kubik 1982).

The most important question is this: Does the span process as a matrix for chord formation survive in African American music, and in jazz particularly? If it does, it can only be found in homophonic multipart styles, both vocally and instrumentally. We have to look at some spirituals, as Kirby noticed in 1930, at vocal quartets, and instrumentally at 1930s to 1940s big band swing, , such as arrangements of the horn/reed sections in Jay McShann's fabulous orchestra (cf. CD *Early Bird*, Stash Records ST-CD-542).

More recently it appears in R&B/soul music "horn" sections (alto and tenor sax, trumpet and sax, sometimes with added trombone or baritone sax). Where classical European rules of harmony seem to be "broken," such as by parallel fourths or fifths, the explanation often is the underlying span process.

Many of Count Basie's arrangements present a case in point. The famous theme of "One o'Clock Jump," for example, transcribed by my friend, jazz musician Helmut Hillegeist, in Figure 9.10 is set for five saxophones (two alto, two tenor, and one baritone) predominantly in harmonic parallelism, itself a feature of African harmonic techniques. The first alto sax and the baritone sax create a frame in parallel octaves within which the four-part homophonic texture evolves. The reed and brass sections are in a responsorial relationship as chorus (reeds) and leader (brass). The theme for reeds is then repeated three times in an almost

Fig. 9.10. Count Basie, "One o'Clock Jump," transcribed and transposed into the key of C by Helmut Hillegeist, Vienna.

identical melodic shape through a twelve-bar blues form. In each repetition, it is "illuminated" or "floodlit" by different accompanying chords (on piano and guitar)—in the first line, tonic chords; in the second line (first half), subdominant; and in the third line (first half) dominant. One would call this four-bar theme a cycle in the African tradition. In its vertical dimension the theme is a harmonic progression in added sixths/minor seventh chords. But because it is–so to speak–interpreted from three harmonic standpoints consecutively, the voice lines of the five saxophones are slightly adapted in their repetitions to fit into tonic, subdominant, and dominant harmonies (see Fig. 9.10).

The means by which this is accomplished by Basie follows structural and aesthetic principles that are very different from Western music. It might also confirm something about the history of the blues form. If it is possible to repeat a compact harmonic set of voice lines in quasi-identical shape through the three lines of the twelve-bar blues form, and it sounds fine, then this also brings to light something about the deep structure of the blues, namely, that there is an underlying idea of theme development with no progression at all through "degrees," let alone to a dominant chord—something still treated as somewhat alien in the rural blues. At some time, voice and instrumental parts of certain songs within the blues genre would have unfolded over a bourdon-like basis and short riff-like accompanying and responsorial passages. This is not to say that such a tradition should be considered as "older." It is even very likely that through contact with nineteenth-century church hymns and popular songs in the European-American tradition, some African American musicians first embraced the Western common chords enthusiastically, as has also happened in the development of guitar styles in Africa. But gradually, the African concepts crept in like a "return of the repressed," and younger musicians, more assertive in demonstrating a different cultural identity, ventured increasingly into nonconventional, non-Western expressive techniques. At that stage, a music called blues became known to the broader public and was eventually also recorded. And ever since, no opportunity has been lost to subvert the Western progressions, as is also the case in Count Basie's masterful arrangements. Bebop musicians continued along that path and elaborated on the swing jazz models of presenting a blues theme in three repetitions with small melodic changes. See for example, Dizzy Gillespie with Frank Paparelli on the piano in "Blue n' Boogie" on *Dizzy Gillespie and His Sextets and Orchestra*, Musicraft MVSCD-53, or Parker's fantastic "Cool Blues" on *Jazz & Blues*, BN 207, disc 2, track 8.

At first hearing, one might not detect any unifying structural principle of African provenance in Count Basie's "One o'Clock Jump," although the auditory impression is regularly described by some of my musical acquaintances in southeast Africa as stunningly familiar. This concerns in particular the compact set "as if the saxophones were singing *makwaya*" (in a choir) and the static quality of the added-sixth (respectively, minor seventh) chords that involve the performers in intonating parallel seconds and fourths in several places.

At first, this compact sound seems to defy analysis, until one realizes that some of the semitone modifications, for example, e♭ versus e, might express adjustments similar to those I have described in vocal music of eastern Angola (see Fig. 9.9). The remaining work is almost routine. We now arrange the theme's notes as composed by Basie in the form of a scale and compare them with the slight modifications of the chords formed by the five saxophones, thereby discovering which notes can be understood as single tonemes. If we then apply the span process to this condensed scale, we discover that it explains the chords. I was able to detect that in this scale, e/e♭ and a/a♭ each form a single toneme (see Fig. 9.11). These tones are interchangeable thirds over c and f, respectively.

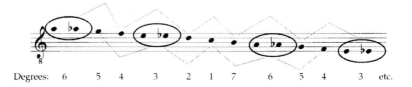

| Degrees: | 6 | 5 | 4 | 3 | 2 | 1 | 7 | 6 | 5 | 4 | 3 | etc. |

Fig. 9.11. Scale underlying Count Basie's "One o'Clock Jump." Notes encircled are interchangeable and function as the same toneme.

Thus, it can be observed, for example, that the first chord in measure 1 (see Fig. 9.10), g-e-c-a-g (from top to bottom), derives from the span 5–3–1–6 in Figure 9.11. The lower g, as an octave transposition of the higher one, can be ignored (as a duplication). When this chord is repeated in measure 5, the e is lowered to e♭, which makes no difference structurally because both e and e♭ are the same toneme and therefore interchangeable within the span process. Also, when checking the spans in Figure 9.11, one must be aware that it is structurally a four-voice arrangement; one note in the voice-line cluster of the five saxophones is always duplicated. It then forms the interval of a second with its neighbor.

All the chords in Basie's arrangement follow the span process except one—the penultimate chord in the theme, in measures 3, 7, and 11: g-e-b-a♭. Its deviant structure probably derives from its function as a substitution chord of some "dominant" quality; it can be split into the components g plus e and b plus a♭, both impressing upon the ear their minor-third quality. The auditory trick is that, thereby, g and b are prevented from fully unfolding their conventional dominant function. Figure 9.12 shows the ten different chords in Basie's theme and its repetitions. To make them comparable, I have rewritten them uniformly in seventh-chord positions by octave-transposing one or two notes. Succeeding chords in the row are often obtained through minimal alteration: lowering one pitch by a semitone.

Fig. 9.12. Structural layout of the tonal repertoire of simultaneous sounds in the reed part of Basie's "One o'Clock Jump," as obtained by the span process.

The African tinge in Count Basie's arrangement of "One o'Clock Jump" can be summarized as follows:

1. Homophonic treatment of voices, predominantly in parallelism.
2. Creation of a lush compact harmony in homogeneous sound clusters reminiscent of eastern Angolan harmonic singing as well as that of some places on the Guinea coast (Alberts and Alberts 1950). It is not by chance that Ghanaian bandleader E. T. Mensah embarked on a similar aesthetic in the 1950s (see, for example, "O hentse mi lo," Decca Records WAL 1002 I/3, also analyzed in Kubik 1999a: 164–65).
3. Use of a modified diatonic scale with two flexible tonemes, e/e♭ and a/a♭, interchangeable in chord formation.
4. Triple application of the span process to the scale, resulting in seventh chords. However, in their distribution to the individual saxophone players, the composer has introduced appropriate octave displacements and duplications that can veil the underlying structure.

Although it seems that the span process as a harmony-generating compositional principle is much more prominent in homophonic styles, such as in big-band swing jazz, spans are not absent from bebop, for example. Sometimes they can even be seen in a bop pianist's hand movements. In addition, the African aesthetics of harmonic parallelism have been recovered even more rigorously in bebop than in any previous jazz style. While oblique motion (with some intervals modified in their repetitions to fit into the structure of underlying chord changes) abounds in big band swing (e.g., "One o'Clock Jump" in Fig. 9.10), it seems to me that bebop marks a decisive turnabout, reinstating the strict parallelism cultivated in some African traditions. In some areas, such as among the -Nsenga in Zambia, it is parallelism in fourths (Jones 1959), in other places in thirds, and in yet other places both combined to form triads. Of many possible examples that could be transcribed from recordings, I am giving one that was already available in print in 1948. Because I am concerned not with improvisational variations but with recurrent structural patterns, there is no need for elaborate transcriptions from historical recordings by ear (sometimes even more subjective than the sheet music). Condensed printed versions by some of the original exponents may demonstrate the matrices much more eloquently. In Dizzy Gillespie and Charlie Parker's "Anthropology," for example, whose earlier manifestation was the title "Thriving on a Riff" recorded by Parker, the piano part, in an arrangement transcribed by Frank Paparelli, starts off in diatonically ascending fifth plus third plus fourth clusters (see Fig. 9.13). The chord implications are B♭maj⁷ to Cm⁷ to Dm⁷, while the clusters' actual content is quite economic. There are in the same arrangement many other instances of parallelism and spans. In combination with Gillespie's presentation of the "Anthropology" theme on the trumpet, there emerges an aesthetic totally different from anything that was common at the time in contemporary European art-composed music. Bebop has no debts in that sense. In any such analysis, it is important to study chord progressions not at their face value, as if they were lexical items, but as part of an intraculturally meaningful syntax.

Fig. 9.13. Extract, Dizzy Gillespie and Charlie Parker's "Anthropology." Trumpet and piano parts transcribed by Frank Paparelli. Published by J.J. Robbins & Sons, New York, 1948.

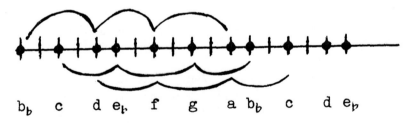

Fig. 9.14. The spans

II. The experience of partials-derived systems

African tonal systems can be divided into three broad families: (1) those developed from the extrapolation of the formants of human speech, (2) those developed from the recognition of partials of the natural harmonic series on tools (instruments), and (3) those developed from projection of the idea of equidistance upon auditory materials. Each category contains an impressive array of possibilities that have led to different tonal systems: tetra-, penta-, hexa-, or heptatonic systems with specific interval relationships (see Kubik 1985, 2010: I). We perceive harmonics in the sounds generated by natural forces such as wind, the wheels of a train, a broken water pipe, or someone's vacuum cleaner. These human experiences are independent of culture-specific musical enculturation, but they can form an ever-present resource for experimentation, especially among children, that begins with a desire to manipulate those sounds, alternating their timbre and reinforcing some of the partials selectively. In speech, it occurs naturally, as Benjamin V. Boone (1994) has shown with reference to blues-like speech in Jelly Roll Morton and Alan Lomax, generated by the use of higher partials. Someone brushing his or her teeth while altering the size of the mouth's cavity has rediscovered the natural harmonic series by the method of using the mouth's cavity as a resonator for sound modification and amplification. It is like playing a friction mouth-bow, a chordophone that is common in Angola and Moçambique. (See, for example, Moya Aliya Malamusi's recording on the CD *From Lake Malawi to the Zambezi*, track 23.)

When playing a wind instrument with an inserted mouthpiece, such as a saxophone or clarinet, the mouth's cavity also functions as a variable resonator. Saxophone players, including Coleman Hawkins, Lester Young, Charlie Parker, Stan Getz, John Coltrane, and others, explored these instruments' physics to modify timbre. In jazz, timbre shaping is one of the most important areas of individual expression. John Coltrane's timbre alterations and manipulations of overtones on the soprano saxophone (e.g., in "The Promise," recorded at Birdland on October 8, 1963) can be seen as the rebirth on American soil of reed techniques of *alghaita* oboe music in west-central Sudan. It is worthwhile to compare Coltrane's aesthetics and techniques with those of musicians in the court of the Fulɓe ruler of Toungo in northeastern Nigeria and also with the solo performance by a Hausa musician and trader, Amadou Meigogue Garoua, with a small *algeita* whom I recorded at Yoko, Cameroon, in February 1964. Both recordings have been published on the compact disc that accompanies the Italian 2007 translation of *Africa and the Blues* (Kubik 1999a), tracks 19 and 20.

The manipulation of nonharmonic overtones is one area of expression. Another, of course, is the systematic amplification of harmonics. When brushing one's teeth, one can reinforce harmonics up to partial 8 quite easily. With a small electric shaver in front of one's mouth one can reproduce the scale of the Wagogo, Tanzania (cf. Kubik 2016), reinforcing harmonics up to partial 10. The lowest partial in a harmonics column is called the fundamental. In prehistory, humans used toothbrushes from split plants, we assume, but there were also ample opportunities to discover the harmonic series through the use of other tools. Eventually, some techniques, such as reinforcing the harmonics of a stretched string by mouth or an external resonator, became established. In Africa such discoveries probably took place in several places simultaneously within a few thousand years. Until recently, the so-called bushmen in Angola and Namibia have been part of an ecologically determined hunter-gatherer economy, with the hunting bow a central tool. Not surprisingly, therefore, it also became a central musical tool. The tonal system of the !Kung', which I studied in Angola in 1965, was developed from experiences with the stretched strings of hunting bows. For us today, it is no longer important, as it was at the turn of the twentieth century, to speculate about which might have been first, the "hunting bow" or "musical bow." Psychologically, it is evident that someone discovering one usage is likely soon to experiment with the other one as well. Thus, it can be inferred that "bushmen" tonality and polyphony were developed thousands of years ago, long before the specific thirteenth- to fourteenth-century developments of polyphonic techniques in Europe. A totally different issue, however, is the subsequent transmission and diffusion of the ideas, always depending on circumstances. Musical bows seem to have had very little development among Native Americans, for example, although the hunting bow was widespread. Thus, while the hunting bow is nearly universal, musical bows are not. The separation occurred at an early stage, and in some parts of the world they were replaced by complex stringed instruments and/or Jew's harps. No "bushmen" were deported to the Americas. The slave traders in Angola despised them.

But southwestern Angola was a major slave-raiding area in the eighteenth century, and Bantu-language speakers such as the -Nkhumbi, -Handa, -Cipungu, and others, had been living in an economic symbiosis with the !Kung' for hundreds of years and—as is testified by the research of my Angolan colleague Marcelina Gomes—musicians adopted essentials of "bushmen" musical-bow techniques. Some may have taken their knowledge to New World destinations. To my surprise, when undertaking a systematic trait-by-trait analysis of an African American musical-bow player, Eli Owens, recorded by David Evans in 1970 and 1973 in Bogalusa, Louisiana (Evans 1994: 333–34), we discovered that the closest African parallels that emerged were to be found in bushmen-related bow techniques of Angola and Namibia (cf. Kubik 1999c).

There are several partials-derived tonal-harmonic systems in use across Africa. What they sound like depends on multiple variables: first, whether the system comes from vocal discoveries (formants of human speech or overtone singing) or from the use of an instrument; second, if its origins are in instrumental techniques, whether it is based on one or more than one fundamental; third, if there is more than one fundamental, what their interval relationships are; and finally, how high up the series of partials the tones are selectively reinforced.

African musical cultures that incorporate a strong awareness of a basic reference tone often operate from a tonal system that has its origins in the selective use of partials over a single fundamental. Of course, not every bourdon-based style can be linked to such a background. By now, several single-fundamental systems have been identified, for example, among the Wagogo of Tanzania (Kubik 2010: I: 175–84) and the !Ko of the Kalahari in Namibia and Botswana (see video document no. 6, tuning of a pluriarc by Dena Pikenien, 1991, Kubik and Malamusi, Namibia). Such a tonal system is easily identified by the fact that it does not provide any possibility for so-called root progressions (see Blacking 1959), that is, movement between tonal steps (degrees) with harmonic implications.

In other areas of Africa one can encounter a very different approach to harmony and form: the so-called shifting tonality. Two roots, usually a whole tone apart, are needed to establish musical events shifting between two focal points. In Luba and Kanyoka culture in the southern Democratic Republic of Congo (see, for example, Hugh Tracey's [1973] recordings on AMA-TR 15), the hexatonic material was laid out in the form of two contrasting tonal compounds, transcribed as c-e-g shifting to d-f-a and back. Translated into Western music theory, it could be described as shifting between two chords, C major and D minor. Such systems, usually hexatonic, can be found in abundance in Africa, with or without associated homophonic or polyphonic devices. In jazz, shifting tonality is the hidden African matrix in some of the so-called modal jazz propagated at one time by Miles Davis and by John Coltrane.

But most forms of shifting tonality in Africa include chords. They derive from the exploration of harmonics over two fundamentals. This is the case among the Faŋ in Gabon, whose type of mouth-bow survived into the 1950s in at least one New World tradition, at Palenque, Colombia (List 1983); it is also the case of

Fig. 9.15. Nkhumbi/Handa musical-bow-derived harmonic clusters.

the Xhosa in South Africa, and the -Nkhumbi/-Handa in southwestern Angola. The tonal system used by these peoples is based on two harmonic columns up to partial 6 over fundamentals that are a whole tone apart. It generates a hexatonic scale. Spectacular use of this kind of scale for multipart singing can be observed in *ekwenje* initiation songs, which I recorded in southwestern Angola (cf. LP *Humbi en Handa*, Musée Royal de l'Afrique Centrale, Tervuren 1973) (see Fig. 9.15).

In the Caribbean, there is a strong memory of shifting tonality associated with chords of this kind. On guitars, in Venezuela and elsewhere, they are usually represented (in transposition) as shown below, resulting in a kind of "dual fundamental" harmony.

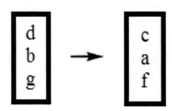

In the recording "Bo Diddley," made in Chicago on March 2, 1955, the early rock 'n' roll guitarist and singer Ellas McDaniel, known as Bo Diddley, can be heard with a passage on the electric guitar in a shifting harmony between f and g (relative pitches) with wow effects. To me, this passage sounds as if it has been played on a *beŋ* mouth-resonated musical bow in a *bwiti* cult meeting in Gabon. McDaniel is unlikely to have had any knowledge of such recordings in 1955 because they then rarely existed. Most certainly however, his preference for such shifting triads on his electric guitar was not a random choice. Even if he adopted this practice from Caribbean styles, it represents a rediscovery of musical-bow harmonies out of some need. But what pushed him to use these harmonies when other blues performers of the time did not? It is perhaps significant that he was born in a place on the border between the states of Mississippi and Louisiana. His birthplace, McComb, Mississippi, is only about thirty-five miles from Sandy Hook, where Eli Owens was born and raised. Bo Diddley was mainly raised in Chicago, with frequent visits back to McComb. His "Bo diddley" playing draws on "Latin rhythms," children's rhymes, hoodoo lore, and the "dual fundamental" harmonic idea. The latter technique is aided by use of open tuning and shifting the barré chord between frets 12 and 10.

Studying African tonal systems comparatively, one can discover yet another significant relationship: the number of roots used in a musical system and the range of harmonics exploited is inversely proportional. Tonal systems built over a single fundamental tend to go high up, at least to partial 9. The reason is obvious: one cannot form melodies from lower partials over just one fundamental. It would result in disjunct intervals of octaves, fifths, and fourths. For melodic formation, one needs the higher partials with their narrower intervals, at least from 4 to 9. But if a second or more roots are added, then tonal resources increase, eventually to an extent demanding restrictive measures. Over two fundamentals, one usually goes up to the sixth partial, very rarely up to the seventh, attaining a heptatonic system. But that is the limit. Neither in Africa nor in the blues can any "octatonic" scales be found, an idea (occasionally encountered in the blues literature) that comes from compulsive counting of variations of blue notes.

Tonal systems over three fundamentals do occur in Africa, but the most prominent case is European folk tonality over fundamentals c, f, and g, generating the "three common chords." By contrast, tonal systems built on four fundamentals, that is, with tonal shifts between four degrees, are prominent in Africa. In some areas, such as Busoga and Buganda (East Africa), the four-root cycle is not associated with any harmonic device; tonality in a song simply shifts between degrees. In other musical cultures of Africa, four-root cycles are associated with harmonic sound derived from partials. One such case is the Shona tonal system in Zimbabwe, based on four roots, each constituting a column of harmonics up to partials 3 and 4. The result is the characteristic Shona bichords in fifths and fourths over the roots c, e, g, and a (cf. Andrew Tracey 1970; Kubik 2010: I: 235–39, track 26 on CDI, Beulah Dyoko).

Modern adaptation of the Shona chords can be found in the music of Thomas Mapfumo, especially in his early recordings such as on the LP *Hokoyo*, Afro Soul, ASLP 5000. Although the Shona chords are responsible for the characteristic sounds to be heard in Shona music of Zimbabwe, and also in Sena music of the Lower Zambezi Valley, the pitch values of the four roots are not rigorously fixed. Sometimes there is considerable margin for variation, especially in the Lower Zambezi Valley, where xylophone and *bangwe* zither players long ago introduced an equiheptatonic temperament. That this must have had considerable influence in conditioning auditory perception in children is evident. Certainly it could have been better studied sixty years ago, when radios were still rare in local houses. And yet we can tentatively assume that growing up in a musical culture in which "perfect" fourths and fifths have been tempered to create an equiheptatonic scale with a standard interval around 171 cents widens the margin of tolerance in pitch recognition. It can easily make semitone progressions acceptable to the ear. And this is why, besides other factors, I find a strange cognitional affinity between some Zambezi music and modern jazz forms. Listen, for example, to Suze's development of improvisatory variations with his group on the *valimba* gourd-resonated xylophone recorded in 1967 and his bebop-like ending in the standard theme "Panagona Diminga" (Where Diminga was sleeping) (cf. LP *Opeka Nyimbo*, Kubik and Malamusi 1989, track A3, Ethnological Museum, Berlin). Suze could not have heard bop records.

To our great surprise, also in May 1967, when Maurice Djenda and I recorded in a village on the Malawi/Moçambique border, we came across a corn-pounding Sena woman, Fainesi, about age twenty, who was singing a worksong to yodel syllables, modulating in semitone steps through a four-bar cycle. The last "chord" of her cycle was then a perfect modulation to a tonal basis a semitone lower than her start (see Fig. 9.18).

Pounding strokes: X . . . . X . . . . X . . . . X . . . .

Fig. 9.17. *Chingolingo* (Yodel). Work song by Fainesi, recorded at Ndamera, Nsanje District, Malawi, May 1967 (Kubik and Malamusi, *Opeka Nyimbo*, track B2).

Fig. 9.18. *Chingolingo* (Yodel) rewritten as a chord progression.

Because this is yodel, with the lower partials implied in the process, one can rewrite Fainesi's tonal material as a progression through four chords to see what is revealed. We add a thought experiment here: In a science-fiction story, Fainesi, with her tonal understanding, travels through time and settles in the United States with a piano teacher. After learning to play piano, she is taken (with her memory still intact) to Minton's Playhouse in 1941. Charlie Parker asks her to make a contribution to his music based on one of her songs remembered since

Fig. 9.19. Vocal technique (*chingolingo*) employed by Fainesi, about twenty years old, during her work pounding maize. Ethnic group: -Sena. At Ndamera, Nsanje District, on the Malawi/Moçambique border, May 1967. Photo: author

childhood. She plays the progression shown in Figure 9.18 with her right hand and later asks Thelonious Monk to add a bass line. Which bass notes would he have added? (This riddle is for the jazz reader to solve. It is my challenge to those who have marked "true" on the *Garland Encyclopedia*'s leaflet! It remains to be seen how many solutions will result.)

III. Blues tonality: Higher partials, difference tones, blue notes, and the interference pattern

Why do certain forms of African music sound "bluesy" while others do not? In the early 1960s, when I began recording all over the continent, Africa was not yet totally connected to Western mass media. There were still traditions that developed and changed responding mainly to internal forces and intra-African streams of influence. Listeners to my early recordings often detect blues-like music, some of which is now published (CD accompanying Italian translation of *Africa and the Blues*, 2007). These listeners are of the most varied background, come from many different countries, and all have their specific ideas about blues. Yet a tendency is discernible. The music they qualify as "bluesy" mostly comes from within specific language families in a region extending from Burkina Faso, northern Ghana, and northern Togo to northern Nigeria, into Cameroon, and across the continent as far east as the Ingassana Mountains in Sudan. It comes from peoples speaking Mande, Voltaic, or Adamawa-Eastern languages (Kutin, Chamba, Zande); Hausa; "Bantoid" languages within the Benue-Congo family (such as Tikar); and eastern Sudanic languages such as those spoken by the Ingassana and the Berta with their spectacular horn ensembles recorded by Artur Simon (CD *Waza*, Museum Collection Berlin, SM 1708/2, 2003). Because of characteristic patterns of rhythmic organization, we call this large chunk of land across the geographical Sudan the swing belt of Africa. It extends to the south as far as the Luo and Abaluhya of western Kenya, especially among lyre players with their declamatory, melismatic vocal style.

The second bluesy area seems to cover northern Moçambique into Malawi—a much smaller territory than the first—especially as concerns log xylophone music, songs accompanied by fiddle or zither, and so on, mostly by performers within Bantu language Zone P, Yao, Shirima, Lomwe (Guthrie 1948). A third bluesy area emerged after our research in Namibia in 1991–93. Audiences in my lectures usually find the pastoral Herero bluesy, especially the *oucina* pentatonic women's songs to handclaps on the off beat (video document no. 6, recorded by Kubik and Malamusi in Namibia, Ethnologisches Museum, Phonogrammarchiv, Berlin).

Can one make anything out of such a cursory assessment? I concluded that it was best not to ignore their reactions. I decided to find out what exactly these audiences (with a variety of cultural backgrounds but some familiarity with jazz and blues) had found to be so bluesy. I discovered that in many cases, the impression was created by just a few traits that appeared in those musical styles in various configurations: (a) music with an ever-present drone (bourdon); (b) intervals that included minor thirds and semitones; (c) a sorrowful, wailing song style; and (d) ornamental intonation. Songs with a prominent minor seventh in a penta- to hexatonic framework also sometimes received this designation, as did pieces that featured instrumental play with a clash between a major and minor third or with a specific vocal style. Never did they consider bluesy music with much percussion. One can take a closer look at some of these traditions. My earliest such encounter was in October 1962 in the Mitukwe Mountains of northern Moçambique. I was studying a small Shirima log xylophone with six slats played by two boys out in the fields to chase away birds and monkeys from damaging the crops. Under the impression of those fast sound sequences over a kind of constant drone, it occurred to me that the tuning perhaps followed the natural harmonic series as far as partial 15 (Kubik 1965: 39). Earlier, in 1960, in southwestern Tanganyika I had recorded two small girls of the -Kisi ethnic group whose voice combinations could only be explained if one assumed that they proceeded from a scale that was constructed from partials 6 to 11 over a single fundamental ("Oyire," recorded at Lupingu, May 1960, on the companion cassette to Simon 1983).

It will perhaps be helpful to recapitulate some of the characteristics of the natural harmonic series. It is important to understand that the upper harmonics are audibly different from Western twelve-tone tunings. The "natural" major third formed between partials 4 and 5 is only 386 cents wide, that is, 14 cents narrower than the tempered third of 400 cents. Further up, the "natural" minor seventh stands at 969 cents, that is, 31 cents lower than the minor seventh (b♭) on a piano. And the eleventh partial stands at 551 cents, just between a tempered f and f♯. The thirteenth harmonic at 840 cents is positioned between a and a♭, if we take the fundamental to be c.

It is likely that individuals who grow up exclusively in a tradition where the exploitation of upper harmonics is important tend to hear any sonic material as approximations to or deviations from that tonal memory ingrained during childhood and adolescence, much as conservatory-trained musicians will inevitably project the Western scale on non-Western tonal systems, detect flats and sharps where there are none, and hear nonmodal Angolan singing in terms of major and minor. After my start in 1962 in the Mitukwe Mountains, I had the opportunity, over the years, of studying many more musicians playing log xylophones, their tunings, and their music in the same cultural region that extends across northern Moçambique into Malawi. There are clues that can help one discover the ideas behind this music. One is that the two performers, sitting opposite each other, play interlocking patterns from a relative beat standpoint, which allows them to create very fast music—after all, it is supposed to frighten the birds! How-ever, watching the performers, one soon discovers that their themes are based on a central tone that is also produced in the interlocking manner, both play-ers striking the same key with their right-hand beaters in fast alternation, each from his side. The effect created is that of a bourdon. Because the sounds emitted are of short duration, they are sustained by that method. (This is illustrated on some recordings of expert performers in Mangochi District Malawi, LP *Opeka Nyimbo*, tracks C1–C3.)

The second observation one can make is that there are no root progressions; the bourdon is the unique permanent reference tone. And the third observation is that any note on the xylophone can be played together with any of its other notes; it always sounds agreeable. To Western-trained musicians, this observation may seem stunning, but having gotten this far, we have almost cracked the code of the tonal system of *mangwilo, mangolongondo*, and similar six- to nine-note log xylophones in that region. There is actually only one music system conceiv-able in which such extravagance could be allowed and in which "all have won," as Alice in Wonderland would say: a scale that is derived from higher partials over a nonobjectified single fundamental—nonobjectified because it is so deep down that it cannot be used as part of a scale. But why can any note on such a xylo-phone be struck together with any other? Why is there no distinction between consonance and dissonance, a concept familiar from other African culture areas, where a local tutor will inevitably point out to a student which sounds do not go together and which do? For a long time during fieldwork, I tried to figure out why that should be so. The solution that finally emerged was this: neighbor-ing sounds in a partials-derived scale, if struck together with emphasis, reinforce their common fundamental through the phenomenon of the so-called difference tone. If one strikes those two notes together rather hard, one can hear it.

In the northern Moçambique xylophone styles that are based on a bourdon-like basic reference tone or, alternatively, riffs filling the cyclic structure of a song, the underlying tonal system incorporates the exploration of higher partials over a single fundamental. The area explored usually includes the seventh, ninth, and eleventh partials, more rarely beyond. In these style areas, songs and instrumental parts can be constructed either strictly on the unison/octave principle, or they can allow for chord clusters, in which any notes of the tonal scale can be sounded simultaneously. It always sounds agreeable.

Boogie-woogie pianist Jimmy Yancey made use of the idea of difference tones, says Alexander Opatrny (2002), one of my former students, who observed this phenomenon of "sonic illusion" in Yancey's music independently, unaware of southeast African xylophone styles. Mathematically, a difference tone is defined as the vibration number (in Hertz) obtained if one subtracts from each other the Hertz (cycles per second) values of two notes struck together. It remains to be analyzed (by Opatrny) which notes Yancey preferably used to create this effect (see *The Unissued 1951 Yancey Wire Recordings*, Document Records, DOCD-1007).

Gradually I discovered how musicians were tuning their log xylophones "listening to the wood." If such an instrument is played by three people, one striking a timeline pattern, as in Waisoni Msusa's group, fascinating sound clusters emerge. (See tracks C1–C3 on the Kubik and Malamusi double album *Opeka Nyimbo*.)

The harmonic sense of these musicians and their acute perception of higher partials put them on a par with jazz musicians of the 1940s who were using increasingly upward extensions of chords. There are, of course, divergent principles behind this that can only be studied case by case in jazz. One principle is to create homophonic sound clusters by stacking thirds on top of each other, and shift them chromatically. I would call this the Mpyɛmɔ approach and refer to our example from Central Africa given earlier (see Fig. 9.1) But other upward extensions and some alterations of common chords, with which bebop musicians in particular were experimenting, may implicitly draw upon remote partials, as closely as they can be rendered on Western instruments. Some of these extended chords are often positioned within the mold of semitone progressions and can be understood as representing clusters of upper partials, as do the notes struck simultaneously on a *mangwilo* log xylophone.

How can we explain such analogies? Contemporaneous borrowings by jazz musicians can be excluded, because the first recordings ever made in northern Moçambique were cut in 1957 by Portuguese ethnomusicologist Margot Dias, and my earliest research there dates from October 1962. It is likely that African American musicians in the 1940s, a period of fascinating experimentation in jazz harmony, independently arrived at partials-based clusters in their quest to detach themselves from Western diatonicism and try something else on the basis of blues tonality. Jazz of the 1940s was intimately rooted in blues tonal ideas and therefore, the idea of partials-based tonal systems is deeply engrained. More than a third of Charlie Parker's compositions were in the blues form. Listen, for example, to "Bird Feathers," "Parker's Mood," or "Relaxin' at Camarillo" on Parker's *Jazz and Blues*, Biem Stemra BN 207, 1998. Blues was still a living force in the United States during that period, and the blues tonal system based on two integrated columns of harmonics up to partial 9 over two fundamentals a fourth apart (cf. Kubik 1999a: 139–44) became pervasive, not Arnold Schönberg or Igor Stravinsky. Benjamin V. Boone in an unpublished paper (1994) points out that there might be a linguistic basis in the development of those tonal structures in blues and jazz that deviate most prominently from the Western diatonic scale. He argues:

> Could it be that blue notes evolved from the interaction inherent in processing the English language through a West African linguistic template? Could the creators of

354

the blues with a heightened awareness of pitch due to their native language traditions . . . have intuitively utilized pitch relationships from the upper harmonics of
the overtone series? This series has as its seventh, eleventh and nineteenth members
none other than the blue notes mentioned above. Furthermore, the blue notes are
generally played out-of-tune when compared to the Western tempered scale, but
in-tune with the harmonic series. In fact, the pitches used in a blues more accurately
and more completely represent the first nineteen harmonics of the overtone series
than do the pitches of the Western major scale. (8)

Although we do not have to take recourse to the nineteenth harmonic to explain
the lower blue note, usually transcribed as e♭ in the key of C—it can be better
understood as partial 7 over a second fundamental (F) (cf. Kubik 1999a: 138)—
Boone's point of a connection between the blues and speech patterns of certain
African languages intuitively using upper partials of the harmonic series is to be
taken seriously. And this is learned and transmitted with language, irrespective of
an individual's ethnic background.

Concentrating on West African savannah cultures, my own research in 1963–
64 has confirmed that a majority of the traits of the blues can be traced to areas
in West Africa that represent a contact zone between an ancient Nigritic culture world developed by millet agriculturalists and an Arabic/Islamic culture
world that began circa 700 AD. I found that some of the people in remote central
Sudanic mountainous areas—for example, the Adamawa plateau on the Nige-
ria/Cameroon border (the Kutin, Chamba, Zanganyi, and others I researched in
1963)—had pentatonic systems that derived from the formants of human speech
with an awareness of harmonics up to partial 9.

Eventually I proposed a simple theory of how the blues tonal system was
structured in its beginnings and where it clashed with the Western diatonic scale
in America (Kubik 1999a). There is agreement today concerning the nature of
the upper blue note (written as b♭) that it represents partial 7 over a single fundamental. But in West Africa, notably among savannah agriculturalists such as
the Kutin of northeastern Nigeria, I detected clues that the section from partial
6 to 9 (range of a fifth) can be used in combination with its own transposition a
fifth downward to form a scale, as if the same melody were first articulated by a
woman, then by a man. The lower blue note, e♭, is therefore the upper blue note's
counterpart over fundamental F. The oscillating quality of blues intonation then
emerges as an interference pattern of the two columns in an integrated scalar
layout (cf. Kubik 1999a: 139).

In the days of bebop, the existence of a third blue note was increasingly discussed by musicians and jazz critics. It was called a flatted fifth. Actually it is more
accurately described as being within the pitch area of a fourth that is augmented.
This tone, represented as f♯ in the key of C, may have its origin in African tonal

traditions that incorporate a projection of partial 11 at 551 cents, although I would not generalize (see Kubik 1999a). Ongoing research on the "flatted fifth" in blues should focus on how this note functions melodically and harmonically in a large sample of recordings.

What is certain so far is that partials-based tonal ideas from eighteenth-century West African savannah cultures, and possibly southeast Africa from where people were clandestinely deported to the United States during the final stages of the slave trade, have survived and been perpetuated in the United States. They have decisively influenced tonal-harmonic developments in blues and jazz.

IV. Flexible pitch areas and tonal collision

David Evans (1982) draws our attention to the fact that blues musicians in their intonation often proceed from flexible pitch areas rather than rigidly defined pitches. Criticizing the concept of "neutral thirds" used by some in the description of blue notes, he writes:

> In fact, "neutral" probably would best represent an area between major and minor where notes can be sung, rather than any specific point between them. Blues singers often waver at the third or seventh or glide from a lower to a slightly higher pitch. The lower part of the third and seventh areas tends to serve as a leading tone respectively to the tonic and fifth below, the upper part as a leading tone to the fifth and tonic above. (24)

Evans's concept is compatible with the interference margin of 119 cents I proposed in my model of the origin of the blues tonal system. But the validity of Evans's concept can be extended to include jazz, and the pitch area concept certainly is present in several African musical traditions, although its specific origins and function within a musical system can only be unraveled case by case. I observed in Zande harp music in 1964 that there was considerable variation in the tunings from musician to musician, and even from day to day in the same musician. For example, the highest note on a *kundi* harp, which I transcribed as an e, was sometimes flatted to the extent of approaching an e♭. To someone who has grown up in the jazz tradition, this gives the strong impression of a blues-like intonation, if the vocalist also follows it. Two Azande harp players I recorded as they were playing together, Bernard Guinahui and Francois Razia, even had the top note of their two harps tuned 58 cents apart, that is, more than a quarter tone. The harps were then played in unison, with those notes generating an enormous friction effect; but the musicians and their audience showed no sign of finding the 58-cents discrepancy uncomfortable. Questions I posed elicited the answer that the harps were "in tune," so I recorded these tunings.

The harp tuning and singing of another of my harpist friends of 1964, Ray-mon Zoungakpio, also strikes listeners as bluesy because of the same flatted e♭ tuning layout (cf. track 8 on the CD accompanying Kubik 2010) This impression is reinforced by the singer's delight in a descending harp passage (from a blue third, e♭-c, into an open fourth, d-a, resolved downward to c-g) and by his somewhat raspy voice. Any kind of knowledge of blues or jazz, or other African American music, was excluded in Raymon's case.

It is significant that the flexibility in intonation and tuning involved only string no. 1 (the highest tuned), not the other four strings, which were always tuned in perfect fourths (no. 2 to go with 4, no. 3 with 5). This is perhaps a key observation. Concepts of simultaneous harmonic sound, based on simple ratio, work against flexible pitch. The two conflicting principles can be present in the same musical tradition, and even affect different sectors of a musical scale, as is also the case in blues and jazz.

What is the origin of pitch flexibility? A single, universal formula cannot be found. There may be quite different causal links in different historical circumstances that favor or inhibit elasticity. However, it has to be stressed that the concept of flexible pitch areas is inherent in African tone languages, especially in those (like the I.A.4 Kwa group in West Africa) that are extremely tonal. Speech tone is not based on rigid intervals; a broad margin of variation is allowed between intonations of a high tone, low tone or mid-tone. The nature of the language then allows pitch fluctuation within a margin of comprehensibility. I observed in Yoruba-speaking communities of Nigeria, when I learned àló story songs, that it was possible to render the same song with different intervals in the overall pentatonic scale. In vol. 2 of *Theory of African Music*, I have transcribed an example of two renderings of the same story song by two different singers in which minor thirds and seconds were used alternately to express the text's tonal patterns. The song was "Erò ti nr'Ojeje" (Travelers are going to Oje market). Yoruba is a distinctively tonal language, and in this musical culture it is therefore most important that the melodic ductus be maintained in representations of the same song so that the words are unambiguous in their meaning.

Without interference of harmonic principles—the Òyò Yoruba sing in uni-son—the intervals can change, however, strictly within the anhemitonic penta-tonic tonality which in this case includes a contrast between seconds and minor thirds. In areas where tonality is merely an extension of speech tones, one gets the widest possible margin of pitch flexibility, and that is usually the case within those traditions based on the unison/octave principle, with no multipart homo-phonic harmony.

In some African musical cultures the use of a tuning temperament can be a factor relaxing intonational rigidity, by extension also in instrumental tunings. It is evident that in societies whose tonal materials are constructed from lower partials, as on musical bows, intonation will tend to follow the harmonics that can be reinforced. But if, in the course of history, someone has introduced a system of temperament, as was the case in the Lower Zambezi Valley among the -Sena, children's auditory memory will be conditioned by both the "perfect" fourth and fifth relationships derived from partials and the near-equidistant tunings of instruments such as xylophones. In these cases, a margin of tolerance in pitch perception and reproduction will evolve. It can be relatively wide, as the example of Fainesi demonstrates. In her yodel song (see Fig. 9.18), she arrived at a chromatic modulation. In a culture that had exposed her to equiheptatonic tunings from childhood on, she reacted in her vocal adjustments with a compromise: while maintaining the key harmonic intervals of the Sena system, fifths and fourths in perfect shape, ideally at 702 and 498 cents, she adapted her tonal progressions through the four steps (degrees) of the system in a direction toward equiheptatonic tunings. Memory of the perfect intervals being strong, she did not actually reproduce equiheptatonic progressions of 171 cents in her descending movements; instead, she arrived at semitone intervals and produced a perfect modulation. This example should make clear that the processes of auditory adaptation and conditioning are subject to complex audio-psychological and cultural factors. Sometimes conflict between two or more tonal-harmonic traditions provokes reactions of auditory adjustment, and if the tonal ideas of the people in contact are not too different, those attempts often result in ambiguity. Intonation a little higher or lower would satisfy either system.

I point out that jazz in the 1940s—besides the social conflicts well covered in the literature—also existed within audio-psychological conflict. Bebop musicians, particularly Dizzy Gillespie, Thelonious Monk, and Charlie Parker, found ingenious solutions to accommodate their personal tonal-harmonic understanding, which was strongly based on blues tonality plus several hidden Africa-related structural ideas, with a musical and cultural environment that had significantly changed since the 1930s. In their reactions to and adaptations of the expanded sound repertoire conquered on the instruments they played, they followed a path that was intertwined with, although not necessarily dependent on, contemporaneous developments in European art-composed music. In jazz, pitch area flexibility is expressed in many ways: not only if a soloist plays slightly off-pitch or with a wavy intonation, but also if he deliberately constructs in his variations a phrase which only in part follows the accompanying chord changes. Within Western music the result would be described as a dissonance. For jazz musicians and African musicians alike, a better term might be friction sounds, i.e., simultaneous sounds distant from each other in narrow intervals within a margin of 100 cents (semi-tone) down to 20 cents.

In many African xylophone, lamellophone, and other tunings, there are what we now call friction octaves. Roderic Knight also describes this phenomenon in tunings of instruments in Gambia and Senegal (Knight 1991). Octaves in many xylophone traditions, including in Buganda, are deliberately tuned up to 20 cents apart irregularly throughout the instrument's range. This is an audio-psychological trick on perception designed to prevent those octaves from forming a merger of sound, so that polyphonic lines at different levels would come out prominently.

In jazz, a friction interval of ca. 100 cents is formed if a pianist expresses a blue note by hitting, for example, e and e♭ (in the key of C) simultaneously. Another example of a friction sound that was common in early jazz is the one that arises when a trumpet player (or any other improvising soloist) intonates a d over an F7 chord in the accompaniment, before the latter is resolved into a B♭ subdominant chord, as I shown in Figure 9.20.

Fig. 9.20. Friction sound: trumpet melody intonating d over an F⁷ chord.

One of the most notable constants in jazz history from the 1920s to the late 1940s, especially in Kansas City jazz and bebop, is an even larger area of collision that arises from the fact that sometimes two different tonal systems are juxtaposed within the same musical piece. This was inherited from blues in which often two different tonal systems clash, for example if the blues singer clings to a pentatonic blues scale with a specific interval structure, but the accompaniment is based on Western common folk music chords. Such archetypal collisions recur throughout jazz history.

Management of collision between different tonal systems operating simultaneously was significantly refined in Kansas City jazz, especially in the big band of Jay McShann, one of the most undervalued giants in jazz history, and later in various bebop combo formations. Here the tonal collisions are often handled in a subtle way by using ambiguous chord extensions, avoiding simple dominant → tonic relationships altogether, and by soloists who create their melodic variations bypassing some of the underlying chords. When they do so, auditory perception does not register the arising friction sounds as "wrong," i.e., alien to the system. It is, as Thomas Brothers says (1994: 490), an African conception of syntax, involving two levels, whereby the supplemental can move in and out of agreement with the fundamental.

I have used an improvisational passage from our own group (see Fig. 9.21) in a test for students both in Africa and Europe. No one hearing the passage on tape finds anything "wrong" with measure 28, although the descending melody of the horn does not follow the Ab_m7 chord of the guitar accompaniment completely, but rather pursues its own scalar structure melodically, thereby colliding with the chromatically descending harmonic progression of the guitar chords. In its last part—the triplet—the phrase anticipates an upper extension of the Gm7 chord which, however, is not contained in that chord. And yet the listener does not feel that there is any collision at all. This is another example of the "supplemental" in Afrologic syntax, as formulated by Brothers (1994).

Fig. 9.21. Soloist's melodic improvisation diverging in part from the underlying guitar chords. Theme: "Lover." (copyright: Sinosi Mlendo)

Sometimes there is a hidden tonal conflict between the melodic structure of a theme and its harmonic interpretation in the chords of the pianist, using extended altered chords, chromatic passages, etc. A case in point is "Cherokee." Perhaps not by chance is this composition often cited as having inspired Charlie Parker to develop his characteristic melodic lines and phrasings that would later be trademarks of bebop. What is so special about "Cherokee"?

The antagonism lies in the fact that "Cherokee" as a popular hit song (composed by Ray Noble in 1938) is pentatonic throughout the main theme, probably because the composer, following stereotypes about Amerindians, wanted to create a "Native American" atmosphere in the song. But the chords used underneath the theme by jazz pianists are anything but pentatonic. Charlie Parker may have been attracted by this inherent conflict, to develop a way to accommodate the two conflicting levels.

Charlie Parker's pronouncements in an interview with Levin and Wilson (1949) have been quoted in almost every publication about the origins of bebop. Although their exact wording has never been authenticated, they can still give us a hint about what was going on in Parker's mind. Parker had performed "Cherokee" at Clark Monroe's Uptown House, New York, in early 1942. He was accompanied by an unknown band of eight or nine people, including Allan Tinney on piano and possibly Ebenezer Paul on the bass (cf. *Early Bird*, Stash Records ST-CD-542). Parker is quoted as having said:

I'd been getting bored with the stereotyped changes that were being used . . . and I kept thinking there's bound to be something else. I could hear it sometimes. I couldn't play it. . . . I was working over Cherokee, and, as I did, I found that by using the higher intervals of a chord as a melody line and backing them with appropriately related changes, I could play the thing I'd been hearing. It came alive.

"Higher intervals" can only mean that he alluded to chord extensions upward. But these can be generated by following one out of several principles: (a) creating a friction sound (see Fig. 9.20) by transposing down the 13th of an extended seventh chord to collide with the 7th, as in the column c-e-g-b♭-d-f-a, or (b) stack thirds in the diatonic system on top of each other and create static progressions in major seventh chords, chromatically descending, or (c) explore the spectrum of remote upper harmonics. Parker may have tried out all of them, alternatingly. In any case, this short paragraph testifies to Parker's constant probing into the auditory spectrum.

A remark Parker is reported to have made in an interview for *Down Beat*, July 1, 1942 with Bob Locke (cf. Feather 1949 [1980: 12]) may throw further light on his statement. Talking about his stay in New York, "hanging around" with guitarist Biddy Fleet, he said: "Biddy would run new chords! For instance we'd find that you could play a relative major using the right inversion against a seventh chord, and we played around with flatted fifths." Parker's use of the language of Western music theory indicates that he may have had the triad d-f♯-a in mind, if the basis was a C⁷ chord.

As Dan Morgenstern observes (1991), soon after the McShann sessions in which Parker first performed "Cherokee" there was a change in his intonation, a harder, more lifting sound": "that throat inflection, almost a growl, that became a key color in the Parkerian tonal palette."

"Using the higher intervals of a chord as a melody line" could also mean that Parker wanted to follow the higher partials of various chords in his melodic constructions, but that he could not yet do so effectively because the chord basis jazz musicians used at that time was limited. Not so long before, even the added sixth chord had been a novelty.

By the 1940s, jazz would increasingly use "substitute" chords and alterations on the basis of inherited blues tonal-harmonic principles. Jazz reasserted itself as an African American tradition, recreating African extensions along structural principles still transmitted clandestinely on American soil, but with materials—Western instruments and their tunings, contemporary harmonic patterns, popular songs, and so on—that were available to be used as clay. Thus, the strategies that made bebop harmonic developments feasible were different in purpose and meaning from the experiments in harmonic, atonal, and serial development made by European and European-American composers in the early twentieth century.

V. Equiheptatonic concepts

Equiheptatonic tunings of musical instruments, e.g., xylophones, lamellophones, and zithers, were once widespread in several distinct areas of Africa. Developed on instruments, they also affected vocal music and singers' intonation. A German traveler, Eduard Peschuël-Loesche (1907), encountered such music among the Bafioti along the Loango Coast (Cabinda); he described compact vocal sounds in three- to four-part harmony that he was unable to identify as either major or minor.

A prominent area of equiheptatonic xylophone tunings is central and southern Moçambique with the -Chopi *timbila* (cf. Tracey 1948 [1970]) and the *valimba* of the Asena in the Lower Zambezi Valley (cf. Malamusi 2011, DVD of Nchoncho's group). Characteristic recordings can also be heard on our LP *Opeka Nyimbo* (Kubik and Malamusi 1989).

Equiheptatonic vocal intonation was common in the 1920s around Benin City, Nigeria, as is documented by the 78 r.p.m. record "Ihore" (Amuyun, with vocal and instrumental accompaniment). It was present on the Gold Coast (now Ghana) and on the Ivory Coast, as demonstrated on the record *Pondo Kakou*, by Gilbert Rouget. Another prominent area with non-modal harmonic singing and a tendency toward neutral-third intonation and equidistance was the east Angolan culture area, as is demonstrated by some of my recordings of 1965, published on the album *Mukanda na Makisi* (Kubik 1981).

What is the concept behind equiheptatonic tunings? It is important to understand that such tunings (as much as the equipentatonic tunings of southern Uganda) are forms of temperament which were developed—possibly first on xylophones—out of certain needs, particularly the need of transposition of melodic patterns to neighboring steps of the keyboard without compromising their identity. That must have happened at some stage far back in history. A. M. Jones (1970) believes it happened in response to xylophones imported from Indonesia, across the Indian Ocean, starting around 600 AD. The concept of tuning temperament was introduced into some African music in that manner, according to Jones.

In equiheptatonic tunings, the octaves on a xylophone or other instruments are approximately divided into seven equal steps. Approximately, because the human ear cannot achieve pitch accuracy down to fractions of an interval, and also for reasons I have explained in the previous section, friction octaves were sought on every step of the new scale of, for example, a twenty-two-note gourd-resonated xylophone such as the Sena *valimba*. The ideal interval, of equiheptatonic tuning is 171.4 cents wide, obtained by dividing an octave into seven equal parts: 1200 (octave) ÷ 7 = 171.4. As a rule, tuning fluctuations are in the region of ± 10 to 20 cents for each tone and are acceptable to auditory perception.

An equiheptatonic system has no modality. There is no concept of major or minor intervals; all thirds are alike, about halfway between Western major and minor thirds, while fourths and fifths are minimally different from perfect fourths and fifths, allowing the ear to "correct" the difference in perception as it also accommodates, for example, within Western tunings, the considerable deviation of the "tempered" major third (400 cents) from the "natural" major third of 386 cents derived from the harmonic series.

An illustration (see Fig. 9.22) can show the difference between equiheptatonic tunings and the Western twelve-tone equidistant tuning (since 1625). The arrows show the notes of the Western scale nearest to the equiheptatonic tones. Apart from the octaves at which I have anchored the two systems, it turns out that equiheptatonic fourths and fifths are only minimally different (by ca. 14 cents) from their Western tempered counterparts. This is important to keep in mind; the difference is audible, but easily tolerated. On the other hand, an equiheptatonic third is about halfway between a major and minor third, therefore called "neutral" (since Hornbostel introduced that term). The same applies to the sixth: halfway between a and a♭ (in the key of C). The remaining two tones, equiheptatonic seconds of only 171 cents width, tend to be perceived as close to a whole tone, but if in the tuning process the interval is tuned 20 cents narrower, about 150 cents wide, listeners can easily perceive it as a "sort of" semi-tone.

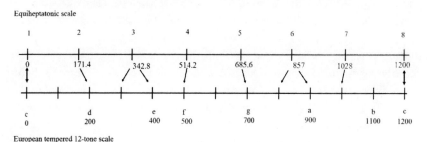

Equiheptatonic scale

European tempered 12-tone scale

Fig. 9.22.

In New World cultures, as is also the case in Africa today, factory-manufactured musical instruments tuned to the Western diatonic/chromatic scale have erased equiheptatonic tunings almost everywhere. In Africa they have survived, as far as I know, in the xylophone styles of Moçambique, among the -Chopi and the -Sena. During the 1950s, xylophone tunings in many other parts of Africa, whatever their previous nature was, were changed to the European heptatonic

Fig. 9.23. Johnny Zuze and his *valimba* group, recorded at Ntoma Mbini, near Ndamera, Malawi/Moçambique border, May 1967. Photo: author

scale, for example, in southern Cameroon, where a new *merengue*-based xylophone style became popular with the (now historic) Richard Band de Zoételé. In formerly equiheptatonic areas, as elsewhere in Africa, the younger generation has become diatonic in its auditory conditioning (particularly in the Congo and in East Africa) or was conditioned by the African American reflux: jazz in South Africa, calypso on the Guinea coast, then soul across Africa, and more recently rap and blues in some places in Mali and Senegal. This is the third African generation under massive influence by the media. Auditory conditioning, tunings, scales, tonal relationships, intervals, and so on are matters of early acquisition during childhood and adolescence. Once learned, habitual auditory reaction patterns are projected onto any familiar and unfamiliar music. This is why Western-trained individuals inevitably "hear" equiheptatonic tunings in terms of major/minor, although if warned, for example, in ethnomusicology classes as students, they may become aware of the auditory adjustment.

And yet, despite what has been the most incisive area of acculturation—because tonal systems are like languages, and a first language leaves behind much deeper engravings in human memory than those learned later—I think that the concept of tonal equidistance has survived in the Americas, notably in some forms of jazz. This is probably so, because throughout jazz history, but particularly in bebop of the 1940s, there has been clandestine rebellion against the Western diatonic system and its functional relationships based on a hierarchical order: dominant, subdominant, and tonic. The implicit symbolism in "classical" harmony, in spite of many sidetracks that obscure its nature, can in itself be repugnant; it reflects too obviously the nature of an authoritarian bourgeois society.

Despite the massive exposure of African Americans in the nineteenth century to folk-music harmonic patterns in ballads, church songs, and other works as well as popular late nineteenth-century harmonic patterns adopted in the ragtime piano from waltzes, quadrilles, marches, and polkas, some other forms of aesthetic experience continued. These included an auditory sensibility to timbre sequences, spatial imagination based on equidistance in decorative art (Vlach 1978), an array of African-derived polyphonic devices, the call-and-response organization, cyclic form, and many other behavioral traits that survived in African American communities. Why they survived is an issue that touches on processes of enculturation, group psychology, and depth psychology. It is certain, however, that small-scale circumstances, such as intrafamily transmission and exposure to movement and sound experiences contradicting the mainstream culture, provided much of the humus.

These innermost secrets, "privacies" in behavior, were hard to identify; in any case, they were resilient, and as long as they did not threaten the larger society, the latter often decided to ignore their existence. And yet it would happen that some of those "Africanisms" considered unworthy by their carriers under pressure from the dominating social group would attract the attention of outsiders. In the nineteenth and early twentieth centuries, it would often happen that young European Americans, in reaction to encrusted conventions of their own communities, set out to appropriate the "Negro" stuff—a trend that began with blackface minstrelsy and continued to the Original Dixieland Jass Band to rock 'n' roll and beyond. But there was also interest based on appreciation and a deep sense of identification with African American culture. Bix Beiderbecke learned jazz to achieve personal transformation and, in his piano work more than on the trumpet, contributed something unknown before, reinterpreting Claude Debussy from a standpoint one could qualify as internalized African American. "Africanisms" also did not fail to impress American composers who had grown up in the Western tradition, and were quickly adapted. Song composers mostly of Jewish ancestry were the most successful and made an undeniable contribution to jazz. They experimented with their perception of blues tonality and responsorial form. George Gershwin and others reacted to the new tonal material, reinterpreting it from their own background of musical upbringing; but they thereby also contributed to its reinforcement. Jazz would be poorer without "Body and Soul," "How High the Moon," "Lover Man," "I Got Rhythm," and other works by various Tin Pan Alley composers.

Where can we detect equitonal, and particularly equiheptatonic, retentions in jazz? The answer is that by the 1940s it was not so much retention but rediscovery, reconstruction of an alternative path. The major discovery in jazz harmonic practice even before the advent of bebop was that through tonal alteration by a semi-tone and modulatory transposition of melodic phrases in their precise interval structures, one can get away from the I-IV-V "classical" functional harmony. Jazz musicians, in contrast to Latin American musicians, achieved that transition with the help of the blues tonal system and its increasing importance, for example in Kansas City jazz, boogie-woogie, and later bebop.

African equiheptatonic tunings—originally developed as a temperament—were aimed at facilitating melodic transposition across the keyboard of xylophones. In jazz of the 1940s, analogous problems arose in motives based on blues tonality, even entire themes that were to be transposed in small steps, as occurs in Dizzy Gillespie's "Groovin' High" (on *Dizzy Gillespie and His Sextets and Orchestra*, MVSCD, track 2) and to an extent in "Early Autumn," a composition by Ralph Burns recorded by Woody Herman's Second Herd with the unforgettable Stan Getz on tenor saxophone. A similar situation can occur melodically, by stepwise shifting, mostly downward, of a phrase in narrow intervals, as can be heard most beautifully in Gillespie's solo trumpet backing on Sarah Vaughan's performance of "Lover Man" with his band (recorded May 11, 1945, MVSCD, track 6). Of course, like everyone else, jazz musicians of the time were still captives of the Western tunings of instruments made in corporate factories. But the way they began to handle the system melodically and transpose phrases a whole tone or a semitone lower, often without altering their interval structure—dismissing Western harmonic rules—demonstrates the resurgence of a kind of approach to handling melodic and harmonic patterns that is familiar to those of us who have worked in African communities with nonmodal, near-equiheptatonic melodic material.

The Irredeemable Monk

Blues tonality and the derivation of tonal-harmonic patterns from partials are interconnected. In our streamlined industrial world, however, an ear that has learned to be alert to overtone structures (perhaps in some other musical cultures) is inevitably confronted sooner or later with the chromatic division of the octave in Western contemporary tunings, as well as their diatonic core idea. How does it adapt and process the discrepancy?

Blues and, by extension, bebop share a centralized tonality. Modulatory deviations in the B part of a jazz chorus, known as the bridge, can disguise but not suppress this concept (see also Berliner 1994: 76–88). Here bebop stands at the opposite end of the spectrum from the bitonal and atonal experiments in Western art-composed music during the first half of the twentieth century. Bebop is decisively tonal, and so are its successors, hard bop and free jazz. A clue to decoding the internal structure of some cluster chords in jazz can be found in the fact that in the buildup of such a column, the "banal" harmonics are often left out. From what is left out we can reconstruct the fundamental. Notes representing partials 8, 10, and 12, for example, are often omitted. However, because partials-derived pitch patterns can only be objectified approximately on a piano or guitar, the analysis of such chords boils down to this question: Which note represents which partial? In the key of C over the tonic chord, partial 7 can be rendered as b♭, although it is 31 cents lower than the tempered value; partial 9 at 204 cents is virtually identical with a d, while partial 11 at 551 cents is rendered as f♯ on a piano, and partial 13 (at 840 cents) as a♭. Remarkably, when jazz pianists began to lay out cluster chords, they also often followed the order of partials in the natural harmonic series, from bass to treble, thereby revealing the underlying (often unconscious) auditory basis. The fact that the banal partials in the series tend to be omitted, unless the fundamental is to be reinforced, is familiar to me from the tunings of *mangwilo* and other log xylophones in the northern Moçambique cultural area. Thus, some of the cluster chords in bebop are simply the nearest possible representations of selected partials from the natural harmonic series, extended high up. The famous flatted fifth in bebop represents partial 11; to make that clear, it is often struck together with its fundamental, for example, f♯ with c, or g with c♯ to be resolved into c. The accurate intonation of the bebop flatted fifth would be 551 cents; the approximation played on a piano is at 600 cents. The C⁺¹¹ chord in its common layout on a piano by bebop musicians plainly reveals its partials-derived structure (see Fig. 9.24).

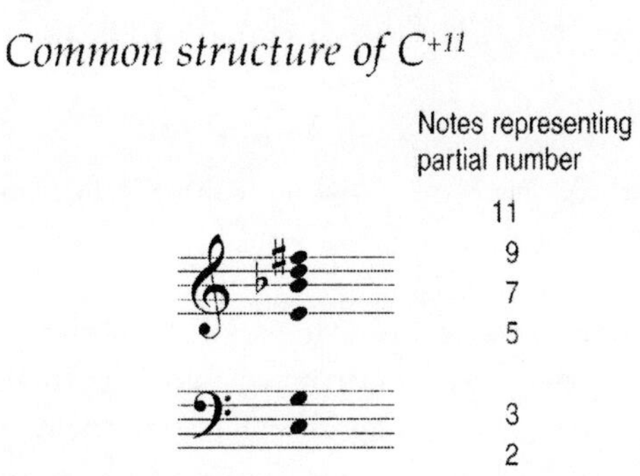

Common structure of C^{+11}

Notes representing
partial number

11
9
7
5

3
2

Fig. 9.24. Common structure of C⁺¹¹.

An intriguing question relating to audio-psychology arises here: If the jazz "flatted fifth" really derives from a representation of partial 11 of the harmonic series—falling halfway between f and f♯—why is it not represented by f? The answer is this: Since the b♭ blue note representing partial 7 sounds 31 cents too sharp on the piano, the note representing partial 11 on the piano must also be raised. Expressed in cents the interval from b♭ to f♯ on the piano is 800 cents; if the latter were replaced by f it would only be 700 cents, a perfect fifth. But the interval between partials 7 and 11 of the harmonic series makes 231 + 551 = 782 cents. That is very close to the 800 cents, and the ear accepts that interval on the piano as representative.

A quite different act, cognitively, is to shift such partials-based harmonic columns to other pitch levels, thereby creating progressions. In bebop, they are often shifted by a semitone, which recalls the Mpyɛmɔ multipart example discussed earlier (see Fig. 9.1). Bebop pianists had a liking for such progressions.

A very common ending progression is demonstrated in Thelonious Monk's "52nd Street Theme," in a transcription by Frank Paparelli (Monk 1948). "52nd Street Theme" may not testify to Monk's well-known and much-admired idiosyncrasies as a composer and pianist—his wife once described his "marvelous sense of withdrawal"—but I am not concerned here so much with the individual genius of bop and bop-related musicians of the 1940s as with typical pathways they all walked from time to time, revealing the hidden African matrices.

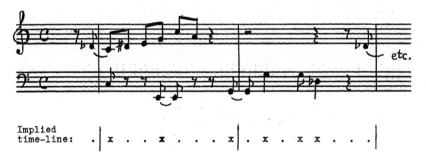

Fig. 9.25. Extract from Thelonious Monk's "52nd Street Theme," transcribed by author.

"52nd Street Theme" is based on a swing-style riff motive in call and response with the pianist's left-hand bass constructed upon the rhythm of an African timeline (see Fig. 9.25). The closing chords of the theme (measures 15–16) progress in the left-hand bass in a major triad from d♭ to c, a semitone downward. But in the right-hand part, there is an augmented chord b-e♭-g apparently "resolving" into a flatted-fifth chord with the tones b♭-f♯-c (see Fig. 9.26). What sense does this make? Some observers might be misled and postulate "bitonality"—until one discovers the matrix. Both combined chords in this progression represent columns of harmonics, incorporating representations of upper partials; the first column with fundamental d♭ resolves into a second column with fundamental c, finding a rest. Characteristically, the $D♭^{+11}$ chord includes representations of partials 2, 3, 5, 7, 9, and 11, suppressing the banal, even-numbered partials 4, 6, 8, and 12, which would only duplicate lower ones. And the tonic chord at the end—and this is what it is—nominally C^{+11}, includes its own partials 2, 3, 5, 7, 11, and also 16, this last note reinforcing its fundamental.

Fig. 9.26. Analysis of Monk's "52nd Street Theme," measures 15–16.

As if there were still doubts to be removed, the progression is then stripped of all harmonic embellishment and (in measure 16) reduced to its core idea (see Fig. 9.27), which is the final resolution.

Fig. 9.27.

Thanks to European national TV from the late 1950s and through the 1960s, when television stations were government-owned and therefore not dependent on revenue from advertising, visiting American jazz musicians were extensively filmed on stage. European TV archives contain invaluable materials on jazz history. From 2006 on these films have become increasingly available for home-viewing on DVDs issued in the series *Jazz Icons* (Reelin' in the Years Productions, www.jazzicons.com). There are gems of jazz history that can now be viewed, for example *Sarah Vaughan Live in '58 & '64* with concerts she gave with her group in Sweden and Holland. And there is also a unique DVD document of *Thelonious Monk Live in '66* with concerts he gave in Norway and Denmark. The shots contain full performances with his group (Charlie Rouse on tenor saxophone, Larry Gales on bass, and Ben Riley on drums) of some of his most remarkable compositions and adaptations: "Lulu's Back in Town" (two versions played on two different occasions to be compared), "Blue Monk," "'Round Midnight," "Don't Blame Me," and the celebrated "Epistrophy."

Fig. 9.28. Thelonious Monk. Courtesy
of the Institute of Jazz Studies, Rutgers
University Libraries.

Each DVD in the series is accompanied by an informative booklet, the one
on Monk written by Don Sickler, who is arranger and trumpet player in Ben
Riley's Monk Legacy Septet. Writing about Monk's piano playing, Sickler recalls
his first encounter with him in New York:

> I didn't get to New York until I was 23, and it wasn't until I got a chance to see Monk
> performing live in New York City that it really hit me as to why his music was so
> unique. In person, I saw that he played the piano very differently than I had ever
> seen it played before. He attacked practically every note, mostly with an unorthodox
> flat finger approach, maybe better described as a percussive stiff finger method on
> the keyboard. Sometimes he would even cross hands (left over right), attacking his
> melody notes usually with either a stiff first or second finger of his left hand, while
> his right hand fingers comped the sparse harmonic elements. . . .
>
> Another major difference in Monk's music is his harmonic approach. Most
> often, Monk plays very open harmony. There is no clutter inside Monk's chords. For
> example, he often leaves the third (and fifth) out of his dominant seventh chords, play-
> ing just the root and seventh of the chord. If you are not a musician, ask any pianist, or
> any musician with knowledge of the piano keyboard, to play just two notes—the root
> and the minor seventh (otherwise known as the dominant seventh) of any chord. This
> is a common Monk dominant seventh voicing. When Monk wants a thicker dominant
> sound, instead of adding the conventional third or fifth, he will leave those out, and

instead, make a three-note chord by adding only the flat nine. What a different harmonic concept this must have been back in the 1940s when people first heard Monk. To further illustrate the concept, play a Monk C7 (flat 9) chord—a C with added upper notes B flat and D flat. That is a true Monkism, one of his favorite dominant seventh chord usages. If you do the normal thing and add the third (E), or the fifth (G), to this chord of course it will harmonically make that same chord, a C7 (flat 9) chord, but it won't sound like Monk and it loses that Monk edge. (Sickler 2006: 8–9)

The style of body movement displayed by Monk is familiar to those of us who have worked with xylophone players in southeast Africa, for example, including the crossing of hands (in xylophone styles, the crossing of the playing sticks), and also the different weight given to individual notes. Without direct contact with the art of xylophone players on another continent, thousands of miles away, Monk recreates some of their behavior and techniques because of a learned, specific approach to movement and attack transmitted through generations within the United States. That this includes his harmonic experimentation should be of no surprise. "Open harmony" is common precisely in traditions of the region mentioned earlier, e.g., *valimba* xylophone music with equiheptatonic tuning.

In Monk I see a tendency to recreate a likeness of equiheptatonic passages, even chords, besides other simultaneous sounds that evoke representations of remote partials (see above). I have no other explanation for Monk's aesthetic delight in the use of a C⁷ flat 9 chord, reduced to a basic c with added upper notes b♭ and d♭, as described by Sickler. Why was this so attractive to him? Probably not just because it is unusual and slightly dissonant, but because it exemplifies a system. That system is not based on the concept of a "dominant function" of the C⁷, as Sickler suggests. If Monk had not lowered the ninth, the b♭ and d together would form a major third fitting into a partials-based system. By lowering the d to d♭, however, and thinking of the b♭ as a blue note representing the 7th partial of the harmonic series over fundamental C, i.e., an interval of 969 cents (31 cents lower than the tempered b♭ on the piano), he creates the illusion of an equiheptatonic third between the two notes, at 1300 minus 969 cents = 331 cents. That value is very close to the equiheptatonic neutral third of 342.8 cents.

The hidden model behind passages such as the one in Figure 9.29 is progressions as played on a xylophone, not a dominant into tonic resolution. That is why Monk would abstain from including an e (leading note) in the first chord.

Fig. 9.29.

Modern jazz is full of intended ambiguities and auditory puzzles. The use of auditory illusion effects is, by the way, another important heritage from African music (Kubik 2010: II: 107–30). The maize-pounding woman in the Zambezi Valley, Fainesi, has shown us how easily a musical mind grown up in an equiheptatonic environment can arrive at representing its harmonic progressions chromatically. I think that this was also taking place in bebop and that, in the 1940s, patterns of auditory perception linked historically to African equiheptatonic systems were activated through a variety of stimuli in the small avant-garde circle of bebop musicians who were trying to find "something else." Here, we need not assume that artists always consciously decide on their own creations. Much simply happens. Because the equiheptatonic tones are not found on a Western piano, someone with an idea or aesthetic tendency in that direction—however vague it may be in its initial stages—will seek intuitively to represent those "in-between" pitch values by alternatives, for example, "double strokes" of neighboring keys or pitch alterations. Chord extensions and pitch substitutions (altered chords) created the sort of ambiguity that was needed to dismantle the exclusive reign of the Western tonal system. Bebop musicians eliminated Western-style functional harmony in their music while retaining the strong central tonality of the blues as a basis for drawing upon various African matrices. While, for an outside observer, the harmonic innovations in bebop would appear to be inspired by experiences in Western "serious" music, from Claude Debussy to Arnold Schönberg, such a scheme cannot be sustained without reservations, by the evidence from a cognitive approach. Debussy did have some influence on jazz, and it is also true that Duke Ellington adopted and reinterpreted some harmonic devices in European contemporary music. West Coast jazz would run into such debts, as would several forms of cool jazz. But bebop has few such debts in the sense of direct borrowings. On the contrary, ideologically, bebop was a strong statement of rejection of any kind of eclecticism, propelled by a desire to activate something deeply buried in self. Bebop then revived tonal-harmonic ideas transmitted through the blues and reconstructed and expanded others in a basically non-Western harmonic approach. The ultimate significance of all this is that the experiments in jazz during the 1940s brought back to African American music several structural principles and techniques rooted in African traditions.

The Earliest Jazz

It can be shown by experiment that, for someone who has grown up exclusively within African musical traditions and would want to play jazz or is encouraged to do so, the greatest initial challenge is to be found not in the areas of harmony or melodic structure and variation but in form. That is where jazz is intrinsically different from African music. Most African music is constructed within cycles; sometimes they are quite long, as for example in *kukuwa* initiation songs in eastern Angola (Kubik 1998b; Tsukada 1990), or in some *valimba* xylophone playing in the Shire/Zambezi Valley, southeast Africa, e.g., by Johnny Suze (see Fig. 9.23); but more often they are relatively short, embracing twenty-four, thirty-two, thirty-six, or forty-eight elementary pulse units within which various combinations of polyrhythm, multipart alignments, and variation find a terrain of expression.

Conversely, early jazz was characterized by the retention from European music of a wide panel of strophic and other long forms including their organization in multiple strains, as inherited from marching bands and other ensemble traditions of nineteenth-century popular European music. For African Americans in the post–Civil War era with opportunities of training for playing this music from notations, the challenge manifested itself from the moment they decided to depart slightly from strict reproduction of the scores. Would it be possible for African ideas about timbre, accent, variation, and melodic phrasing to be inserted into such strophic forms?

Many African Americans trained in the performance of European music were nevertheless cultural carriers of a memory of Afrologic principles assimilated through enculturation in their families, or in peer groups, through auditory experience and kinemics, and even other channels of implicit transmission. They would be eager for small-scale experimentation. A melodic line would be changed a little; the combination of instrumental lines in a piece of marching music would be reinterpreted as a responsorial structure, with one or two trumpet or cornet players assuming the function of lead singers.

But an earlier solution to handling strophic forms, such as those inherited from ballads and other European song types, had already been found by blues singers along country roads, along the waterways of the Mississippi, and elsewhere; they would conceptualize a four-bar textline as divided into a vocal statement and an instrumental response, usually on guitar. The twelve-bar blues form was developed in this process, as a sequence of three leader (vocal)/chorus (instrumental) lines, with the singer's repetition of the first textline and the conclusion in the last line both being highlighted by the use of contrasting chords. This model turned out to be applicable to other strophic song forms as well, e.g., with sixteen or thirty-two bars, and eventually also to multi-strain compositions played in bands. As explained earlier, the twelve-bar blues form must be understood as a structure, a three-line arrangement of a basic African responsorial form idea, and separated in analysis from other variables in the blues, such as chord progressions and barlines that are secondary additions.

Solo blues singers, self-accompanying with guitar, were faithful to the form but had not always developed cycle awareness in terms of measures or single beat-units. They would easily shorten a cycle to eleven bars on the guitar, or skip or extend the form by one or two beats, without any discomfort. There are many examples of recordings of blues singers where this happens, too numerous to be cited here. Many solo blues singers actually had a weak cycle awareness in terms of measures or beat-units.

In an ensemble, on the other hand, there has to be agreement on standard lengths between the performers, in order to make it all function. No aspiring jazz musician can afford to be weak at chorus awareness with all the involved chord changes. This is why we say that in these musical cultures there are three simultaneously operating interlaced levels of timing: the elementary pulsation, the reference or dance beat, and the cycle, together forming an indispensable subjective grid in performers of both African music and jazz (Kubik 2010: II: 31–52).

Around 1900 internalization of the call-and-response schema by musicians, from spirituals, blues, and other African American genres, contributed to the development of functional polyphony in emerging New Orleans jazz bands, with the trumpet taking up lead-singer function; the trombone that of "rolling out the carpet" for the leader with initiatory glides and sometimes a powerful deep-voiced affirmative chorus response; and the clarinet taking up responsorial, embellishing (arpeggio) and chorus "rounding-off" functions in relationship to the trumpet's voice lines. Other polyphonic tricks would be used, such as inserting melodic cross rhythms that would interlock with the trumpet, or inserting a riff phrase or a variant contrasting with the trumpet's main theme. Clarinet and trombone would also often shift their phrases polyrhythmically against the trumpet player's accent lines. Sometimes the clarinet would "harmonize" a phrase played by the trumpet, duplicating it a third above, as happens in many African heptatonic song traditions.

New Orleans polyphony, from the moment it embarked on an Africa-based reinterpretation of the voice lines in a marching band, drew on several methods and techniques of heterorhythmic and polyrhythmic combination inherited from organizational principles in various styles of African music. Besides the ubiquitous responsorial schema to be followed by both clarinet and trombone at different pitch levels and with different fluidity, some organizational principles came even from the functional schema in three-drum sets found in some kinds of African music.

In a wonderful recording at the home of clarinetist George Lewis in New Orleans, on May 14, 1945, of a collective improvisation called "Slow Drag's Boogie Woogie" to celebrate the art of bass player Slow Drag Pavageau and the entire rhythm section of the George Lewis Band, Bunk Johnson decided to launch a riff across the twelve-bar blues form, abandoning his leader function temporarily. Although this recording really is "modern" or "revival" New Orleans jazz of the 1940s like the Stuyvesant Casino recordings in New York, and Bunk most definitely imitates a riff as in big band swing, there is no reason to assume that a cornet or trumpet player around 1900 would not also have changed roles sometimes and inserted a stomp pattern or a riff into the interplay by his partners. This emphasizes that no one in New Orleans functional polyphony was nailed down for good to a specific function. In the absence of a trumpet, or when the trumpet paused for a chorus, the clarinet would take over and often take up the theme.

Many themes in New Orleans jazz were first presented in unison with heterophony, i.e., the simultaneous playing of variants of a melody by trumpet, clarinet, and trombone, before the group would split into their conventional roles and functions in the next chorus. For comparison, in African traditions heterophony is particularly prevalent in styles that are devoid of any use of harmony, marked as "unison singing" in A. M. Jones's (1959) "harmony map." Jones distinguished between indigenous African and Arab-influenced unison styles. In such traditions themes are presented either in unison, or in unison plus octaves, with vocal intonation or instrumental tunings slightly divergent to create a friction effect. Sometimes this music sounds harsh, especially the Arab/Islamic-influenced style, and the friction sound may be exaggerated by heterophony in minute variations or voice fluctuations. There are many recorded examples. For listening and study I would recommend one I made in 1963 of the *algeita* (oboe) court music ensemble, with six double-headed snare drums (*ganga*) of the Lamido (Fulɓe ruler) of Toungo in northeastern Nigeria (track 19, CD accompanying the Italian edition of Kubik 1999a [2007]). Heterophony in jazz as a principle of theme presentation can be seen as a direct extension of some West African savannah musical styles, such as court music of the Fulɓe and Hausa rulers in Nigeria and northern Cameroon.

There are many examples from New Orleans jazz in which a theme is presented by trumpet, trombone, and clarinet in heterophony, each acting within the constraints of its own tonal range, the trombone often an octave lower. Everyone among the readers will have their own favorite examples; therefore I want to mention just one recording, which I happened to listen to while writing these pages: Myrtle Jones's (vocal) "My Life Will Be Sweeter Some Day" with the Bunk Johnson Band, recorded in New Orleans, July 31, 1944.

Historically, there are several culture-geographical and sociological factors that had an influence upon which of the structural characteristics of African music would become factors in the shaping of African American genres. Contrary to a widespread popular assumption, the most formative African strands in the confluence leading to jazz in New Orleans cannot be traced to Congo Square culture, because Congo Square did not become a model for young African Americans of the post–Civil War generation after 1865. By the next generation, which was directly involved in the rise of jazz, the memory of Congo Square was largely erased; nevertheless, it existed underground, and some of it resurfaced in later developments (see also the section "Congo Square and jazz" in chapter 2).

In the post–Civil War era the United States had become a large country; the socio-cultural situation varied considerably from place to place, and in some locations it radically changed at the rate of every ten years, the time it takes approximately for a new generation to come up and impose its tastes and fashions upon others. Thereafter, when alternative ways have turned "mainstream," shedding their ethnic valence, they tend to decay quickly and begin to be considered old-fashioned, "corny," or whatever term expressing derision is in vogue. In the 1890s one African American cultural expression had come to the forefront, constantly gaining terrain: the ragtime/jig piano complex, developed from the earlier street banjo culture. Ragtime eventually received important encouragement off-stage at the 1893 World's Columbian Exposition in Chicago, and soon thereafter it appeared in sheet music adaptations. (Heide 2004–2005).

"Music" was then what was written. The very term had adopted the meaning of what otherwise is called a score. Anything else was not music. For young people with ambitions, the attraction would be in the glittery instruments of, for example, a marching band, or in the sounds of the upright piano in some homes, such as was bought for the adolescent Scott Joplin, besides other contemporaneous emblems of social ascent.

Opportunities for learning brass and reed instruments as well as piano were abundant, provided one could pay for it or was lucky to find a sponsor, even on plantations. As an example one can mention the work of James Brown Humphrey, the itinerant African American teacher who used Otto Langey method books to train brass band musicians on rural plantations from ca. 1880 until 1915. We know from oral testimony that some of his students later became jazz musicians, such as Jim Robinson, the Morgan brothers, Chris Kelly, Burke Stevenson, Oscar "Chicken" Henry, and others.

Those who had a chance of instruction were keen on getting access to the once inaccessible other cultural world. This first generation in the new transculturation process could be called the foster generation, a term applied by Jahnheinz Jahn in his book *Muntu* (1958) to the authors of early developments of post-colonial literature in Africa who were willing learners of the culture that claimed superiority. The next generation would not be so subservient and rather would begin to subvert the dominant culture. However, it must not be overlooked that even parallel to the foster generation there was a majority that did not attempt a total crossover. They had internalized the upper-class values, but for various reasons chose to preserve a stronger ethnic identity.

One of the many musical traditions in New Orleans that became accessible to this middle stratum in the sociology of southern African Americans was marching music. It would soon be reconfigured to become an important strand in the confluence leading to the rise of new forms of New Orleans dance music, incorporating ragtime, blues, and other genres, which would later be summarized as jazz. Some individuals, gifted with an excellent imitative memory, and not only musicians from Uptown, began to take shortcuts in performance and play music from the scores in front of them without actually looking at the notations. They had already memorized everything. Gradually, Afrologic principles crept in, introducing timbre variations and shifted accents that in any case were impossible to write down: pitch modification that sounded bluesy, and a bit of off-beat phrasing of melodic lines, which made the steps of the marches less rigid, a little more swinging—processes that not only changed the music profoundly, but eventually gave it a new direction.

It would be wrong to see this as an exclusively ethnically based process, assuming that "the" African Americans or "the" Uptown musicians began to introduce Afrologic aesthetics and kinemics into European marching music. It was a more widespread phenomenon and also more individualistic, and in any case it was not by design. What probably happened was that among twenty, forty, fifty faithful performers of the music as written, there was one at a time who would begin to divert a little from established performance conventions, setting an example for others who noticed it, recognized some advantage for themselves in the new practice, and began to follow the example. Gradually, dissident ideas won. The new approach was also status-enhancing within the peer group for those who were sharing it. After 1902, Buddy Bolden reached such a legendary status in New Orleans that with just a call on his cornet he could easily divert a crowd from attending a performance by his notation-dependent rival John Robichaux. Bolden and others within the new stream would begin to use notations only as a helpful source to be consulted, if necessary, by their C-clarinet player, rather than play from them. For a variety of reasons I have explained earlier in this book, this rejection is also related to kinemic concepts inherited from African music. Like narratives of a folktale, the theme and its prevalent variations would be memorized and then modified a bit from performance to performance, in the manner an African storyteller modifies his orature and even a story's plot. This promoted the creation of a musical culture in New Orleans in which ensemble performance would be based on memorized outlines of a theme and its instrumental parts, serving as a recipe for personal creative elaboration by each of the interacting group members.

The increasing irrelevance of written pretexts in musical performance also led to a phenomenon jazz shares with forms of African music that are socially informal, non-ritual, etc., and could be summarized as "popular music" in a historical sense. They have a wide variation margin between performances. "Buddy Bolden's Blues," for example, was recorded twice by Jelly Roll Morton (Hobson 2008) and later also once by Little Brother Montgomery (piano and voice) (cf. Heide 1970). The difference between these versions testifies to the margin of variation that was tolerated in a musical piece by audiences. It corresponds with a similar margin of acceptance in African popular songs that were performed by many different musicians. In southeastern Angola in 1965, I repeatedly recorded a popular song called "Manguchata kumufweta" in Cokwe language from many Cokwe- and Lucazi-speaking young men with *likembe*, a box-resonated lamellophone. The instruments were often constructed by the performers themselves and had a recognizable variation margin in their timbre depending on many factors, such as the size of the iron lamellae, the materials used, the type of buzzers, the size of the resonator, and so on. Presentation of the song by the different artists was also highly variant, and yet everyone recognized it, even without the words, from the instrumental performance alone. So there is a clear margin for permissible variation, as there are also boundaries. For comparison, Little Brother Montgomery's version of "Buddy Bolden's Blues" seems to circumvent the third blue note, F♯ over C, prominent in Jelly Roll Morton's piano version, and yet the song is recognizably the same.

A similar margin of variation is detectable even in those cases in which an artist records the same song on different occasions. "Make Me a Pallet on the Floor" is one of the earliest blues in New Orleans jazz, and it probably already was part of the repertoire of the Buddy Bolden Band in the late 1890s, before his valve trombone player Willie Cornish left for the Spanish-American War of 1898. Bunk Johnson, after he was rediscovered in 1938, recorded it on four occasions: a) February 2, 1942, in his home in New Iberia, Louisiana; b) June 11, 1942, with Bunk Johnson's Original Superior Band, at Gruenewald's Music Store, New Orleans; c) May 7, 1943, several times with pianist Bertha Gonsoulin at her home in San Francisco; d) May 15, 1945, at George Lewis's home in New Orleans. All these versions are remarkably different, in the chords for accompaniment as used by different pianists, but also in Bunk's rendering of the theme on trumpet and its variations. And yet, within this permissible span of variants, the song is clearly identifiable. That is also a basic aim in Bunk's renderings.

In New Orleans, one strand in the confluence leading to early forms of jazz was the changes taking place in the brass band culture. Several principles in multipart structuring of ultimately African provenance seem to have been revived or reinvented precisely in the marching music environment. They were tried out there, and—with the associated brass and reed instruments—would become central to early jazz.

Our tragedy today is that we have no original recordings from the 1890s and early 1900s to listen to. Therefore, anything we infer can easily be brushed away as speculation. And yet, personally I think that the best approximation to early jazz around 1900, as played with standard instruments partly taken over from marching bands, is what Bunk Johnson attempted to put on stage in 1942 upon request by Bill Russell and others, whose primary interest was the early history of jazz. I can think of no better examples to discover how exactly polyphony and heterophony were negotiated in an early New Orleans jazz band than the attempted reconstructions by Bunk's Superior Band.

One indication that the intention was serious, as far as one can get in collaboration with personnel born twenty to thirty years later, is that among twenty-one or twenty-two pieces they recorded on two occasions there are songs in complex multi-strain form that Bunk would never be able to record again. Why? Because 1940s New Orleans musicians were not very keen on following him on a historical time trip that would require a lot of work and learning, practicing a complex repertoire. For his partners it was easier to stick to their current repertoire of pieces that had an enthusiastic audience locally such as "Ice Cream," "San Jacinto Stomp," "Just a Closer Walk with Thee"—the kind of repertoire Bunk played with the group in 1945 in New York at the Stuyvesant Casino.

In the first session on June 11, 1942, at Gruenewald's Music Store, the personnel included Jim Robinson (tb), George Lewis (cl), Walter Decou (p), Lawrence Marrero (bj), Austin Young (b), and Ernest Rogers (d). It features the formidable "Moose March" and also William H. Tyers's 1911 composition "Panama," besides a great number of New Orleans standards. But in the second session, which brings to light a different set of Bunk Johnson's remembered repertoire, the trombone player was replaced by Albert Warner, a brass band expert, which perhaps gave the band an even closer approximation to early jazz and allowed Bunk to introduce pieces that Warner played without difficulty. The bass and drum players were also replaced by Chester Zardis (b) and Edgar Mosley (d). In this second session on October 2, 1942, some rags and other pieces from Bunk's inherited repertoire were included that would also be recorded only on this occasion. This is why these first two recording sessions are such an important historical testimony to earliest forms of jazz, even if they are reconstructions. After all, which historical music is not? Mozart as played by our contemporaries is also reconstruction.

In Bunk's recordings one can study pieces of diverse background, some rags, some march-based music, some blues, etc., in minute detail, and learn how strophic and multi-strain forms of nineteenth-century popular European-originated music had been converted into a multipart system of interlacing instrumental voices, recreating and reinstalling a panel of polyphonic principles known from African musical traditions.

How do these voices interact? And what is the underlying concept? Apart from the conversion of parading drum rhythms into something more complex in early jazz, following the chosen song genre, blues, rags, etc., brass and reed instruments install a forum of conversation in their melodic interaction. This principle is also paramount in many ensembles of African music. The idea that instruments do not just play abstract melodic lines, but seem to talk to each other, respond, agree or disagree, even quarrel, is a deeply rooted concept in Africa. It derives from the general concept of verbalization as expressed also in mnemonics, something that is not restricted explicitly to tone languages such as I.A.4 (Kwa) languages, Yoruba, Ewe, Gã, Twi, etc. The same principle is present in the organization of some drumming, with a tripartite division of individual drums' functions as in the *nawansha* dance of northern Moçambique (Kubik 1999a: 108–9).

The interaction of the voices in Bunk's reconstructed style of early New Orleans jazz involving trumpet (or cornet), clarinet, and trombone, the so-called front line, can be understood that way, as a conversation between partners with different roles, functions, and specializations in the "community," the band, Accordingly, a number of multipart organizational principles seem to be inherited from African communal activities. Bunk's trumpet plays lead melodies, stating the subject of the conversation, with slight melodic variations that follow ideas of extension, substitution, occasional phrase shift, and accents in a patterned relationship with the harmonic scheme underlying the piece and the constant drum beats inherited from marching music. The B-flat clarinet alternates between different comments on the statements by the trumpet player; essentially, the clarinet draws upon a large panel of response patterns that are in a way similar to those used by a stringed instrument player accompanying his own voice lines, for example an East African itinerant singer, accompanying himself with a fiddle or board zither.

In New Orleans this role of the clarinet was probably the result of a merger between the system of voice/instrument interaction by itinerant musicians in Louisiana, blues singers and others accompanying themselves, and the clarinet's traditional function in a European-style brass band. Due to its broad tonal range including the registers of chalumeau, clarion, and clarinette, the clarinet in early jazz would tend to enjoy most of the improvisational liberties in the group, although in practice it also follows a strict framework for behavior, like everyone else in the group. No one may actually practice "free improvisation," but everyone proceeds from a prescripted set of possible interventions at appropriate moments of the conversation, with some freedom in phrasing and pattern development. At one point of an evolving theme the clarinet may insert a responsorial comment, confirming the trumpet's statement; at another it may paraphrase or contradict it. More than the trumpet with its often blues-based tonality in the presentation of a theme, the clarinet, however, tends to follow the functional-harmonic system of the European chords in a song, often breaking a chord into arpeggio. At other points, both clarinet and trombone may simultaneously interfere with the trumpet's lead melody, "disagree" with its statement in the manner one interrupts somebody's speech, filling in a rhythmically contrasting pattern, even before the trumpet player has ended his melodic phrase.

My description of the three instruments' interaction in Bunk's reconstructed early New Orleans jazz as a conversation is in itself an indirect acknowledgment of an important Africa-derived concept that survives in jazz: that the instrumental interaction is like a talk between people, and that melodic lines and their variations are conceptualized as somehow verbalized, not only in obvious demonstrations such as by the celebrated scat-singing duo of Louis Armstrong and Ella Fitzgerald (cf. "Stomping at the Savoy" Ella and Louis Armstrong, Verve MGV 4017 Matrix no. 21138–1, recorded July 23, 1957).

This conversational background also explains why accents can fall on any division of the drum beat, mostly off-beat due to the melodies' speech-line structure, because in speech, especially in African languages, there are morae and syllables with standard timing; one mora corresponds with one elementary pulse-unit in music. This affects phrase formation particularly by the trumpet and the clarinet. In a different way it also applies to the trombone, which draws on a broad panel of functions, changing between them; playing bass lines, reinforcing them, playing fill-ins, rhythmic variations with a "grandfather's voice," etc. The relationship of the three instruments with each other is best described as three people with different voice ranges talking to each other, one having leadership function, deciding about the topic (theme) to be discussed, the others contributing their views and supplementing the leader's statements.

The choices available to the participating instruments also depend on those instruments' technical capabilities and range of tones. The trumpet as leader operates in the middle range; the trombone at a lower voice range (in Africa one would say with a "bigger" voice) can choose between two basic functions. This is demonstrated by comparing the styles of Jim Robinson, who was obviously a conversationist in his playing and would even argue with the leader, with Albert Warner, who stuck to the other basic function of trombone in early jazz: to provide a fundament of basic notes, tonal-harmonic "pillars" that support the others, reminding them of ensuing chord changes. Warner's style was closely related to the trombone's function in marching music.

Preference for certain makes of musical instruments was also steered in part, if only unconsciously, by Africa-related aesthetics and technical and other considerations. The cornet as a lead instrument was preferred to the trumpet in early New Orleans jazz. It has a softer timbre and as such is more supple as a conversational partner of the two other instruments of different voice range, all three of equal standing like members of a family, but each with a different function. Later the cornet gave way to the trumpet, when in the 1920s, macho-style behavior and showbiz began to estrange the leader from the "family," raising the trumpet player to stardom and thereby isolate him and reduce the others from the role of partners to sidemen.

For reasons of timbre and aesthetics, the choice of Albert system clarinets over Boehm system instruments can be explained in a similar manner. Albert system clarinets, named after the Brussels maker Eugène Albert (1816–1890) are different in bore, mouthpiece, and reed from later models. They seem to have a "deeper" timbre quality. The choice was perhaps mainly motivated more by the sound spectrum than by differences in mechanics. In all clarinets the tone color is determined largely by the virtual absence of even-numbered partials of the harmonic series. But it is also influenced by the choice of materials for construction (normally, African blackwood is most suitable), and by many other factors such as type of reed, distance of the reed from the slot-like opening of the mouthpiece, and choice of embouchure of the player. Albert system clarinets tend to have a sound spectrum that resonates more deeply and fully than other types, and sub-jectively, they seem to combine favorably with cornet or "flügelhorn" and trom-bone. What I mean is perhaps best demonstrated if one compares the recordings George Lewis made in the 1940s using his old clarinets, and then in the 1960s on European concert tours playing instruments of contemporary make. One can also compare the sound of another important New Orleans clarinetist, Albert Burbank, recorded in 1949, with his contemporaries, e.g., Benny Goodman, Artie Shaw, or Woody Herman—very different sound worlds. A recent "muta-tion leap" is the modern jazz clarinet played by Don Byron, exclusively using Buf-fet clarinets and Vandoren reeds (cf. Don Byron, *ivey-divey*, CD, recorded May 23–24, 2004).

There was one more opportunity for Bunk to convey his two basic messages to us as his legacy: (a) the value of reconstructions of music he had played with Buddy Bolden and others, in marching bands, and in his own band during the first decade of the twentieth century; (b) his composers' right to adapt contem-porary popular song titles (of the 1940s) within his own style.

Bunk did not allow critics to reduce him to a "canned" zombie of early jazz, mysteriously revived. He insisted on being acknowledged as a contemporary art-ist who would creatively merge the past with the present. This was the essence of his message in the recordings for his *Last Testament*, December 23–26, 1947 (Delmark DD 225), with musicians who were willing to learn from him, follow-ing his instructions.

Four of these recordings—"Hilarity Rag," "Kinklets," "That Teasing Rag" and "The Entertainer"—give us a fairly authentic picture of the style of music he cherished in the early twentieth century. Composed by Arthur Marshall, "Kin-klet" (1906) is probably the most successful example. "The Entertainer" is well arranged, but has one performance flaw: clarinetist Garvin Bushell's timbre and phrasings belong definitely to another era. But generally, Bunk's choice of co-performers was a lucky undertaking. Ed Cuffee on trombone and the others are doing their best in helping reconstruct the music Bunk had in mind.

One can compare these last recordings with the first in New Orleans, 1942, when Bunk Johnson had an initial magic spell over the New Orleans musicians who then were trying to live up to his expectations, even embarking on titles they were not familiar with. Both attempts at reconstruction of the music Bunk had played in the early 1900s overwhelmingly demonstrate principles of functional polyphony, variation techniques, etc., inherited from various forms of African music that Bunk could not have known but that had survived transatlantically in some coded, abstract form. The innovation of it all is that these principles were successfully implanted into nineteenth-century European popular forms of music with customary chord changes and multi-strain arrangements. But even the form and the chord changes were in part also reinterpreted: the form due to a line-by-line leader/chorus approach in some pieces, though instrumentalized; the chord changes by often circumnavigating them in the melodic variations of the front-line instruments, particularly the trumpet following blues tonality in developing its themes.

SUMMARY AND CONCLUSIONS

For a variety of reasons, some of them technical, the original computer-typed manuscript had to be split into two separate books. With 543 pages and a typeface large enough for both older and younger eyes to read, the original volume appeared to be "overweight."

I realized, however, that radical dietetics can also be dangerous, because it tends to eliminate precious information that kindles interest in the reader and may stimulate ideas for additional research. Therefore, I decided upon a minimally invasive procedure, splitting the overweight person into two.

The present volume, *Jazz Transatlantic I*, focuses on the African undercurrent in the twentieth-century jazz culture, navigating through transatlantic history, sociolinguistics, kinemics, musicology, and the biographical study of personalities in jazz.

Jazz Transatlantic II concentrates on the African "return trip": how various forms of jazz from the period of the Swing Era to bebop and post-bop became an inspiration to a minority of creative musicians in Africa after World War II, into the 1970s, and later; and how this feedback was processed into something that now stands as an indelible part of a universal jazz history.

I am trying to take the reader on a multi-channel trip through history, learning about patterns of change in people's culture-historical environment and the arts. This necessarily entails a broader strategy than merely looking for African "traits" or Africanisms in jazz and some other, related forms of African American music. We engage with methods and concepts drawn from linguistics, cognitional studies, psychology, and more, besides musicology and culture history, resulting in the unfolding of a wide range of subjects for discussion: spirituality, magic and sorcery, kinemics, Africa-based ideas in harmony, and multipart patterns in jazz, etc.

All this evolves from our theoretical awareness of interconnectedness, transcending the construction of dichotomies, as we move forward to a more balanced, multilinear interpretation of processes of cultural interaction and change. Within the confines of our topic we investigate historical strands leading to musical phenomena transatlantically, and their background in various parts of Africa. Here, however we have to limit ourselves geographically, while not neglecting strands that lead to other continents. Although I do not use currently fashionable terms such as "creolization," let alone "hybridism," I am fully aware of the intricacies and different outcomes of processes of transculturation (to use Fernando Ortiz's term).

In contrast to conventional jazz histories, which tend to focus on well-delineated topics, queries and sets of data, my option has been to pursue a methodology of branching out, as if on a field research trip. Like the young Japanese art student in Akira Kurosawa's celebrated film *Dreams* (1990) who walks through landscapes painted by Vincent Van Gogh, I try to walk with you to meet creative individuals, and learn about their destinies, achievements, fears, and transformations in the context of culture history as an interlaced framework.

BIBLIOGRAPHY

Abbott, Lynn
1999 "Mr. E. Belfield Spriggins, First Man of Jazzology," *78 Quarterly* 10, November.
Abbott, Lynn, and Doug Seroff
2002 *Out of Sight: The Rise of African American Popular Music 1889–1895*. Jackson: University Press of Mississippi.
2007 *Ragged But Right: Black Traveling Shows, "Coon Songs," and the Dark Pathway to Blues and Jazz*. Jackson: University Press of Mississippi.
2008 "'They cert'ly sound Good to me': Sheet Music, Southern Vaudeville, and the Commercial Ascendancy of the Blues," in David Evans, ed., *Rambling on My Mind*. Urbana: University of Illinois Press, 49–104.
Adamo, Giorgio
2008 "An 'African' perspective applied to the analysis of South Italian dances," in Regine Allgayer-Kaufmann and Michael Weber, eds., *African Perspectives: Pre-colonial History, Cultural Anthropology, and Ethnomusicology*. Frankfurt: Peter Lang, 49–70.
2012 "Music in the Body: Video Research in Central and Southern Malawi (2008–2011)," in Mitchel Strumpf, ed., *Readings in Ethnomusicology: A Collection of Papers Presented at Ethnomusicology Symposium 2012*. Department of Fine and Performing Arts, University of Dar es Salaam, 173–86.
Alberts, Arthur S., ed.
1950 *Tribal, Folk and Café Music of West Africa*. New York: Field Recordings.
Albrecht, Theodore
1979 "Julius Weiss. Scott Joplin's First Piano Teacher," *College Music Symposium* 19: 89–105.
2008 "African, autobiographical, and earlier operatic element in Scott Joplin's *Treemonisha*," in Allgayer-Kaufmann and Weber, eds., *African Perspectives: Pre-colonial History, Cultural Anthropology, and Ethnomusicology*. Frankfurt: Peter Lang, 215–40.
Allain, Hélène d'Aquin
1883 *Souvenirs d'Amerique et de France, par une Creole*. Paris: Bourguet-Calas.
Allgayer-Kaufmann, Regine, and Michael Weber, eds.
2008 *African Perspectives: Pre-colonial History, Cultural Anthropology, and Ethnomusicology*. Vergleichende Musikwissenschaft, Volume 5. Frankfurt am Main: Peter Lang.
Alpers, Edward A.
1975 *Ivory and Slaves in East-Central Africa: Changing Patterns of International Trade to the Later Nineteenth Century*. London: Heinemann.
Amagbenyō, Danhin
1989 "Das Fō-Königreich Dahomey" in Gerhard Kubik, *Musikgeschichte in Bildern: Westafrika*. Leipzig: Deutscher Verlag für Musik, 126–45.
Ambrosio, P. Antonio
1989 "O danço Congo S. Tomé, e as suas origens," paper presented at the *I Reunião de Arqueologia e História pré-Colonial*. Lisboa, 23–26 October 1989.

Ames, David W.

1973 "A Social-cultural View of Hausa Musical Activity," in W. L. D'Azevedo, ed., *The Traditional Artist in African Societies*. Bloomington: Indiana University Press, 128–61.

Anderson, Lois

1977 "The Entenga Tuned Drum Ensemble," in *Essays for a Humanist: An Offering to Klaus Wachsmann*. New York: Town House Press, 1–57.

1984 "Multipart relationships in xylophone and tuned-drum traditions in Buganda," *Selected Reports* 5: 120–44.

Anonymous

1917 "The Appeal of the Primitive Jazz," *Literary Digest* 55: 28–29, August 25.

1918a "Why 'Jazz' Sends Us Back to the Jungle," *Current Opinion* 65: 165, September.

1918b "Jass and Jassism," *Times-Picayune*, New Orleans, June 20.

1919a "Where the Word 'Jazz' Started," *Music Trade Review* 68/50, May 3.

1919b "Jazz Origin Again Discovered," *Music Trade Review* 68: 32–33, June 14.

1945 "Origin of Term Jazz," *Jazz Session* 8: 4–5, July–August.

1958 "It Comes Out Jazz," *Down Beat* 25: 10, May 29.

Anthony, Arthé Agnes

1978 *The Negro Community in New Orleans 1880–1920: An Oral History*. Dissertation. Irvine: University of California.

Armstrong, Louis

1954 *Satchmo: My Life in New Orleans*. Englewood Cliffs, NJ: Prentice-Hall.

Asbury, Herbert

1936 *French Quarter: An Informal History of the New Orleans Underworld*. New York: Alfred A. Knopf.

Ashforth, Alden

1985 "The Bolden Photo—One More Time," *Annual Review of Jazz Studies* 3: 171–80.

Baily, John

1988 "ICTM Colloquium on Film and Video," *Yearbook for Traditional Music* 20: 193–98.

Baraka, Amiri (LeRoi Jones)

1963 *Blues People: The Negro Experience in White America and the Music That Developed from It*. New York: William Morrow.

1967 "Jazz and the White Critics," in *Black Music*, 11–20. New York: William Morrow.

Baraka, Amiri, and Amina Baraka

1987 *The Music: Reflections on Jazz and Blues*. New York: William Morrow.

Barth, Thomas

2013 *Wer Freud Ideen gab*. Eine systematische Untersuchung. Psychotherapiewissenschaft in Forschung, Profession und Kultur, Band 6. Münster: Waxmann.

Baskerville, John D.

1994 "Free Jazz: A Reflection of Black Power Ideology," *Journal of Black Studies* 24 (4): 484–97.

Béhague, Gerard H., ed.

1994 *Music and Black Ethnicity: The Caribbean and South America*. North-South Center, University of Miami. New Brunswick: Transaction.

Bender, Wolfgang

1991 *Sweet Mother: Modern African Music*. Foreword by John M. Chernoff. Chicago and London: University of Chicago Press.

2000 *Sweet Mother: Moderne afrikanische Musik*. Mit einem Beitrag zur Musik Äthiopiens von Andreas Wetter. Wuppertal: Edition Trickster im Peter Hammer Verlag (enlarged edition of 1985 book).

Bender, Wolfgang, Ed.

1991 *Chéri Samba*. München: Trickster.

Berlin, Edward A.

1980 *Ragtime: A Musical and Cultural History*. Berkeley: University of California Press.

Berliner, Paul F.

1994 *Thinking in Jazz: The Infinite Art of Improvisation*. Chicago: University of Chicago Press.

Bergquin-Duvallon, Pierre-Louis

1806 *Travels in Louisiana and the Floridas, in the Year 1802, Giving a Correct Picture of Those Countries*. Translated by John Davis. New York: I. Riley.

Bethel, Tom

1977 *George Lewis: A Jazzman from New Orleans*. Berkeley: University of California Press.

Bilby, Kenneth

2007 "The Legacy of Slavery and Emancipation: Jamaica in the Atlantic World," paper presented at *Ninth Annual Gilder Lehrman Center International Conference*. Chicago: Center for Black Music Research.

2011 "Africa's Creole Drum: The Gumbe as Vector and Signifier of Trans-Atlantic Creolization," in Robert Baron and Ana C. Cara, eds., *Creolization as Cultural Creativity*. Jackson: University of Mississippi Press.

Blesh, Rudi

1949 [1958] *Shining Trumpets: A History of Jazz*. London/New York: Cassell.

Blesh, Rudi, and Harriet Janis

1950 [1971] *They All Played Ragtime*. New York: Alfred A. Knopf.

Boone, Benjamin V.

1994 "A New Perspective on the Origin of the Blues and Blue Notes: A Documentation of Blues-like Speech," paper presented at the Conference on America's Blues Cultural and Heritage, University of North Florida, Jacksonville, April 1994. Unpublished manuscript.

Boone, Olga

1951 *Les Tambours du Congo Belge et du Ruanda-Urundi*. Annales du Musée du Congo Belge, Nouvelle Série in-4°. Tervuren: Musée du Congo Belge.

Borneman, Ernest

1969 "Jazz and the Creole Tradition," *Jazz Research* 1: 99–112.

Boroditzky, Lera

2011 "How Language Shapes Thought," *Scientific American*, February, 43–45.

Bowdich, Thomas Edward

1819 *Mission from Cape Coast Castle to Ashantee*. London: John Murray.

Braga, Lourenço

1961 *Umbanda é magia branca, Quimbanda magia negra*. Rio de Janeiro: Edições Spiker.

Breuer, Joseph, and Sigmund Freud

1895 *Studien über Hysterie*. Leipzig and Vienna: Franz Deuticke.

Brenner, Klaus-Peter

1997 *Chipendani und Mbira. Musikinstrumente, nicht begriffliche Mathematik und die Evolution der harmonischen Progressionen in der Musik der Shona in Zimbabwe*. Göttingen: Vandenhoeck & Ruprecht.

Brisbin, John Anthony

1990 "Jay McShann: The Intersection of Blues and Jazz," *Living Blues* 93, September/October: 31–33.

Brooks, Tim

2004 *Lost Sounds: Blacks and the Birth of the Recording Industry 1890–1919*. Chicago: University of Illinois Press.

Brown, Ernest D.

1991 "The Africa/African American idiom in music: Family resemblances in Black music," in Jacqueline Cogdell DjeDje, ed., *African Musicology Current Trends* (2). Los Angeles: African Studies Center, University of California, 115–34.

1994 "The Guitar and the *Mbira*: Resilience, Assimilation, and Pan-Africanism in Zimbabwean Music," *World of Music* 36 (2): 73–117.

Brothers, Thomas

1994 "Solo and Cycle in African American Jazz," *Musical Quarterly* 78: 479–509.

2006 *Louis Armstrong's New Orleans.* New York: W.W. Norton.

2014 *Louis Armstrong: Master of Modernism.* New York: W.W. Norton.

Browne, Kimasi L.

1999 "The Introduction as Signature: An Analysis of Western Musical Instruments in Chimurenga, Mbaqanga, and Motown," in Jacqueline Cogdell DjeDje, ed., *Turn Up the Volume! A Celebration of African Music.* Los Angeles: UCLA Fowler Museum of Cultural History, 220–29.

Browne, Kimasi L., and Jean N. Kidula, eds.

2013 *Resiliency and Distinction: Beliefs, Endurance, and Creativity in the Musical Arts of Continental and Diasporic Africa.* A Festschrift in Honor of Jacqueline Cogdell DjeDje. Point Richmond, CA: MRI Press.

Brunner, Natalie

2009 "Mulatu Astatke—Interview," *Die Bunte Zeitung* 5: 54–55.

Buel, J. W.

1882 *Metropolitan Life Unveiled, or the Mysteries and Miseries of America's Great Cities.* San Francisco.

Burgess, Richard James, ed.

2010 *Jazz—The Smithsonian Anthology.* Washington: Smithsonian Folkways Recordings.

Burns, Ralph (with Charles L. Granata)

2001 Liner notes to the CD *Woody Herman—Blowin' Up a Storm! The Columbia Years 1945–47.* New Jersey: Sony Music.

Cable, George Washington

1886a "The Dance in Place Congo," *Century Magazine* 31, February: 517–32.

1886b "Creole Slave Songs," *Century Magazine* 31, April: 807–28.

Carney, Judith A.

2001 *Black Rice: The African Origins of Rice Cultivation in the Americas.* Cambridge, MA: Harvard University Press.

Castagneto, Pierangelo, ed.

2007 *L'Oceano dei Suoni.* Migrazioni, musica e razze nella formazione delle società euroatlantiche, with CD. Torino: Otto Editore.

Cavin, Susan

1975 "Missing Women: On Voodoo Trail to Jazz," *Journal of Jazz Studies* 3 (1), Fall: 4–27.

Charlton, Blake

2013 "Redefining What It Means to Be Dyslexic," *International Herald Tribune*, May 24: 6.

Charters, Samuel

1963 *Jazz New Orleans, 1885–1963: An Index to the Negro Musician of New Orleans.* New York: Da Capo. Second edition, 1983.

2008 *A Trumpet Around the Corner: The Story of New Orleans Jazz.* Jackson: University Press of Mississippi.

Chambon, C. M.

1908 *In and Around the Old St. Louis Cathedral of New Orleans.* New Orleans: Phillippes Printery.

Chase, Gilbert

1987 *America's Music from the Pilgrims to the Present.* Urbana: University of Illinois Press.

Cieply, Michael

2007 "The Elusive Man Who May Have Invented Jazz," *International Herald Tribune*, April 24: 11.

Cleaver, Eldridge

1967 *Soul on Ice.* Introduction by Maxwell Gleismar. New York: McGraw-Hill.

Cockrell, Dale

1997 *Demons of Disorder: Early Blackface Minstrels and Their World.* New York: Cambridge University Press.

Cohen, Roger

2007 "What France Can Learn from Its 'Lost Province,'" *International Herald Tribune*, April 11: 2.

Collins, John

1986 *E. T. Mensah: The King of Highlife.* London: Off the Record Press.

1987 "Jazz Feedback to Africa," *American Music* 5 (2): 176–93.

Courlander, Harold

1960 *The Drum and the Hoe: Life and Lore of the Haitian People.* Berkeley: University of California Press.

Creecy, James

1860 *Scenes in the South.* Philadelphia: Lippincott.

Cuming, Fortescue

1810 *Sketches of a Tour to the Western Country.* Pittsburgh: Cramer, Spear and Eichbaum.

Curiel, Jonathan

2004 "Muslim Roots of the Blues," *San Francisco Chronicle,* August 15: E6.

Curtin, Philip D.

1969 *The Atlantic Slave Trade: A Census.* Madison: University of Wisconsin Press. 3rd edition 1973.

Dalzel, Archibald

1793 *The History of Dahomy, An inland kingdom of Africa. Compiled from authentic memoirs, with an introduction and notes.* London: T. Spilbury and Son.

Dauer, Alfons M.

1985 *Tradition afrikanischer Blasorchester und Entstehung des Jazz.* Beiträge zur Jazzforschung. Graz: Akademische Drück-und Verlagsanstalt.

Davidson, Basil (with F. K. Buah and J. F. A. Ajayi)

1965 *A History of West Africa 1000–1800.* The Growth of African Civilization (series). London: Longman.

Davidson, Basil (with J. E. F. Mhina and Bethwell A. Ogot)

1967 *East and Central Africa to the Late Nineteenth Century.* The Growth of African Civilization (series). London: Longman.

Davis, Martha Ellen

1994 "Music and Black Ethnicity in the Dominican Republic," in Gerard H. Béhague ed., *Music and Black Ethnicity: The Caribbean and South America.* Miami: University of Miami, North-South Center, 119–55.

Davis, Miles, with Quincey Troupe

1990 *Miles: The Autobiography.* New York: Simon & Schuster.

DeVeaux, Scott

1997 *The Birth of Bebop: A Social and Musical History.* Berkeley/Los Angeles/London: University of California Press.

Dias, Margot

1986 *Os instrumentos musicais de Moçambique.* Instituto de Investigação Cientifica Tropical. Lisboa: Centro de Antropologia Cultural.

DjeDje, Jacqueline Cogdell

1980 *Distribution of the One String Fiddle in West Africa*. Monograph Series in Ethnomusicology no. 2. Los Angeles: Program in Ethnomusicology, Department of Music, University of California.

1982 "The Concept of Patronage: An Examination of Hausa and Dagomba One-string Fiddle Traditions," *Journal of African Studies* 9 (3): 116–27.

1984 "The Interplay of Melodic Phrases: An Analysis of Dagomba and Hausa One-string Fiddle Music," *Selected Reports in Ethnomusicology* 5: 81–118.

2008 *Fiddling in West Africa: Touching the Spirit in Fulbe, Hausa, and Dagbamba Cultures*. Bloomington/Indianapolis: Indiana University Press.

DjeDje, Jacqueline Cogdell, ed.

1998 *Turn Up the Volume! A Celebration of African Music*. Los Angeles: UCLA Fowler Museum of Cultural History.

Djenda, Maurice

1968a "L'arc-en-terre des Gbaya-Bokoto," *African Music* 4 (2): 44–46.

1968b "Les pygmées de la Haute Sangha," *Geographica* 4 (14): 26.

1994 "De la croyance religieuse des Mpyɛmɔ̃. Precis d'une analyse en ethnologie de la religion," in August Schmidhofer and Dietrich Schüller, eds., *For Gerhard Kubik Festschrift* . . . Frankfurt am Main: Peter Lang, 73–82.

Elie, Louis E.

1944 *Histoire d'Haiti*. Port-au-Prince: Droits de Traduction, de Reproduction.

Epstein, Dena J.

1977 *Sinful Tunes and Spirituals: Black Folk Music to the Civil War*. Urbana: University of Illinois Press.

Erlmann, Veit, ed.

1991 *Populäre Musik in Afrika*. Veröffentlichungen des Museums für Völkerkunde Berlin. Neue Folge 53. Abteilung Musikethnologie VIII. Berlin: Staatliche Museen Preußischer Kulturbesitz.

Evans, David

1970 "Afro-American One-stringed Instruments," *Western Folklore* 29 (4): 229–45.

1971 *Tommy Johnson*. London: November Books.

1972 "Black Fife and Drum Music in Mississippi," *Mississippi Folklore Register* 6: 94–107.

1978a "African Elements in Twentieth-century United States Black Folk Music," *Jazz Research* 10: 85–110.

1978b "Structure and Meaning in the Folk Blues," in Jan H. Brunvand, ed., *The Study of American Folklore*. Rev. ed. New York: W. W. Norton, 421–47; 3rd ed. 1986: 563–93.

1978c *Afro-American Folk Music from Tate and Panola Counties, Mississippi*. LP with notes. AFS L67, Library of Congress.

1982 *Big Road Blues: Tradition and Creativity in the Folk Blues*. Berkeley: University of California Press.

1990 "African contributions to American Musical Heritage," *The World & I* 5 (1), January: 628–39.

1994 "The music of Eli Owens. African music in transition in southern Mississippi," in August Schmidhofer and Dietrich Schüller, eds., *For Gerhard Kubik. Festschrift* . . . Frankfurt: Peter Lang, 329–59.

1996 "Robert Johnson: Pact with the Devil," *Blues Revue* 21 (February/March), 22 (April/May), and 23 (June): 12–13.

1999 "The Reinterpretation of African Musical Instruments in the United States," in Isidore Okpewho, Carole Boyce Davies, and Ali A. Mazrui, eds., *The African Diaspora: African Origins and the New World Identities*. Bloomington: Indiana University Press, 379–90.

2000 "Musical Innovation in the Blues of Blind Lemon Jefferson," *Black Music Research Journal* 20 (1): 83–116.

2008 "From Bumble Bee Slim to Black Boy Shine: Nicknames of Blues Singers," in David Evans, ed., *Ramblin' on My Mind* . . . Urbana: University of Illinois Press.

2012 "Moses 'Doorman' Williams: One-String Master," in Dwight DeVane et al., liner notes to CD *Drop on Down in Florida*. Atlanta: Dust-to-Digital, 78–113.

Evans, David, ed.

2008 *Ramblin' on My Mind: New Perspectives on the Blues*. Urbana and Chicago: University of Illinois Press.

Evans, Freddi Williams

2011 *Congo Square: African Roots in New Orleans*. Lafayette: University of Louisiana at Lafayette Press.

Eyre, Banning, and Brett J. Bonner

1999 Liner notes to CD *Mali to Memphis: An African-American Odyssey* PUTU 145–2, Putumayo World Music.

Falceto, Francis

2001 *Abyssinie Swing: A Pictorial History of Modern Ethiopian Music*. Addis Ababa, Ethiopia: Shama Books.

2002 "Un siècle de musique moderne en Éthiopie (précédé d'une hypothese baroque)," *Cahiers d'Etudes Africaines* 42 (168): 711–38.

Fanon, Frantz

1952 *Peau Noire, Masques Blancs*. Paris: Editions de Seuil.

Farmer, Henry George

1924 "The Arab influence on music in the western Sudan," *Musical Standard*, N.S. 158.

1966 *Musikgeschichte in Bildern: Islam*. Leipzig: Deutscher Verlag für Musik.

Feather, Leonard

1949 *Inside Bebop*. New York: J. J. Robbins.

1957 *The Book of Jazz: A Guide to the Entire Field*. New York: Horizon.

1979 "Piano Giants of Jazz: Jay McShann," *Contemporary Keyboard*, October: 80–81.

1980 *Inside Jazz* (originally titled *Inside Bebop*). With a new introduction. New York: Da Capo.

Feld, Steven

2012 *Jazz Cosmopolitanism in Accra: Five Musical Years in Ghana*. Durham and London: Duke University Press.

Ferris, William R.

1974/75 "Black Prose Narrative from the Mississippi Delta," *Jazz Research* 6–7: 9–138.

1989 "Voodoo," in Charles Reagan Wilson and William Ferris, eds., *Encyclopedia of Southern Culture*. Chapel Hill: University of North Carolina Press, 492–93.

Festinger, Leon

1957 *Theory of Cognitive Dissonance*. 6th ed., 1968. Stanford: Stanford University Press.

Fiehrer, Thomas

1979 "The African Presence in Colonial Louisiana: An Essay on the Continuity of Caribbean Culture," in Robert MacDonald et al., eds., *Louisiana Black Heritage*. New Orleans: Louisiana State Museum, 3–31.

1991 "From Quadrille to Stomp: The Creole Origins of Jazz," *Black Music Research Journal* 4. 22–59.

Fields-Black, Edda L.

2008 *Deep Roots: Rice Farmers in West Africa and the African Diaspora*. Bloomington: Indiana University Press.

Floyd, Samuel A. Jr.

1995 *The Power of Black Music: Interpreting Its History from Africa to the United States.* New York and Oxford: Oxford University Press.

1999 "Black Music in the Circum-Caribbean," *American Music* 17 (1), Spring: 1–37.

Floyd, Samuel A., ed.

1999 *International Dictionary of Black Composers,* vols. 1 and 2. Chicago: Fitzroy Dearborn.

Floyd, Samuel A. Jr., and Marsha J. Reisser

1984 "The sources and Resources of Classic Ragtime Music," *Black Music Research Journal* 4: 22–59.

Fortier, Alceé

1888 "Customs and Superstitions in Louisiana," *Journal of American Folklore* 1 (2) : 136–40.

1904 *History of Louisiana 1512–1768.* Vol. 2. New York: Goupil and Company of Paris.

Fortune, George

1962 *Ideophones in Shona.* London: Oxford University Press.

Foster, George (as told to Tom Stoddard)

1971 *The Autobiography of Pops Foster, New Orleans Jazzman.* Berkeley: University of California Press.

Frazer, Sir James G.

1910 *Totemism and Exogamy,* 4 vols. London: Macmillan.

1890 [1907–1915] *The Golden Bough,* 12 vols. London: Macmillan.

Freud, Sigmund

1923 [1997] "Eine Teufelsneurose im siebzehnten Jahrhundert," *Imago* 9: 1–34.

Friedwald, Will

1992 *Jazz Singing: America's Great Voices from Bessie Smith to Bebop and Beyond.* New York: Collier.

Gansemans, Joseph, and Barbara Schmidt-Wrenger

1986 *Musikgeschichte in Bildern: Zentralafrika.* Leipzig: Deutscher Verlag für Musik.

Gara, Larry

1959 *The Baby Dodds Story.* Los Angeles: Contemporary Press. Reprint: Baton Rouge and London: Louisiana State University Press, 1992.

Gates, Henry Louis, Jr.

1988 *The Signifying Monkey: A Theory of African-American Literary Criticism.* New York: Oxford University Press.

2011 *Black in Latin America.* DVD, four-part series, approx. 240 min. WNET.ORG Properties, Wall to Wall Media, and Inkwell Films.

Giddins, Gary

1994 "Charlie Parker: An Overview," *Library Chronicle of the University of Texas* 24 (2): 52–103.

Gillespie, Dizzy

1948 "Anthropology," transcribed by Frank Paparelli (trumpet and piano parts). New York: Robbins and Sons.

Gillespie, Dizzy (with Al Fraser)

1979 [2009] *To Be, or Not . . . to Bop.* Minneapolis: University of Minnesota Press.

Goffin, Robert

1946 *La Nouvelle-Orleans Capital Du Jazz.* New York: Éditions De La Maison Française.

Gold, Robert S.

1975 *Jazz Talk.* New York: Bobbs-Merrill.

Gomes, Marcelina

2015 "Cantigas de José Emanuel Virasanda com *embulumbumba* (arco musical)," in Anja Brunner, Bornelia Gruber, and August Schmidhofer, eds., *Transgressions of a Musical Kind: Festschrift Regine Allgayer-Kaufmann . . .* Aachen: Shaker Verlag, 189–98.

Gourlay, Ken A.

1982 "Long Trumpets in Northern Nigeria—in History and today," *African Music* 6 (2): 48–72.

Graham, Richard

1994 "Ethnicity, kinship, and transculturation. African-derived mouth bows in European-American mountain communities," in August Schmidhofer and Dietrich Schüller, eds., *For Gerhard Kubik. Festschrift* . . . Frankfurt am Main: Peter Lang, 361–80.

Graves, Tom

2008 *Crossroads: The Life and Afterlife of Blues Legend Robert Johnson.* Foreword by Steve la Vere. 2nd ed. Memphis, TN: Rhythm Oil Publications.

Gray, John

1991 *African Music: A Bibliographical Guide to the Traditional, Popular, Art, and Liturgical Musics of Sub-Saharan Africa.* New York: Greenwood Press.

Greenberg, Joseph

1966 *The Languages of Africa.* Research Center for the Language Sciences, Indiana University. Bloomington: Indiana University Press.

Gunderson, Frank

2008 "Music performance on 19th-century Sukuma-Nyamwezi caravans to the Swahili Coast," *African Music* 8 (2): 6–25.

Gushee, Lawrence

1981 "Would you believe Ferman Mouton?" *Storyville* June-July: 164–68.

1985 "A Preliminary Chronology of the Early Career of Ferd 'Jelly Roll' Morton," *American Music* 3 (4): 389–412.

1987 "When Was Bunk Johnson Born and Why Should We Care?" *Jazz Archivist: A Newsletter of the William Ransom Hogan Jazz Archive* II, no. 2: 4–6.

1994 [2002] "The Nineteenth-Century Origins of Jazz," *Black Music Research Journal* 14 (1), Spring: 1–24. Reprinted 2002, vol. 22, Supplement: 151–74.

2005 *Pioneers of Jazz: The Story of the Creole Band.* New York: Oxford University Press.

Guthrie, Malcolm

1948 *The Classification of the Bantu Languages.* London: Oxford University Press.

1967–1971 *Comparative Bantu: An Introduction to the Comparative Linguistics and Prehistory of the Bantu Languages,* 4 vols. Farnborough: Gregg International.

Hair, William Ivy

1976 *Carnival of Fury: Robert Charles and the New Orleans Race Riot of 1900.* Baton Rouge: Louisiana State University Press.

Hall, Gwendolyn Midlo

1992 *Africans in Colonial Louisiana: The Development of Afro-Creole Culture in the Eighteenth Century.* Baton Rouge: Louisiana State University Press.

2001 "Myths about Creole Culture in Louisiana," *Louisiana Cultural Vistas* 12; Summer: 79–85.

2005 *Slavery and the African Ethnicities in the Americas: Restoring the Links.* Chapel Hill: University of North Carolina Press.

Halloway, Joseph E., ed.

1990 *Africanisms in American Culture.* Bloomington: Indiana University Press.

Handy, William Christopher

1916 "How I Came to Write the 'Memphis Blues,'" *New York Age,* December 7.

1926 *Blues: An Anthology.* New York: Macmillan. Reprint 1974.

1941 *Father of the Blues: An Autobiography.* Toronto: Collier-Macmillan.

Hannerz, Ulf

1992 *Cultural Complexity: Studies in the Social Organization of Meaning.* New York: Columbia University Press.

1996 *Transnational Connections: Culture, People, Places.* London: Routledge.

Hansen, Deidre Doris

1981 *The Music of the Xhosa-Speaking People*. Dissertation, Faculty of Arts. University of Witwatersrand.

Hazeldine, Mike

1994 Review of "Bunk Johnson—Last Testament" (Delmark DD 225), *New Orleans Music* 5 (2): 28.

2008 "Bunk Johnson: The Story So Far." *New Orleans Music* 14 (1): 12–17.

Hazeldine, Mike, and Barry Martyn

2000 *Bunk Johnson: Song of the Wanderer*. New Orleans: Jazzology Press.

Hazzard-Donald, Katrina

2013 *Mojo Workin': The Old African American Hoodoo System*. Urbana: University of Illinois Press.

Heide, Karl Gert zur

1970 *Deep South Piano: The Story of Little Brother Montgomery*. London: Studio Vista.

1999 "The Case of the Missing Years," *New Orleans Music* 8 (2), June: 16–18.

2004–2005 "Chicago, 1893 Part I and II," *Doctor Jazz Magazine*, 42 (187): 9–19 and 43 (188): 1–16.

2010 "Ma Rainey—Part I" and "Ma Rainey—Part II," *Doctor Jazz Magazine*, no. 208 and 209, 6–13 and 8–15.

2012 "Origin of the Rag Time"—Part 1 and 2, *Doctor Jazz Magazine*, no. 218: 9–17 and 219: 9–18.

Herskovits, Melville J.

1938a *Dahomey: An Ancient West African Kingdom*. 2 vols. New York: J.J. Augustin.

1938b *Acculturation: The Study of Culture Contact*. New York: J.J. Augustin.

1941 *The Myth of the Negro Past*. Boston: Harper & Brothers.

1949 *Man and His Works: The Science of Cultural Anthropology*. New York: Knopf.

Heywood, Linda M., and John K. Thornton

2007 *Central Africans, Atlantic Creoles, and the Foundation of the Americas, 1585–1660*. Cambridge: Cambridge University Press.

Hillegeist, Helmut, and Gerhard Kubik

1989 *Multipart Singing in East and South-East Africa*. Selected recordings of the Hillegeist/Kubik fieldtrips August 7, 1961, to January 10, 1963. LP published by Phonogrammarchiv of the Austrian Academy of Sciences, Vienna.

Hillman, Christopher

1988 *Bunk Johnson: His Life and Times*. New York: Universe Books.

Hirschberg, Walter

1988 *Neues Wörterbuch der Völkerkunde*. Berlin: Reimer.

Hobson, Vic

2008 "Buddy Bolden's Blues," *Jazz Archivist: A Newsletter of the William Ransom Hogan Jazz Archive* 21: 1–18.

2009 "The Blues and the Uptown Brass Bands of New Orleans," in Howard T. Weiner, ed., *Early Twentieth Century Brass Idioms*. Studies in Jazz No. 58. Langham, MD: Scarecrow Press, 133–42.

2011 "New Orleans Jazz and the Blues," *Jazz Perspectives* 5 (1): 3–30.

2014 *Creating Jazz Counterpoint: New Orleans, Barbershop Harmony, and the Blues*. Jackson: University Press of Mississippi.

Hobson, Vic, and David Sager

2010 "Letters to the Editor," *Jazz Archivist: A Newsletter of the William Ransom Hogan Jazz Archive* XXIII: 37–39.

Hodeir, André

1956 *Jazz: Its Evolution and Essence*. Transl. David Noakes. New York: Grove Press.

Hoeptner, Fred

2010 "Crittenden's Rag," *American Music Review* XL (1), Fall: 11–15.

Holbrook, Dick (Richard)

1973/74 "Our Word Jazz" *Storyville* 50, December/January.

1976 "Mister Jazz Himself—The Story of Ray Lopez," *Storyville* 64, April/May.

Hood, Mantle

1983 "Musical Ornamentation as History: The Hawaiian Steel Guitar," *Yearbook for Traditional Music* 15: 141–46.

Hooper, Joseph

1990 "Stan Getz, Saxophone Virtuoso, Dies," *International Herald Tribune,* June 8–9, 1, 8.

Hopkins, Donald R.

1983 *Princes and Peasants: Smallpox in History.* Chicago: University of Chicago Press. New edition with a new introduction by the author, 2002.

2008 "Smallpox in History: A Contribution to Pre-colonial History of Africa," in Regine Allgayer-Kaufmann and Michael Weber, eds., *African Perspectives: Pre-colonial History, Anthropology, and Ethnomusicology.* Frankfurt am Main: Peter Lang, 43–48.

2011 "A Slave Called Saint Jago," *Rhode Island History* 69 (1): 30–39.

Hopkins, Donald R., and Cherry Fletcher Bamberg

2011 "Where Did Ship Carpenter Lewis Hopkins (~1810–1850) Come From?," *Journal of the Bahamas Historical Society* 33, October: 51–58.

Hornbostel, Erich Moritz von

1913 "Die Musik der Pangwe," in Günther Tessmann (Hrsg.), *Die Pangwe,* vol. 2. Berlin: Ernst Wasmuth AG, 320–57.

Hunt, Alfred

1988 *Haiti's Influence on Antebellum America.* Baton Rouge: Louisiana State University Press.

Hyatt, Harry M.

1970 *Hoodoo—Conjuration—Witchcraft—Rootwork.* Washington: Western Publishing.

Jackson, Rachel

2012 "The Trans-Atlantic Journey of Gumbé: Where and Why Has It Survived?" *African Music* 9 (2): 128–53.

Jahn, Jahnheinz

1958 *Muntu. Umrisse der neo-afrikanischen Kultur.* Düsseldorf: Diederichs.

Janata, Alfred

1975 *Musikinstrumente der Völker.* Wien: Museum für Völkerkunde.

Johnson, Jerah

2000 "Jim Crow Laws of the 1890s and the Origins of New Orleans Jazz: Correction of an Error," *Popular Music* 19 (2), April: 243–51.

Jones, Arthur M.

1949 *African Music in Northern Rhodesia and Some Other Places.* The Occasional Papers of the Rhodes Livingstone Museum 4. Manchester: Manchester University Press.

1951 "Blue Notes and Hot Rhythm: Some Notes on Africanisms in Jazz, Both Melodic and Rhythmic," *African Music Society Newsletter* 1 (4): 9–12.

1959 *Studies in African Music,* Vol. 1 and 2. London: Oxford University Press.

1971 *Africa and Indonesia: The Evidence of the Xylophone and Other Musical and Cultural Factors.* Leiden: E. J. Brill.

Jones, Claire

2012 "A modern tradition: The social history of the Zimbabwean marimba," *African Music* 9 (2): 32–56.

Jones-Jackson, Patricia

1987 *When Roots Die: Endangered Tradition on the Sea Islands.* Athens: University of Georgia Press.

Jung, Carl Gustav

1961 *Memories, Dreams, Reflections*. Ed. A. Jaffé. Translated by R. and C. Winston. London: Fontana, 1972.

Kastin, David

2011 *Nica's Dream: The Life and Legend of the Jazz Baroness*. New York/London: W.W. Norton.

Katz, Bernard, ed.

1969 *The Social Implications of Early Negro Music in the United States*. New York: Arno Press and the New York Times.

Kayombo kaChinyeka

2008 "Konkha vya vanda . . ." in *African Perspectives: Pre-colonial History, Cultural Anthropology, and Ethnomusicology*, Regine Allgayer-Kaufmann and Michael Weber, eds. Frankfurt: Peter Lang, 103–20.

2013 *Konkha vya vanda—Search for the Hidden*. Blantyre, Malawi: Oral Literature Research Programme.

Kazadi wa Mukuna

1979/80 "The Origin of Zairean Modern Music: A Socio-economic Aspect," *African Urban Studies* 6 (Winter): 31–39.

1992 "The Genesis of Urban Music in Zaire," *African Music* 7 (2): 72–84.

Kelley, Robin D. G.

2009 *Thelonious Monk: The Life and Times of an American Original*, New York: Free Press.

Kernfeld, Barry, ed.

2002 *The New Grove Dictionary of Jazz*. London: Macmillan.

Kingsley, Walter

1917 "Whence Comes Jass? Facts from the Great Authority on the Subject," *New York Sun* III, 3, August 5: 6–8.

1925 "Jazzbo Washed Up, and Gravy," *New York World*, Editorial Section, October 25, 3: 1.

Kinzer, Charles E.

1996 "The Tios of New Orleans and Their Pedagogical Influence on the Early Jazz Clarinet Style," *Black Music Research Journal* 16/2, Fall: 279–303.

Kirby, Percival R.

1930 "A Study of Negro Harmony," *Musical Quarterly* 16 (4): 404–14.

1934 [1953] [1965] *The Musical Instruments of the Native Races of South Africa*. London: Oxford University Press.

1959 "The Use of European Musical Techniques by the Non-European Peoples of Southern Africa," *Journal of the International Folk Music Council* 11: 37–40.

1961 "Physical phenomena which appear to have determined the bases and development of an harmonic sense among Bushmen, Hottentot and Bantu," *African Music* 2 (4): 6–9.

Kmen, Henry A.

1966 *Music in New Orleans: The Formative Years, 1791–1841*. Baton Rouge: Louisiana State University Press.

Kmen, Henry A., and John Baron

2013 *Concert Life in Nineteenth Century New Orleans: A Comprehensive Reference*. Baton Rouge. Louisiana State University Press.

Knauer, Wolfram, ed.

2008 *Begegnungen: The World Meets Jazz*. Darmstädter Beiträge zur Jazzforschung, Band 10. Darmstadt: Jazzinstitut.

Knight, Roderic

1991 *Vibrato Octaves: Tunings and Modes of the Mande Balo and Kora*. Baltimore: Sempod Laboratory, Department of Music, University of Maryland.

Bibliography

Koelle, Sigismund W.

1854 *Polyglotta Africana* ... F. E. H. Halr and D. Dalby, eds. Sierra Leone, 1963. First edition: London.

Krehbiel, Henry Edward

1914 [1967] *Afro-American Folksongs: A Study in Racial and National Music*. New York: Frederick Unger.

Kremser, Manfred, ed.

1996 *Ay Bobo: African-Caribbean Religions*. Part 2: Voodoo. Vienna: WUV.

Kubik, Gerhard

1965 "Transcription of *mangwilo* xylophone music from film strips," *African Music* 3 (4): 35–51. Corrigenda in *African Music* 4 (4) [1970]: 136–37.

1973 "Helmut Hillegeist's Bunk-Johnson-Transkriptionen 1960/61," *Jazzforschung—Jazz Research* 5: 103–18.

1979 *Angolan Traits in Black Music, Games, and Dances of Brazil: A Study of African Cultural Extensions Overseas*. Lisboa: Junta de Investigações Cientificas do Ultramar. (Reprinted 2013 by Diasporic Africa Press, Inc. New title: *Angola in the Black Cultural Expressions of Brazil*.)

1981 *Mukanda na makisi—Circumcision School and Masks*. LP with booklet. MC 11 Museum Collection. Berlin: Ethnological Museum.

1985 "African Tone-systems: A Reassessment," *Yearbook for Traditional Music*, 17: 31–63

1986 "Hubert Kponton (1905–1981), Erfinder, Künstler und Begründer eines ethnographischen Privatmuseums in Lomé, Togo," *Archiv für Völkerkunde* 40: 157–71.

1988 Review of the film by Paul Henley, *Yearbook for Traditional Music* 20: 255–57.

1990 "Drum Patterns in the 'Batuque' of Benedito Caxias," *Latin American Music Review* 11 (2), Fall/Winter: 115–81.

1991 *Extensionen afrikanischer Kulturen in Brasilien*. Aachen: Alano Verlag. English translation: *Extensions of African Cultures in Brazil*. New York: Diasporic Africa Press, 2013.

1993 "Die *mukanda*-Erfahrung. Zur Psychologie der Initiation der Jungen im Ost-Angola-Kulturraum," in Marie-José van de Loo and Margarete Reinhart, eds., *Kinder. Ethnologische Forschungen in fünf Kontinenten*. München: Trickster, 309–47.

1994a "Ethnicity, Cultural Identity and the Psychology of Culture Contact," in Gerard Béhague, ed., *Music and Black Ethnicity: The Caribbean and South America*. North South Center, University of Miami. New Brunswick: Transaction, 17–46.

1994b "Namibia—Survey 1991—1993 Gerhard Kubik/Moya A. Malamusi...." *EM. Annuario degli Archivi di Ethnomusicologia dell'Accademia Nazionale di Santa Cecilia*, II: 151–200. Sintesi in italiano di Giorgio Adamo, 200–209.

1995 *African Guitar*. Solo fingerstyle guitar music, composers and performers of Congo/Zaire, Uganda, Central African Republic, Malawi, Namibia, and Zambia. Audio-visual field recordings 1966–1993 by Gerhard Kubik. Sparta, NJ: Stefan Grossman. DVD and booklet.

1998a "Intra-African Streams of Influence," in Ruth M. Stone, ed., *The Garland Encyclopedia of World Music. Volume 1: Africa*. New York and London: Garland, 293–326.

1998b "Central Africa. An Introduction," in: Ruth M. Stone ed., *The Garland Encyclopedia of World Music. Volume 1: Africa*. New York and London: Garland, 651–80.

1998c "Analogies and Differences in African-American Musical Cultures across the Hemisphere: Interpretive Models and Research Strategies," *Black Music Research Journal* 18 (1/2), Spring/Fall: 203–327.

1998d *Kalimba, Nsansi, Mbira,—Lamellophone in Afrika*. Berlin: Ethnologisches Museum.

1999a *Africa and the Blues*. Jackson: University Press of Mississippi. Italian translation with CD: *L'Africa e il Blues*, A Cura di Giorgio Adamo. Subiaco/Roma: Fogli Volanti Edizioni, 2007.

1999b "African and African-American Lamellophones: History, Typology, Nomenclature, Performers and Intracultural Concepts," in Jacqueline Cogdell DjeDje, ed., *Turn Up the Volume! A Celebration of African Music*. Los Angeles: UCLA Fowler Museum of Cultural History, 20–70.

1999c "Reflections on Eli Owen's Mouth-bow: African American One-stringed Instrumental Traditions and Their African Backgrounds," in Jacqueline Cogdell DjeDje, ed., *Turn Up the Volume! A Celebration of African Music*. Los Angeles: UCLA Fowler Museum of Cultural History, 186–93.

2000a "Masks from the Lands of Dawn: The Ngangela Peoples," in Frank Herreman, ed., *In the Presence of Spirits*. New York: Museum of African Art, 123–43.

2000b "Symbolbildung und Symbolhandlungen. Ethnopsychologische Forschungen bei den Mpyɛmɔ (Zentralafrikanische Republik, 1966)," *Anthropos* 95: 385–407.

2001 "Das Versinken eines Kindes im Boden—Yoruba Märchenmotive aufgezeichnet 1960," in Karin Richter and Thomas Trautmann, eds., *Kindsein in der Mediengesellschaft. Interdisziplinäre Annäherungen*. Weinheim: Beltz Verlag, 251–61.

2002a *Lamelofones do Museu Nacional de Etnologia*. Lisboa: Instituto Português de Museus/Museu Nacional de Etnologia. Book and CD with notes in English and Portuguese.

2002b "Mukanda—Boys' Initiation in Eastern Angola: Transference, Counter-Transference and Taboo Symbolism in an Age-Group Related Ritual Therapeutic Intervention," in Alfred Pritz/Thomas Wenzel, eds., *Weltkongreß Psychotherapie. Mythos Traum—Wirklichkeit*. Ausgewählte Beiträge des 2. Weltkongresses für Psychotherapie, Wien 1999. Vienna: Facultas, 65–90.

2003 "Konversionsphänomene. Theorie und Materialien im Kulturvergleich," in *Hysterie*, Wiener Psychoanalytische Vereinigung, ed., 77–159.

2007a "Flux and Reflux: Jazz and Blues Analogies and Reinterpretations in Africa," in P. Castagneto, ed., *L'Oceano dei Suoni*. Torino: Otto Editore, 17–30 and CD tracks 3–8.

2007b *Tabu. Erkundungen transkultureller Psychoanalyse in Afrika, Europa und anderen Kulturgebieten*. Studien zur Ethnopsychologie und Ethnopsychoanalyse Band 7, Münster/Wien: LIT.

2008a "Zur Mathematik und Geschichte der afrikanischen time-line Formeln," in Albrecht Schneider, ed., *Systematic and Comparative Musicology: Concepts, Methods, Findings*. Frankfurt am Main: Peter Lang, 359–98.

2008b "Small Voices Doomed—A Keynote," *Yearbook for Traditional Music* 20: 1–4.

2008c "Bourdon, Blues Notes, and Pentatonism in the Blues: An Africanist Perspective," in David Evans, ed., *Rambling on My Mind: New Perspectives on the Blues*. Urbana and Chicago: University of Illinois Press, 11–48.

2009 "The Mystery of the Buddy Bolden Photograph," *Jazz Archivist: A Newsletter of the William Ransom Hogan Jazz Archive* 22: 4–18.

2010 *Theory of African Music*. Vol. 1 and 2. Chicago: University of Chicago Press.

2013a "South African Contributions to Jazz History," in *Generations of Jazz. At the Red location Museum*. Exhibition catalogue, ed. Diane Thram. Grahamstown: International Library of African Music, 10–16.

2013b *Extensions of African Culture in Brazil*. New York: Diasporic African Press.

2015 "The 18th and 19th century African presence in Brazil. What we can learn from musical iconography," in Anja Brunner, Bornelia Gruber, and August Schmidhofer, eds., *Transgressions of a Musical Kind: Festschrift Regine Allgayer-Kaufmann . . .* Aachen: Shaker Verlag, 125–61.

2016 "The Gogo tonal-harmonic system. Structure and continuity in Tanzanian music history," in Bernhard Hanneken and Tiago de Oliveira Pinto, eds., *Mambo Moto Moto: Music in Tanzania Today*. Berlin: VWB, 23–46.

Kubik, Gerhard, and Moya Aliya Malamusi

1989 *Opeka Nyimbo—Musician-composers from Southern Malawi*. Double LP with pamphlet. Museum Collection Berlin MC 15. Berlin: Museum für Völkerkunde.

2002 "Formulas of Defense: A Psychoanalytic Investigation in Southeast Africa," *American Imago* 59 (2): 171–96.

Kubik, Gerhard, et al.

1982 *Musikgeschichte in Bildern: Ostafrika*. Leipzig: Deutscher Verlag für Musik.

1989 *Musikgeschichte in Bildern: Westafrika*. Leipzig: Deutscher Verlag für Musik.

Kubik, Gerhard, Moya A. Malamusi, and András Varsányi

2013 *Afrikanische Musikinstrumente*. Katalog und Nachdokumentation der Musikinstrumente aus Afrika südlich der Sahara in der Sammlung Musik des Münchner Stadtsmuseums. Berlin: Nicolai.

Kuper, Adam

2005 *The Reinvention of Primitive Society*. London: Routledge.

2008 "Changing the Subject—About Cousin Marriage, Among Other Things," *Journal of the Royal Anthropological Institute* 14 (4): 717–35.

La Chance, Paul

1992 "The 1809 Immigration of Saint-Dominique Refugees," in Carl A. Brasseaux and Glenn R. Conrad, eds., *The Road to Louisiana: The Saint-Domingue Refugees, 1792–1809*. Lafayette: Center for Louisiana Studies, 245–84.

Latrobe, Henry Benjamin

1819 [1905] *The Journal of Latrobe*. New York: D. Appleton and Company.

1980 *The Journals of Benjamin Latrobe 1799–1820. From Philadelphia to New Orleans*. Vol. 3. Edited by Edward C. Carter II, John C. Van Horne, and Lee W. Formwalt. New Haven: Yale University Press.

LaVere, Stephen C.

1986 [1990] *Robert Johnson: The Complete Recordings*. Columbia C2K 46222. New York: Sony.

Law, Robin

2004 *Ouidah: The Social History of a West African Slaving Port, 1717–1892*. Cumbria: Long House Publishing Services.

Lems-Dworkin, Carol

1991a *Africa in Scott Joplin's Music*. Evanston: C. Lems-Dworkin.

1991b *African Music: A Pan-African Annotated Bibliography*. London/New York: Hans Zell.

Levin, Michael, and John S. Wilson

1994 "No Bop Roots in Jazz: Parker," *Down Beat* 61, no. 2: 24–25 (originally published September 9, 1949).

Lévi-Strauss, Claude

1958 *Anthropologie structurale*. Paris: Plon.

1964 *Mythologiques I: Le Cru et le Cuit*. Paris: Plon.

1967 *Mythologiques II: Du miel au cendres*. Paris: Plon.

Lewis, George E.

1996 "Improvised Music after 1950: Afrological and Eurological Perspectives," *Black Music Research Journal* 16 (1), reprinted *BMRJ* 22 (supplement) 2002: 215–46.

Ligeti, György

1988 Interview in *Die Zeit*, Feuilleton 57, no. 5, Frankfurt.

List, George

1966 "The Musical Bow at Palenque," *Journal of the International Folk Music Council* 18: 36–49.

1983 *Music and Poetry in a Colombian Village: A Tri-Cultural Heritage*. Bloomington: Indiana University Press.

Littlefield, Daniel C.

1991 *Rice and Slaves: Ethnicity and the Slave Trade in Colonial South Carolina.* Urbana: University of Illinois Press.

Lomax, Alan

1952 [1959] *Mister Jelly Roll: The Fortunes of Jelly Roll Morton, New Orleans Creole and "Inventor of Jazz."* London: Pan Books.

1968 *Folks Song Style and Culture.* Publication no. 88. Washington: American Association for the Advancement of Science.

1993 *The Land Where the Blues Began.* New York: Dell.

Lomax, Anna Wood, and Jeffrey A. Greenberg

2005 *Jelly Roll Morton: The Complete Library of Congress Recordings.* Cambridge: Rounder.

Major, Clarence

1994 *Juba to Jive: A Dictionary of American Slang.* New York: Penguin.

Malamusi, Moya Aliya

1984 "The Zambian Popular Music Scene," *Jazz Research* 16: 189–98.

1991 "Samba Ng'oma Eight—The Drum-Chime of Mario Sabuneti," *African Music* 7 (1): 55–71.

1992 "Thunga la ngororombe—The Panpipe Dance Group of Sakha Bulaundi," *African Music* 7 (2): 85–107.

1997 "Two panpipe ensemble traditions," *Kalinda: The Newsletter of Afro-Caribbean and U.S. Black Music Interconnections* (published by CBMR, Chicago), Fall: 22–24.

1999a *From Lake Malawi to the Zambezi: Aspects of Music and Oral Literature in South-East Africa in the 1990s.* CD with pamphlet, pamap 602, LC 07203. Frankfurt/Mainz: Popular African Music/ African Music Archive.

1999b *Ufiti ndi Using'anga. Witchcraft and Healing Practice.* A Culture and Personality Study of Traditional Healers in Southern Malawi. M.A. thesis, University of Vienna.

2003 "Identifying Witches: A Performance by Sing'anga Jonasi Masangwi," in Daniel K. Avorgbedor, ed., *The Interrelatedness of Music, Religion, and Ritual in African Performance Practice.* Lewiston, NY: Edwin Mellon Press191–218, photos 12–13.

2004 *The Nyau Masking Tradition in Central and Southern Malawi.* Field observations 1983–2003 on meanings, social context and recent developments. Ph.D. dissertation, Institut für Ethnologie, Kultur- und Sozialanthropologie, University of Vienna.

2008 "Sounds of a Ventriloquist," in August Schmidhofer/Stefan Jena (Hrsg.), *Klangfarbe. Vergleichend-systematische und musikhistorische Perspektiven.* Frankfurt am Main: Peter Lang, 199–203 (with CD example).

2011 *Endangered Traditions—Endangered Creativity . . .* A CD/DVD documentation. Frankfurt: Popular African Music.

2015 *The Banjo Bands of Malawi.* Field recordings by Moya Aliya Malamusi. DVD with PDF booklet. 78 minutes. Vestapol 13135. Sparta, NJ: Stefan Grossman's Guitar Workshop.

2016 *Za Using'anga Ndi Ufiti—About Healing and Witchcraft.* A Culture and Personality Study of Traditional Healers in Southern Malawi. Studien zur Ethnopsychologie und Ethnopsychoanalyse, track 9. Münster/Wien: LIT Verlag.

Malamusi, Moya Aliya, and Mose Yotamu

2001 "Zambia," in Stanley Sadie, ed., *The New Grove Dictionary of Music and Musicians.* London: Macmillan.

Marquis, Donald M.

1978 *In Search of Buddy Bolden: First Man of Jazz.* Baton Rouge: Louisiana State University Press. Revised edition, 2005.

Martin, Florence

1994 *Bessie Smith*. Paris: Edition du Limon.

Mauss, Marcel

1925 *Essai sur le Don. Forme et Raison de l'Echange dans les Sociétés archaiques*. Paris: Les Presses Universitaires de France (edition 1968).

McCusker, John

2012 *Creole Trombone: Kid Ory and the Early Years of Jazz*. Jackson: University Press of Mississippi.

McDonald, Mark

2010 "Mike Zwerin, trombonist and a writer on jazz, 79," *International Herald Tribune*, April 6, 3.

Meadows, Eddie S.

1999 "Africa and Jazz: The Melo-Rhythmic Essence of Warren 'Baby' Dodds," in Jacqueline Cogdell DjeDje, ed., *Turn Up the Volume!* . . . Los Angeles: UCLA Fowler Museum of Cultural History, 194–209.

Mensah, Atta Annan

1971/72 "Jazz—The Round Trip," *Jazz Research* 3/4: 124–37.

Merolla da Sorrarto, Girolamo

1692 *Breve e succinta relatione del viaggio nel regno di Congo*. Napoli: Mollo.

Merriam, Alan P.

1960 "Jazz the Word," *Jazz Review* 3, March–August.

Merriam, Alan P., and Fradley H. Garner

1968 "Jazz—The Word," *Ethnomusicology* 12 (3): 37.

1998 "Jazz—The Word," in Robert G. O'Meally, ed., *The Jazz Cadence of American Culture*. New York: Columbia University Press, 7–31.

Merwe, Peter van der

1988 "Shifting Tonal Levels in Africa, Europe and America," *Papers Presented at the Sixth Symposium on Ethnomusicology*, 1–3 October 1987. Grahamstown: ILAM, 53–56.

1989 *Origins of the Popular Style: The Antecedents of the Twentieth-Century Popular Music*. Oxford: Clarendon Press.

Minton, John

1996 " West African Fiddles in Deep East Texas," in *Juneteenth Texas: Essays in African-American Folklore* 54. Denton: University of North Texas Press, 291–313.

Mohamadou, Eldridge

1965 *L'Histoire de Tibati. Chefferie Foulbe du Cameroun*. Yaoundé: Éditions Abbia avec la collaboration de CIE.

Monk, Thelonious

1948 "52nd Street Theme," arranged by Frank Paparelli (piano part). New York: Robbins and Sons.

Moreau de Saint-Méry, Médéric Louis Elie

1797 *Déscription . . . de la partie française de l'isle Saint-Dominique*. 3 vols. Rev. par B. Maurel et E. Taillemite, Paris, 1958.

1985 *A Civilization That Perished: The Last Years of White Colonial Rule in Haiti*. Translated, abridged, and edited by Ivor D. Spencer. Lanham, MD: University Press of America.

Morgenstern, Dan

1991 CD liner notes, *Early Bird: Charlie Parker and Jay McShann and His Orchestra*, Stash Records ST-CD-542.

Morton, Jelly Roll

1938 "I Created Jazz in 1902, Not W. C. Handy." *Down Beat*, August.

Muir, Peter C.

2010 *Long Lost Blues: Popular Blues in America, 1850–1920*. Chicago: University of Illinois Press.

Murray, Jocelyn, ed.
1981 *Cultural Atlas of Africa*. Oxford: Elsevier, Phaidon Press.
Mushlitz, Dick
1997 CD liner notes, Jimmy and Mama Yancey & Guests, *The Unissued 1951 Yancey Wire Recordings*. Recorded at the Yancey apartment by Phil Kiely and Dick Mushlitz, June 16, 1951. Document Records DoCD-1007.
Narváez, Peter
1994 [2002] "The Influences of Hispanic Music Cultures on African-American Blues Musicians," *Black Music Research Journal* 14 (2). Reprinted *BMRJ* vol. 22 Supplement 2002: 175ff.
Ngumu, Pie-Claude
1975/76 "Les mendzaŋ des Ewondo du Cameroun," *African Music* 5 (4): 6–26.
Nketia, J. H. Kwabena
2010 Preface to Freddi Williams Evans, *Congo Square*. Lafayette: University of Louisiana Press.
Nkosi, Lewis
1966 "Jazz in Exile," *Transition* 5 (24): 34–37.
Nooter, Mary H., ed.
1993 *Secrecy: African Art That Conceals and Reveals*. New York: Museum for African Art.
Nurse, George T.
1968 "Bush Roots and Nyanja Ideophones," *Society of Malawi Journal* 21 (1): 50–57.
1974 "Verb Species Relationships of Some Nyanja Ideophones," *African Studies* 33 (4): 227–42.
O'Brien, Fr. Peter F.
2004 *Mary Lou Williams presents Black Christ of the Andes*. CD liner notes. Washington: Smithsonian Folkways Recordings.
Oliveira, Ernesto Veiga de
1964 [2000] *Instrumentos Musicais Populares Portugueses*. Lisboa: Fundação Gulbenkian/Museu Nacional de Etnologia.
Oliver, Paul
1970 *Savannah Syncopators: African Retentions in the Blues*. New York: Stein and Day.
1991 "That Certain Feeling: Blues and Jazz ... in 1890?" *Popular Music* 10 (1): 11–19.
2002 "Blues," in Barry Kernfeld, ed., *New Grove Dictionary of Jazz*, 2nd ed. London: Macmillan, 247–54.
Opatrny, Alexander
2002 *Afrikanische und europäische Elemente im Ragtime-, Blues- und Boogie-Woogie-Piano*. M.A. dissertation, University of Vienna.
Ortiz, Fernando
1952 *Los Instrumentos de la Musica Afro-Cubana*, Vol. I–V. La Habana: Cardenas.
Osgood, Henry Osbourne
1926 *So This Is Jazz*. Boston: Little, Brown.
Owens, Thomas
1974 *Charlie Parker: Techniques of Improvisation*. Ph.D. dissertation, University of California, Los Angeles.
1995 *Bebop: The Music and its Players*. New York: Oxford University Press.
Panassié, Hugues, and Charles Edward Smith
1942 *The Real Jazz*. New York: Smith & Durrell.
Parin, Paul
1983 *Der Widerspruch im Subjekt*. Ethnopsychoanalytische Studien. Frankfurt am Main: Syndikat.
Parin, Paul, et al.
1980 *Fear Thy Neighbor as Thyself. Psychoanalysis and Society among the Anyi of West Africa*. Chicago: Chicago University Press.

Parker, Charlie

1949 *Be-bop. Instrumental choruses for Alto Sax.* 6 original choruses on outstanding Be-Bop themes transcribed by "Gil" Fuller. London: Bosworth & Co. (Copyright J.J. Robbins & Sons Inc.).

Pearson, Emil

1970 *Ngangela–English Dictionary.* Cuernavaca, Morelos: Tipografica Indigena.

Pechuël-Loesche, Eduard

1907 *Die Loango-Expedition.* Stuttgart: Strecker & Schröder.

Pike, Kenneth

1954 "Emic and Etic Standpoints for the Description of Behavior," in K. L. Pike, *Language in Relation to a Unified Theory of the Structure of Human Behaviour.* Glendale: Summer Institute of Linguistics, 8–28.

Piras, Marcello

2012 "Treemonisha, or Der *Freischütz* Upside Down," *Current Research in Jazz* 4, Dan Morgenstern Festschrift, www.crj-online.org.

2013 "Garibaldi to Syncopation: Bruto Giannini and the Curious Case of Scott Joplin's *Magnetic Rag*," *Journal of Jazz Studies* 9 (2), Winter: 107–77.

Porter, Lewis

1997 *Jazz: A Century of Change.* New York: Schirmer Books.

Prögler, J. A.

1995 "Searching for Swing: Participatory Discrepancies in the Jazz Rhythm Section," *Ethnomusicology* 39 (1): 21–54.

Purdue, Charles, Jr., Thomas E. Barden, and Robert K. Phillips, eds.

1976 *Weevils in the Wheat: Interviews with Virginia Ex-slaves.* Charlottesville: University Press of Virginia.

Raeburn, Bruce Boyd

2004 *Psychoanalysis and Jazz.* Panel held at the 43rd Congress of the International Psychoanalytical Association, New Orleans, March 11, 2004. Panelists: Steven Rosenbloom (Montreal), Richard Karmel (Montreal), Michael White (New Orleans), Sergio V. Delgado (Cincinnati). *International Journal of Psychoanalysis* 85: 995–97.

2009a *New Orleans Style and the Writing of American Jazz History.* Ann Arbor: University of Michigan Press.

2009b "Stars of David and Sons of Sicily: Constellations Beyond the Canon in Early New Orleans Jazz," *Jazz Perspectives* 3 (2), August: 123–52.

2012a "Bix Beiderbecke in New Orleans," *Current Research in Jazz* 4 (Dan Morgenstern Festschrift), www.crj-online.org.

2012b "Beyond the Spanish Tinge: Hispanics and Latinos in Early New Orleans Jazz," in Luca Cerchiari, Laurent Cugny and Franz Kerschbaumer, eds., *Euro Jazz Land: Jazz and European Sources, Dynamics, and Context.* Boston: Northeastern University Press.

2012c "New Orleans Jazz Styles of the 1920s: Sam Morgan's Jazz Band," in Anthony M. Cummings, John J. Joyce Jr., and Bruce Boyd Raeburn, eds., *Sam Morgan's Jazz Band: Complete Works.* Music of the United States of America, vol. 24. Ann Arbor: American Musicological Society/Society for American Music.

Ramsey, Frederic

1951 "Baby Dodds: Talking and Drum Solos in Footnotes." Liner notes, *Jazz* vol. 1. Folkways Records FJ 2290: 1–4.

Ramsey, Frederic Jr., and Charles Edward Smith, eds.

1939 *Jazzmen.* New York: Harcourt Brace.

Rawick, George, ed.

1972 *The American Slave: A Composite Autobiography.* Westport, CT: Greenwood Press.

Rego, Waldeloir
1968 *Capoeira Angola: Ensaio Sócio-Etnográfico*. Rio de Janeiro: Editôra Itapuá.
Reisner, Robert G.
1974 *Bird: The Legend of Charlie Parker*. London: Quartet Books.
Roberts, John Storm
1972 *Black Music of Two Worlds*. New York: Praeger.
1979 *The Latin Tinge: The Impact of Latin American Music on the United States*. New York: Oxford University Press. 1985 edition: Tivoli, NY: Original Music.
Rose, Al, and Edmond Souchon, M.D.
1967 *New Orleans Jazz: A Family Album*. Baton Rouge: Louisiana State University Press.
Rouget, Gilbert
1969 "Sur les xylophones équiheptaphoniques des Malinké," *Revue de Musicologie* 55 (1): 47–77.
1972 *Musique malinke: Guinée*. LP, Vogue LDM 30113.
1980 [1990] *La musique et la transe. Esquisse d'une théorie générale des relations de la musique et de la possession*. Paris: Gallimard.
1996 *Un roi africain et sa musique de cour: Chants et danses du palais à Porto-Novo sous le règne de Gbèfa (1948–1976)*. Paris: CNRS Eds.
2001 *Initiatique vôdoun. Images du rituel*. Santi-Maur: Editions Sépia.
Rugendas, Johann Moritz
1835 *Malerische Reise in Brasilien*. Paris: Engelmann.
Russell, William (Bill)
1994 *New Orleans Style*. Compiled and edited by Barry Martyn and Mike Hazeldine. New Orleans: Jazzology Press.
1999 *"Oh, Mister Jelly:" A Jelly Roll Morton Scrapbook*. Copenhagen: JazzMedia.
Safire, William
1981 "On Language," *New York Times Magazine*, April 26.
Sager, David
2009 "Louis Armstrong, Bunk Johnson, and Jules Levy: The Art of 'Tonation,'" in Howard T. Weiner, ed., *Early Twentieth-Century Brass Idioms: Art, Jazz, and Other Popular Traditions*. Lanham, MD: Scarecrow, 143–54.
Sahlins, Marshall
1976 *Culture and Practical Reason*. Chicago: University of Chicago Press.
Santelli, Robert
1993 *The Big Book of Blues: A Biographical Encyclopedia*. New York: Penguin.
Schafer, William J.
1977 *Brass Bands and New Orleans Jazz*. Baton Rouge: Louisiana State University Press.
Schmidhofer, August
1991 *Xylophonspiel in Madagaskar. Ergebnisse der Feldforschungen 1986–89*. Ph.D. dissertation, Institute of Musicology, University of Vienna.
Schmidhofer, August, ed.
2009 *Central African Guitar Song Composers: The Second and Third Generation*. Field Recordings 1962–2009 by Gerhard Kubik and associates. Liner notes by Gerhard Kubik. Vienna: University of Vienna.
Schmidhofer, August, and Stefan Jena, eds.
2011 *Klangfarbe. Vergleichend-sytematische und musikhistorischen Perspektiven*, Frankfurt: Peter Lang.
Schreyer, Lowell H.
1985 "The Banjo in Ragtime," in: John Edward Hasse, ed., *Ragtime: Its History, Composers, and Music*. New York: Schirmer Books, 54–69.

2008 *The Banjo Entertainers: Roots to Ragtime. A Banjo History*. Mankato: Minnesota Heritage Press.

Schuller, Gunther

1968 *Early Jazz: Its Roots and Musical Development*. New York: Oxford University Press.

1989 *The Swing Era: The Development of Jazz, 1930–1945*. New York: Oxford University Press.

2002 "Jelly Roll Morton," in *The New Grove Dictionary of Jazz*, vol. 2, 828.

Schultz, Christian

1810 *Travels on an Island Voyage*. Vol.2. New York: Isaac Riley.

Schweninger, Loren, ed.

1984 *The Autobiography of James Thomas: From Tennessee Slave to St. Louis Entrepreneur*. Columbia: University of Missouri Press.

Schwerke, Irving

1926 "Le jazz est mort! Vive le jazz," Guide du Concert 12, March 19: 679–82.

Scott, Rebecca

2003 "Se batter pour ses droits: écritures, litiges et discrimination raciale en Louisiane (1888–1899)," *Cahiers du Brésil Contemporain* 53/54 : 175–210.

Shapiro, Nat, and Nat Hentoff

1955 [1966] *Hear Me Talkin' to Ya: The Story of Jazz by the Men Who Made It*. New York and London: Jazz Book Club.

Shermer, Michael

2013 "Logic-Tight Compartments: How Our Modular Brains Lead Us to Deny and Distort Evidence," *Scientific American* 308 (1), January: 71.

Sickler, Don

2006 Liner notes to the DVD *Thelonious Monk, Live in '66*, Reelin' In the Years Productions, ww.jazzicons.com.

Silvester, Peter J.

1989 [1990] *A Left Hand Like God: A History of Boogie-woogie Piano*. New York: Da Capo.

Simon, Artur

1989 "Trumpet and Flute Ensembles of the Berta People in the Sudan," in Jacqueline Cogdell DjeDje and William G. Carter eds., *African Musicology—Current Trends*. A Festschrift presented to J. H. Kwabena Nketia, Vol. 1. Los Angeles: Crossroads Press, 183–217.

2003 *Waza: Die Musik der Berta am Blauen Nil—Sudan*. CD & booklet. Museum Collection Berlin. Mainz: Wergo.

Simon, Artur, ed.

1983 *Music in Afrika. 20 Beiträge zur Kenntnis traditioneller afrikanischer Musikkulturen*. 2 Kassetten. Berlin: Museum für Völkerkunde.

Simon, Artur, and Ulrich Wegner, eds.

1999 *Music! 100 Recordings—100 Years of the Berlin Phonogrammarchiv 1900–2000*. Berlin: Museum für Völkerkunde.

Singer, Barry

2008 "History Softens Toward a Baroness of Jazz," *International Herald Tribune*, October 21, 17.

Skipper, James Jr.

1986 "Nicknames, Folk Heroes and Jazz Musicians," *Popular Music and Society* 10: 51–62.

Soko, Boston, ed.

2002 *Nchimi Chikanga: The Battle against Witchcraft in Malawi*. Kachere Text no. 10. Blantyre: CLAIM.

Sonderegger, Theo

1998 *Psychology*. Cliffs Quick Review. Lincoln, NE: Cliffsnotes.

Spencer, Frederick J.

2002 *Jazz and Death: Medical Profiles of Jazz Greats*. Jackson: University Press of Mississippi.

Spencer, Jon Michael

1993 *Blues and Evil*. Knoxville: University of Tennessee Press.

Spriggins, E. Belfield

1933 "Excavating Local Jazz," *Louisiana Weekly*, April 22.

St. Cyr, Johnny

1966 "Jazz As I Remember it," *Jazz Journal*, September 6–9.

Stoddard, Tom

1982 *Jazz on the Barbary Coast*. Chigwell: Storyville. 2nd edition, 1998.

Stone, Ruth M.

1982 *Let the Inside Be Sweet: The Interpretation of Music Event among the Kpelle of Liberia*. Bloomington: Indiana University Press.

1988 *Dried Millet Breaking: Time, Words, and Song in the Woi Epic of the Kpelle*. Bloomington: Indiana University Press.

Storb, Ilse

1989 *Louis Armstrong. Biographie mit Selbstzeugnissen und Bilddokumenten*. Reinbeck: Rowohlt.

1991 *Dave Brubeck—Improvisationen und Kompositionen: Die Idee der kulturellen Wechselbeziehungen*. Frankfurt am Main: Peter Lang. 2. Auflage, Münster: Lit, 2000.

2014 *Untersuchungen zur Erweiterung der funktionalen Harmonik in den Klavierwerken von Claude Debussy*. Münster/Berlin: LIT.

Stuart, Jay Allison

1961 *Call Him George*. London: Peter Davies.

Sublette, Ned

2004 *Cuba and Its Music: From the First Drums to the Mambo*. Chicago: Chicago Review Press.

2008 *The World That Made New Orleans—From Spanish Silver to Congo Square*. Chicago: Lawrence Hill Books.

Szwed, John, ed.

2005 "Doctor Jazz." Notes to *Jelly Roll Morton: The Complete Library of Congress Recordings*. Cambridge: Rounder Records.

Tallant, Robert

1968 *Voodoo in New Orleans*. New York: Macmillan. Reprint, Pelican, 1983.

Tamony, Peter

1939 "Origin of Words," *San Francisco News Letter and Wasp* 5, March 17.

Taylor, Billy

1982 *Jazz Piano*. Dubuque, IA: Winston C. Brown.

Teffera, Timkehet

2009 *Aerophone im Instrumentarium der Völker Ostafrikas*. Berlin: Trafo.

Tessmann, Günter

1913 *Die Pangwe*. Berlin: Reimer.

Thacker, Eric

1973 "Ragtime," *Jazz and Blues* 3 (9): 4–6.

Thornton, John

1998 *Africa and Africans in the Making of the Atlantic World, 1400–1800*. 2nd ed. Cambridge: Cambridge University Press.

Titon, Jeff Todd

1977 *Early Downhome Blues: A Musical and Cultural Analysis*. Urbana: University of Illinois Press. 2nd edition 1994, Chapel Hill: University of North Carolina Press.

1993 "Reconstructing the Blues: Reflections on the 1960s Blues Revival," in N. V. Rosenberg, ed., *Transforming Tradition*. Urbana: University of Illinois Press.

Townsend, Peter

2000 *Jazz in American Culture*. Jackson: University Press of Mississippi.

Tracey, Andrew

1961 "Mbira Music of Jege A Tapera," *African Music* 2 (4): 44–63.

1970 *How to Play the Mbira Dza Vadzimu*. Roodepoort: ILAM.

1971 "The Nyanga Panpipe Dance," *African Music* 5 (1): 73–89.

Tracey, Hugh

1948 [1970] *Chopi Musicians: Their Music, Poetry and Instruments*. 2nd ed. London: International African Institute.

1953 Review of Alan Lomax: "Mister Jelly Roll," 1952, *African Music Society Newsletter* 1 (6), September: 76–77.

1961 "Tina's Lullaby," *African Music* 2 (4): 99–101.

1973 *Catalogue of the Sound of Africa Recordings*. 210 Long play records on music and songs from Central, Eastern and Southern Africa by Hugh Tracey, Vol. I and II. Roodepoort, South Africa: International Library of African Music.

Triandis, H. C.

1990 "Theoretical Concepts That Are Applicable to the Analysis of Ethnocentrism," in: R. W. Brislin, ed., *Applied Cross-Cultural Psychology*. Newbury Park, CA: Sage, 34–55.

Tsukada, Kenichi

1988 *Luvale Perceptions of Mukanda in Discourse and Music*. Ph.D. dissertation, Queen's University of Belfast. Ann Arbor: University Microfilms no. 8917245.

1990a "Variation and Unity in African Harmony: A Study of *mukanda* Songs of the Luvale in Zambia," in Usaburo Mabuchi et al., eds., *Florilegio Musicale. Festschrift für Professor Dr. Kataoka Gido* … Tokyo: Onagaku no Tomo, 157–97.

1990b "*Kukuwa* and *Kachacha*: The Musical Classification and the Rhythmic Patterns of the Luvale in Zambia," in Tetsuo Sakurai, ed., *Peoples and Rhythms*. Tokyo: Tokyo Shoseki, 229–75. (in Japanese)

1998 "Harmony in Luvale Music of Zambia," in Ruth M. Stone, ed., *The Garland Encyclopedia of World Music, Volume 1: Africa*. New York and London: Garland, 722–43.

Tucker, Sherrie

2000 *Swing Shift: "All-Girl" Bands of the 1940s*. Durham, NC: Duke University Press.

2001/2002 "Big Ears: Listening for Gender in Jazz studies," *Current Musicology* 71–73: 375–408.

2004 *A Feminist Perspective on New Orleans Jazzwomen*. New Orleans: Jazz National Historical Park Online (January 12, 2015) www.nps.gov/jazz/historyculture/upload/New_Orleans_Jazzwomen_RS-2.pdf.

deVane, Dwight, and Blaine Waide, eds.

2012 *Drop on Down in Florida: Field Recordings of African American Traditional Music, 1977–1980*. With contributions from Peggy A. Bulger, Doris J. Dyen, and David Evans. Georgia: Dust-to Digital.

Vansina, Jan

1965 *Oral Tradition: A Study in Historical Methodology*. London: Routledge and Kegan Paul.

Verger, Pierre

1968 *Flux et reflux de la traite des nègres entre le golfe de Benin et Bahia de Todos os Santos du dix-septième au dix-neuvième siècle*. Paris: Mouton.

Vlach, John Michael

1978 *The Afro-American Tradition in Decorative Art*. Cleveland, OH: Cleveland Museum of Art.

Wallerstein, Immanuel

1976 *The Modern World System: Capitalist Agriculture and the Origins of the European World Economy in the Sixteenth Century*. New York: Academic Press.

Waterman, Richard A.

1948 "'Hot' Rhythm in Negro Music," *Journal of the American Musicological Society*, Spring: 24–37.

1952 "African Influence on the Music of the Americas," in Sol Tax, ed., *Acculturation in the Americas*. Chicago: Chicago University Press, 207–18.

Wegner, Ulrich

1990 *Xylophonmusik aus Buganda* (Ostafrika). Musikbogen 1. Booklet and audiocassette. Wilhelmshaven: Florian Noetzel.

Weinstein, Norman C.

1992 *A Night in Tunisia: Imaginings of Africa in Jazz*. Metuchen, NJ: Scarecrow Press.

Welch, David

1977 "West African Cult Music Retentions in Haitian Urban Vaudou: A Preliminary Report," in *Essays for a Humanist. An Offering to Klaus Wachsmann*. New York: Town House Press, 337–49.

Welding, Pete

1971 [1966] "Hellhound on His Trail: Robert Johnson," *Blues Unlimited* 83, July: 16–17.

Welle, Jean

1952 "Rumbas congolaises et jazz americain," *African Music Society Newsletter* 1 (5), June: 42–43.

Werner, Otto

1992 *The Latin Influence on Jazz*. Dubuque: Kondall/Hunt.

Weseen, Maurice H.

1934 *A Dictionary of American Slang*. New York: Thomas Y. Crowell.

West, Steve

1985 "The Devil Visits the Delta: A View of His Role in the Blues," *Mississippi Folklore Register* 19 (1), Spring: 11–23.

Whiteman, Paul

1924 "What Is Jazz Doing to American Music?" *Etude* 42, August: 523–24.

Wilkison, Christopher

1994 "The Influence of West African Pedagogy upon the Education of New Orleans Jazz Musicians," *Black Music Research Journal* 14 (1): 25–42.

Williams, Linda

2005 "Reflexive Ethnography: An Ethnomusicologist's Experience as a Jazz Musician in Zimbabwe," *Black Music Research Journal* 25 (1/2), Spring/Fall: 155–65.

Williams, Martin

1985 "Jazz: What Happened in Kansas City?" *American Music* 3 (2): 171–79.

Wills, Geoffrey I.

2003 "Forty Lives in the Bebop Business: Mental Health in a Group of Eminent Jazz Musicians," *British Journal of Psychiatry* 183: 255–59.

2004 "Creativity, Mental Disorder and Jazz," *British Journal of Psychiatry* 184, February: 185.

Wilson, Olly

1974 "The Significance of the Relationship Between Afro-American and West African Music," *Black Perspective in Music* 2 (1): 3–22.

1977 "The Association of Movement and Music as a Manifestation of Black Conceptual Approach to Music Making." Paper presented at the 12th Congress of the International Musicological Society, Berkeley, August 21–27, 1977.

Winans, Robert B.

1982 [1990] "Black Instrumental Music Traditions in the Ex-Slave Narratives," *Black Music Research Journal* 10 (1), Spring: 43–53.

1993 "The Banjo: From Africa to Virginia and Beyond," *Blue Ridge Folk Instruments and Their Makers*. An exhibit of the Blue Ridge Institute Museum, Ferrum College, VA.

Winick, Charles

1970 *Dictionary of Anthropology*. Totowa, NJ: Littlefield, Adams.

Winston, Justin (assisted by Clive Wilson)

2009 "The Bolden Photograph: A Photographic Examination," *Jazz Archivist* 22: 19–24.

Wolf, Paul P. De

1983 "Xhosa," in Hermann Jungraithmayr and Wilhelm J. G. Möhlig, eds., *Lexikon der Afrikanistik*. Berlin: Reimer, 270.

Work, John

1940 *American Negro Songs and Spirituals*. New York: Bonanza Books.

Zemp, Hugo

1971 *Musique Dan. La musique dans la pensée et la vie sociale d'une société africaine*. Cahiers de l'Home, Nouvelle Série XI. Paris: Mouton.

2001 *Masters of the Balafon: Funeral Festivities*. Sélénium Film. Videocassette.

Zwerin, Michael (Mike)

1979 "Remember Bird," *International Herald Tribune*, September 19, 20.

1983 *Close Enough for Jazz*. London. Quartet Books.

1994 "Bird Stars in Bebop Garage Sale in London," *International Herald Tribune*, September 7, 8.

2001 "Mighty Miles and His French Band of 1957," *International Herald Tribune*, May 25, 22.

2004 "Remembering Dolphy, 'undisciplined genius,'" *International Herald Tribune*, October 6, 10.

INDEXES

413

AFRICAN ETHNIC-LINGUISTIC DESIGNATIONS

SONG TITLES

GENERAL INDEX

CPSIA information can be obtained
at www.ICGtesting.com
Printed in the USA
LVOW11*0038301117
557883LV00010BA/254/P